PANTHEON

Pantheon

A NEW HISTORY OF ROMAN RELIGION

JÖRG RÜPKE

TRANSLATED BY
DAVID M. B. RICHARDSON

PRINCETON UNIVERSITY PRESS
PRINCETON & OXFORD

Copyright © 2018 by Princeton University Press

This is a translation of *Pantheon*, by Jörg Rüpke, © Verlag C. H. Beck oHG, München 2016

Requests for permission to reproduce material from this work should be sent to Permissions, Princeton University Press

Published by Princeton University Press,
41 William Street, Princeton, New Jersey 08540

In the United Kingdom: Princeton University Press,
6 Oxford Street, Woodstock, Oxfordshire OX20 1TR

press.princeton.edu

Jacket design by Chris Ferrante

Jacket photograph © Pino D'Amico

All Rights Reserved

Library of Congress Cataloging-in-Publication Data

Names: Rüpke, Jörg, author.
Title: Pantheon : a new history of Roman religion / Jörg Rüpke ; translated by David M. B. Richardson.
Other titles: Pantheon. English
Description: Princeton, N.J. : Princeton University Press, 2018. | Includes bibliographical references and index.
Identifiers: LCCN 2017015360 | ISBN 9780691156835 (hardcover : alk. paper)
Subjects: LCSH: Rome—Religion. | Religions—History. | Religion—History.
Classification: LCC BL803 .R84513 2018 | DDC 292.07—dc23 LC record available at https://lccn.loc.gov/2017015360

British Library Cataloging-in-Publication Data is available

This book has been composed in Arno Pro

Printed on acid-free paper. ∞

Printed in the United States of America

10 9 8 7 6 5 4 3 2 1

CONTENTS

LIST OF ILLUSTRATIONS

ACKNOWLEDGMENTS

AT THE CORE OF THIS BOOK lies the conviction that a survey of the history of ancient religion that does not take collective actors such as Rome or "the Romans" as its starting point, but rather individual actors and how they lived religion, produces not only a different view of religion, but above all a new awareness of the mutability of religious conceptions and practice. My own research and the chance to work with the team comprising Marlis Arnhold and Benjamin Sippel (who supported me in the selection of illustrations), Christopher Degelmann, Valentino Gasparini, Richard Gordon (whom I owe thanks for more than a decade of intense exchange), Maik Patzelt, Georgia Petridou, Rubina Raja (who co-directed the project), Anna-Katharina Rieger, Lara Weiß, and finally Emiliano Urciuoli and Janico Albrecht, made possible by an Advanced Grant from the European Research Council (no. 295555), enabled me to put that conviction to the test. That team's share in the outcome distinctly exceeds what I have been able to indicate in the notes and the bibliography. This also applies to the many colleagues who have collaborated in this undertaking, as contributors to meetings, as guests at the Max Weber Centre, as fellows of the research group "Religious Individualization in Historical Perspective," financed by the Deutsche Forschungsgemeinschaft (German Science Foundation, no. KFOR 1013), or as co-editors of the journal *Religion in the Roman Empire*, which arose from this project. I mention by name here Roberto Alciati (now preparing an Italian translation together with Maria dell'Isola), Clifford Ando, Michal Bar-Asher Siegal, Eve-Marie Becker, Elisabeth Begemann, Anton Bierl, Malcolm Choat, Nicola Denzey-Lewis, Ulrike Egelhaaf-Gaiser,

Esther Eidinow, Cristiana Facchini, Harriet Flower, Jonas Grethlein, Ingvild Gilhus, Simon Goldhill, Manfred Horstmannshoff, Maria dell'Isola, Julia Kindt, Karen King, Patricia McAnany, Harry Maier, Teresa Morgan, Maren Niehoff, Vered Noam, Valeria Piano, Ilaria Ramelli, Federico Santangelo, Günther Schörner, Seth Schwartz, Marco Francisco Simón, Christopher Smith, Darja Šterbenc Erker, Guy Stroumsa, Ann Taves, Zsuzsanna Várhelyi, Jutta and Markus Vinzent, Katharina Waldner, and Greg Woolf. Collaboration with the latter was supported by the Alexander von Humboldt Trust with its funding for research on sanctuaries. Jan Bremmer, Max Deeg, Martin Fuchs, Valentino Gasparini, Bettina Hollstein, Ute Hüsken, Antje Linkenbach, Katharina Rieger, Veit Rosenberger (who died just a few weeks afterward and is still missed at the Center), and Michael Stausberg took the trouble to discuss the entire text with me in July 2016. My sincere thanks to all those named!

Ursula Birtel-Koltes and Diana Püschel created the organizational infrastructure for the work. Katharina Waldner took over more than my teaching duties, so freeing me of other obligations. The management team at the Max Weber Centre for Advanced Cultural and Social Studies, Bettina Hollstein, Wolfgang Spickermann, and then Hartmut Rosa, and the presidents and chancellors of the University, Kai Brodersen and Michael Hinz, Walter Bauer-Wabnegg and Thomas Gerken, supported the project in every conceivable way. My sincere thanks go to them all, and to the staffs at the funding organizations. Sarah Al-taher and Karoline Koch tirelessly sought out literature and incorporated it into the bibliography. I thank them too, and the British School at Rome with its director Christopher Smith, who provided me with a safe harbor during the final editing process.

David Richardson has again undertaken the translation of the text from its original German. I am grateful to him for his care and critical feedback. The same holds true for Eva Jaunzems who smoothed the text for an ever broader audience. My thanks to Maik Patzelt and Janico Albrecht for compiling the index.

The book would not have taken its present form if Al Bertrand of Princeton University Press and Stefan von der Lahr at C.H. Beck had not persuaded me that it should be configured both as a narrative of religious changes and as an examination of the mechanisms of religion in antiquity in general.

Erfurt
Summer 2017

PANTHEON

I

A History of Mediterranean Religion

1. What Is Meant by a History of Mediterranean Religion?

It is the intention of this book to tell the story of an upheaval epochal in its impact. This is the story of how a world well beyond the understanding of most of us was transformed into a world very like our own, at least in one particular. To put it succinctly: we will describe how from a world in which one practiced *rituals*, there emerged a world of *religions*, to which one could belong. This is no straightforward story. The changes I shall relate were not inevitable; no one could have foreseen them. Nor were they irreversible: quite the contrary.

To speak of religions—in the plural—seems to us today quite normal. We may in fact define ourselves in terms of *a* religion. A religion may open doors for us—access to officialdom, to the mass media, to tax offices when it is a question of tax exemptions—or in some cases the doors of a prison. But, although we as individuals may belong to one religion, we can no longer "unthink" the plural form of the term as a concept for describing both present-day and historical societies. And yet, with ever-greater frequency, trends arise that defy such categorization. "New Age" has been one such concept. "Spirituality" increasingly appears to be another, and "mysticism" has a long history as a phenomenon of this kind. Countless Christians, Muslims, and

Hindus talk quite straightforwardly of themselves as belonging to one (only rarely several) of many religions, but there are good grounds for wondering whether, in many cases, we should not speak of culture and cultural differences rather than of membership of different religions.

When a concept has many different meanings, windows of comparison are opened across space and time, and in many cases it is only then that a meaningful conversation becomes possible. A history, moreover, can be communicated successfully only when the number of concepts in play is limited, when recognizability is vouchsafed to all participants, despite small differences; otherwise, we are faced with a multitude of disparate, sometimes conflicting histories, with results that may be entertaining (think only of the "Thousand and One Nights"), and thoroughly informative and revealing (a thousand everyday stories adding up to a "microhistory"), but with no end, no "moral." This is all the more true of a long history such as the one being attempted here, where the actors change repeatedly, or at least often more frequently than the parameters of religious practices and concepts.

Conceptual harmonization can, of course, add to the difficulty when an effort to achieve such harmony superimposes an appearance on continuity that masks on-going changes and transformations. It then becomes critical to refine our concepts, to notice differences. We begin to see that the world we are describing comprises many geographical spaces, where many different kinds of development are underway: a change that we note in one location may also have taken place elsewhere, but there is no guarantee that it had the same consequences in both settings. Thus, although a history of Mediterranean religion is not a universal history of religion, it must nevertheless always take into account other geographical spaces, must ask what happened there, and must notice instances where ideas, objects, and people broke through those walls erected in our imagination by the metaphor of separated spaces.

My Mediterranean narrative recognizes that comparable transformations with similar outcomes (in religions, in assemblages of practices, in concepts, and in symbols) took place in other epochs and in other realms, where they were perceived by the peoples they affected as being distinctive. I think particularly of western, southern, and eastern Asia. And yet, in the past half-millennium, religion in many of these regions was very different. I maintain that the institutionalization of religion characteristic of the Modern Period in many parts of Europe and the Americas, and the conflict-ridden rigidity of the "religions" or "confessions" of which one may be a member—but only one at a time—rests on the particular configurations of religion and power that prevailed in antiquity, and on their legal codification in Late Antiquity. Not only the Islamic expansion, but above all the specifically European developments of the Reformation and the formation of national states, reinforced the confessional character and institutional consolidation of supraregional religious networks. This model was exported to many, but certainly not all parts of the world in the course of colonial expansion, and frequently in a spirit of arrogance.[1]

It is circum-Mediterranean and increasingly Euro-Mediterranean history post-antiquity that draws our attention to Rome. But our choice of Rome as a hub is mistaken if it is origin myths that we seek. Ancient polytheism and its narrative worlds did not develop anywhere near Rome, but rather in the Middle East, Egypt, and Mesopotamia. The monotheistic traditions of Judaism, Christianity, and Islam connect in Jerusalem, not in the city on the Tiber. Moreover, we have Athens to thank, not the Seven Hills, for the polemical separation of philosophy and religion, virtually a unique marker of Western religious thinking. Even the Latin-language codification of the law, the *Corpus iuris civilis*, which left its mark on many modern legal systems, emerged from Constantinople, the Rome of the Byzantine Empire, and not from its Italian predecessor. Certainly, the word *religio* had its origin in Rome. But that has only slight relevance to the change that is the subject of this present narrative.

Origin is not everything, however. Rome was situated in a part of the world with a long history of absorbing cultural impulses rather than initiating them. From the end of the 1st millennium BC onward, the city exported multiple conceptions of religion throughout the Mediterranean.[2] And with the destruction of Jerusalem, Roman power politics became a central factor in the history of various religious identities. The growth of the empire into a multicultural space with a newly stratified power structure, the accelerated exchange of ideas, goods, and people within such a space, the attraction its center had for prophets no less than for philosophers, all of these factors combined to assure that Rome would be a focal point of the first millennium AD. In the centuries prior to this, Rome is to be seen more as one *instance* of Mediterranean development, one with its own history and timeline, with the consequence that we must constantly question what is to be regarded as typical and what is untypical for other regions. The distinctive strand that will be represented by Rome in the present narrative will thus only slowly emerge from a consideration of Italian and Mediterranean beginnings.

Our attention is thus set free to range widely over religious conceptions, symbols, and activities, an entire spectrum of cultural practices from ancient oriental high cultures to Late Antiquity (and beyond), viewing them all as they undergo substantial processes of development, and all with a multitude of facets in common. From a long-term and global perspective, the development of particular forms in the fields of architecture and the media here assume considerable importance. The Buddhism that emerged from India owes a considerable degree of its imagery to Greek modifications of Egyptian archetypes as can be seen in the art of the Gandhara region. Moreover, the concept of a "pantheon" of deities interacting in a hierarchy, a concept that once again originated in western Asia and the ancient Orient, played an important role in defining the form and personification of Greek and Roman conceptions of the divine, and their adoption in Christianity. The religious history of the Roman period had far-flung ramifications. In the Mediterranean world we have the formation of Judaism with the emergence of Christianity from it, and the dissemination of Christianity's Romanized form via Rome and Constantinople, while Islam arose at the southeastern periphery of the same world, and, with its expansion across the south, increasingly toward the east and even the northeast of that space, in many ways marked the end of antiquity. The processes of dissemination, or more precisely those of mutual exchange on the eastern frontiers and along routes of contact—the Silk Road to Central Asia, shipping routes to southern India[3]—still lie in the shadowy regions of scholarship, and frequently lack even elementary appraisals: a situation that cannot be altered by a focused history such as is intended here.

In any event, however, one decided advantage attaches to a focus on Rome. Already in the Hellenistic Age, the final two centuries BC, Rome was probably the biggest city in the world, growing in the early Imperial Age to a population of half a million, many say one million inhabitants. Such numbers would not be equaled until the High Medieval Period, with cities such as Cordoba in Moorish Spain and Bian (now Kaifeng) in central China, or Peking in the Early Modern Period. When it comes to the function of religion in the life of the metropolis and the role of megacities as intellectual and economic motors, Ancient- and especially Imperial-Age Rome provides a historical "laboratory" with which few other cities in the ancient world can compare. The closest would be Alexandria, the new foundation of Alexander the Great and cultural melting pot on the Nile Delta, and perhaps Antioch, with Ptolemaïs and Memphis next in size. The Latin pejorative term *pagani* did not describe people merely as non-Christians, but also identified them as country folk. The sentiment that whatever is important takes place in cities—and especially metropolises—is not new, but it has never been thoroughly studied in the case of religions. And so my story of religion here ventures onto new ground. But what exactly *is* religion?

2. Religion

When it comes to describing transformations in religion, unexamined preconceptions should not be allowed to stand. We normally base our thinking about religion on its plural, "religions." It is even maintained by some that religion actually exists only in terms of that plural form. Religions are understood as traditions of religious practices, conceptions, and institutions, in some contexts even as business or business-like enterprises. According to an important strain of sociological thought that goes back to Émile Durkheim (1858–1917), we are dealing here with social products, products of societies[4] comprised of groups of people normally living together within a territory, for whom the central core of their common existence, their shared orientation, is shielded from daily discussion by being vested in symbolic religious forms. There emerges a system of signs whose immanence is safeguarded by the performance of rituals, and which seeks to explain the world in images, narratives, written texts, or refined dogma, and to regulate behavior by the use of ethical imperatives or by an established way of life, sometimes by recourse to an effective apparatus of sanctions (for instance through the power of the state), but sometimes even without that implied threat.

Such a conception of religion can explain a lot; it meets its limits, however, when it seeks to explain religious pluralism, the enduring coexistence of different, mutually contradictory conceptions and practices. It can find itself at a loss also when it must decipher the quite distinctive relationship between the individual and his or her religion. It is repeatedly accused of being too closely oriented to "Western," and above all Christian religious and conceptual history, and criticized for its unquestioning "colonialism" in superimposing Western concepts onto other cultures.[5] There are similarly problematic ramifications when we seek to apply this conception to antiquity.[6] The reason for this, too, lies in the present. The dissolution of traditional allegiances that we so frequently observe in our time is read as religious individualism or as the decline of religion, or even as the displacement of collective religion by individual spirituality.[7] This perspective then becomes associated with the complementary assumption that early societies and their religions must have been characterized by a high degree of collectivism. We shall see how this assumption, already problematic in respect of the present day, creates a highly distorted picture of the past.[8]

This does not, however, compel us to abstain from speaking about religion. What we need, rather, is a concept of religion that enables us to describe, with precision, changes both in the social aspects of religion and in its significance to individuals. This can be achieved successfully by conceiving of religion from the standpoint of the individual and of his or her social environment. I shall not focus on the mental systems that have been constructed by both insiders and external observers, for these can in any case never yield more than fragmentary and incomplete particulars about a religion.[9] Instead, my starting point is lived ancient religion—in all its variants, its differing contexts, and social configurations.[10] Only in rare instances—and these will, of course, be given due attention—do the activities of people dealing with one another coalesce into networks[11] and organized systems, or find their way into written texts, so that they take on a life of their own and develop into the massive, autonomous, and often long-lived structures that we normally categorize as religions.

How, then, is religion to be comprehended? We can only hope to gain a perspective on changes in religion, on the dynamics embodied in it and how these produce changes in the social and cultural contexts of religious actors, if we do not assume at the outset that what religion is self-evident. We must, then, seek out boundaries for our subject that take in what it is about religion that interests us—namely those aspects of it that conform to our view of the subject—but at the same time the boundaries must be broad enough to include the deviant, the surprising in the religious practice of a particular time. I see the religion of the epoch we are considering from a situative perspective, as including actors (whether they be described as divine or gods, demons or angels, the dead or the immortal) who are in some respect superior. Above all, however, their presence, their participation, their significance in a particular situation is not simply an unquestioned given: other human participants in the situation might regard them as invisible, silent, inactive, or simply absent, perhaps even as nonexistent. In short, religious activity is present when and where, in a particular situation, at least one human individual includes such actors in his or her communication with other humans, whether by merely referring to those actors or by directly addressing them.

Even in ancient cultures, communicating with or acting in relation to such beings was not simply accepted as a matter of course. In respect of the present day, this will scarcely be disputed: the assertion that transcendent actors[12] are participants, either actual or to be invoked, would be viewed askance in many parts of Europe, would indeed appear quite implausible to many people. Even when a particular human actor is firmly convinced of the immanence of a god, or of something divine, in the presence of others he or she will frequently abstain from making such a claim, in either word or action, for fear of inviting ridicule. Since, in my view, religion consists primarily in communication, I would have to say that in such a situation religion does not occur. The reluctant modern European believer I have described is, however, not a universal figure. The presence of the transcendent is entirely noncontroversial in other regions, and was so in other epochs.

Nevertheless—and this is my point—making such an assertion and/or taking actions compatible with it would be problematic even in the ancient world. It would risk damage to the credibility of the speaker and might put his or her competence into question. This is because the assertion would never be couched as a general statement that gods exist. Instead it would take the form of a claim that one particular deity, whether Jupiter or Hercules, had helped or would help the speaker or other individuals, or that Fortuna (fate) stood behind the speaker's own actions. Such a claim might be borne out, or it might not. "You of all people?," "Venus?" "We want to see that for ourselves!" "But you're not normally so very pious!": the possible demurrals were legion. And religious authority could not simply be acquired by mere prayer: some individuals were successful in their claims and earned a livelihood by them; for others, priesthood remained a spare-time occupation, and in the end might not even secure election to the local council. Ascribing authority to invisible actors and exercising corresponding circumspection in one's actions appears, as postulated by evolutionists, to have been conducive to survival and accordingly favored in human development;[13] but it was a tactic that provided an opening for challenges by fellow humans and its systematic use could provoke organized dissent.[14]

In a Germany (and to some extent a Europe) that, with either satisfaction or horror, sees itself as largely secularized, it is easy to forget that regular church attendance and church marriage, knowledge of the catechism, and generalized church tax were not widely imposed until the nineteenth century, and that this was done in an attempt to use religion as an instrument of social discipline, to instill in all and sundry the awareness of belonging to a particular Confession, and to make church membership and services available and obligatory for everybody, even in far distant places.[15] It is not simply the case that the past was more pious. Countless thousands brought small gifts to Roman temples to show their gratitude or to give emphasis to their requests; millions did not. Millions buried their deceased children or parents with care, and even provided them with grave goods; countless millions contented themselves with disposing of the corpses.

The question we must ask in respect both of present-day religion and the religion of the past, of the ancient Mediterranean world, is: In what ways did religious communication and religious activity enhance the individual's agency, his or her ability to act, and to carve out a space for initiatives? How did it strengthen his or her competence and creativity in dealing with everyday problems and with problems that went beyond the everyday? In other words, how did reference to actors who were not indisputably plausible contribute to the formation of collective identities that would enable the individual to act or think as part of a group, of a social formation that might vary greatly in its form and strength, no matter whether it existed in actuality or only in the imagination or fevered awareness of a few people? If we are speaking of strategies here, however, we must think not only of dealings with other people, and of implied learning processes and gains (or losses!) in social status, but also of strategies for dealing successfully with those who stood outside the everyday, or who intervened unbidden in that everyday; namely, of the transcendent actors, the gods. Their attention must be sought. They must be called to listen. A divine "power" about whom and with whom nobody speaks is not a power. Without invocations or ritual, inscriptions and religious infrastructures, visible images and audible priests, religion does not happen. And this has consequences. In a society without institutional memory, religious developments (and not religious developments only) can very quickly dissipate.

To look back into the past from the standpoint of the present and detect traces of such developments is no simple matter. We must keep our eyes and ears open. A religious history of the ancient Mediterranean world must use multiple approaches and consult a wide range of sources. To unearth a lived ancient religion demands that we pay attention to the voices of individual witnesses, to their experiences and practices, their distinct ways of appropriating traditions, to the way they communicate and innovate. For example, the use of a god's name in a particular situation does not mean that there was a structured "pantheon" with fixed names and roles, although of course we must search carefully for other, similar utterances overheard by our particular witness, for comparable utterances known to him or her, and for later imitations or variations. Such information may be gleaned from ancient histories, poetry, memoirs, and plays; it may often comprise the imaginings or inferences of ancient authors, rather than direct attestations of other people's thoughts. Ancient religion, too, was rooted in individual experience and agency. At the same time, it was subject to constant change, in a constant state of becoming. In spite of the impressive traces it has left to us in the form of texts and monuments, and information about religious institutions, it stubbornly eluded attempts to freeze it, to fix it as a ritual system with a stable pantheon of gods and a rigid system of beliefs. Only by narrative can this ancient Mediterranean religion be called forth and given shape.

Before the advent of Judaism and, especially, Christianity, both religions that are strongly oriented to the individual,[16] the notion of an individual religion was so foreign that some further clarifications may be in order.[17] Ancient religion consists in what is said about it, what we tell of it. It does not simply lie to hand in the debris of archaeological digs, or in inscriptions and literary texts, waiting patiently to be expounded and revisualized.[18] A description of what the lived religion of antiquity looked like, and how far its reach extended, will begin in chapter 2. Some readers may wish to jump ahead to this discussion.

3. Facets of Religious Competence

It is difficult to catch sight of an individual at a distance of two thousand years. It is only with difficulty that we can fathom the innermost soul of someone still living, even though we have available to us interviews and journals. The surviving remnants of an ancient everyday life and of its attempts at communication present us with far greater challenges. It is all the more important to develop at least a model conception of how ancient Mediterranean people went about developing strategies of religious behavior in their constant interactions with one another, to determine what facets of that process were of particular significance, and how these came to define religion in the final centuries of the first millennium BC and the first centuries of the first millennium AD. I will next look more closely at three facets of "religious competence," by which I mean the experience and knowledge necessary for successful religious action, and the authority hence attributed by others. These facets—religious agency; religious identity; and techniques and media for religious communication—while closely linked, allow us three different perspectives from which to examine what appears to us as familiar and what seems alien in ancient religion.

Religious Agency

Interpretive social and cultural sciences have characterized human agency as a meaningful process, to be understood against a background of socially created meaning.[19] The socio-philosophical theory called Pragmatism has refined such analyses: agency is claimed to be above all a process of problem-solving. The individual is constantly confronted by new situations, which he or she attempts to overcome in ways that are not entirely based on preconceived notions. The meaning of agency and its goals evolve in the very course of exercising agency, undergoing some measured degree of change despite the fact that the agent is restricted by social contexts and traditions. Within this concrete yet changeable arena of possibilities, creativity in actions is possible.[20]

Competence in the exercise and scope of agency is developed in the course of exercising agency.[21] Agency is in this sense "the temporally constructed engagement by actors with different structural environments . . . through the interplay of habit, imagination, and judgment, both reproducing and transforming those structures in interactive response to the problems posed by changing historical situations."[22] It is the constantly renewed and also repeated interactions between people that create the structures and traditions that define and limit the subsequent exercise of agency, which in turn also alters or even challenges those same structures and traditions.[23]

It is characteristic of religion that, by introducing "divine" actors or authorities, it enlarges the field of agency, offering a wider range to the imagination and a wider choice of ways to intervene in a given situation. By attributing agency to "divine actors" (or the like), religion enables the human actor to transcend his or her situation and to devise correspondingly creative strategies for action—perhaps by initiating a ritual, or as a person possessed. But the converse is also possible. The same mechanism can also trigger a renunciation of personal agency, resulting in impotence and passivity, with agency being reserved for the quite "special" actors. Over time, agency thus comes to be delineated along increasingly definite lines and is enhanced in its effectiveness, so that ever more successful and sophisticated "schematizations" are undertaken. These are predicated on past exercises of agency; routines are thus established that facilitate ever more sweeping projections as to the future consequences of agency. This process happens in the context of hypothesis-framing and yields ever more apt "contextualizations" that aid in the practice-oriented assessment of the present state of the facts on the basis of social experience.[24] It is not the single actor who "has" agency. Rather, in concrete negotiation with his or her structural environment, the individual finds spaces for initiatives and is imbued by others with the responsibility to act. Structures and the individual as actor reciprocally configure one another.[25]

On the basis of such reflections, we might now feel prompted to sift the evidence for forms of religious learning and means of acquiring religious knowledge. Where could young people observe religion, and participate in it?[26] How did they learn to interpret experiences as religious? Where was training in self-reflexion, the contemplation of an autonomous self, to be obtained?[27] How could new religious roles or a religious name be assumed, so as to influence one's further interactions?

These and other questions will be addressed in the following chapters with an eye to opening new perspectives on religious agency.

Religious activity was also closely connected to the structuring of time by means of calendars, month-names, and lists of feast-days, a structuring based on "hypotheses" that designated particular days as especially suitable for communicating with the gods and reflecting on the affairs of the community. Contrary to common assumptions, we shall see that none of this was carved in stone; rather it was ever susceptible to innovation and adjustment.[28] Prophets and prophetic movements were able to exert enormous influence on future expectations, both individual and collective. But it is also true that "contextualizations" in the here and now provided considerable scope for the creative exercise of religious agency. The character of space and time could be changed by acts of sacralization; distant actors, too—enemies behind city walls, fugitive thieves, travelers—could be reached remotely by means of rituals, oaths, and curses, or by inserting pins into dolls.[29] By the transfer of religious capabilities and authority or the invocation of oracles, new directions could be given to political decision-making processes.[30]

Religious Identity

The individual seldom acts alone. More often, he or she has the notion of acting as a member of a particular group: a family, a village, a special-interest group, or even a "people" or "nation"; a notion that may be strongly situation-dependent, emphasizing now the one, now another identity, as a mother, a worshipper of Bona Dea, an adept of the Bible or of Stoic philosophy.[31] Such notions, even when vaguely formed, can influence individual behavior.[32] But we must always be clear that these are first and foremost *notions* of belonging, often failing to take into account whether the group in question exists in the notions of others, or whether others count this person as belonging to the group. It is thus a matter of self-classification; of the individual's assessment of his or her membership and the significance he or she assigns it, in common with others insofar as such membership is discernible by them. It is an identity forged from a felt emotional connection and dependence (to the extent of a considerable overlapping of the personal and this collective identity), and its importance rests in the degree to which membership is embedded in everyday practice and characterizes personal behavior. Finally, it consists in the narratives associated with such notions, and a knowledge of the values, defining characteristics, and history of the group.[33] In view especially of the gradual character of the development of religions in antiquity, it must be stressed that the term "group" does not imply an established association. A situation-dependent grouping of (not only human!) actors, among whom the individual in question does or does not number himself or herself, is sufficient. The many ancient inscriptions recording family relationships, citizenship, or place of origin can also be read as declarations of membership.[34] For many, of course, this could lead to highly complex collective identities, involving various affiliations (and also dissociations).[35]

It is precisely when our evidence of "religion" is confined to a few archaeological traces, a statuette here, fragments of a vase there, dogs' bones, or the post-holes of a suspected temple, that we must beware of reifying and essentializing these groups and communities. They are not simply defined by the close distribution of houses, identical practices, the same language, or similar votive gifts or gods. "Community is . . . something that you do," and it is individuals who do it: ". . . how people feel linked to particular places, just as who people think they are, and equally who they are not, determines how they associate themselves with others in space and through time, over generations, in shared memories or in agreed forgettings."[36] The apparently archaic stability of the social context, of the locality, is often deceptive; it is only a snapshot of a reality in flux.[37] The history of ancient religions cannot be described as a process that turned "tribal religions" into "world religions," as handbooks have had it until very recently.

Religious Communication

The issue of competence in communication provides a third way of looking at how an individual brings "religion" into play in his interaction with other people.[38] But the fact that religion may at the same time be understood to *be* communication allows us to associate enhanced possibilities for communication with the growing variety of religious practices that existed in antiquity.

We do not know how and how often the majority of the inhabitants of the Roman Empire spoke with their gods or their God, or what they spoke about. But we have a considerable number of ancient texts that describe such communication, and tens or rather hundreds of thousands of direct witnesses to it, in the form of the remains of gifts, as well as visible documentation, intended to be permanent, in the form of votive inscriptions and dedications. This points to the dual character of much, although not necessarily all communication with the divine: the religious act is also a message to the actor's fellow humans, his audience or readership, to give witness by eye and ear. To cry *O Iuppiter, audi* ("Oh Jupiter, hear"), also means: "Look. I am pious. I am in league with the gods. Jupiter listens to me. Whoever is against me is also against the god and the divine order!"

We shall have to return later to the interpersonal functions of religious communication. It suffices at the moment to understand that this reaching out to the divine by participants in an action gets attention and creates relevance. In this latter term lies the key to understanding communication. In order for a communication to be successful, attention must be created by the promise of relevant information. This must be given credibly and audibly by the speaker, whose audience must indicate to him or her that they apprehend and believe the promise before the communication can proceed. In the rush and tumble of everyday affairs, only the promise of relevance (whatever form that promise takes) can attract attention to a communication that then changes those addressed (in ways that are never predictable!), and in this sense meets with success.[39] It is not surprising that human beings extend these ground rules of communicative success to their communications with nonhumans.

To reach the gods, then, it is necessary to attract and retain their attention. The religious history of antiquity is also the history of how formal strategies were developed and employed in the Mediterranean world, in Italy and in Rome, to achieve that end, and how they were then refined or even radically questioned. In order, however, to understand these practices and the alterations they underwent, we must keep one ground rule in mind: "Hey, you . . ." is more effective than "I should like to say . . ." The key to success does not lie in making the correct selection from a catalogue of prayers, vows, offerings, blood sacrifices, types of processions, and circus games (all according to the size of one's purse), but in how effective a combination of such communicative techniques one adopts. Here, the categorizations in classic Religious Studies texts give a quite false impression. Addressing a deity almost never involved merely a prayer, or only a sacrifice.

The very first consideration seems to have been location. An already established sanctuary testified to the success of others' efforts to communicate. It suggested the proximity of a deity, who lived in this place, or at least visited it quite frequently. Naïve confidence in the presence of the deity might in rapid order be replaced by philosophical considerations as to what conditions were conducive to the presence of an omnipotent deity: repeated reports of statues nodding to a supplicant do not mean that the deity and the statue were equated in conversation outside the temple. It was common for a deity to be invoked in another's sanctuary, and not considered unthinkable to document that successful act of communication by means of, say, an image of the alien god in that same place. On the other hand, it must be pointed out that the choice of an established time, perhaps the feast day of the particular sanctuary or god, was a far less important issue. The critical considerations were how urgent a need was, when a cult site could physically be reached, and whether one was even available. In many towns, for example, cult spaces dedicated to Mithras were not accessible for individual worship, or certainly not all of the time; if someone nevertheless wished to turn to this god, other public sanctuaries were available, as dedications to Mithras left in them testify.

Well-nigh every choice of location was preceded by the question as to how the divine was to be brought into the place. Systematizers like Fabius Pictor in the second century BC and the subsequently much-cited Marcus Terentius Varro in the mid-first century BC sought to assign a specialized deity to cover every possible source of danger, sometimes perhaps inventing them for the purpose (or perhaps, more precisely, inventing names of divinities that could readily be invoked), but in everyday reality recourse was held to a manageable number of popular deities that were present either at cult sites or in the form of images. The situation might remain even more amorphous, especially in rural areas and in the northwestern and western European provinces, where the divine might always be addressed in the plural, as a set of related figures (*Iunones, Matres, Fata*), depicted in an idiosyncratic combination of iconographically standardized (and only thus recognizable to us as "identical") figurations.[40] Accessing the divine in an architectural sanctuary, moreover, was not the only option, for a spring or a painted house-altar within one's own four walls was still a viable and in some situations preferred venue.

The invocation to the god or goddess was not just one of several elements within prayer, but rather the very foundation of the act of communication. It required intensification and could be extended in many ways so as to arouse increased attention and further charge the act with relevance. Foremost among the methods used was acoustic enhancement. The invocation was isolated from the bustle of the everyday by stillness. It was not made in everyday language. Formal speech helped to ritualize the act of communication, elevating it above the ordinary. The effect was furthered by singing instead of merely speaking, and by instrumental music. By the choice of instruments, it was possible to connect with particular traditions, attract the attention of a specific deity, and signal that special connection to those present. We often come across the double-reeded *tibia*; but trumpet-like instruments, organs, and percussion instruments were also used. It seems that there were actual musical themes connected to certain sanctuaries.

Care was taken over choice of clothing, especially when the act of communication involved a high degree of public visibility. What was critical might be the color of the clothing, as for example the wearing of white in processions dedicated to Isis; or the type of garment chosen, such as the toga worn by Roman officials in the late Republic and early Imperial Age, and probably by Roman citizens generally on festive occasions. These very examples show that it was less a question of indicating a specific affinity than of signaling simply that a special kind of ritualized communication was in process; the toga was in fact normally white. But, on the other hand, even the choice of foliage for wreaths worn on the head was capable of expressing fine distinctions.

The attention of both the deity and of any passers-by could also be attracted by coordinated movement. Processions, either small or large, walking in step, were common. In the larger cities there was scarcely any other way of drawing large crowds of both participants and onlookers. Dances of highly varying degrees of exuberance, such as the "three-step" dances of the Roman *salii* (jumpers), and the more abandoned dances to Isis depicted on reliefs in Latium, also played a role. Self-flagellation, sometimes in public, was first practiced by monks in the eastern Mediterranean; and writers reported the castration of priests of Cybele; although this was surely not a public ritual open to observers.

Wide scope for communication was also provided by the custom, borrowed from the interpersonal realm, of bestowing gifts, which, by their material value, would heighten the relevance of the spoken message. These were chosen with a view to the intent of the communication (the fulfillment of a request, a demonstration of gratitude and praise, enduring harmony with the divine) and they had the capacity to secure that message in lasting form, at least until the object was cleared away. Both aesthetics and material worth could play a part in

the choice of gift, but mass-produced miniaturizations were not unusual, and were apparently sufficient to attract divine attention. But
lasting visibility was not necessary. Small gifts (accompanying the utterance of an oath, or documenting its success) might also be directly
deposited in pits, sunk into rivers, or thrown into the fire and so destroyed or melted down. These practices will be treated in the next
chapter on the early period. Unlike inscriptions, written messages (on
stone or wooden tablets) in such cases would no longer be legible to
others, excepting deities. On the basis of a specifically theological
judgment as to what religion should be, modern scholarship has wrongly
postulated that the term "magic" could be applied to these variant
practices.

The gift did not have to be durable. The burning of incense, the
presentation of selected foodstuffs (many different kinds of cakes,
for example), the odor from the preparation of animals that had been
slaughtered and dedicated to the deity: all these were performance,
enactments underlining the importance of the attempt at communication. Theatrical performances as gifts to deities were a specialty of
the Greeks and then the Romans from the fifth century BC onward.
They became quite elaborate, but were not without parallels in Central
American and Southeast Asian cultures. In addition to dance and song,
we should mention the phenomenon called in Latin *ludi* (games).
These were competitions offered to the gods, usually to whole groups
of gods, whose busts would be brought in procession to the circus and
placed on special seats. Scaenic games (*ludi scaenici*) were dramatic
productions staged for the gods; in Greece, and soon afterward in
Rome also, we even find structures erected especially for these
occasions.

We must keep in mind that such enormous architectural (and, of
course, financial) endeavors were not funded by religious organizations, but as a rule relied on the initiative of individuals who wished,
by such an undertaking, to give proof of their exceptional gratitude to
and intimacy with a deity. Authorities such as city councils had to
give their support for the projects and there was public wrangling
over building sites, but it was individuals who took it upon themselves

to donate some of their war plunder or other gains to cover the costs, and it was they who decided on the architectural forms structures should take, and which particular deity would be honored. They thus established the religious infrastructure, and by their choices shaped the cult and decided which gods would be most easily accessible. In a word, they defined the "pantheon." We must also inquire into the social rules that determined which particular forms of communication should be employed. Who had access to these modes of communication? Did access depend on ethnicity, the office an individual held, prestige, or simply financial means? What monopolizing forces were operative, from the burning of unauthorized oracles to decisions regarding the architecture of amphitheaters?[41] We must never forget, however, that the broad range of religious practices we have just surveyed offered a wide field in which individuals could obtain success, authority, respect, or even simply a living that was not available to them in other areas of social, political, or merely domestic activity.

As ancient religion increasingly came to comprise visible public acts, the private religious communication of individuals also began to draw audiences, who might either be present at a proceeding or, if absent, could hear about the event through metacommunicative means, through discourse about the proceedings by word of mouth or via secondary media (such as inscriptions or texts). The animal sacrifice required a feast committee; vows were spoken out loud; and many forms of divination took place in public. As a result, the act of communication in addressing a deity was received by an audience beyond the intended addressee. The vow spoken aloud by the army commander not only reached the deity, but also demonstrated the commander's religious competence to his soldiers, who were likewise his intended audience.

But the public character of religious communication not only had the effect of giving further levels of meaning to communication between humans and gods. Public exposure also played the role of a witness, lending extra weight to a communication that was otherwise so asymmetric and so liable to failure, or at least subjecting it to the scrutiny of socially tested rules of obligation, reciprocity, and deference.

Where the element of public witness was absent, written forms were available quite early in the Greco-Roman world, as is attested by curse tablets and inscribed votive texts.

4. Religion as a Strategy at the Level of the Individual

I have defined religion as the extension of a particular environment beyond the immediately plausible social milieu of living humans: and frequently also animals. Such an extension may involve forms of agency, ways of structuring identity, and means of communication. What enters into any given milieu that is beyond the "immediately plausible" can vary in ways that are entirely culture-dependent; plausibility, "worthiness of applause," is itself a communicative rhetorical category. In one instance it might apply to the dead, in another to gods conceived as having human form, or even to places whose location is not fixed in terms of mere topography, or to humans beyond a sea. What in a particular culture may be understood as not normally plausible depends on the boundaries drawn by the student of religion observing that culture. This is evident in the concentration on "gods" discernible in my own examples; but it can also be seen in demarcations such as my radical rejection of a boundary between religion and magic.[42]

A high degree of investment in the construction of initially implausible actors as "social partners" consistently produces in the person making that investment an "excess" of confidence, power, or problem-solving capacity, an outcome that in turn becomes precarious on account of the way it disadvantages others, who may then seek to defend themselves against it. Sacralization, declaring objects or processes in the immediately plausible, visible environment to be "holy," is one element of such an investment strategy.[43] The investment metaphor can easily be illustrated by the enormous outlay religions regularly devote to media, cult images, and sanctuaries, as well as to complex rituals and texts as strategies for communication, a topic I touched on above, under the heading "Religious Communication." We should also, however, think about the ways in which religion reinforces *inferior* status. This is a process that some affected individuals counter by efforts at social change within the religious context, while others turn their backs on religion to pursue social mobility on their own (when they do not turn to quietism).[44]

With these introductory observations, I have not sought to provide answers to the question of the great religious transformations, but rather to indicate the questions that still remain to be posed, the observations that yet need to be wrung from source material that is often all too sparse. I have also hinted at interdependencies and mechanisms of reinforcement in the field of religious development: the acquisition of competencies both strengthens communication and lowers the thresholds confronting it,[45] and a denser communication network intensifies the need on the part of the individual actor to develop more complex collective identities.[46]

This is not to say that this model describes a stable pathway, a definite evolutionary trajectory, or a system in equilibrium. Rather, over the course of time in many of the areas we need to consider, it is possible to observe movement in different and even contradictory directions. The processes we observe—individualization, mediatization, and institutionalization—are all commonly regarded as indicators of modernization rather than as facets of the religious history of the ancient Mediterranean. But, by observing these processes, and working with the concept of religion as we have defined it, we shall be able to accomplish our goal; namely, to observe and explicate the highly unstable phenomenon that is the religion of the ancient Mediterranean world in all its guises: the entire Pantheon.[47] Time after time in the following chapters, we shall see how each of these facets turns into an epochal process.

Our attention will turn first from the Mediterranean and Italy to various locations in central Italy and Etruria (chapters II–IV), where evidence is to be found that will ease our understanding of Iron Age religious practices. Only then will the narrative turn to Rome under the middle and late Republic (chapters V–VI) and in the Augustan Age (chapter VII). But Rome was never isolated, as will be made clear time and again in these chapters. It engaged in exchange and competition with other central-Italic centers and with actors around the Mediterranean. We will therefore turn our attention increasingly to this wider arena as we come to consider the Imperial Age, beginning with religious practices during the early part of that period (chapter VIII). Many developments regarding both the available store of religious signs (chapter IX) and the evolution of religious expertise and authority can be understood only in the context of the Mediterranean region as a whole, and the exchange of people, goods and knowledge that was given extra impetus by the Roman Empire (chapter X). This same broader context also becomes critically important when it comes to the self-conceptions and orientations of individuals and local groups, and continues to affect their religious conceptions and practices into Late Antiquity (chapters XI–XII). My narrative ends in the mid-fourth century: not with the end of Roman religion, nor with the privileging of Christian groups, nor with the expansion of Islam. Rather, the end-point, the culmination of all the far-reaching changes undergone in the course of history by the practices, conceptions, and institutions covered here, consists in the phenomenon now associated worldwide with the concept of "religion." And yet my epilogue (chapter XIII) seeks to demonstrate how open the situation still was in the fourth century, and how contingent has been the historical course since taken.

II

Revolutions in Religious Media in Iron Age Italy

THE NINTH TO SEVENTH CENTURIES BC

1. The Special

In the beginning was the house. And the house was inhabited: not by a god, but by people; and not by many people. In central Italy at the turn of the first millennium BC, the house, or rather the hut that is discernible to us through the spyglass of archaeological research, is small. The older longhouses, able to accommodate dozens of people, have gone out of fashion.

What is religion in this house? We adjust our focus, but still we do not yet see religion. No domestic altar, no statuettes, no sacrifice pit. A woman enters our field of view. She is perhaps in her mid-twenties, so she does not have so very much longer to live. She will probably die in childbirth. For us she has no name; of course, she has a name, but we do not know it. Without writing, history remains nameless: and in this region it will remain so for another two hundred years. But, as we speak of the woman, she begins to take on form, feelings, actions, a will of her own; so, why not also give her a name, one that she could have borne here in the hills of the west coast of central Italy? Let us call her Rhea.

We shall not ask Rhea about religion, but rather about what she wonders at, what goes beyond, transcends her everyday life, what she feels
is "special." She will probably begin with the loom. Here clothes for
protection and adornment are created from the wool of sheep. The
skill is passed on from generation to generation, but the patterns that
emerge are always new, varying from village to village, often from
family to family, and they are often the product of individual invention. This is the high technology of the hut, and it is special.[1] Rhea
will then probably point to the tableware: a few wooden vessels, but
above all ceramics. These too are high technology, but still homemade. Ceramics made by specialists will not be available for purchase
in the marketplace until the seventh century BC, a division of labor
that will prove momentous. As with weaving, the technical risk is
considerable. Just as the warp of a garment on the loom may tear, so
the wall of a pot may be too thin, its firing temperature too low, or the
firing time too long. Inclusions in the clay may harm not only the outward aspect of the vessel, but also its solidity, and faults in firing may
detract from its aesthetic effect.

Risks lurk in such vessels, however perfect, and in the route taken
by foodstuffs to reach them. This is probably the third area to which
Rhea will draw our attention. The things that can go wrong! Rooting
quadrupeds and foraging birds can forestall germination; rain and
wind, cold, drought, and heat can harm a whole variety of field crops,
reducing the yield dramatically, even life-threateningly. The necessity
to set aside a substantial part of this year's crop as seed for next year's
subsistence allows scant margin for error in the case of grains such as
einkorn. The same applies to many horticultural crops. When it comes
to animal husbandry, transhumance (the transfer between winter
and summer pastures) can be difficult and involve losses; and it may
take Rhea's man away from the hut for weeks at a time. Life is always
under threat; but it does not do to dwell on that.

When Rhea looks around her again, she may linger on the space
itself, the architecture, the hut. This form of dwelling, which provides
room for only a quite small nuclear family and its possessions, is not

merely a pragmatic alternative to living in a longhouse, a tent-like structure, or a cave (a much-practiced lifestyle, wherever easily worked volcanic rock made that form of dwelling—or rather that negation of an architectural form—possible). The many depictions of which I will soon speak suggest that the hut also has strong emotional meaning for Rhea, representing both the most substantial refuge in her uncertain life, and at the same time a technological miracle that has made a stable—although still precarious—whole out of a systematic assemblage of fragile components.

Whom should Rhea thank for this? Perhaps she would not understand the question. She has seen how the hut was built, how it has been repeatedly repaired; she knows what tasks she herself and others must perform outside, is aware of the difficulties involved in weaving, potting, and cooking, in transforming the unpalatable and thus unusable into the edible and useful. But she could also tell us that there are neighbors who say that success does not depend merely on one's own efforts, that there are others who have names but cannot be seen, whose help, or at least goodwill, is important or even vital. Many of these neighbors even take the trouble to set aside a part of their crop, as they do with seed, for those invisible aides and supporters, and they bring these gifts to special places where, although the "others" are still not to be seen (so say, at least, most of those who concern themselves with such matters), they can at least be contacted and addressed: in the caves or the foul-smelling springs at the fringe of the settlement. Rhea's words do not tell us much about what she thinks of all this; but we may imagine that, if times were really to become difficult, she might perhaps bring herself to ask those with more experience for names, and for the effective action to take.

The Religion of the Early Iron Age: Methodological Considerations

Rhea's story gives us access to an epoch in which the sources are thinly distributed, scattered, and above all not drawn together in contemporary written accounts. My narrative is a fiction, of course. It is my interpretation of the archaeological evidence, my attempt to develop a model for a religion that embodies situation-related action, is optional by nature, and above all—and this is the main thing that makes it graspable to us—represents a particular form of media-intensive communication. The story presents us with Rhea's "wonderment"; and certainly religious practices are quite apt to arouse wonderment. Our first task, however, is to discover those religious practices.

The situation in the latter part of the Bronze Age, roughly the twelfth and eleventh centuries BC in the western Mediterranean, differs very little from the scenario we can reconstruct for post–Mycenaean Greece: both are cultures without images of gods, without temples or priests. In the absence of writing and of contemporary accounts from literate Eastern cultures, any reconstruction remains dependent on archaeological sources. The evidence they provide is, however, rather limited. We may perceive intensified or more institutionalized religious activity in practices that differ from normal eating, in deposits that differ from normal deposits of waste, and in evidence that sites were used in ways that are inconsistent with everyday settlement patterns. But what is it about these features that makes them religious? What can we sensibly claim to be comparable with something that today, in the guise of religion, constitutes so important and dramatic an element of our lived experience, whether in the Americas, India, or Europe? The classic view recognizes very little as unquestionably "religious" beyond deposits that might be interpreted as "sacrifices." And such deposits, both because of the limits of archaeological technology and because so much of what might help us is perishable, are confined to a narrow range of offerings. Animal offerings are difficult to identify as "religious," unless the contexts in which the bones are found have already been interpreted as such on the basis of architectural remains.[2] Buried offerings or votive deposits are likewise scarcely discernible as such if their location has not already been interpreted as a site of ritual. Deposits in caves and springs, along watercourses or bodies of standing water, thus dominate the archaeological evidence until the Early Iron Age, into the tenth (and on into the ninth) century BC.[3]

What we find in such contexts are the very objects that we met in Rhea's story. Everyday items, some of them in miniaturized form, predominate. Only occasionally do we find accumulations of prestige objects such as weapons. This circumstance confounds attempts (and there have been many) to identify divine addressees by means of the specific qualities of objects or places: spindles do not indicate gods of weaving, any more than ceramics point to potter-gods. It is not that the evidence is inadequate here, but that the question is falsely posed. Archaeological discourse has taught us to see objects differently, especially in the context of the history of religion.[4] We read them as instruments of ritual, but also as objects that give rise to experience, such as that of wonderment at encountering an unfamiliar form; or as challenges to action, as in the case of a jug that "wants" to be filled with a liquid. People become attached to objects, associate memories and feelings with them; their production and care require effort, processes of exchange are involved, perhaps even the requirements of mobility; the biographies of humans and things become entangled. Under the perspective of religion, we can see how modes of activity, power, and personality are ascribed to objects. If under normal circumstances we perceive objects as special only by virtue of their extraordinary forms or materials, that is to say as a reflection of the exceptional financial means and perhaps cultural contacts of their donor, we must nevertheless assume that individuation,[5] or the subjectification of the individual, always occurred in specific contexts, in accord with a particular individual's acquired degree of sensibility in dealing with objects.[6] In this way, ancient religion too is capable of being reconstructed as "lived religion."[7]

2. The Transition from Bronze Age to Iron Age in the Mediterranean Region

The Space

Italy, Sicily, and Malta, together with Tunisia, form a central chain across the Mediterranean that was at various times less a dividing line than a bridge.[8] That bridge extends far to the north: the arc of the Alps was penetrable in multiple ways, canalizing rather than hindering cultural and economic exchange. This chain by no means stands alone: the Adriatic is a narrow body of water and did little to hinder contacts, often enduring ones, in the third and second millennia BC,[9] while at the same time Italy's east coast was inhospitable to coastal navigation and offered few harbors.[10] At the beginning of the second millennium BC, the main maritime routes out of the Aegean, both between what is now Greece and Turkey and from the Levant, the eastern Mediterranean, ran only to a few locations on Italy's south coast, through the straits to the Aeolian Islands, to Sicily, and from there to Sardinia or Malta. From that point on transport was indirect, with goods being carried via local coastal navigation. The degree of ease with which regions were accessible influenced the level of their cultural integration into the wider Mediterranean region. The large islands of Sicily and Sardinia[11] present a very different picture from the situation on the Italian west coast, only stretches of which are easily navigable (the Gulf of Naples and then, further to the north, in the central region of Latium and Tuscany).

Routes and destinations could change if winds and currents permitted. The involvement of Malta and the Aeolian Islands in the flow of traffic across the Mediterranean had clearly declined by the latter part of the Bronze Age at the end of the second millennium BC, while there was easy access to the northern Adriatic and so also to the Po estuary.[12] After the Minoans left the scene at the close of that millennium, these routes were taken up by Cypriot, Phoenician, and—beginning especially in the eighth century—also Greek merchants and craftsmen, who extended them into southern Spain and the valley of the Guadalquivir (Tartessos),[13] and of course to the Tunisian coast (Carthage!) and its hinterland. By the end of the second millennium and beyond, both the cultural and the material traffic along these routes appears to have been imbalanced, generally flowing more intensively in an east-to-west direction than from west to east. The extent of cultural exchange at individual locations depended greatly on the degree to which foreign goods were accepted by local groups and by the level of initiative shown by these groups, especially by their elites. With the exception of relations within the realm of Greater Greece, the degree of connectivity between the Levant and Greece was without parallel.[14]

The routes outlined here are significant in view of the rather short distances involved in the case of Italy: a situation very like that of Greece and the coast of Asia Minor. These routes gave rise to a disparate multitude of developments; particularly momentous were changes that they wrought in the few larger cultural and political spheres. In the wider Italian sphere, besides Sicily and Sardinia, the plain of the Po and the Etruscan region of central Italy are noteworthy; and, on the Iberian peninsula, the extreme southern sector (later to be Baetica). Southern France was long involved only indirectly, via regional contacts along the coastline, but itself played a highly significant role in exchanges with the more distant regions of northwestern Europe. A phase of extreme regional fragmentation, when there were no major political formations or corresponding monuments, can be detected about 1200 BC.[15] The megalith cultures, with their massive stone circles and stone structures, were gone, as were the social groups associated with them. This can be demonstrated for Malta in the south, and in the north for the British Isles.[16] The persistence of a megalithic sanctuary (fig. 1) such as Tas-Silġ on Malta is exceptional. At the same time, the dedication there of an only slightly older Mesopotamian import, a gilded crescent moon with a cuneiform inscription, shows that extra-regional influence at particular locations can easily be underestimated.

Developmental Models and Outcomes

Owing to highly varied regional social structures and levels of interaction, the transition from the Bronze Age to the Iron Age was also highly variable, in terms both of chronology and intensity. I intend to focus especially on two processes—social differentiation and urbanization—that have left their traces in the archaeological record. A wide range of factors determined whether a particular settlement

1. Mnajdra (Malta), Neolithic temple complex of the late fourth millennium BC.
akg-images / Rainer Hackenberg.

acquired the character of a city. Increases in the population of the
Mediterranean region may have underlain this process, and this demographic expansion may have been favored by the end of a very dry
period at about the turn of the millennium.[17] In every period, major
climatic changes have far-reaching consequences; and the highly disparate local consequences of global warming observable today suffice
to heighten our awareness of the problems involved in taking the sedi-
ment layers of a lake here, or the growth rings of a forest there, as a
basis for statements about other locations in such a physically varied
region as the Mediterranean.

   Differences do not, however, arise solely from the interpretation of
climate data. Alongside local evidence, research traditions in particular fields of study also play a significant role in the reconstruction of
social and cultural developments. In the case of Greece, the formation of social hierarchies and the foundation of cities are viewed
against the background of Homer's epics and the concept of the autonomous *polis*, familiar from ancient writings on political theory. In

Italy, on the other hand, a central role is ascribed to the Roman model of city-formation and monarchy, involving an aristocracy organized around great families, and on-going opposition between patricians (*gentes*) and plebeians (clients, a middle class).[18] Such tropes of scholarship have had an impact extending to the details of archaeological interpretation.

By the same token, religious practices, and burial practices in particular, are normally read as reflecting or expressing social differentiation. Alternatively, they can be understood as responses to the dictates of religious conceptions and beliefs, always with a view to the social position attained by the particular actor. Usually, religion is not perceived as an autonomous dimension, or in some circumstances even as a motor of social differentiation. Modern histories concentrate as a rule on technological challenges and property relationships, along with the long-term relationships of dependency that these engender.[19]

It must, though, be borne in mind that at this period changes in social organization were more rapid than technological advances, and were often short-lived. So far as the archaeological evidence allows us to judge, rituals and the religion-related manipulation of space and (even harder to perceive) time must have been among the most effective means of communicating an enduring message and guaranteeing the persistence of a social arrangement. What was critical was not that a prince should receive a princely tomb, but that the person who constructed the "princely" tomb should be seen as the son of a prince by his contemporaries (and by us). This perspective offers us an insight into "lived religion." It is significant that such tombs precede palatial houses by a span of some generations.[20]

Although the central concern of the first chapters of this book is Italy, and especially developments in central Italy, for purposes of comparison I must pay brief attention to developments in the Greek world. The example of "princely tombs" has once again brought us to surmise that, in such contexts, religious communication provided the actor with new competencies and options that could then find expression in his social position and perhaps also in his power. Confirmation in the case of Greece might lie in the fact that metal objects were manufactured for specifically religious uses, so that the use of the object in religion, in a funerary context, for example, was primary rather than secondary.[21] In the central sanctuaries of the palace period, we find rulers using the same objects as are used in many other settings, thus providing us with a link between such different contexts. Indeed, after the palace culture had ended, as early as the eleventh century we find cult sites of the palace period occasionally being reused.[22] More lavish and evolved cult practices more commonly took place in the houses of petty chieftains, although not in specifically designated cult spaces, and this usage appears to have persisted for a period after the establishment of larger public cult settings, a development begun in the ninth century.[23] Such structured locations coincided with the enlargement of political units, and provided a space for public celebrations marked not least by the communal consumption of meat.[24] In some instances, no substantial settlement formed in the vicinity of such cult sites, so that the sites did not come under the control of regional outposts of power until about 600 BC.

As in Italy, we see differentiation in the area of Greek burial practices. Here, religion offered opportunities either to create or consolidate social differences, or to mitigate them. Cremation spread rapidly from the twelfth century BC onward. It became associated with burial mounds of widely varying size, and burial goods of highly disparate quantity and quality. But the degree of variation never reached the proportions that we find in Etruscan-Latin burials of the same period. Beginning about 750 BC, there was a shift that saw the preponderance of religious outlay going to the erection of monumental stone sanctuaries, initially styled after contemporary domestic structures.[25] This is seen at first in only a few locations, of which Samos is a prominent example, but the trend spread quickly throughout the Greek and then the Greater Greek world. It had reached Rome by the sixth century BC.[26] At about this same time, and with equal speed, we see an increase in the production of large-format, often greater than life-size votive offerings. These were for the most part fully three-dimensional depictions (if not portraits) in wood,[27] bronze (*sphyrelata*),[28] clay, or stone, and may have represented donors, both male and female. These locations became sites for aristocratic self-promotion, and began to compete with one another. In several cases, their rivalries found expression in actual competitions, such as the games at Olympia (traditionally founded in 776 BC) and in Corinth.[29]

If we turn our attention from the eastern to the western side of Italy, to Sardinia, we observe the marked continuity[30] of the originally Early Bronze Age Nuragic culture, with its multitude of local stone structures, which perhaps also had ritual functions. These continued in use, but after about 1000 BC, no new examples were being built.[31] The use of exotic materials distinguishes a small number of them as projects built by elites able to obtain materials from distant sources, but they nonetheless served at the local level as foci for identity formation. This was associated with a particular practice. Individuals, or groups in ritual contexts, maintained a tradition of inserting small bronze figurines into the cracks in the walls.[32] The figures and the scenes they represented may have referred to oft-told stories, and seeing the visible parts of the figurines would have reminded viewers of these tales. This not only gave assurance of a shared narrative world but, combined with the occasional use of scenes with reference to current events and personal motifs in a building constantly renewed and under constant use, would have invested both the structure and its location with a sense of permanence, of being eternally there for the use of the people. Here too, religion appears to have played its part in enabling and stabilizing a developed sense of territoriality: it is hard to imagine that just anyone would have been entitled to contribute his or her figurine. We do not know the content of the stories linked to the figurines; but we can establish that clearly recognizable deities are represented by at least a minority of the anthropomorphic figures.[33] The stability of both the practice and the local culture may be gauged by the fact that local development appears to have been largely unaffected by an influx of imports and the presence of Phoenician traders or craftsmen.[34]

3. Ritual Deposits

We will return now to the subject of the "special" as exemplified in central Italy at the beginning of the Iron Age. In southern Latium, some sixty kilometers south of Rome on the little river Asturia, lie the sites of Campoverde and, a few kilometers further south and downstream, Satricum. The people of this area, which must surely have constituted a political unit, had the custom of throwing ceramic vessels, both miniaturized and of normal size, into pits dug into earlier habitation levels and into the Laghetto del Monsignore, a small spring-fed lake near Campoverde. Not all shapes are found in both sizes, but it can be demonstrated in at least some instances that vessels of both sizes were manufactured at the same place and by the same techniques.[35] Although ceramics form the bulk of the surviving finds, inhabitants of the surrounding settlements also deposited pearls and bronze items, such as fibulae and metal figurines.[36]

Handmade ceramics, the dominant component of these deposits, may well seem commonplace, but they stand for a complex technology, a nonintuitive manufacturing process, whose products are, ideally, used and repaired over periods of years. The use of items of pottery as a means to communicate with actors whose presence is not beyond dispute (to return to my earlier theme) was frequently associated with the offering of food, which required preparation that may have been no less complex. Garden and field produce often required processing before it could be used in the home. The same technological complexity would apply to the manufacture of textiles, and, although these do not normally appear in the archaeological evidence, spindle whorls and other implements associated with looms and spinning are not uncommon.[37] The rare metal objects are the products of yet another complex production process.

All these objects can be understood not only as items of exchange,[38] but also as representing the female or male donor, both in and beyond the act of deposition. Longstanding familiarity prior to deposition—many of the objects show signs of long use[39]—cause the "biographies" of object and donor to become intertwined. This shared history bestows meaning on the act of separation and the object's continuance (although invisible) at a particular place, giving relevance to both.[40] Miniaturizations, which is to say the production of objects specifically for deposition, creates that relevance at the very moment of production, anticipating their later use.

Closer to Rome, and also in Latium, lies Gabii, where a collection of huts marks a settlement that dated from the ninth century BC at the latest. This site, too, is one example of a widespread phenomenon that saw cult sites moving from the outer edges of an agricultural area to sites closer to domestic settlements. Beginning at the end of the eighth century, one location here took on special significance as a place where objects were regularly deposited.[41] No temple was erected at the location, however, until the first half of the sixth century. The inhabitants of Gabii again frequently used miniatures in order to communicate with their (spiritual) counterparts; even miniature loaves of bread have been found.[42] The small size may indicate that the objects were never meant to be used before being deposited in a pit; or, at the very least, that the actors renounced any prospect of continuing to have them in sight, which was certainly the case at Laghetto del Monsignore. The archaeological evidence is not always clear in this regard. In many cases, the objects must surely have been displayed in the open air, or, later, in temple structures, then to be cleared away and buried at lengthy intervals. Miniaturizations are in any case to be found from the Neolithic period onward, and their use was widespread in the Late Bronze and Early Iron Ages.

What aspects of life in the Early Iron Age led to this use of specifically domestic objects as media for communication between human actors and their not-quite-tangible counterparts, communication that often took place in unusual natural spaces such as caves, or, in the Bronze Age, in "contaminated water" from volcanic contexts,[43] and then, increasingly, in special locations closer to settlements? Such objects presumably embodied associations with manufacture and the risks of material faults in the manufacturing process—in firing or weaving—as has already been mentioned, and were likewise liable to destruction, breakage, and loss. How did these factors contribute to the use of such objects as media for communication with beings who were not quite accessible by normal means? What violations of every-day experience, what "transcendences" of varying degree[44] were being addressed, memorialized here, and at the same time rendered accessible not only to the gods, but also to the archaeologist? Or were these direct attempts at intervention in such events? To what extent was there a connection between these rituals and the extreme tran-scendences that might be encountered within the limits of a particular human life—for example famine, accident, illness, or a child's death? These questions do not admit of answers for this period. Only centu-ries later does a fundamental change in the form of communication become discernible. The intensive spread of healing cults, made man-ifest in the deposition of replicas of parts of the body,[45] emerges only in the latter part of the fifth century BC, when it may be read as the expression of a new relationship to the body and a new concept of self.[46]

The extension of communicative activity to addressees and actors who are not indisputably plausible in everyday terms, but are none-theless addressed in a form of communication that signals a high degree of relevance, is characteristic of the religion of this period and this geographical area. Relevance is signaled by the deployment of objects with which the religious actors are intimately associated, whether through their use in the home and contribution to the per-petuation of the family,[47] or by the difficulty and high degree of risk involved in their manufacture. Worth mentioning here are the few in-cidences of animal sacrifice in the Italian Middle and Late Bronze Age that do not accompany burials; these typically involve dogs closely associated with the home, or game animals whose killing involved risk, or at least an unusual degree of effort.[48]

But religious communication is not limited to confidential conver-sation between human initiators and their more problematically tangible counterparts. The expansion of active options created by the attribution of initiatives and influences in concrete situations to nonhuman actors, whose involvement need not be entirely, or even at all, accepted by all human actors, gives rise to a form of *religious* action that also changes interhuman relations, either increasing the power and creative ability of the actor, because he is supported by those nonhuman actors and sees himself as their instrument, or consigning him to passivity. We are aware of such quietism in more recent religious history,[49] but it leaves no archaeologically discernible traces. Thus, while we cannot exclude the possibility that the phenomenon also existed in antiquity, this cannot be proven.

In both cases, religious action can also be strategic action. The religious actors perform a dual role in the situation, defining a religious identity and at the same time entering into a dual contest: for social prestige and for the highest degree of attention from the divine counterpart. Both contests can assume an entirely paradoxical form: a demonstrative renunciation by the actor of his or her personal power to dispose of things as he or she desires, or conspicuous consumption, involving considerable expenditure of material resources.

The equating of ritual distinction with social differentiation is one of the key concepts underlying the interpretation of early ritual practices, especially those discernible during the transition between the Bronze and the Iron Age, which are in fact seen as periods of social and ethnic differentiation.[50] The underlying social picture is one in which property, external and social contacts, and aesthetic and religious practices march in step with power, status, and prestige, leading to a unified hierarchy. This fundamental assumption is problematic. The alternative perspective is that of a heterarchy, in which the positions of individuals can vary on different scales, so that precedence in any particular circumstance becomes a matter of negotiation. This opens new, and in my estimation more fruitful, perspectives on the evidence that we have from antiquity.[51] I would, however, like to stress that the degree to which ritual acts of religious communication are visible on a lasting or even a short-term basis is often slight. As a rule, we know little about the audience. The absence of a geographical correlation between pre- and Early Iron Age sites of religious activity and specific settlements affords no grounds for assuming communal activities that would confirm the reality of such acts of witness. We should accordingly be cautious regarding claims of collective activities. These are only occasionally discernible, as, for example, in some cases of animal sacrifice connected with collective burials.[52] This has implications. It will be difficult for "traditions" to develop if, frequently, only a few people are present. Thus, while on the one hand the practice of deposition shows us that people used this method to enter into communication with their invisible counterparts, on the other hand, owing to a scarcity of evidence, our ability to interpret their specific intentions and thoughts is likewise restricted.

4. Burials

Burials are among the oldest of practices that afford a tangible view of religion, and they are also distinguished by their great variety and by the rapid rate at which they can change, even within restricted geographical areas and brief periods of time. In Italy, cremation and the deposition of ashes in urns spread from the north, beginning in the twelfth century BC, probably under the influence of the Urnfield Culture of central and northwestern Europe.[53] The burial of urns in close proximity to one another, in what were probably family graves, became more systematic and was coordinated with settlement areas. At the same time, there was a longstanding tradition of infant burials close to or within houses. Bronze Age cave burials ceased almost entirely,[54] although deposition at remote spring sites continued. Where they buried their fellows was evidently not a matter of indifference to the inhabitants of these settlements. In establishing a burial location, a space for the dead, at an accessible distance, they were also saying something about the space devoted to a community that comprised both the dead and the living. An established location for the one implied an established location for the other. They thus laid claim to and demarcated an entire territory as theirs, as opposed to the territory of others. Of course, this arrangement was not fundamentally new. The same method of establishing territoriality through the placement of cemeteries, that is to say burial sites maintained by several people over a certain period, had already been developed at several locations

2. Ash urn in the form of a hut, bronze with lead in the double floor; 28.5 cm high,
40.5 cm long, 35.7 cm wide, ca. 800–750 BC, from the Osteria Necropolis
at Vulci, Tomba della Cista litica. Rome, Museo Nazionale di Villa Giulia,
inv. 84900/01. akg-images / Andrea Baguzzi.

in the world by the ninth millennium;[55] but concrete instances had
never endured for more than limited periods.

How did burials occur? The use of hut urns (fig. 2) became standard from the ninth century onward[56] in many places in the area of
the Villanovan culture (northern Italy south of the plain of the Po), and
subsequently in Etruria and Latium. That the residents of eighth-century
Vulci, an Etruscan center and by no means a remote settlement, could
opt instead for direct cremation in a longitudinal pit (*fossa*)[57] indicates the availability of a spectrum of choices even in the context of
funerary "fashions." When people model vessels in the form of huts
for the cremated remains (ashes and incompletely burned remnants
of bone), we are reminded of Rhea contemplating what was "special"
in her life, a life always threatened by imminent death, especially for a

REVOLUTIONS IN RELIGIOUS MEDIA   41

woman of child-bearing age. Final accommodation for the dead is designed with the domestic sphere very much in mind.[58] One could not think of the dead without calling to mind that the living share their fate.

Alliances of settlements based on kinship, proximity, or some broader criteria brought into play other decisions regarding burial sites—decisions that might either precede or follow those regarding residential alliances. In a series of locations, we see how dispersed settlements on a tufa plateau united from the ninth century BC onwards. The decision of such a larger united settlement either to use a common burial site or to continue to maintain distinct sites, might give expression both to the complexity of the integration process and to persistent conflicting claims.[59] Competition between burial districts can be read in entirely contrasting layouts set completely apart from settlement areas, or in the use of settlement areas.[60] We see the various options available for this form of religious activity exploited in Orvieto, where a necropolis was laid out in the mid-sixth century on a systematic plan of parallel streets, the same pattern chosen in Cerveteri in about 530 BC (fig. 3), while settlements in Marzabotto did not adopt such a layout until the end of that century.[61]

However, it is not local circumstances alone that are articulated by the way forebears or children are buried. Grave goods point to intensive trans-Mediterranean exchange during the so-called Orientalizing Period, from the late eighth through the mid-seventh century BC. This is evidence of trading contacts extending as far as Spain, and also presupposes close collaboration and intensive learning on the part of craftsmen, as well as a transregional orientation on the part of indigenous elites who were in communication with incoming colonial elites. In the field of religion too, interaction was at play, and not mere reception.[62]

As I have suggested above, an element of instability is introduced to ritual traditions when there is a high degree of variation between locations[63] and, in the case of more densely spaced burials, within the same location. In Pontecagnano, situated north of the Sele in Campania, repeated attempts were made to regulate burial practices between

3. Tumuli tombs in the Banditaccia Necropolis at Cerveteri/Caere,
sixth to fifth century BC. Photo: J. Rüpke.

the late eighth and second quarter of the sixth century. The intent was
to standardize practices and to curb ostentatious assemblages of grave
goods. At the same time, however, contrasting changes can be seen
taking place in topographically distinct areas of the necropolis. One
group chooses to express male exclusivity, while another extends the
same kind of lavish burials to women and children of every age.[64]
Here too, the question arises as to how extensively any particular
practice was used by a population. Who, in fact, made the investment
underlying the burials detected by the archaeologist? What proportion of the local population is attracting our attention in this way? An
evolutionary perspective on history, the sort commonly taken by researchers with a cognitive orientation, often assumes perfect uniformity in the propagation of cultural practices: what is successful in an
individual case is adopted by all, or at least by all those who survive
long-term; and the adoption process is typically rapid. Ritual burial
(as opposed to the mere disposal of a corpse) would under this

perspective have long been a universal practice. The concept of religion developed at the beginning of this chapter, which places emphasis on the risk, even the possibility of failure, involved in religious action, makes such a scenario less likely, and this is supported by the archaeological evidence. Skepticism is called for in the face of the widespread assumption that any particular burial practice was common to all members of a society, and thus suffices as a comprehensive documentation of that society in so far as its cemeteries are concerned:[65] a comparison of settlement sizes on the one hand with documented burials on the other suggests that, here too, we see a range of particular classes and individuals who opted for or against an investment that exceeded the strictly necessary level, and for or against the corresponding visible practices. Even social pressures need not be homogeneous.

The concept of religion that we outlined at the outset requires that burial practices be included in the category of religion. In outward appearance, these practices seem to consist in methods of subterranean deposition, and it would seem that their aim was to establish or further a relationship with actors who were no longer indisputably plausible. Once again, we must remember that it remains unclear what precise ontological view of the status of these actors was associated with the practices in question. Some participants may have had concerns for the "care" of the dead or for their "survival after death," but such metaphors cannot be deemed adequate to explain fully what was going on. Our purpose, however, is not to ascertain what conceptions were current regarding the actors at the other side of the situation, the dead, but rather to explore the actions, identity, and means of communication of those actors indisputably present within the situation: that is, the living. Where direct sources are lacking, we must turn to historical and ethnographical comparison, while avoiding the pitfall of confounding the evidence with modern practices that, though they may coexist within the same space that contains the ancient, the Judeo-Christian, and the Islamic, are nonetheless products of a markedly different technological environment, one that also bears the stamp of rationalism.

The main problem after a death may well have resided in the necessity to redefine and reshape social relationships, sometimes to a radical extent.[66] The more central the deceased was to the internal organization of the family group and its external relations, the more urgently this problem posed itself to the people of the Early Iron Age (and far beyond). The death of a small child or an aged parent (40 or 50+ years old) may have been emotionally harrowing. From the perspective of its significance for relationships, however, the death of an important person such as a mother or father would have had more consequences for the family group. The father's death turned wives into widows and children into partial orphans, or full orphans if, as is probable, the mother had died in her final childbed. A son would then become the "head of the family." More radical still for members of the wider settlement group, the death of such a significant figure may have entailed a loss of prestige, influence, property, or shares in income. The continued presence of the deceased might avert these threats, if his continued relevance was thereby rendered plausible. An individual enjoying intimate communication with the deceased could then, conceivably, lay claim to the respect, authority, and property that had belonged to that deceased, could see to it that these were transferred to himself as the deceased's intimate, and then could instill this new status into the memory of the wider group, and perhaps monopolize it.[67]

The corpse per se can play only a very brief role in such interactions, unless the technically complex and costly option of mummification is employed. But individual body parts can be preserved more easily, whether by desiccation (as shrunken heads in western South America) or skeletonization. In some cases the loss of soft tissues—by cremation, by a temporary so-called primary burial,[68] or by exposure in the open air—might even be reversed by subsequent remodeling, of the skull for example. Sustained and substantial manipulation of parts of the corpse, such as the skull, is widely attested in the eastern-Mediterranean Neolithic.[69] By possessing the ancestors, and keeping them to hand in one's own house or on one's own land, communication with them might be controlled and even, again, monopolized. This circumstance might persist for generations or it might end after a few years or even months, with perhaps a secondary and final burial. Burial of the entire corpse within the shortest possible time predominated in Italy in the first millennium BC. A few hours or days of "lying in" apparently obviated the need for longer-term communication with the body parts of the deceased. Only a few instances of secondary burial are to be found in Late Bronze Age burial sites; these suggest a more prolonged use of bones,[70] and would signal dramatic differences in the way some families managed their public dealings with their dead. Such dramatic differences may be due to the fact that some, perhaps many individuals were already reluctant to employ conspicuous burial and continued care of the burial site, preferring instead to secure the continuing relevance of deceased family members for communication within the local community, or as a means of asserting their own identity as members of a family. These differences, and also the rapid rate of change in ways of dealing with the dead—now full inhumation, now cremation, now deposition in an urn, now burial of the remains of the funeral pyre, or the burning of bodies in a pit grave— have led to the surmise that it was not a question of giving ritual and material expression to conceptions of the "being," the ontology of the deceased; but rather, that these varying practices reflect highly uncertain conceptions of death, notions that were always subject to revision.

What is there to say about these conceptions, these assumptions that are made over and over again in various situations, though perhaps only implicitly? Those who introduced "relics" of their deceased forebears or family members as relevant objects into their actions and communications may have been trying to reference the individual's status within the family or the locality, or perhaps to summon something of his or her personal qualities. Primary and secondary burials in our own day, however, only rarely allow us to draw conclusions as to prior perceptions of the deceased. They provide no basis for generalizations. The notion that the contents of a solitary burial are meant to individualize the deceased runs up against the fact that grave contents are often of a rather generic, conventional nature. Moreover, grave markers may be absent or they may fail to include a portrait of

the deceased. Grave goods were in any case rare in the Italian Late
Bronze Age. Where they later became more frequent, the question
remained open as to how far generic-seeming objects should be associated with this specific buried person, perhaps as personal equipment or because the individual made them. While the cremation
and subsequent collection and deposition of cremated remains in
urns permitted a brief though intensive manipulation of the corpse
between the gathering up of the ashes and the burial of the bones
(and that period may have lasted longer in individual cases), that
same process then removed the remains once and for all from further dealings, and from any possibility of being presented in its earlier likeness. Here we may speculate about conceptions. Was it
thought that the highly distinctive and conspicuous act of cremation allowed the individual to become one with the ancestors? Was
there an ontological transition in play, one that was further referenced by the frequent use of miniaturizations, which are especially
common in cremation burials?[71] From this stage of the ritual process onward, communication with these actors, whose presence was
now less than certain, would then take on the same form as communication with "gods."

We can in fact even observe this in the case of particular individuals. L. Velchaina from Caere used the same objects to communicate
visibly with gods at cult sites as he did to communicate at graves with
the dead.[72] We owe this information to the fact that, in both cases, by
inscribing the objects, he made it clear to posterity that it was he
who had entered into communication in this way, and he who had
something important to say. That this was important to him and to
others is indicated by the selection of the objects, but what exactly
that importance consisted in still eludes us. The items of crockery and
the spindle whorls we have already mentioned are to be found both
in graves and in other deposits; replicas of amphoras or of other
objects represent risky production processes, which gives added
weight to their link with the donor's person. These "exclamation
marks," these references to the actor, are characteristic of religious

communications: that is, with the process of making a connection between the living and the dead, in the same way as in communication with other actors whose presence is less than certain.

5. Gods, Images, and Banquets

It is in the miniaturization of grave goods that we find a parallel between these objects and other means of relating to nonhuman agents who were not one's own ancestors but rather "gods." Without images and dedicated sites, clearly distinguishable representations or symbols, reliable texts or established teachings, the differentiation and personalization of these actors is both difficult and uncertain. The naming-practices of a later period are accessible to us in written form in both Etruscan and Roman sources, and these make it clear that there were groupings of gods called by the same name and variations between singular and plural forms of names. The gender of these actors is not constant; their relationships to one another are also unstable, expressed in adjectival or genitival forms:[73] Turms of Hades (*turmś aitaś*); Thesan of Tin (*θesan tinś*); Lasa, Acolyte of the Demiurge (*lasa achunanu*).[74]

On phonological and semantic grounds, however, it is certain that the names of gods and goddesses had already stabilized within language groups by the Bronze Age, prior to renewed contacts in the Iron Age, and that these names were in widespread use. Examples of such ancient names from the Etruscan are Menerva, Uni (Italic), Nethuns, Suri, Tinia, and Turan.[75] As they were regularly used in religious communication during the Bronze and Early Iron Age, they came into use in interpersonal communications as well and thus achieved both currency and stability. "Come, Tinia," "Menerva has appeared," "Sacrifice to Veive," "Usil has come," "dedicated to Maris." With such an array of possible invocations, affirmations of presence, petitions for intercession, and calls to worship, it would seem that participants had freedom to choose whatever mode of address they thought best suited the occasion or would best meet their needs, and then pass these along to others for their own use. For all its instability, what we have here is a cultural apparatus that both delimits individual religious behavior and lends credibility to religious communication, while at the same time depending on individual acts of appropriation.[76] There was by no means a structured "pantheon," but a shared knowledge base came into being that could be expanded by incomers, especially if they brought compelling religious elements into the conversation. The names of *Menerva*, Juno, and *Nethuns* reached Veii by this route. They arrived in both Greek and Latin forms, and then took root, acquiring their own cult sites.[77]

Images

As far as we know, large-format images play no role in Italy before the 6th century BC. We know of anthropomorphic faces in ceramics as early as the Early Neolithic, especially on vessels not intended for daily use. Images of people were clearly quite special.[78] In the Italian Bronze Age too, people made images of people. These took the form of urns fashioned anthropomorphically, depicting facial characteristics in particular; later, sculptors and ceramicists began to decorate bronze and clay vessels with small-scale reliefs depicting human or animal figures (fig. 4).[79] Despite a predilection for such images at various locations (and often only at defined periods), the impetus for life-sized representations appears to have come from outside: perhaps reaching such places as Cerveteri from the region of Syria in the first half of the seventh century.[80] The adoption process was surely a complex one, for life-size objects could not have been transported. It must instead have been ideas, concepts of representation, and schemes of design that made the necessary journey over thousands of kilometers. Traveling craftsmen were no doubt crucial, as were patrons interested in the new and unusual, especially if it might add to their prestige. We have legends, recorded in the first centuries BC and AD, to the effect that Demaratus, father of the Roman king Tarquinius Priscus, fled from Corinth and brought Corinthian craftsmen with him to Tarquinia.[81] If the seated pair of tomb occupants depicted in the Tomba delle Statue at Ceri near Cerveteri (fig. 5) is representative of this

4. Benvenuti Situla, detail with animals and returning warriors. Bronze, embossed and engraved; 25.5 cm high, 25.5 cm diam. at the mouth, ca. 600 BC, from Este, Villa Benvenuti, tomb 126. Este, Museo Nazionale Atestino, inv. 4667. akg-images / Cameraphoto.

process, then the translation was not merely a matter of reinterpreting sculptures of royals as funerary sculpture: what was a Syrian expression of hegemonic power had to be recast in a plausibly Etruscan guise. The notion of projecting one's status and perhaps power by means of monumental architecture provided the needed context.[82] In Etruria this began in the field of funerary structures, for there were ancient precedents in the form of *tumuli* (massive funerary mounds) to serve as models.

The willingness of rich Etruscans to risk such far-reaching experiments indicates how attractive this mode of portraying those who were geographically absent or no longer among the living must have been. It reveals perhaps a certain common feeling between these Etruscan actors and the Greek patrons who, at about this same time, and after a period largely lacking in representational images,[83] began to

5. Stone figures, under life size, from the Tomba delle Statue, Cerveteri/Caere, 700–650
BC. Drawing by Giovanni Colonna, reproduced with her kind permission.

commission the life-sized and over-life-sized Korai and Kouroi. Many
visitors to the cult site at Lavinium, from the mid-sixth century onward, had themselves portrayed in the form of clay statues; but the
practice was still far more widespread in Latium.[84] This was certainly
a genre with a great deal of appeal, for there is evidence that it pene-
trated the Celtic world north of the Alps. The life-sized terracotta figure
from the Glauberg in Hesse, adorned with its crown of leaves, probably
also dates from the 6th century BC.[85] (And here again we are reminded
that, thanks to the passes that traverse them, the Alps were not the
hindrance to communication that one might imagine.) It was probably thanks to their knowledge of large-scale Greek sculptures that the
Etruscan elites not only produced their first monumental domestic
architecture, but also surmounted these houses with statues of their
ancestors. The palace at Murlo (fig. 6) was one of the earliest large

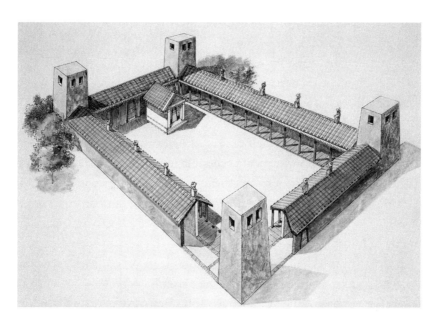

6. Palace of Murlo/Pioggio Civitate, reconstruction with statues on the roof. 7th/6th century BC. Drawing by Giovanni Colonna, reproduced with her kind permission.

private buildings to be adorned in this way. Its owners perhaps used its inner courtyard in the same way that later Roman senators used atria: for rituals and communication with the gods.[86] But to interpret the whole structure as a cult venue would not be justified.[87] The miniature houses and urns in the form of huts were also provided with such images.[88] It was not until this time that we begin also to find statues of gods on the roofs of buildings that can be interpreted as temples, and only sometime later that such statues were placed inside temples as cult images.

Temples and Religious Differentiation

In ever more densely populated settlements, inhabitants now lived in close daily contact with one another. Religious activity, too, moved from the edges of the territory into the center, and, by the seventh century BC, some individuals had introduced into urban spaces the form of religious messaging that in this period spoke the loudest, namely performance at monuments. By the sixth century BC, they had erected freestanding temples in central Italy.[89] If their intent in making such investments was strategic, then they certainly succeeded in stealing a distinct march on their competitors, whether it was a case of rivalry between individuals and families in the same town, or between towns. But such initiatives also established standards of religious practice. Through their choice of dedications, they determined which god would now be most accessible to people, and they imposed the ritual forms that best suited the unusual elevated, stage-like architecture of the temple with its frontal orientation and strong circuit walls.[90] Presumably familiar with Greek temple structures, either directly or indirectly, the residents of Francavilla Marittima in Calabria had already built their first verifiable temple in the early seventh century BC, out of wood initially, and then later in stone.[91]

By the sixth century BC, isolated monumental structures no longer held sway. Settlements with their carefully laid out streets and stone buildings were coalescing into what could without reservation be called cities, whether Tarquinia[92] or Rome. As we have already seen, there had previously been a dearth of architecturally designed central spaces for religious communication, with the exception of leveled-off areas at tomb entrances and similar but much larger leveled areas on burial mounds.[93] At the latter locations, the principal individual actors would probably have been chosen on the basis of family status, or because they had attained status by assuming religious responsibilities. The city lacked not only the spatial infrastructure of religion, but also the human infrastructure. There was no permanent force of religious actors, nothing like a hierarchy of priests. Religious activity was situation-based, even though it involved considerable repetition. Priest-like figures arose now and then, but there was little continuity. In Etruria in the Early Iron Age and Archaic Period, local magnates drew on the sacred symbolism of the eastern Mediterranean monarchies by, for example, adopting sphinxes in their imagery,[94] but any efforts they may have made to establish a permanent religious authority were rare and short-lived. Such initiatives might become visible to contemporaries when, in real situations or in imagery, systematic use

7. *Lituus*, bronze; 36.5×2.5 cm from a chamber tomb at Caere. Rome,
Museo Nazionale di Villa Giulia. akg-images.

was made of a *lituus*, the bent staff of a
priest (figs. 7, 8), instead of an axe pointing to the power of a magistrate. Was the
lituus a symbol of priesthood? The axe?
Revealingly, we first see experimentation with such symbols in the context
of burials, and only later in iconography
outside of necropolises.[95]

8. Denarius of Pomponius Molo,
Numa with *lituus* on obverse, 97 BC.
Photo: Classical Numismatic
Group (CC-BY-SA 2.5).

In sixth- and fifth-century Rome too,
there were claims to religious authority. These were raised on various
grounds and, again, only occasionally. As we shall see, there was no
conception of stable priestly roles, nothing like a coordinated hierarchy.[96] But where was the basis for a sustained, overarching system of
religious authority to be found? Communication by individuals with
their own ancestors was certainly significant, but merely at the local
level; it would have been of marginal relevance in the context of increasingly fortified and complex cities. As for the Latin tombs, some
were indeed so sumptuous that we can call them "princely," but we do

not know whether they, let alone their opulent contents, even remained visible after what must have been equally opulent funerary ceremonies.[97]

We know neither the extent nor the visibility of another social practice of this period. The consumption of wine, which began in the ninth century, developed during the "Orientalizing Period," into a banquet culture, with goblets and pitchers finding their way to cult sites and into tombs.[98] The enjoyment of wine remained a luxury activity, its regular use being confined to wealthy households. In the following period, it became associated with Dionysian imagery.[99] This may have been an ancient legacy, or perhaps an attempt to give legitimacy to a criticized lifestyle by giving it a religious patina. In any event, prominent depictions of banquets were avoided in Latium from the fifth century onward. In Veii and even Anagni, on the other hand, there were many who found fit to draw attention to their attachment to the culture of wine by displaying banqueting paraphernalia in cult sanctuaries.[100] At least when it comes to Latium, however, we may dismiss the notion that this particular brand of religious activity supported the establishment of sustained religious roles and forms of authority. It can be assumed, however, that drinkers (and in Latium this included females) continued undaunted to pursue this cultural ritual, which was surely conducive to the maintenance of their social networks.

Italian religion also deviated from the pattern set in the ancient Orient, in that it did not produce a religious literature; this although writing had been adopted, further developed, and disseminated by the second half of the eighth century. This was not due to any restrictions on written scholarship. More likely the literate and priestly *Etrusca disciplina* simply came late, as a reaction to Roman expansion rather than an original mark of a revealed religion. But that will be the subject of a later chapter.[101]

III

Religious Infrastructure

THE SEVENTH TO THE FIFTH CENTURIES BC

1. Houses for Gods

The settlement identified today with Satricum sits on a spur of a steep escarpment a good hundred meters to the west of the little river Astura, some fifteen meters above its bank and downstream from Campoverde (which featured in the previous chapter).[1] In the late ninth century BC, several small groups, probably families, came together at this spot and built huts around a small body of water formed by a spring. Within a hundred years, communal life had stabilized so that closer attention was paid to the position of the huts relative to one another, and common areas and access ways had been reserved and gradually paved. By the second half of the seventh century, the huts were not only of differing sizes, but now also had walls of wattle and plaster and were roofed with tiles.

The dead were buried in the near vicinity, and those who wished to converse with invisible named actors presumably also went to nearby locations. These remain unknown to us, but they were probably not as remote as Laghetto del Monsignore. A new possibility arose at some time around 600 BC. Over what was probably a rather long period of time, objects had been finding their way into a pit within the

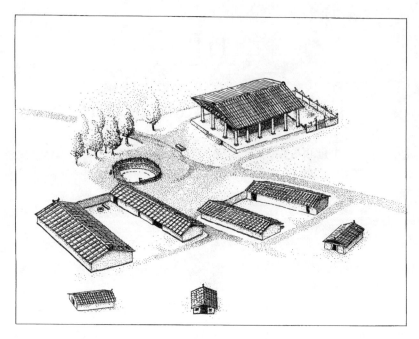

9. Plan of Satricum, the archaic phase of the acropolis. Reconstruction by Marianne Kleibrink, reproduced with her kind permission.

settlement, close to the main street, which had meanwhile been well paved. A rectangular house was now built in front of this pit (fig. 9). The house, with a solid roof and terracotta decoration, was of a type that was standard for only a few decades before larger houses of horseshoe design became the norm.

Who was responsible for this new building? What did it contain? As the answers to these questions lie beyond the scope of archaeology, the only tools that are left to hand are comparison and speculation. The structural finds indicate that Satricum was a community engaged intensively in communication, but not a community of equals. Economic inequality was not concealed; it was in fact given a kind of deliberate staging in the necropolis situated to the northwest of the settlement.[2] But this inequality did not prevent the development of an infrastructure from which all profited: the network of streets, and above all the road that enabled connections beyond the immediate region. Enduring, visible religious activity, on the other hand, came late to the settlement, and developed during a phase of intense social differentiation.

Innovation

Those who erected this new building devoted to religious communication—and they may as well have been female as male—were clearly engaged in competition with other locales at the settlement's periphery. Theirs was not an action calculated to express a common identity. Their aim was to ensure that the building would be appealing, both by its proximity and, even more, by its architectural design. While space was still reserved within or outside the building for the traditional practice of deposition, the building itself offered something entirely new, an innovation that was at once architectural and religious. "Monumentalization"[3] lent an immediately perceptible aura of authority to the building as a religious structure, as did its optimal setting. The entrepreneur (or entrepreneurs) who, in about the year 600, undertook this project, was perhaps concerned less with sheltering an image of a god[4] than with providing a location where objects could be displayed that would then finally be deposited in the pit, in a gradual process or as need arose. We do not know, however, whether all objects reached the pit via the building.

Unfortunately, we cannot identify the builders of the new structure with any precision. The evidence provided by Satricum's dwellings and graves is insufficient to indicate either an acephalous or an autocratic regime. What we do know is that our first evidence of religion and religious innovation comes from the central core, the focal point of settlement, on the so-called acropolis. Did the initiative come from the richest family, or from the genius who saw to the paving of the streets? Was it perhaps a benefaction from the lady who owned the most beautiful house? Or maybe the act of some individual or some small group that feared losing its position in the community? We cannot know the answer. What *is* self-evident is the innovative spirit that this undertaking demonstrates, and the degree of risk involved.

The example of Greece makes it clear that only local significance can be attached to the term "innovation." The number of locations recognizably designed to receive depositions increased markedly over the course of the eighth century BC. At the beginning of the century, these sites were normally open to the elements; by its close, approximately half were provided with structures of some kind.[5] Three types can be distinguished. First, in the region of the Cyclades, for example on Delos and on Crete, we typically find a rectangular dwelling furnished with a bench, probably intended to accommodate objects for use in communicating with superhuman agents possessing (ancient)[6] names but (as yet) no form. Such objects have frequently been found in the gap behind the bench in such dwellings. Common on the Greek mainland and in western Asia Minor is a second structural type: a long, narrow house with a rounded apse at one of the narrow ends. The interior was accessed via a vestibule or veranda that opened into a hall with a steep roof, and there is sometimes a separate room at the rearmost, rounded end. In these buildings too, users deposited objects for communicating with gods. A pitcher-sized clay model of such a building (fig. 10) was used at Perachora on Cape Melangavi in the Gulf of Corinth as a means of communicating with Hera. The third and most prestigious type of structure referred back to the hegemonic tradition of a long, rectangular building with a vestibule, central space, and rear room. Early Greek temples were built on this plan by about 800 BC; an example is the first Heraion on the island of Samos, which had a length of some 30 meters (100 feet), and was completely surrounded by a row of wooden columns.

In all these instances, and surely in many others independently of one another, innovators decided to use a dwelling layout as the model for a structure intended for religious communication. This was surely a masterstroke. It would be easier to attract the attention of superhuman addressees if they were regularly addressed at one specific location. Where, if not at such a site, could humans be sure of finding their faceless counterparts? The trick, perhaps, would lie in successfully tying the addressee to the location. Beautiful, attention-catching architecture might work, especially if it was of larger than normal size.

10. Terracotta model of an early Greek temple, ca. eighth century BC. From Perachora, Greece. Athens, National Museum of Archaeology, inv. 16684. akg-images / De Agostini Picture Lib. / G. Nimatallah.

Cult images would reinforce a sense of possession, and the right furnishings would suggest a home. Ever more lavish objects might in the long run have a part to play. Visitors would surely be prepared to invest in aesthetically appealing tokens liable to attract attention (and perhaps increase in value over time), because the spatial context offered a guarantee that the offering would have a prolonged presence and high visibility. Objects were displayed above ground and for long periods, while being protected from theft. However visible, though, objects could be recognized as the offerings of a particular actor only if that actor had succeeded in attracting a larger public to witness the process of communication in which he or she was engaged, thus anchoring the association between the person and object in the memories of third parties. In this way, the objects would constitute memorials of a shared experience. And this would remain the case when donors began to render the context "visible" to non-participants as well by means of painted or engraved inscriptions (although these did not yet play a role in the eighth century).

In at least some places in Greece, on Samos and perhaps also Delos,[7] the practice of deposition progressed to such an extent that, as early as the end of the eighth century, treasuries enlarged their display areas. Visibility was an issue in relation not only to supernatural beings, but also fellow humans: an ancient religious practice provided a path to social prestige that was more direct now, no longer being merely a by-product of pious action. In a society that was still scarcely monetized, accumulated surpluses were increasingly[8] channeled toward religious practices, in the form of building projects as well as objects.[9]

Before returning to Satricum, we must again consider the question of innovation, a concept that does not fit comfortably with the traditional image of religion. A monumentalized cult site already existed on Kea in the second millennium, at the location now called Ayia Irini, and it continued in use, at least sporadically, despite the destruction of the associated settlement. When the head of a much older terracotta statue was found in the eighth century BC, someone positioned it in such a way as to make it serve as a divine counterpart.[10] In the present state of our knowledge, the use of one cult site over such a long span of time is highly unusual, and here we see not only the continuation of religious practices, but also traces of older practices being incorporated anew into later religious activity. Innovation was thus not some kind of counter-movement within a religious practice that was by its nature traditional, but the actual motor driving new practice.

Investments

To return to central Italy: a religious undertaking may come with risks, but the initiative of the princely patrons in Satricum—and we must not forget that "princely tombs" were also built for women![11]—paid off handsomely. The new site, or at least the enormously enhanced visibility afforded the old pit by the new structure, attracted many visitors. Why, people may have begun to ask, should we continue to invest substantial wealth in visible burials and tombs in the far-off northwestern necropolis?[12] Growing households (and we must remember that this does not include all households) were increasingly inviting one another to ceremonial banquets, and they recalled these occasions to mind with increasingly frequent deposits not only of drinking vessels and pitchers, but also of articles associated with personal grooming. Perhaps the vessels had last been used at a symposium where spouses and friends were present, which would have enhanced their significance. A second pit was opened on the other side of the street and used from the fifth century BC onward. Its contents suggest that people often celebrated together in the area and made contact with the gods. One analysis suggests that the pit's contents represent the remnants of sixty-seven such parties.[13] The participants, comprising both men and women, did not confine themselves to drinking on these occasions but partook also of the meat of domesticated animals: cattle, sheep, and pigs.[14] Perhaps the house beside the pit afforded them some protection from the elements, especially at cooler seasons of the year or in the event of rain. This may in fact have been the primary function of the structure, as also of the apsidal structures in Greece.[15]

The long-term success of the model combining a pit with a building was mirrored in other developments in Satricum. Some decades after the construction of the first structure, in the third quarter of the sixth century BC, it was replaced by the structure referred to as Temple 1. Those who undertook this new venture clearly intended to dazzle the onlooker, and it was the roof, they decided, that would be the foremost attraction; in Etruria too, roofs were designed to make a dramatic first impression. But it was not Etruria that provided the model for the first (or perhaps only the second) version of the structure in Satricum, as we will soon see. The terracotta tiles at the eaves and gable were provided with coping stones, or antefixes, representing palmettes, heads, and *gorgoneia* grimacing and displaying their tongues

11. Terracotta from the Temple of Mater Matuta at Satricum, ca. 490 BC.
Rome, Museo Nazionale di Villa Giulia. akg-images / Pirozzi.

(fig. 11). Among the decorative features on the ridge were predatory
felines. At the base of the pediment were terracotta representations of
cattle.

These embellishments to the roof followed a fashion recently developed in Campania, a district further to the south and more exposed
to Greek design concepts. Craftsmen from Capua could perhaps have
produced on-site in Satricum designs that their patrons had seen on
trading journeys to the south. But it appears that those same patrons
finally opted for a simpler but considerably more expensive procedure:
they had the entire roof produced in Capua, and the consignment of
some 2,500 tiles, weighing in total about forty tonnes, shipped to Satricum via the coastal searoute and the river Astura.[16] Such a radical
course may have been motivated by the construction of a second
temple at Satricum, probably about 550 BC, thus shortly before the

construction of Temple 1.[17] For this temple, a three-element *cella* was commissioned, proof that extra-regional fashions were sufficiently familiar to be employed in this building erected at Macchia Santa Lucia—and it was perhaps not the first temple at that location. That a number of people in Satricum had far-flung contacts is attested also by imported wares from Italy and Greece, based in part on Cypriot and Egyptian models. These were paraded at funerals before being deposited in rich seventh-century tombs.[18]

As we have already mentioned, reorientations could be quite rapid. Within a few generations, the collections of objects deposited in tombs and pits would change, and along with them the structural components of those same tombs and pits. In the fifth century BC, after the abandonment of the northwestern necropolis, burials were even carried out on the acropolis itself, at the center of the settlement. These perhaps represented ripostes to rivals, innovations in the competition for status, influence, marriage opportunities, and economic or even military alliances. And religious communication was one weapon in the arsenal available for such competitions.

2. Temples and Altars?

The entire eastern Mediterranean world, and especially ancient Greece—of which Ionia, the coast of Asia Minor, must always be counted a part—was fascinating to the Italian elites, and especially to the moving spirits of the Etruscan-Latin region and the southern Italians of the coastal zone, with its Greek colonies. Witness to this is the Orientalizing Period of the second half of the eighth and early seventh centuries BC, when those who had access to overseas imports by virtue of their economic status and contacts put such objects on show to enhance their social standing at home.

Our discussion of large-format images showed how complex such contacts and imports could be.[19] And this serves to remind us to take care when comparing Greek and Italian developments in religious buildings. I have on purpose largely avoided the term "temple," which carries with it a connotation based on Greek material: namely, that a temple is the house of a deity, or, more precisely, of his or her statue, to which sacrificial activities at the altar, located in front of the temple, refer. Scholarship accordingly sees animal sacrifice as the quintessence of Greek religion, and this has broadly speaking also been the operative conception in respect of Italy and Rome.

This view of the centrality of the sacrifice has opened numerous avenues for religious theorists to follow.[20] In their critique of the reductionist implications of this view, some researchers have concentrated on broadening their perspective on religion to include banquets, games, and trade. But they nonetheless do not question the temple-sacrifice-altar construct just outlined,[21] even though rich displays of "votive gifts" are found not only in temples, but as religious foci in their own right, a fact that might well have raised some doubts. The paradigm does not work at all in the case of Iron Age Italy, which also puts into question the utility of the concepts derived from it. The fact that *aedes*, the Latin equivalent of "temple," means "house" would seem to invite us to view a "temple" as the "residence of a deity," but in fact the word tells us little. Like the terms *ara* and *altaria* for "altar," *aedes* and its definitions derive from late Republican texts that attempted to systematize Italian religious practices under the influence of Greek discourses. We find no word in Latin texts for the pits that served as primary locations for the direct accommodation of objects within a process of ritual communication with the invisible world. *Favisae* and *stips*, often used in this sense in modern literature, did not have that meaning in antiquity.[22]

Religious Communication

We saw in the first chapter that human communication with actors whose existence was not beyond doubt was a widespread religious activity far beyond the bounds of ancient Italy. This choice of strategy affected the options available in respect of practices, social identities, and modes of communication, along with the choice of media employed for such communication. Religion is not an assemblage of practices based on conceptions of gods and notions concerning their capacities for consuming food, receiving gifts, and revealing their presence. All these notions, practices, and media are variables within a range of human options that may or may not be activated in a specific situation. If they are so activated, they become embodied in successful, or relatively successful, processes of communication with the aforementioned special actors, be they the dead or gods. They are also variables in a form of competition that, in the event of success, may lead to their being temporarily consolidated into traditions, and, in the context of continuing competition, may in turn constitute a threat to those very traditions. Competition, however, is not the only valid perspective on a religion conceived in these terms. Resonance, the attempt to form successful, satisfying, and stable secular affiliations, and also to manage and restrict them, is scarcely less important.[23] This last perspective was important when it came to duplicating or extending the reach of an actor's own person by means of objects that would represent him or her in a lasting way before those special others (as we saw, for example, in Rhea's attempt to assure herself of her own being in a world that, although very small, contained risks that seemed to point to another realm). This perspective highlights the importance of statues and statuettes of patrons. It is when we seek a paradigm to explain the changes, the dynamic, and the rates of innovation displayed by ancient religion that competition comes to mind.[24] Thus the patrons who commissioned archaic statues such as Kouroi and Korai were entering into competition even with temples and altars.[25]

We must not forget that house-like structures were not the only sites designated for contact with the "gods." The mineral-rich water found in volcanic regions, with its unusual smell or high temperature, was a constant draw for humans. Springs and the pools fed by them, and locations by rivers and lakes, were also sought out as places for communicating with the divine, and this remained true throughout antiquity.[26] Here it was not merely a question of keeping up ancient cult sites, or extending monumentalized cult complexes by means of pools or cisterns.[27] Locations distinguished by their natural form could also be remodeled, as must have happened in the case of Pantanacci near Lavinium, where objects were deposited in the fourth and third centuries BC.[28]

And it was not only the natural setting that was critical. This is demonstrated by a well-excavated complex further to the south, the Torre di Satriano in Lucania. On the summit of a pass between Salerno and Potenza, at a height of some 950 meters, a complex ritual site was established in several stages over the course of the fourth and third centuries. Its inhabitants probably came from a distinctly older settlement, dating from at least the Early Iron Age. Three terraces were constructed parallel to the hillside. A small ditch was dug from the east, leading to the uppermost terrace from a spring about 100 meters away, along with a second channel from the west. As is so often the case, the archaeological remains provide no clue as to the actual function of these watercourses. In the process of a fundamental reconfiguration of the site, however, the western channel was simply filled with the resulting spoil, including objects that had been deposited. The closure of the stream from the east, on the other hand, was accompanied by intentional depositions, made in a ritual fashion.[29] As in the case of Satricum, the position of the complex on an interregionally significant road should be stressed. But yet another aspect may apply to southern Italian and central Italian sites alike: the choice of site provided the builders with a high degree of local visibility, and, by addressing the gods from such an elevated setting, they also provided the entire location with a face to the outside world. The local inhabitants were offered an enhanced collective religious identity, while travelers were invited to enter into contact with the place and its people, perhaps even to trade with them. On the basis of a religious identity, common ground was established that was accessible to and shared by both sides.[30]

This new common reference had little to do with the deity worshipped at the site. In fact, in the absence of images and written testimony, we have no idea what deity was worshipped at Satriano. In this we only share the situation of many people in many places in antiquity. The external aspect of a site, whether or not it took the form of a building, normally indicated only that this was a location for communication with superhuman actors. Neither the absence of images at natural locations altered only slightly by human agency, nor the number and variety of such images in the case of cult structures, was an aid to reaching a more precise identification. But this was presumably not (yet) important. The deities invoked could remain nameless, or could be addressed by various names. Wherever invocatory traditions and names became stabilized and translated into plastic images, many people nevertheless felt free to use other names in their attempts at communication, to invoke other superhuman agents in other ways, even to the extent of giving them an enduring face in that same location. Minoan cult sites of the second millennium BC did not fundamentally differ in this sense from Italian sites of the first millennium BC.[31]

Locations for human communication with "not indisputably plausible actors" included cemeteries, where communication with the dead was beset with the same uncertainties and choices that we saw in respect of communication with "gods." The family groups involved with the necropolis at Cerveteri, or their representatives (or maybe the builders of the complex), provided the tops of their great tumulus graves with accessible surfaces. In the seventh century, these platforms took a carefully flattened form. Ramps were constructed to enable access to the platforms, while at the same time care was taken to emphasize the character of these ramps as bridges overleaping the boundary between the tombs and the network of paths.[32] Family members[33] did not use these ramps only during the burial ceremony.[34] The custodians of Tumulus 2 *della Capanna*, constructed at Cerveteri at the beginning of the seventh century BC, constructed a new ramp in the second half of the sixth. In later tomb structures, the ramp was replaced by a set of steps, as in the construction of the cuboid tombs of the fifth century. Tumulus graves in Tarquinia were also provided with steps. In the Monterozzi necropolis there, these did not lead onto the platform, but merely enabled it to be used as a gigantic table-top by someone standing on the top step. These various configurations were used repeatedly in cemeteries over subsequent centuries, with many variations, and they are depicted in images of the period that record the actions of both men and women.[35]

But what took place around and on these surfaces? The archaeological evidence is highly inconsistent. This is why I am very careful not to use terms such as "altar" or "sacrifice" in evaluating such evidence, for applying these terms would preempt the question. Although well established and apparently neutral, they presuppose a particular interpretation. In Pisa, a bronze dagger and a trident were left behind on top of a tomb, after which the surface was covered over, having been used only once. The woman depicted on a stele at Marzabotto is smelling a flower (fig. 12). Common to both ritual configurations is a pronounced aesthetic dimension, whether open to conjecture or clearly depicted: the act involved its participants in intense processes of seeing and smelling. At the same time, the elevated location of the act made it visible to others. The actors also made evident the fact that they were communicating with special addressees here. Who these were, whether the dead or gods, the human actors may have learned by aural means, in spoken or sung texts; but it is hard to believe that the form given to the place itself would have revealed the identity of the addressees. The designers of the structures appear, in fact, to have consciously avoided any immediate optical perspective onto the entrance to the tomb; thus the ramp and the entrance to the chambers containing the bodies of the dead do not as a rule coincide.[36] In many cases, a person who wished to be on a level with the buried person, and desired a platform for such communication, could use small blocks placed at the entrance or in a vestibule for that purpose. A vertical relationship with "not indisputably plausible actors" (whether downwards in the direction of the dead or upwards and away from them) was occasionally evoked by a stele on the platform. However, the clearly demarcated upper surface of either a platform capable of accommodating religious actors or the smaller, "table-top" model, were clear markers that pointed to "special" addressees. In assembling or in presenting something on such a surface, actors clearly aligned themselves and their offerings with their communicative act.

Other sites confirm this conclusion. If Italic travelers to Greece had seen monumental ash altars heaped high with the remains of burnt animal sacrifices, such as might be viewed at Olympia, or long altar tables (like that at Isthmia near Corinth, which in the seventh century BC had already reached thirty meters in length),[37] or if Greek

12. Stele with relief from Marzabotto. Original: Museo Nazionale Etrusco Pompeo Aria (Archaeological Museum). Drawing by Giovanni Gozzadini, 1870.

architects had recommended such altars to them, they had evidently not been moved to imitate them. Monumental surfaces of this kind appear to have exercised no attraction, even though it would perhaps have been possible to remodel tumuli along these lines. One of the few exceptions, although much smaller than the Greek examples, is the archaic feature within the podium of the later "Temple of the Winged Horses" in Tarquinia, probably erected in the seventh century BC.[38] As in the case of the later *Ara maxima* of Hercules in Rome, these altars took the form of large platforms (and the term *ara* was current, with this meaning, in the language of late Republican architects[39]). Otherwise, however, Italic peoples erected and used small-scale structures, capable of being configured both to drain away fluids used for libations and to accommodate a small fire. They came in both round and square variants, later frequently miniaturized, and often had a large base and top (fig. 13; see also the podest in fig. 12), and pedestals that were sometimes slightly concave, and in some cases extremely constricted, suggestive of an hourglass.[40]

These lavish installations were evidently employed in communicating with special actors when food or similar products were being used instead of durable objects: in other words, when it was contents and not receptacles that were in play. When the intervention of not indisputably plausible actors was invited by offerings of food, agricultural products were deemed to have enhanced value because they had been technologically processed, brewed or baked, or specially selected. The fragrant flower might stand for the latter category, and for the former not only cakes—a broad spectrum of terms for cakes is found much later in Latin sources and in the Oscan Iguvine Tablets—but also the bakeware discovered[41] by archaeologists in the House of the Vestals.

Those actively engaged in religious communication could use it to perpetuate both the mutual increase in agency signified by their attribution of power to superhuman addressees and the gain in power to themselves set in train by the agency of those same addressees. The human actors in the process would be drawn to the notion of compensating for the transitory nature of the foodstuffs used in sacrifices

13. Arula from Roselle, Etruria, fourth–second century BC. Museo
archeologico e d'arte della Maremma. Photo: Sailko (CC-BY-SA 3.0).

by means of enduring structures that were built for the exchange. The
term used for those structures—*āsa, āra*—had widespread currency
in Italic languages. We have no testimony to inform us how contemporaries understood the term, but, etymologically, it belongs unambiguously to the sphere of ashes and fire, and may long have been
understood in the sense of "hearth" (a fireplace used for processes of

drying).[42] A later concern to restrict the term to its religious connotation gave rise in Latin to the bold neologism *focus* for the domestic hearth.[43]

The linguistic background clarifies the extent to which the Greek focus on animal sacrifice—if a well-founded assumption[44]—represents a special case. Italic peoples occasionally killed animals in order to attract the attention of their gods. But disassociated bones in archaeological deposits do not prove that such instances of slaughter had central significance in religious communication. If such a communicative act was associated with a celebratory meal for the human participants, it was as appropriate for the bones to be left in place as for the crockery used in the preparation of the meal, for both were elements of special significance with respect to the overall event. This form of ritualization set off the addressing of special (superhuman) actors from the activities of the everyday.[45] The same conceptualization might apply not only to the terminology used—as already demonstrated in the case of the hearth—but also to the design of implements down to knives and ladles, not to mention the food itself that was consumed, whether it was a kind of porridge, meat, or drinks. Many banquets in such settings are thus associated with the ritualization of slaughter, a feature that can be traced into the Imperial Age.[46] But all acts of ritual slaughter were not followed by a banquet. Where wine was a luxury item, and milk a demonstration of successful dairy production, libations—both communicative and demonstrative for those present—could acquire a significance that has been obscured both by ancient polemic against animal sacrifice and by modern theories of sacrifice that react to that polemic.[47]

The most important objective for those who organized such ceremonial banquets was to underscore, through every aspect of the proceedings, the differences between such meals and domestic banquets. While asserting the importance of the superhuman actors and their particular significance with respect to the situation at hand, and perhaps also to the social dimension of the event, the human actors also remained aware of the otherness, the alterity of their supernatural counterparts: they ate for them, but not with them.[48] Only when representational images became widespread did the idea of actually feeding the gods emerge. In the fifth century BC in the city of Rome we see magistrates, eager to gain attention, assembling onto couches portable busts from various cult sites, placing food before them, and holding ceremonies of *lectisternium,* "the draping of a couch."[49] Methods used for communicating with not indisputably plausible actors thus assumed disparate forms. The act itself, and the fact of its visibility, gave added credibility to the proceedings.

3. Dynamics of the Sixth and Fifth Centuries

The sixth century BC was the decisive period for the monumentalizing of sites of religious communication in the emerging cities and beyond. The dynamics of the process can be witnessed at some locations in central Italy and Campania. Monumentalization had not been important in the previous century, even in Greek-oriented Sicily.[50] Greek colonists constructing the colony of Poseidonia (Paestum) in southern Campania in the early sixth century first built an ash altar nine kilometers away, then complemented it in mid-century with a stone cult structure, built on the initiative of the same city. There were parallel developments at Metapontum in southern Italy and at Kroton (Crotone),[51] although at Poseidonia, unlike the other two locations, a second, smaller platform was added. Was this perhaps a distinctly Italic feature? Another structure arose at about the same time within the city of Poseidonia. Greek temples might be built at a nodal point in the hinterland, at a territorial frontier, or in the middle of a city itself. The position of the cult site at the mouth of the Sele north of Paestum belongs to the first-named category.

The images of the goddess Hera produced by craftsmen at the latter location, which include the characteristic feature of a pomegranate, seem to us to be hybrids of Corinthian types. However, this representation of the goddess, which shows her wearing a head-covering (*polos*) and veil, and seated on a throne with winged sphinxes, did not become her standard iconography until the beginning of the fifth century BC. The same process of figurative standardization had parallels in other places such as Argos, Tiryns, Corinth, and Samos.[52] As this stabilization of identity proceeded at a gradual pace, it is difficult to establish the specific form of "special" agency to which a cult site referred at its founding. At Punta della Campanella on the Sorrento peninsula, the religious use of images certainly began as early as the third quarter of the sixth century BC, but there is no evidence that images in the form of statuettes were produced until the end of the fifth, perhaps by craftsmen from the Greek colony of Naples.[53] By this time, an Athena is clearly identifiable as the main addressee.

The inhabitants of Etruscan Veii were making strides toward urbanization as early as the first half of the eighth century BC.[54] A first rectangular building with walls of tufa, presumed to have served cult purposes, was erected in the decades immediately before or after 600 BC, on an important street in the extreme south of the settlement. The area of 15 × 8 meters contained by the walls was extended to 20 × 10 meters by a roof supported on columns. Its builder or builders protected the wooden structure with terracotta plaques, which, at the beginning of the second half of the sixth century, acquired images of a procession involving a leading political figure. The whole assemblage became paradigmatic in both Etruria and Latium. Much later Latin sources relate that the terracotta sculptor Vulca was called from Veii to Rome, where he created the cult statue for the Temple of Capitoline Jupiter and a statue of Hercules.[55] A building that may have served for banquets was added at this period in the vicinity of the Piazza d'Armi on the heights of Veii.

A site already existed in the seventh century BC at Portonaccio, about two kilometers up the Piordo at the western foot of the plateau on which the city of Veii stood. Contemporaries must have felt that the location favored successful religious communication. Many objects were deposited here, some of them manufactured locally, some outside the region, coming from as far away as the eastern Mediterranean. People from Caere, Tarquinia, Falerii, and perhaps also Cortona left objects along with their own names: Vestricina and Teiθurna, Velkasnas, Hvuluves, Qurtiniie.[56] Aulus Vibenna deposited an incense burner here. He was from Veii, but by the time in question may already have moved to Rome. The great attraction of the place region-wide may have rested on oracular sanction.

It was the final third of the sixth century BC before persons unknown ventured to make a monumental contribution to the site. This involved cutting a watercourse through a platform and erecting a small building dedicated to Minerva, as well as a monumental structure that featured iconography familiar from Rome and Velletri, namely a representation of the account from Greek mythology of the deified Hercules' introduction into the circle of the Olympian gods.[57]

Subsequent developments reveal the extent to which the location became a setting for various activities and rivalries, and the degree to which this in turn attracted region-wide attention. At the end of the sixth century BC, the large structure was replaced by a building that would become the prototype for the "typical" Etruscan temple: a high podium with three *cellae*, friezes that were ornamental in nature rather than narrative, and a deeply recessed gable end,[58] the whole constituting a stone stage that offered a totally new context for ritual actors.[59] The so-called Temple B from the cult complex at Pyrgi, likewise located outside a city, was built on the same principles.

Producers of terracottas and roof tiles evidently responded rapidly to the new demands. The enormous scale on which the agricultural surplus was diverted into cult architecture opened up opportunities for such entrepreneurs to go into commercial production. This applied equally to manufacturers of small-scale objects for use in the cult (perhaps occasionally originating in neighboring settlements),[60] including those that might be inscribed to order. The particular style of script that was used at Veii, with marks separating the syllables, became widespread.[61] On the site itself, a large water tank was constructed that fed from the little river. It is possible that this was associated with a healing facility for physical disabilities.[62] Changes in structures were not always major or strategic in nature; it may, for example, have been the destruction of statues by a lightning strike that led someone to carry out alterations to the temple in the course of repairs.[63] A location outside the walled areas of a settlement, and thus beyond the strict social control typical of small communities, appears to have favored religious innovations. These might prove successful, but they equally well might not—or, at least, not in the long term: by the beginning of the third century BC, we find Veii's water tank filled with objects, and the temple's decorative features buried.[64] Other cult sites had long been established within the city bounds of Veii, for example at Macchiagrande to the northeast, and above Portonaccio in the area of Campetti: shrines that drew thousands of people who deposited objects over the years. Sites within the city also competed with one another.[65]

Even in Rome, however, the most innovative decorative programs for religious structures are found at peripheral sites. It is at the Forum Boarium marketplace,[66] at the bend in the Tiber, that we first see a decorative program that could also be found at the same period in Veii and Velletri. The complex in question was discovered adjacent to and beneath Sant'Omobono. In a phase of construction dated prior to the mid-sixth century, the wooden roof and gable end of the complex had already been protected with terracotta plaques depicting lions, perhaps descended from Assyrian motifs.[67] A thorough remodeling of the decorative scheme was carried out in about 530 BC.[68] It was probably a workshop in the city of Rome that received the commission to provide new decorative features for the roof.

It is possible that the craftsmen in this workshop came from Veii; they were at least familiar with the Etruscan themes of chariot processions and races, riders, and banquets that were to be seen there, which perhaps corresponded to narratives about the heroic past. During the next two decades, these craftsmen worked in a highly organized manner to produce high-quality terracotta plaques that adorned the eaves of all the prominent buildings, palaces, and cult structures. Their repertoire also included terracotta statues for the roof ridges and crowns; by degrees, from about 500 BC onwards, this type of decoration came to be reserved solely for cult structures.[69] Here too, we see a process by which particular media became so closely associated with religious communication that traditions developed, limiting the options of subsequent actors. Only an overview encompassing fragments from Veii and Rome, and especially from Velletri and the neighboring Cisterna di Latina (more precisely Caprifico di Torrecchia, probably

the Volscian city of Suessa Pometia) in northern Latium, would reveal the full range of the imagery. Also common to all these sites is a
program of statuary depicting Minerva (Athena in Greek myth) leading Hercules to his place among the gods. It follows that the choice of
motif must have lain with the craftsmen, which precludes our analyzing the iconography as reflecting in any way the different ethnic and
political circumstances in the various towns involved. Patrons were
dependent on the patterns offered by their suppliers. This also applied
when, as in the case of the Sant'Omobono temple, the patron is said
to have been the Etruscan Servius Tullius, king of Rome, who according to Roman tradition dedicated the temple to Mater Matuta
and Fortuna.[70]

This temple was completely destroyed shortly before 500 BC, and
replaced on the same site by a complex of two temples on a substantially higher platform: the one on the left to Fortuna, the other on the
right to Mater Matuta. We do not know the reasons for this change.[71]
Rapid successions of structures can be observed at other locations
too. All over western central Italy, actors with the means and/or the
power[72] grew accustomed to this new medium of religious communication, and further developed it in a spirit of keen competition. As a
rule, they associated themselves with already-existing sites of religious
activity, both centrally located and at the peripheries of settlements.
Reference to a particular deity[73] facilitated a new form of dynamic
continuity: so long as the deity remained the same, a previous building
or its decor could be replaced after only a short time. Bigger, higher,
more impressive: whatever the nature of the enhancement, it could be
justified, and a spiral was set in motion that quickly led to enormous
temple structures, and then, in Rome already by the early fifth century BC, to a collapse of the competitive spirit. Sixth-century patrons,
both male and female, had presumably financed their projects from
surpluses previously sunk in luxurious tombs and burials. These rich
farmers (for that is how the group must be characterized)[74] then gave
up almost entirely on flamboyant funerals and the marked invisibility
of wealth concealed in graves.[75] Following on the collapse of extensive
Etruscan rule in the aftermath of defeat to a Greek fleet at Cumae

(494 BC), and pressure from groups from the Abruzzo, this class could no longer muster a level of surplus adequate for construction projects.

A multiplicity of cult sites existed in Rome at the end of the sixth century BC.[76] Many of these remained without recognizable monumental structures, but they did boast rich deposits.[77] Others were in the process of being provided with open hearths, as was the case at the deposit site on the Clivus Capitolinus with its sixth-century tufa platform (the Ara Saturni),[78] or were furnished with built structures, such as the mid-sixth-century building on the northeastern slope of the Palatine,[79] and the early-fifth-century construction in the southeastern sector of the Palatine.[80] Many of these were local initiatives undertaken by small neighborhoods. They were used largely by locals,[81] and not infrequently only for short periods of time. Some never breached the horizon of the historiographical tradition.

None of this applies to the Capitoline Temple of Jupiter. Here, the Etruscan princes of the Tarquinii family, described in Latin as *reges* (kings), appear to have seized the initiative in monumentalizing a site that had been distinguished by cult depositions since the early sixth century BC.[82] The family's involvement in religious projects promised to broaden the base of their political dominion, which was above all of a military nature. Accordingly, they were said to have financed the gigantic project over its long period of construction mainly from the proceeds of plundering expeditions. The foundation itself, on the peak of the hill, was a mighty structure, fifty-four meters wide by a length of sixty-two meters, all of it covered by a superstructure.[83] The building itself combined many Italic developments, and so became a rich source, if not necessarily a model, for later temple architects.[84] Its terracotta revetments were in the main executed by craftsmen from Veii using materials from Veii. The major concern, above and beyond the aesthetic, was with religious definition. There is not the slightest room for doubt that the deity addressed by the structure was identified as Iuppiter Optimus Maximus, "the best and greatest Jupiter." This name was given a face by means of a great clay statue by the Veiian coroplast Vulca.

The complex was not destined to remain isolated. A rival group of rich farmers, who called themselves "plebeians," built a structure dedicated to Ceres, Liber, and Libera on the Aventine and entrusted its decoration to the Greeks Damophilos and Gorgasos.[85] More than a decade later, in reaction to Rome's victory over a menacing Latin alliance at *lacus Regillus*, a "house" (*aedes*) was built for Castor and Pollux, the sons of Zeus (*dioscuri*), now conceived as cavalrymen. The main instigator of the construction, dated to 484 BC, was the son of the Aulus Postumius who had won the battle as dictator, and who was said to have promised not only booty to the soldiers, but also a reward to the gods for their help.[86] Despite a lengthy construction period, the project remained a family affair, winning the family the nickname *Regillensis*. In the end, the temple measured more than twenty-seven meters in width by a length of almost forty meters, a scale comparable to that of Temple A at Pyrgi. The podium was designed to equalize the slope of the terrain, and so stood between one and a half and five meters above the level of the Forum. The rear section of the building was laid out as three *cellae*, in this too following a tradition developed elsewhere, and also followed at Pyrgi.[87]

What the Postumii were embarking on here was an entirely Etruscan structure. The architecture presented them as the military saviors of the city and recipients of divine support, a position further secured by the temple's position on the Forum Romanum, long since configured as the city's central square. It was the first time (in a tradition that is perhaps reliable) that a monumental structure was founded on a successful religious communication, one that had led to victory in an actual military conflict. This would become the norm one and a half centuries later. But most of the few fifth- and early-fourth-century construction projects in Rome that are mentioned in Augustan-period histories and the narrative traditions connected with them arose from different circumstances.

Investment in Religion

It must have required courage and strong convictions to found a site where objects could be deposited for the sake of invisible agents. One imagines that the requisite degree of administrative ability and financial means was not in over-abundant supply, so it is probable that only prominent and well-to-do families could afford such ventures. Those who then undertook the monumentalization of such a site, augmenting its capacity for religious communication in a highly public manner and with significant outlay of funds, were in effect appropriating it. It was the kind of project that only rich farmers could manage, and it allowed them, perhaps for the first time, to make use of wealth that would otherwise have disappeared into graves or hoards. The local markets offered only a very restricted range of possibilities for exchange, but commissioning substantial buildings over a wide geographic area opened plentiful avenues for investment.[88] Various practices overlapped, and often persisted in parallel. We know nothing of the discussions that must have gone on about the character and boundaries of such sites; but the strategies of the actors themselves suggest that all participants profited from a certain fluidity, as when areas of convergence predominated over clearly drawn boundaries.

Using the various means at their disposal, those who initiated such processes of appropriation engaged in frequently furious rivalries to develop distinctive and effectual "religious" sites and signs. In many places in the sixth century BC, the competition amounted to a stampede. There was plenty of room here for innovation. However, competition between farmers who wished by their religious undertakings to enhance their social reputation, perhaps even their political standing, or to gain a reputation as good trading partners, could not rely solely on ingenuity. They had to employ what was ready to hand in the way of methods and symbolism: architectural elements, such as terracotta roofs that were also used for dwellings, and decorative motifs that were familiar from tombs, or from settings where self-promotion was a motivating factor.

Characteristic were the motifs of the terracotta plaques that protected the timber components of these new cult structures. These plaques show a very narrow section of social reality. The rich farmers (for the economic base of these people must be sought in agriculture) became charioteers; no longer landlords, they were depicted as aristocrats and nobles (fig. 14). And frequent reference was made to the

14. Terracotta plaque showing galloping horsemen; 21.5×64×4 cm, ca. 530 BC.
Borgia-Velletri collection. akg-images / De Agostini Picture Lib. / L. Pedicini.

imagery of the eastern Mediterranean monarchies. It was not a question of championing a pan-Mediterranean "sacred kingship," but simply
one of borrowing images, frequently taken out of context and misun-
derstood. The plaques, with their potential to refer to heroic legends,
also positioned these religious buildings erected by prosperous farmers as the property of "aristocrats." Many of the same motifs either
already decorated or soon would decorate their manor houses (more
accurately, farmhouses).[89]

Practical necessity and the interest of patrons in promoting these
ennobling associations led to numerous hybrid forms, and not only in
the area of decoration. The Regia, the "royal house" on the Roman
Forum, evidently belonged to this eclectic breed of architecture. The
builder of the "third Regia," in the mid-sixth century, gave the "house"
a very early terracotta roof with decorative features of the same material, thus positioning it in a group that includes not only palaces such
as the one at Murlo, but also the contemporaneous cult building at
Sant'Omobono. The "fourth Regia," in the third quarter of the same
century, was decorated after the style of Veii, Velletri, and Rome, also
found in the subsequent phase of the Sant'Omobono building.[90] Its
plan was so configured as to accommodate cult functions (subsequently taken over by new priests) in a residential complex.[91] This
brings to mind the link mentioned previously between political and
religious roles in Archaic Greece.[92] Evidently, prior to the banishment

of burials to sites outside the city, the foundation of this same building, in its earliest phase at the end of the seventh century, had rested
on an infant burial.[93]

Against a background of parallel attempts in Etruria to differentiate the religious from the elite political sphere,[94] it comes as no surprise
that, after banishing political rulers bearing the title *rex*, Rome marked
that separation by anointing a *rex sacrorum*, a "king of religious acts,"
whose role, as the title implies, would be confined to the religious
sphere. It was a radical move about which we know nothing further.[95]
Perhaps the sequence of thirteen or even fourteen altars at Lavinium
should also be understood against such a background. Whatever the
aim behind this particular gradual accretion, it is plain that those who
organized it carefully avoided giving the religious space any hint of
aristocratic coloration; which would seem to support the notion that,
in their own peculiar way, these "hearths" paid homage to a communal
project: the foundation of Latin colonies.[96]

IV

Religious Practices

1. The Use of Bodies

Most of what constituted ritual during the mid-first millennium BC, especially in the realm of religious practice, lies beyond any possibility of reconstruction. This applies to words, and more so to words formulated rhythmically, and most of all to melodic formulations; that is to say, songs and music.[1] Occasionally, a wind instrument deposited in a grave points to the element of sound. The same strictures apply to smell, which is only rarely hinted at in imagery (we have already seen the example of the figure smelling a flower). Special forms of movement, such as dancing or stamping, aimed at attracting the attention of the supernatural agents being addressed, while at the same time representing the special form taken by communication with them. But they are documented only in late, ritual-related references and images.[2] The central role played by the body in religious activity is again shown by those objects brought to a site by human actors, objects they had interacted with and finally left at a religious site.

Whose Head Is That?

As early as the beginning of the seventh century BC, some inhabitants of Trestina on the upper reaches of the Tiber threw bronze figurines

83

in human form into pits and shafts as a means of communicating with the unseen.[3] This practice was copied in the following century by quite a number of individuals in northern Etruria, often in small, remote settlements not unlike Trestina. The people making the depositions used the figures to represent themselves as they wished to appear. They occasionally marked their local status by means of weapons, but more frequently by precise representations of their own dress.[4] In Rome too, in the pits of Sant'Omobono, people used this means to mark clearly their continued and lasting, although not necessarily visible, presence at special locations.

More was possible. In the escalating interplay of initiative and imitation, insofar as affordable, at a few larger cult complexes such presence was expressed in life-size form. At Lavinium at the beginning of the fifth century, a tradition was established—probably by young women and men—of having themselves represented as life-sized (or somewhat smaller) clay figures (fig. 15), possibly in the context of local customs marking the end of childhood. The tradition was kept up by subsequent generations into the second century BC.[5] In northern Etruria, splendid bronze figures continued in production into the second and perhaps the first century BC, and were set up by individuals in cult buildings in the context of religious communication.

This was a practice that many could ill afford. Perhaps as early as the end of the sixth century BC, a cheaper option became available, which we see first in the Campetti district of Veii.[6] This was the use of heads modeled in clay and perhaps mounted on wooden posts. At first the practice was only sporadically imitated, but it became quite popular at the end of the fifth century BC. Ceramicists could cater to the new demand because a novel technology had probably been available in Italy from the end of the sixth century: the mass production of ceramics using either a single- or a dual-matrix mold.[7] Throughout central Italy, especially at the bigger cult locations, people could purchase ceramic heads, either fully three-dimensional or, no doubt at a lower price, as half-depth reliefs that they could use for religious communication. The heads were fashioned to meet the particular display purposes to which they would be put. Many had ring bases that

15. Terracotta statues of women, near life-size, from Lavinium–Pratica di Mare, fifth century BC. akg-images / De Agostini Picture Lib. / G. Nimatallah.

kept them stable when they were positioned on podia or benches, in chests or showcases, or even on the ground if that was appropriate. The half-reliefs had provision for being hung.[8]

The quality of these heads often left something to be desired. The backs and edges remained unworked. After several hundred castings, the molds would be worn, sometimes showing faults that had been only superficially retouched. They were unpainted, and almost always uninscribed: suggesting customers with limited purchasing power and a deficient level of literacy. Many were fashioned as need dictated by the purchasers themselves, while others were individually finished to show individual traits, after the manner of a portrait. Notwithstanding such differences, the message conveyed to both gods and humans by displaying the heads was of a similar nature: for all the splendid architecture and decoration, for all that we know about the patrons of this place and their position as members of economic, military, political—and now, to top it all, religious—elites; despite all that, the message was, "We too are still here!" It cannot have escaped many of these actors that their heads would at some point be cleared away or taken down, then thrown into pits or shafts, but they nevertheless appropriated to themselves these locations redolent of superhuman powers and human potentates. Legitimated by the fact that they were performing religious acts, in this way they took ownership of these extraordinary places where it was possible to communicate with divine beings.

While religious activity afforded some individuals the opportunity to achieve self-representation by creating architectural splendor, and at the same time to influence religious practices, guiding them in particular directions, it allowed others to appropriate the very same spaces by performing modified versions of elite practices, and, in so doing, to claim recognition for their own concerns and desires. Such appropriation had to be justified, and it is precisely in Rome and Latium that we frequently find traces of veils covering the backs of clay heads, as clear evidence that the ordinary people who left the heads were in fact engaged in religious communication.[9] Both clay heads and construction projects grew in importance until the end of the second century BC. In central Italy, a broad spectrum of social strata joined with the elites in what amounted to an indirect, mutually rein-forcing game: masses of objects deposited by a multitude of hands en-abled their donors to appropriate the religious infrastructure for themselves, but at the same time these objects by their presence strengthened that infrastructure by contributing crucially to the sa-cralization of structures and precincts.[10] Clay statuary was a me-dium that served quite different purposes in many parts of Greece. Although the same medium often underwent similar processes of popularization, in Greece clay reliefs mainly pictured gods, or gods together with humans.[11]

But it was not heads only that were depicted. If a head could stand *pars pro toto* for the whole person, the same role might be assigned to other body parts as well. Eyes, feet, arms, and legs might be said to be of a public nature, but the same could not be said of the external sex-ual organs, breasts and penises, or of internal organs such as the lungs, intestines, or a uterus (fig. 16). Any representation falling within the latter category of body parts, offered in the public space of a cult struc-ture, most definitely indicates an understanding that such spaces were primarily settings for intimate communication with those that were to be addressed there, as well as constituting a form of personal appropriation of the space. The precise content of such attempts at communication necessarily remains hidden to later observers. Was the intent to express quite specific concerns by means of quite specific objects, and to impress these concerns on the memory of the inter-locutor? There is no doubt at all that the practice entered into medical discourse of the kind where a specialist provides ever more specific representations, perhaps as part of a consultation or as an aid to diag-nosis; although these representations were by no means anatomically reliable.[12] It was perhaps as a consequence of such a conversation and diagnosis that, in the third century BC, a woman from Etruria com-missioned a female torso showing, between small, taut breasts and thick folds of fabric draped over the thighs, a large, ovoid opening in the belly displaying the details of internal organs, including a loop of intestine at the lower extremity.[13]

16. Terracotta intestines and uterus, third to second century BC. From Etruria. Prague, National Gallery, HM10 3374. Photo: Zde (CC-BY-SA 3.0).

Keeping Up the Conversation

The woman from Etruria, and many others, would have accompanied their offerings of such highly specific representations with words. And we may be sure that the oral petitions they presented were comparably precise. The same may have been true of earlier religious communication practiced and witnessed at the same place. While the media used in such cases did not reproduce the subject matter of a communication, they were not without influence on it. The heads had presumably provided the impetus for bringing problems relating to particular body parts into this type of religious communication. While this step had rested on a misapprehension, in the sense that the clay heads did not refer to head pains, it was a productive misapprehension of the kind common in learning processes that depend on observation-led imitation, the kind of imitation that is characteristic of religious communication in general. A banqueting utensil in traditional use became the vehicle of a curse deposited on the Quirinal in Rome by a man who called himself (or was called) Duenos (the good), and was perhaps trying to establish a marriage contract. It was evidently the discrepancy between the object, a *kernos* combining three small food vessels in a ring, and his intended curse that moved him to reach for his stylus and produce one of the earliest Latin inscriptions.[14] The interpretation of the inscription is highly disputed, and I am not intending here to enter into that dispute. The important point I wish to make is that the cultural technique of writing was used to communicate via material objects that were not employed simply to evoke their most widespread context of use, and was further shaped by that process. In this way, ritual presentation, and the local and social contexts of ritual performances, operated alongside continuous display and readable text to enlarge the repertoire of religious communication.

The monumentalizations that were so characteristic of the sixth century BC afforded new opportunities for display, and gave rise to associated demands that prompted the use of new objects. Prominent among these were nonperishable baked goods made of clay strips and balls.[15] Use of these items implied a decision that they should be a gift to the invisible counterpart. The notion of a "gift," however, remained only one option among others. The use in religious communication of bronze ingots (*aes rude*), a form of weighable money that preceded the introduction of bronze and silver weights, and finally of coins, constituted a similar custom as early as the sixth century BC.[16] It was the habit to remove any possibility of a misunderstanding by inscribing these objects with words: first *donom*, and then later *donum* or *donum dedit* (He/she presented this as a gift). This is the oldest formula in common use. Lucius Salvios Seios, son of Lucius, inscribed it on a stele at Samnite Superaequum in the third century BC, adding the Sabelline-Oscan formula "upon receiving favors."[17] At the beginning of the third century at the latest, Orceria, probably the wife of one Numerius, wrote *donom dedi* on a bronze tablet at Praeneste, describing the recipient in the triple form typical of central Italy as "Fortuna, daughter to Jupiter, Primigenia."[18]

This tablet accompanied a gift that has not survived. Was it of use to Fortuna? One of the most popular gift ideas took the form of what were called *arae* (hearths). We find them used as gifts as early as the fifth century BC, at Satricum among other places.[19] Some actors were prepared to use a miniaturized *ara* instead of a full-scale one, and not solely when making a deposit in a grave. Their intentions may have been various. By the duplication or even multiplication of existing hearths, donors also altered the religious infrastructure. In Italy, the establishment of new *arae* was one of the most frequent measures taken when further developing cult complexes;[20] and, judging from the expense involved, the actors concerned were probably among the wealthy of a locality. Quite apart from this form of appropriation, however, the multiplication of hearths made the special communication itself the theme of the act of communication: one talked with the gods about talking with the gods, and made this explicit by making the altar as a sign of that type of communication; a gift accompanying a prayer. In the donated object,[21] the lasting presence of the unique ritual act appeared in a form that invited repetition and actualization. At the same time, the actors involved were no longer presenting themselves as domestic technicians, as Rhea had done, but as actors taking part in the actual field of religious activity, much in the way indicated by the veiled clay heads. In iconographic terms, the hearth, being the place where libations were poured, long occupied the role in Rome that in Greece belonged to the libation cup (*phiale*). Large numbers of these ceramic cups are found in Athenian deposits of the fifth century BC.[22] The figure of a woman identified as *Pietas* is represented on coins from the late Republic onward as a woman with a covered head standing beside a small altar or pouring a libation from a bowl (fig. 17).

Others too used such over-determined symbols. At more than one hundred sites in all, traditions developed that called for the erection or deposition of animal figures of bronze or clay—or at least offered these as options.[23] Representations of pigs and cattle were used at Fregellae during a period that lasted from the fourth to the second century BC. Doves were favored at the Minerva complex at Lavinium, while at the so-called Minerva Medica sanctuary in Rome we find cattle, a wild pig, a horse, a lion, and birds. Local traditions restricted what one could represent without giving offense; in other instances, local diversity invited individual experimentation. The most common

17. Pietas sprinkling incense on an altar. Reverse of
a sestertius of Antoninus Pius minted in Rome, AD
138 (*RIC* 2.1083a). Photo: Classical Numismatic
Group (CC-BY-SA 3.0).

animals consumed at meals at these locations, sheep and chickens,
were rarely represented among the figurines. Some individuals might
associate such an object with a request for fertility, or for the end of a
pestilence in their own flock; for others the miniatures may have been
important as a way of showing themselves to be cattle-owners, successful hunters (and keepers of hunting dogs), or people who followed
local religious practices (such as the killing of doves). Boasting may
have been no more or less a factor here than in representations of young
or richly-adorned individuals. Only in the rarest of cases would a rep-
lica of a slaughtered animal be deposited: a private feast of a thousand
portions of beef (as might be provided by a single, full-grown animal)
was certainly not a religious act that frequently took place at sites
where we find representations of cattle.[24]

The practices we have described may have been oriented toward the
kind of religious communication that was maintained long-term, in
the interest of acquiring, for the long term, the sorts of benefits that
religious communication could bring; this in contrast to the sort of
communication conducted, for example, at Asclepius complexes, which
were mainly visited in times of special need. (In any case, even in the
third century BC, Asclepian sites were not yet abundant in central
Italy.)[25] What expectations would then have arisen on the part of our
not indubitably plausible actors? Anyone interested in exhibiting an
association with a deceased individual, and in drawing continued

advantage from the respect due to him or her, may have sought out frequent opportunities for "religion"; someone who wished to obtain support from a "god" may likewise have made repeated visits to a special place, or in some other way nurtured a special relationship. The calling may have been even stronger for an individual whose connection with a site was quite public, if for example he or she had been responsible for constructing a building at the site. In all other instances, the question of what deities or the dead might expect in the way of continuing worship was presumably resolved by mere forgetting: in much the same way as occurs today in comparable instances where worshippers have only the vaguest notions of what the rather shadowy "others" might want. An awareness that such expectations existed increased, however, as the unseen agents received a form and a face through the media of architecture, noteworthy rituals, or images. Those who had established a more intimate relationship, perhaps on account of specific infirmities that reminded them of their need, might also feel more strongly the reciprocal needs of those from whom they sought help. Such personalized images were increasingly visible, not only on and in temples, but also in the streets during processions in the form of statuettes, busts, or litters bearing symbols.[26]

Vows

The comic playwright Plautus, and after him Titinius, addressed the theme of vows with terminological precision at the turn of the third century BC: a character would be "condemned" to "redeem" a vow (*votum*) and so would be obliged to its fulfillment.[27] This language was of rather recent vintage, appearing first in inscriptions of the third and second centuries BC. The rather legalistic feel of the proceedings, and the language to which it gave rise, suggest that what was at issue here was a breach of the dialectical bounds appropriate to individual humans and deities respectively; that is to say, it was a situation where demands on the public purse were involved.[28] This assumes a developed state system, which was nonexistent in central Italy in the sixth and fifth centuries, arising first in Rome in the second half of the fourth century BC.

We are given an insight into the process by a bronze tablet from Falerii Novi, a new foundation established after 241 BC. The wording, in a local script but in the regional variant of Latin,[29] is important. The local praetor was careful to establish down to the last detail that the religious act he had undertaken had its origin in an order issued by the local Senate:

> *Menerva sacru / La. Cotena La. f. pretod de / zenatuo sententiad vootum / dedet cuando datu rected / cuncaptum.*

> Sacred to Minerva. Lars Cotena son of Lars, praetor, issued a vow by a decision of the Senate. When it was issued, it was correctly formulated.[30]

So as to treat this new Latin institution with perfect rectitude, he went so far as to indicate the length of the vowel in its name by doubling it (*vootum*).

A pair of well-educated, eloquent brothers, Marcus and Publius Vertuleius, addressed the new institution in one of the earliest private inscriptions to mention a *votum*. It was found near Sora and dates to around the second century BC. Here, too, a period of time has elapsed since the father, finding himself in a desperate situation, assumed the obligation of the vow, and his sons must now see to its fulfillment. This they will do by means of a tithe in the form of a sumptuous meal for Hercules Maximus, "Hercules the Greatest." At the end, the brothers cannot resist begging that Hercules, who has now obliged them once, might in the future frequently sentence them, or perhaps a more appropriate expression would be "condemn them" to fulfill a *votum*:

> *M(arcus) P(ublius) Vertuleieis / C(ai) f(ilii) quod re sua difeidens asper(a) / afleicta parens timens / heic vovit voto hoc / soluto [d]ecuma facta / poloucta leibereis luben/tes donu(m) danunt / Herculei Maxsume / mereto semol te / orant se voti crebro / condemnes.*[31]

"Marcus and Publius Vertuleius, sons of Gaius. That which, de-
spairing for his shattered affairs, squalid, fearful, the father vowed
here, the sons—when this vow was fulfilled by means of the tenth
set aside and offered as a sacrifice—happily give as a gift to Hercules especially meritorious. Together they pray that you frequently
condemn them (to the fulfilment) of a vow." Tr. Meyer, *Legitimacy*,
2004, 53.

The concluding witticism draws attention to the issue of how legaliza-
tion changes religious communication. Whereas both the request to
Hercules and the thanks promised were embedded in a full and enduring communication, in the context of the *votum* institution they
became discrete events in time. Once the obligation incurred by the
vow had been made good, the tie binding the two parties in mutual
responsibility was loosed.

In Rome itself, up to the time of the Second Punic War in the third
century (218–201 BC) there appear to have been only two, or maybe
three circumstances when a *vota* might be used: at the departure of a
commander to a war (*vota nuncupare*), at the construction of a temple,
and at the inauguration of "great games" (*ludi magni*). Livy's Roman
history offers no accounts of personal *vota* prior to the end of the Second Punic War. It is not until 200 BC that the issue appears to have
been raised as to how the body politic can be bound to regular acts of
religious communication by means of *vota*, and how *vota* in general
can be detached from concrete causes (and resources). The ("great")
votive games were periodically recurring events, and the expenditures were directly tied to a consul's preceding "five-year vow."[32] The
comedies mentioned at the beginning of this section dealt with situations of this kind.

The *votum* was not an embodiment of Roman piety, but rather a
special means of securing, by means of religious communication,
substantial resources under public jurisdiction. This device was in
place by the end of the third century BC, and its purpose was to deal
with questions such as: how exactly are the hundred cattle promised
by one Scipio in Spain,[33] but which have to be slaughtered in Rome,

going to be paid for? The background for the *votum* as an institution in Latium, and perhaps more directly in Rome, was the increasing centralization of state administration. The *votum* also tackled disputes arising from more common sorts of religious communication. It did create some new problems, and it might give rise to ridicule, but it quickly became popular. Already under the Republic, use of the *votum* had become so formalized that, in Rimini, Pupius Salvius was able to assume that the acronym *V S L M* in his inscription[34] would be understood by all: *votum solvit lubens merito* (He gladly fulfills the vow as merited by the god).

2. Sacralization

Classifications

Land bought and marked out in the *uhtur*ship of C. Vestinius son of V. & Ner. Babrius son of T. (in community X), in the *maron*ship of Vols. Propertius son of Ner. & T. Volsinius son of V. (in community Y). I (the stone) stand as sacred (marker?).[35]

With this inscription, composed in Latin script but in the Umbrian language, and dating to the first quarter of the first century BC, the named magistrates marked the place where land owned by one community abutted the border of the neighboring community. *Sacre* (Latin *sacer*) indicates the status of the stone. It is something that cannot be moved; it is shared public property: and, for this reason, the name of any individual landowner is expressly not mentioned. There can be no doubt that the term has its origin in the sphere of religious communication in the broadest sense. Like *donum*, *sacrum* is written on objects with increasing frequency everywhere in the Imperial Age. The two terms in fact often occur in combination. To those capable of classifying any item of property—slaves included—it fell easy to designate neutral ground as a divine possession,[36] although its legal classification as such, first formulated in textbooks of the second century AD,[37] was another matter, amounting to squeezing the gods into a schema that even the Roman jurists who created it limited to the territory within the borders of what was "Roman" in the narrowest sense of the word: the city and its immediate Latin environs. What could it have meant, in another instance, for Jupiter to possess a sanctuary at Gubbio?[38]

What it meant from the viewpoint of the laws of property was then, as now, one perspective among many, inculcated or initiated though it may have been since archaic times (or even earlier) by the *lapis niger* on the Forum Romanum[39] and, at other sites, by warnings not to disturb the location. In reality, the property of superhuman agents, gifts deposited at a site for example, were not always left undisturbed. They might upon occasion be brought back into circulation, so to say, by a thief, or "repurposed" by the local political overlord.[40] And, as we have seen, anyone who found it incumbent upon him- or herself to upgrade a complex, did so without hesitating to encroach upon the existing assets. It was precisely such construction projects, the intensity with which sites were used, and the objects deposited in them that furthered the sacralization process, determining both the focus and the extent of complexes that were for the most part not restricted by boundary stones or walls, or acquired them only very late.

Strategies

All these pits, objects, and structures formed part of a strategy aimed at separating action defined as *religious* communication from action that, as it ascribed no relevance to those special actors, had no need to assert its relevance to them. To this extent, it was the objects and communicative practices that gave the divine a concrete presence at a specific location.[41] But there were also detailed practices of sacralization. The use of incense, sourced from the eastern Mediterranean (and it was already an imported product there), was one preferred way in which a desire for distinction, for standing out socially, could be satisfied, not least in the quest for sacralization. The "discovery" of incense was a feature of the Orientalizing Period, when an entire complex of innovations and imports derived from overseas contacts reached Italy. The utensils necessary for burning incense were copied from Phoenician models and produced primarily in local bronze-work. The forms thus arrived at underwent further development in the fifth and subsequent centuries, until a simplified bowl-like incense burner became standard.[42] Unlike in Greece, the association of incense-burning with libations—*ture et vino*—became a dual marker designating activities as sacred; the round Etruscan incense *pyxis* or the rectangular Roman *acerra* became accessories that marked an individual as the temporary bearer of a religious role.[43] The two-handled pitcher shape of the *olla* or *urna*, being ill-suited for pouring, was frequently replaced by the three-handled Greek *hydria*; however, the more cumbersome ancient form long persisted in central Italian cult, and was used by Rome's Vestal Virgins even into the Imperial Age. The Vestals, being highly visible in the middle of Rome, also long used archaic forms of banqueting utensils and storage vessels.[44] In particular ritual contexts, their costume included bronze fibulae of a kind known from as early as the La Tène Period in central Europe.[45]

Anyone who made his actions somehow special, while speaking to special addressees and signifying relevance to them, was at the same time addressing himself, assuring himself of his own significance.[46] And, as we saw in chapter 1, both sides in such a conversation must also have been addressing yet another, wider, human audience. In inscribing objects intended for religious communication, whether in temples or in tombs, early users of first the Greek, then the Etruscan and Latin scripts, took advantage of a quality inherent in all three of these: consisting as they do of both consonants and vowels, they reproduce the very sounds of words. Donors and objects were thus able to "speak," but only if they could count on the cooperation of readers who would respond to the challenge implicit in the phonetic signs by reading them aloud, as was normal in antiquity.[47] The famous early-fifth-century BC inscription *[——]iei steterai Popliosio Valesiosio suodales Mamartei* (. . . as companions of Poplius Valesius, erected this for Mars) from Satricum[48] was intended to be declaimed, and it must have been aimed at such an audience.

That an audience must have been present is self-evident when it comes to other forms of ritualization. Why would aristocrats bother to stage chariot races or gladiatorial contests if there were no audience to see them? The element of sacralization, the reference to the dead or to gods, which gave such events their special importance, and thus presumably also assured a still larger audience, is somewhat more problematic. Individual competitors may have invoked named deities on such occasions, but sacralization was more evident and impressive if the entire event made such a reference. New religious media offered various solutions. A choice of location was one such. An event might be held on the Capitol in Rome near the Temple of Jupiter; or an entire complex might be built for the purpose, as at Olympia on the Peloponnese. Another means was to involve statues, in which case these had to be fetched in procession from the temples. In addition to contests, funerary paintings of the sixth and perhaps even the seventh century BC attest to parades and processions in Etruscan cities; in various locations these feature in the repertoire of motifs designed for the representation of aristocratic prestige. We have already seen two-wheeled chariots, of the kind used in races and processions, featuring in rooftop terracotta friezes, their presence suggesting that such events were not uncommon in Italy;[49] and they can be seen in Rome in clearly sacralized contexts from the end of the sixth century onward.[50] Watching such spectacles, hearing the clatter of hooves and armor, smelling the sweat of horses and contestants (or the oil with which the contestants anointed themselves), perhaps even running with them: all this turned mere spectators into participants in the ritual.[51] And it caused another transformation as well, for it made the aristocratic activity of "play" (ludi), recast as religious communication, into public action. The same could not be said of every activity. The aristocratic enactment of a hunt was common in antiquity, and persists into the present day. Such hunts were staged on an immense scale in the Early Modern Period, and were an important subject of stories and images at all periods, but they were seldom sacralized until the Romans acquired the organizational and architectural skills necessary to relocate the hunt to the amphitheater.[52]

The ritualization and sacralization of some activities had implications that had to be taken into account. First, particular days of the year had to be designated for such events. The roles of the actors involved were also affected. Once participants and competitors, aristocrats now had to become organizers and promoters as well. And things got even more complicated when aspects of a performance had to become markedly "special" in order for it to be perceived as religious: the victorious horse in the *October equus* race in Rome was killed, and the winner of the Capitoline race had to drink absinthe.[53] Such excesses were perhaps omitted when an event was less prominent. Dancing may have been a frequent element, but we have only indirect means of knowing.[54] It was not only children who rode on the swings at the *feriae latinae*, the holidays that brought Latins from outlying towns to Alba.[55] Ritualization and sacralization, the reiterated characterization of communication as "special," as religious communication, changed the character of the everyday, added new forms to the spectrum of religious activity, and in many ways rendered it more visible, more "public".

3. Complex Rituals

Great rituals required great numbers of participants, and interested parties flocked to the places where they were held to make their particular contribution. Even though the roles of host and guest were in each case clearly defined, such rituals were regarded as belonging to an entire town or even region; Greek cities made of them a complex diplomatic, but nonetheless religious, occasion.[56] In the growing city of Rome, interest increased with the population. The "games" began to last longer from the third century BC onward, and "scaenic games" (spectacular productions) were added. The occasions on which games were celebrated also multiplied, and permanent architectural forms were eventually created to accommodate them, following the model of the Greek theater at first, and then elaborating it further. Eventually, the Roman theater and amphitheater became synonymous with Mediterranean life, and it remained so until far into Late Antiquity.

But this takes us far ahead of the historical account. The traces left by rituals are difficult to read. It is not until the end of the first century

BC that Dionysius of Halicarnassus, a Greek from Asia Minor, provides for us a detailed description of a circus procession, with participants and gods marching to the *circus* (the Roman equivalent of the Greek hippodrome), where races will take place.[57] In Italy, we have only the *Tabulae Iguvinae*, bronze tablets from Gubbio near Perugia inscribed in the second and early first century, to give an impression of how lavish ritual processions in the smaller cities could be. They tell us that a ritual, perhaps performed for the protection of the settlement, could not be held unless successful auspices had been observed by two individuals working in collaboration. There then followed an inspection of the three gates, with animals being sacrificed to various individual deities both before and behind each gate, plus an additional offering. The leading priest, distinguished by holding a staff, slaughtered another three animals in the sanctuaries of Jupiter and Coredius, each time delivering lengthy prayers.[58] The use of writing had obviously enabled ritual to become more complex.[59]

In Rome too, landowners, magistrates, and military commanders held comparable processions in the form of circuits around a locality. They might involve the whole city, a particular group of persons, voting citizens, or a military unit. In this way, they added an element of religious communication to the identity of groups or localities constituted politically or militarily, or on the basis of property ownership. We do not know when this practice began. As a stable ritual it may have dated from no earlier than the third century, having derived from a ritual confirming citizenship.[60] A group of three animals—a pig, a sheep, and a bull (the *suovetaurilia*)—accompanied the procession, indicating the ritual status of the actors involved, and making the ritual itself recognizable as such as it passed by. The intention was doubtless to disambiguate a group or location and the corresponding relation of ownership.[61] The Iguvine text makes this very clear with regard to the role played by the people of the city in another ritual. In this case, evidence comes from the wording of a prayer used in the rural ritual *agrum lustrare*, described in the first half of the second century BC by the elder Cato in his handbook on agriculture. Conscious of the risks of damage to the harvest posed by everything from disease to war, the actors in this ritual sought to make contact with another world that was hard for them to comprehend. Seeking to define that world as fundamentally benevolent, these administrators of a farm focused their risk-management strategy on their own misdeeds, which were predominantly of a ritual nature, and thus potentially redeemable only by dint of ritual repetition. It was therefore critical to precisely define both sides of this relationship, requiring exact specification of the group of religious actors involved and the relevant members of the other sphere, the latter through the use of quite specific names of gods.

In the event of a catastrophe that had already happened (such as a military defeat), or following an instance of general good fortune (a victory by the city's own forces), those in Rome who were affected pursued a diametrically opposite strategy. The "entreaty to the gods," the *supplicatio*, now called for the widest possible mobilization of participants, including women and dependants. For an entire day (and increasingly longer: eventually, in the first century BC, for as long as fifty days at a time), the gods were to be beseeched or thanked in all the temples, which were thrown open for the occasion.[62] Resonance, in the sense of connectivity between suppliants and the not indubitably present others, was either celebrated as having been strengthened or lamented as being absent in a non-specific, general sense. Competitive, architecturally- or theologically-based distinctions no longer played a role. So sacralization burgeoned, became total; and, in thus expanding, it came to typify what was in the mid-first century BC an increasingly absolutist regime, set to control even religious communication.

Calendars

Our examination of the sacralization of spaces has led us to examine broad expanses of time. This has been due not only to the limited availability of sources, but also to the fact that there would probably be details that differed in every individual performance of a ritual, and many such changes—although, at the time, they would usually be perceptible only at a microscopic level—made themselves felt only in the long term. On the other hand, changes in people's involvement with the sacralization of time, the calendar in other words, have frequently been revolutionary, and at the very least the objects of heated debate. Here we must focus our attention tightly on Rome, as the Roman calendar played a decisive role in the history of religious practices, especially in terms of sacralization, which has been the focus of my attention in this chapter.

That we view the Roman *fasti* virtually as a fact of nature has solely to do with the circumstance that many modern calendars are direct descendants of the format established in Rome. (I have given a full account of its history elsewhere.[63]) In brief, by the end of the fourth century the phases of the moon had ceased to be the central units by which time was measured, and were replaced by months of similar length, with adjustments to the existing intercalary mechanism. Rome thus departed from all the systems used elsewhere in both the Italian and the Greek worlds, where the course of the months from new moon to new moon was understood to reflect essential fractions of the solar year, and the moon's phases were observed accordingly; sun and moon stood for the ordered course of time, and provided the framework for ascribing certain qualities to certain days, thus sacralizing them.[64] As a technical measure, local rulers inserted intercalary months from time to time: on astronomical and thus climatic grounds; although they often did this simply because a lengthening of the year appeared politically opportune.[65] The aim in Rome was to alter this situation.

Whether as a cause or as a consequence of the renunciation of empirical lunar months, the written form of the calendar was changed to a format that represented all the days of the year in monthly columns. This initiative clearly surpassed that undertaken, for instance, in the *tabula Capuana* at the beginning of the fifth century BC, where ritual duties, probably of a priesthood, had been set out in a list of the days affected.[66] While the new, convenient layout made the calendar easier to use in the legal, political, and economic spheres, it at the same time made clear the extent to which, in analogy with the sacral ownership of land (space), time too had been sacralized. There is no doubt that this project formed part of a political process in which various strata of society, especially the patrician and plebeian elites, coalesced into one unified political elite, and were obliged to extend their attention to one another's religious commitments.[67] In the epoch termed the Republic, the claim of the "patricians," that they alone possessed the requisite competence to communicate with the gods, was increasingly contested.[68] Not for nothing was the new graphic representation named after the days whose use was *unconstrained* by religion, the *dies fasti*. The main historical models used by the Romans were calendars from Attica that listed all days when financial obligations arose from cult commitments, along with the names of benefactors.[69] Those actively concerned with the Roman project, among whom sources name in particular the *censor* and pontiff Appius Claudius (who subsequently acquired the cognomen "Caecus")[70] and his probably pontifical scribe, Gnaeus Flavius, treated the calendar as a municipal instrument intended to define the boundaries of a "public" religion relevant to all. Their efforts incorporated numerous errors that had to be resolved by the so-called *lex Hortensia* of 287 BC.

Perhaps publicly available in the shape of only one copy, the calendar text was of no use to individuals in organizing their religious practice. Even when, in the Imperial Age, private editions of the calendar were widely available, its indications of holidays reserved for the gods (*feriae*) and temple-foundation days appear not to have been used by individuals for allocating time to their own religious activities.[71] The complex rituals and the sacralization of time beyond the weekly and monthly rhythms, as revealed by the calendar, reflect the increasing complexity of life in the city of Rome. For those below the aristocratic level, the whole intricate round of special days represented opportunities for entertainment and occasional self-identification rather than a schema for personal religious activity.

4. Stories and Images

Communication with the realm of those I have referred to as "not indubitably plausible actors," but whom the Italics of the time would have been well able to address with individual names—much as *we* would address the gods or the dead by name, sharply distinguishing the one from the other—was normally not confined simply to words. The meaning of the words was reinforced with bodily movements, gestures, or representations of the bodies of the living actors. Such words and actions were embedded in stories about the addressees. The stories related to the storytellers themselves, their children, neighbors, and certain others, but they were also concerned with those special actors, be they gods or dead ancestors. They may have comprised reminders of the lives of the deceased; experiences of the living, such as dreams involving those who were long dead; or just stories about similar actors: thus harking back to authentic religious experiences, or mere fictions. Even when they concerned the past, such narratives offered important guides to the present and the future, no matter whether they explained, drew limits, or taught how one should or should not behave.[72]

That storytelling was (and still is!) important everywhere does not mean that it was everywhere equally important, or that it was everywhere important in the same sections of society, or, of course, that a particular story was everywhere the same. We have no texts, other than those from the ancient Orient and *Magna Graecia*, that can be traced back before the third century BC. What we do have are images that appear to relate to stories or to be calculated to invite storytelling. Typically, they represent scenes that can be understood only as single acts within a whole series of acts. As early as the seventh and sixth centuries, consumers in northern Etruria and Lombardy, who were wealthy in terms of exchange power rather than buying power (for there was as yet no money economy in which to be cash-wealthy), were ordering large bronze vessels depicting not only scenes of hunting and fighting, but also landscapes and banquets. Such out-of-the-ordinary objects were intended to be flaunted, not least because they represented the human qualities and virtues connected with the activities depicted,[73] and thus differentiated those viewing the objects as either equals or inferiors. Such vessels were most probably shown off in the context of banquets, and in such a context, centuries later in Rome, youths or professional storytellers performed stories in verse form and sang encomiums to ancestors.[74]

Whereas the prose narratives of one's grandmothers or hunting partners were prone to constant revision in the telling, in the rhythmic form of poetry the wording of a story would likely acquire stability. Poetry was suited to repetition. Images, on the other hand, were unique pieces. But they too tended toward stability, at least in particular details, and, in these as in their overall composition, they invited imitation. We have already observed this in the case of narrative friezes and gable groups on temples. A similar process was occurring in Etruscan tomb painting, and was later adopted in Rome as well, at the latest by the time of the Scipios in the third century. A further consideration of Etruscan burial chambers is called for if we are to understand this later Roman development.

The architects or commissioners of the above-mentioned tombs created spaces in which the dead were present: as statues of stone or clay, in the—seldom archaeologically recoverable—form of wooden heads, perhaps mounted on posts, on textiles, or in the shape of urns incorporating elements of the human figure.[75] Plastic forms could change according to changing fashions, and surely also changing conceptions as to the precise existential parameters of the dead; or they might remain unaltered by any such influence. In any event, relevant ideas were eagerly adopted from all over the Mediterranean region.[76] In the final analysis, whether ontology was consistent or not was immaterial; all that counted was that, in these spaces, it was possible to interact with dead ancestors,[77] or to enact such interaction and thereby demonstrate to others that an enduring link remained in effect.[78] In the process, the figures represented became associated with prototypes, and transient traditions were formed in a search for intelligibility and acceptance, then again to dissolve, either in a return to past forms or in pursuit of something new.

Stories can accomplish the same function as images; they can produce coherent accounts, although they may not be able to answer every question. Grandfather appeared to me in a dream, but was gone when I awoke: what is there to dispute in that? More important, however, is the ability to register that it was *my* grandfather who, when he was alive back then, drove out the enemy; and he *is still* my grandfather. While the narrative lives by progressing consistently through consecutive time, an image allows a succession of scenes to be given a synchronicity that forgoes temporal markers without positively asserting that they are entirely absent. Games, banquets, and processions are frequently not clearly marked as belonging to the one sphere of time or the other, the before or the after, even while the available repertory of such temporal markers increases. The custom of setting food before the dead progressively decreased, beginning as early as the sixth century.[79] The journey into the underworld was increasingly understood as being final and irreversible; painters interposed winged beings designated as nonhuman between the two realms. In the fifth century in particular they adopted Greek, especially Attic motifs depicting farewell scenes at an archway that stood for the passage between life and death.[80] The sequence of images in their locally defined setting reveals no clear conceptions of a hereafter, or even of a clear direction of progress toward such a destination.[81] For many, however, the idea of a journey to one's ancestors was critical.[82] The stress placed on genealogical lineage was in fact so important and so widespread a phenomenon that, by the sixth century at the latest, it led to a remodeling of the system of personal names, with the introduction of the gentilic or family name.[83] Tomb design subsequently gave this concern new forms and possibilities of expression. Through the medium of paintings, it was even possible to refer to ancestors buried elsewhere,[84] and the use of a tomb over several generations[85] would reinforce its function as a setting for the appropriation of the status and respect due to ancestors. At this time in history there was no other location where a broad cognatic family link, that is to say a link defined by a common ancestry (or understood to be so defined), could be as effectively expressed.[86] This process too was subsequently adopted in Rome.

The motif of an ancestor processing with magisterial honors went beyond a mere reference to the rank that ancestor had achieved: it further justified that rank by the telling of its public enactment.[87] Some families in the fourth century went one step further, using their tombs

18. Mural painting from the François tomb at Vulci (Latium): Achilles slaughters
Trojan prisoners in revenge for the killing of Patroklos, ca. 320–310 BC. Florence,
Soprintendenza per i Beni Archeologici della Toscana. Drawing by Augusto
Guido Gatti, 1931. akg-images / Rabatti–Domingie.

to tell more precise stories of concrete, usually warlike services; it is
probably to such models that members of a branch of the Roman Cornelii, the Scipios, referred in decorating their tomb.[88] The owners of
the François Tomb at Vulci went to particular pains for such a project
at the end of the fourth century, filling the tomb's walls with an upper
and a lower register of paintings depicting both mythical Greek and
historical Etruscan stories (fig. 18).[89] This program of illustration
broke with the parochial orientation typical of the isolated city states
of central Italy, which was reflected in tomb paintings that concentrated
entirely on a patron's own family. It may well itself have reflected increasing social and political confrontation among the Etruscan cities

and between them and Rome. The Greeks, whose constantly expanding world embraced almost the entire Mediterranean, had freed myths of their local contexts, making of them a virtually international medium of communication. Greek myths became essentially universal themes, with potters depicting the most popular of them on the wares they produced for export.[90] Such narratives provided a chronological and topographical grid that embraced that wider world, and upon which the early histories of the Greeks' trading partners and those of their enemies could be superimposed. The private iconographies, and even the individually produced mythological narratives, that are found on the polished metal backs of Etruscan mirrors, with their frequently very specific references, scarcely bore comparison. Family accomplishments and the deeds of an individual's own ancestors were important in the struggle for distinction and social position in an Italian city, and accordingly had to be represented. Descent from gods, as regularly narrated in Greek myths, was—as yet—too high-value a coin for the purpose.

V

The Appropriation and Shaping of Religious Practices by Religious Actors

THE FIFTH TO FIRST CENTURIES BC

1. Heterarchy and Aristocracy

The religious activity I described in the previous chapter always involved actions of individuals in social contexts. These contexts varied greatly in spatial, temporal, and social terms, and were inherently complex. The ritual in or on a tomb was on some occasions visible only to a few people, on others to many, perhaps extending beyond actual participants to mere onlookers. Processions allowed and even compelled the attention of large numbers of such onlookers. Durable media such as stelai or entire buildings generated observers beyond the time of the ritual activity, and motivated both those near to the event and those far from it to compete for distinction on their own account. The sacralization of a location might focus religious activity: the tomb served as a medium for the family, enabling it to communicate with its deceased members, and at the same time essentially bringing the family into being by providing a location, images, and narratives that others could adopt as a collective identity, thus also assigning themselves to the family, and perhaps exclusively so. Other cult locations performed similar functions, as we have seen. They also encouraged members of other houses and families, perhaps even incomers, to participate in religious activity, normally without any absolute insistence on a particular divine addressee.

Religious communication thus provided an opportunity to create or reinforce collective familial identities extending to the large associations of families, or clans, that we identify under the Latin concept *gentes*.[1] Its effect on geographically defined associations was similar. The latter in the case of central Italy were probably the *curiae*, perhaps to be understood as extended neighborhoods. In Rome, they functioned as one of the oldest political units; their assemblies (*comitia curiata*) not only invested commanders with unlimited military authority, but also ruled on the religious duties of families and on adoptions.[2] The rituals of these neighborhood associations were presumably too mundane to become the subject of historiography. What little we know of them comes in part from Carolingian extracts of extracts dated to the Imperial Age, which tell us that these *curiae* chose not only a leader (*curio*) but also a *flamen* for ritual functions; it was in such a context that they also sacrificed on their own tables to a deity named Juno Curis.[3] During the Augustan Age, at the end of the first century BC, a Greek observer, Dionysius of Halicarnassus, wrote of their having buildings specifically for dining.[4] The "senior" *curio* had the status of a high-ranking priest, and, until the end of the third century BC, it was required that he be a patrician; Gaius Mamilius Atellus (d. 174 BC) was the first plebeian to hold this office, from 209 BC.[5]

We know still less about other geographically defined groups. There were the "hills" (*montes*), the "tribes" (*tribus*), and later the "streets" or "neighborhoods" (*vici*). Although we know little that is reliable about them, it is evident that they, like the *curiae*, underwent pronounced changes over time.[6] Thus, according to later sources, the first of these groups celebrated rituals, perhaps going back to a very early period, peculiar to each of the hills of Rome (*Septimontium*).[7] We know nothing of any religious activities of the *tribus*, whose membership extended deep into Rome's environs. The existence of such groups, however, indicates that it would be quite unwise to confine our attentions too narrowly to the city of Rome (and this applies to other Etruscan cities as well): important groups that participated in the life of the city not only had their economic bases in the surrounding territories, but also to some extent their real places of abode.[8] Nonetheless, and perhaps for this very reason, religious communication was important for the formation of political links that transcended local allegiances, and for the delineation of geographical coherence and a corresponding collective identity.

We may speak of the "state" and of the "city," but at least the first of these concepts is highly problematic at this period. Great clans decided the political fate of Rome, and into the medieval papal era provided its cohesion, on the one hand confronting one another and competing for positions (even to the extent of seeking consulships for small children), and on the other being prepared to tolerate or support the centralized administration. The extent to which such clans cooperated in particular instances varied dramatically, as did the social imaginaries that they developed as collective identities, which then became institutionalized. The Roman Republic, we must constantly keep in mind, was a "precarious statehood."[9] By the second half of the fourth century BC, the development of Rome's strong imperialist orientation toward the external world,[10] and the growing conception of broadly based, shared interests, a common ethos, and a division of power,[11] ran up against efforts to anchor the conceived interests of groups—of landowners, veterans, the landless, and others— ever more strongly within the institutional fabric, while also conflicting with increasingly manifest and undesired concentrations of power: the Gracchi, Marius, Sulla, Pompey, and Caesar come to mind.[12]

The limits of Rome's statehood become even more palpable when we consider their effect in the field of warfare. While perhaps appearing to have been the central function of the city's coalition of forces, war remained a sphere of clan activity: plundering expeditions served exclusively to increase the wealth of those who carried them out.[13] But what happened when the resulting counterattacks did not distinguish as precisely as they might between particular Roman actors? Envoys of the *res publica*, the "common cause," were sent out to resolve such situations, and they might either demand the return of plundered goods, or arrange for the perpetrator to be delivered up. Religious communication was the element that reduced the potential for internal conflict in such circumstances, and lent greater weight to the proceedings in the eyes of outsiders. Jupiter was invoked as a witness. The envoys, the *fetiales*, were sacralized, looked upon as *pater patratus* and "priests," and given sacral legitimation: a tuft of grass with earth from the Capitol showed quite plainly that the central concern was the common soil of Rome.[14]

The common cause found everyday visible expression in the magistrates identified by their purple-striped togas; these were elected always for one year only, and were thus constantly changing figures of authority. They were "those who walk in front," the "counselors" (according to contemporary etymology), and the "builders" (*praetores, consules, aediles*), who, along with their personal assistants and slaves (figs. 19 and 20), in principle saw to routine official business. We do not see them acting as departmental heads, but rather engaging in dealings with the plenary assembly of hereditary or conferred nobility, in other words with the Senate, and with the various types of popular assemblies; and of course as military commanders. This was where their presence was felt. Religious activities—praying aloud, leading a procession, or presenting a gift to a deity—formed an occasional or ancillary part of their duties.[15] In some cases, the rituals they performed took place outside Rome: the *feriae latinae* on the Mons Albanus, and occasional rituals at Lavinium;[16] thus out of sight to most Romans. But they were rendered all the more visible in the city of Rome by communication via inscriptions and poetic recreations,[17] creating the classic conditions under which a culture of secrecy becomes established.[18] At the same time, the magistrates entered into religious communication with inhabitants of more remote parts, which was a practical impossibility for other city-dwellers.[19]

These men also used religious activities within their own homes or clans, in the context of important gatherings. Games, sacrifices of meat, simply the distribution of meat out of the stock or the surpluses held by this agriculturally active elite, or demonstrations of its power

19. Ritual functionaries, such as *popae* and *victimarii*, in the center of the procession on
the so-called Altar of the Vicomagistri, second quarter of the first century AD. Original:
Rome, Museo Gregoriano Profano. Copy Römisch-Germanisches Zentralmuseum
Mainz; reproduced with the museum's kind permission. Photo: Jörg Rüpke.

of disposition over building material and labor, were an important element in the construction of a *res publica*. And, in the broad context of
the free citizenry, this "public thing" was less a matter of conducting
political deliberations in common than—as was usual in politics well
into the Early Modern Period—a forum for giving and receiving.[20]
Thus were inequalities, obligations, and the recognition of shared
values assured in the long term. At the same time, it was only the opportunities for competition, for gaining distinction, and for mutual
point-scoring offered by these rituals that made the expense involved
worthwhile from the viewpoint of the individuals who initiated
them.[21]

The question arises as to what circumstances might have called
for these services to be offered, services that, together with those

20. Bronze statuette, ca. 13 cm, of a *victimarius* with loincloth and knife (*culter*), crowned with laurel, probably grasping a rope to lead the animal; early first century A D. Kestner-Museum Hannover. Published with the museum's kind permission.

provided by small-scale merchants and craftsmen, went into the making of a "city."[22] The original core around which Rome urbanized had certainly been the harbor and its ancillary workshops.[23] This area attracted the palace-like dwellings of the nobility, who chose to demonstrate their wealth, forsaking—in Rome at any rate—the ostentatious tombs of an earlier period.[24] The necessary infrastructure for the city's water supply and drainage, and for flood prevention, was undertaken early on, while facilities to ensure the supply of grain did not follow until the end of the third century BC. Temple structures—we know of about ten built in the period of the Sant'Omobono sanctuary alone—had already acquired (renewed) importance prior to the institution of the *cura annonae*.

2. Priests

As in Rome's Etruscan-Latin environs, permanent specialists in religious roles played no perceptible part in the early life of the city, whether as partners in or counterparts to political or economic power. We have already noted the occasional experiments that were made in Etruscan locations to associate such roles with a symbol in the form of the later Roman augur's staff, or in Latium with a statuette and a knife;[25] and the story of Attus Navius circulated in Rome, telling how his arts of divination and magic brought Tarquinius Priscus to despair, as the seer always remained one step ahead of the king, and was finally able to split a whetstone with a razor.[26] The augur Cicero liked to tell the story in the first century BC, but the picture of priestly power it projects is one that the institution of Cicero's time would scarcely have been able to conceive of.

The flamens were an exception. These were men with long-term ritual functions that also extended to their wives (*flaminica*).[27] Use of the name, perhaps linguistically(!) kin to the Indian *Brahmin*,[28] suggests an ancient religious title related to particular gods, identified by the use of adjectives such as *Dialis, Martialis, Quirinalis*, and *Carmentalis*. The flamens' specifically religious role was marked by a distinctive and striking costume. Marcus Popillius, consul in 359 BC, earned himself a nickname when, wearing the cult costume of the *flamen Carmentalis*, he hurried straight from the ritual into an assembly.[29] The attendance of the different flamens together at the sanctuary of Fides, who stood for keeping one's word even to inferiors,[30] may, like the obligation that they should be married, have indicated a particular role that flamens played in ancient clans. It was in the flamen's role in particular that the aristocracy as a whole demonstrated how extraordinary and demanding it was to be in such close and continuous communication with a deity. At the same time, individual flamens repeatedly rebelled against the resulting constraints on their freedom of movement and social liberty, such as the injunction against leaving Rome overnight, the requirement that the *flamen Dialis* should wear an extravagant head-covering at all times, and the obligation that they should choose a wife only from within a restricted circle. Waivers were granted in individual cases.[31]

Vestal Virgins

Although conveying no political power, the above high-profile positions, monopolized as they were by the old inherited aristocracy (*patricii*), played as much of a role in the conflict between that aristocracy and more recently ennobled families (the *plebeii*) as the constant threat of loss of office and life, on the grounds of alleged sexual contact, directed against the Vestal Virgins (fig. 21), who came from plebeian families.[32] In the event of doubt in such cases, recourse to an appeal procedure was possible, such as the one in 113 BC undergone by Licinia and Marcia, who, unlike their colleague Aemilia (sentenced in 114), had been acquitted the previous year.[33] Having already as children been withdrawn from family structures and from the marriage track, the Vestals lived in a state of apparent retirement in their own complex of buildings on the Forum in the center of Rome; this gave them scope to exercise a variety of functions, such as storing volatile political testaments, granting temporary asylum, and riding with their own father on his triumph to protect him from being manhandled.[34] Their day-to-day functions remained unaffected: they tended

21. Relief with four vestal virgins and, at right, a priest (Pontifex maximus?) standing before altars; the priest addresses Vesta who is seated at the left. From Mistretta, Sicily, first century A D. Palermo, Museo Archeologico Regionale. akg-images / De Agostini Picture Lib. / A. Dagli Orti.

the fire in the circular sanctuary of Vesta, produced and stored the blend of salt and grain (*mola salsa*) with which every animal sacrificed in Rome was ideally sprinkled before being slaughtered (*immolatio*), and kept watch over the household gods, who, by later interpretation, originated from Troy (the *penates*).

If a "state religion" is to be found anywhere in Rome, it is here in the Atrium and the Aedis Vestae. The "common cause," the *res publica*, was enacted here, directly opposite the Regia, on the marketplace, which had been drained by the efforts of several *gentes*. And, what is more, it was enacted as an institutionalized religious act: daily visible, and yet with its most important aspects hidden from view. Here was produced the *mola salsa*, a collective identity transportable in a casket or bag. We do not know who actually fetched and used this substance shared by all, and thus assumed the role of the archetypical Roman. The Vestals promoted the same common cause through their participation in the Fordicidia, held on the 15th of April. The slaughtering of pregnant cows in the *curiae* was supplemented by a central ritual in the form of a similar killing performed on the Capitol (more precisely at its highest point, which was dedicated to Juno) in the presence of the supreme pontiff. The oldest Vestal (*virgo Vestalis maxima*) cremated the fetus, and then six days later at the Parilia (April 21) distributed its ashes as ingredients for a purification ritual for both animals and humans, held on the very day when the birthday of Rome was celebrated.[35] Alongside its overt materiality, this performance also incorporated a reference to geographical and metaphysical transcendence, a narrative of commonality that was not ethnically based, but rather a tale of migration (from Asia Minor), and of a connectivity beyond the actual social space (perhaps involving the miraculous rekindling of the fire of the goddess, and objects fallen from the heavens): the first of these elements, though, did not transpire until Rome itself was already functioning as a great power in the Mediterranean. The scale of values of the actors involved is revealed by the fact that they chose young girls and women for this task that involved such a harsh subordination to rules. Another aspect of gender role as it appears in this context was that the Vestals themselves did not perform animal sacrifice, but presented bloodless gifts instead, such as cooked grains and cakes. They were accordingly backed, not by *victimarii* (butchers), like other ritual actors, but by their own baker (*fictor*),[36] a post that was highly respected in the Imperial Age. Flavius Apronius, one of these ritual bakers, expressed his gratitude in 250 AD with a statue honoring the *vestalis maxima* Flavia Publicia, so acquiring for himself an indirect but durable presence in the Atrium among the statues of the Vestals.[37] In the persons of the Vestals can thus be read the manner in which religion itself was able to alter gender relationships.

Pontiffs and Augurs

The most powerful of Rome's religious specialists are scarcely to be compared with the groups we have mentioned up to now in terms of the roles they played. Later historiography may well be correct in assuming that two small *collegia*, probably comprising five augurs and five pontiffs respectively, representing important clans, and each headed by its longest-serving member, had already existed during the so-called Age of Kings in the seventh and sixth centuries. Insofar as they themselves identified and co-opted successors for deceased members (without the popular elections that would have been held for magistracies), they perpetuated not only knowledge, but also established lines of compromise and personal and family relationships.

The "bridge-builders" (a term that can scarcely have been meant as a metaphor for the relationship to the divine) appear to have dealt mostly with problems involving the validity of norms across clan or family boundaries, primarily claims that had been raised concerning locations and times, and, where important, backed up by religious action. Am I permitted to use land where your forefathers are (allegedly?) buried? Is a promise valid even when it is given outside the social control of the clan? Must I respect your feast day by refraining from activity? Is your marriage ritual also binding for my daughter? Can you assign my land to a god, and so deprive me of its use? These may have been burning questions for a "political" coalition that had built its new center, the Forum, over an old cemetery. Claims formulated in religious terms were not a separate category; but they thereby acquired particular cogency. It may have been inevitable that the arbitration committee itself, being representative of all clans, also used religious communication, and was a participant in the rite that constituted the most elaborate of all mechanisms for resolving inter-clan problems: the plebiscite. According to this hypothesis, the bridge that the pontiffs built would have been the walkway (*pons*) leading to the poll. The nomenclature is suggested by the fact that it was here that their function became most visible. If this primary hypothesis is true, it explains the pontiffs' later function as experts in, even inventors (or translators) of what was emphatically nonreligious law (*ius*). And it would explain as well their assumption of a statutory role (if I may be permitted the anachronism) supervising important categories of religious activity and religious actors, in a sphere that they themselves were helping to define as *publicum*, as distinguished from *privatum* and *sacrum*.[38]

While the pontiffs often explored the boundaries of religious action, and also set those boundaries, the augurs constrained political and military action by religious means. Here too, though, the initiative belonged to the *collegium augurum* functioning as an instrument of all the clans, and not to one seer or, specifically, augur acting alone.[39] Partly a protagonist, and partly an expert consultant, an augur consulted the auspices before important acts of the highest magistrates, such as the convening of public assemblies. He went before dawn to an appropriate location, choosing a vantage point that would be as undisturbed as possible. The observation point was demarcated, and then a determination made as to which bird-songs or bird-flights would constitute a positive answer. Our detailed knowledge of the techniques employed comes from the later Republic, the procedure given here being that recorded on the Iguvine Tablets. Lightning too was observed, using techniques that have also been attributed to the Etruscans, although not in every detail.

From the standpoint of the magistrates affected by such decisions, religious action in a particular sphere was bound up with political action. Their own activities involved elements of religious communication, but at the same time they also consulted expert knowledge that was imputed or even publicized as such, but which manifested itself in practice in the persons of specialists who were themselves distinguished by intensive religious activity. This dual structure of reference, to the gods and to the experts, permitted religious actors to present innovations in the context of a traditionally legitimized activity. Success did not, however, reside in either the pragmatic flexibility or traditionally maintained rigidity of these religious practices in the public sphere. "Civic religion," as this category of religious practice is often called, was precisely *not* the binding smallest common denominator, but rather the largest common multiple that covered the fragility of compromises with the vision of an additional level of religious communication, while not casting doubt on the religious practices of individuals, families, or clans, or networks based on trade, commerce, ethnicity, or gender. These latter networks were not controlled, but appropriated.[40]

The importance of institutionalized religious roles grew alongside the proliferation of "common" institutions along with a common administration, all these being steps in the formation of statehood. An increase in the memberships of the existing *collegia* (colleges, "professional institutions"), and the extension of the *collegium* model to interpreters of the collection of Greek oracles called the Sibylline books (*duoviri sacris faciundis*), initially ad hoc appointments, was thus to be expected. It paralleled the phase of enormous state growth that reached early and significant high points with the *Lex Licinia Sextia* on plebeian consuls, and Rome's victory in the Latin Wars. That same set of laws (dated 367 BC and named for the people's tribunes who proposed them, Lucius Sextus Lateranus and Gaius Licinius Stolo) extended the committee overseeing the oracles to ten members. In about 300 BC, the membership of both the pontifical and augural colleges was also increased to nine priests by the additional election of plebeians.[41] With the increasing consolidation of group interests, the election of additional priests to these colleges (and to the initially three-, then seven-strong *epulones* [aides to the pontiffs]) became a contentious issue. Initiatives to carry out the appointments by popular vote failed, then passed, were revoked, and then reinstated; in the Imperial period, the choice was left to the Senate. Only the appointment of the *pontifex maximus*, who, after the reforms of the fourth century, had acquired extremely broad authority, was made subject to consensus from the second half of the third century onward. As in other elections, optimum geographical participation was probably achieved through election by the tribes; Augustus in 12 BC boasted of having been elected by people "from all Italy." And yet priests were not treated in the same way as magistrates. Of the thirty-five tribes, only seventeen, chosen by lot, were able to participate in the vote, amounting to what might be termed a "negative quorum" of *less* than one half.[42] Privileged communication with the gods was not a matter to be decided by majority rule.

3. Distinction

And how did the candidates see this? Membership in a priesthood does not play a central role in the few autobiographical texts that have come down to us from the period of the Republic; and this does not change until Augustus's publication of his *Res Gestae* (Deeds). But the occasional letter that mentions the careers of magistrates and priests reveals how important membership in a college was for male aristocrats seeking distinction within the senatorial class.

Priestly Careers

M. Aemilius Lepidus (ca. 230–152 BC) had already been appointed to his first post as legate in 201. He was co-opted as *pontifex* in 199, became curule *aedile* six years later (193), consul for the first time in 187 (after an unsuccessful candidature in 189), and consul for a second time in 175. In the meantime, he was elected as *pontifex maximus* in 180, nineteen years after his co-option, and became *censor* immediately afterward in 179. As *censor*, to finance the renovation of the Capitoline Temple of Jupiter he used proceeds from the sale of votive weapons actually dedicated to the gods (it will be remembered that the repurposing of votives was not unusual). He was *princeps senatus* from that same period. In the same year, 179, as *pontifex maximus* he had a vestal flogged. More biographical details on the life of Lepidus have come down to us than is usual for priests. We know further that in 172 he recited the prayer before the magistrates at the *vota decennalia,* and that in 159 he resolved a conflict of unknown nature by fining the former people's tribune and *praetor* for that year. In 156 a lightning strike hurled the roof of his official residence, along with its pillars, into the Tiber. Four years later, in 152, by decision of the college he refused the *censor* the right to a valid *dedicatio* of a statue of Concordia. Finally, on his deathbed, he is said to have requested a modest funeral, without purple, and costing no more than a million *asses*.[43] With such an amount, he could have fed the entire freeborn population of Rome on the day of his funeral.

L. Cornelius Dolabella was a somewhat younger patrician contemporary who came into conflict with Lepidus's predecessor in the office of *pontifex maximus*, the plebeian C. Servilius Geminus. Geminus, in his final year of office (180), had selected Dolabella for the office of *rex sacrorum*, in succession to Cn. Cornelius Dolabella. The younger Dolabella refused, even though it was perhaps—we do not know for certain—a question of succeeding his own father. Although Geminus fined him, Dolabella refused to resign as *duumvir navalis* (fleet commissioner, 180–178) in favor of the office offered him, which was subject to political restrictions. P. Cloelius Siculus therefore had to be appointed in his place.[44]

The reaction of Gaius Valerius Flaccus was quite different when, entirely against his will, he was made *flamen Dialis* in 209. Much to the satisfaction of imperial writers, he demonstrated the extent to which a man was capable of changing, and set about his new functions with a will: so much so that he was able successfully to petition for a senatorial seat for the *flamen*, and for his right to hold municipal office.[45] A solution was even found for the problem that arose when he was appointed as *aedile* (199), and had to swear an oath (a binding act that was not permissible for a *flamen*): his brother spoke the oath on his behalf.

The life of Gaius Iulius Caesar (13 July 100–15 March 44 BC), likewise a patrician, can also be described in terms of priesthoods. While still a boy he had probably already become a *salius*, one of a group of priests who progressed through the city performing a kind of springing, three-step dance. They were especially active in March, when, armed with shields in the form of a figure 8 (regarded as an archaic form), they took part in a number of rituals. Appointment to this role was normally granted at an early age, to females as well as males, and the office may have developed from initiation rituals. In the Imperial

Age, members retired as a rule upon first assuming higher office.[46] Caesar was probably nominated, and presumably also inaugurated, as *flamen Dialis* at Cinna's instigation at the beginning of 84, at the age of fifteen, after his separation from his first wife Cossutia and marriage to Cinna's daughter Cornelia. When, in the course of a restructuring of the priesthoods, Sulla wanted to force him to separate from his adversary's daughter upon pain of supreme pontifical sanction, Caesar seized the remedy of *provocatio ad populum* against the measure, but lost his case before an assembly dominated by Sulla, and so could no longer fully carry out the functions of the prestigious office. A compromise was arrived at on the initiative of Caesar's fellow members of the pontifical college: the earlier determination that Caesar held the office wrongfully would become moot, and the flaminate would for his lifetime remain unoccupied. It remained vacant until 14 BC. Caesar was also offered the prospect of resuming his place in the pontifical college, to which he had belonged as *flamen Dialis*. He was co-opted as *pontifex* in his absence in about 73 BC (the popular vote had again been annulled at this time, although Sulla had increased the membership of the colleges from nine to fifteen); Caesar's co-option as pontiff preceded his quaestorship (69/68), and this with a majority of Sulla's associates in the college. In 63, thus prior to being appointed praetor in 62, Caesar was elected as *pontifex maximus* over his older and better-known fellow candidates, Quintus Lutatius Catulus and Publius Servilius Vatia Isauricus. He was consul for the first time in 59, but it was not until after his victories in Gaul, his second consulate in 48, and his second dictatorship in 48/47 in the middle of the Civil War that he was elected as augur. He assumed the post at the end of 47 or the beginning of 46 at the latest (the popular vote had in the meantime been reintroduced, and the colleges increased in size, although only by one seat—perhaps for Caesar himself—to sixteen members). Caesar as dictator now implemented a thoroughgoing reform of the calendar. By his authority as *pontifex maximus* he added intercalary months that lengthened the year to 445 days in all. A book, *De astris*, published at the same time, demonstrated the knowledge behind this act, just as his *Commentarii de bello Gallico* presented the details and rationale of his earlier military activities; but he made no mention at all of the supreme pontificate,[47] or of his steps toward claiming god-like veneration.

As our examples show, religious activity, even in its institutionalized forms, amounted to more than the rational use of a resource that was entirely calculable, for the not indubitably plausible actors hardly ever intervened of their own accord, and ritual action required that exacting rules be followed.[48] Human beings used religious action as a special form of problem-solving:[49] they reacted to the widest imaginable array of problematic situations by resorting to a plethora of addressees, chosen from the long list of deities that arrived as newcomers to the sphere of religious communication during the middle and late Republic. These ranged from deities embodying social values, such as Concordia and Virtue, to gods and goddesses of healing and protection, such as Asclepius and Isis. This company was not the organized "pantheon" of a "civic religion," but the unsystematic consequence of individual decisions arrived at on the basis of what was known and what was acceptable at the level of one's family, region, or intellect. On these grounds, for example, the choice was made as to whether one should continue with one cult or neglect another. The actors concerned perceived past actions and former addressees as traditions to be reinforced by repetition, altered by modifications, or creatively (and on occasion subversively) appropriated.

The new institutionalized religious roles posed entirely new challenges, for in the expanding territory under imperial domination there were now positions that called for service by and large beyond the bounds of Rome, whereas particular priestly obligations were tied to the city. As such cases arose sporadically over the course of a half century, a consensus was reached, around 200 BC, that priestly offices requiring such absences should not be held by patricians. No explicit rule to this effect was ever formulated, but the injunction came into effect via a long exploratory process. A number of persons resigned from the office of *flamen*; plebeians at one time were eligible for the post of *rex sacrorum*, then again not; the *flamen Dialis* received a seat in the Senate without having been able to fill any magistracy before; a *pontifex maximus* voluntarily took on an Italic constituency instead of a province. As much as the distinction of a priestly office was valued, there was little willingness to forsake other chances for its sake.

Temple Construction

The actors engaged in temple construction quite consciously left behind distinctly more visible traces than those left by debates over ritual rules. This more concrete field of distinction by religious activity became even more important in Rome after the close of the fourth century BC. The list of confirmed addressees of temple structures from that time to Caesar's death shows both the variety and the limitations discernible in the selection of deities by those who vowed or dedicated such buildings:

Aesculapius (292), Bellona (296), Bona Dea (second century), Castor and Pollux (second century?), Clementia Caesaris (44), Concordia (216), Consus (272), Diana (179), Faunus (194), Felicitas (151), Felicitas Feronia (225), Flora (240), Flora (3rd century), Fons (231), Fors Fortuna (293), Fortuna Equestris (173), Fortuna huiusce diei (168), Fortuna huiusce diei (101), Fortuna Primigenia (194), Fortuna Publica (241), Hercules (third century), Hercules Invictus (292), Hercules Magnus custos (223), Hercules Musarum (189), Honos (233), Honos (third century), Honos and Virtus (222), Honos and Virtus (early first century), Hora Quirini (third century), Janus (260), Juno Curritis (241), Juno Regina (179), Juno Sospita (194), Jupiter Fulgur (third century), Jupiter Invictus (ca. second century), Jupiter Libertas (246), Jupiter Stator (294), Jupiter Stator and Juno Regina (146), Jupiter Victor (295), Juturna (242/1), Juventas (191), Lares (third century), Lares Permarini (179), Luna (third century), Mars (138), Mars Invictus (second century?), Mater Magna (191), Mens (215), Minerva (263/2), Neptunus (257), Ops (third century), Ops Opifera (250), Pales (267), Penates (3rd century), Pietas (181), Pietas (91), Portunus (292), Salus (302), Sol and Luna (third century), Sol Indiges (third century), Spes and Fides (258/7),

Summanus (276), Tellus (268), Tempestates (259), Tiberinus (third century), Vediovis (194), Vediovis (192), Venus Erucina (215), Venus Erucina (181), Venus Genetrix (46), Venus Libitina (temple construction uncertain, third century), Venus Obsequens (295), Venus Verticordia (114), Venus Victrix, Honos and Virtus and Felicitas (55), Vica Pota (third century), Victoria Virgo (193), Volcanus (252), Vortumnus (264).[50]

But the identity of the particular divine addressee does not begin to reveal the complex reality of the diverse processes of religious communication occurring at each of these locations. The addressee, male or female, is only one element of the bigger picture. Even in the case of the central Capitoline Temple of Jupiter, we find references to Juno in Jupiter's *cella*, and appropriate tales to explain this.[51] The architecture itself was a more visible and more effective factor. Collaborating with the architect, those who commissioned a temple could communicate their desires as to its external size and shape, the spatial effect and decoration of its internal design, and the size, design, and positioning of the image of the god in the inner room.[52] The choice of unusual forms, such as the round temple, is especially noteworthy.

A few years after 146 BC (the confirmed date for the first marble temple in Rome), after a successfully foiled pirate attack, a merchant called Marcus Octavius Herennus, who had once been a flute-player, built a round temple on the Tiber and dedicated it to Hercules Victor (fig. 22). In so doing—and this was confirmed by Masurius Sabinus in the early first century AD—he established a link between his own experience and Hercules's general identification with successful commerce.[53] It is possible that he was supported by the prominent architect Hermodorus, who was active at this period. The structure—if we are talking of the round temple still visible on the Forum Boarium, and if that is not to be identified instead with the temple, also dedicated to Hercules Victor, built by Lucius Mummius, the victor over Corinth[54]—was unusual in many ways. It had neither a podium nor a clearly defined frontal aspect. The twenty columns stood so close together that they entirely obstructed the view of the core structure,

22. Temple of Hercules on the Forum Boarium, Rome,
mid-second century BC. Photo: J. Rüpke.

the *cella*, and from a distance also obscured the entrance with its two
flanking windows. Only from close up, with the door and windows
open, would the statue placed at the center have been sufficiently lit to
be visible. The foundation was built of common Grotta-Oscura tufa,
but the superstructure emphasized innovation and a sophisticated
aesthetic. The internal walls were built of travertine, a newly fashionable building material that was available locally, while the slender
columns, almost ten-and-a-half meters in height, were fashioned of
Pentelic marble from Attica. This was surely a demonstration of superior wealth, and of the appreciation of Greek culture that is so evident
at multiple locations around the city, in Rome's institutions and its
theatrical productions; it testifies both to cultivation and to plunder.

It was probably a few decades later that Quintus Lutatius Catulus
undertook yet another experiment with round sanctuaries by building a temple to "Fortuna of the Present Day" (*Fortuna huiusce diei*) on
the Field of Mars, today to be admired as Temple B on the Largo

Argentina (fig. 23). The importance that the consul of 102 assigned to religious communication is shown not only by this temple, built in the year following his consulate, but also by the fact that, while he himself probably did not hold a priestly office, he succeeded in having his son co-opted by the pontiffs in the following decade, and that son went on to become celebrated by completing in lavish fashion the restoration, begun by Sulla, of the Capitoline Temple of Jupiter.[55] Quite unlike Herennus, Catulus set his round structure on a two-and-a half-meter-high podium, and surrounded it with eighteen more substantial pillars, also on Attic bases and with Corinthian capitals that reached an overall height of nearly eleven meters above the podium. The builder gave this structure, one of a series of temples[56] at the same location on the Field of Mars, a clear orientation and frontal aspect. A broad stairway leads up to the podium, and the approach to the entrance is in alignment with a widened intercolumnium. Catulus had the colossal cult image placed in such a way that it faced the visitor, in living color, at the opposite end of the internal space; its visible body parts were of white marble (perhaps with a painted surface), while the rest of the figure may have consisted of bronze body armor. When the entrance-way was open, this eight-meter-high deity filled the space so that it was visible from a great distance. In his choice of addressee, Catulus, too, refers back to tradition, which identified Fortuna as the force of fate, and linked her with a radically personal twist of his own fortune. She is the power who helped him at a particular moment, and his purpose in honoring her in this highly visible, even insistent way is entirely polemical. For, in honoring Fortuna, Catulus is also celebrating his own victory over the Cimbri at Vercellae (in June of 101 BC), won by him *together with* Gaius Marius, the already celebrated commander: an assertion to which the construction of the temple gives monumental relevance. We must not forget that Catulus is doing this at a time when the presentation of votive objects is still a widespread form of popular ritual practice. The marble structure gleams in contrast with the clay objects left on benches and in pits,[57] emphasizing that the temple is not just a building, but a representation and perpetuation of a specific religious communication aimed at higher

23. Circular temple of Fortuna huiusce diei at the Largo Argentina, Rome,
second century BC. Photo: J. Rüpke.

powers. Of course Quintus Lutatius also broadcast his version of
events by word of mouth and the written word, but, in the heightened
competitive atmosphere of the late Republic, mere tales or assertions
were not enough.[58] Any individual with the necessary wherewithal
saw to it that buildings dedicated to the gods would stand as witnesses
in stone to his own importance.

4. Banquet Culture

Distinction was, however, also sought within the growing ambit of
the colleges, and a Roman aristocrat's prime locus for self-representation
was his own house, that palace-like structure for which the term
"villa" today easily awakens confusing associations.[59] This strategy
was publicly advocated. In the first century BC the Roman architect
Vitruvius advised aristocrats to construct for themselves houses com-
mensurate with their prestige. High, regal entrance halls were required,

broad courtyards and arbors, and generous wooded areas and paths, where a man could relax from the burdens of his office and the services he provided to the citizenry. Private libraries, art galleries, and reception rooms should conform in scale to those in public buildings, as they had to offer space enough for public as well as private consultations.[60] These requirements also applied to members of priestly colleges. And the houses could not be built just anywhere. Into the first century BC, the Roman Forum was a prime location for such residences, and for a few shops as well.[61] What imperial development made into "public space," comparable to the Greek *agora*,[62] comprised primarily the common forecourts of aristocratic palaces interspersed with a small number of facades, such as those of the Temple of Castor and Pollux and the Atrium Vestae. Here old and new aristocratic families built and maintained their residences; behind these facades they held daily receptions for their clients, or received fellow college members. As elsewhere, the owners of these houses added an open courtyard with a surrounding colonnade (peristyle), and reduced the older, frontally positioned atrium to a more austere space for meetings with people of more modest rank. The atrium was further traditionalized by the display of ancestral portraits. The brighter peristyle with its murals and herms became the venue for more intimate, higher-status meetings with people of the owner's rank and cultural orientation, and in addition served as a location for various religious practices.[63]

We know that, at least in the first centuries BC and AD, acceptance into a college entailed the obligation to provide a lavish meal for its members; this was the *cena aditialis*, the enrollment meal. The *Saturnalia* of Macrobius, a work of the early fifth century AD that derives— needless to say not directly—from the pontiffs' *commentarii*, gives us a contemporary, first-hand description of such an event (while at the same time representing the longest direct quotation from any of the *libri sacerdotum*.)

On the ninth day before the Kalends of September [22 August, probably 70 BC], on which day Lentulus was inaugurated as flamen of Mars, the house was decked out, the dining rooms laid with

ivory couches; the pontiffs reclined in two dining rooms—Quintus
Catulus, Mamercus Aemilius Lepidus, Decimus Silanus, Gaius
Caesar, . . . the priest in charge of sacrifices [rex sacrorum], Publius
Scaevola sixth, Quintus Cornelius, Publius Volumnius, Publius
Albinovanus, and Lucius Iulius Caesar, the augur who inaugurated
him—in a third dining room there were the Vestal Virgins Popilia,
Perpennia, Licinia, and Arruntia. Publicia the wife of the flamen
Lentulus, and his mother-in-law, Sempronia. This was the dinner;
as a prelude, sea-urchins, raw oysters (as many as they wanted),
cockles and mussels, thrush over apsaragus, fattened hen, a dish of
baked oysters and cockles, white and black acorn-mollusks; mussels
again, clams, jellyfish, fig-peckers, loin of roe-deer, loin of boar, fattened fowl wrapped in dough, fig-peckers, murex and purple-shell; for
the main courses, sows' udders, boar's cheek, a dish of baked fish, a
dish of baked sow's udder, ducks, boiled water-fowl, hares, fattened
fowl roasted, gruel, and bread of Picenum. (Robert Kaster, trans.,
pp. 93 and 95, my additions in square brackets).[64]

Lentulus's bill of fare is a compendium of the culinary favorites of the
day. An entire litany of items served at such tables can be found in an
epigram by Martial[65] that describes the fussily gluttonous conduct of
an impoverished epicure at table: loin of boar, doves—although others preferred thrushes, also a table delicacy[66]—hares and oysters are
a must, udder (sumen) was a first-rate delicacy (and also a popular
term for a gourmet).[67]

Surprisingly, there is almost a complete absence of typical sacrificial meat. Insofar as Lentulus served meat in the narrower sense at all,
it was largely game, precisely not the kind of meat that was normally
used as an animal sacrifice. Even the loin was from a roe-deer or a
wild boar rather than a domesticated pig. For the rest, fish and shell-
fish, fowl and poultry predominated; and these too would have been
unusual in either elite or public sacrificial rites. The selection in fact
characterizes not only Lentulus's personal preferences, but fine
Roman cuisine generally: to be a gourmet meant not eating the meats
that were regularly used in a sacrifice. Only the prominently cited

sows' udders *might* have been used in sacrifice. It was much more important that such a feast should also be a feast for the eyes. This may especially be seen in the two opening courses, which show attention to a chromatic logic. While not free from repetition, they comprise dishes that achieve quite differing effects so far as color is concerned. The first series ends with a combination of black and white crustaceans, the second with *murices* and *purpurae,* two kinds of purple snails, that is to say with red tones. This sequence corresponds to a color scheme that is also found in the decoration of interior spaces, although only occasionally. Black and white signifies simplicity and occurs in domestic contexts;[68] purple indicates high status.[69] The palette chosen for the table, of course, does not indicate a social scale, but it does appear to introduce a temporal logic, a before and after sequence, into the variety of the dishes. As we do not know how the walls of the dining room in Lentulus's house were decorated, however, it may be that important color references of particular dishes have escaped us.[70]

Sumptuous banqueting thus provided priests with a fruitful field for economic and culinary competition: it is said that the peafowl was first served as a delicacy by an augur named Hortensius;[71] and moray eels may also have been introduced first at priestly dinners. Here too, it may be apposite to consider the location of the priestly banquet: it was an indoor occasion, but highly ritualized in comparison with the normal run of such events. And more was involved than a private meal around a table. Not only did banquets enter into the annals of a college, but they became topics of public discourse. Observed by very few in Rome, they were talked of by many: they became, in fact, shared knowledge. Their lavishness was proverbial. And there would seem to be only one route by which they might make their way into the common sphere, and that would be from the tales told by the insiders, that is, from the writings and talk of the priests themselves. Prestige was awarded where it was due, but frequent reminders were required; and those best qualified to see to this were the partakers themselves. "Public" and "private" thus became categories that were deliberately constructed and just as deliberately deconstructed.

Bacchus

What is missing from the fragment that remains to us of an account of a banquet given by the *pontifex maximus* Quintus Caecilius Metellus Pius[72] is any indication of the wine that was drunk. Wine had been *the* prestige beverage of the Italic aristocracy since the Early Iron Age. Men reserved it for their consumption alone, so that at this stratum of society it also served, down to the very vessels used, as an important instrument for the construction of gender differences.[73] Religious intoxication with pure, undiluted wine (associated with the older, chalice-shaped *kantharos*) may lie behind representations that became popular in Tarquinian tombs after the 6th century BC.[74] Images of the Greek Dionysos/*Bakkhos* (Latin *Bacchus*; Etruscan *Pacha*)[75] appear to have been favored motifs for the interpretation and perpetuation of these experiences. The demand for Bacchic images on vases apparent in the fourth century BC[76] was not, however, an isolated phenomenon, not least in the wine-producing regions that constituted one of the most important economic sectors in the Roman Empire. That sector's reach no doubt helped to spread the Bacchic imagery of the Roman Empire far beyond the Mediterranean region, arousing interest in its fantastical motifs, and inspiring house-owners to invest in mosaic floors and murals that brought this imagined world within their own walls.

As soon as markets came into being, wine, like vases, became a commodity that was accessible even to people who were not aristocrats, so long as they had the wherewithal to purchase it. These same people of means may also have been familiar with wine's cultural, or, more narrowly, religious connotations through contacts with the same Greek sources, at least by the Hellenistic Age. The greatest interest arose when the consumption of wine became available to city-dwellers as a social experience, open to both men *and* women, and the ecstatic outdoor experience moved indoors to domestic settings. This "nouveau bourgeois"[77] form of religious activity, which gave free rein to laughter[78] and opened up new roles for women,[79] was also sought after in Italy, where, however, it is much harder for us to detect. At the period in question, Italy lacked Greek culture's prominent means of public communication via inscriptions, which gave visibility to religious activity even in the absence of monumental architecture and durable votive deposits.

As in Greece, groups involved in such rituals in Italy may also have become embedded in the networks of locally powerful individuals: perhaps when members of such groups took part in prominent rituals,[80] or through the medium of urban altars or temples dedicated to the new worship.[81] Social approval would have rendered the new forms of religious agency acceptable, and speeded their dissemination. This does not mean that there were no social conflicts. In Rome in 186 BC, the suspicion arose that involvement in Bacchic networks was reaching far beyond small enclaves of the citizenry, and that the new groups were becoming a breeding ground for political opposition. Reaction to this fear unleashed a persecution that amounted almost to civil war. The critical factor may have been less the formation of religious groups per se than the general climate of discord. After the rather disordered and ad hoc nature of government during the Second Punic War (218–201), debate about the institutionalization of rule both over and within the "common realm" was intense. How was a ruling authority to be organized so as to function in an orderly and efficient manner, while at the same time restricting the power of individuals? When might an ex-consul stand again for consular office? When might a *praetor* stand for the first time? The underlying question concerned the prerogatives that might be secured by communication with the gods, and the limits that must be set to this kind of religious activity. Priestly roles were opened up to new groups, or they were closed; new priesthoods were created.[82] In 190 BC, a commander, Publius Scipio Cornelius Africanus, had justified a perhaps controversial military stand-down in Asia Minor by referring to religious obligations incumbent upon him as a *salius* in Rome.[83]

Drastic measures, extending to the burning of Numa's sacred books, were the order of the day.[84] In such an atmosphere, the crackdown on the Bacchic societies was an equally harsh measure, and one that had ramifications far beyond Rome.[85] The senators who prevailed in this instance fully acknowledged the special character of the practices of these groups, using terms such as *sacerdos* (priest) and *caerimonia* (rituals), and saying not one word against the god.[86] Their tactics consisted in limiting the social institutionalization of the rites to women, and making it necessary for any group that wished to use an enclosed space on a regular basis to have the support of senatorial patrons: in other words, the rite would have to be integrated into an elite network, or made dependent on such a network. This last point, obligatory dependency through patronage, was not in the text of the decree in so many words, but was implicit in the requirement for senatorial approval, which was indeed explicit. The personal conception of being a *mystes* of Bacchus remained unaffected, although it might now be confined to the form taken by a sarcophagus, or the decoration of a living room.[87] The authors of the resolution that settled the case did not address religion as a concept, but they do seem to have reached an understanding that religious practices were necessary to some individuals, and an outlet that they ought to be able to pursue unmolested, so long as the practices did not develop into something like an institution. As was normal in Rome, this was a one-off decision, directed at the particular circumstances of the cult of Bacchus as understood by the authorities involved. But the decision nevertheless demonstrates a line of thinking to which recourse might again be had in the future, in such matters as the regulation of religious practices in colonies.[88]

5. Mass Communication

Games

Also unaffected was the theater, which was an enormous arena of religious practice. And, while in Greece theater was inseparably associated with Dionysos, it had shed that association in Latium (leaving aside organized troops of Greek players). Leading members of the clans in Rome had increasingly found that, in organizing games *for the gods*, they had also discovered a medium of communication *with the citizenry* that made use of theater.[89] Under southern Italian/Greek influence in the fourth century BC, the classic form of *ludi circenses,* which centered on aristocratic chariot races,[90] became associated with theatrical farces and, in the final third of the third century, with comedies and tragedies in the Greek style. As well as broad themes of Greek city life, the subject matter of these productions included Roman history and pan-Mediterranean mythic history. The stage as an institution was more for those projecting themselves as patrons and benefactors than for the players, who, being of low social standing, were kept as far as possible concealed behind anonymizing masks;[91] anyone who had donated toward games was taken up and advanced socially. The expectations thus given rise to were, at the end of the Republic, an aspect of electoral campaigning highly prized by and useful to all involved.

Above all, however, games were a valuable gift to the gods, who were to be entertained according to the highest sporting and aesthetic standards (if I may use these adjectives anachronistically). New games were typically introduced in situations of crisis, promised as rituals that would be implemented after a favorable outcome. The *ludi plebei, ludi Ceriales, Apollinares, Megalenses,* and *Florales* were introduced in this way in the context of the war against Hannibal, and became more or less rapidly established as annual events (fig. 24).[92] Demand also had a part to play in the frequency of religious spectacles. That the political elite was prepared to bear the enormous costs involved shows how seriously they took this form of direct communication, in a city that was increasingly becoming a metropolis.[93] Although the construction of temples remained a field of activity, the games were more important.[94] The large, elevated podium of a temple might offer a kind of exposure to its donor, but the circus, in the form of a racetrack, and the theater offered opportunities to be seen and to be associated with spectacles that were of quite another order. Temples could also serve as stages, and they were occasionally designed or altered accordingly; but temple podiums in central Italy also stressed exclusivity, going so far sometimes as to incorporate screens to conceal a ritual space.[95]

24. Three of a series of five *denarii* of M. Volteius M.f., 78 BC. On
the reverses: Cybele in a *biga* drawn by lions (Ludi Megalenses);
Ceres in a *biga* drawn by snakes (Ludi Cereris); a tripod with
snake, perhaps with an inscription referring to a collection of
money: S(tips) c(ollata) d(ei) t(hesauro). Museum August Kestner,
Hannover. Photo: Christian Rose.

In the Greek cities with their elite citizen bodies, permanent theaters were widely constructed, and had served as places for common
celebration and reflection since the fifth century BC. Beginning with
Syracuse, in the following centuries the governments of Italian cities
on the Greek model also decided in favor of such structures, first in

Sicily, but then also in Metapontum and Locroi Epizephyrii, in the second century in Campania, and at the end of that century also in Nuceria and Pietrabbondante, and perhaps in Lanuvium.[96] By the early second century, Plautus's Roman audiences had tired of standing for long hours, and were asking for somewhere to sit in the theaters; but the elites blocked the creation of a permanent space where audiences might be able to communicate freely among themselves, and even with the players. They went so far as to forbid sitting altogether, although the frequent practice of constructing temporary stages had long been extended to include more durable structures providing audience space.[97] The architecture was of course also a part of the gift to gods and humans alike. The elite may have taken the initiative, but they did not have full control over what happened in the ritual institutions and architectural spaces they financed. This held true both for theaters and for circuses. Players like Decimus Laberius were becoming highly paid solo performers already in the first century BC, and chariot drivers in the Imperial Age were like pop stars. The aphorisms in Publilius Syrus's *sententiae* informed the morals of several generations, and the fan clubs of the racing teams delineated divisions between the political loyalties of city-dwellers in late antiquity. These developments were among the most momentous in Rome's religious history. Even to say this, however, is to recall that, while religious communication provided the occasion and the context for an entertainment, defined its timing, and decided which gods' busts would be brought in *pompa circensis* (with lavish spectacle) into the circus, to occupy the places of honor represented by the *pulvinar*,[98] religious communication did not determine the substance of these productions. We owe the major part of our detailed knowledge of ritual performances to later attempts by hostile Christians to gauge the religious character of the event as a whole. Tertullian's main accusation against readers of his *De spectaculis* was that they were oblivious to this.

"Gods" were merely one class of "not indubitably plausible actor," and this is the reason I have persisted in using this clumsy expression. We can only understand much of ancient religion in many areas around the Mediterranean if we see that gods, dead ancestors, demons and the like were thought of and dealt with in much the same ways. A tomb was also a *locus religiosus*, a fact that the grammarian (or antiquarian) Aelius Gallus declared in the late Republic to be self-evident, seeking perhaps to justify his opinion on the basis of the protection given to tombs by the gods.[99] That the tomb was *sacrum* to the *di manes* of the deceased was a standard sentiment increasingly expressed on gravestones, first in the city of Rome, then also in the provinces. These particular divine agents too, although they were effective and powerful only to a degree, were honored in Rome from the third century BC onward with spectacular contests. Decimus Junius Pera, consul in 266 BC, and his younger brother Marcus first organized gladiatorial contests in 264, on the occasion of the cremation of their father Decimus Iunius Brutus Pera.[100] Not quite a century later, in 174, Titus Flamininus's funeral games in honor of his father comprised three days of gladiatorial contests, involving seventy-four gladiators, a distribution of meat (*visceratio*), and four days of plays.[101] For the distribution of meat, a practice attested in Rome since 338 BC, the origin of the meat and therefore the context of slaughter appears to have been so immaterial to both donors and recipients that no reference is made to any preceding sacrifice or hunt, or—surely the norm—to the city slaughterhouses.[102]

There were scarcely any limits to the variations possible in orchestrating such events. At the end of the same century, and on a similar occasion, in the context of games promised by him in war, Marcus Scaurus staged athletic contests of the kind that Marcus Fulvius Nobilior had already organized in 186, in combination with a lion and panther hunt.[103] And the family of Lucius Aemilius Paullus, in presenting Terence's *Adelphoe* at the great general's funeral games, were making it clear that on this occasion they invited reflection on the roles of commanders and those committed to obey.[104]

One unifying term, *munus*, was used to describe all these undertakings. It refers etymologically to mutuality and exchange as well as "obligation" and "duty of office," or "gift." In seeking a better moment for "going public," the survivors of a deceased honoree often did not balk at allowing a considerable period to elapse between the actual funeral and the games in his honor. Like the organizers of games for the gods, they transposed ritual elements from one context to the other, and in both directions.

Wars

Games were not only vital means of communication between a political elite and an ever more diffusely structured and constantly growing urban population. They were also one of the most important services offered by Rome to people present in the city, and at the same time a means, using seating order and a preliminary roll call, of articulating and cementing inequality. Religious activity played no lesser a role when it was a question of mobilizing the urban population in order to produce the vital benefit of military security, or to apply that same strength of military organization to geographical and economic expansion. This applied not only to those military personnel involved in combat—even in ancient warfare often only a small proportion[105]—but also to many other groups and individuals, from clan members and clients of commanders to dependents and slaves. As in many ancient city-states, obligatory military service was a defining element of political identity in Rome: only Roman citizens (*cives Romani*) were allowed to serve in the Roman legions.[106] However, the military apparatus was not confined to this group. Even disregarding the baggage train, which probably comprised mainly non-Romans, there were non-Roman units that played a major role in warfare itself. Under the Republic one thinks first of all of the Italic allies, and in the Imperial Age there were the auxiliaries, who were awarded citizenship only upon leaving service.

Both Romans and non-Romans were made subject to military discipline by an unconditional oath sworn to the person of the commander (later the emperor as notional commander). This, like other oaths, was called *sacramentum*. The term related to a kind of "wager" that, in other forms of this oath, required that a security deposit be left at a temple, and become forfeit to the god concerned in the event of failure. The relationship between the leader and members of the organization was in this novel way accorded religious sanction.

That same relationship was also given expression in the *lustratio exercitus* performed upon departing for war. In this elaborate boundary ritual, referred to as *suovetaurilia*, a special group of sacrificial animals—a sheep, a pig, and an ox—was led around the assembled army or camp, accompanied by musicians and sacrificial assistants (fig. 25). The animals were then sacrificed. This ritual would have been familiar to a Roman citizen from the similar five-yearly *lustratio populi* census ritual, which required the presence of the entire citizenry on the Field of Mars, and to a Roman peasant in the form of the *lustratio agri*, in

25. Procession of sacrificial animals during a *lustratio exercitus* of the First Dacian War, AD 102. Above, inside the camp, the emperor Trajan conducts a ritual. 90–125 cm high. The photo is of an 1861 plaster cast of the marble original on Trajan's Column, Rome, AD 113. Rome, Museo della Civiltà Romana, inv. 3061. akg-images.

which the sacrificial animals were led around the boundaries of the farm.[107] Although this is never explicitly attested, the *lustratio exercitus* may have been seen against this familiar experiential background, so that the unity of the active armed force, hierarchically structured under its commander, was demonstrated to its members by a reference to the gods. War service, and service as such in the case of the professional army, which developed from the end of the second century BC onward, came to an end only upon release (*missio*).

I have no intention of providing here a complete inventory of rituals performed in war, or even of all cults practiced in military establishments.[108] Such ritual activities, regulated by the calendar, and centered on a room in which battle standards and portraits of the emperor were stored and displayed, did not exist until the Imperial Age. This room, typically at the central axis of an administrative complex grouped around a courtyard in a camp, was regarded as a temple, although religious activities carried out by officers and guard details may also have taken place at other locations, such as parade grounds. A list of days for obligatory rituals, as featured in the so-called *Feriale Duranum* of the early third century AD, was probably issued early on by Augustus. It is not, of course, possible to see in all this a specific, religious conceptualization of war.[109] In other respects too, the religious practices pursued by soldiers, individually or in groups, were primarily derived from regional and local traditions of "provincial religion," and as such were of course marked by their own experiences in their region of origin or on earlier assignments. There is no question here of a specific "army religion."[110]

As for rituals specifically related to wartime operations, the first that should be mentioned belongs to the unspectacular, routine category of rituals carried out by the commander, probably within the narrow circle of his staff, or even delegated to specialists, such as the accompanying musicians and sacrificial assistants. For the soldiers, such actions, as a rule combining sacrifice with divination, augury, or the examination of entrails, nevertheless defined dispositions, especially of a geographically related kind, as when a river was crossed or a camp set up.

It is difficult to evaluate the public nature of the rituals performed in the context of a battle, a focal point in warfare. What is certain is that augury was used in the Republican period. In historical time, it was regularly performed in the field in the form of *tripudium*, the observation of the feeding behavior of the chickens that traveled along with the army. The procedure—greedy feeding indicated approval—was complemented or replaced during the late Republic by the examination of entrails. As ancient critics already remarked, commanders knew that hungry chickens ate more greedily, and that very dry feed was more likely to fall from the beak during such greedy eating. The ritual could probably not be directly observed by the soldiery, but it would surely have been described to them by the commander's address before the battle, a scene frequently depicted in the literature and in graphic imagery.

It was probably uncommon for such a performance to be resorted to before battle, after the manner of the general Sertorius, who, to remove uncertainty as to the probable result of an upcoming battle, released a white hind so that it rose up out of a place of concealment as if god-sent.[111] Just as the positive outcome of divination could fire up an army eager for the fray, a hesitant consul might postpone a battle by announcing that his communication with the gods he had chosen as addressees had been negative. It is hard for us to imagine the acoustic conditions for such an address. It would surely not have been possible to address the entire army en masse; those standing closest to the consul would more than likely have reacted to his words, and their reaction would have spread outward, gathering impetus as it traveled. The same would apply to communication in yet more difficult conditions—in the battle itself, where, in moments of crisis, the commander might urge the gods at his side to greater efforts by making a vow. So long as he proclaimed his vow loudly and visibly—with raised arms—the soldiers would learn that they could now expect the support of the gods.

We are still in the realm of vows when it comes to challenges addressed to the protecting deities of cities that the Romans were besieging. During the middle Republic these deities were usually understood to be aspects of Juno,[112] and they would be promised temples and cults in Rome if they forsook their city, for this would of course make the city's capture easier. As late as the first century BC, Publius Servilius Vatia performed such a ritual at Isaura Vetus in Asia Minor.[113] In earlier times, it was likely normal to remove the cult statue of the captured city, and this procedure may have been the model for the triumph that began to figure from the end of the fourth century BC onward. The religious dimension of war was here demonstrated in the most concrete terms, as first the army and then the citizenry would see with their own eyes the superiority of Rome's gods over those of the enemy.

Only a few elements of sacralization strategies in warfare can be traced so far back. The display of trophies, for example, became established practice only in the course of the second century BC; earlier, the enemy's weaponry was normally collected together and burned; but the new practice, adopted from Greece, proved to be attractive.[114] Weapons won in single combat, especially those of the enemy commander, had long been given special treatment. They might be displayed in temples back in Rome, or hung up on the victor's own home, where they would witness to his individual share in the glory.[115] The treatment of the dead also remained an individual affair. They had to be cremated and buried after the battle, but this was treated as a private matter; only in exceptional cases, and not until the Imperial Age, were there public burials and public memorials to the fallen.[116]

A victorious battle ended with another address by the commander to his army. This was a moment to announce commendations and distinctions; we hear no mention of offerings of thanks. It was also the occasion for the troops to acclaim their general as *imperator* (commander); this was an honorific title during the Republic, later to be applied exclusively to emperors, with the acclamation of a different commander as imperator becoming the crucial act of usurpation, the mechanism for imperial succession that would conclude with the killing of the ruling emperor.[117] Such an acclamation gave retrospective recognition—either voluntarily or as the result of effective staging—to the religious legitimation that the commander had gained when his vow met with success.

War in Rome

In Rome too, there were rituals marking the beginning of a war. Comprising the usual requests for success and divine favor, they centered on the commander, with an emphasis on establishing his legitimacy, though within the limits of his powers as a magistrate. Neither the army nor the city's wider population observed the proceedings. Fundamental again were the auspices, observed before daybreak by the commander so as to establish Jupiter's approval for whatever action was planned for the day just beginning. These auspices upon departure did not cover the entire campaign. They were comparable to the auspices observed upon taking up office, in that their significance lay in their enabling a whole series of actions, each of which would require its own acts of divination, but which would nevertheless follow logically from the initial act and its auspices. It was not unknown for a general to have to return to Rome in order to renew the departing auspices (*auspicia repetere*).

Consulting the auspices did not in itself constitute divine legitimation. It was instead a kind of test. The act of augury was not something that could be easily viewed, although it might be conveyed through various media, as for example augural symbolism on coins of the emperors. The augural veto (*obnuntiatio*) at most was publicly enacted: so long as the priests and magistrates authorized to declare the veto refrained from doing so, they indicated consent, and a military campaign might continue, sometimes even when defeat was seen to be inevitable, as in the case of Cannae.[118] The religious legitimation of a failed commander, the likes of a Gaius Flaminius after the catastrophe at Lake Trasimene, might of course subsequently be cast into doubt.[119] A specific statute, the *lex curiata de imperio*—which did not bestow the right to consult the auspices, but merely confirmed the result—also assured the commander's extraordinary legitimation within the system of plebiscites.[120]

The departing commander then registered vows on the Capitol before Jupiter Optimus Maximus, the foremost custodian of the common cause by virtue of his towering Capitoline Temple, and promised to fulfill them upon his victorious return home. The actual ceremony of departure then occurred at one of the city gates. The commander exchanged the toga, the costume of peace, for the cloak of war, and trumpet blasts communicated the event to an audience whose make-up is unknown to us. War was primarily a spatial category, called *militiae* (in the spatial realm of the military), which began just outside the city walls. Trajan's Column depicts the opening of individual campaigns by means of processions through gates and crossings of bridges.

At some time before this moment, the commander would have gone to the Regia on the Forum and there brandished a lance-shaped idol of the god Mars, while exclaiming *Mars, vigila!* (Mars, awake!). This ritual was practiced until the beginning of the first century BC at the latest, but it continued thereafter to be reflected in omens and portentous events that had to do with the spears of Mars, such as mice attacking them or sounds as if the spears were clashing. These were then discussed publicly and ritually compensated for, in a form perhaps calculated to preserve a sense of the *presence* of the departure ritual for the benefit of a wider public. These rituals did not constitute a fixed system, but made use of various traditions of religious activity that might repeatedly be reappropriated, modified, or simply ignored. Their treatment in the Augustan age will make this clear.

When a campaign had ended, it was once more made *present* to the awareness of the city's population. Even before the commander's return, the Senate might react to the news of the victory by voting a *supplicatio*, a festival of thanksgiving, for which all the temples would be opened.[121] Thanks were directed to the gods "in the name of the commander," but the latter was himself honored directly in proportion to the duration in days of the festival. After a gradual increase in length to five days, the number increased dramatically in the final years of the Republic: Pompey received *supplicationes* of ten days' duration, Caesar of fifteen, twenty, and finally fifty days; Augustus mentions in his *Deeds* a total of 840 days of thanks decreed for him personally. By this simple additive process, the medium eventually exhausted its power of expression and escalation. It no longer played any great role after the reign of Augustus.

The central and most complex ritual of return was the triumph, which, probably from the second half of the fourth century BC onward, regularly concluded a victorious campaign. The decorated army entered the city in a long procession featuring prisoners and plunder, and including scenes of the war in the form of living tableaux or paintings.[122] I suggest that the *triumphator*, arrayed like the statue of a god in his chariot at the center of the proceedings, anticipated as a living image the erection of an honorific statue in the city center.[123] Before the massed public lining the streets, this (one might almost say) gestalt-forming ritual reprised the elements of the departure to war. After a breakfast furnished for the soldiers by their commander, the procession formed up on the Field of Mars outside the sacral city limit, the *pomerium*. The Senate awaited the *imperator* at the Porta Triumphalis, where it would join the triumph and thus appropriate the victory. The *imperator* donned colorful triumphal robes and the procession set off. It was headed by a display of war booty and representations of the campaign (fig. 26), and, as it crossed the city limits, was brought to a close by the soldiers crowned with laurel. Not until selected prisoners had been garroted in an underground room did the *triumphator* step up to the statue of Jupiter Capitolinus and lay his crown in the god's lap. Decorated animals brought along for the purpose were then sacrificed, fulfilling the vow made before Jupiter at the campaign's outset. Games and banquets followed.

Triumphal processions in the Republican period were often preceded by prolonged and robust negotiations over the form, financing, and temporal limits of the celebrations. The commander's prerogative was assumed in principle, but in every individual case it could be contended, for there were risks involved in deviating from the established form for such a prestigious public ritual. Moreover, constraints on the

26. Triumph of Titus, presentation of booty (including the Menorah), in the passage
of the Arch of Titus, Rome, after AD 81. Photo: J. Rüpke.

lavishness of the ceremonials constituted a form of control by the elite
in the face of a victorious commander, now standing before the city at
the head of an armed force. The presentation of plunder, the representation of events from the war in the form of paintings or *tableaux vi-
vants* of course constituted a bid for prestige; but the appearance of
the proceedings as a whole made possible a straightforward categorization: either the victor was a *triumphator* or he was not; in the latter
case, he was a second-class victor or no victor at all. The monopoliza-
tion of the triumphal procession by the emperor from the time of Augustus onward makes it clear that the difference was of considerable
significance. Celebrations of the *adventus*, the formal arrival of an emperor into a provincial town, and the triumph remained cornerstones
of Roman victory propaganda beyond the end of the Western Empire.[124] The emperor could count on a ceremonial entrance at any stage
of his progress, whether before or after a victory.[125]

Plunder provided the means for more victory celebrations of various forms, conceived of as the fulfillment of vows formulated on a campaign, and especially on the battlefield. Here we might point especially to games (*ludi votivi*) dedicated to the deity whose aid had been called upon, for they were a particularly flamboyant use of plunder that would surely have persisted in the collective memory. Defeats were not ritually addressed; at most, they were assessed as portentous events, signs of divine anger, and the date of their occurrence would be noted on the calendar so that battles might be avoided on that day in future. In extremely exceptional instances, especially if a member of the imperial house such as Germanicus were involved, the report of a defeat might become the immediate occasion for a *iustitium*, a temporary suspension of public life as a form of mourning ritual.[126] There do not appear to have been rituals of expiation, or declarations of guilt.[127]

The rituals celebrating the end of a war created a large public for communication with the gods. At the center of everything, of course, was the victorious commander; but in the triumphal procession at least, the troops brought back to Rome likewise became subjects of the ritual, and they were thus able to appropriate publicly an individual share in the victory, either by the display of plunder or by wearing decorations. These "transference mechanisms" broadcast loud and clear in the very innermost heart of Rome the positive effects of military endeavor that a soldier might hope to achieve. The killing of enemy leaders and the spectacular display of the arms of fallen enemy commanders (*spolia opima*) must have been impressive, and then, finally, the games that consumed plunder, animals, and humans reinforced that impact. The incorporation of the vow into religious vocabulary legitimized the pomp and the public extravagance. The exaltation of a member of the leading elite, who demanded military obedience far beyond what was economically thinkable for an individual of more humble station, both required the (literally) spectacular consumption of plunder and combined with it to enlist the participation of the whole of the Roman people. Competition within the aristocracy found both its territory and its limits here. But aristocratic competitiveness and cooperation found both these elements again in the horizontal links that tied local elites in all the towns and tribes whose military contribution had been vital in assuring the military effectiveness of the "Roman" army. We are incapable, however, of gauging the role played by familial obligations and "private" friendships in the success of Roman military adventures.[128] This element of collaboration did not become visible in the ritual enactment of a military victory.

6. The Divine

In every instance of religious communication, it appears to be vital to the plausibility of the actors addressed as gods that they are neither entirely nor at all times at the disposal of human actors, and that this aspect of their "presence" is apparent to onlookers. In the period under examination here, this condition found expression in the form of discussions as to whether gods were present in statues and temples, and in measures enlisted by human actors to demonstrate the uncertainty of the outcome of, say, a sacrifice that required studying the inherently very individual liver of a sacrificed animal, or observing the form taken by flames after incense had been thrown into them. The Republican aristocracy emphasized the empirical aspect of portentous events called "prodigies." These were unsought-for signs, classified as abnormal, that often took the form of meteorological or biological events.[129] They could be observed and reported by anybody, and the Augustan historiographer Livy noted heightened receptiveness to such signs in periods of crisis. The prodigy had to be recognized as such by the Senate, which entrusted the interpretation to religious specialists, the pontiffs or the *decemviri*, or later the *quindecimviri sacris faciundis*, the interpreters of the Sibylline books. These in turn suggested remedial measures" (*procuratio*) that might be implemented by the priesthoods themselves or by the magistrates to improve the chances of a happy outcome. *Haruspices*, Etruscan examiners of entrails, occasionally became involved in an expert capacity. Their presence in Rome is documented at both the official and the private level from the third century BC onward, and the alien knowledge that they possessed may well have been judged especially credible. Their influence grew, less from their participation in public sacrifices, which was at first minor, than from their close personal associations with members of the elite.[130] Lucius Cornelius Sulla reported in his autobiography that he was guided by the recommendations of the *haruspex* Gaius Postumius.[131] Astrology played a similar role, although not a significant one until the Imperial Age; it had no public function, but astrologers were increasingly consulted by private clients from the end of the second century BC onward.

Efforts to find a means of direct access to divine will and divine knowledge did not end here. As Plautus attests, there was an awareness of the existence of non-Roman oracles. In special circumstances, sites such as the shrines sacred to Fortuna in neighboring Praeneste, where divination by lot was practiced (*sortes praenestinae*), offered their services.[132] Set against the paucity of explicit sources, the probable impact of prophet-like figures (*vates*) who came to prominence in Republican Rome is striking. Horace and Propertius were among them.[133] Moral exhortation appears to have been their particular stock in trade. Although this socially marginal fount of religious authority does not seem to have enjoyed the esteem of the elite, instances such as the adoption of the *Carmina Marciana* by the populace in the Second Punic War suggest that its influence may have been considerable in individual cases. We have literary texts, dating from the final years of the Republic, in which the author assumes the role of a *vates*. Collections of oracles, *libri Sibyllini* or *Etrusci*, also circulated in great numbers; one survey of such oracles conducted during the reign of Augustus is said to have turned up two thousand volumes in rapid order.[134]

Auspices

At the beginning of the first century BC, after the Civil War, the Roman Senate seems gradually to have lost interest in receiving reports of portentous events and dealing with them as "prodigies." Given the increasingly personalized conflicts of this period, such information may have seemed too broad-spectrum to be of much use. The practice of taking auspices flourished in its place. The normal procedure, quite unlike the complicated process of interpreting portentous events, was largely independent of empirical elements. The flight of birds or even the pecking of chickens was observed, and the conclusion reached was either unambiguous approval or rejection. Each sign had one plain meaning, which magistrates or priests could create, fake, or disregard; typically, interpretation was no longer called for. In the classic chicken oracle (*auspicium ex tripudiis*), greedy feeding marked by the spilling of grains indicated strongest approval, but the sign could readily be manipulated by previously feeding or starving the chickens, as well as by controlling the consistency of the food (damp or dry). But nothing of the kind was really necessary. There was no provision for public verification; only the outcome was announced to the public. This meant that the consultation could come down to a routine dialogue between the assistant whose job was to observe the chickens and the magistrate undertaking the procedure. Real signs and fabricated signs thus became practically equivalent, and were generally indistinguishable by "end users." A sign was valid as long as a magistrate accepted it, and taking auspices was a core element of the magistrate's vocation: the right to undertake auspices was a prerogative expressed in Roman terminology by the dualism *imperium auspiciumque*.[135] The downside of this form of legitimation was the constant obligation placed on the magistrate to consult the auspices. During his entire period of office, the thoroughness of a magistrate's legitimation depended on the perceived validity of his election, and was thus contingent, constantly in need of renewal,[136] and precarious. Divine approval could be sought only case by case. But magisterial power was strictly circumscribed; the tribunes had the right to intercede, and colleagues of equal rank could veto decisions. Moreover, the augurs had the right of *obnuntiatio*, meaning that they could report contrary signs and thus put a stop to political actions. These potential sources of intervention forced magistrates, despite the apparent power at their disposal, to seek consensus. In the dying years of the Republic, despite attempts to institutionalize standards, religious practice remained a field where negotiation was the name of the game, and opportunities for an individual to increase his own standing were rife.

A look at Cicero's Second Philippic (said to have been written in September of 44 BC, but not published until that November) makes this point clear. Marcus Antonius, as consul and presiding electoral officer, had prevented the election of Dolabella (preordained by Caesar as suffect) to the consulate by reporting contrary signs with the summary deferring formula *alio die*, "at another time," in the final phase of the electoral procedure (Cic. *Phil.* 2.82–83). Cicero claims that Antonius had already anticipated this impediment on January 1st (2.80), trusting to his authority as augur (2.81). It is on this that Cicero founds his criticism: the anticipation showed that the supposed auspices were fallacious; Antonius had specified neither what he had heard nor what he had seen (2.83), and, moreover, had later declared the election to be valid (2.84), which amounted to a political *volte-face* on Antonius's part.

If Cicero is correct in his accusations, then Antonius had evidently offended against the code of conduct. But was this code mainly a perpetuation of the fiction that divination was based on the genuine, empirically substantial observation of signs? If religious communication was capable of signaling the special relevance of the intentions and message of a particular human religious actor, then the purpose of *obnuntiatio* was to terminate all negotiation. At a very late juncture, Antonius had cast doubt on the validity of the entire process of communication up to that moment, by citing a divine "no." To a narrow circle comprising the highest-ranking magistrates for the current year (elected the previous year) and the college of augurs with its long-standing constitutional status, this form of disavowal constituted a legitimate means. It was an act expressing a principal disagreement—"I demur"—not an exercise in interpretation for experts.[137] But this opened the door to the counter-criticism: Cicero charges Antonius with not being able to say whether Jupiter had thundered or cast lightning. But *alio die* speaks for itself, as Cicero himself concedes elsewhere (*Leg.* 2.31). Cicero is therefore obliged to escalate his accusations; he accuses Antonius of having breached certain other rules of procedure.

On January 1, it had been a question of resisting Caesar's imperious determination of the next year's consuls; it had been Antonius's task as serving *consul*, not Caesar's, to demand that the process be set in motion whereby the nobility nominated candidates and presented them for election or selection by the *populus Romanus*. With his announcement, as *augur*, of a reported sign, however, Antonius had signaled his departure from the political decision process, only later to resume it arbitrarily by withdrawing his own objection.

It is characteristic of the interplay of political institutions in Rome at this period that the way in which a break-off of negotiations was handled had quite different consequences depending on the matters involved. It must first be understood that the moment when this particular *obnuntiatio* was imposed was the precise moment when the decision-making process was about to leave the purview of the nobility and enter into the *comitia*, where affairs were at their most public. The restricted circle of people who were entitled to make a declaration of *obnuntiatio*,[138] and the potentially momentous consequences of contesting it, made it abundantly clear to the *populus* (to those who had the right to vote) that there could be no question of popular sovereignty.

In this case, however, the *obnuntiatio* must have gone beyond a statement on the locus of authority, as the augural protest had vastly different consequences. Laws were promulgated in spite of it, yet elections were delayed. Unlike the creation of laws, elections were not regarded as one-off decisions. The "stigma" of augural error (*vitium*) persisted even when a decision had been positively implemented. The college of augurs might take up the objection at any later time in retrospect, evaluate it, and lay it before the Senate, which would then make the decision whether to retain or rescind the former popular outcome.[139] Cicero says (*Phil.* 2.83): "So as not to give the impression of declaring invalid Dolabella's actions as magistrate, as these will at some time have to be laid before our [augural] college, I do not wish to take matters further at this time." In the case of laws, the outcome of the augural protest was only to render more fluid even those decisions that ought to be given the higher dignity of *lex*. Even such decisions as these were thus denied the quality of norms created in perpetuity. The consequences were more serious in the case of elections, as is indicated by the passage from Cicero: when the fundamental legitimacy of a particular decision was questioned, it was not only that decision that became the subject of grave reservations, but every decision made during an official's entire term of office.[140] This was insupportable. Consensus was not only desirable in such a situation, but necessary. The overweening power of the magistrates, although limited geographically (e.g., the limitation of the right of *provocatio* to within Rome or within the borders of provincial jurisdiction), temporally (by the restriction of the period of office to one year), and personally (by the obligatory sharing of power with a colleague of the same competency), was nevertheless prodigious, and was necessarily reined in by the requirement for a broader consensus of officeholders who were also endowed with religious competencies. Thus the political efficacy of aristocratic competition was maintained. As an available alternative to consensus there was always force; the use of force in the final years of the Republic was ever more frequently associated with strategies of obstruction.[141] No administrative jurisdiction was ever supplanted by religious activity alone.

Civic Religion

Members of the elite used the possibilities offered by religious communication for various purposes. For political actors, vertical reference was ideally suited to the creation of a communicative space beyond the *gens*, one that would emphasize shared interests and yet enable them to use religious activity as a field in which to compete and, potentially, obtain distinction. This flexibility helped ritual activity and religious architecture to achieve a high degree of dynamism: ever new possibilities of religious communication were invented, or existing Mediterranean-world traditions appropriated and altered in order to circumvent the problems thrown up by the increasing geographic area over which Rome had dominion, by the growing city, and by increasing social differentiation and competition. It was not only the significance of religious practices that grew with the increasing complexity of the institutions required to administer the "commonweal," but also the pressure to create fixed practices and rules. The strategy of tacit modification proved inadequate to the new conditions. It may have been this situation that triggered a new way of reflecting on such practices, a kind of reflexivity that was altering "religion," or possibly even creating it for the first time.

VI

Speaking and Writing
about Religion

THE THIRD TO FIRST CENTURIES BC

1. The Textuality of Ritual

Slaughtering a number of unblemished white bulls or depositing a
large-scale bronze figure in a temple was expensive, to be sure, but—
setting aside the practical difficulties of butchering or bronze-casting—it
was not complicated. What was operative in such rituals was not,
however, any aspect of religious innovation, nor did they showcase
the ability of human actors to accentuate their importance by doing
something unexpected in this area. Even those who themselves performed such traditional acts to win success at the hands of gods and
humans were people who had learned religion by watching and participating. No special training was needed. As we shall see below, not
until the Imperial Age, long after the idea had arisen that religion
could also be knowledge or a field of learning, do we come across the
idea that noble youths growing up far from Rome might need instruction in "Roman religion."[1] If we think of religious communication as
a kind of language (with the reservation that it is spoken far more rarely
than a mother tongue), we can apply insights from linguistic studies
to the character of orally transmitted religious activity. Contrary to the
assumptions of seminal nineteenth-century studies, what we have

here is not a *system* possessing an inherently *stable* vocabulary, shared by a particular generation and used to produce change *according to set rules*. We must rather assume systemic, local, social, and gender-determined *variations* within a community, each of these *differentially appropriated* by children, not least in view of the difficulties of phonetic reproduction, and *continuously altered* as a function of changing contexts and the varying contacts of the groups of speakers concerned.

In central Italy as in Rome, practical knowledge about religious activity was widely shared. This continued to apply to most areas of Hellenistic religious practice, even at a later period. Where ritual actors produced texts, they tended to do so in order to deliberately introduce and implement standards that would have the effect of stabilizing and homogenizing changes in practices.[2] Even when the *lex Ogulnia* of 300 BC opened Roman priesthoods to plebeian members, many of whom lacked relevant family traditions, the priesthoods saw no need to provide them with procedures in written form. Demands on the time of college members had to be kept within limits, for, like most of their Greek equivalents, they were in fact only "part-time priests."[3]

Wherever internal records began to be kept—and it is assumed that the Roman Senate did keep some such records from around 300 BC onward—the main concern was to document cult membership.[4] A further interest in the documentation of the successive courses served at enrollment meals, which gave rise to the longest known fragment from the pontifical records, has been discussed in detail above. It was probably the *pontifex maximus* and consul in 280, Tiberius Coruncanius, who began keeping this type of continuous record in 249; this is the same Coruncanius who is supposed to have introduced a public legal consultation service, and who, in about 254, when perhaps in any case the longest-serving (*maximus*) pontiff, may have been the first plebeian and the first elected in the *comitia* to become *pontifex maximus*.[5] The pontiffs had already introduced written records shortly before 300 by writing down and publishing the calendar and the list of court days and holidays (*fasti*). It is possible that already at this time they were the only priesthood to have its own scribes, who

later became so important that they were referred to as "minor pontiffs."[6] The other priesthoods did not develop anything comparable.
By displaying extracts from the full records on whitened wooden
tablets outside his home (not the Regia, his "place of business"), a demonstrative form of written publication, the *pontifex maximus* underlined his claim to an authority that was quickly to be expressed in
conflicts with other priesthoods.[7] But neither a pontifical doctrine
nor a *ius pontificum* was thereafter developed.[8]

Disciplina Etrusca

It is, hypothetically, possible to reconstruct how such a process may
have worked in Etruscan cities. In about 340 BC, Larth Velcha and his
wife Velia Seithi, or their children, had the Tomba degli Scudi near
Tarquinia decorated, not only with representations of themselves and
the husband's parents, but also with an inscription giving his magisterial offices in great detail.[9] Other contemporaries acted similarly, and
in the process may have had increasing recourse to family records,
which then in the first century AD facilitated the production of the *Elogia
Tarquiniensia*.[10] The family's familiarity with written texts was in any
event so important to them that they had themselves portrayed holding book rolls.[11] Some Etruscan nobles took this indication of learning further, broadening the repertory of images for their burial urns
with scenes of murder at the altar, and so providing us with a warning of
how far religious power and religious error might go.[12] These third- and
second-century tombs, with their impressive temple-like facades, were a
further means by which such claims could be communicated.[13]

Collaboration with Rome, a tool evidently adjudged valuable in internal social conflicts, as instanced in 302 by the use of Roman help to
put down a rising of the lower classes in Arretium (Arezzo), could
become a strategy in structurally no less problematic situations. Some
members of Etruscan elites sought actively to work with Rome in its
phase of expansion. Not only did they bring to this endeavor their
own experiences, economic power, and client base (in order to take
on functions and offices in Rome itself), but many chose to describe

themselves as experts in religious communication, especially in divination of the sort that conveys knowledge of the future.[14] It was a genre that offered substance, in contrast with the rather formalistic style of communication that characterized Rome's own dealings with auspices.[15]

On the basis of old ritual traditions, influenced by Greek narratives and thinking on the subject of divination, and above all with an eye to the prestige to be gained with their Roman clientele, they invented and elaborated an *Etrusca disciplina*, a book of "Etruscan doctrine," which may not previously have existed as an organized body of knowledge.[16] Images of instruction in hepatoscopy, and such items as the model of a liver made in Piacenza about 100 BC, gave visible substance to the new knowledge (figs. 27 and 28).[17] Texts in the form of *libri rituales* and *fulgurales*, or "thunder calendars," provided the basis for practical instruction in divination from lightning strikes, and at the same time evidence for the very existence of such a discipline.[18] It is possible than many a writer of a Latin text, such as Tarquinius Priscus, may have passed off his own original rendition of Etruscan teachings, worked up in Latin, as a translation from the Etruscan. Nigidius Figulus's thunder calendar, dated to the mid-first century BC, and preserved for us in a late antique Greek translation by the scholar Johannes Lydos, perfectly reflects conditions in first-century BC Rome.[19]

The prophecies of Vegoia, who in 88 BC intervened in conflicts between Rome and the Italic peoples, were able to emerge and function only against the background of such a body of written knowledge.[20] With the exception of the Sibylline Oracle, earlier Roman attempts to claim authority for written prophecies or texts of any kind had always been problematic: this applied to the *carmina Marciana*, the late-third-century prophecies of Gnaeus Marcius or the brothers Marcius, which, although contested, nevertheless prompted the establishment of the *ludi Apollinares* in 212.[21] The city praetor was more skeptical in the case of the pseudepigraphical Books of Numa, which were found in 181. Their reference to Pythagoras was insufficient to prevent them from being burned.[22] The Sibylline books, even if the originals had been destroyed together with the Capitoline temple by a fire in 83 BC,

27. Bronze model of a liver, second century BC, from Piacenza. Piacenza, Musei Civici, Museo Archeologico. akg-images / De Agostini Picture Lib. / A. De Gregorio.

represented such a broad textual field in the late Republic that they could easily inter-refer, while no other texts existed that were capable of supporting written prophecy as an exegetic phenomenon in the manner of the Old Testament.

Certainly no such basis was provided by those sets of rules that could be encountered in inscriptions based on the Greek model, in Italic sanctuaries among others, from the late Republic onward. Any patron or magistrate publishing such rules, mistakenly referred to as *leges sacrae*, did so with the intention of guiding the behavior of the users of cult sites in matters beyond the purview of architecture and images. These sets of rules were essentially pragmatic in nature, and even in the Greek period had not sought to create a separation between religious and profane directives.[23] By issuing them, however, their authors claimed the ability successfully to impose limits on

28. Model of a sheep's liver with cuneiform inscriptions, tool for divination. Terracotta, 14.6×14.6 cm. Probably from Sippar, Iraq, ca. 1900–1600 BC (Text: ANE 92668). London, British Museum. akg-images / Erich Lessing.

religious activity. Especially in situations where such claims had to be newly negotiated, as in the early years after the foundation of a colony or province, these texts could become important components of meta-communication. The rules governing mourning rituals for Germanicus in the early 1st century AD are a good example.[24]

2. Observation of Self and of the Other

Anyone visiting a dramatic presentation in Rome not only became a participant in ritualized "scaenic games," but frequently also observed enacted religious activities, and took part in conversations about such activities. At the beginning of the second century BC, tragedies presented versions (frequently mythical) of a Greek world, referring obliquely to the history and rituals of the city of Rome. *Praetextae* and in later periods mimes made such references directly and expressly.[25] The knight and writer of mimes Decius Laberius, highly regarded by Caesar and an exact contemporary of Cicero (106–43 BC), wrote works with titles such as *Anna Perenna, Augur, Compitalia,* and *Saturnalia.*[26] A few of his lines, often isolated, have survived because they were cited by later grammarians interested in single words or expressions, but they convey hardly any sense of the content of these pieces. The augur in the mime of that name interestingly speaks on stage about the ample profit he earns,[27] possibly from divination services performed for private clients.

It was due especially to their vigorous (and sometimes critical) moral statements and comments that mimes were popular, as is shown by the better-preserved sayings of Publilius Syrus, a still more popular and probably somewhat younger exponent of the art.[28] Jerome in his school years in the second half of the fourth century was acquainted with Publilius's dictums.[29] These writers' works were aimed directly at an urban audience that was interested in hearing (and ultimately appropriating) traditional values explicitly spelled out. *Ex hominum questu facta fortuna est dea*—"out of the laments of humans is fate made a goddess [Fortuna]" (180)—is one of Publilius' dictums, not necessarily of his own creation. It is entirely disparaging of religion. "I think the gods laugh when a lucky man fulfills a vow" (169) has a similar tenor, but is not inimical to religion. "He wrongly blames Neptune who is shipwrecked a second time" [having failed to learn the dangers of the sea the first time] (331), and "No herb is effective against lightning" (640) tell of a world in which gods exist, but worshipping them is not seen as necessarily changing reality. Such dictums were, however, mere aperçus, not the stuff of which mimes were made. A collector or publisher of such aphorisms shared both the intent and the polemical motivation of authors of popular philosophical texts like the *Golden Verses of Pythagoras* (first century BC) or the—perhaps contemporaneous—tract *On the Universe* (*De mundo*), put in the mouth of Aristotle.[30] As the authors of these texts left them anonymous or pseudonymous, they essentially forsook a persona for the sake of achieving consensus. They differ in their anonymity from the mime who appears without a mask, or the likewise mask-free director of a drama who expresses himself in similar manner in a prologue.

In Plautus's dramas, by contrast, the gods too are present: either appearing directly in the form of actors or as figures not present but spoken about, addressed in prayers, or even on the receiving end of brief curses. Occasionally, reference is made to an actual ritual conducted locally.[31] Drawing perhaps on the cultural differences embodied in these plays—based on Greek-Hellenistic models, but viewed by Roman-Italic audiences—the authors occasionally went beyond the mere portrayal of gods. In the prologue to *Rudens*, Plautus has Arcturus, the main star in the constellation Bootes, deliver substantial reflections on the gods: on Jupiter as ruler over gods and humans; on his interest in particular values and the rejection of false oaths; and, of course, on the desire of the makers of such false oaths to placate this very Jupiter with gifts and sacrificial animals.

Ennius, who also wrote dramas at the beginning of the second century BC, went further still, and in several of his plays inquired into the foundations of divination.[32] But it was not the practice of the *sacerdotes publici*, the augurs, that he so openly addressed. Rather, his critique centered on astrologers, prophets, and examiners of entrails (*harioli*), practitioners the author seems to have associated with the lower classes. Lucius Accius took up the same themes nearly two generations later. Far from mocking, he even used the rhythmic song and speech of his drama to accommodate terminological precision, asking under what conditions divination could succeed. He accordingly has his characters combine different techniques of divination, asserting that this is necessary if they are really to take it seriously. In the sharpness of his critique, however, he was no weak precursor of a Laberius. Mercilessly, he exhausts the assonant possibilities of *aurum* (gold), *aures* (ears), and "augur."[33] Like Ennius before him, he frequently uses "heaven-dwellers" (*caelites*) instead of "gods," especially in passages concerning earthbound cult sites, or addressing the question of whether the heaven-dwellers on high really bother about humans on earth.[34] The theater was no place, however, for the step-by-step arguments of philosophical investigation. Its function was entertainment. But in the course of the drama questions were posed, observations were made, and a public—mixed in social class, age, and sex—could not help but take note.

Myth and the Critique of Myth

Mythic material was staged even more frequently than historical subjects from the more recent Roman past. Myths were narratives.[35] Aristotle in his *Poetics* concerned himself simply with the content, the themes of such narratives. Herodotus and Thucydides further refined the concept so as to set their own work apart from myth-writing. "Myth" and "history" became antonyms. This is not to say that a myth was a lie: it was a narrative that should not be examined for historical truth. Such stories could serve a purpose when other information was lacking, although it would be unwise to claim that the events they relate actually took place in exactly the way they are told. Plato contrasted "myth" with *logos*. A *logos* (pl. *logoi*) was first and foremost an utterance, a representation, in many cases even a history. It might be about gods or religious matters. Or it might explain the meaning of a ritual, as Ennius did in his translation of a tale by the Sicilian Euhemerus. In his *Sacred History* (*Hiera Anagraphe*), Euhemerus had portrayed Zeus's (or Jupiter's) travels to the island of Panchaea in the Indian Ocean, and the many good deeds he performed there, thus explaining how a human being might become the object of a cult.[36]

One could take almost anything and make it into a myth, and that myth might then become the subject of a drama. Beginning with the origin of the world (cosmogony) and the origin of gods (theogony), there was no limit. The majority of the narratives ready to hand, however, dealt with the period of the Trojan War and the generations immediately preceding it. What most interested audiences, it seems, was interventions by the gods in the human world and, conversely, visits by humans to the world of the gods. A great number of characters and stories could be woven into narratives set against the backdrop of major military events like the campaign of the Seven against Thebes, or the Achaeans' ten-year campaign against the Trojans. These myths, which involved the mobilization of the whole of Greece, permitted writers to involve and so to connect in their stories many different places and tribes, goddesses and gods.

The foundation myths of cities, such as Pergamum's Telephus myth (monumentally depicted on the Pergamum Altar), formed another layer of this textual genre. In presenting such myths, authors and tellers of tales created links with other narrative cycles through the gods and heroes whose actions they depicted. Their primary concern may have been their particular town, but in telling its story they also helped its inhabitants find a worthy place in the Greek world. In the end, this also applied to Rome, whose own narratives concentrated more on the history and immediate prehistory of the city of Rome and Latium. At the same time, Romans with a more cosmopolitan outlook preferred to seek common ground with the Greeks.[37] The chronologies recorded by historians of Rome from the end of the third century BC onward therefore took account of Greek chronologies.[38] They dated Rome's foundation with reference to the fall of Troy, so that it became effectively a date in Greek history. There was apparently no urgency about separating mythology and history. While the Augustan historian Livy at the end of the first century BC expressed skepticism over Rome's foundation stories, his contemporary Dionysius of Halicarnassus, a Greek writing in Rome, dealt with the same period in great mythic detail. Just a few centuries later, Judeo-Christian historians even contrived historical chronologies of the world going back to Abraham, and in some cases to the Creation. All of these chronologies had one thing in common: they assumed that a very short period of time had lapsed between the creation of the world and their own time, no more than a few centuries. In this they differ radically from Asiatic histories, which saw a past that stretched back eons.

Those who promoted such narratives about the founders of the city and of their own native city were at the same time composing a self-portrait of that city. But recalling common ancestors did more than strengthen the ties between citizens; it could also constitute a bridge between cities. When Rome entered the ambiance of the Greeks settling in southern Italy and Sicily, leading Romans were moved to create a place in the narrative cosmos for their own Etruscan-Latin settlement.

As always when it comes to myth, the storytellers, working under the patronage of particular families, the producers of vase paintings and the like, did not necessarily unite around one version of a tale. Various tellings could live amicably side by side, thus opening a wide field of possible story lines. Hercules was always a great favorite in the tales that circulated throughout Magna Graecia; he was integral to local myths from quite early on, as instanced by his portrayal among the gable figures of the sixth-century-BC temple at Sant'Omobono. Stories of the Trojan refugees scattered after the downfall of their city offered other possibilities. Vase paintings show that the story of Aeneas carrying his father Anchises out of the burning city of Troy (fig. 29) was known in Italy from an early date. The Greek historian Timaeus in the early third century interpreted a horse sacrifice in the city of Rome, performed with a spear, as an act of revenge on the Trojan Horse that had made possible the conquest of Troy.[39] At the end of the same century, the Romans saw in their struggle against the North African stronghold of Carthage a legacy inherited from mythical times: the refugee Aeneas had, after all, forsaken the Carthaginian queen Dido. It was not until the following two centuries, however, that the Romans appropriated the myth as their own in a more preemptive fashion. Asia Minor was bequeathed to Rome in 133 BC, and in 129 become a Roman province. With their incursion into the region the Romans acquired new access to this variant origin myth. They were now, and rightfully, in the place they had come from, and they underlined this fact by visiting Ilium and making offerings.[40] Thus embedded in the Greek narrative network, they created a parallel, specifically Latin network that not only gave Rome an address in the wider Greek world, but also gave Latin-speakers and their diasporas a sense of place in a Roman world.[41]

29. Aeneas fleeing from burning Troy together with his father Anchises and his son
Ascanius. Black-figure amphora, ca. 520 BC. Boulogne-sur-Mer, Château-Musée.
akg-images / Erich Lessing.

For all the success of such narratives, a success that the Roman stage made abundantly clear to contemporaries, myth was accompanied from the beginning by the critique of myth. This is not to say that the critical deliberations of a few philosophers became common knowledge. Philosophical schemes that replaced the multitude of gods with a single first principle, or at most with four such, could make little headway against the superior weight of institutions that enacted myth in structures and statues, in theaters, and in songs at popular festivals. In any event, these new schemes had no superior insights to offer. They did, however, pose questions that would be raised again and then brought back to the stage by such writers as Plautus, Ennius, and Accius.

Already in the sixth century BC, Greek thinkers had come up with fundamental critiques aimed at religious practices as well as narratives. Greek natural philosophy represented a first fundamental denial of myth, but it still couched its arguments in markedly mythic language. Distinct principles replaced the many divine agents. For Thales of Miletus it was water, for Anaximenes air, for Anaximander the "undefinable." Then Xenophanes of Colophon, at the end of the sixth century, came out with an explicit polemic against myths: "Homer and Hesiod," he wrote, "have foisted upon the gods everything that is, in the world of humans, blameworthy and a source of dishonor: theft and adultery and mutual deception." But his critique extended beyond issues of morality: "Mortals suppose that the gods were born, and had clothes and a voice and form like themselves. And yet, if oxen and horses and lions had hands, could paint with their hands and produce works like those of humans, the horses would paint horse-like and the oxen ox-like divinities, and each species would portray bodies with a form like its own."[42] Not the gods, but earth and water were the basis of everything; the sea sufficed to explain the formation of clouds, winds, and currents.

To this were added the critiques of historians, beginning with Hecataeus of Miletus, a contemporary of Xenophanes. He bluntly asserted that mythic narratives were legion and ridiculous. In his history of the Peloponnesian War between Athens and Sparta, Thucydides at the end of the fifth century BC went further. He made lofty claims about his use of historical method, contrasting this with the tendency of poets to embroider their stories because, he believed, their pleasure in telling a good tale exceeded their concern for the truth; and he did not hesitate to accuse his historiographical predecessors of falling prey to the same habit. This repository of criticism would suffice for the whole of antiquity up to the Christian polemic against myths.

But there were other voices as early as the sixth century BC, speaking from the philosophical camp, who portrayed myths in a more positive light than was suggested by the critique of myth that arose at the same period. Theagenes of Rhegium read the quarrels of the Homeric gods as testimony to the conflict of the elements: Apollo, Helios, and Hephaistos stood for fire, Poseidon and Scamander for water, Artemis for the moon, and Hera for air; Athene was reason, Ares unreason, Aphrodite attachment, and Hermes speech. This form of interpretation has been referred to as allegoresis, the idea being that the ancient purveyors of myth systematically replaced natural elements and forces with the names of gods; the same approach was soon extended to the human actors in Homer.[43]

It was not just any texts that were treated in this way.[44] The epics of Hesiod and Homer had evidently become highly significant by the end of the sixth century. They could no more be removed from the cult than from the Greeks' conception of themselves. In many cities, they had become something in the manner of canonical texts, and themselves served as a baseline from which further myths could be spun. Such a text might present a target for ridicule and criticism; but it was also worth defending. Defenders relocated the critical level of meaning through their allegorical interpretations, so that it was no longer the actions of the characters portrayed, their battles and quarrels, that were paramount. Admittedly, contradictions had quickly to be exposed, offensive elements condemned: the poet had really wanted to say something else, so the argument ran, and this was precisely what the allegorical meaning revealed. Practitioners of the genre often derived their equivalences from similarities in sound; but, from the third century BC onward, Stoic philosophers had instead invented the field of etymology as a tool in their quest for the origins of words. The Stoic Cornutus at the end of the first century AD described this attempt as something of a rescue mission. At the conclusion of his treatise on opinions regarding the teaching of Greek theology, he wrote: "And, child, convinced that the ancients were no mean people, but possessed sufficient capacities to understand the nature of the cosmos, as well as a predilection to philosophize about it in symbols and cryptic expressions, you may well now be able to trace to the elements I have mentioned those other traditions too that appear to have come down to us in mythic form regarding the gods."[45]

Not all critics were as kind as Cornutus. Philodemus, a first-century-BC Epicurean, for example, soundly refuted the idea that stars were gods, although he conceded that the gods, who were distant, and visible only behind the heavenly bodies, might well be confused with them; the confusion was understandable. His point, however, was to allow more legitimacy even to this confused perspective than to temples, dwellings of the gods constructed by human hands.[46] The central strategies for the representation of gods met with constant criticism: temples, images, and, above all in Greece, sacrificial rites.[47] The motives behind the critique of myth and the critique of ritual here coalesced.

3. Systematization

Interpretation did not necessarily denote criticism. The author of the fourth-century-BC *Derveni papyrus* demonstrated how individual elements of a ritual, described sympathetically and interpreted meticulously, could cast the ritual practices in terms that conformed to a broader philosophical world view.[48] The text was cremated, and thus preserved by carbonization, in Thessaly along with the deceased, for whom it had perhaps been especially written. It displays a degree of complexity that would not be achieved in Rome before the second century BC. Even Ennius's *Euhemerus* had no progeny and presumably made no great impact, despite the reflections formulated in the dramas mentioned above.

Historiography and Statute

Others found more consequential options in the rich store offered by available Greek texts. At the beginning of the third century BC, Appius Claudius Caecus had improved the Latin script so that it better reproduced the sound of Latin speech, by using the letter "G" to stand for the hard, guttural "C," and adjusting the script to the altered pronunciation of intervocalic "S" as "R" (rhotacism). But it was Quintus Fabius Pictor who, having found in Greek a model for relating a chronological history of a city, wrote what is the first extant and substantial historical work in the Greek language written in Rome.[49] He devoted much space to the portrayal of the religious activity of the Roman political elite, probably because such rituals were, to his mind, the most important element of what for him had to be the subject of the narrative: the "commonweal" (*res publica*) of the city of Rome.[50] Subsequent Roman historians, including those writing in Latin from the mid-second century onward, retained this focus.[51]

This does not mean that clans' memories of their respective achievements played no role. Families and their male young had no doubt long made heroes of (male) ancestors in their own song traditions. Families began to provide accounts of such heroic deeds in highly truncated form in tomb inscriptions, such as that in the François Tomb and those on the sarcophagi of the Scipios. And these memories did not remain within the circle of the family. From at least as early as the second half of the fourth century BC, Roman aristocrats adopted the somewhat older Greek practice of erecting statues outside their homes, representing not only their celebrated ancestors, but also living family members with claims to glory.[52] Occasionally, these were erected even in spaces devoted to public monumental architecture.[53] Once it had been victorious commanders who were driven into the city in the guise of living statues, and subsequently honored with an actual statue on the Capitoline Hill. The granting of such a triumphal procession depended on a decision of the clans assembled in the Senate. This constraint, tying permission to erect a statue in a public space to particular military services or the exercise of senior magisterial functions, was gradually relaxed, owing to the exacerbation of social differences and competitiveness during and after the Second Punic War. But restraint was reinforced in other fields. In 158 BC, an attempt was made to forbid women the use of excessively ostentatious jewelry; and, in the same year, the censors removed from the Forum any statues that had not been authorized by senatorial decision.[54] At about the same time, the Greek Polybius observed how, during funerals, aristocratic families in Rome displayed "living statues" of ancestors, celebrated for (real or supposed) victories or magisterial posts, at the place of assembly of the *comitium* on the Forum. Embodied by actors, they would thus be virtually at their own front door but also in the public gaze. Speeches were made in their honor, and they were led in procession through the city to the place of burial, usually via the cremation site.[55] It was such statues, these very rituals, and the wax masks used in the funeral procession and displayed alongside inscriptions, or the speeches that were were read on such occasions in the semi-public space of the atrium, that kept alive or perhaps awakened for the first time memories both of family members and of those outside the family circle. They quite likely would have inspired upcoming generations and perhaps swayed voters.[56]

The first attempts to write a common Roman history coincided with a period of intense conflict and confrontation with more distant societies and cultural practices. Roman commanders and their troops had advanced beyond Sicily and Sardinia, as far as Spain and North Africa. After the Second Punic War they ventured into Greek territories near and far, and already in the second century BC had established themselves in southern Gaul (France), Asia Minor, and along the Mediterranean seaboard of Spain. Direct or indirect contacts extended as far as Palestine and Egypt, and slaves, merchants, and ambassadors, occasionally even fighting soldiers from those areas, came to Italy. Cultural diversity was not something the Romans learned about merely by reading Herodotus or Hellanicus of Mytilene;[57] it became part of a victor's triumphal self-representation, inherent in the exotic spoils of foreign wars displayed either in temples erected especially for the purpose or in his own villa, perhaps in the peristyle. Greeks came and remained as doctors, or to teach young men who did not know whether they would be able to emulate their fathers in positions that would enable them to bring home fortunes surpassing those of other clans.

These circumstances contributed to the popularity of Greek narratives such as those that Philochorus provided for Athens, linking the complex present condition of a city with its simpler beginnings.[58] Writers active in Rome who wished to find a common history behind the present-day collaborations and rivalries of the clans were drawn to the model of Greek foundational histories, and attempted to trace the establishment of as many important institutions as possible far back into the city's early years.[59] Ennius in his hexametric history of Rome introduced a second principle prominent in Latin-language historiography: annalistics, the recording of history as a yearly sequence of events. Such "annals" used the annual offices of senior magistrates as their basis, and the pattern thus established enabled writers to identify, year by year, the first instance of anything that was new or different. This included innovations in the religious sphere, such as new temples, new rituals, and new priesthoods.

No less interested in the past were those who, from the mid-second century BC onward, compiled statutes describing in detail particular institutions or procedures on the basis both of the records of magistrates or priests and of their own intuitions. Quintus Fabius Maximus Servilianus wrote about "pontifical law," Marcus Iunius Congus about the "prerogatives of office." Sergius Fabius Pictor too wrote about "the law of pontiffs," listing "the following deities invoked by a flamen when he performs the Ceres sacrifice to Tellus and Ceres: the field-sweeper, the one who ploughs again, the furrow-maker, the sower, the over-plower, the harrower, the hoer, the weeder, the cutter, the collector, the storer, the one who brings forth stored grain."[60] The records of the pontiffs must have been accessible, not only to Pictor, who as *flamen Quirinalis* was a member of the college,[61] and those records would likely have been a general stimulus to systematization. Subsequently, augurs too wrote about auspices and augural law.[62]

Knowledge and Authority

Anyone "producing" knowledge in this way would be likely to alter traditions at the same time as determining them, coming down on one side or the other in uncertain cases, or suppressing alternative versions. Unlike historians, these writers themselves claimed ownership of this knowledge, for they belonged to the class of functionaries who carried out the practices that were the subject of their texts. Attempts to regulate by statute conflicts over specific questions might contribute to systematization; but they could also work against it, especially if political considerations turned a question of knowledge into an issue of power.[63] The area of divination was especially affected.[64] Historians, by contrast, whether they wrote in prose or recited hexameters, were for the most part not themselves senators. They did, however, seek and find the support of patrons belonging to that circle.[65] A professional historian might be hired to write one's biography, for example, although there remained, of course, the alternative of writing it oneself, as did Sulla, Cicero, and Caesar, with varying emphases on the religious aspects of their lives.[66]

The suspicion of partisanship could more easily be avoided by refraining from the narrative form, with its tendency to take a particular standpoint. Chronicles inscribed on stone with no mention of authorship could achieve this, typically being chronicles of the place of display. In Greece as in Rome, these assigned great significance to religious data as a particular token of the "commonweal." Roman authors accompanied chronicles such as those produced in the Hellenistic Period on Paros and Lindos with representations of the calendar; the earliest of these was the work of Marcus Fulvius Nobilior, or perhaps of Ennius, in the Temple of Hercules and the Muses in the 160s BC, to be followed by examples at Antium and Ostia in the first century BC.[67] This Roman invention was particularly influential, in that, besides an added chronological list, it used the schema of the twelve months of the calendar itself to bring reminders of both Roman successes and the successes of families into the calendar's text, along with the dates of temple foundations. This pattern would be taken up frequently in the Late Republic, by Marcus Antonius, Cicero, and Augustus himself.[68]

Ritual actors too demonstrated their knowledge through religious communications in this public form, and not only in Rome. In the course of the second century BC, the *fratres Atiedii*, a priesthood in Umbrian Iguvium, produced a total of seven bronze tablets, the *Tabulae Iguvinae* mentioned earlier.[69] They ranged in size between tabloid and double demy (A3–A1). Inscriptions in the bronze indicated codified knowledge or unchangeable instructions describing the ritual first in Etruscan, and then, on the later tablets, in Latin script. The perhaps contemporary Etruscan *Liber linteus*, a linen book with rituals arranged in calendar order, suggests venerability by the very material of which it is made, and it likewise may have enjoyed a visibility and public presence beyond the expert circle of its authors.[70] So far as we can tell, however, such first steps were not taken in Rome until the Augustan Age, when they were cast in the form of monumental inscriptions in the sanctuary of the reorganized Arvals, and a short time afterward for the "saecular games" of 17 BC.

"Religion"

The few protagonists able to write, whether magistrates or priests, poets or historians, systematized: they arranged, they filled in gaps, they wrote things down. This they did for particular places or procedures: it did not occur to them to do it across the entire field of "religion" (whether or not they would now have called it "religion"). There were exceptions. In Caesar's final year, the founder of the Roman colony of Urso in Spanish Baetica set himself the task of decreeing rules for various areas of life in the settlement (44 BC). A relevant "need" may have existed before this, but nobody appears to have addressed it; and the author of the *lex Ursonensis*, who came from Caesar's circle, naturally fell back on older norms where they were available.[71] Cicero's *On the laws*, an unpublished attempt to compile rules for religious practices modeled on those governing magisterial posts and competencies, was only a decade older, and itself referred extensively back to

Plato.[72] Although a *lex Iulia municipalis* had been passed, probably on Caesar's initiative, immediately before the colony's foundation, perhaps as a model statute for civic "constitutions,"[73] the author of the law in respect of Urso did not refer to it; "religion" was not a category of the *lex Iulia municipalis*, and the statutes of Urso were themselves seen as archetypal by later generations. When the constitutions of Salpensa and Malaca were being written more than a hundred years later, during the Flavian dynasty at the end of the first century AD, in Urso the *lex Ursonensis* was merely republished on bronze tablets, the very ones that survive to this day.[74]

All three of the above bodies of law contain rules governing religious activities, but in all three cases alike these rules are dispersed throughout the texts, falling under different headings. What we would call religion is treated in chapters 64 to 72 and 125 to 128 of the *lex Ursonensis*. These chapters do not exhaustively cover what we know of ancient religion and of ancient religious practices, but there is no reason to assume that this text or one of the other collections of statutes originally contained chapters addressing other religious matters.[75] Chapters 64 to 72 govern the financing of the cult (62–65), describe pontiffs and augurs (66–68) and the procedure for financing ritual consumables (69), the organization and financing of games (70–71), and administration of the cash donated to temples (72). The most inclusive term that the author uses is *sacra*, "public rituals." The rules set out here are addressed to the *duoviri*, the colony's most senior magistrates; they are followed, from Ch. 73, by norms that apply to others. The later chapters concern the rules for seats at games, obligations regarding priests' places of residence, and restrictions on donations to temples.

The author, or the committee set up for the purpose, must have had in mind a two-layered model of religion. One level was made explicit and regulated. It was here that religious activity had an established place in the social and political fabric of the *colonia*. As a public cult (*sacra publica*), it was financed and organized by the council and its magistrates; accordingly, the financing of the cult is the theme binding together the entire passage on religion.[76] The precise content of the public ritual, with its emphasis on commonality, was the responsibility of the political decision-makers and would be financed by them. At this public level, the primary cults were those of the Capitoline Triad and, to a lesser extent, Venus, probably Venus Genetrix. This choice ensured that every magistrate who sought prestige for himself as the organizer of games had to do so with reference to Rome and Caesar.

The second level of religion was precisely *not* subject to explicit regulation, or only negatively so. To this level belonged priesthoods, fines for malfeasance, and burial and the cult of ancestors; perhaps also religious groups if such there were. All this might exist, but it must not impede the administrative functioning of the colony. Even pontiffs and augurs, a traditional element ranking at the first level in Roman religion, were assigned to the second level insofar as they were given no functions so weighty as to be essential to the colony's administration; although their existence was assumed by the statute's authors. Donations given by individuals to cults were seen as belonging to the public sphere, and were to be administered solely within temples; they could not be used beyond the precincts of the temple. Opportunities for independent religious activity were restricted by legal means, but without hampering time-honored traditions. The authors regulated all this with a view to problems that had arisen in the past in one context or another. None of it amounted to anything that might be called "religion."

In another area, however, reflection on what magistrates did went further. A good hundred years after Ennius's "Euhemerus," Greek rhetoric, after enormous resistance, had found supporters in Rome. A number of senatorial and wealthy "equestrian" families firmly entrusted with judicial duties were even sending their adolescent sons to receive appropriate instruction in Greece itself. Not only rhetoricians, but also Greek philosophers and Greek philosophy were finding favor or a ready hearing among the Hellenistically inclined Roman elite. But even as prominent an advocate, orator, and theoretician of oratory as Marcus Tullius Cicero waited until the presumptive end of his political career before he undertook to make Greek *theologia* systematically accessible in the Latin language.

When he did, he demonstrated its principles in fictional dialogues.[77] Even in Cicero's dialogues *On the nature of the gods, On divination*, and *On fate*, reflection on a general concept of "religion" was allowed to progress only so far. What may at first sight have appeared to his readers to be a definitive position[78] was revealed on closer inspection to comprise standpoints taken up by the various disputing participants in a dialogue. Thus, in *On the nature of the gods*, the trinity *pietas, sanctitas*, and *religio*, by means of which Cicero juxtaposes religiosity and the gods' involvement in religion, is not so fundamental as at first appears. It is used only in the introductory section (1.3 and 1.14), and is not clearly defined. The most stable of the relationships involved is that between *pietas* and *religio*. *Pietas* describes the relationship of a person to a human or divine other who is his or her superior. *Religio* on the other hand is a particular consequence arising from a relationship to the gods, perhaps expressed in terms of the cult. The existence of the gods is thus the prerequisite for any piety or religiosity toward them.[79]

Despite its original context in a trinity with *pietas* and *sanctitas*, *religio* thus emerges as a central concept in the dialogue. It is not frequently employed, but when it is it occurs at introductory or summarizing sections of an argument. Its distribution between the participants is uneven. Velleius, Epicurus's disciple, hardly ever uses the term *religio*; Quintus Lucilius Balbus the Stoic uses it rarely; Cotta the academic and pontiff, on the other hand, employs it frequently, in both its singular and plural forms. He juxtaposes the plural *religiones* with *caerimoniae* (1.161), as well as *sacra* with *caerimonia* (3.5), and qualifies *religiones* as "public": these it is the pontiff's duty to defend. *Religio*, for Cotta, is not merely a vague sentiment (for this he criticizes his adversary) or an "empty fear," like *superstitio* (1.117), but a human disposition, a habit, a part of the social order that follows from acceptance of the gods and finds expression in appropriate rituals (*cultus deorum*, 1.117); here the argument takes a quite normal Greek bent,[80] in which the existence of the gods is a prerequisite for *religio* (ibid.), whereas *religio* may be imperiled by an unbridled multiplication of gods. Cotta sees *religio* as a social factor of great utility for the stability of the community (3.94), but not as an argument that can be introduced into philosophical discourse (see 1.118). Cicero himself set great store by the notion that *religio* tends to be constrained by *ratio*, and this is the purpose of his entire book.[81]

Religio in the singular in Cicero's argument is a necessary consequence of any belief in a god, and finds its expression, as also its limits, in various feelings of religious obligation: *religiones*. It is possible to argue as to the existence or the relevance of the gods; that is, about theism, which is a theoretical problem or tenet. But it is not possible to question *religio*. As a pontiff, and a man inclined to academic skepticism, Cotta mentions Romulus's institution of the auspices, and the foundation of other cults (*sacra*) by Numa, with an air of approbation; he does not, however, accept it as the philosophical justification claimed, but in Cotta's opinion not provided, by the Stoic Balbus: "As you are a philosopher, I must require of you a justification for religion (*rationem . . . religionis*); I, though, must concur with our ancestors, even if no justification is forthcoming" (3.6). Such a justification would of course amount to no more than evidence as to the gods' existence; it could not validate historical cult forms. Cult practice imposed limits on theory, and vice versa.

Faced with a choice between no god and too many gods as a basis for religion,[82] the figure of Cicero in the dialogue chooses the latter. It is admittedly a weak theoretical position, but it proves the best among the options given. And it is a serious option notwithstanding its shortcomings, for it avoids the split, indicated by Cotta, between a public and a private, a philosophical and a traditional *persona*. The social status of the participants in Cicero's fiction is not unimportant. Setting aside the Epicurean arguments (as Cicero invites his readers to do), the central role in each of the dialogues is given to the person with the highest social standing and highest avowed religious function: the pontiff Cotta in the earlier work *On the nature of the gods*, and the augur Marcus Tullius Cicero in the later work *On divination*. The authority thus lent to their statements ensures that their critical arguments are taken seriously, and their positions seriously tested. This does not mean that everyone is compelled to support that position, as the author's voice demonstrates at the end of *De natura deorum*, pronouncing against Cotta, even though Cotta is the host and the oldest participant. The characters demonstrate the norms of Roman philosophical discussion.[83] Philosophizing was as honorable an activity as trading in the Forum, and its conventions were similar. This was important, and not only to a figure such as Cicero. If philosophy led to a good life, a *vita beata,* as all schools maintained, then the practice of philosophy must itself follow the norms of such a life.[84]

Unlike religion, philosophy offered a comprehensive model for the conduct of a life. Religion was one object among others that one could reflect about, but it could not be separated from everyday religious practices. Could it be that its dignity was of a loftier sort, even for theoretical purposes, than Cicero allowed Cotta to assume? The traditional cult, touched upon only anecdotally by Cicero, is exhaustively portrayed by his contemporary Marcus Terentius Varro (116–27 BC) in *Antiquities of things human and divine.* In one sense an accumulation of historical-ethnographical scholarship, this latter work is also driven by the assumption that religion itself might become a philosophical resource, and might at its earliest historical levels contain philosophical insights.[85] The original absence of imagery in Roman cult (no matter how much Varro might apply his imaginative powers to some details) argued in support of this view.

It therefore transpires that "religion" as a concept was not a topic of theoretical reflection until the late Republic, and even then only in rudimentary terms. But the very fact that some individuals had applied themselves to systematizing religious experience and religious activity and the interpretations thereof had a pronounced effect. It fundamentally altered traditional activity and authority. It is scarcely possible for us, then, to imagine the greater impact that would be felt when religion all at once took written form and became a matter of record.

VII

The Redoubling of Religion in the Augustan Saddle Period

THE FIRST CENTURY BC TO THE FIRST CENTURY AD

1. Restoration as Innovation

In his *Antiquitates rerum humanarum et divinarum*, probably dedicated to the *pontifex maximus* Gaius Iulius Caesar in 47 BC, Varro's intention is not merely to sum up older "traditions." Rather he intends to present philosophical reflections on the nature of deities, and organizes his work so as to treat the subject with encyclopedic thoroughness. After an introduction, he writes about human actors (priesthoods), about cult places, about the times and types of feast days, about rituals, and finally about gods, both established deities and those whose shape or personality is less certain.[1] Varro himself had held various magisterial posts, and as recently as 49 BC had led a legion as Pompey's *proquaestor*, but he had never held a priesthood. He relied, then, neither on his own experience nor on practical knowledge, but on the investigation of sources and on etymology, and on what he could glean from these about changes in religion over the course of history, and, finally, on philosophical reflection. Who, where, when, what, and above all for whom: these were the fundamental themes of his inquiries into religious activity.[2]

The knowledge that Varro sets out, while systematized, is no longer dependent on the approval of other aristocratic actors, although he places it at their disposal, and intends it for them.[3] It is now—and this is critical—the learned specialist who decides what has taken place in the past and how the knowledge of it ought to be presented. It is no longer the ancestors (*maiores*) who speak, their mouths made to utter contemporary claims that are alleged to be *mos maiorum*, "tradition."[4] Such a critique as Varro's could not be restricted to developments in Rome alone—such as the early abandonment of the aniconic cult postulated by Varro—although Rome is where its author, through loyalty, grounds it. And it could also address itself to other specialists, even those whose field was religion, as when Varro proposes to enlighten the priests in Samothrace as to the character of the *penates* venerated there.[5] What Cicero had already touched upon in his universalizing project *On the laws* is now consistently implemented, and without reliance on priests as arbiters: religious knowledge is no longer the property of the aristocracy, or even of patricians.[6] Caesar—priest and patrician but above all dictator—seized the occasion and appointed Varro to head his library project: which, however, came to nothing owing to Caesar's assassination and Marcus Antonius's persecution of Varro, whom Augustus was then to take more thoroughly under his wing.

Why was knowledge increasingly claimed and generated by specialists? The fact that Cicero refers to the problem of newly imported or immigrant cults in the very first paragraphs of his religious laws shows the extent to which his contemporaries were aware of changes, and of the forms those changes took. It was not only a question of cult practices from outside the Aegean orbit, such as the worship of Isis, a goddess indigenous to Egypt, or the occasional banishment from Rome in previous decades of philosophers, rhetoricians, specialists in Jewish cult, and finally the astrologers;[7] other factors probably came into play, less visible, but productive of long-term changes just the same. Such were the consequences of the Second Punic War and above all the Social War, with its rapid effects on migration and linguistic developments, for social and economic development in Italy. The

increasing Roman presence in Greece was to have similar consequences, motivating intellectuals to reinvent their traditions.[8]

In Italy, the slow changes in religious practices, such as the decline
of votive offerings, owed perhaps more to a reorientation of the manufacturers than to a reduction in demand.[9] At the same time, throughout Italy, terracotta reliefs depicting scenes from Greek mythology
were becoming increasingly prominent as donations in temples. In
the context of religious communication, these aided in the dissemination of the Greek themes they depicted. Catullus's epithalamium
(*carmen* 64) relating the marriage of Peleus and Thetis may have reflected such developments;[10] and the groups of statuary with Niobids
at Sosius's Temple of Apollo in Rome are also symptomatic of this increasing presence of things Greek.[11] Roman aristocrats borrowed
from the Etruscans as well, installing marble candelabras in their houses
in free imitation of archaic Etruscan bronze incense burners.[12] There
was a superabundance of the old and the utterly new, and it was no
longer possible to keep them within bounds by mere assertion of the
vague code of conduct as yet still shared by the elite. Varro himself
arranged to be buried in the style of the Pythagoreans.[13]

Augustus

Gaius Octavius, the future Augustus, was eighteen years old when
Caesar was assassinated in 44 BC, and he became Caesar's heir and
adoptive son, Gaius Iulius Divi filius Caesar. Even as his generals were
defeating his opponents at Philippi, Naulochus, and Actium, he kept
constantly in mind his own plans for dominance, set against the background of the fate suffered by Caesar. He appears to have concluded
that success in ending the civil wars and establishing his own position
could not be achieved by further political upheaval, but would be better served by restoring the common cause, the "Republic": a political
program that even figures as a rallying call in the Civil War texts
belonging to the *Corpus Caesarianum*.[14] A lengthy process led to the
creation of a position of power within the framework of the old, established offices and rules that governed the exercise of power until

Augustus's death in AD 14. Authority was informal or granted only on a temporary basis.[15] Against this backdrop, the "restoration" was both a program and a path of least resistance that, in individual instances, led to surprising results. At the same time, in view of the abundance of available traditions and tendencies, the correlations with the basic outlines of Varro's approach are striking. This orientation toward the antique, toward Greek models defined as "classical," belies the radical nature of the innovations concealed within the proclaimed "restoration of freedom to the republic."[16] In view of the comparatively healthy state of our sources for the late Republic, it is noteworthy that what was represented as tradition by actors in Augustus's circle in many cases had no actual antecedents, or at least none that were convincingly similar to what was being put forward.

Augustus and his contemporaries no doubt made very conscious use of religious communication in this process, but they did not speak of any clearly delimited field called "religion." In *The Deeds of the Divine Augustus*, written at the end of his life and promulgated in the form of monumental inscriptions in Latin and Greek—parts of which from Ankara, Antioch, and Apollonia survive—Augustus speaks of his priesthoods in the course of listing his offices, mentions vows pledged to him and altars dedicated to him under the heading of "honors received," names temples built and restored by him in the context of disbursements from his own purse, and likewise the games and theatrical productions that he sponsored.[17] When, however, it is a question of honors and expenditures visible in Rome, of communication with the populace (especially the citizens of Rome), religious practices and institutions offer by far the broadest field of action. Setting aside political assemblies with their modest infrastructure of *comitium* and *curia*, it was primarily religious activity that constituted the "public" domain in any substantial sense. It is clear from the framing of Augustus's account that his unchallenged military power and a world empire were the prerequisites for the Augustan project, for they were the source (we are to understand) of the necessary financing. We shall come to speak of this imperialist effect and the religious strategies of victors and vanquished in the next chapter.

Networks

Knowing the right people was central to success. But how did networking function in Rome? Military functions were performed outside of the city. And magisterial offices within the city were merely annual appointments. The most consistent support for network-building was to be found in lifelong senatorial offices and priesthoods. The latter operated in a tandem fashion, members of priestly colleges having normally served in magisterial offices that then brought them a seat in the Senate. But priestly colleges were also family affairs, meeting in private houses in circles of manageable size. Augustus was appointed pontiff at Caesar's instigation when he was still Gaius Octavius, probably at the end of 47 BC. He continued on the same course after Caesar's death, having himself co-opted as augur in the course of his consular year (43). He became *quindecimvir sacris faciundis* after the Treaty of Misenum, perhaps as early as 39, at the latest in 37, and subsequently *epulo, arval,* and *sodalis Titii*.[18] He thus obtained admission to the most important colleges, and, once arrived at this level, enjoyed contacts with the families of the Aemilii, Antonii, Appulei, Caninii, Claudii, Coccei, Cornelii, Domitii, Fannii, Fonteii, Iunii, Licinii, Marcii, Mucii, Munatii, Pompeii, Scribonii, Sempronii, Sosii, Statilii, Tullii, Valerii, and Vipsanii.[19] This was certainly a deliberate strategy, and a definitive change from the time when the pontifical college was dominated by Marcus Antonius and M. Aemilius Lepidus, installed by Antonius in 44 BC. As early as 38 BC, however, having meanwhile been promoted to the status of *Divi filius*, he gave a demonstration of how this same college functioned by asking it for an opinion clarifying the inheritance implications of his marriage to Livia, who was pregnant by her former husband, Tiberius Claudius Nero. What Tacitus later described as "derision" on the part of the college[20] may have been as much a demonstration of power as an unprecedented expert opinion: Nero, like Augustus, had been a member of the college providing the opinion. In any event, personal affairs had in this way become a subject of public debate, and were decided by a process of religious communication.

The same strategy was also apt to be pursued in less prominent priesthoods. In 32 BC it impacted the college of the fetiales; initially a diplomatic institution, by the end of the Republic the fetiales were regarded as a priesthood, and had increasingly developed into an instrument of control for magistrates acting ever further from Rome. At the latest under Cicero, the *ius fetiale* had become a medium for reflection on international law and the "just war," while the role of the fetiales was largely taken over by ambassadors.[21] During his conflict with his rival Marcus Antonius, Caesar's heir remembered this priesthood, mentioned by Varro; we do not know who had been its members in the preceding decades, or to what extent it had been active or even staffed at all during that time. His ritual experts associated with the institution of the fetiales an antiquarian account of earlier military commanders hurling a lance to open a campaign, mentioned in one of Varro's treatises that had only just appeared at this time. The young Caesar as fetial declared war against Cleopatra by hurling a blood-colored lance into a piece of mock enemy land at the temple of the war-goddess Bellona (a civil war against Antonius could not have been a *bellum iustum*, a just war). The accompanying propaganda claimed a long pedigree for the ritual, asserting that it could be traced back to ancient Latium, and had been moved to the Field of Mars as early as the time of Pyrrhus.[22]

The older Caesar himself had used similar strategies to enact and legitimize severe measures by religious actions. After his triumph in 46 BC, he had forestalled a rebellion by having the two ringleaders ritually executed with lances.[23] Ritual action and ritual actors had been mutually defining in this case, for the active parties had been the pontiffs and the *flamen Martialis*, the latter belonging—like Caesar and his future adoptive son—to the pontifical college. Those who watched the ritual would have had in mind a comparable custom: the killing by similar means of the winning horse in a race during the October festivals, the so-called October Horse. Contemporaries disagreed in their interpretation of this ritual; but one version, in circulation since the third century BC, cited a connection to the Trojan War: the lance-thrust into the October Horse was punishment for the horse that had enabled the Greeks to enter Troy and destroy the city. That myth was reprised in scaenic games in Rome, so impressing one contemporary, the poet Virgil, that he invented the scene in the Aeneid where the priest Laocoön throws a lance at the wooden horse: an occurrence not found in the Greek epic tradition.[24] In both cases, the suppression of the rebellion and the declaration of war, the ritualization remained without sequel, for at least two hundred years in the case of the fetiales.

The future Augustus, who in the meantime presided as a perpetually reappointed consul, made a similarly profound and probably also original reference to "tradition" (or, more precisely, to Varro's conception of it) with the reorganization of the Arval Brethren. Until now, he had confined himself to finding ways to pack the membership of existing priesthoods, and, by having himself co-opted as a member, turn them into a network with himself in a controlling position.[25] At the time when he wrote the Deeds, he was still able to boast that some 170 priests stood at his side at the time of the Battle of Actium (31 BC).[26] So as to be able to continue proactively filling priestly offices at the end of the Civil War, in 29 BC he obtained the right to appoint new patricians from plebeian families, thus at the same time underlining the special status of religious authority; this in parallel with his "purge" of the Senate, which excluded 190 members. The reorganization of the sanctuary of Dea Dia at the fifth milestone of the road leading from Rome to the southwest gave Gaius Octavius occasion to put splendid shape to his designs.[27]

The contractor charged with the project saw before him a sanctuary fronted by a temple of Dea Dia, dating to before the second century BC.[28] The redevelopment would occupy more than two hundred years. Probably from the Flavian period onward it also included a complex referred to as a Caesareum, and from the Severan period an ever-lengthening axis comprising the sanctuary, a temple of Dea Dia, an altar, the Caesareum, a portico, and a bathhouse, the latter extending toward the Tiber and skirted by a hippodrome (fig. 30). One of the earliest elements of incipient monumentalization was the erection of marble steles on which the records of the Arvals were inscribed at the end of each year, beginning perhaps in that very year of 29 BC, and thus preserved in perpetuity. So as not to begin with blank tablets, an initial ensemble of four steles, each 86 cm wide by 220 cm high, offered a calendar (*fasti*) with a list of magistrates in the space beneath.[29] What was to become the largest surviving coherent collection of inscriptions in Rome was, from the beginning, the ritualization of a cult space in which "brethren" newly recruited from the first families of Rome would play roles, the status of which (compared to the older priesthoods) was not yet known. Even the new priests had yet to be convinced. They received lavish assurance, at a superficial level at least, in the form just described: marble plaques bearing their own names.[30] But it was not merely a question of monumentalization. Tents (*papilliones*) were erected at the entrance of the entire complex to serve as accommodation for the Arvals. These made plain at the level of felt, personal experience that the purpose here was not urban, sited in this rural place by some happenstance, but deliberately agrarian. The complex was intended for communication with Dea Dia, and its aim was to bring about successful seedtimes and harvests. The main festival was movable in relation to the calendar, although variations were only slight, and accomplished by the magistrates through the medium of public announcements. In this sense, the occasion imitated the similar movability of other festivals of seedtime and harvest, expressing graphically in terms of a universal experience of time what was in terms of space a private matter confined to the Arvals themselves.

It is to be assumed that the *Divi filius* was pursuing still further-reaching strategies when he reorganized a priesthood that boasted mythical connections with Romulus. Romulus, founder of the city, was at this time a figure with whom Augustus was in many ways keen to associate himself, one whom he favored as prefiguring his own role.[31] It was perhaps the critical emphasis under Caesar on Romulus's role as a king that eventually disabused him of the idea, even though Romulus himself remained important.[32] *Rex* was a concept diametrically opposed to *libertas*, and one that late Republican historians, relying on Greek theories of the state, had proscribed in respect of Roman history. In the end, in January of 27 BC, Octavian's advisors

30. Plan of the sanctuary of Dea Dia in La Magliana, Rome. Drafted by
John Scheid. Copyright École Française de Rome. Reproduced by
the kind permission of the École Française de Rome.

brought off the brilliant gambit of offering him the honorific epithet
augustus, an adjective with numerous sublime religious echoes, of *augur*
and *augurium,* but unburdened with historical allusions to kingship.[33]
It was to become his proper name, and eventually the descriptive term
for the leading position in a new Roman monarchy.

There was nothing honorary about priestly office. It carried with it
an obligation to action, to religious communication. In this way it afforded connection to a network upheld by regular interaction among
its members. For the Arvals as in the case of other colleges, formal
meetings and rituals were often held in the house of their annually
changing *magister.*[34] This both enabled and defined contacts between
male members of different clans, and it did not only affect those individuals whose election had brought them to prominent positions
within the senatorial class. Perhaps already in the context of his new
interpretation of the fetiales, Augustus had also given renewed

attention to the groups of the *salii Palatini* and *Collini*, formed of young aristocrats, and presumably now differentiated for the first time one from the other. The same attention was given to the *Luperci*, from now on occupied by members of the equestrian class, and perhaps (after Caesar's attempts at differentiation) consolidated and reduced in numbers. Finally, Augustus was interested in the various priesthoods of fictitious or defunct Latin communities whose priests were appointed from Rome.[35]

The reorganization of Rome's districts into fourteen regions comprising 265 neighborhoods (*vici*), begun after Augustus's election as *pontifex maximus* in 12 BC and completed in 7 BC, allowed him to confer important aspects of network formation to persons from distinctly lower social strata. By treating the *vicomagistri* as priests, he enabled them to find their own respective publics and roles in religious communication with the local *lares*. This did not involve the kind of hierarchical chain of communication that would have led from the 265 times two *magistri*, via the regional *curatores*, to higher magistrates, and finally to Augustus: the link with Augustus was direct, and it too was maintained through religious communication. It had been Augustus who had transferred the cult to these communities in his role as *pontifex maximus*; they remembered this as a historical event, and recognized it each in their own particular reckoning of eras, which sometimes varied from neighborhood to neighborhood, with lavish marble altars, and on occasion in their own lists of incumbents.[36] If Augustus had no actual presence as a member, he was symbolically present in the form of the *Genius Augusti*, which was included in the cult of the *lares*: at an appropriately large number of small, sacralized sites at crossroads (*compita*), Augustus himself was iconographically visible above the heads of his functionaries performing their rituals.[37]

Rituals

Not every religious innovation required new personnel. Many simply brought new narratives, installed along with claims as to their antiquity. For the Augustan poet Virgil, the mere opening of the doors of the

Temple of Janus was symbolic of war.[38] The opening of a *porta Ianualis*, a gate adjacent to the Forum and spanning the Argiletum, may once have been carried out as a ritualized gesture by a military commander upon setting off for war, or at least some such story may have been told. Varro in any case knew about such things, and he could also cite older writers.[39] As no one, after passing through the gate, would have inquired whether it was open or closed, this gives rise to the question as to why a door should be opened during a war, when caution would surely have dictated that it be kept closed. There were no other temporal tokens of such a thing as a state of war in Rome. The entire religious construct of war aimed, in fact, not at a temporal distinction, but at a spatial one between *domi*—Rome, the permanent sanctum of peace—and *militiae*, where the rules of war applied: a distinction that could be lifted only in a few exceptional instances such as a triumph. With the early removal of the Janus gate from the vicinity of the city wall, together with an understanding, perhaps arrived at in the third century BC, that allowed a war to consist in a series of annual campaigns of varying outcome, ending only once a Roman victory had been achieved, new interpretations were possible. As early as 235 BC, the gate had supposedly been closed in circumstances of victory.[40] It was important to Augustus to use such a ritual to load the end of the Civil War in 29 with religious significance, and he would repeat it twice more (once as early as 25 BC); but, again, there were only occasional later repetitions, for example by Nero and Vespasian.

These were not isolated relics, fetched from the drawers of antiquaries, or from their think tanks, to be used by a detail-obsessed ruler seeking to make his mark on the Zeitgeist.[41] The ideas were already there, already developed and reflected on; and they would continue to be reflected on, by authors of prose narratives and epics, stage-plays, and poetry. As for Augustus himself, however, wherever possible his aim was broad. The best example of this is the "saecular games," the *ludi saeculares* (fig. 31). In a mixture of different temporal conceptions no longer fathomable to us, the initiators of these games were manufacturing the start of a new Golden Age. Central to the

31. Reverse of a denarius of Domitian, struck for the saecular games of AD 88. A herald holding a shield stands in front of a stele inscribed *Co(n)s(ul) XIIII lud(os) saec(ulares) fec(it)*. Photo: Museum August Kestner Hannover, inv. Mü 389. Photo: Christian Tepper.

project was the Etruscan doctrine of a limited sequence of wearisome *saecula*, while at the same time the games were understood to mark the fifth return of the 110-year festive cycle of the city of Rome.[42] It was at least maintained that earlier celebrations of the *ludi Tarentini*, attested for 249 BC and named after the site at which they were held on the Field of Mars, had this same meaning.[43] Simultaneously, the organizers emphasized the *saeculum* as the maximum duration of a human life: no person born in one *saeculum* can experience the beginning of the next but one. They moreover based the holding of the games on an oracle contained in the Sibylline books. Foremost in the texts of prayers, however, was not retrospection, but a new departure: the Golden Age must be vigorously promoted.[44]

Everyone was to attend; there would be no second chance in a lifetime: this was precisely the meaning of the *saeculum*. What the heralds were announcing was not participation in a sacrifice in the form of a meal of meat, but the enactment of a completely new age through the medium of religious communication.[45] The two bulls for Jupiter Optimus Maximus, sprinkled with *mola salsa* by Augustus and Agrippa, would scarcely have sufficed, nor the nine each of sheep and goats of the previous night. The *quindecimviri* who led the complex ritual under Augustus and Agrippa, who were their *magistri*, addressed themselves especially to married women; mourners were encouraged to cut short their period of mourning and take part in the games; incense was provided. The nightly presentations were followed by prayers and offerings, with stage-plays during the day.

The wooden theaters used for the games were certainly lavish structures, but even they could accommodate a few thousand people at most, no more than a fraction of the city's population. And the theaters were the only spaces with optimal acoustics. All the more effort, then, was expended on disseminating representations of the ritual, as would be typical also for later saecular games under the emperors Claudius (AD 47), Domitian (AD 88), and Septimius Severus with Caracalla (AD 204), and then again in AD 247. Event programs, often including the complete texts of prayers and hymns, were displayed in the form of large-format inscriptions. In at least two years, 17 BC and AD 88, series of coins were minted, depicting scenes that could be observed in the city at large, such as the announcement of the games and the distribution of incense. Religious communication on the part of the emperor and his presumptive successor thus preserved their presence in the city beyond the day and hour of actual delivery.

The Reduction of Religion

Augustus redoubled the scope of religion through the everyday medium of the coin and the rapidly spreading medium of the inscription,[46] which spoke its authority loud and clear as it confronted readers in the public realm.[47] But he also reined in some aspects of religion. In those very areas where, in the city's past, religious communication had aroused competition, he sought to monopolize it. The decisive phase was the decade after the victory at Actium (31 BC). Marcus Licinius Crassus, consul for 30 BC, returned home to a triumph approved by the Senate. On the basis of dubious arguments dredged from the obscure depths of history, he was denied the special honor accorded to a victorious commander who had defeated an opposing commander in single combat: he was not allowed to lay down the defeated commander's arms as "rich spoils" (*spolia opima*), after the precedent set by Romulus. But Crassus's aristocratic rivals were allowed to triumph, and they garnered in his stead the immense prestige bestowed by this parade of plunder and military conquest. By renouncing time-honored customs and devising new stratagems, Augustus established what was to become the long-term monopoly of the imperial family.[48] He no longer triumphed at all after his three-day triumph in 29 BC. After a few triumphs by aristocrats subsequent to this date, Marcus

Agrippa, number two in the hierarchy of power, likewise renounced the triumph due to him in 19 BC. [49] What remained for him and other victors were triumphal distinctions and an honorific statue. In this way, the entire civic space that had been so thoroughly affected by the routes of triumphal parades was appropriated by Augustus for his own forms of communication.

2. Religion in Space

The appropriation is clearer still when it comes to built structures. During the years after the victory over Caesar's assassins at Philippi, the allied generals were widely active in restoring temples. How great the actual need for such renovation may have been was quite beside the point. Even when the military and financial basis of political power was to be sought in the provinces, many rivals shared the conviction that a firm foundation was to be gained only in Rome and by a presence in Rome; even if, in particular contexts and at particular times, such a presence could be obtained only indirectly through the use of media. Such presence, again, was expensive, and it necessitated military successes. Even after his unprecedented gains in prestige and power between 29 and 27 BC, Augustus again set off for Spain; [50] only after his return from that theater and the conspiracy of 23 BC did he resolve on a permanent presence in Rome. The balance between the city and the provinces was difficult to achieve, but it inclined toward Rome. And Rome no longer needed to seek balance with other Italic centers, as in the period preceding the Social War. For an increasing number of people Rome had become a "mnemotope," a city laden with memories and meanings. Space had become place. [51]

Temple Construction

The initiatives pursued by the holders of magisterial office in restoring temples need not be seen as reactions to a late Republican decline of religion. Structures have to be maintained, and there was as yet no permanent arrangement for the care of public buildings; this would come later.[52] The many temple foundations of the second century had thus created an unfulfilled need. But, how had the Roman population received these structures, and how did they appropriate them for their own religious practice? From the second century on, ever fewer Romans took it upon themselves to deposit terracotta objects at sacralized locations, and there was a consequent lack of interest in devoting new spaces to this purpose. To many, it seemed more important and more appealing to participate as spectators at the great *ludi*, especially the circus, and (although in much smaller numbers) in the theaters. Monumentalized sanctuaries like the one dedicated to Fortuna at Praeneste, or to Hercules at Tibur or Tusculum, offered the appropriate spaces, and were doubtless used for such events.[53] It was only around a few sanctuaries that groups crystalized, or themselves undertook to carry out the building process, sometimes even at odds with the powers that be. There were repeated attempts, for example, to establish a cult of Isis on the Capitol, and also to prevent its establishment. It was a conflict that even Varro in his encyclopedic and normative representation of Roman religion could not abstain from describing.[54]

The interest of a family in maintaining a little-used sanctuary may have been slight, even when the sanctuary had been founded by its own ancestors. But a victorious and booty-rich general might welcome the chance to join the elites in a restoration project, so long as it was affordable and would lead to a lasting association between temple and restorer. The first of these conditions, cost, depended on the nature of the project, and on whether or not the builder confined himself to traditional materials. These restorations were not the occasion for making Rome a city of gold or marble. Even for what amounted to a new building, the prominent temple of Mater Magna on the Palatine, renewed recourse was had to *peperino* tuff, its surface stippled for decoration.[55] As for an enduring connection with the elite, this could be contrived if a project was represented as being so fundamental that a rededication with the appropriate festival day and building inscription was justified. This could be realized most effectively by moving the date of the foundation day, and that is precisely what is reflected in subsequent calendars.[56]

In the case of a new build, the patron was both inclined and obliged, in the spirit of competition, to reach further into his pocket and come up with a more innovative plan. In 36 BC, the young Octavian built on the Palatine a temple to the god Apollo that was only later linked with the victory at Actium, ascribed by the victor to Apollo. He not only sheathed this temple's exterior with gleaming white marble, but also furnished it with gold. A combination of yellow paint and gold ensured that, from a distance, the pediments seemed to sit on the shimmering white building like a golden crown. Golden acanthus leaves crowned the individual columns, while the dentils beneath the cornice were picked out in silver and ochre. While earlier uses of gold, for example in decorating temple ceilings, succeeded in impressing someone actually entering the structure, the color scheme described here was also central to the temple's appearance as one approached from a distance.[57] Contemporary observers reported being profoundly impressed (fig. 32).[58] The effect of the marble was soon to be even further enhanced by the addition of tints.[59]

More lavish still, and destined to be the central element of Augustus's own Forum, was the Temple of Mars Ultor, vowed by the elder Caesar's adoptive son in 42 BC for the victory over his father's assassins. The material Augustus used for the building's construction, not to be completed until 40 years later in 2 BC, was Carrara marble, newly exploited by him as a building material for Rome. Two adjacent porticos defined a garden-like courtyard, while at the same time providing space for statues of historical personages, presented in two semi-circular bays (exedrae) as the most important Romans.

Augustus had only limited competition at this point. In the city of Rome—and there only—he had established that only he himself and his continually redefined family were qualified to endow public building projects. This relegated the entire senatorial class to projects in other towns in Italy and the provinces, where patrons who were local or only occasionally present were not seen as competing with a remote

32. The so-called Campana terracotta from the temple of Apollo Palatinus, Rome,
showing two girls decorating an aniconic *baitylos*, an archaic symbol of Apollo,
75×61 cm, ca. 36 BC. Rome, Antiquario Palatino. akg-images / Erich Lessing.

ruler.[60] Competition in Rome was thus confined to older buildings
and to Augustus's own earlier projects. This was in any event enough
competition to create a pressure for increasing the size of porticos,
baths, and structures designed for games: a venue for sea-battles (*nau-machia*); a circus and theaters; and, not least, temples.[61] Here, specifically public recreational spaces were created to complement the streets,
which were the liveliest places in the city, and had already been given
an Augustan aura by the *Genius Augusti* and *Lares Augusti*. These common spaces were locations for relaxation, conversation, pleasures of
the eye and—time and again—of the memory. Already in the late Republic, Varro had met with friends in the Temple of Tellus for the purpose of contemplating a map of Italy.[62] Augustus's development of such
an imperial monopoly, beginning in the 20s BC, also forced the clans
to make adjustments to their prestige-seeking strategies. Perhaps the
most distinctive of these was the invention of table-sized equestrian

statues. These permitted friends and relations still to be honored in the stance that was the most appropriate for many kinds of distinctions, but in a domestic space.[63]

It was perhaps the feeling that it was no longer necessary to think within the standard guidelines governing the construction of temples, or even theater-temples such as Pompey had built, that inspired the designers of Augustus's building program to take up and radically alter yet another ancient form of cult structure. Whereas the common circular altar was scarcely suitable as an object of public prestige, especially in its slender form reminiscent of an hourglass, platform altars bearing no cult images opened up almost unlimited possibilities of scale. It was with such an *ara* that Fortuna Redux, "the Fortune of return," was thanked for Augustus's return from Hispania in 19 BC; the annual games of the *Augustalia* on 12 October consistently lavished attention on her. What coins, our only surviving record, show to have been rather a modest structure[64] was far surpassed by the Ara Pacis Augustae, likewise commissioned by the Senate acting in concert (fig. 33). The three wings of the altar table, whose interior was accessed by a total of seven steps, were more than four meters high; the altar table itself stood in a space measuring more than eight times nine meters, defined by walls that were themselves decorated with marble reliefs, and interrupted only on the two longer sides.[65] The form and site of a further Ara Numinis Augusti are unknown, but it must have been a significant altar, as four great priesthoods operated there on the feast day.[66] Augustan-period actors thus adopted patterns of Greek court altars, as erected at Samothrace, Priene, Magnesia on the Menander, Ephesus, and of course Pergamum, that had long been established in Italy. Such an enclosed altar was erected in the second century BC at Lucan Rossano di Vaglio, perhaps as a sanctuary of the Lucan federation on the territory of the later *municipium* of Potentia.[67] The appropriation of this space by Augustus and the Senate thus referred back to non-Roman forms of sacralization. Religious innovation anchored the power of the *princeps* more firmly in the urban space.

33. The marble Ara Pacis Augustae, viewed from the southwest, with a glimpse into the interior altar, 9 BC. The dimensions of the outer wall are 10.5×11.6×7 m. akg-images / Pirozzi.

3. The Redoubling of Religion

With developments—more religious than cultural—centralized in Rome and driven by the aforementioned actors, and the territorial expansion systematically pursued by those same actors (and destined to continue for a further century), the Augustan Age represented a "saddle period," not least in the history of religion. One way this expressed itself was in the appropriation of religious forms of aristocratic competition for the purposes of imperial patronage, initially monopolized in Rome, but, step by step, often after inexplicable delay, and never without local rivalry, spreading across the entire Roman Empire. I have already spoken of the building of cult structures and the holding of large-scale games and rituals; the dissemination of the emperor's image beyond Rome will be covered in the next chapter. Perhaps to a still greater extent, however, this lengthy period (truly a saddle, not merely a narrow mountain pass) was central to the media presence of religion and its redoubled importance to contemporaries when dealing with the tension between the political center and the empire, new elites and the inhabitants of a metropolis.[68] It can be attributed in part to strategic initiatives, but was also a consequence of situation-driven intensifications or multiplications of familiar practices, as will now be shown by a few examples.

Coins

The mass media available for the project were on the whole already well embedded. Since the final third of the second century BC, first the moneyers—the *tresvir monetalis* was an entry-level annual office in a magisterial career—and then later the mints controlled by civil-war generals had struck highly individual and programmatic coins commemorating achievements of the moneyer's family or even celebrating the moneyer himself. This was a convenient precedent to follow.[69] Such coins would now instead bear honorific references to Augustus, his priesthoods, the temples he had built or merely planned, and (not least) his achievements in the field of ritual, for example the saecular games that have already been mentioned.

But it was possible to take the use of coins even further. On very rare occasions, late Republican moneyers had already used the dative case on coins. This might be part of a graphic image, for example when *DIVO IVL(IO)* can be read on a temple architrave pictured on a coin, and perhaps also in the case of the legend *CLEMENTIAE CAESARIS* encircling the image of a temple facade.[70] Occasionally, however, such formulations appear to have been used in analogy with dedicatory inscriptions, making the coin itself into an offering without giving its users any reference to a more "real" gift. This applies to the legend *CONCORDIAE* that accompanies a head in 52 BC, and, strikingly, to the head of Cleopatra with the legend *CLEO-PATRAE REGINAE REGVM FILIORVM REGVM* in 32 BC.[71] In

16–15 BC in Rome, Gaius Antistius Vetus had coins minted with the legend *APOLLINI ACTIO*, which was copied for example in Lugdunum (Lyon) in 15–13 BC on an aureus bearing the legend *ACT*, probably to be integrated as *(Apollini) Act(io)*.[72] Prestige and performance coincided here.

Statues and Calendars

Less mobile, but more durably visible and less susceptible to being copied, were ceremonial inscriptions. Here we might think of the protocols of the Arval brethren, mentioned above, in the sanctuary of Dea Dia before Rome's gates (from about 29 BC) and those of the *quindecimviri sacris faciundis* concerning the saecular games of 17 BC; also the gradually expanding phenomenon of the marble calendars (*fasti*), which began as space-fillers within the ensemble of the Arval Acts, but went on to carry all before them in presumably quite unintended fashion; and finally the monumental *Res gestae divi Augusti*, the account of the deeds of Augustus. Included in the same category are murals and reliefs such as adorned the Forum Augusti and the Ara Pacis, with their graphic portrayals of religion. Artists in these media cast religious practice in durable form, going beyond the short-term spectacles provided by victory games and triumphs. This redoubled presence of religion was not in itself entirely new, as can be seen from the substantial sequence of ritual inscriptions from Umbria, the *Tabulae Iguvinae*. Owing to its concentrated occurrence in the period under discussion, however, this redoubling changed the character of religious communication in and beyond Rome. Ensemble copies of the Summi Viri, either statues of the same historic Romans as in the portico of the Temple of Mars, or at least the *elogia* from the statues' bases, reached Pompeii, Arretium, and several locations in Hispania.[73] The *Elogia Tarquiniensia* were formed under the same influence.[74]

The calendars merit a second look. With their feast days (*feriae*) and temple foundation days (*dies natales templorum*), they became increasingly widespread in Latium as a medium of religious memorialization from as early as the beginning of the second century BC. But it was only Caesar's calendar reform (46 BC) that gave the graphic form of the calendar, the *fasti*, sufficient popularity that it inspired some local actors to erect the Italic marble calendars of the Augustan and Tiberian Age, some of which were enormous.[75] While these initially recorded the traditional religion of the city of Rome writ large, especially the new dedication days relating to the numerous temple restorations,[76] such examples as the Tiberian-age Fasti Amiterni demonstrate that the calendar was rapidly coming to be dominated by the growing number of imperial festivals, listed with comprehensive historical notes (". . . because member X of the imperial house performed Z on this day . . ."). By the end of the reign of the first Augustus—admittedly a long period—the Senate had approved some thirty new *feriae*. The lengthy wording of new entries affected the appearance of the calendar. The clear layout of columns of numbers and letters, and the ample space between the columns representing the months, became cluttered with quantities of small letters, all pointing to some detail of imperial genealogy, emperors' biographies, or their achievements. The monarchy took visible shape even beyond the distance at which the small characters could actually be read. If the Ides, the traditional mid-month *feriae* (usually given to Jupiter on account of his connection with the bright sky of the full moon) are excluded from the count, imperial festivals started to outnumber the old feriae even in the city of Rome. For purposes of reception throughout the Empire, the old dates could easily be set aside; but they too, to the urban dweller familiar with the genre, bore the savor of the Principate. Restorations of temples were frequently combined with a change in the dedication day noted in the *fasti*.

By reproducing the detailed inscriptions of the Roman calendar, the leaders of voluntary associations and magistrates in central Italic towns enabled their populations to imagine public Roman rituals beyond any possibility of actual local imitation. This representation of religious practice was not a guide to the rituals, but rather a performative act in its own right. For Augustus, whose presence in the calendar grew ever larger as his memorial days and festivals multiplied, the calendar offered an ideal medium for projecting his double role as god and source of local legitimation. For those endowing these calendars, the details of the contents played only a minor role. This is evident from the frequent errors. In similar fashion, especially in Greece from the second century BC onward, individuals installed clocks in sanctuaries, not to regulate cult ceremonies, but as a demonstration of their technical sophistication.[77] The *fasti* offered an alternative in Rome, but patrons drawn to the connection between the sun and theology might instead erect solar clocks, as many did in the Iseum Campense.[78]

It is through such dealings with the calendar that we are able to pursue in detail the redoubled presence of religion.[79] But the effect that the focus of attention on Augustus and his successors had was not inconsequential when it came to the physical media: marble was not the most suitable material in which to list the rapid proliferation of imperial festivals, or to purge the list of festivals eliminated upon a change of regime. The sumptuous marble calendars disappeared from public view after Tiberius, to be replaced by painted mural forms, while book calendars resumed a prominent position, initially in roll form and later as codices.

Texts

A third genre gives an even clearer picture of the interplay between individuals' perceptions and initiatives and their productive appropriation of impetuses from above. The redoubling of religion in purely visual terms, in coins and calendars, was joined by textual representation. Historians like Dionysius of Halicarnassus in Greek and Livy in Latin should be mentioned here, whose work, although entirely critical in some detailed respects, was marked by a concern to integrate contemporary practices into a view of the past that explained such practices as vestiges of ancient Roman norms, and viewed them from the perspectives of historical actors.[80] In the coinage of the city of Rome, bronze medals, showing Augustus and the mythical king Numa on the obverse and reverse respectively, were struck in the very years around 23 BC when Livy's first books, and passages of Virgil's epic treatment of Aeneas and Rome's beginnings, were just coming into being.[81] At almost the same time, some of Tibullus's published poems included conceptions of ritual practice from Rome's origins.[82]

This discourse was not a Roman invention either, but it did open up purely Roman material to a literary exchange that, while always incomplete, increasingly spread throughout the Empire. The narratives of the victors were here joined by the interpretations of those on the losing side, militarily and politically, where these were not already part of the discourse (e.g., in the form of the first two books of the Maccabees), along with the comparative perspectives of Hellenistic Jews like Philo of Alexandria, who described the role of Moses as founder of a religion, analogous to Numa, a founder figure in Roman texts.[83] To forestall misunderstandings: the "redoubling of religion" addressed here did not lead in the Greco-Roman world to anything like that long development of religious texts in various genres, largely based on fictitious historiography and the social criticism and visions of prophets, that in Persian-Hellenistic Judaism culminated in narratives and collections of maxims and psalms. However, Hellenistic texts in Athens, Pergamum, and Alexandria, together with products of the late-flourishing of late Republican and Augustan literature, made it possible for intellectuals *to speak of* a religious tradition of their own, and to conceive of it as capable of being viewed apart from actual constellations of historical and political circumstances. Only now could administrators export their constructs in the form of statutes such as the *lex coloniae Iuliae Ursonensis*, and embark upon the kinds of religious comparisons that might form a basis for acceptance or rejection.

Just how specific the reactions of intellectuals could be is revealed to us by two poets of the mid and late Augustan Age. Shortly after 16 BC, Sextus Propertius published a collection of poems on the theme "cults and festivals." The thread running through these poems was not the calendar, however, but localities either in Rome or, like Lavinium, within the ambit of Rome's religious activity. At the central point of the book, the poet celebrates the victory at Actium, in the process referring to the Palatine Temple of Apollo, the subject a poem he had written in an earlier book.[84] What is, however, important to him is not to turn his attention constantly toward Augustus, but to express the multilayered quality of the Roman memory-scape: historical, social, and sexual. This may be illustrated by a poem toward the end of the book. It relates how Hercules one day drives his cattle to the Palatine Hill in Rome. A local thief, Cacus, steals them from him, driving them—backwards, in order to conceal the hiding place—into a cave. The lowing of the cattle betrays him, and Hercules strikes him down. On the "cattle pasture" where he has driven his herd, Hercules is smitten by thirst. A shady grove promises him refreshment, but the girls playing there refuse him entry: no admittance to men. In a speech interspersed with mythic instances, Hercules begs to be allowed in; but he is unable to persuade the priestess in charge of the place. He finally forces his way in, quenches his thirst, and builds a "very large altar" in thanks for the recovered cattle. He then imposes the condition that no female should be allowed to worship there, thus avenging for all time his unslaked thirst.[85] The topographical reference is unmistakable. Close to the Roman "cattle market" on the bank of the Tiber was an *ara maxima*, a cult site called "very large altar," at which Hercules was worshipped. Here, successful merchants and generals each dedicated a tenth of his profit or plunder, and magistrates performed important sacrifices. The exclusion of women from this cult demanded an explanation. The myth provided a reason and gave the place a special significance, while binding the Italic past with the local present.[86]

Some two decades later, Publius Ovidius Naso embarked on a virtually encyclopedic opus: a record, with a commentary in elegiac distiches, on the Roman *fasti*. Completed in exile only up to the sixth book, June, it provided a day-by-day chronicle of the festivals of the Roman year, along with the poet's own emphases. Augustus was already a very prominent figure, and the book was originally dedicated to him. Going beyond religious practice, however, Ovid also used the calendar as a framework for the presentation of cosmic myths, concentrating on the risings and settings of constellations: Augustan self-reflection and self-representation surpassed the realm of the city, and aimed for the stars.[87] The first astrological manual in Latin verse, the epic work of Manilius, is also to be assigned to this period; it may have been published shortly after 9 A.D.[88]

Reactions and Reflections

Writing during the reign of Tiberius, that is to say in the immediate aftermath of the Augustan Age, Valerius Maximus collected "memorable deeds and sayings" by sifting through quantities of late Republican and Augustan historiographic literature. He chose a topical arrangement rather than a continuous narrative, and in this way made the "documents" of earlier people of virtue easily accessible.[89] Valerius relied for his authority on his skills as a historiographer, not on any moral stance. He assigned foreign examples second place in every category, but "deeds and sayings of the city of Rome and of foreign peoples worthy of memory," to quote the very beginning of his book, were all documented in a series comprising a history part homemade and part the work of immigrants.[90] For the empire of the early Principate, only a universal history would suffice, and Valerius dedicated it to Caesar Tiberius, the person in whom lies the "consensus of men and gods and the ruling of sea and land."[91]

From the point of view of observers in the very late Republican and early Imperial Age, the complexities of the divine were a branch of learning, as I have shown above; and knowledge learned was the basis for successfully tapping the religious resources offered by the divine in the shape of numerous propitious deities. The gods were present as actors about whom something could be known. Their presence persisted in the form of narratives, but they could be multiplied, pinned down, and given better shape by being "known about."[92]

In the first chapter of his first book, Valerius presents a selection, and by his very choices he constructs his particular image of religion. Valerius's selection forms the basis of many modern accounts of Roman Republican religion; but as a selection it is far from traditional, and thus cannot be consequential for later understanding. It describes a religion where rules take precedence over all else, and public priests are at the very center of things by virtue of their total control of religious knowledge. However, knowledge about religion was not purely an academic enterprise. Augustus burned two thousand oracular books because they were concerned with divinatory knowledge.[93] Astrological knowledge was intensively tapped by the emperor Tiberius himself, employing specialists like Scribonius and Tib. Claudius Thrasyllus.[94] Divinatory knowledge was also potentially dangerous.[95] In AD 17, *mathematici* were driven out of Rome together with Jews,[96] and in the preceding year some had been executed for taking part in an alleged conspiracy.[97] According to Suetonius, Tiberius demanded that no *haruspex* be consulted except in public and in front of witnesses.[98]

For Valerius, religion was not a fixed code to be learned by heart. Tradition, or "ancient custom," was not a fixed resource either. Tales of exemplary behavior from some kind of past—even one that was not chronologically fixed—show that religious knowledge was to a great extent practical in nature, encoding the actions of virtuous men.

Valerius shared with his contemporary Velleius Paterculus[99] a fundamental belief in the continuity of a Rome that we tend to divide sharply into "Republican" and "Imperial." To emphasize that continuity, he focused on persons and virtues rather than explicit rules and offices. The primary source of continuity was, in his view, religious practices, which in part dated back to the founding of the city, as he stated in the case of the auspices.[100] A past composed of values was made concrete in "documents" and "lessons taught," universalized in narratives from both home and abroad, profiled by a few contrasting moral tales, and finally naturalized and immunized by the mysterious effects of Nature herself: by miracles.[101] Like Varro, Valerius gives a list of gods, but he presents it in the form of stories from history. Starting with two stories about Castor and Pollux,[102] Valerius then lists Aesculapius, Juno, Fortuna, Silvanus, Mars, the Penates, Divus Julius, Fortuna, and Apollo. This was a religion based on learning, and on people adhering to a knowledge that was capable of facing the extraordinary challenge of the divine presence.

Valerius's religion is centered on "the emperor as a living god."[103] Castor and Pollux must have been prominent in Tiberius' self-representation, for he had dedicated their temple as early as AD 6.[104] Valerius narrates a religion that, centered in but no longer confined to the city of Rome, offers carefully ordered historical proof of the benefits of divinization. Religion is based on rules, controlled by priests, but above all subject to a virtuous quality exemplified and deified in the person of the living emperor. The individual actor is scarcely present, except as a reader. But literary texts made both the cultural and the natural cosmos accessible to the individual, and it is such individuals who must now take center stage.

VIII

Lived Religion

THE FIRST TO SECOND CENTURIES AD

IT IS EASY TO BE SEDUCED by the sources into concentrating on elite actors, or even on the emperor and his advisors alone. But the significance and success of their religious activity developed against the background and within the spectrum of the patterns of activity and conceptions of the population as a whole. To this elite actors responded by maintaining that their own mode of action was oriented by norms, by the *res publica* and the *mos maiorum,* in other words by the goals of a common good and tradition. Where Plato favored religious control coming from Delphi over "democratic" city governance, Cicero asked private individuals to turn to the "public priests" recruited from the ruling elite.[1] Their utterances proved much more durable than popular conceptions, with the result the these two individuals facilitated an appropriation of antiquity that was constitutionalist and legalist in the second half of the nineteenth century, and structuralist in the second half of the twentieth.[2]

But how did lived religion look in antiquity, not from the perspective of the (city) state or even the Roman imperium, but from below? What were the experiences, conceptions, and practices that people, whatever their social position, made their own and used, each according to their circumstances?[3] What did the individual take from magnificent public spectacles? How did his or her own domestic or neighborhood customs combine with notions received at first-, second-, or third-hand from literary deliberations? To what extent did their views reflect the new and different kinds of religious practice that led to the formation of new institutions, associations, religious sites, and religious actors? How, again, did these new formations alter the behavior of professionals and the mighty, of the wealthy and the educated? How did all this manifest itself, not as "religious system," but as "lived religion"?[4] Such questions must be addressed in this and the following chapters, with especial reference to chapters II and IV. It will be necessary to consider combinations of circumstances typical of Rome in the final years of the Republic and the early Imperial Age, and to make our initial field of inquiry the relations between the social world, the natural world, and the individual. This will bring us back into domestic and familial spaces. We must consider actions that could arise only from a superabundance of interpretations of the world, and from assumptions variously arrived at as to its order and purpose. Only then can we devote some space to the introduction of novel practices and signs, to new gods, and to the constant stream of discrete changes brought about by the growth of the Roman imperium.

1. Individuals in Their Relationship with the World

To speak of the individual may be to invite misunderstanding; and this applies from birth onward. A multiplicity of cultural practices, even some statutory rules, reveal the extent to which a Roman child was a social being. According to antiquarian theory—and we can never know for sure how far theory reflects actual practice rather than merely seeking to formulate norms—it was the midwife who lifted the child from the ground in order to check its vitality, not the father![5] Only then did the question of name-giving arise; and yet, really, it did not arise at all. A son, whether he was the first-born son or the last-born after the father's death, as a rule received not only the name of his father's gens (*nomen*), but also his first name (*praenomen*). A third element, the *cognomen*, distinguished branches of families rather than individuals. Gaius Iulius Caesar was the son of Gaius Iulius Caesar; even of the few current first names, always abbreviated when written down, only a still smaller number were used in any particular family. Girls in Gaius Iulius Caesar's family were often called Julia, "female Julian."[6] It was important to know her family, and anyone in the know would also have been able to divine membership of the patrician nobility on the basis of gens names and cognomens. But a person's name gave no information about his or her provincial origin or ethnic identity, or the precise status of his or her family; and, in the course of time, the name came to contain no dependable information on the family at all.[7]

A person's name did, however, provide further information. In its most complete form, it indicated the identities of that person's father and grandfather, and membership of an electoral constituency. If the man was a Roman citizen, it distinguished whether he was free-born ($f. = filius$, "son of"), or a former slave ($l. = libertus$ "freedman of"): with the franchise, but with no father worthy of mention.[8] In the case of a woman, such connections were established by mention of her father or husband. In other words, even a person's relationship to a rudimentary administrative structure, his or her status under criminal and civil law, in the strict sense even right to life, were mediated by the family; the new status of a freedman was also represented in the name, in terms of genealogical incorporation into the former owner's *familia*, which also embraced enslaved members. The male head of a family was entitled of his own judgment to execute the death penalty on his sons (not to mention his slaves); a son could not own property on his own account before his father's death.

Many of these tokens of status were immediately evident upon direct observation of an individual's body, and not only in respect of nutritional status. The freeborn male child reminded himself and the world[9] of his status by means of a *bulla*, an amulet in the shape of a ball or bulbous bottle, worn on a neckband. This marked his status until he reached adulthood, and in formal dress it was underlined by a narrow purple stripe on the toga. A slave's tattoo was likewise physical, although irremovable. The right (for free women) to ride in a carriage within the city bounds, or on special occasions (for knights, and aristocratic youths) to accompany the carriage mounted on horseback, was another physical reflection of status, an extension of a person's own body, of the kind represented in images of centaurs. The opposite circumstance, that of a slave, was also represented in his body, which was constantly exposed to punishment; or, if he was a gladiator, to death as a public spectacle: in short, he was merely a "tool with a voice" (*instrumentum uocale*).[10] Reflection on, and in individual cases experience of, such contrasts gave rise to notions of a body separate from the soul or the "self."

But this principle applied in both directions. The body's presence in society might be separated from the very ego that experienced that body; statues enabled a body to be duplicated; even a statuette or merely a bust made "me" present to others, in, say, a sanctuary.[11] And, as in the case of my own body, whether emaciated or well-tended, it was a question not only of form but of material aspect. Just as, in China, jade was a preferred material for early cult implements, so in Roman statuary gold was reserved for gods, and marble and bronze created an association with wealth that was not produced by either wood or terracotta.[12] This element was not necessarily contradicted by the simultaneous desire to establish a living effect by the use of color. The mixture gold and ivory, for example, could both express status and enhance the life-likeness of a statue.

Self-world relationships, as a sociological concept, are a useful starting point for any inquiry that looks beyond social status and its mediated representations to ask how people experience their situation in space and time, and how they relate emotionally, intellectually, and morally not only to other humans, but also to objects, to the world as a whole, and finally to themselves.[13] Here it is possible only to mention ideal-typical cultural conditions that make the function of religious activity more understandable in the context of the self-images and worldviews of religious actors. For it has often been made clear to us in this account that it was not only social status and political identity that were key. Objects themselves provided important means of access to the world, regardless of one's social context. This was true of raw materials and finished products, painted ceramics and colors typical of marble, as well as wine and milk. In the specific case of religious activity in the early Iron Age, we clarified the extent to which it reacted to the natural environment, economic forms, and technology, and to the spatial and social aspects of the environment. It was no different in the Imperial Age. The house snake, constantly appearing and disappearing, defied instrumentalization. The ox might be treated as a creature in possession of rights, allowed to rest from work on holidays, while exotic animals served only briefly as entertainment in the arena before being dispatched. In the culinary arts, Roman cooks experimented to discover which animals were fit to appear as food on Roman tables, leading astute contemporaries to raise peafowl, moray eels, and dormice.[14] The elite thus appropriated the world to the utmost possible extent: even mussels and pearls became part of the mix.[15]

This became *habitus*, custom. And it was an easy matter to find comparable customs in older empires: among the Hellenes, the Persians, the Neo-Babylonians. The world within which Romans saw themselves situated was one that, in its cosmic dimension, did not seem too remote from them; it was, on the contrary, relevant. Vitruvius, Ovid, Germanicus, Manilius, and in the second half of this first century AD the older Pliny, continued in their astronomical and astrological passages, books, or entire works the process that such figures as Aratus (and Cicero his translator) and many "Chaldean" specialists had begun.[16] Even Manilius's detailed didactic poem, written in the Augustan Age, was to its contemporary readers more of a mood-piece on universal harmony than a textbook for astrologers: the erratic paths of the planets, the "wandering stars," scarcely feature in his representation of cosmic order.[17] But humans, whatever the extent of their freedom or constraints, were tied into this order. It would be the third century AD before the world picture presented by Manilius was significantly challenged, and then it would be the intellectuals among the followers of Christ who did so.[18]

On the basis of the reflections ventured in my introductory chapter, I suggest that ancient religion enabled leaps between disparate social, material, and transcendent relationships with the world, leaps that became commonplace. Religious communication transcended the indubitably plausible context of real situations, and altered that context. Actors who were not indubitably plausible were construed as relevant; whether the dead, "spirits," or "gods," they altered conceptual and emotional relationships with the "other," with objects, with the world, and combined those changed contexts into a transcendent worldview. These new situations, too, were culturally informed. Religious actors appropriated for the most part handed-down names and linguistic formulae; they also appropriated communicative techniques, techniques peculiar to hierarchical social relationships between children and parents, slaves and slave-owners, subordinates and masters. No "theology," in the sense of a systematic pattern of thought regarding the actors addressed, was implied, but the possibility of giving further thought on a case-by-case basis, and of involving new actors, or perhaps the same old actors for new purposes, was presumably left open. A multitude of objects and instruments for further creative development in challenging new situations was accessible through experience, through memory, and through observation within the network of multiple small-scale cultures characteristic of the Mediterranean;[19] this was especially true in the great hubs, not only ports and trading centres but also military camps and veteran settlements, and even in the smaller towns. In this way, social and geographical mobility on a regional, for some even a supra-regional scale, facilitated cultural exchange.

2. Home and Family

We became acquainted with the home as a site of production[20] and consumption in the second chapter. The homes of the Imperial Age, which we are about to consider, postdate that situation by six or seven centuries of urbanizing processes. For a minority, those processes created the new living space represented by the city, and for a small minority—in Rome, Alexandria, and Antioch—an entirely new kind of living space, perhaps comparable to the later heydays of Mexican Teotihuacán, Baghdad, and Chinese Kaifeng: the metropolis. Here too, the home remained an important space, for lived religion as well as other things.[21] We must, however, always remember the immense range that existed, from the small single room to the workshop, or the retail unit in an apartment block (*insula*), serving as a mere refuge for children and journeymen who spent major parts of the day in the surrounding city, to the separate and complex landscape of urban villas, with their gardens that brought the countryside into the city. The stately urban villa with its gardens was then exported to the actual rural space of the countryside.

Even as a basic social space, the "home" was by no means a simple structure. The juxtaposition of generations, with gaps and role-displacements occasioned by mortality, the perhaps disparate geographical origins of men and women sometimes passing through serial relationships, and the linguistic and ethnic diversity that characterized the unfree members of households, meant that this primary social space was embedded in a neighborhood that was in some areas highly heterogeneous in structure, and in many ways a melting pot.[22] Here, social and territorial boundaries tended to collapse. Greco-Roman cities were sometimes further structured or complemented by groups resembling clubs or associations, which often formalized cooperation that rested on familial, neighborly, or economic ties.[23] The regular or occasional use of further areas of the urban space as a service sector was defined in the cities of the Roman Empire by the facilities offered by particular venues: markets; entertainment in the case of amphitheaters and theaters; baths; occasionally also law courts, and spaces where one could express political preferences (rather than actually participate in decision-making); and, of course, architecturally defined spaces for religious communication. Economic activities or the search for work, interaction with relatives or friends, military service, an administrative career, or plain curiosity, might lead one far beyond this urban space, into the city's closely-connected environs or perhaps into the wide world itself, to experience all the perils and vicissitudes inherent in travel.[24] Cicero, the legislator of religion, saw only danger arising from this: the worship of "personal," "new," and "foreign" gods would lead to a *confusionem . . . religionum*: a confusion of sentiments of religious obligation, and rituals unknown to the priests.[25] However, his polemical approach, articulating in a rather predictable way a loss of control in the area of domestic religious practice, brought the argument no further.[26]

But the "confusion" went further. There was no simple congruence between the home and its social environs. The dwelling space of the living often took in dead family members, in ways that were becoming increasingly visible. Selected ancestors themselves occasionally had a presence in the home, for there was an elite tradition of displaying their wax busts, which was spreading beyond the confines of the city.[27] A narrow space in one of the rich terrace houses in Ephesus, for instance, contained funerary reliefs next to the image of a snake.[28] Otherwise, tombs were situated outside the city, many placed quite prominently along the roads leading out of town. This meant that the approaching traveler would initially encounter dead family members.

The elaborate homes of rich individuals always included public areas. A widespread house type, known in many variations, featured an entrance area that gave into an *atrium* that sometimes even encroached on the living room or dining room, the *triclinium*, that lay beyond it. This accommodated the owner's clients and fellow members of his class or association, allowing their admiring and appraising eyes deep into the home.[29]

The home was without a doubt the most important location for individual religious practice, for the consumption of objects distinguished as instruments or reminders of religious communication because they represented gods and myths, or referred to sacral architecture or symbols associated with it. The home was also where literature was to be had that offered or discussed mythical narratives (which must continue to preoccupy us too). The infinite variety displayed by extant objects and the few surviving substantial ensembles bear witness to individual patterns of appropriation.

Combinations of Objects

In the fourth century AD, the owners of the house near the Roman forum in Corinth, known as the *Panayia domus*, set up a small side-room as a cult space, painting it in red and white with a floral frieze and red garland. In this room were placed costly painted and gilded marble statuettes, representing among other deities Artemis, Asklepios, Herakles, Europa, Dionysus, and Pan (the latter perhaps only in the form of a bust); entirely unusual in such a private context is the inclusion of a statuette of Roma. The objects themselves derive from the period between the late first and late third centuries. We must assume that, as precious objects, they had previously been displayed in a more visible space; but we might suggest that image-related religious practices achieved more intimacy in the new setting of the smaller space.[30] Such alternatives for realizing a cult space would scarcely have been open to the owner of another location in Corinth, this time a shop, who juxtaposed a marble statue with terracotta figures.[31] These extant ensembles of statuettes are not typical of the period; it was usually bronze or even silver objects that were carefully hidden and survived for that reason, only to become accessible again as hoard finds; of the (perhaps) numberless wooden figures that once existed we have scarcely a trace. In the same way, in what is now Clermont-Ferrand, someone hid statues together with other valuable objects, probably from a domestic-cult niche-shrine; the group of objects was found in 1985 during an excavation at the *Confiturerie Humbert*. All together they comprised eleven bronze figures, among them Fortuna (fig. 34, an example from another collection), Diana, Mars, Mercury, Cernunnos and Sucellus, and a bull and a deer, as well as a terracotta figure.[32] Already in the first century AD, the owners of House VIII.5.37 at Pompeii (*Casa delle pareti rosse*) had assembled comparable objects in a miniature temple projecting from a wall: six bronze figures of *lares*, Mercury, Apollo, and Hercules.[33] These were all common religious symbols, but occurring here in new combinations, not defined by any local norms.

Even if, in addition to statuettes, we include a greater number of figurative representations, mostly small murals, that have survived *in situ*, the finds at the various locations are consistent.[34] The actors concerned were not innovative in their choice of the individual deities. They likely made their choices based on the roles commonly ascribed to these deities, and surely on what they themselves were able to see

34. Bronze statuette of Fortuna from Hirschling, Bavaria. Gäubodenmuseum, Straubing. Photo Wolfgang Sauber (CC-BY-SA 3.0).

in local temples.[35] Where they displayed creativity was in the combinations of deities and above all objects. The range of materials, different ages, and varying provenances of the statuettes in any one house show the collectors to have been acting autonomously.[36] These individuals, or possibly groups of collaborators, did not of course choose at random from a catalogue of the pantheon. In a newly acquired home, family heirlooms and inherited objects stood next to new acquisitions that could only have been selected from readily available stock, which is to say from local traders and producers. The presence of a particular deity in the local public cult may have played a major role in the choice, more decisive than knowledge of the gods gained from texts. Personal travel and experience played a part. What appears to us in the form of an archaeological snapshot was the result of a lifelong process, sometimes lives-long, during which choices had been both made and inculcated. Perceptions of different collections in other houses may have played an important role; one exceeded, however, by the publicly available choices made by other people for dedications, votive gifts and inscriptions in temples, or by an individual's knowledge gained from actual participation in rituals where vows were redeemed. Such encounters and experiences might happen by chance. Thus, according to his own testimony, in the second century A D Aelius Aristides was told by Asclepius to enter the latter's sanctuary in order to "make a full sacrifice . . . and to have sacred bowls set up, and to distribute the sacred portions of the sacrifice to all my fellow pilgrims."[37] Children also took part in such rituals, perhaps as choristers in the performance of hymns,[38] and they learned in doing so.

As we would expect, decisions about dedicatory inscriptions or figurative elements on marble urns were arrived at in a similar fashion.[39] The formulation of a vow, and, in the event that the request was granted by the deity addressed, the redemption of that vow by the endowment of a monument (however small it might be), either as a gift to the god or to memorialize an ephemeral ritual of thanks, were frequently crisis rituals. But the crisis and the way it was handled did not have to be "highly individual." A response to an illness, a bad harvest, the perils of an imminent birth, marriage, or manumission (of a slave) were all matters of social routine. And yet those concerned made it clear, by the broad range of measures that they took and the different ways in which they combined them, that they claimed—and were allowed to exercise—personal competency in such matters. They achieved this as clearly in their invocation of gods foreign to the locality (an activity negatively remarked upon by Cicero) as in the texts of their inscriptions, which characterized the endower on the basis of family position and career. All this was done with careful consideration. Combinations that were politically symbolic at the level of the imperium remained rare in the private realm, at least in any demonstrative form. This applies as much to the above-mentioned Dea Roma as to the Capitoline Triad of Jupiter, Juno, and Minerva.[40]

Religious competency came most prominently to the fore in the way different deities were linked and original nomenclatures applied to them.[41] In both matters, the main interest of the actors concerned in the act of religious communication may have been to secure divine assistance in as specific a way as possible. The singular combination of Juno, Minerva, and Bellona was chosen in one instance in Carthage, for example, and in another a Diana Caelestis Augusta was addressed. Dedications were also made to deities who were most probably not present at local cult sites, such as the Venus of Mount Eryx in Sicily, or the Thracian Heros.[42] These testify as much to individual religious experiment as to practices that were no longer defined by the immediate locale.[43] Here too, however, individuality must not be understood as solitary initiative.[44] We cannot know the extent to which priestly advice and craft traditions and skills contributed to the final product.[45] In the very group of inscriptions by individuals that has been most thoroughly studied, the so-called "confession inscriptions," propitiatory inscriptions from Asia Minor, the principals and priests at the sanctuaries concerned make their close collaboration particularly clear.[46] In the Asclepion at Epidaurus, the priests maintained an archive that enabled them to monitor and restrict the signs used.[47] And yet a Nestorius, at the end of the fourth century, was able, against the declared will of his entire circle, to take a statue of Achilles (as he had been commanded to do in a dream) and place it next to a statue of Athena Parthenos (because this seemed to him, according to his own competency, to be the most reasonable course to take).[48]

But we should return to the home. There is no possible way to know when or to what extent actors or observers understood the use or even the mere contemplation of these statuettes as religious communication or as assertions of a religious identity. The objects mentioned, especially the many utensils and lamps, and the coin banks decorated with figures of gods (fig. 35), were only *potentially* the implements or foci of religious acts. As Athenaeus reminds us in the second century AD: when necessary, even a clay jug might represent a divine addressee.[49] Situations and competencies were highly varied.

35. Terracotta moneybox with representations of numerous altars, Imperial Age. Gotha, Museum, inv. AVa 199. Photo Museum Gotha, reproduced by kind permission of the museum.

3. Learning Religion

Was it only visits to local religious sites, travels abroad, and chance meetings that determined which religious alternative a person claimed as his or her own? By no means. The ancients were of one mind that the vital spark was most readily kindled at a tender age.[50] In Athens in the fourth century BC, Plato had spoken of the tales that were heard time and again, initially from mothers and nurses, told or sung, in fun or in earnest; and these were the same tales that were then acted out in performances or worked into the formulas of prayers.[51] Prudentius too, in his fourth-century-AD polemic *Against Symmachus*, took tales about gods as his starting point, then went on to decry the virtually hereditary pollution of "heathen" children by false images and practices. These they took in with their mothers' milk, and all the senses played a part in the seduction: drinking, tasting, seeing (and presumably also smelling the rancid oil on statues), watching and touching, even kissing. And in the process children unconsciously appropriated the practices, until finally they themselves participated in the bloody sacrifice of lambs.[52] Prudentius reserved his most severe anathemas for "errors" (*errores*) and vain superstition (*vana superstitio*) that involved images and sacrifices: in other words, idolatry. His analysis was nevertheless acute; like Plato, he seized upon early cognitive influences, and above all bodily and behavioral imprinting. Like Seneca and Plutarch, who in first-century Rome criticized a piety that was at odds with their philosophical conception of the gods,[53] Prudentius seized upon the emotional dimension. He imagined the child seeing its mother pale in prayer, and described how, outside its own home, the child was stunned (*stupuit*) by the extravagance of public feasts and games, by temples that soared heavenward, opulently-attired cult actors, the roaring and howling of sacrificial animals, and then the sight of towering three-dimensional figures that the child believed were "real" and the "rulers of the heavens." The child's mind, his or her cognition, was overwhelmed by the coordinated effects of aesthetic over-stimulation and emotional agitation.[54] What Prudentius described as a tradition of a thousand generations was at the same time for him an evolving phenomenon, as exemplified by the cult of the Augusti.

Despite differences in the details, the mechanisms by which tradition was created remained the same. Poets and other writers laid great stress on rhythmic and melodic speech and song,[55] typically overvaluing content and undervaluing the physical and emotional experience of song accompanied by movement that, while in principle minimal, also embodied elements of dance.[56] Theologians' and scholars' emphasis on the text and its cognitive content unduly stressed the function of hymns to create confessional identities, and the role of hymns in stressing the boundaries of religious tradition. Such a view is, however, mistaken. It was mainly persons and not dogmas that featured in such texts; and this applied as much to the singer David and the sung Christ[57] as to the persons addressed by Plato and Prudentius.

Persons and names once heard could be reencountered in image form, and vice versa. More widely available than sculptures were representations on ceramics and coins, in glass paste, and in the form of wall paintings, all of which quickly found their way into more humble settings,[58] and were just as likely to reproduce entire, complex scenes as to extract individual elements from them.[59] Those who commissioned these works placed few limits on the precise use of domestic spaces thus ornamented.[60] Narratives and themes were clearly identifiable, but the meaning of the images and scenes was not fixed. Diverse interpretations were possible, shifting with the age and status of the viewers.[61]

This interpretive openness was not simply a given. It was in fact both a goal and a problem. The Augustan writer Ovid, in his magnum opus *Metamorphoses*, set himself the task of producing a complex web of hermeneutics to counterpoise the dominant, contemporary Augustan culture that he perhaps perceived as inflexible and one-dimensional. His variations and combinations of mythic material favored the transformative possibilities of stories over an orderly fixedness.[62] Many painters' workshops of the period brought to Roman walls a similar play of illusions created and dispelled, reality simulated and denied.[63] At the same time, however, those commissioning works were concerned to impose their own particular interpretations on familiar material, for example by combining image with inscribed text. This strategy was of central importance in certain genres, especially for representations of individuals in statuary and similar honorific works.[64] The existence of such contested discourses suggests that people by no means trained their perceptions by simply appropriating a standardized set of signs to represent the figures and attributes of gods;[65] on the contrary, they were continually exposed to surprise, to new ways of seeing,[66] in a process that might have a wide variety of outcomes, depending on the viewer's preparedness and experience.

4. Places Where Religion Was Experienced

It was only in rare cases that householders reserved a domestic space exclusively for religious communication, such as occurred in the Panayia Domus at Corinth. When they did so, they referenced those signs in the public realm that helped to sacralize spaces, giving them durable form and a special status; paramount among these public spaces was the "temple," to which we must turn our attention before we return again to the home.

In the temples of Iron Age Italy, the relevant signs included especially lavish architectural decoration, a high podium, roof figures, and grotesque masks at the eaves.[67] These served the strategy, regularly employed by temple builders, of exposing visitors to particular experiences mediated by visual stimulation: as, for example, the experience of confronting an oversized statue; or witnessing the power of a deity displayed in a space in such a way as to emphasize its dynamism. Temple interiors were planned with this goal in mind, either at the time of construction or in later restorations.[68] Great store was set by doorways and entrances, which were positioned to surprise the visitor with novel sightlines or confusing reflections. Inside the temple, architects oriented visitors by means of floor mosaics or curtains, thus making the act of entering a process of a certain duration.[69] Particular care was taken with the installation of a cult statue. The power of motion might be simulated in a statue by placing it directly on the mosaic floor.[70] The impression of vitality could be enhanced by combining different materials: classically gold and ivory, but also metal alloys.[71] Images and mural paintings gave the already extraordinary atmosphere added impact.[72] An awareness of the religious experiences of a great many earlier visitors and of their successful acts of religious communication was aroused by the appropriate positioning of votive gifts, or by the sheer quantity of deposited objects.

That the public temple was itself a location for intense religious experience is suggested by the acerbic critiques of the philosophers Lucius Annaeus Seneca and Plutarch, in their treatises *On superstitions*, to which I have already referred. They were troubled by religious experiences that exceeded the bounds of social control. The publicly accessible temple, the most strongly institutionalized and most visible venue for religious activity, perhaps even financed by the city, was not reserved exclusively for ritual activities of a normative nature, rites performed by political elites or even by particular religious specialists. Even the statue—commissioned by the authorities, as Prudentius stressed, and in which the god could *even* be construed as being present[73]—enabled individual religious experiences, which critical observers saw as inimical to the special character of the place. In the eyes of such observers, individual religious practice could amount to deviance, and might occasion general mockery. As in the case of Aristides, it might not meet with the approval of temple personnel or be acceptable to other temple visitors.

Private cult spaces also came under critical scrutiny. From Late Antiquity onward, what was no more than suggested in Cicero's polemic on the *sacrarium* of the conspirator Lucius Sergius Catilina led to a conflict that, owing to power relations in the real world, was never resolved. In one camp were those who claimed that ecclesiastical institutions should have sole control of religious spaces; in the other were proponents of the intensification of religious communication that could be experienced by private individuals on their own premises. It was precisely by adopting elements of the public formal vernacular of sacral space that designers of domestic structures could reproduce the sacral character of spaces in private contexts. Choir screens then no longer served to differentiate ritual spaces and to guide processions, but merely lent to the domestic setting something of the special character of an episcopal basilica. A temple facade might feature as domestic mural decoration or as the motif on an urn, so as to indicate a domestic space intended primarily for religious activity.[74]

Bedrooms

Inscriptions on temple walls or on free-standing stelae allowed those who commissioned or directed religious communication to report on the success of their endeavors. Often they told of claimed personal appearances by deities, and frequently, although not always, those appearances took place in dreams.[75] A variety of deities were accessible in this way, and to achieve the requisite vision it was not necessary to visit a temple and sleep there, as was the custom in such places as Epidaurus.[76] One could dream, as a rule, in one's own bedroom (*cubiculum*). This form of communication might be quite intense, as we learn from the orator and Asclepius-worshipper Aelius Aristides. In his *Hieroi logoi*, he reports the commissioning of a silver tripod and its associated dedicatory inscription; but he also relates that the third and fourth lines of the inscription were corrected by the god himself shortly before morning. After awakening, Aristides repeated the lines until he had committed them to memory. His account continues: "After this, when we took counsel in common about the dedication, it seemed best to us, the priest and the temple wardens, to dedicate it in the Temple of Zeus Asclepius. . . . And the inscription is inscribed, and it has been added that it is from a dream. I also dedicated to Olympian Zeus the inscription and another dedication, so that the oracle was in every way fulfilled."[77]

An almost contemporary visionary in the city of Rome, describing himself in his writings as Hermas, reports having important visions not only on lonely roads or at workplaces remote from the city, but also in his own bedroom.[78] It may well be that he mentioned this last, familiar locale in order to gain credibility, for in the same text he presents a rather remarkable array of visions and apocalyptic revelations, and the apparition he describes has no fixed place in tradition.

Gardens

Important as particular springs, hot or "contaminated" water, caves, and mountains had remained as cult locations since the Early Iron Age, they were tied to particular regional networks and to local populations in villages surrounding the water source or in a city very nearby.[79] They were accordingly always under threat. In the case of Rome, Varro established in the mid-first century that numerous groves previously considered sacred (*lucus*) now survived only as place names, or, through greed (probably on the part of property developers), had drastically shrunk in size.[80] The designers of temples compensated, at least in part, for this loss. The builders of the Temple of Juno at Gabii in the mid-second century BC had not flinched from the laborious task of digging trenches for trees in the stony subsoil—thirty-four in the first phase of construction, seventy smaller examples in the second. Trees may also have surrounded the Temple of Hercules Musarum, and may have stood in the Porticus Octaviae. In other complexes, the planners were probably satisfied with establishing planting beds and water features.[81] For Italic urbanites of the Late Hellenic and the Imperial Age, whose offerings have survived at these sites, religious experience did not require travel to remote wilderness locations, but was available closer to hand in serene parkland settings.

But the desire for such an experience was real, and among the wealthier members of society it was quite the rage. It was, moreover, a desire that could be satisfied by an appropriately designed private garden. Roman landscape planners accordingly produced explicit imitations of sacred groves for their clients, and the use of such gardens for religious communication in the context of festive rituals was not mere poetic fantasy.[82] Pompeii's inhabitants sited a fifth of their domestic shrines in gardens surrounded by walls or even a peristyle.[83] The last inhabitant of the Casa degli Amorini dorati at Pompeii (VI.16.7), perhaps Gnaeus Poppaeus Habitus himself, installed in the garden of the approximately 800-square-meter complex two regular temples about two meters in height, furnished with statuettes, including a Horus, and a movable stone altar 57 cm in height (fig. 36). In addition, the walls bore many reliefs showing deities, and masks representing Silenus, Bacchantes, and Dionysus, figures that recur in the form of herms alongside herms of children and portrait herms. The garden layout, dominated by a central, three-meter-long pond with a fountain, was completed by more marble statues, both great and small, some of animals.[84] Despite the large number of objects, Habitus was not aiming to make an encyclopedic collection. The sacralizing elements had a few clear foci, both spatial and thematic. This wealthy merchant chose to define his desired setting by Dionysian imagery with all its orgiastic, alcoholic, and sexual associations (fig. 37); within that context, he presumably combined specific religious practices having to do with Horus and Fortuna on the one hand, and on the

36. A reconstruction of a statue group in the garden of the Casa degli Amorini dorati, Pompeii. Photo taken in 1904.

other with Jupiter, Juno, Minerva, and Mercury, together with the
lares in Roman dress that were virtually ubiquitous in the town.[85]

In this way Habitus established his place in a world that reached
from his house to Rome, and was quite obviously Roman in all its
facets. By adding Mercury to the mix, Habitus underlined the mercantile dimension. Simultaneously, he referenced a world that, in relation to his own welfare, was of greater moment, more solid, and yet,
even to this merchant, unfathomable. At the same time, however, one
specific form of worldly experience was quite available to Habitus and
to at least a few other male and female members of his household: with
the help of masks and the garden setting, wine, and sex. That Habitus
also referenced a Greek dedicatory relief shows that he nevertheless
conceived of this directly experiential world as a sacralized space,[86]
embodying a guarantee of the presence of not indubitably plausible actors in the form of gods and satyrs, Silenus and the Bacchantes. Habitus
was not alone in this.[87] To anyone proposing to erect an altar adorned
with reliefs, his or her own garden was the first setting to come to mind.[88]

The idea of creating spaces for such experiences, and the reality of
making them happen, might need to be helped along.[89] And for both
of these purposes, appropriate texts, whether read aloud, sung, or lis-
tened to, might prove useful. A whole category of poems or songs—
bucolics—thus assumed the task of facilitating intense and religious
experiences in rural settings. In the third century BC, the Greek poet
Theocritus, who had lived in the city of Cos as well as the metropolises of Syracuse and Alexandria, founded the genre with his "idylls."
Roman poets of the Augustan Age and after followed him with individual texts (Tibullus, Propertius, Ovid) or entire books of poetry
(Virgil, Calpurnius Siculus). The garden as an experiential space might
be further enhanced and sacralized by means of sweet-smelling flowers or the burning of incense or aromatic types of wood.

Such a world was to be had more cheaply than by traveling to the
great sanctuaries. It was available on a smaller scale, and even on
rainy days, but without the necessary cultural background it was not a
world easy to comprehend. "Sacred idylls," painted landscapes in
which rural surroundings were combined with ancient cult places (often

37. Faun and Bacchante in a mural painting from the Casa dei Dioscuri, Pompeii, first century AD. Naples, Museo Nazionale Archeologico. akg-images / Nimatallah.

marked as such by their ruinous state) (fig. 38), free-standing statues or herms, garlanded pavilions, occasional dancing peasants, and votive gifts. Such images were to be seen everywhere: in the Villa Farnesina in Rome, at Boscotrecase, and at the Villa Oplontis.

Painters' workshops[90] (and the sculptors of reliefs) emulated the spaces depicted in the written idylls, and even exceeded in their depictions what was realizable in the larger gardens. These images existed in parallel with painted Dionysian imaginaries, as configured in spaces created in other Roman and Pompeiian villas.[91] They were accompanied by Dionysian motifs on tableware that not only referred

38. Mural painting in the fourth style: an Egyptian scene showing pymgies and a woman at an altar in front of a temple, a tower in the background. From the House of the Pygmies at Pompeii, ca. AD 50–75. akg / Bildarchiv Steffens.

to Dionysus, but contributed in a utilitarian sense to the Dionysian cult of eating and drinking.[92] The images used were thus more than decoration; they were an integral part of Dionysian activities, even if those activities may have been set in motion by other objects or gestures, or the music of lutes. They became part of an emotionally charged atmosphere. In this way, the garden as a space for religious communication formed part of a larger fabric that extended into interior spaces, where its themes were picked up in decor, pictures, and other objects. Through frequently repeated activities and the sacralization of particular corners and objects, this ensemble extended a constant invitation to renewed religious communication and experience.[93]

Tombs

Gardens were not designed only to grace houses, or as rural parks. At least in Italy, anyone designing a tomb, whether their own or that of a deceased family member, might conceive the idea of setting it in a garden or surrounding it with a garden.[94] Even without a garden, however, tombs were held in much regard as spaces for religious experience and activity.[95] The enormous significance of these particular spaces demands to be closely examined.

One stricture that applied to the hundreds of thousands living in a metropolis like Rome also held good for the owners of large urban gardens, and for residents of small towns: dead bodies must be removed from the habitation area, and cremation or the disposal of the corpse in some other way had to ensue outside the city limits. This was an obligation, dating in Rome certainly from the fifth century BC, and laid down by statute in some Campanian towns in the early Imperial Age;[96] anything further was optional. In principle, rules governing the treatment of deceased dependents permitted exhaustive use of all those opportunities for distinction, self-definition, and self-assertion that we were able to observe in the Early Iron Age. These opportunities, combined with social pressure to fulfill "obligations" to the dead, had certainly become established standards in the upper and middle social strata, whence they were appropriated by quasi-familial group structures among the better-situated slaves, and, especially, by freed persons. We do not know what percentage of the population comprised freedmen, nor do we know how many, after death, were consigned to what Varro in the second half of the first century BC described as *puticuli*, "small holes," on the Esquiline.[97] In about AD 200, at a time when a plague or some other catastrophe had caused many deaths, a mass grave was used even for members of the elite.[98]

Whether the tomb was new or a regular place of burial for a family or for a club or association, relationship to the location was proclaimed publicly when associates of the deceased processed with the corpse from the home to the cremation- or burial-site. A crematorium (*ustrinum*) was among a city's usual utilities; at Puteoli in Campania it was one element of a full set of funerary services offered by a monopolistic franchise, which also offered use of an altar and a hall (*chalcidium*). Removal of the body might occur at night, for example in the case of children, or, in the case of executed slaves, in a demeaning fashion using a hook; but it was normally the most visible part of a procedure that was highly ritualized, and therefore easily recognizable by both observers and participants. In the first century BC, the funeral processions of members of the political elite, including females, even halted at the Forum, where an oration was delivered.[99] The family also arranged for "living statues" to accompany the procession; these were actors wearing the masks of important ancestors who had themselves been honored with public statues. By these means, which endured into the Imperial Age, descendants created a publicly visible representation of their families and their position in society.[100]

How did surviving associates and relatives mark the exceptional nature of a funeral? On the one hand, they did it by ostentatiously neglecting their own outward appearance, leaving their hair unkempt (or at least without ornament), and wearing ragged, "dirty" (or at least dark) clothing. In sum, by renouncing signs of social distinction.[101] At the same time, however, the opportunity for public exposure that the mourning ritual provided was not to be missed, for it was yet another opportunity to showcase the personal status or the prestige of the family or group. The deceased person accordingly became a

medium for the projection of that message. The Law of the Twelve
Tables, Rome's supposedly most ancient collection of laws, which was
said to date to the fifth century BC, had already prohibited the use of
more than three *ricinia* (large shawls) and a small purple *tunica*, presumably for clothing the corpse.[102] Mourning too presented an opportunity for conspicuous display. At this period, the hymn of praise for a
deceased member of the senatorial class was not to be sung by young
men from his or her peer group, but in a plaintive style by female sing-
ers; although, as in the case of the funeral oration, a higher-quality
rendering might be obtained by the use of professional performers. In
the Twelve Tables, again, the senatorial class had already attempted
to limit ostentation by families at funerals by setting an upper limit
of ten flautists.[103] There was in consequence a continual struggle between efforts at control and endeavors to overstep or avoid controls.

Attempts to mark the death of an important family member visibly
by well-practiced traditional actions, and at the same time to exceed
those traditional practices, resulted in constant innovations, and even
gave rise to funerary fashions. We can observe this process as it played
out among Rome's elite. Families in the late Republic and the earliest
part of the Imperial Age usually practiced cremation, but they gradually returned to the use of burial from the second century AD onward.
Overall, in the signs and practices employed, they remained true to
traditional means of ritual communication with gods by means of deposits and cremations.[104] Similarly rapid changes were to be observed
elsewhere, and led to major differences between geographical regions
and individual burial sites alike.[105]

Cremation, being a multistep process that included the laying out
of the corpse on a bier, an incineration lasting many hours, the securing of the cremated remains, and only then burial, offered a particularly attractive context for the self-representation of families on a
stage that was readily adaptable. The ruling Republican elite reacted
to this *en bloc* with laws restricting luxury and addressing the particulars
of the cremation ritual. Late Republican and Augustan laws regulated
the use of particular kinds of wood, the sprinkling of perfumes, the
use of oversized wreaths for the deceased, and altars of a particular

kind that dispensed incense and other aromatic vapors.[106] The smell associated with the burning of bodies could be reduced by the use of cypress wood.[107] On the most ostentatious of such occasions, other objects besides sumptuous litters were thrown into the fire, including sacrificial animals.[108] Contemporary authors persuaded aficionados of Greek literature to see in these practices reflections of Homeric burial rites.[109]

The cremation rituals of the Augusti had to compete with these practices and to outdo them, and they began the attempt by founding individual and monumentalized crematoria. Later imperial generations, in making their plans for the next funeral ritual, had to compete with memories of earlier rituals before engaging with the contemporary practices of the elite, and as a result they often lagged well behind changes. When, for example, a fashion for sarcophagi spread throughout the city of Rome in the second century AD, the Augusti initially demurred.

But intimate experience was also possible within the framework of the older rituals. An Augustan poet was able to imagine the high emotions that would have been aroused by the collecting and touching of bones that had failed to fully incinerate, a scenario at a late stage in the cremation process, and one that prohibitions expressly discouraged.[110] In fact, only minimal amounts of the cremated remains were normally gathered into burial urns, less than 100 grams in many places, and this in the early Imperial Age.[111] The deceased's persona was reckoned not to reside in his or her particular physical remains,[112] but rather to emerge from successive stages in the handling of them.[113] This was the case in both Gaul and Palestine, where, in the Hellenistic Period, ever more frequent use was made of ossuaries, containers for bones, as a form of secondary burial.[114]

Tomb-Building Projects

In countless cases, the tomb itself served mainly as the scene of the closing act for the organizers of the funeral ritual. Depending on whether a new grave was being established in the course of the ritual, would not be established until afterward, or had long been in place and now perhaps must be reopened, activities during the funeral might take very different forms. Those who cared enough acquired a monument in their own lifetimes. This constituted a public showplace, while, inside the tomb—whether this internal element was marked by an actual structure or not—a site was created for funerals and subsequent memorial feasts, thus comprising a path for religious communication.

It was not only contemporaries who were impressed by the competing projects of the first century BC,[115] which did not always require the construction of enormous edifices. To Varro (who died in 27 BC), *the* systematizer of Roman religion, it was more important that his grave be lined with olive, myrtle, and black poplar, in accordance with neo-Pythagorean ideas.[116] A little later, Gaius Cestius Epulo, a member of the priesthood of the *septemviri epulonum*, had a pyramid built for himself on the Via Ostiense,[117] which, at a height of almost thirty-seven meters, was nearly double the size of the round structure for Caecilia Metella on the Via Appia, built in the first half of the century. What, for senators in Rome itself, would soon be restricted by the primacy of the Augusti nevertheless remained a model for the economically successful of other classes, and especially for freed persons.

In the second half of the first century BC, it was still possible for the baker Marcus Vergilius Eurysaces to build himself a funerary monument at the fork of the Via Labicana and Via Praenestina (fig. 39). He incorporated columns resembling dough-making machines,[118] and crowned the approximately ten-meter-high structure with a figural frieze, the details of which were difficult to decipher from below, in which he represented his trade as a master baker and bread wholesaler. He had himself and his wife Atistia depicted by life-sized statues, positioned on the side of the monument facing outward from the city. An urn in the form of a small breadbasket may have contained his wife's remains; the monument does not appear to feature any other cavity where ash and bones might have been kept.[119] Eurysaces's trade would seem to have served him not only as an instrument of social recognition, but as an entire lived and symbolic world.[120]

39. Tomb of the baker Eurysaces, outside of the Porta Maggiore, Rome, second half of first century BC. Photo: J. Rüpke.

Petronius may have had such projects in mind when, in his *Satyricon*, he has Trimalchio plan, at the top of his voice, a funerary monument two hundred square feet in area, with a sundial to attract the curious, as a representation of his commercial success and his family fortune, while at the same time he voices apprehensions that his family might abuse the monument or put it to another use, and accordingly declares that he wishes to have it safeguarded by a third party, appoints a watchman, and excludes it from his estate.[121] Alexander of Hierapolis (and subsequently Abercius from the same city, according to his biography) must have had a magnificent tomb built for himself in his lifetime, for he stipulated a fine of three thousand gold coins for its abuse.[122]

Most projects were smaller. Even gravestones and funerary altars were not used extensively in Rome until the first century BC, and then above all by freed persons, in an example that was then imitated throughout the Empire.[123] Tombs in the form of houses were popular from the end of the first century AD onward, erected along the roads leading out of Rome and in the necropolises of the Roman harbor town of Portus (fig. 40). External inscriptions were brief, internal ones very rare: urns were perhaps positioned hierarchically, so that it was not only the repositories of deceased slaves (perhaps at least occasionally admitted to these family fastnesses) that remained uninscribed.[124] In a manner more precise than was possible in the constant hurly-burly of a home, such a space offered the possibility of constructing and reconstructing the family. A rudimentary coat of paint may have been commonplace; its renewal would offer repeated opportunities to adjust the space to the family's continuing needs, or to a change in the tomb's ownership.[125] The interior spaces of these tombs were often equipped to accommodate not only communal funeral feasts, such as those indicated on various calendars, but also birthday meals and family celebrations (e.g., the *Parentalia*); names like *Rosalia*, which are used in many provincial inscriptions or literary texts, may be associated with a customary practice of bringing in flowers.[126]

There is no doubt that such mausoleums were above all personal projects; and nothing indicates this more clearly than the incredible

40. Necropolis along the Isola sacra, first through second century A D. akg-images / Pirozzi.

variety of the remains.[127] Even if many in the provinces combined elements of Roman with local models in their funerary structures,[128] it was nonetheless their own individual solutions that they communicated in this way. Interestingly, it was not the Romans but the provincials who, in the second and early third centuries, most often looked outward for their solutions. In many cases, the living designed tombs for themselves *se vivo* ("while still alive"). Wills were common, written early and often amended.[129] Occasionally, the death of a child or a partner appears to have triggered a tomb construction project.

The principal, either male or female—the latter more rarely, but in significant numbers—here entered into a relationship with his or her own self in the guise of the future dead. It was a cultural practice that, while to us peculiar, seems to have been a phenomenon with mass appeal.[130] This does not mean that the actor failed to construe him- or herself in terms of family relationships, as a mother or wife, a son or a father. In fact the contrary was often the case.[131] The frequent use of the dative in funerary inscriptions—"for so-and-so"—implies a subject, someone acting, even if this person is not explicitly named. The principal of such a construction project during the final years of the Republic—and of many subsequent tombs both large and small—quite clearly acted with the intention that the interred individual (perhaps him- or herself, as in the case of Eurysaces) should remain socially present beyond death. The tomb would bring him or her securely into the compass of social memory, and an inscription, a statue, or a portrait would perhaps prolong their presence even beyond the memory of those in attendance at the feast.[132] In the case of a family tomb erected *se vivo*, as well as in setting up tombs for somebody else, the writer of such an inscription moved into a specifically religious mode of communication with those who were yet to die or were long dead, just as if he or she were the subject of a funerary inscription written by another. The writer thus gained the opportunity of defining him- or herself, configuring him- or herself socially, presenting him- or herself as a citizen or a migrant, a landowner (even if only of a tiny grave), or a benefactor, while at the same time performing the self-same service for another. Typically, the size of the letters naming the person who erected the tomb was no smaller than that of those naming the one buried.

Particular beneficiaries of this new cultural practice[133] were those whose inferior status barred them from other means of self-articulation and -representation. In the altered public realm outside the city, they were able to appropriate with impunity the methods used by the elite.[134] Freed persons especially celebrated agency over their own bodies and those of their dependents. Only now could they represent for themselves, in funerary inscriptions and portraits, an established family, and a status as fully-fledged human beings: privileges that accrued to them by virtue of their manumission.[135] But slaves too, together with the less wealthy, had formed lasting associations that enabled them to enjoy occasional shared meals and celebrations, and they too now used the funds of their patrons, as well as their own contributions, to

41. Fresco of children at play. Columbarium inside tomb B of the necropolis of the Via Portuense, Rome, ca. AD 150–200. Rome, Museo Nazionale Romano delle Terme. akg-images / Nimatallah.

realize tombs that provided themselves and their large families with internal spaces where they could pursue their particular forms of religious experience. Here, in the uniformity of urn-niches in *columbaria*, subterranean spaces with dovecot-like compartments, they appear to have created a degree of social equality they had not found elsewhere (figs. 41 and 42).[136] In the extreme instance, 1,800 places were made available and filled.[137]

If Roman funerary inscriptions and tomb-building projects became instruments of self-representation, beginning in Rome itself with its specific legal, social, and spatial arrangements, this does not mean that the grave could not also be a scene of intense emotions. Only rarely did those affected make this as clear as did one of the two lovers of Allia Potestas, a woman who probably died in the second century AD. He not only wore a ring bearing the image of his dead lover, but also described both her body and his grief in a highly

42. Columbarium of Pomponius Hylas on the Via Appia at the Porta Latina, Rome, first century AD. akg-images / De Agostini Picture Lib. / G. Nimatallah.

emotional poem.[138] Children who had died young might excite similar attempts by their parents to preserve their social memory against their own feelings of loss.[139]

In the city of Rome at the end of the first century AD, child burials seem to have provided poignant impetus for especially lavish and at the same time presumably more intimate forms of interment. Of the first stone sarcophagi commissioned in Rome—and we must reckon with earlier wooden or clay forms that have not survived—a larger proportion were designed to accommodate children at this time than is the case in later periods.[140] Those wishing to use sarcophagi for interments from the mid-second century to about the end of the third could select from among the products of a supraregional market spanning the Roman Empire (fig. 43). Something like fifteen thousand examples survive to this day.[141] Importers, local suppliers, and those who commissioned the sarcophagi created together an enormously

43. Marble sarcophagus from Rome, displaying biblical motifs; in the center, the swallowing of Jonah. Third century AD. Original, Rome, Vatican Museum. Copy in the RGZM. Photo: J. Rüpke, with the kind permission of RGZM.

varied supply. This recalls the situation of fourth-century-BC Etruscan clay sarcophagi, which had also reached a point in their history where they could offer individualized and quite moving images on their lids, including depictions of married couples; this market was also region-wide, and commanded a following into the first century BC.[142] A concentration on portrait depictions also enabled sarcophagus designers to achieve a high degree of personalization even without recourse to inscriptions.[143] The equally wide selection of mythic subjects available for additional reliefs further increased possibilities for the individualization of sarcophagi.[144]

But the most influential developments were not in the area of motifs. Location was more important. Presumably so that their projects would not be seen as competing with those of the Augusti, the elite of the Empire, beginning in the latter stages of the first century AD, no longer erected their lavish tomb structures within the immediate environs of Rome.[145] While it is true that the wealthiest Romans had been moving their domiciles out of the cities of the western part of the Roman Empire and into palatial country seats ("villas"), a trend that began in earnest in the third century BC, there was another factor that affected the choice of locations for tomb projects. Wealthy Romans were for the most part turning their backs on architectural designs of the kind that had characterized the first century BC. In common with other members of their class, Marcus Servilius Silanus, Marcus Nonius Macrinus, and Publius Cluvius Maximus Paullinus, all three

of them consuls in the second half of the second century AD, built
funerary monuments in the form of rectangular temples.[146] Unlike
many freed persons, they avoided expressing an overt desire to be regarded as gods; but when it came to the form and costly execution of
their funerary monuments, they too were defining their positions
in the debate about deification that was being pursued so intensely in
the Senate with regard to deceased members of the imperial family.

An inhabitant of Rome who lacked a horse and wagon, but wanted
to visit his tomb without staying away overnight, would have to build
that tomb within walking distance, at roughly the fourth or fifth milestone from the city. The same radius applied to other great cities. From
the end of the second century onward, however, space in this "subur-
ban" area was becoming increasingly scarce.[147] Existing graves were
put to intensive use, with urns carefully positioned and multilayered
burials. Even the smallest gaps between graves were used, which produced a rather vibrant intermingling of forms and styles.[148] Even
elaborate sarcophagi were squeezed into small spaces, with lavish
furnishings and mural decoration as partial compensation for the
crowding. In the third century, the free-standing sarcophagus was
sometimes designed as a miniature mausoleum. New, terraced tombs
provided small, discrete plots. Just as urban villas and apartment
blocks might provide living units in a great variety of sizes,[149] so too
in the world of tombs appropriate plots might be acquired by inves-
tors. A market had arisen, and with it developers who increasingly
traded in underground sites to satisfy a variety of demands, for individual graves as well as family vaults and interment complexes for
associations.

Religious organizations, whether "pagan" associations, synagogues,
or churches, played no part in this development until far into the
fourth century: boundaries between religious identities were still of
no importance when it came to burial.[150] Differences in status, however, were as much reflected here in the world below as in the design
of houses in the upper world. The upper classes favored sarcophagi
that, like the mosaics of their villas, were so thoroughly steeped in
mythology that interpreting them called for a high degree of *paideia*

("cultivation"). This was a commodity that few could acquire, but that, once obtained, could open doors throughout the Empire.[151]

From the early Imperial Age onward, an increasing number of people used their tombs as places for religious activity and religious experience. A degree of personal discretion was allowed in the details of tomb design, in the uses to which tombs were put, and in the beliefs to which they gave expression. Comparable license was rare in the case of other kinds of sanctuaries. An idiosyncratic cult rule, formulated by Lucius Numisius L.f. Vitalis at Thuburbo Maius in North Africa, required that those wishing to step onto the little podium Lucius had established should abstain from women, pork, beans, haircuts, and public baths for three days.[152] Tombs in the Imperial Age were the most important locations for individual religious communication and innovation.

5. Domestic Gods

In terms of outlay, deceased relatives—parents, partners (and in the case of freeborn and freed persons, spouses), children, siblings, but also fellow slaves or association members—were normally the most important not indubitably plausible actors with whom a person might engage in private religious communication. This was as true at the end of the first century BC as in the fifth century AD. The meal held at the gravesite was, accordingly, one of the most persistent and widespread of funeral customs: even radical critics in Late Antiquity could not abolish it, but had to be content with reinterpreting it.[153] Pipes were regularly installed to allow liquid to be delivered directly to the grave's occupant.[154]

Ideas about this custom varied greatly. In a fictitious forensic speech, probably from the second century AD, a lawyer represents a mother who saw and felt her deceased son next to her in bed at night, kissed him, and spoke with him. When after some time she admitted this to her husband, he had the tomb sealed while a specialist chanted incantations. The apparitions ceased, and the distraught mother accused her husband of (we would say: psychological) cruelty (*mala tractatio*).[155]

Although the differences here were within a family, the lawyer had to tread carefully where the judges were concerned: while admitting the husband's position that the cremation, which occurred on the day of the son's death, should have put an end to things, the lawyer nonetheless accuses the husband of cruelty. He explicitly represents the mother's apparitions as a woman's subjective experience, yet argues that the cessation of what were desired apparitions after the tomb was sealed shows that this was more than a case of mere imagination. Gender-specific reactions are assumed here, and yet criticized in their radical form. Similarly contradictory positions may have led to an imperial rescript of the second half of the second century, determining that a grave without physical remains, a cenotaph, was not a *locus religiosus* inalienable for all time.[156]

The case of the "bewitched grave" saw a father upholding a prohibition against his deceased son, at enormous expense, while an account of the first century shows that same rule being upheld at the Lemuria by a son who throws beans in an effort to chase away his deceased father's "spirit," which evidently has tried to enter the house.[157] Ovid and the anonymous father upholding the prohibition against his son understood the need for a separation between home and tomb. It was not merely a pragmatic matter, but—unlike in many cultures—programmatic: ancestors might be acknowledged in the home; their presence in the form of wax or marble portraits was acceptable, even a source of prestige. But as permanently lodged actors they were unwanted. As a structural consequence of this distinction, urban space was freely alienable and alterable, so long as it had not been declared to be the property of deities by a political decision of the *res publica*. In Rome at least, this division reflected a cultural disconnect that marked one instance of the monumentalization of public space: the Forum Romanum as a separate public space had been established on top of the familial spaces of old graves.

But did the dead in their graves become gods? There was a growing sense in first-century-BC Rome that they in fact did. Cicero gave expression to the notion, couching it as a cautionary norm, at the end of his religious legislation: *suos leto datos divos habento* (deceased family

members should be treated as having been deified).[158] This is consonant with the contemporary custom in the cult of ancestors of addressing the dead as *di parentes* or *divi parentum*; in the singular, for
women too, *deus parens*.[159] From the latter part of the first century BC
onward, a grave was frequently dedicated to the *Di Manes* of the dead,
or, with both terms side by side in the dative and without grammati-
cal connection *Dis manibus Gaii* or *Dis manibus, Gaio* .... In the Latin
West, but occasionally even in Greek-language inscriptions, the living quickly adopted this wording and held fast to it, even when they
included elements with a Christian connotation in their texts. By
using the plural *di manes*, and thus by-passing any connotation as to
the gender of the deceased when alive, the living created a distance
between the tomb occupant and the social persona of the deceased
(although that persona was unmistakably identified in the rest of the
inscription), while at the same time creating a close tie between both
aspects of the person commemorated.

No conceptual clarity was offered as to whether the multiple persona was divisible or indivisible. This created scope for narrative solutions that required a separation between *animus* (soul) and body, as in
the case of journeys to the underworld or to the heavens by both the
living and the dead. The authors of such first-century-BC texts as Cicero's *Dream of Scipio* and the encounter between Aeneas and Anchises in the sixth book of Virgil's *Aeneid*, or the *Apocalypse of Paul* or
of Peter in the second and third centuries AD, made disparate fears and
expectations vividly actual, and thereby aroused much interest.[160]
The names of the supposed authors, and especially of the witnesses,
were in themselves enough to cast doubt on the narrators' credibility,
about which Lucian was scathing in his *Dialogues of the Dead*. Women
came off even worse than men: in the only gospel ascribed to a woman,
the *Gospel of Mary*, the eponymous author speaks of disciples who
doubted whether Jesus could have entrusted anything of importance
to her as a woman.[161] Others, in Rome too, made ritual use of noncor-
rosive precious metal for the period following death, leaves of gold
bearing brief texts as a pass to the other side;[162] here it was reference
to the "age-old" tradition of Orphism that brought credibility in the

midst of doubt.[163] Conceptions of a post-mortal existence remained vague, however, and varied even within families. This applied even to a eulogy for an Augustus.[164] In consequence, builders of tombs preferred to stick to what was traditional, thus safeguarding a kind of "main-stream" standard for the social groups they served, as well as their own financial prospects. Often graves differed from one another only in terms of their decoration and in the details of the inscriptions. This applied in Rome as in Judaea.[165]

Lares

If, for many outside the home and even the city, communication with the *manes*—since the final years of the Republic frequently classified as deities (*di manes*)—was the religious activity most firmly anchored in the everyday, in the immediate vicinity of the home this was true of communication with the *lares*. The conceptions entertained in the process were similarly vague; dual and plural forms happily alternated with the singular *lar*, frequently understood more as a generic title in a complex ontology, situated somewhere among gods, nymphs, he-roes, demons, *manes*, and *penates*. Plautus at the turn of the third century BC, in the prologue to his *Aulularia*, profiles a *lar familiaris* that, residing in the hearth, comports itself as the family's observant super-ego. Two hundred years later, Dionysius of Halicarnassus, a Greek visi-tor to Rome, brings together the prolific actor in the hearth of a Roman royal palace and the *Lares Compitales* celebrated on Roman streets, understanding them as heroes bound to the home but venerated out-side it, at the curbside.[166] After a further four hundred years, the Virgil commentator Servius reconstructs the *lares* cult as a mode of ancestor worship predating the prohibition on home burial. From a historical perspective this is perhaps the most plausible hypothesis for the ori-gins of the domestic cult: that the *lares* and *manes* resulted from an enforced separation between home and grave as locations for com-munication with the dead, a separation that had been in effect since before the fifth century BC.[167]

During the centuries of the Republic and the Imperial Age, however, this remained merely one among many interpretations. It was more important during this period that communication with an agency associated with a particular place and its inhabitants was capable of producing negotiating options within groups and solidarity between their members. In narratives of the birth of King Servius Tullius, versions of which we know of from authors of the latter part of the first century BC, this perspective tended to confirm the assumption that the king had been conceived behind closed kitchen doors. In first-century Pompeii, it allowed slaves to have a cult that connected them to the *familia* as a whole in their workplace, the kitchen.[168] Here, mural painters chose to portray these deities as two identical, often dancing youths, corresponding with the linguistic collective plural, thus excluding the possibility that the figures refer to a particular person (fig. 44). Their association with a sacrificing *togatus*, and often also the purple stripes (*clavi*) on the youths' tunics, constitute a reference to the homeowner in his quality as a Roman citizen, which is also to say as freeborn. A snake clarifies the location: it is the kitchen of this same house that is portrayed here.

Let us imagine the scenario. As in the case of the Dionysian images and the landscapes in other rooms, these are first and foremost murals. Unlike the Dionysian images, however, these stand in clear contrast to the space: the hard-working domestics here have before their eyes a festive ritual, the quintessence of non-work. The image is "activated" in many ways. An architectural frame, or niche—the most minimal way to sacralize a space in a house with stone walls[169]—accentuates the painting. The painting does not act as a backdrop for a cult location, nor does the cult address the painting. In fact the painting represents the cult. It is not the potential addressees that are central here, but the very medium of religious communication, normally an altar. The image of the cult perpetuates the action,[170] but it can also be further activated by those present. Bringing light into what was no doubt a dark, internal room would be the easiest and most obvious means to this end. The domestics light a small lamp and its flickering

44. Mural painting in two registers: above, two young men in tunics flank a sacrificial scene in which a libation is sprinkled over an altar by a *genius* with cornucopia (instead of the master of the house); below, two serpents flank an altar. Pompeii, Casa VII.6.3, first century AD. Naples, Museo Nazionale Archeologico, inv. 8905.

brings the fire on the painted altar to life, also animating the figures in the painting through the play of light and shadow. The painting further encourages them to pour a small libation; this at least is the stereotypical activity of the youths featured (and at the same time an indication of typical festive celebration). Finally, the hearth as the biggest fire in the room might be used metonymically to receive small offerings of food. If the narratives current in Rome were also known in Pompeii (and we cannot assume this), then actors in this scenario doubtless understood the transference in its converse sense: the portrayed altar represents the hearth in which Plautinus's *lar* was concealed, and the place where the *lar* was revered with the likes of wreaths, incense, and wine. But the spatial context of the kitchen was not necessary as a set figurative element; in Pompeii, either the image or a niche might be configured in some other location, and sometimes even given monumental expression.

The accepted iconographic formula of two figures was "set in stone" by Augustus in 7 BC when he furnished each of Rome's neighborhood cult shrines (the *Compitalia*) with two statuettes.[171] However, many Romans did not think of the *lares* "in twos," but as "many." Whether Pompeiians faced with an image of two youths, a snake (or snakes), or figures holding cornucopias or a herald's rod and thyrsus thought of *genii*, Mercury, Bacchus, or simply of *lares*, or sometimes of one and sometimes of another of these alternatives, we cannot know. Distinctions were possible when the written form called for precision.[172] When the term *lararia* is first used in an extant literary text, in the fourth century AD, it refers to household collections of statuettes, which may perhaps *also* have been used for purposes of religious communication; no distinction was made between statuettes of humans and statuettes of gods. On the other hand, small cult locales for *lares* were most often referred to as *aedes* or *aedicula larum*. [173]

To use the term *lararium* was merely to perpetuate an overlap between this term and the term *penates*. In Rome, the latter were associated with the idea of just such a group of statues as had been assembled in the Casa delle pareti rosse.[174] It was under this term that a group of this kind was understood as marking the sacral heart of the home in the late Republic and the early Imperial Age; in a worst-case scenario the statues might be removed from the house—like Anchises of yore on the shoulders of Aeneas—or possibly even discarded.[175] But there was a difference that lay in the character of the plural: in the case of *penates,* the *dei patrii*, it was possible to speculate about the identity concealed within each statue.[176] Contemplating the *penates* at the publicly inaccessible hearth of Vesta in the Aedes Vestae had therefore been a favorite exercise for intellectuals since the late Roman Republic. In the home, too, whether *penates* or *lares* was the preferred term could be merely a question of taste, in terms both of language and of fact: or it could be a choice based on one's notions of religious communication and the interpretation of religious experience. If a person favored and addressed an amorphous collection of superhuman actors, he or she was likely to address them as *lares*. If, however, they preferred to address a self-assembled collection of objects that could actually be held in the hand and individually recognized as divine actors, a mix-your-own granola of gods rather than porridge as mother makes it, then (presuming of course that the person's means allowed such a collection) *penates* was the word.[177]

Against this background, Augustus's genius in standardizing veneration of the *Lares Compitales* in Rome's 265 neighborhoods in 7 BC again becomes apparent (fig. 45). For it was not the prerogative of the villa-owners joined together in their local associations to address the *Lares Compitales* (as was perhaps the case in respect of the *curiae*), but that of the majority of the population of the metropolis for whom house walls, streets, and crossroads were not just transit spaces, but their main living spaces. They belonged to these *vici* (streets) as

45. So-called Frieze of the Vicomagistri, showing the handing over of the statuettes of the *lares*, ca. AD 25–50. Original Rome, Museo Gregoriano Profano. Copy in the RGZM. Photo: J. Rüpke, reproduced with the kind permission of the RGZM.

thoroughly as to a family group, and the "streets" accordingly made an appearance in the guise of puppets or disembodied heads in the festival ritual. For this class of Romans, the *Lares Compitales* were the equivalents of the "powers" of home and family. Here, the presence of the under-defined figure of the *Genius Augusti* was particularly unproblematic, for it combined with a neighborly solidarity whose celebration had to await a sign from the *praetor urbanus*; it was this that was concealed behind the definition of the Compitalia as a movable, "mandatable" feast (*feriae conceptivae*). It was for this very category of politically instrumentalized religious communication that an arena of religious activity had been sought here in the streets, where barriers both internal and external might be removed, and the distinction between the "private" and the "public" erased.

6. Lived Religion Rather Than Domestic Cult

There was no *religion privée*, no "domestic religion" in Roman antiquity.[178] The type of communication that is treated in this book as religion was first and foremost a network of practical strategies, experiences, and conceptions, also acts of institutionalization and shared signs, that came into use or had traditionally defined communication in different social spaces. The various elements of this religion had to be learned and applied in ever-new spaces and situations, and so further developed. Above all, however, it was forever confronting religious communication as practiced by others. Religious competency—which comprised knowledge, experience, and also courage and the will to experiment—traveled as the people possessing it traveled through different spaces. Such journeys or displacements, flights or abductions were themselves only rarely motivated by religious concerns; but, to a varying extent and through the agency of various actors, the spaces to which they led were already "occupied" by religious signs and actions.

For many in the great cities and metropolises of the Imperial Age, the street was a "house," comprising different rooms that constituted the primary living-spaces. However, the few home-occupiers who were able actively to configure the architectural features and furniture of their homes created an "infrastructure" that could also be used by others in a multitude of ways. What we saw in the example of the garden could also be projected into internal spaces. Lighting played a large role here, not only the decision as to which space should be lit and used, but which of its elements, whether mural decoration or furniture, should be moved into the light. Lamps themselves were instruments of religious communication of the first order (fig. 46).

46. Terracotta oil lamp, 10.5 x 8.9 x 3.0 cm, with illustration of a man in a mantle (*sagum*) approaching a burning altar, followed by a person with head covered, first century AD. Kestner-Museum Hannover, inv. 967. Reproduced with the kind permission of the museum.

Sculptured objects arranged around the wick of either bronze or clay lamps produced a corresponding shadow.[179] But the lamp also illuminated itself, so that the figures of gods that decorated its aperture might appear brightly illuminated.[180] These images of gods, in common with other decorative options—circus scenes, erotic motifs, etc.—became literal "eye-catchers," stimulating the vision. The lamps streaming light might well give the viewer the illusion that they were themselves brilliant "eyes," and that he or she was being watched by them. Each day brought its own possibilities and experiences.

The same applied to another, vital religious instrument: the altar (figs. 47 and 48). The slender, delicate, and often richly decorated Italic altar, and perhaps also its portable and collapsible equivalent in bronze, also had a place in the garden.[181] It was an unmistakable emblem of communication with a presence that was not otherwise immediately obvious to the eye, whether it be the presence of gods or of the dead. Its use was unthinkable without a flame or a libation, for the very shape of its upper surface invited just this mode of activation. Even in this respect, however, the altar was not merely an instrument to be used, but, with its decoration depicting ritual procedures and other instruments and materials being used in such procedures, it was itself an act of religious communication and ritual continually in progress. It could be still further activated with a minimum of effort, by placing a lamp nearby, or by providing a bit of speech or song. More might of course be done: baked items of various forms, aspect, taste, and smell were commonly placed on the altar, as were flowers.

More was always possible, but rarely necessary. This was true in the home, at the street corner, in the temple, and at the gravesite. The mere representation of a bull would suffice, an image that cost nothing. Dogs, on the other hand, were sacrificed more often than has been documented.[182] The provision of meat was a marginal aspect of Roman religious practice, for a meal was specifically *not* consumed in the company of the gods.[183] On the other hand, providing feasts of meat was a highly regarded "liturgy" and a means to prestige.[184]

Strategies practiced in houses (or in the street) might also be effective in institutional spaces designed for religious communication,

47. Wall painting in the fourth style: the sacrifice of a hind, from the Casa dei Vettii, Pompeii, ca. AD 63–79. akg-images / Tristan Lafranchis.

such as temples and their precincts. If graffiti were welcome in the home, as the enthusiastic expression of some invited guest, this minor but durable form of linguistic communication might also play a role in the precincts of temples. Such was demonstrably the case at Dura-Europos in the east of the Roman Empire. There, in the temples and assembly buildings of Jews as well as worshippers of Christ and Mithras, users of graffiti endeavored to leave a lasting memorial of their requests to be remembered or blessed: as close as possible to the focus of religious communication, in the vicinity of the cult image, on mural paintings, or in corridors;[185] in this way were also appropriated the great two- or three-dimensional signifiers of religious communication provided by other actors. And of course altars both great and small and increasing numbers of lamps left as offerings continued to play a large role in the Imperial Age, to the detriment of other kinds of depositions.[186]

But religious communication could take on a much more intimate guise, next to a person's own skin. Where the mighty, the Augusti,

48. Oil lamp, Imperial Period. Cybele seated on her throne, flanked
by two lions. Badisches Landesmuseum, inv. B1703. Photo
Badisches Landesmuseum Karlsruhe, reproduced with the
museum's kind permission.

used lavish media in their communications with a personal protective
deity, many others achieved the same goal by the use of amulets made
of glass paste or cut stones, or in the form of jewelry[187] manufactured
according to traditional expert knowledge of the effective properties
of stones, and with the addition of figurative or textual references to
protective superhuman actors (fig. 49).[188] This form of communication might be practiced continuously or on a particular occasion, for
example when a woman was experiencing a gynecological problem.[189]
These objects too were carried into temples and placed there,[190] in

49. Gold ring with image of Serapis. Badisches Landesmuseum, inv. F2129.
Photo Badisches Landesmuseum Karlsruhe, reproduced
with kind permission.

order to bind this additional location into the wearer's own scheme of
religious communication.

There were a very few members of the highest stratum of society
who were able to compete with fifth- and sixth-century bishops in the
realm of domestic architecture, adding basilica-like rooms to their
villas, and free configurations of ecclesiastical architecture in the
form of private chapels,[191] but tombs remained the configuration in
which religious communication reached its most individual level.
In the long term, with the cult of martyrs and relics, these would become the most important locus for innovation in Christian churches
into the Early Modern Period.

Graves and tombs were also preferred sites for the deposition of
written prayers, demanding of superhuman actors the restoration of a
justice that the power relationships in society could no longer

guarantee.[192] Here precisely, where religious communication arose from a situation of subjection that could not otherwise be altered, those affected mobilized their entire store of knowledge, their grasp of rhetoric, literary skills, and any scraps of institutional knowledge that were available to them. With all this, however, they also dared to use temples when they thought it necessary. In the words of a supplicant, imprinted on a little lead tablet in the Temple of Mater Magna in Mainz:

> Mater Magna, I beg you, by your sanctuaries and your divine power: Gemella, who stole my brooches, I beg you that they cut her so that she is nowhere whole. Just as the *galli* cut themselves . . . so let her [do], and let her not cut herself in such a way that she can no longer cry out in pain. Just as . . . they deposited the holy objects in the temple, so should you also not be able to redeem your life and your health, Gemella, from the mother of the gods, neither with sacrificial animals nor with silver, unless the people witness your death.[193]

IX

New Gods

THE FIRST CENTURY BC
TO THE SECOND CENTURY AD

1. Background

The religious changes described in the previous chapter were no longer restricted to the city of Rome. The Roman Empire was not a territorial state; it was precisely an empire, whose governability relied on its ability to obtain the cooperation of tribal elites and, above all, that of the elites of the innumerable cities surrounding the Mediterranean and located in its hinterlands: these local elites thus provided the first level of authority within the mechanism of imperial rule; the second and third levels resided with provincial jurisdictions and imperial rescripts and decisions; even interventions by the standing army (whose size is exceeded by many modern national armies) provided only the final imperial resource. The degree to which the direct export of religious symbols and practices from the city of Rome was politically or administratively orchestrated was correspondingly slight; it paled into insignificance beside the slow diffusion and frequently active adoption of religious conceptions and practices, and often even their intentional dissemination by third parties.[1] As an effect of this lively process of cross-pollination, changes occurred in Rome just as in other cultural centers within the same geographical space, such as Alexandria, Antioch, and Carthage. One evidence of this is religious communication with the gods Isis and Serapis, originally Egyptian but already very widespread in the Hellenistic Period. The appearance of these names in the borderlands of the Empire is almost a more certain sign of Roman influence than the name *Jupiter*, which was used in many and various analogous forms.[2]

People transported religious signs, often practices too, and, to a varying degree, the conceptions associated with them. This happened via shipping routes and the great military roads, such as the Via Egnatia to the north of Greece, and reached even thinly populated provinces and border regions, as well as islands large and small. Such transference might occur through the medium of material objects and texts, or craft skills and pattern books.[3] Soldiers, merchants, slaves, and craftsmen were as likely as the occasional religious specialist to be the responsible agents. There is, however, no doubt that slaves, economic migrants, and soldiers (who also went on leave, and wrote letters) differed in terms of their mobility from officers, members of the senior provincial administration, senators, and orators, as well as other "intellectuals,"[4] especially those who produced texts. But all this remained ineffectual so long as others did not appropriate these signs, gestures and actions, narratives and interpretations, and incorporate them into their own modes of religious communication. Their intentions in so doing, and the effects of such acquisitions, might vary radically: some used them to renew links with their place of origin, while for others they represented exotic options that demonstrated the width of their horizons, enabling even those who had remained in their place of birth to claim the broad expanse of the Roman Empire as their own. Both chosen paths were as important for personal identities as for communication with others.[5] Already in the late second century AD, both Lucian in his *Alexander the False Prophet* and Irenaeus in *Against Heresies* composed satirical analyses of processes such as these.[6]

Lucian portrayed an interplay of individual initiatives, of vague familiarity with equivalent gods or gestures, of patronage and networks of adversaries. But could individuals be successful agents in transporting and implanting new religious signs merely by virtue of having something rather extraordinary to offer,[7] or did success require the mobility of entire groups? Third- and fourth-century writers of fictitious narratives about the early missions of followers of Christ surmised that success required obtaining access to local authority figures and an ability to connect with local ideas and institutions.[8] The interplay between individual initiative and the customary ways in which the social strata operated *in situ* decided the end picture. In the light of these processes, we will in what follows consider some of the new religious signs that emerged from the first century BC onward.

2. Isis and Serapis

To invoke a deity such as Isis was to configure a divine addressee who was known to be widely invoked in Egypt. Her cult was that of an attractive female figure devoid of animal features. In narratives, she was ascribed the role of a mother (of Horus) with her child at her breast, and of a devoted wife (of Osiris), and endowed with great power. Isis had enjoyed a particularly avid following in the third century BC in Ptolemaic Egypt, and was readily imported as a religious sign into the Greek world, where she was often associated with the figure of Aphrodite; from the first half of the third century BC onward, she also served as a patron goddess of seafaring.[9] She appeared on Sicilian coins from about the end of the third century. Temples of Isis were built in Campania, at Puteoli, and in Pompeii from the end of the second century onward (figs. 50 and 51). At the same period, a space in the sanctuary of Fortuna complex at Praeneste was provided with a mosaic depicting a Nile landscape, which would serve to demonstrate, in a religious context, the attractiveness of Egyptian culture.[10] The first institutional evidence of the worship of Isis in Rome appears at the latest under Sulla, in the first quarter of the first century BC, when we hear of individuals who were engaged long-term in her worship, and of patrons who financed cult sites dedicated to her; one such patron, the *pontifex maximus* Quintus Caecilius Metellus Pius, funded the construction of the Iseum Metellinum.[11]

50. Mural painting in Pompeii, depicting a priest and priestess of Isis, first century A D. Naples, Museo Nazionale Archeologico. akg-images / Erich Lessing.

The port cities mentioned above—and they included Rome—had close links not only with Egypt, but with the entire Mediterranean region. This circumstance may account for the presence of a great variety of images of Isis in these cities. Certainly she appealed on many grounds: a powerful goddess widely revered within the Mediterranean region (her name was the same in Egyptian, Greek, and Latin); an attractive element of Egypt's exotic culture;[12] and the female deity associated with Serapis, that divine combination of Osiris and Apis invented by Egypt's Ptolemaic rulers. In the Rome of the late Republic, the invocation of Serapis and Isis was part of a religious strategy pursued by groups critical of the Senate. At the beginning of the 50s BC, at the latest, they countered aristocratic usurpation of Jupiter (as *the* god of the polity) and Venus (as personal patron of many aristocrats, among them Sulla, Pompey, and Caesar) by attempting to install the ruling partnership of Serapis and Isis on the Capitol, or more

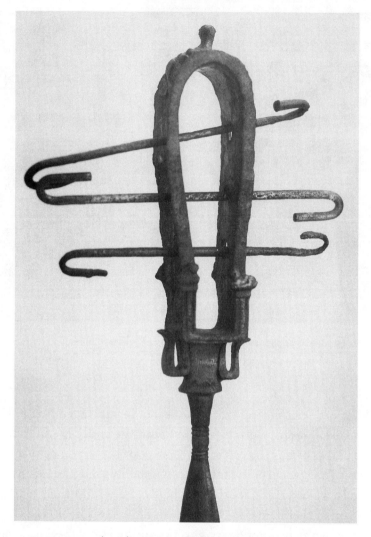

51. Bronze *sistrum* (rattle) used in rituals addressing Isis; from the grave of a
priestess on the island of Rheneia. Mykonos, Archaeological Museum.
Photo: Zde (CC-BY-SA 3.0).

precisely the Arx.[13] In so doing, they incurred not only the opposition
of the Senate, but also the hostility of members of the Etruscan nobility operating in Rome as *haruspices*, specialists in the inspection of
entrails.[14] Isis's cult site was evidently used above all as an oracular
center, a function no doubt suggested to contemporaries by the

significant oracular function of Isis and Serapis in Alexandria, Canopus, and Menouthis. Cicero, who in one essay polemicized against
the two gods as harbingers of Egyptian animal worship, makes only
one further reference to the goddess when he mentions "soothsayers
of Isis."[15] The contemporary poet Catullus saw the child god Harpo-
crates, associated with the pair, as the god of silence,[16] suggesting
perhaps some sort of oracular function. This makes it easier to understand the bitter struggle surrounding the cult site, which not only
involved its development, destruction, and redevelopment, but extended even to its decontamination by the removal of buried traces of
sacrifice.

It was, however, precisely the exoticism of this oracular cult, which
embraced even the dog-headed Anubis, that legitimated it as alien
wisdom, in a Latin-speaking world that, after the "Etruscan discipline"
and Pythagorean speculation surrounding numbers, was now also
beginning to embrace the "Chaldean" lore of astrology.[17] The various actors concerned must have judged communication with foreign
gods, more beset with risks though it was, to hold advantages in circumstances of political confrontation. Its rapid appropriation by Antonius and later Augustus shows how highly its potential was judged.
That the vow by the triumvirs to endow a temple, reported by Cassius
Dio for 43 BC,[18] was not realized, and followers of Isis were again ex-
pelled in AD 19,[19] makes clear the risk entailed by such communication. It was only with the Flavian Augusti, and especially Vespasian,
whose ascent to power was founded not least on Alexandrine oracles,
that Serapis and Isis in their exotic variant became a mainstream phenomenon in the city of Rome. By presenting the veneration of Isis and
Serapis as more exotic, more Egyptian, it was possible to create a geographically extensive claim to hegemony and an ecumenical identity
for figures like Hadrian, or for the Severan dynasty, come out of Africa.[20] The Iseum Campense, attestable for the most part archaeologically, was constructed under the Flavians.[21] Egyptian motifs were incorporated in its design: from hieroglyphs to colored stones, water
features to obelisks; all in monumental style, and enlivened by theatrical rituals (fig. 52).

52. Wall painting in the fourth style, depicting priests conducting a theatrical ritual of the cult of Isis and Serapis; ibises and sphinxes reference Egypt. Herculaneum, ca. AD 62–79. Naples, Museo Nazionale Archeologico, inv. no. 8924. akg-images.

Such a context prepared individual visitors for those "mysteries" that constituted the attraction of many shrines of Isis, especially in Rome, where professional priesthoods resided in the sanctuary. A subsequent initiation ritual, possibly enhanced by repetition, involved an epiphany that was experienced at an emotionally intense level. Similar experiences marked climactic moments for members of Mithraic cult groups. In respect of Isis, however, the most intensive form of membership might also be manifested visibly and lastingly at a physical level by special clothing and a shaved head.[22] In the middle of the second century AD, Apuleius published a description of such a ritual as the climax and conclusion of his eleven-volume work *Meta-morphoses*. The goddess was addressed and celebrated in so-called aretalogies (hymns of praise), or even celebrated herself in the first person: *egò eimi* ("I am . . ."). These litany-like texts, which contributed to the emotional power of the ritual, were already being published in epigraphic form one or two centuries before Apuleius.[23]

The nature of the exotic to be experienced under these conditions always depended, of course, on the particular follower's standpoint. For Apuleius's follower of Isis (as for Lucian), the "Syrian deity" (Dea Syria) was the exotic "other," and, like Isis, an irresistible attraction.[24] But only a fraction of those who added Isis to their religious portfolio actually underwent initiation into her mysteries. In many places the attraction was more in the nature of theater, with temples putting on enactments of such spectacles as the Nile floods, or dramatizations of the stories of Isis and Osiris.[25] It must not be forgotten that Apuleius's longest description is of a procession that was visible to all-comers.

But "Isis" too, despite her enormous architectural and priestly apparatus, was open to a great many different and personalized forms of appropriation, even in Rome. This was not a unique circumstance, but typified the ways in which "new gods" were received. In the early Severan Age, Lucius Ceius Privatus erected a statue of Isis Regina after achieving a significant advance in his career.[26] He publicized his promotion twice over on the statue's marble base, proclaiming it to be a dedication both to Isis and at the same time "to the well-being (*pro salute*) of the Augusti." In a wordy sixteen-line formula, Ceius constructs parallels between his own promotion from *subprinceps* to *princeps castrorum* and the functions of Geta (AD 189–211) as *princeps iuventutis* and of Iulia Domna, the Augusta, and Geta's mother (*ca.* AD 165–217), as *mater castrorum*. He had created the occasion and the opportunity to publicize this analogy by enlarging the baths of his military unit, the *Peregrini*, and himself delineated the specific form that the act of religious communication was to take by swearing a vow to a deity favored by the imperial house. This allowed him to enter publicly into a triangular relationship with the imperial family and the goddess.

At some time between AD 140 and 160, one Astralagus dedicated a marble altar to Isis (fig. 53). Judging by his name and his function as temple guardian, this was someone of humbler social station than Lucius Ceius.[27] The five-line inscription *Isidi / sacrum / Astragalus / aeditimus / D. M.* ends with what is otherwise the abbreviation normal for the first line of funerary inscriptions. A contemporary observer would have been confused, and likely have felt compelled to look more closely at the object itself. One side shows a man holding a dove above an altar laden with fruit. Opposite him, on the other side of the stone, stands a woman crowned with a diadem (perhaps of lotus), holding a *sistrum* (a rattle typical of Isis) and ritual vessels (a libation bowl and a pitcher). This is the goddess herself rather than one of her priestesses. With the formulaic *D(is) M(anibus)* (there would have been space enough to write out any other, less common formulation!), Astralagus makes clear the link binding the two persons in the inscription and the images: their relationship will last beyond death. In the relief, the goddess and the ritual expert (and the man is represented as such, not as a custodian) approach one another. The channel of communication between them is the altar, firmly set between them on the stone. The ritual for which altar and relief stand is fixed for all time. Religious communication likely provided Astralagus with a degree of agency that his social status could never have given him.

Decimus Valerius Chaereas chose another field of action. With his son of the same name and a Publius Aelius Alexander, whom he addressed as "brother," he presented a silver bust of Serapis to an unnamed college, perhaps that of Serapis or Isis.[28] Vanity was not what motivated him here, but, as the fragmentary inscription makes clear, an apparition of the deity (*ex visu*). The beginning of the inscription is not exactly unassuming, however, stressing as it does the distinguished position held by the dedicant in the college: he styles himself *quinquennalis perpetuus* and *quinquennalis*; something like "honorary president." That he took the two laymen along with him on this first-class ticket may have been due less to their financial participation than to the purpose of the statue's presentation: it probably constituted a kind of "letter of recommendation" for them. Even religious groups had administrative

53. Marble altar of Astralagus, Rome, mid-second century AD, *RICIS*
501/0122. Photo: Laurent Bricault, *Recueil des inscriptions concernant les
cultes isiaques* 3 (Paris, 2005), pl. lxxxvi. Reproduced by kind permission
of L. Bricault.

expenses, and required inputs of money and social prestige. And here too, religious communication opened new pathways.

In many of these contexts, Isis and Serapis were no more or less useful than other religious "signs" or addressees. The conditions under which actors might choose them in particular frequently depended not so much on stories making the rounds or on inscriptions testifying to the success of this or that god or goddess—that is to say, on their reputations—as on the situation of the moment or the matter in hand. In many respects, the persons and concerns that evoked calls for divine helpers by various divine names were similar. Even a Varro, who spent fifteen of the books of his *Antiquitates rerum divinarum* clarifying the historical and systemic differences between the gods, in the end concluded that these gods amounted to no more than secondary variants of the one divine principle. He shared this opinion with most other philosophers.

The principle of free choice did not fully apply in everyday religious life. The options in any particular situation might be limited, or one option might be preferable to another on account of a circumstance or a person's station in life, and many carried strong associations of one kind or another. When religious specialists, either male or female, engaged in such undertakings as forming groups or developing cult sites—and here the reference to both sexes is important—enormous importance was ascribed to their particular level of "knowledge." It was critical to know the right practices and signs, the correct attributes for statues, and the proper kinds of gift and ritual that should be offered. Such knowledge was particularly important for creating a sense of recognition, of familiarity, of a kind that would invite Roman worshippers of Isis to worship the goddess in Thessaloniki as well. Whether visitors from the next town shared the same perceptions is another matter.

3. Augusti: Initiatives

New gods did not have to be imported from Egypt. It was a certain Gaius Amatius who provided the impetus for the posthumous worship of Caesar, assassinated on March 15, 44 BC, and then cremated to great tumult on the Forum. Along with some followers, Amatius had an altar erected on the site of the funeral pyre. This Amatius was no blank page. He had earlier appeared on the scene claiming to be the grandson of the popular military commander and multiple consul Gaius Marius. Although it was said that he was in fact a horse doctor, or maybe an eye doctor, called Herophilus (the textual tradition is not clear), he amassed many followers in his guise as a relative of Caesar, who had a fair share of trouble ridding himself of the fellow.[29] Cicero himself used the name Marius when speaking of him.[30] In this role, he swore revenge against Caesar's assassins, but was himself removed from the scene by Marcus Antonius before the altar could come into use. The people, having occupied the Forum after Amatius's murder, accordingly demanded that the altar be dedicated and the first sacrifices made to Caesar.[31] There was evidently a widespread desire to worship Caesar as a god, but such a step nevertheless involved a risk. A rival entering the contest for power, and summoning Caesar to his side as a god, was still quite inconvenient for Caesar's successors. The tradition tells us that the murder of Amatius had to be backed up with character assassination.

A good thirty years before, events had taken an opposite course. The nephew of Gaius Marius, who, as Marcus Marius (Gratidianus), had twice been city praetor, had been revered in his lifetime by Roman citizens with offerings of candles and incense. Sulla in response had him seized by Catiline (Lucius Sergius Catilina). His legs were broken, his eyes put out, his tongue and arms severed, and then, still alive, he was cut limb from limb. More than a century later, the whole grisly business was described by Seneca, with abhorrence, in his essay *On Anger*.[32] Here again, the possibility of the involvement of a god in the everyday activities of Roman citizens constituted a risk that was punished after a change of regime. Such a thing could happen in the wink of an eye. Plautus in his comedy *Asinaria* has his characters argue about which traditional god's name they should use to address their benefactor. They are in agreement that offerings before a statue and an altar will constitute him a god, and so spare him the risk of being killed.[33]

Religious communication with a new addressee was thus easy to set in train. All it took was a few conventional signs or activities, either alone or in combination, to make it recognizable as such. Whether it would be judged appropriate by those attending or observing was far less simple to foresee. For the initiative did not have to lie with social or political elites. Quite the contrary: such initiatives could, as we have seen, alter existing power structures in various respects. The involvement of living or recently deceased individuals (in possession of relatives) as new addressees in religious communication was to that extent no less charged a project than the introduction of established deities who perhaps belonged to some enemy group or to another ethnic group. It is just such turns of events that feature in the texts that serve us as "sources": not only in terms of their outcomes, the establishment of a new cult site, for example, but also as processes. Themes such as "ruler worship" or "imperial cult" are of less concern to us than the means by which new addressees become protagonists in religious communication.

While a religious initiative might markedly enhance the agency of the principals concerned, it was important to win allies for such ventures, perhaps even beyond the immediate circle of one's followers. Before 15 BC at Beneventum, the *arriviste* Publius Veidius Publii filius Pollio, remembered in literature for his gruesome habit of feeding slaves to moray eels, erected a "Caesareum" for Augustus and the colony.[34] Some time later at Ferentinum, Sextus Hortensius Clarus erected not only an "Augusteum," but a forum and an ancillary building for the citizens. He celebrated the dedication of the building, erected at his own expense and on his own land, by throwing a great banquet.[35] It was *arrivistes* in particular who were set to gain a new measure of public presence by establishing a cult locale or instituting an annual ritual, and success made them ever more ready to cover the costs of such projects, and to commit their own time to performing associated functions. This is demonstrated by the many examples of Augustales (*seviri Augustales*) in Italy.[36] There was much to be gained from promoting religion.

Institutions

And yet, to begin something new in societies that owe their perceived stability to preserving what has "always been so"—traditions of action, thought, and speech—was always risky. Imitating the actions of the powerful and successful among Roman or, rather, Mediterranean merchants and administrators, was one way. But acts of resistance could occasionally also prove effective. The imitation of Roman religious practices produced enormous quantities of inscriptions and temples in the western Roman Empire. If religious communication was to open opportunities for agency and central positions in existing provincial societies, it was important that the addressee, the designated "divine" counterpart, was plausible to onlookers and capable of eliciting their consent; although there was no reason why he or she should be in principle immune to all doubt.

To make this addressee the Augustus in far-away Rome was doubtless a rather odd choice at first glance; but it had much in its favor. His existence could scarcely be doubted. His power too was undeniable, even if the assertion of its relevance to any particular situation may not have been *indubitably* plausible in every case. It was presumably more readily disputed by the denizens of distant, wealthy provincial cities or remote rural districts than by Italics, men with Roman citizenship, or those newly subjected. To all, however, the *princeps* of the moment, the "first taker" (which is the literal meaning of the Latin term), offered an unambiguous point of reference. He was a person whose face could be seen here and there. One could read his name, and there were reports of his doings.[37]

How claims of relevance were projected in particular instances, and how this or that male or female addressee was determined upon, depended on various factors: on the knowledge and skills of the actors in question, on their originality, and on local traditions of religious discourse. When, after the death of Lucius Caesar (17 BC–AD 2), Augustus's adoptive son, the town council of the colony of Pisa decided to erect an altar and endow an annual ceremony for Lucius's *manes*, it went so far as to omit the term *di manes* from most passages of the resolution, increasingly frequent though it was in contemporary inscriptions.[38] The committee and the clerks involved—Quintus Petillius, Publius Rasinius Bassus, Marcus Puppius, Quintus Sertorius Pica, Gnaeus Octavius Rufus, and Aulus Albius Gutta, all named in the founding document—took as much care in setting out the requirements for the actions to be performed as in designating the addressee. Those admitted to prominent roles in the death ritual had to wear black togas. The ox and the sheep to be slaughtered were similarly to be adorned with black bands, a bluish black being the color of deepest mourning in Rome.[39] A pitcher full of milk, honey, and oil was to be poured over each animal's cremated remains. Those persons who lacked the legitimation conferred by a public office were allowed to participate, but they were restricted to holding a candle, a torch, or a wreath, which they might throw onto the burning pyre. Further rules were merely taken from the relevant resolution of the Roman Senate for this particular ritual.[40] According to the epigraphic version of the Pisan resolution, all of this was to be recorded in an inscription erected next to the altar. Religious communication with Lucius's *manes* was at its most impressive at the August 20th performance, but its renown outlasted that occasion, if only by virtue of the carefully positioned altar, in front of which a burnt offering was regularly made after the Greek fashion.

Widespread reflection on what it meant to be human had found expression in the emergence of the term *di manes* on large numbers of gravestones since the latter part of the first century BC. Against this background, an answer also emerged to the question as to whether—and if so *how*—rulers should be addressed in political or religious communication. Within the field of possible responses to that question, the term *divus* marked a transition in terms that indicated a sharp distinction. Formally speaking a personal title, the word's use asserted the identity of the human being and the god. The two were one. Just as senators during the Republic had debated whether observed omens were to be considered portentous for the *res publica*, they would now discuss whether the human being they had themselves observed could have become a god.[41] At the same time, the fact that the title had also occurred in older names of gods—Diva Palatua, Diva Angerona, Diva Rumina, Bona Diva[42] (also Bona Dea)—pointed to the world of established deities. But the inherent ambiguity of the term is demonstrated by the fact that Cicero himself appears to have used *divus* as a designation for ancient deities and *deus* for such new ones as had arisen from the deification of humans (although the textual tradition here is uncertain).[43] In short, when used in relation to a formerly living person the term *divus* suggested a perceptible change of status.

In Rome, the senators or the heirs of the deceased laid the necessary groundwork for the transition by means of the consecration ritual. In figurative and partly also ritual terms, the metaphor of the ascent to heaven was central, whether in the form of a soaring eagle or of a journey in Sol's chariot (fig. 54).[44] The ascent could be observed, and, like the appearance of a new star—a comet in Caesar's case, the empty tomb with the rock pushed aside in the case of Jesus—it was empirically comprehensible or authenticated by eyewitnesses. In the Roman world, the established ritual referred back to ancient narratives, beginning with that of Romulus, and repeated them reliably and openly. It always took place on the Field of Mars.[45] The organizers released an eagle, whose ascent everyone could observe. There was always a funeral pyre, even when the corpse had long been disposed of.[46] This theology of ascent or "ascension" was unsophisticated. As we shall soon see, however, it made oversight possible. In the longer perspective, the Augustan Age signified a time of radical change in the West, where, for the first time, rulers—alive or dead—were addressed wholesale in religious communication as *divi*. This phenomenon lost ground over the course of the following centuries, but it was not a steady decline; there were movements and counter-movements.[47]

The same cannot be said of the alternatives to this sharply marked ascent from human being to god. They lacked both the elements of possible oversight and ritual standardization. The most viable

54. Marble relief displaying the apotheosis of Augusta Vibia Sabina, wife of
emperor Hadrian (c. AD 86–136). Hadrian observes the scene in seated position,
on the left the personification of the Field of Mars as indicator of the place
of the ritual. Shortly before AD 138. 268 cm high. Rome, Musei Capitolini,
Palazzo dei Conservatori. akg-images / Pirozzi.

possibilities for new praise or ritual derived from the conception that the "other," and above all the ruler, might be the epiphany of a known god. To incorporate such a notion into one's own project of religious communication was not only to honor the individual thus identified (in case a malevolent observer wished to raise an accusation of *maiestas*); it also opened up a rich spectrum of images and narratives that could be called upon to further enhance the plausibility of that project. But the contrary dynamic may have operated more commonly in everyday reality: the importance and contingent relevance of an address to a known god might be enhanced by association with the personal and political facets of the individual identified with the deity. An obvious choice was the figure of Hercules: energetic, a creator of order, and himself a human being promoted to divine status; thus an exemplar of the matter at issue here.[48] But the spectrum was broader. It extended from Jupiter, the main political god of the city of Rome, and Zeus, who played a comparable role in many cities of the Eastern Mediterranean world, via the triumphant Dionysos (translated as Liber Pater), to Apollo and Romulus Quirinus. In many instances, the individual concerned suggested the identification himself, by choosing the god as a particularly important personal addressee, sponsoring temples or games in his or her honor, or dressing the part.

The ways in which the relationship could be signaled were many and various. Geographical proximity to a cult site, a genealogical reference, the experience of an epiphany or of the internal presence of the divine: all were possible, and demand for precision was on the whole rare. Here too, resort was had to older reflections on the relationships of gods to one another, which had found expression in copious juxtapositions and subordinations of gods' names. At the beginning of the second century BC, Ennius mentions Nerio or Nerie Mavortis, as well as a Hora Quirini, in his epic *Annales*; and Gellius in the second century AD explains the alternative understandings that might lie behind those names. The power of Mars? The Nerio in the sphere of Mars? Nerio, wife of Mars? A peaceful Mars?[49] So the dead Livia was addressed (in the dative denoting her as the recipient) in rituals so important to their principals that they were also given epigraphic form, as *Livia Augusti dea, Iuno Livia (Liviae?) Augusti*, and *Ceres Iulia (Iuliae?) Augusta/ae*.[50] What in linguistic terms remained ambiguous could be clarified figuratively. The instigator of the religious communication might, for example, place two statues next to one another. (Dea) Roma and Augustus were a favorite pairing, Venus and Caesar a controversial one. The choice of material might introduce a nuance, uniting or polarizing observers, as we have seen earlier in the case of gold or ivory used for a statue of a human. The clearly established autonomy of a human personality might itself raise the question as to its ontological status, its place in an order in which angels, demons, and gods, while self-evident players, were in detail enigmatic, and in their situative identification controversial.[51]

Of the possible positions on the relationship of the divine to the human dimension, two were popular and rapidly institutionalized as divine figures in their own right. One of these was the *Numen Augusti*, a *numen*, a divine "power of assent," attaching to the Augustus. According to Varro, qualities such as this were assigned above all to Jupiter.[52] The concept now provided a possible formulation for an addressee located beyond a situation and yet ascribed effective power within it, just like an Augustus, who was not present but evidently wielded power in any provincial locality. In its precise imprecision—quite clearly divine, but in unclear relation to the person of the Augustus, which is to say making no assertion as to the latter's ontological status—this concept was propagated by provincial administrations and elites. In the context of prominent religious activity, for example in founding and operating central cult locales, they invoked the *Numen Augusti*.[53] Theological systematization followed only later, against the background of the wide dissemination of this concept in connection with the Augusti.[54] The second popular option was likewise popularized from the bottom up. The concept of the *genius* was rapidly appropriated by many individuals on their own account, and the divine dimension of the emperor might be addressed as *Genius Augusti*. The *genius* was occasionally used in domestic religious practice in order to associate the father, around whom the family centered, with the divine. This usage too, however, did not become popular until the notion of the *Genius Augusti* became widespread. Once established, the tactic to give a divine dimension to a place or group by addressing a *genius loci* or a *genius* of some military group became widespread. It seems to have been used to capture the common element, the binding power inherent in a human group by employing it as an addressee of religious communication. No such far-reaching use was made of the *numen*.[55] But the concept of the *genius* was also limited by linguistic boundaries. Like the *numen*, it remained confined to Latin.

But the desire to encourage reflection on the person of the Augustus or his family was at most—at most!—of secondary concern in the choice of such addressees in religious communication. The central strategy underlying the choice lay in the enormous boost to the relevance of a communication that an indubitably potent empire-wide actor brought into the local context. Onlookers might well have regarded such a step as "unnecessary," but that did not alter the fact that the principal had thereby enhanced the status of his or her petition. It also meant, of course, that the petition, now associated with the Augustus, would have to be couched in suitably lavish form. This also applied should the Augustus (or Augusti) not be directly addressed by the principals, but included, perhaps along with the imperial family, as beneficiary of a communication with divine addressees: *pro salute Augusti* ... ("for the emperor's well-being ...") was a formula used frequently across all religious orientations.[56] While not rendering necessary any more precise description of the projected "well-being," at the same time it permitted more specific benefactions to be named, such as the wish that the Augustus might remain "unharmed," or a wish for his safe "departure and return," and the like.[57] Strikingly, the formula was almost never abbreviated, and then only when the principal's own welfare (*salute sua*) was meant: the full, easily recognizable form was required in view of the complex relationship between actor and beneficiary. The choice unmistakably implied a claim to a relationship with the ruler as a person; its extension to the entire imperial family, the "house of the *divus*" (*domus divina*), was accordingly unproblematic.[58]

Including the Augusti in local religious communication was a gesture that made sense, because they were in fact present in many ways. They communicated, through the uncommon medium of the letter, with town councils and officials; and they were present in images, not only images of themselves, but also those of their growing children. In some cases, for example in imperial villas such as that at Chiragan (Martres-Tolosane in southern France), imperial family members were even on view in the form of true-to-age portraits. Moreover, when a local customer or donor commissioned such portraits, they often entered into correspondence with the imperial court. This served both to ensure the quality of the portrait (and perhaps also to ascertain the subject's current appearance and correct titulature) and to draw the imperial family's attention to the personal initiative being undertaken.[59]

However, in making known their desire to establish religious veneration of the emperor on a permanent basis, it was not only with the center in Rome that city representatives entered into more intensive communication. Such ventures were at the same time competitive forays launched against other cities of the region. This was true especially in the densely urbanized areas of Asia Minor.[60] In the cities of the Greek East, such initiatives were very carefully monitored, not least by the systematic exchange of festival delegations, and judged to be an element of competition for renown. A delegation from Ptolemais-Barca in North Africa, sent in AD 154 to the feast of the Capitolia established by Domitian, was warned by Antoninus Pius that its visit created a precedent for yet more (unnecessary) competition.[61] The warning appears to have helped. And besides, there were alternative avenues available. The title *neokoros*, "guardian of the imperial cult," was an official distinction that might be granted in this competition between cities for prestige.[62] Coins minted centrally, distributed above all through the medium of military wages, and bearing the portraits of the Augusti, brought the emperor's figurative presence, which underlay all these activities, into the everyday.[63]

Control

Religious activity involving the introduction of new gods was, perhaps more than any other aspect of life, subject to the interplay between local actors, who had their own preconceived notions, and the administrative leadership of the Empire, which sought to keep control of the symbolism surrounding the emperor. The priests of the cult of deceased and deified emperors were the chief instruments in this area of control, and they were themselves the object of contention among the senators. In the text of the speech Cicero maintained he delivered in the Senate on September 19th, 44 BC (the so-called *Second Philippic*), the speaker takes Marcus Antonius, appointed *flamen* in Caesar's very last days, sternly to task. He accuses Antonius, now acting in the role of *flamen* to the god Julius (*divo Iulio*), of setting himself up as the equal of the priests of Jupiter, Mars, and Quirinus. Cicero goes on to ask why Antonius has not yet been inaugurated (been ritually introduced into priestly office), and calls for a mechanism of oversight for this new type of priesthood.[64] That ritual was not in fact brought into being, and the role thus institutionalized, until 40 BC,[65] whereas the *luperci Iulii* were established by Caesar himself, and were evidently regarded as his priestly "bodyguard." Their demise in 43 BC also meant the end of Antonius's leading role as their *magister.*[66]

The "son of the god," soon to be called "Augustus," regarded the position of the *flamen* as so seriously in need of monitoring that, after Antonius's death, and probably as early as 29 BC, he transferred it to his (still young) nephew Sextus Appuleius,[67] whose father became consul in that year. We may assume that it was at this same time[68] that the *de facto* sole ruler established alternative forms for the religious veneration of rulers. The Arval brethren preserved the memory of Romulus, and made important moments in the life of the family of the current Augustus and in his reign the central subjects of their rituals.[69] The future Augustus directed the *sodales Titii*, which had already existed in the Republican Age and probably embodied a reference to the ancient *tribus Titiensis*,[70] to hold an annual cult commemoration at the supposed tomb of the mythical Sabine king and five-year colleague of Romulus, Titus Tatius. About twenty years later, Dionysius of Halicarnassus as a newcomer to Rome accepted this public cult as an established fact.[71]

Terms such as *fratres*, "brethren," or *sodales*, "companions," unlike *flamen*, left the status of the revered person uncertain. When Augustus died in AD 14 after an unexpectedly long life, recourse was had to the model of the *sodales Titii* in establishing his priesthood, although with some modifications imposed by Tiberius. Thus the *sodales Augustales* would follow the pattern set by Titus Tatius, who had enjoined his "companions" to perpetuate Sabine cults. Tacitus's account leaves the actors of AD 14 and their particular positions entirely unclear. The lottery for the twenty-one places in the new priesthood included the entire elite, and was then filled out by the appointment of Tiberius, Drusus, Germanicus, and Claudius, the dynastic core of the Claudians.[72] The family's shrine at Latin Bovillae was considerably enlarged. Whether the *sodales Augustales* exercised any ritual function there prior to the completion of construction work is unknown to us. With the lavish furnishing of the new locale, which included inscribed membership lists,[73] the actors involved aimed to blend the non-public character of the site as the *sacrarium* of the *gens Iulia* with the cult of the *divus Augustus*, whose statue was erected there.[74] Maintenance of the cult of the *gens Claudia Domitiaque* at Antium was subsequently transferred to the same group.[75] Logically enough, the name was then extended to become *sodales Augustales Claudiales*. These meticulous incremental adjustments carried out by Tiberius did not prevent the *sodales* from being perceived as a "proper" priesthood. As early as AD 22 Tiberius had to allow the *Augustales*, as the priesthood of the *domus Augusta*, the family of Augustus, to host games pledged by the Senate, in common with other highly regarded priesthoods.[76] The opportunities for both Augusti and senators to assert their positions for the long term were evidently limited. Those limits were to be found in the perceptions of third parties and in the internal dynamic of the new institutions, and even in the readiness of individual members of the priesthoods or their dependents and clients to reproduce the detail of titulatures when they had honorific or tomb inscriptions set up for them. So the following two centuries saw the emergence of the *sodales Augustales Claudiales*, the *sodales Flaviales Titiales*, *sodales Hadrianales*, and the *sodales Antoniniani* (which took in all of the deified emperors from Antoninus Pius to the Severans). Isolated attempts in the second half of the second century to curb or centralize this apparatus by establishing a union of personnel between sodalities or a new group of *sacerdotes domus Augustae*, perhaps a kind of court priesthood, enjoyed no long-term success.[77]

The flaminate priesthood, however, which in Rome was embedded in the pontifical college and thus allowed little freedom for autonomous initiatives, was exceedingly successful. In many places in the Roman Empire, the role of *flamen* (and, for deified female members of the ruling house, *flaminica*) became an important opportunity to practice and configure the ruler cult. From Britannia to Africa, Hispania to Syria, members of local elites and those seeking advancement used the chance afforded by religious communication with the *divi Augusti* (and *Augustae*) to enhance their own agency and religious experience. The officeholders of course became the subject of major expectations; but the fact that they were normally appointed for a year somewhat restricted the range of such expectations. The office nevertheless provided scope for personal initiatives affecting the spatial and architectural as well as the ritual face of these new gods, extending into the realm of "mysteries."[78] Into Late Antiquity, the figure of the *flamen*, and even the lifelong office of *flamen perpetuus*, became a hallmark of Rome-oriented towns. It was even held by individuals who saw themselves as Christians.[79] As in Rome, its presence might be augmented by groups whose members were seen as priests or magistrates by virtue of their cult role. The *Augustales* were recruited partly from the ranks of *arrivistes* and freedmen, and partly from existing local economic or political elites, and to some extent they constituted a distinct social class.[80]

Presence and Absence

The ruling Augustus stood for a great many things. He might appear as a military victor and protector, or, in a pose of sacrifice, as the quintessence of piety, a generous patron, a savior in natural catastrophes, or as a general source of well-being. His name could, accordingly, be invoked for a great number of possible reasons, and by a great many means. Far from Rome the Augustus was named in building inscriptions documenting individual interventions and donations. His image appeared on military standards, he was present in the form of statues, and in both images and legends on coins. The invocation of an emperor thus became plausible, because although he was perhaps a person never seen, he was nonetheless ubiquitous. He was unambiguously existent. Calls on the emperor also made sense because of the special "divine" quality of his presence in the minor rituals and major festivals celebrated by Roman administrators and soldiers. Every subject of the emperor thus had a reference point that made his or her relation to the ruler at one and the same time individual and socially plausible.[81]

However, the increasing sacralization of the Augusti, through the images they disseminated and the etiquette by which they increasingly formalized access to their persons, also restricted the scope and flexibility of such a reference.[82] The possibility of considering and discussing the particular qualities of a particular ruler—especially after his death—were therefore limited. It was principally the senators and intellectuals of the Principate who were able to debate the boundaries of human potential, calling up the emperor as an example, without having to await the passage of a great interval of time before doing so.[83]

As early as the twenties of the first century BC, the Apulian poet Quintus Horatius Flaccus (Horace), a protégé of Augustus's confidant Maecenas, wondered whether it was a god in human form that had been sent to Rome's aid. Not until the last lines of his poem does he propose a solution to the puzzle by identifying this savior as the young Caesar.[84] The same poet went further a decade later. In the

fourth book of his *Songs*, which may have been published in about
13 BC, he addresses Caesar as a son of the gods, comparing his presence
in the city with the light and the spring, and remarking that he made
the day more fair and the sun brighter.[85] But it is above all Caesar's
military successes that Horace repeatedly celebrates. Against this
background, so the songs relate, Caesar is invoked in prayer with libations of wine, and his divine power (*numen*) revered along with the
Lares. To him are compared Castor and Hercules, adoptees of the
gods.[86] A bare half-century later, it was self-evident to the historian
Valerius Maximus, who belonged to roughly the same social stratum
as Horace, that a review of world history had to begin with an invocation of the ruling *Caesar*: the name had long since become generic for
the imperial ruler. The foreword to Valerius's collection of *Exempla*
ends aphoristically with the assertion: "We received the other gods;
the Caesars we gave to the world."[87]

This particular take on the half-century of Augustan rule that had
turned the oligarchy of the Republic into a different world was not
necessarily a viewpoint that others shared.[88] At around the turn of
the first century, the senator and ex-consul Cornelius Tacitus was
able to complete ten chapters of his historical text, which began with
the death of Augustus, without a single hint at the emperor's divine
status. He devotes only one rather matter-of-fact remark to the deification: "As for his burial, once it had been completed according to
custom, a temple and rituals typical for celestial beings (*caelestes religiones*) were decreed."[89] The expression *divus Augustus* does not
occur for the first time in this text until the following chapter.[90] We
see clearly in Tacitus's choice of terms the political and religious control represented by the ritual of consecration and the decision to perform it. At roughly the same period, Plutarch, a Greek and a long-time
resident of Rome, was able, in his 113 *Roman Questions*, to unfold a
panorama of cultural and especially religious practices, and a Roman
topography in which the Augusti do not feature at all. He presents his
predominantly Greek readership with an entirely contemporary
Rome, with a culture that, while continually reacting to particular
events, and therefore profoundly defined by its history, nevertheless

remains substantially local, untouched by the kind of Romanization that could in fact be observed everywhere in the Mediterranean region at the time.[91]

It is difficult to accept that literary representations such as Plutarch's reflected reality. Images of the Augusti increasingly dominated the cityscape. Independently of all other considerations, the material used for, say, statues itself tells us what the agenda was: a statue made of gold and ivory had to represent a god. Nobody after Gaius Iulius Caesar, other than the Augusti, drew on such materials for representations of himself during his own lifetime.[92] The prominence of religious practices related to the Augusti and their families[93] is unmistakable, as much in the array of great festivals held under the aegis of the public priesthoods as in anything else. Calendars in the Roman mode of *fasti* conveyed this year-round imperial presence to places outside Rome as well, to towns that did not themselves enact all of these rituals. In the manner of the short narratives published in calendars of the Early Modern Age, the brief entries in small letters to be found in calendars such as that at Amiternum referred to the biographies and successes of the Augusti. Here too, the physical material played a role: in particular, the use of marble by those who erected these "narratives" underlined their perceived importance. Marble, though, was resistant to the rapid additions and corrections that might be necessitated by conspiracies, victories, births, and deaths, and the very fact of its permanence turned local patrons against the medium as early as the mid-first century AD.[94] Even the dissemination of epigraphic copies of Augustus's *Deeds*, which in its introduction presented local Roman elements as part of the imperial culture to which everybody belonged,[95] was not repeated. Roman dates, even those in the religious sphere, were in any case rarely mentioned in calendars outside of Rome,[96] except where they were legally required, as in the case of the dates of legal proceedings.

Despite all the possibilities offered by this new god or gods, in the everyday world and outside of Rome the emperor was very far away. The disconnect between lived reality and conceptions of a new age as celebrated in the saecular games, not only by Augustus (17 BC) but also by Claudius (AD 44) and Domitian (AD 88), left its mark. Titus Calpurnius Siculus, a writer of pastoral verse at the beginning of Nero's reign in the second half of the 50s AD, portrayed that optimism as well as his own disappointment.[97] Reference to this new god was a risky business, and always controversial. Constant effort was required in order to render the divinity of the emperor plausible. In many towns the elite made such efforts, in others they did not. The substantial presence of the imperial cult in Pompeii and Ostia reflects their direct relations with Rome, and not diffusion.[98]

4. The Self

No separate discussion will be devoted here to the numerous deities of the Roman Empire. Entire monographs have been written on each of them, and, as I stated at the end of the section on Isis and Serapis, they did not, in any case, constitute distinctly profiled "personalities" whose "essence" would explain their use in religious communication. As religious signs, while central, they were also often interchangeable. The very names of these gods were the result of contingent naming strategies, permitting choices calculated to highlight the character of the principal's personal experiences of the divine, or to profile him or her as a human religious actor, and so potentially playing a part in a strategy to acquire a following. In almost every province, Jupiter (or, in Greek texts, Zeus) was the most frequently used god's name. This was due to the fact that many relied on this name, on the one hand descriptively, to formulate a Roman identity, and on the other hand functionally, to achieve as high a profile as possible in local hierarchies without yet presenting themselves as state actors (which invoking the Capitoline Triad would have implied).[99] So far as we can tell from our sources, followers of Mithras did not differ sociologically from followers of Silvanus. It was merely that the former frequently belonged to groups organized around the god, whereas the latter did not.[100] Some attempts were made in antiquity to systematize the gods, attempts that tally with the image of a circle of functionally differentiated deities who were turned to only in the context of a particular request, while occasionally fitting the need for creative new arrangements. Only in these limited contexts does the picture resemble a well-ordered pantheon. If we are to tell the story of religious changes in antiquity, we must understand "pantheon" differently, as a vision of the entirety of the religious landscape.

In contrast to the many deities that cannot be mentioned here, there is one whom we entirely overlook, and that is the self. Initially, the self was not a focus of religious practices, apart from marginal phenomena such as the "Orphic gold tablets" already mentioned, which were placed into the mouths of dead bodies, and the narratives connected with them.[101] Contemporary philosophers reflected on the precise position of the individual in the world (*oikeiosis*), and made both the soul and the self key concepts. It is in Seneca the Younger in the first century A D that we discern an outright biographical interest beyond abstract agents;[102] but here it is to a fundamental concern of philosophical schools that we are referred:[103] it was philosophy,[104] and not religion, that offered a path to self-reflection that amounted to a real program. The aim of Stoic self-examination was to achieve consistency in the conduct of one's own life.[105] Stoicism was not a form of enhanced individualism, but based itself rather on the analysis of one's own situation in nature[106] and in society. Roman followers of the Stoa stressed a person's obligation to dependents and even to the world at large.[107] The soul was precisely *not* an individual phenomenon that perhaps even survived physical death, but a general concept of the divine in human beings.[108] We see this same exercise, this *askesis*, again in late antiquity, in monastic journals concerned with personal passions.[109]

The figurative language used, and the topography of the inner self formulated by intellectuals in various genres nevertheless remained complex.[110] From Plato to Plotinus, the figure of the *daemon* constituted a lens through which to examine the relationship between two aspects of the self that were equally difficult to access. These were, on the one hand, the inner (comparative) and innermost (superlative) self, which was thought to determine one's thinking and acting, and on the other hand the divine "Other" (or "Others"), which exerted an influence on the first, dual self that constituted the innermost essence of the human.[111]

But the field of religious communication also and above all embraced practices that cleaved to a specific, material logic that was medical in character. Important actors found an institutional framework in a network of sanctuaries of Asclepius, which were established from Epidaurus outward to the limits of the Hellenistic world. Here, illnesses were treated as individualized phenomena that were more than disruptions of a natural social order or sequence of generations.[112] Aelius Aristides in his *Hieroi Logoi*, an account in several books given by an invalid of his dreams, pilgrimages, and encounters with Asclepius, not only plumbs the depths of his own self, but extols that self, which in its excellence, despite frightful illnesses, stands as supreme evidence for the power of his god.[113] Even beyond the bounds of expensive sanctuaries of Asclepius, however, where invalids like Aristides established themselves as worshippers, deities were implored for good health or recovery from illness.[114]

Dreams became more important, and were taken seriously at all social levels.[115] Manuals were either available for their interpretation or could be especially written.[116] The popular deities were precisely those who appeared in dreams. Asclepius did this, Silvanus did it regularly. Their demands in dreams instigated religious activities in the waking life of the dreamer, so that the dreaming itself became a religious behavior.[117] The Imperial Age also saw the revival and proliferation of small, local oracles, available for individual consultation.[118] Ready-prepared portions of text were used for divination by lot, which made the procedure both straightforward and cheap. This measure of accessibility also meant democratization. Even where the self had not become the central locus for direct communication with or even manifestations of the divine, it had become an object of interest, capable of religious communication with addressees who, while external to the soul, could be accessed in sanctuaries and oracular sites, and could be addressed in various ways about a multitude of concerns.

5. Résumé

The dissemination of gods' names, and the naming strategies employed in different localities and by different individuals in their religious communications, was in the Imperial Age embedded in a cultural context that was so vast geographically that it could not really be *experienced* by most people. The imperial context was nonetheless present, a constituent element of their relationship to the world. This very element might exert influence over a person's choice of divine addressees, as perhaps in the case of dedications to *Victoriae* in the Roman province of Africa.[119] That people in frontier regions and strategically important locations frequently addressed a goddess of victory is not in itself surprising. But they did this in North Africa by addressing a *Victoria Parthica* or *Armeniaca*, thus defining their particular situation with reference to other frontiers of the Roman Empire thousands of kilometers distant.[120] It was just this kind of realignment of local activity to the imperial level that was critical for the involvement of the Augusti in religious communication, if only in dedications *pro salute imperatoris*.

And yet many developments remained regional in character. Typical of Egypt was a broad absence of cities, but with structured clerical bodies that tended to coalesce into temple-related, centralized priesthoods.[121] The cult of the Senate flourished in Asia, discernible for example in the youthful *Genius Senatus* represented on coins.[122] Not even the supra-regional cult locales of the imperial cult that spanned entire provinces or groups of provinces—the *ara trium Augustorum* (Lugdunum/Lyon), the *ara Ubiorum* (Cologne), or the Greek *koina* (provincial structures)—were set up as part of a comprehensive strategy.[123] The cult of the *domus divina* flourished in *Germania superior*.[124] This situation need not surprise anyone, for the geography of the Mediterranean shoreline favored small-scale polities, while the sea facilitated rapid links (at least from spring to autumn). We saw isolated instances of this dynamic already functioning in the second millennium BC, and it developed further in the wake of Alexander the Great. Small-scale settlements, combined with opportunities for contact, led to regional differentiation.[125]

The most widespread religious medium in which these differentiations occurred was the ritual of the vow, in its various textual and material forms. Countless individuals embraced it. Elites in competition among themselves invented other rituals as well, rituals that required far more infrastructure but remained part of an all-embracing culture of religious communication. Contests and enactments (*ludi circenses, gladiatorii*, and *scaenici*), which necessitated the construction of venues, initially improvised, but eventually taking the formal, often monumentalized shape of theaters and amphitheaters,[126] became popular from Africa to Britannia (fig. 55).[127] In only a few cities, notably in the Syrian region, did the elites reject this form of religion.[128] Further architectural signs, such as temple construction and the

55. Amphitheatre at Thysdrus (El-Djem), Tunisia, third century BC. Photo: Institute for the Study of the Ancient World (Graham Clayton) (CC-BY-SA 2.0).

anthropomorphic statue, were now taken up in regions they had not hitherto reached, despite intensive contacts since the middle of the first millennium BC. Even old and complex religious traditions adopted new elements. What appeared at first sight to visitors from the center of the Mediterranean world to be classically Greco-Roman structures in central Syria proved upon closer examination suggestive of unfamiliar rituals, and perhaps alien theological concepts. In Etruscan-Roman temples, the roof was designed as protection against rain and as a support for the display of figures of gods. In both Syria and Egypt it formed an important platform for cult activities.[129] The Gallic circumambulatory temple, a closed space with a four-sided colonnade, was an innovation of the Roman period.[130]

In the field of gods' names, too, the acceptance of the new and the adoption of new media were not without consequences. When it came to the question of how to address the gods, public literacy enabled a precision that the vagueness and variability of an oral approach could not easily achieve. Anyone wishing to write had to name the elusive deity.[131] Whoever wished to do this in Latin, employing the Mediterranean technique of the dedicatory inscription, had to pursue that naming process using a strategy of differentiation and identification, in an intercultural context of two if not more cultural, linguistic, and religious traditions. Outcomes varied. Many Aramaic-speaking Jews in the Syrian region rejected these Greco-Roman practices.[132] Many in northwest Spain now put into written form the addresses to deities they had already been in the habit of using, so producing, within the regional idioverse, an enormous number of gods who were seldom to be addressed again, not even for a second time.[133] More frequently, the creators of these nomenclatures, having an eye to various conventions, produced outlandish name-image combinations, as well as names that added locally generated adjectives or cognomens to Roman gods' names, so creating new local possibilities of religious action. Such a "translation" (*interpretatio*) did not merely presuppose reflections as to the very recognisability of gods;[134] it also demanded a mastery of the media and of the various rules governing formulation and invention, and this in a context characterized not only by cultural difference, but also by asymmetric power relationships.[135] It was possible, too, to balk at translation, as Caesar emphasizes in his attempt to describe the religions of both his *Germani* and his *Galli*;[136] or, as in the case of the "Indian Dionysus," to fall very wide of the mark.[137] And naming strategies might reach their limits when the usual medial practices for visual depiction of an entity were absent.[138] Not everything adhered to the model of "the gods."

X

Experts and Providers

THE FIRST TO THIRD CENTURIES AD

1. Religious Authority

In the chapter just ended we saw the importance of religious competence in the context of *interpretatio Romana*. One thing is quite clear, and that is that religious competency was unevenly distributed. Everyone, of course, was allowed a certain degree of it. All might perform the religious act that was fundamental to ancient Mediterranean culture: all might pray.[1] This applied both in the home and in public. It applied if actors reinforced their prayer not only by the pitch at which they set it, but also by the use of devices, by their choice of time and place, by gifts to a deity whose presence was contingent upon an invocation. It applied if they subsequently spoke about their prayer, or, having performed it, lastingly documented it by means of a wooden tablet, some other kind of textual record, or an inscribed or anepigraphic stone altar. Enhanced agency accrued to the human actor precisely because religious communication was considered to entail a gain in authority: this is the person who brought the god (or dead person or demon) on stage as a personal ally, with all his or her own potential agency. But the opposite might be the case if that person then knowingly renounced a mode of action imposed on him or her by society, refused to go to war, to marry or assume an office, to eat some normally accepted foodstuff: in sum no longer wished to be a good daughter or son, a good subject.

That religious action was used, and surprisingly often, to give authority to acts of resistance does not mean that it was not also used to reinforce existing social or political authority. The *pater familias* or householder often presided at important acts of ritualized religious communication in the home, as did patrons of both sexes before their clients. Landowners brought their dependents, leaseholders, and neighbors together for rituals that served to demonstrate their religious initiative and economic superiority, at least this time: to correct the asymmetry, neighbors with the necessary means were of course free to issue return invitations to the same kind of event.[2] The option was regularly used by political actors, and it was accordingly laden with prestige.[3] It is precisely the "footprint" that it left, in the form of literary mentions, stone reliefs, and monumental inscriptions that, down to the most recent past, has cast ancient religion as "state religion" or "civic religion."

On May 17, AD 81, the Arval brethren met in the house of their chief (*magister*) Gaius Iunius Mefitanus, in order to begin the *sacrificium*. They noted in their protocols that freeborn children of senators, sons "with fathers and mothers," carried incense and wine to the altar in libation bowls while the priests banqueted. The latter met three days later at the sanctuary of Dea Dia, their headquarters, and sacrificed two pigs in propitiation of the goddess, and two cows. They dined, sacrificed a plump lamb, returned to the table, and then initiated games with four-horsed chariots and mounted acrobats. On the following day, May 20, the "sacrifice" was concluded in the house of the *magister*, and the children now brought grain to the altar. The priests met again on September 14, this time on the Capitol to sacrifice for the *imperium*, the dominion of Domitian: to Jupiter Optimus Maximus they offered a male ox, to Juno Regina a cow, to Minerva a cow, to both Salus and Felicitas a cow, and to Mars a bull. Unfortunately, only the deputy chair, the *promagister* Lucius Pompeius Vopiscus Gaius Arruntius Catellius Celer, could be present (such names arose when one took pride in both one's father's and one's mother's lineage).[4]

The pattern was not new. In their internal cult practice, the priesthoods consistently sacrificed a cow, a female animal of such a size being imperative for a goddess one had no wish to offend; but priests dined on pork or a "plump lamb." For those active in mid-city temples, on the other hand, oxen of either sex (consistent with the sex of the invoked deity) were standard: here there was no question of a meal. By a blood sacrifice with no food-related purpose, the priest underlined the ritual character of his action and the religious authority of his person. The choice of a large sacrificial animal evidently suggested itself to the social and political elite as a strategy for indicating a high level of religious authority, such as would suggest economic means and the capacity to deal with the practical problems of slaughtering the largest routinely available domesticated animal. Oxen were emblematic of this strategy. Even those who could not rise to the slaughter of a bull operated by the same yardstick, for instance in representations.

Many ritual roles were required for these complex performances, and other even more complex rituals. Not only senators' sons, heralds, and slaves were involved. There were also the *popae*, who performed the actual slaughter, and the ladle bearers, the *simpulatrices*; the latter perhaps exclusively women, while the former are attested to have included women.[5] Complexity was also dictated in respect of the implements required. The jurist Antistius Labeo, a contemporary of Augustus, needed four lines just to list the various materials required for a sacrificial knife.[6]

Political authorities displayed their religious power by installing in plain sight in public sanctuaries a quantity of floor-rings for the slaughtering of oxen. They extended the life of the same message beyond the event with reliefs depicting subordinate personnel—slaves and lower-ranking priests[7]—engaged in the elaborate preparatory phases up to and including the act of slaughter itself. Of more critical import, though, was attracting onlookers to observe them as the principals in such rituals. Augustus took pains to establish a connection between himself and such representations—of how the powerful, the magistrates, communicated with the gods through sacrifice—and thereby to acquire, in addition to his many other roles, that of the state's premier celebrant of sacrifices, a role he publicized through images in different media, and in particular on coinage.[8]

Besting the Augusti in a contest at this level might be impossible, but the effectiveness of an effort depended above all on presence. The feeding of whole towns by local patrons was not the kind of act that would be outdone by an image on a coin, and no conflict of loyalty was entailed in organizing such a project, if it was done in the emperor's name. Anyone who was not content with performing a single benefaction of this sort could fall back on the time-honored strategy of investing in religious infrastructure, in constructing buildings as locations for particular kinds of religious experience and communication. This too was often performed by women.[9]

A fundamentally different riposte to power gained in terms of religious capital by lavish acts of sacrifice was to relocate the question of religious authority to a different level. For centuries, those who termed themselves "philosophers"[10] had shifted the focus to the *meaning* of the activity itself, the question being not whether a sacrifice could be afforded, but whether it was an activity capable of being explained. There was reason enough for speculation, interpretation, and reinterpretation: by their very actions, actors in the field of religion seemed to maintain that they were pleasing invisible gods by the killing of animals, and feeding them by the act of incineration. It was again Lucian, in the second century AD, who succeeded in summing up centuries of critiques and attempts at interpretation in his satire *On Sacrifices*.

Lucian's critique was extreme. It relied on the great number of those who did not polemicize against sacrifice, as the Cynics did, but sought instead constantly to reinterpret it, even when they themselves did not practice it. Even those who had lost their central (if not sole) place of sacrifice with the destruction of the Temple in Jerusalem normally argued along this line.[11] To speak out against sacrifice signified direct criticism of the establishment, the Augusti. In an apology *Legatio pro Christianis*, at least formally addressed to Marcus Aurelius and Commodus in AD 177, Athenagoras as a follower of Christ proposed the notion of "bloodless sacrifice," taking up an idea that Plutarch about a hundred years earlier had put in the mouth of Numa, the purportedly peaceful founder of Roman religion.[12] In many parts of the Roman Empire after the third century AD, animal sacrifice in images was replaced by bloodless sacrifice.[13] This had nothing to do with the prevention of cruelty to animals. Staged animal hunts (*venationes*), a celebration of slaughter that included exotic animals, were not forbidden in Rome until 523, and the practice continued for the whole of that century in the East.[14] But acquiring or maintaining authority in the context of religious communication by means of actual or metaphorical slaughter persisted in forms that continued to evolve.

2. Experts Male and Female

Sacrifice was no panacea. It was primarily seen as reinforcing oral communication, prayer. Even then, quantity was only one among many parameters, and did not in itself suffice in order to establish the correct communication strategy. It was no less complicated to communicate with the gods than with people, but in the former case a systematic rhetorical theory was lacking. Attempts, not only by individuals but by entire groups, to change actual behavior and not merely to reinterpret it by means of new theories of religious communication are not seen until the third century AD. Such attempts were legislated by the "masters" (*rabbanim*), the "overseers" (*episkopoi*), and the Augusti (interpreted as "increasers of empire") as norms to be followed, although the degree of obedience they could command was another question.[15] Intellectual monitors were no more successful than those who invented elaborately patterned practices for "public"[16] rituals, unless they managed to translate their positions into criminal law and then also to apply that law. Endeavors in this direction remained ineffectual and isolated until the fourth century AD.

Religious knowledge was by its very nature precarious. It was widely but unevenly distributed. What was known was stored above all in constantly changing practices and narratives, as well as in conventions having to do with space and time, finding expression in the architecture of particular places and in calendars, but varying greatly from house to house and from town to town. Activities undertaken during the Hellenistic and late Republican periods, and not only by the elites, had altered the conditions of religious communication. Imperial expansion, aristocratic competition, and migration (both forced and voluntary), had led to an explosion of religious experiences and options. Intellectuals—court poets or retired magistrates, prisoners of war or arrivistes—made religious practices a topic of their discourse, and shaped religion into a form of "knowledge" that posed new challenges for knowledge in its everyday guise.

Routine situations apart, good advice was now expensive; but the assumption that such advice was needed was more widespread than ever. In many places this circumstance created an opportunity for those whom anthropologists describe as "primitive philosophers" or "primitive intellectuals."[17] In situations where social hierarchies offered individuals little hope for betterment—where, alongside a yearning for what was inaccessible, there was dependence on the powerful, and unjust treatment before the law—effective religious communication, while deemed particularly necessary, was hard to achieve. Marginal practices thus came into being, not only in the form of self-help emerging from personal experiment, but also as clandestine strategies in the context of small networks, such as we encountered in the Temple of Mater Magna in Mainz.[18] Such practices, however, were taken further, with new addressees, new uses of language, new character sets (magical letters), new locations that increased the probability of successful communication with deities. A local provider of such resources in Rome—whose name was common currency among the "racing drivers," the charioteers—systematically deposited his offerings in the urns of a collective tomb, a *columbarium*, on the Via Appia.[19] In many other instances, those affected turned to their own creativity and knowledge. The resulting stratagems have survived in many literary texts, but in terms of both content and form they were *prekäres Wissen* (precarious knowledge).[20] In this area, only the specialist Egyptian priests, with their institutional bases in temples and their long-standing but no longer easily comprehensible systems of knowledge, were able to develop regular traditions of expertise.

In other fields, expert knowledge was more openly developed and called upon, but in many ways also more easily grasped (fig. 56). Female experts in expiation, *piatrices*, offered various services, providing, for example (under many labels), substances such as resin or sulfur that could be burned for cleansing purposes.[21] Festus in the second century AD understood as synonymous such descriptors as *saga* (having acute prescience, wise woman), *simulatrix* (capable of producing illusions), and *expiatrix*. This shows how imprecise the boundaries were between the various activities and specializations, whether in practice or only in perception. But it also shows how frequently these services might be used without leaving any further trace. Unlike the ancient observer, who did not hesitate to classify such a woman as a *sacerdos* (priestess), modern analysts have overlooked her.[22] The same applies to those female actors who produced and sold highly

56. Wall painting: an expert in magic offers his services to a traveler, Pompeii, Casa dei Dioscuri VI.9.6–7, first century AD. Naples, Museo Nazionale Archeologico, inv. no. 9106. akg-images / Tristan Lafranchis.

specialized sacrificial cakes. Consistently referred to as "old women," they are mentioned in contemporary accounts but given no particular title. Varro saw them everywhere in the city at the festival of the *Liberalia,* and referred to them as "priestesses of Dionysus."[23] There was a special cake, probably from the same source, for birthdays.[24] The Vestals, of course, had male bakers: gender roles were entirely mutable when it was a matter of emphasizing status.

Ritual competence[25] was also sought when it appeared advisable to fill gaps in one's knowledge of facts relevant to decisions, simply to obtain knowledge of the future, or to seek further confirmation regarding a decision already made.[26] It was possible to procure a wider public by providing such a service, for the demand was presumably very high. Members of the Roman elite, and the authors among them, had already railed against these callings in the first half of the second century BC.[27] Here too, women played a wider role as service providers (figs. 57 and 58); Plautus was aware of *praecantrices* (female cantors or prayer-leaders), *coniectrices* (seers), *hariolae* (soothsayers), and *haruspicae* (readers of entrails).[28] With the exception of the first-named function, men also provided such services. What all these providers lacked was backing by a widely accepted institution, such as a temple or oracle. When they made no claim to having repeated or even enduring direct communication with a deity by means of visions, they often attracted customers by alleging to possess special, often exotic knowledge. As I have already indicated, the groundwork for this new direction in religious practice emerged under the late Republic.[29]

Astrology, the "Chaldean discipline," became popular from the second century BC onward. Backed by the prestige that was accorded anything ancient and Oriental, the discipline was in fact a symbiosis of Greek mathematics and Babylonian astronomic writings, refined by its practitioners on an on-going basis. The spectrum of expertise in this field was broad; at one extreme, astrology was no longer used as a kind of manual for practical divination, but as a model for a philosophical description of the world. Manilius did not write his instructional poem for use by astrological professionals, but with the intent

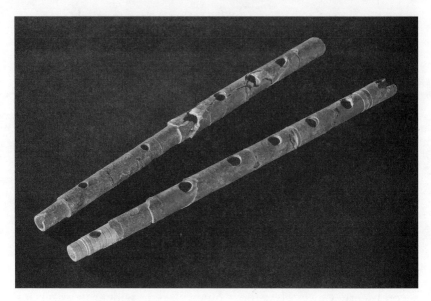

57. Double flute (*aulos*). Bone sheathed in copper, 28.5 cm, second–third century AD.
Photo: Museum August Kestner Hannover, inv. 1976.66, used with the
museum's kind permission.

of making available to philosophy new data and sources, which belonged as much to astronomy as to religion.[30] The Augusti, on the other hand, beginning with Augustus himself, showed a real interest in astrology;[31] but their need for personal advice conflicted with astrology's technical claim to produce results that could be repeated by others, which in principle opened the knowledge obtained to all and sundry. From Augustus into late antiquity, imperial administrations accordingly took pains to prohibit this form of knowledge. Firmicus Maternus in the fourth century even developed the theory that the emperor's life was not subject to the revolutions of the stars.[32]

We encounter the typical astrologer serving the middle tier of society in the fourth of the major practice speeches falsely ascribed to Quintilian. In the account by the fictitious speaker, the astrologer is an honorable person, who must take account of both the positives and negatives in reporting the fate of his clients. Nevertheless, the speaker does not assume that all his listeners share a positive view of astrological prediction; so, in the course of his speech he discusses the

58. Bronze statuette of a woman with a *patera* and perhaps a pyxis containing incense, 11.5 cm, first century A D. Photo: Museum August Kestner Hannover, used with the museum's kind permission.

possibility that everything might depend on chance. In any event, the gist of the case is whether the Senate should allow the client to commit suicide before he kills his father: the first part of a relevant prophecy, that he would be capable in war, having already been fulfilled.[33]

At the other end of the spectrum we see actors operating with simple mechanical procedures, so-called lot oracles. For marginal "experts," handbooks were available, which, as codified stores of presumed knowledge, formed a basis on which to build reputations with their clients. In many instances, the client relationship depended on the astrologer's ability rapidly to analyze the problem and make a diagnosis: for example, from tremors in a particular body part. What documentation there is for the sorts of questions asked at these consultations suggests that they were aimed at low-income clients, such as male and female slaves.[34]

In many instances, contact was not confined to the acquisition of one-off services. If sufficient money and perhaps even space were available, members of the upper classes (not necessarily the political elite) could employ an assortment of specialists. Those available ranged from Greek slaves and immigrants who, from as early as the second century BC, often functioned as domestic tutors, to household poets and philosophers. Polybius, Ennius, and Philodemus fell into these categories. The imparting of knowledge—and this included philosophy—merged with "life coaching." It is easy to imagine the slave Epictetus as just such a "philosopher" in the second century AD before his manumission; that is to say, before he founded his own school, as did Gaius Musonius Rufus, of equestrian stock, in the first century, and Justin, similarly wealthy, also in the second. Whether training took place in the home or the "school," long years of contact were the rule. Religion increasingly became a theme of philosophy, and it was necessarily just one theme among many, as in the case of Epictetus's school.[35] Philosophy and religious authority could scarcely be distinguished one from the other in the pot pourri, so long as both stuck to interpreting accepted texts and to ratiocination, and did not bring personal revelation to the table. But the latter tendency increasingly characterized the field from the second century onward, as is demonstrated by the many later biographical sketches of supposed heretics.[36] Expert knowledge, too, occurred in many forms that enjoyed varying degrees of success, according to circumstance and opportunity. In all cases, people were then enabled to optimize their own experience of religious communication on the basis of the knowledge of others.

3. "Public" Priests and Religious Innovation

What role in this broad spectrum of actors entrusted with specifically religious authority was played by the great Roman priesthoods? What contribution did the upper-class holders of these positions play, besides taking leading roles in great rituals, and advising the Senate? Were the priesthoods a contact point for petitioners or service providers? The Greek senator Lucius Cassius Dio from Bithynia studied biographical documents of the first two centuries AD, which he supplemented with observations from his own experiences in the city of Rome, to produce a quite distinctive picture of the Roman Empire.[37] This he wrote after returning to his birthplace, Nicaea, after his second consulate in 229. By his own account, this undertaking was motivated as much by Severus's praise for his earlier (nonextant) work on dreams and portents, as it was by a command given him in a dream-vision of the divine (tò daimónion).[38] He was accordingly attentive to both dreams and prodigies, exerting thereby a great influence on future Augusti in particular, but also on other actors.

The great priesthoods were in Dio's view primarily a field of imperial activity. This applied above all to the filling of posts, although appointments were almost never controversial. The Augusti themselves took on many priestly roles, in particular that of supreme pontiff; but they hardly ever acted explicitly in this role. The priests themselves enter Dio's narrative when they have to assume the management of new games, often operating within a collaboration between different priesthoods. This applied in the Augustan Age to the Actaean Games and to the common procession around Augustus's pyre.[39] But deifications produced new offices, beginning with the *sodales Augustales*

after the death of Augustus, with Livia as *flaminica*.[40] There appears to
have been no lack of candidates. By contrast, it was difficult to find
sufficient qualified *virgines Vestales*; Dio found it entirely worthy of
mention when, in AD 5, even the daughters of freedwomen are admitted.[41] Regarding priests, he notes changes as no more than a question
of personnel, scarcely differing in impact from the introduction of
new festivals and the removal of the old as the dynasties succeeded
one another.[42]

Were these priesthoods service providers, part of a religious infrastructure such as Cicero had pictured, that enabled private persons
either to continue with ancient cults or to introduce new ones?[43] Their
deliberations took place in private villas, as did their meals. The size
of these gatherings was modest, twelve or fifteen as standard, with
often a few supernumeraries added. The great pontifical college, with
the pontiffs, minor pontiffs, *flamines*, and Vestals, comprised more
than thirty individuals, of whom often only a few were able to attend.
Neither on these occasions nor when performing their rituals were
they available for consultation by the populace. One at least knew
where the Vestals were to be found (as was otherwise true only of
the *pontifex maximus*, who could be located in his palace on the Palatine). All the rest, in their standard *toga praetexta*, could not even be
recognized by their dress.[44] Legal advice had long been sought elsewhere; only questions of burial continued to be regarded as a responsibility of the pontiffs, if they were indeed ever asked. In the only attested instance, in AD 155, a personal acquaintance of a pontiff turned
first to the emperor.[45]

Anyone with religious concerns who sought proximity to the great
priesthoods was able to make contact by other routes, at least in the
case of the Vestals, who had already had personal lictors in the Republican Age. Under the Empire they also possessed "bakers" (*fictores*).
Even these were not of course ordinary people, but often senators. They,
however, were complemented by other personnel, slaves under "public" ownership, and aides (*apparitores*), and going through these offered
other means of access. This was especially true in the case of the "criers"
(*calatores*), normally appointed from among the priests' freedmen.

The *collegium calatorum pontificum et flaminum* had an assembly hall (*schola*) close to the Regia on the Forum Romanum, for which a sponsor, Iulius Anicetus, in 101/2 had a kind of nameplate produced, a list of thirty-six names in the form of a dedication to Trajan.[46] The same person built a portico at Trastevere for Sol the sun god (to whom he had also made dedications elsewhere), noting that he had received the permission of the *calatores*.[47] Whether such permission was at all necessary, or had any legal force, is questionable. It is possible that the man's ability to refer to tangible and at the same time official religious actors might still at this date have been a useful tactic for enlarging the scope of his own agency. The stone and the memory remained. A new dedication was undertaken more than a century later in the same spatial context under Alexander Severus, this time to Iulia Mamaea as *mater Augusti* and *mater castrorum*, and it was likewise marked "with the permission of the *calatores*."[48] The presence of any permanent contingent of relevantly entitled priests (if any such delegation of authority ever existed) is certainly not indicated here.[49]

If an enormous social gulf separated Rome's *sacerdotes publici* from a public outside senatorial ranks, this cannot be extended to apply to circumstances in other locations. In some towns in the provinces of Mysia and Lydia in Asia Minor, male priests stood ready to give intensive consultations to male and female clients in the event of illnesses or family misfortunes, including those of the most serious kind. It must have been by the influence of dedicatory and honorific inscriptions created mostly in cities[50] that these priests developed a specific form of religious communication for their more well-heeled clients. In the process, they steered self-exploration toward self-inculpation, which led to gifts and purification rituals being offered in the appropriate temple, and so brought the problem to an end. Those affected were happy to record this outcome epigraphically on highly visible stelai. Depending on the bargain struck, it appears that priests tended to urge a particular emphasis: how gracious the deity addressed, how successful the procedure. Clients (male and female), on the other hand, found it more important to provide a full list of the services delivered and paid for, and to record the degree of the relief provided and how long it lasted. In many instances, the accounts included family members who were themselves guilty, or shared in the client's guilt, or were innocent, and their descendants.[51]

4. Prophetesses and Visionaries

Cassius Dio, who was as we have seen himself influenced in important decisions by dreams, had understandably overlooked the Asian and rural phenomenon described above. In respect of Rome, he saw religious innovation in the actions of prophets rather than in those of priests. In AD 7, a woman claiming divine possession entered Rome. She had letters scratched into her arm. Augustus saw himself compelled by the general mood to promise games for Mater Magna.[52] At the beginning of AD 38, a slave named Machaon mounted the *pulvinar* of Capitoline Jupiter, proclaimed grim prophecies, killed the dog he had brought with him, and then killed himself.[53] Religious dissent was expressed in later incidents as well. In 217, first an anonymous seer and then a person named Serapio prophesied the end of Caracalla's reign. The oracle of the sun god subsequently foretold the installation of a new ruler.[54]

What Dio found worth recounting in only a few episodes of his political history was at the same time reflected in many other texts. In a tradition already existing in the Hellenistic Age, anonymous or pseudonymous authors in the eastern Mediterranean wrote oracular texts, "Sybilline books," and apocalypses such as 4 Ezra, Enoch, and the Apocalypse of St. John, all of them with a clearly anti-Roman bent, just as their predecessors had had an anti-Hellenistic bent. Their authors were likely members of the former elite, who no longer shared in governing and now therefore branded the regime with the stigma of foreign rule.[55] In order to be rid of unwanted but authoritative texts such as these, Augustus and Tiberius examined and burned thousands of them. But a substantial number were back in circulation by the time of the Great Fire of Rome in 64.[56]

A similarly apocalyptic text "revelatory" of the occult, far less radical but all the more popular, made its advent in Rome shortly before the middle of the second century. It was a substantial text, released in several stages (probably because of continuing demand), and the author—if, that is, we are to believe the first-person narrator (and he set store by being believed)—was the Hermas briefly mentioned above (Ch. 8.4). This Hermas faced the problem shared by every "seer": how to make his message credible as authentic revelation. The problem was all the more acute for an author who was not backed by an institution, such as a shrine of Asclepius or an oracle. And, if his text was destined merely to be read, he even had to forgo the impact of his own persuasive presence as a speaker. It was for this reason that the eponymous John of the Apocalypse, in what was a slightly older text, identified with a probably real name, also supported his claimed authority on prophetic tradition and astrology.[57] Hermas, on the other hand, began on a more aggressively autobiographical note, even down to his frailties and details of his living and working environment.[58] He then developed the idea of apocalypse stage by stage on the basis of contemporary reflections concerning the possibility of divination by visions.[59]

This author allows us a rare insight into the problems of visionary communication in the presence of others.[60] In the spirit of contemporary philosophical tracts, Hermas's text is evidently targeted at individual listeners and readers, to whom he offers the possibility of self-development. It was to this end that he initially sought entry to institutional settings, so as to have his text read out as a heavenly missive within a circle of *presbyteroi* and *episkopoi*.[61] He perhaps used another circle to admonish one Maximus, known to his audience.[62] A woman called Grapte was to read the text out to widows and orphans, and a Clement to disseminate it in letter form.[63] That recipients urged the author on to ever new visions, copied his work, and quickly translated it into Latin and the languages of Syria and Egypt demonstrates the success of this reading therapy aimed at individual transformation within the "congregation" (*ekklesia*), and at both spiritual and behavioral change (*metanoia*). Only occasionally does the author allow the reader to see that he is thinking of followers of Christ, who know what a Sybil is, but perceive her as something other.

Other than whom? Hermas assumed that his first hearers and readers were familiar with Roman institutions, such as the military, and with Italic economy and agriculture. Critical, however, was their being "citizens."[64] As was typical for citizens of an empire, Hermas's audience already had what amounted to double citizenship. They were at the very least inhabitants of Rome, and Hermas was now trying to awaken them to a further relationship with a heavenly city, an alternative to the Jerusalem that was definitively lost. Contemporary texts from the eastern Mediterranean urged their readers to foresee Rome's apocalyptic destruction, which they themselves as individuals might bring about by adopting a new lifestyle.[65]

As opposed to the fantasies he spun for his audiences in distant provinces, Hermas had also to address an audience that lived in this very Rome, and beheld with wonder an infrastructure recast in flawless marble by the Flavians.[66] So, in the images he uses, he relies not on that other city, but on an architectural feature that was universally conceivable in perfect or (at least) perfectible form: a tower. He gives his female oracular figure a Roman magisterial throne, and has her accompanied by six youths after the fashion of official attendants.[67] These were not end-time alternatives, but mental images, conceptions to be nurtured in the here and now. There was not even any need for built structures: the concern expressed is for widows and orphans, and for the winning of souls in this earthly city with which the pastoral habitations of his audience's other city coexist.[68] To increasingly individualized addressees, it was vital not to hold out the prospect of a popular uprising. Such individuals might in any event arrive at unusual, deviant decisions: Perpetua was represented at the beginning of the third century as a visionary who used dream images to legitimize a radical departure from familiar social roles, including that of motherhood.[69]

Visionaries were not an exceptional phenomenon (fig. 59). But the sources of their revelations might vary greatly: they could come from a god in the form of a snake, like Glycon; from the one God; from new interpretations of older inspired texts; and, of course, as per the standard accusation, from the repository of the visionary's own imagination, evil nature, and deceitfulness. Lucian, Celsus, and those

59. Gilded silver *patera* from Parabiago, showing the triumph of Mater Magna/Cybele
and Attis, fourth century A D. Milan, Castello Sforzesco, Civiche Raccolte d'Arte
Applicata ed Incisioni. Photo Giovanni Dall'Orto, used by kind permission.
akg-images / De Agostini Picture Lib. / G. Cigolini.

who understood Montanus and his female acolytes as prophets
(naturally, false ones) were in agreement about the frequency of such
phenomena:[70] religious authority, in both textual and personal form,
was apparently easily obtained: perhaps not more easily than before,
but by people from different social milieus. Observers, in any case, were
seeing religious communication more frequently as dissident.

5. Founders of Religion

Religious authority could be won by others besides the visionaries who
were held in such high regard. New forms of personal communication
proposed by a person (or a group) could be attractive, even though

the content offered might not be at all spectacular. Bearers of religious knowledge need not be prophets or deities, but might instead be organizers and founders of religions. Fronto, in his correspondence with Marcus Aurelius, describes the second king Numa as a founder, in terms that go beyond those used in earlier texts that attribute to him the role of institutionalizing religion. For Fronto, Numa is an "originator of ritual meals," the "first to institute sacred banquets," and a "promulgator of laws establishing feast days."[71] Lucian saw Peregrinus in similar terms, although as someone who exploited qualities instilled in Christians by the "first lawgiver" (*nomothetês*).[72]

Nomothetês in this sense of the word describes those founders of new temples who laid down detailed rules prescribing the way future users should configure religious communication within those establishments. Probably in the second or early third century, in Aquae Flaviae, today Panóias in northern Portugal, Gaius Calpurnius Rufinus established a cult with *mystaria* (*sic*), probably fed by his own experiences in his hometown of Perge. He prescribed in detail how and where animals were to be slaughtered and their blood dispersed, what was to be burned and what consumed.[73] Guidelines already suggested to future visitors by the detailed physical features formed in the rock—they included pits, paths, and what may have been walls—were further specified by the founder in various texts that he inscribed in the rock itself.

What in Panóias remained a unique phenomenon, although it had a lasting effect there, led in other instances to ever new foundation events, spurring on ever new generations of founders. Many of these remained unknown, while others were subsequently regarded as philosophers, "Valentinians" perhaps, not as founders of cults.[74]

To look at a further instance, cult practices for the worship of Mithras were disseminated locally in southern Asia Minor, where they underwent changes in the Hellenistic Period. In the final quarter of the first century AD, they were transported out of that region by a person unknown to us, who gave these practices a form distinctly different from the one that persisted in the empire of the Parthians and then the Sassanids.[75]

This unknown individual brought to the fore the image of an action performed by the god's own hand: the killing of a bull by means of a dagger (fig. 60); he thus satisfied the requirement construed as central to the cult's tradition, the sacrifice of a bull. But at the same time he introduced a clearly countervailing circumstance, for the small size of the cult locale ruled out any reenactment of the sacrifice.[76] Instead, sculpted scenes showed Mithras, the divine actor, killing the bull. On a stele-like cult image he is depicted as foreign, in Persian guise. Secondary scenes, centered on the killing of the bull, relate the biography of the god, including prenatal scenes that identify him as superhuman, while scenes of the struggle with the bull illustrate his extraordinary strength, and others showing him with the sun

60. Relief picturing the cosmogonic killing of the bull by Mithras, from Aquileia, third century A D. Vienna, Collection of Antiquities, Kunsthistorisches Museum. akg-images.

god demonstrate his divine affinities. These all refer to narratives explaining and at the same time enhancing the central scene. The initiator of each new Mithraic foundation may have varied and extended these narratives, which were evidently not subject to control by a written text. The same applies to a great many aspects of the cult, from the cult apparatus to the timing of meetings. However, a common meal in the presence of the cult image remained central. Many foundations are distinguished by lateral podiums flanking a central aisle, surfaces where the diners could recline. But individual sanctuaries varied greatly. Spaces were often configured in rented houses, and here, too, founders adapted the basic narratives and images in highly individual ways. A great variety of forms arose even in one and the same location; the port town of Ostia is a good example. Narrative murals alternate with normal decorative themes, sculptural reliefs with three-dimensional images; and Mithras might be worshipped alone or alongside other deities, such as Silvanus.[77]

Members of these little "societies" met in rooms that could accommodate from eighteen to forty-five people. They were recruited largely from the merchant class and high-ranking slaves, who were in a position to meet the membership fees. So far as food was concerned, the standard meats found on the Roman-Italic table were the norm; and this surely applies to the wine also.[78] In the hymn-like acclamation *Nama* (Hail!), on the other hand, the Persian language was preferred. The shared meal was also styled with an eye to the exotic. Some of the vessels bore representations of snakes or other animals, and some were themselves shaped like animals. Those commissioning these objects were clearly concerned that participants in the cult identify with the mythical protagonists, so as to experience the meal more intensively, and to be able to slip into the role of the snake under the dying bull, or of the lion, animals with central roles in the Mithraic narratives, and frequently depicted. The Mithraic group that had a public presence in Tienen (Belgium) in the third century AD went even one step further. They heated the wine, so encouraging the notion that it was the warm, fresh blood of a bull that was being drunk.[79] Different grades could be attained in the cult hierarchy, and these guided and controlled the experiences of initiates: the "lion" (*leo*) represented the most important rank below the group leader. The founder of the Imperial Roman form of the Mithraic cult transfigured public forms of sacrifice so thoroughly as to completely replace the usual functional ritual titles with mythic references (fig. 61). Mosaic representations in the Mithraeum of Felicissimus at Ostia suggest that the "raven" (*corax*) as cup-bearer was responsible for serving drinks, the young *nymphus* for lighting, while the "soldier" (*miles*) acted as slaughterer.[80] Even though the hindquarter of a bull is depicted, here too the setting excludes the possibility of a literal blood sacrifice. But it seems that the participants construed even their meals of piglet and chicken as the consumption of beef.[81]

In any event, shared activity permitted the cultivation of individual distinction as an imitator of the heroic Mithras, and thus enabled a distinct form of male persona to coexist alongside a Roman civic identity. Mithraic narratives could also be memorized and related outside the bounds of the cult locale and thus of the group. In this wider context too, those same narratives could further activate the sense of belonging to a particular group, of possessing a collective identity shared by only a few. Despite the terminology of different ranks, hierarchization remained slight. The central figure was the *pater*, the "father," who was also the founder, and remained as leader. Renting or constructing spaces, organizing banquets, and occasionally involving the local population, required consistent engagement, not least financially. Levies may have provided a means of refinancing.

An interest in intense, physical experiences of the kind that might be interpreted as religious did not have to involve the formation of stable groups, of the sort described for the Mithras cult, which was established at about 150 locations very unevenly distributed through the Roman Empire.[82] The concept of "mysteries" increasingly signified such intense experiences, sometimes part of a process lasting several days, but also often one-off events, although usually of a kind that could be repeated and perhaps intensified over time. This may have involved acceptance or "initiation" into a virtual community, but not necessarily.[83] More important was a geographical link with an already prestigious cult locale where there was an established infrastructure

61. Relief from the Mithraeum at Dieburg, depicting Mithras as hunting and
carrying a bull, surrounded by other scenes. Dedicated by the shoemaker
Silvestrius Perpetuus, his brother the sculptor Silverstrius Silvnius, and his
grandchild Silvinius Aurelius. Sandstone, late second century AD. Copy
in the RGZM. Photo: J. Rüpke, reproduced with kind permission of the RGZM.

that, while defined architecturally, was above all perceived in terms of
organization and personnel.[84] At Andania (near Messene in the Peloponnese), the complex organizational structure of the cult is recorded
in a substantial inscription dating perhaps from the end of the first
century BC: in order to be attractive, mysteries required predictable
structures even more than secrecy.[85] The highly prestigious and

structured sanctuary of Artemis at Ephesus was enhanced by the addition of mysteries during the Imperial Age.[86] And it was by means of images and narratives that the cult was disseminated.[87]

Apart from local participants, however, mysteries remained the preserve of those few who could afford an expensive journey. All the more important, therefore, were the stories told by people who had undertaken such long and complicated journeys for the sake of religious experience. An example from the first or second century AD is the story of Thessalus, who had traveled to Egypt to acquire religious knowledge.[88] That what he eventually acquired was an advanced knowledge of herbs probably left ancient readers unfazed, for this was precisely the kind of knowledge most people deemed effective. And they were aware too of the limits of its effectiveness when recourse was had solely to local "wise women." Moreover, Egyptian priests knew how to use literary media to advertise the advantages of their unique knowledge, which would, they insisted, fully repay the journey involved: Chaeremon wrote such an "Egyptian History" in the first century AD.[89]

Differ though they might from one another, the examples we have given demonstrate forms of personal interaction, with supply and demand as factors determining success. On the one hand were human beings who had or had imported new ideas regarding the divine, and had institutionalized those ideas in the form of new practices; on the other, human beings who had enjoyed particular experiences of religious communication and wanted to repeat them reliably.

6. Changes

Already in the mid-first century BC, Cicero in his work *On the laws* had attempted to give public priests (literally "public rite-givers," *sacerdotes publici*) influence over the direction of religious innovation.[90] They never, in the three centuries following, achieved this. Although there had still been systematizers and authors of religion-related texts among the priests of the late Republic,[91] in the following centuries, apart from appearances in public rituals, it was at most subordinate members of the college who entered into direct contact with individual religious actors.

The decisive factors here may have been twofold. Acts of religious communication by "public priests" were concentrated more and more around the Augusti, whether in actual collaboration with them or by addressing or at least mentioning them. At the same time, candidates recommended for recruitment as priests by the reigning Augustus, or emerging from his own network, were part of the class that increasingly set itself apart socially and economically and in its self-representation, whether in terms of palaces or tombs. The Augusti themselves employed religious signs in both political argumentation and ceremonial contexts from the late third century onward. Individual priests and entire colleges accordingly acquired a stronger religious orientation, which led them to act as a religious group and to see themselves as religious actors. The pontiffs ended their dependence on the emperor as *pontifex maximus* in about AD 380.[92]

Mediterranean urbanization, considerably increased by the expansion of the Roman Empire into North Africa and northwestern and southwestern Europe, and by city foundations in the Danube region, was also among the many relevant factors. At an ever-increasing number of locations, people opted for communal life in a concentrated space, with all its disadvantages, in order to enjoy the opportunities, both active and passive, offered by this congested lifestyle. During the course of the Imperial Age in these urban societies in the Latin-speaking world, themselves highly specialized, but still oriented to an agricultural hinterland, "intellectuals" articulated something that already had a long history in the East: a critique of cult activity, and above all of sacrifice. In so doing, they at the same time criticized those traditional landowning elites who had at their disposal the resources necessary for grand sacrificial rituals, especially cattle. Often the authors of these critiques themselves stemmed from such milieus or operated under the protection of such families, and thus in committing their objections to writing they gave expression to personal claims to authority.[93] They turned religion into a field of learning, set religious communication free from particular sites and appointed times, and, above all, no longer insisted that it take the form of rituals. Although the Mediterranean alphabetic scripts were in principle easy to learn, the broad influence of such texts remained dependent on their being read aloud or explicated in the presence of audiences. This of course had an economic implication: the activities of those we are here calling "intellectuals" cost little in comparison with the expensive modes of religious communication employed by the older elites. The same applied to inexpensive traditional practices: taking into account a reader's living expenses and the cost of handwritten copies, having a text read aloud, while not in itself cheaper than depositing mass-produced gifts, required no comparable architectural infrastructure.

As religion took the form of knowledge, there was growing fascination with the specialized knowledge developed by or attributed to writers from ancient Oriental cultures. This was the same process as we have already observed in fifth- and fourth-century Greece, third-century Alexandria, and in the second century BC in Rome. It coincided with heightened interest in translations, and in questions of whether local cultural practices and regional bodies of knowledge might contain wisdom of a universal nature. The changes in the political and cultural landscape brought about by the formation of the Roman Empire reinforced questions of this ilk that challenged the religious practices of the old elites.[94] Priests who belonged to those elites and had an interest in intellectual issues came under the influence of philosophers of religion.[95] Where ritual lacked sophisticated interpretation, it took on an insipid cast, even as it continued to be an inexhaustible and thus valuable catalyst for intellectual speculation.[96] Conversely, actors specializing in word and song in late-antique synagogues, as for example at Sepphoris, were able to acquire authority by explicating sacrifice via iconographic or textual reference to practices at a Temple in Jerusalem that no longer existed (fig. 62).[97]

It was not only the great authors of the literary canon, or even just those whose names are known to us, who engaged in speculations of this sort. Much more numerous were the "primitive intellectuals," whose deliberations found expression in the design of gardens and the arrangement of domestic interiors, or in curse tablets. Many did

62. Wall painting from the western wall of the synagogue at Dura Europos (Salihiye, Syria), showing Aaron performing temple cult. New building of AD 244/45 with a frieze illustrating the Tenakh. The frescoes have been transferred to the National Museum, Aleppo. akg-images / Gerard Degeorge.

not advance beyond such strategies; and, even if they did, their contemporaries lost all interest in these "thinkers" once death had silenced them. Here, the ability to preserve one's thoughts in writing constituted the decisive difference.

But these trends did not affect only those people who moved to the nearest city; although this was probably the most common scenario, especially when the move ended in one of the few ancient megacities. Some traveled great distances, either voluntarily or as prisoners of war and then slaves. The effects of travel were compounded by increasing social mobility and separation from society back home, with its established social roles and lived lives, and sometimes also by more dramatic events, such as enslavement and manumission. The latter process by no means necessarily freed slaves from dependency, but at the age of about thirty gave them a radically new status and new perspectives. A long-term consequence was individualization,[98] which in many ways left its mark on religion and was itself considerably marked by religion.[99] Life in congested, culturally diverse urban conditions, and within the most significant vectors of immigration (for instance the army) created new propinquities, encounters with new hierarchies, different values, and unfamiliar languages. Monetization, and the spread of money as a universal means of exchange, opened further options while reinforcing differences.[100] New opportunities were on offer, and personal preferences could develop in matters such as choice of community, or participation in a particular cult of the dead. Self-reflection became more common, and alongside it greater openness to sensual experiences.

Heroic journeys away from rural marginality or slave status might give those affected a taste and desire for recognition. Such a member of the old elites as Petronius might accordingly in his *Satyricon* ridicule the freedman Trimalchio. But such careers as Trimalchio's remained models for many, even if the prospects envisaged might frequently enough prove unrealistic. High expectations might also easily tip over into a sense of self-empowerment, confidence that anything was possible. A visionary like Hermas might not delay in having his first book of visions copied for the export market.[101]

Offering support to others in their assays at religious communication opened up another field of economic activity. This began as early as the fifth century BC in the case of artisans, who produced enormous quantities of dedicatory offerings for consumption at cult locales. From the Hellenistic Age onward, increasing numbers of religious service providers offered divination, healing, knowledge of the divine will, extraordinary religious experiences, and general religious knowledge: all for a price. These small-scale religious entrepreneurs operated mostly in the milieu of freed persons, but also among women and slaves whose opportunities for agency were not, in this area, subject to much constraint. They were perhaps the most innovative element in the religious history of the Imperial Age. They would normally tend to carry out their activities in a rather ad hoc manner, unless they managed somehow to find a way to turn the extreme disparities of wealth to their own advantage, and win clients or patrons from among the well-to-do. That such an entrepreneur might see his work as a full-time "mission" is unlikely given the circumstances. The intellectual and tent-maker Paul (of Tarsus?), whose journeyings are described in the second-century Acts of the Apostles as primarily driven by just such a sense of mission, was probably above all motivated by the continual need to find new customers for his no doubt high-quality products;[102] until, that is, he found himself able to make a living as a philosopher and visionary.

Such religious entrepreneurs were successful when their explanatory models found confirmation in the context of their clients' precarious lifestyles; so long, that is, as those interpretations could be remembered amid the constant vicissitudes ordinary people suffered in terms of food, health, familial circumstances, or even legal status. Owing to clients' deficient social status, the likelihood of any negative feedback reaching outsiders was low, but there may also have been a few positive results that confirmed the efficacy of the techniques employed and of the agents employing them.[103] Dissatisfaction, though, tended to be articulated in political terms, leading to the banishment of entire professional groups.

But why should even those local people who had adequate financial means, who were potential patrons, have retained an interest in supporting both the religious communication of their fellows and the experts who provided the religious services we have mentioned? Perhaps, with the establishment of the Roman Empire and its essentially centralized monarchy, the situation of such relatively privileged groups, and many local elites, had fundamentally changed.[104] On the one hand, they were invited to participate in an at least approximately coordinated administration, in the formation of a single market (although many local taxes remained), and in the pooling of military power (or, more precisely, the centralization of military command). In this sense, they played a vital part in facilitating a central administration whose representation on the ground was extremely sparse,[105] and they thus gained in prestige and agency. This was surely an important reason for their intensive participation in the religious practices that accorded divine honors to the Augusti.[106] The ambition of all concerned to have a presence in a locality through such means as inscriptions remained powerful into the Severan Age.[107]

In time, however, especially in those very cities that were of more recent foundation, it became clear that local elites had lost their monopoly of power. People more often addressed their appeals to provincial governors and to the Augusti, who were now known even in the most remote areas through such media as coins, statues, architecture, and other instances of their munificence. This "mediatization" of what was up to that time the most important level of collective political identities had consequences that became ever clearer as time went on, especially in the third and fourth centuries A D. First, the remarkable, vital, but at the same time so distant construct "empire," tangible only in the persons of the Augusti, was not perceived as a replacement for the degraded middle level of urban political identities.[108]

This appears to have given new impetus to religious practices already long established as forms of public communication. Religion related to the world as a whole and embraced the Empire, but it was rooted in individual experience. Members of the well-to-do classes accordingly found it attractive to form networks and groups through religious communication, rather than continuing to invest in the *sacra publica* of the city.[109] Jewish patrons in the third century concentrated their support on such projects as the construction of synagogues.[110] Slaves might even be manumitted for the benefit of synagogues.[111] The development of religious networks was perhaps more pronounced in the Greek East, with its tradition of multiple regional identities, than in the Latin West.[112] The rhetoric of individual ethnic identity could be heard coming from all sides,[113] but it failed to shake the political dominance of the imperium; this despite the fact that it was the vocabulary of the family and the polity, especially the semantics of ethnic identity, citizenship, and civil law, *civitas*, that furnished the most important metaphors for imagining collective identities that might extend familial contexts. It would, however, be long years before a government from heaven, "of God's grace," such as that of Justinian in the sixth century, could be contemplated.

Those offering new religious practices or bodies of knowledge were moved by an orientation that reached beyond the bounds of their home city to anchor their offerings too, symbolically, beyond that local context. The validity of "Chaldean" knowledge or "Persian" dress did not have to be proven; both, however, were assumed by the same itinerant actors who exploited familiarity with earlier religious systems, and they were helped thereby to manufacture familiarity with their offerings, with the aid of iconographic programs and pattern books, and texts, although the latter did not circulate widely until later on, and then more rarely.[114] We thus have, on the one hand, countless individual invocations of the divine under the names and iconographic signs of Mithras, Silvanus, and Isis. On the other hand, generic forms of religious communication directed at the same addressees were also very popular. Here, opportunities appear to have existed above all for individual actors possessing expertise.

In sum, it is possible to establish that, while competence in the area of religious communication could be gained by and was freely vouchsafed to all comers, there was, below the level of the political elite, a growing number of providers who laid claim to religious authority in one way or another. Their mere presence on the scene, their trading in practice-based knowledge, and also their resourcefulness and competitive zeal, affected and indeed altered what was increasingly understood as an entity specific in itself, namely "religion," which might occur at the level of the Roman Empire or in local sanctuaries, by the agency of old women living locally, or through the medium of wandering prophets. Common to all of these was the claim that they could establish contact with the divine, with those not indubitably plausible addressees, in a way that promised answers to the inquirer, salvation to the hopeful, and healing to the sick.

XI

Notional and Real Communities

THE FIRST TO THIRD CENTURIES AD

SINCE THE HELLENISTIC AGE, it had become increasingly common for people living in the cities of the Mediterranean to join together in societies; during the first two centuries of the Roman Empire, this trend further intensified and expanded beyond the Hellenistic cultural space. Individuals combined together most readily when they shared professional interests, whether as artisans in a particular trade in their home city, or as merchants of common origin in far-flung places. So the "clubs" of the elite, which had often been organized in the form of priesthoods, were now paralleled by *thiasoi* and *collegia* that met occasionally for festive meals, and often guaranteed their members a suitable burial on the basis of subscriptions. The expansion of the artisanal and mercantile trades, which underpinned economic growth, also increased social differentiation, and those who benefitted from higher status, once their gains were secured, might aspire to preserve that new status beyond the grave.[1]

Those who organized themselves in this way were not members of minorities. In Pompeii, about a quarter of the adult population, mainly but not exclusively male, may have been organized in *collegia* with memberships of between fifteen and two hundred.[2] These were private groups only in appearance. They were able to acquire special legal status, and, from the time of Marcus Aurelius at the latest, were registered. As organizations of members employed in the same trade, they undertook to safeguard their own interests along the same lines as medieval guilds.[3] When such interests were at stake, formal distinctions of status between free individuals, freed men and women, and even slaves, might be secondary. To members, it was likely more important to have a presence in a city's public space, and to be recognized by virtue of their group status. This might be achieved by holding a festive banquet in public, such as was organized in the early 130s in Lavinium near Rome by the *collegium* of the worshippers (*cultores*) of Diana and the only recently deified Antinous.[4] To the same end, groups cultivated associations with the emperor or with important local cults.

As an alternative to renting public space, such as the dining halls attached to temples,[5] some groups built and maintained their own buildings, which provided them with constant visibility.[6] As, however, they normally met only a few times in the year, at most monthly, such an undertaking was more a bid for prestige than a practical necessity. A frequent precondition was, of course, an enormous degree of engagement on the part of patrons. All in all, *collegia* were intermediary organizations that strengthened local integration into the third century AD.[7] Members of such associations played a special role in the installation of inscriptions and the implementation of building projects in public spaces. Here too, however, the processes described at the end of the last chapter left their mark from the third century onward.[8]

Slaves in large households might also organize themselves in groups resembling societies. As, however, under imperial law, it was possible to belong only to a *collegium* that was registered, many such groups were more loosely configured.[9] Moreover, religious assemblies were not a central concern of the legislation on associations.[10] To many people, familial, trade-based, and ethnic groups were in any case more important, as has been established, for example, in the case of Jews in Rome.[11] It was thus possible to maintain several specifically religious collective identities at the same time. But how did such groupings come about in the first place?

1. Textual Communities

An initial question: what role did reading and writing play in religious groups?[12] It is in the second and third centuries A D that we find authors of numerous texts formulating polemics that appear to delineate boundaries between groups, and thus to prepare the ground for group formation. There was evidently competition between groups that found expression in claims of exclusivity. On the one hand, rigid positions adopted in a bid for members do not necessarily indicate a background of sustained conflict with other groups.[13] On the other hand, too much competition was regarded as problematic, as Philostratus makes clear in the picture he paints of the biographies of various "sophists."[14] But did these texts belong to such "societies" as we are discussing here?

Some of the texts became foundational, at least in the context of the religious and intellectual history of Europe, and to some extent they continue to color our perceptions of the religious "other" to the present day. This applies not only to the New Testament canon, but also to heresiological works. As a second-order observation, such a work as Irenaeus's *Adversus haereses: Élenchos kaì anatropé tês pseudônúmou gnóseôs* (Examination and rebuttal of gnosis falsely so called), in its Latin translation, was a source of religious-historical classifications into the Early Modern Period. Notions that these authors were writing for "their" group and sharing its "spirit," and that such groups exerted a defining influence on their texts, have seduced commentators into accepting the self-serving claims and individual agendas of such texts[15] without further critique.[16] But writing social history was not at all what the heresiographical authors had in mind. It was often sheer rivalry and an uncomfortable convergence of opinion that led them to manufacture the profound disagreements described in these texts.[17] Such processes of systematic rhetorical exclusion often had social consequences. This was the case with the entourage of the visionary Montanus in Asia Minor in the second century A D, characterized by the label "Montanist" and then treated accordingly in terms of exclusions and polemics.[18] The formation of a community based on a common text was, however, no simple process. It rested on long-term reading in common, and the formation of common modes of interpretation shaped by that reading.[19] It began with the basic elements, texts themselves in their material form, and their mediation within a communicative process.

In the scriptographic cultures of antiquity, where the only means of duplication was copying by hand, each book was a unique entity. There is no doubt that there was commercial production and distribution of books from the early Imperial Age onward, relying on dictation to a number of slaves writing simultaneously, and that there was a book trade. The percentage of texts disseminated in this way may, however, have been negligible, perhaps confined to a few fashionable authors.[20] More vital was dissemination by means of dedications, and subsequently by the dedicatees themselves, and within circles of acquaintanceship,[21] potentially making available the entire libraries of participants in such circles. If the persons involved did not live in close proximity to one another, they may well have overcome distances by means of written inquiries.[22] They would without question have been members of the elite, for they had not only to bear the cost of manuscript rolls and transportation, but needed also to be capable of coping with *scriptio continua* (the writing style in which word follows on word without any space in between). As it took years of experience to read even the simplest of texts, those who had access only to an elementary education, barely adequate for reading the clearly grouped characters and succinct formulas of inscriptions, were excluded.[23]

By the very nature of the architectural infrastructure involved by way of theaters, dramatic productions—whether pantomimes or enactments of myths from the Isis cycle—targeted a "mass public." This was also true of declamations. Readings, on the other hand, took place in smaller, frequently private spaces, where on occasion anonymous listeners might be addressed.[24] Far more often, though, the audience consisted of personal invitees, a community of readers who met a high threshold of eligibility for participation, as they had to be sufficiently sophisticated to take part in recitations and the ensuing critiques.[25] As with the theater, admittance was in the purview of the organizer or patron. Juvenal portrays such a by-invitation-only occasion in the home of a self-styled star poet, not omitting to note the careful orchestration of the public and the applause.[26] It is unlikely that the situation was different for readings of visionary texts. Anyone invited to such a recitation may well have had the sensation of participating in the sort of event that was quite normal in elite circles.

The written word enabled communication with audiences who were not present. The correspondence of the younger Pliny at the beginning of the second century AD is a case in point, and, in compilation and publication, an example of an aristocratic network deliberately maintained by letter.[27] Parallels may be seen in Cicero's posthumously published letters of the first century BC to his friend Atticus, to his brother, to other relations, and to both political friends and opponents, and in the letters of Paulinus of Nola and Symmachus at the turn of the fourth century AD. Outside the growing imperial administration, there was often little separation between the administrative sphere and personal correspondence, and even there, personal and official correspondence was not always clearly differentiated.

Any collector, publisher, or mere writer of letters would not be interested purely in personal recipients. He would more likely be aiming at an anonymous public, or at delivery aloud to a particular circle of recipients. In the early second century AD, the so-called second and third *Epistles of John* point to the problems involved in controlling the recitation space, perhaps by forbidding visitors to read aloud. While the second epistle portrays the good group, which effectively communicates its faith, the third, formally addressed to only a single member, Gaius, describes the bad group:

> I have written something to the church, but Diotrephes, who likes to put himself first, does not acknowledge our authority.
> So if I come, I will bring up what he is doing, talking wicked nonsense against us. And not content with that, he refuses to

welcome the brothers, and also stops those who want to and puts them out of the church.[28]

Finally there were intellectual contests, debates between professionals who lived by public polemic. Antagonists both male and female[29] confronted one another in Rome, Athens, Antioch, and Alexandria, the Empire's chief intellectual centers,[30] and the subjects of their debates included religious knowledge as a sub-section of philosophical discourse. Rhodon, a pupil of Tatian, illustrates this when, in works subsequently cited by Eusebius, he gives an exhaustive account of a discussion with Apelles.[31] Galen compared the arguments of Moses and Plato as if they were known to all present.[32] The new texts that recorded these intense debates were perhaps a pot pourri of earlier materials.

Listeners remembered what they had read, and writers what they had heard (fig. 63). Written texts and oral presentations influenced one another. Publilius Syrus's collection of aphorisms of the first century AD relied on his vivid memory of his success as a mime in the second half of the first century BC. At about this same period, Cornutus's interpretations of myths and allegories similarly functioned only when viewed against a background of narratives that were common knowledge, remembered and reactualized in a mutually dependent relationship with the images concerned. Textual communities did not arise in a vacuum around a particular text. But where exactly were such communities to be found?

The Formation of Groups through Texts

We need only to look back at the period of the Civil War after Caesar's death to see that it was not only for religious groups that texts played a role. Aulus Hirtius, Caesar's colleague and the consul for 43 BC, combined Caesar's descriptions of the Gallic Wars (58–52 BC) and the Civil War (49–47 BC) with his own and other writers' texts to produce a continuous account of Caesar's wars from 58 to 45 BC.[33] The resulting text was not pseudepigraphical, but continued without

63. Silver jug, probably from the Balkan region, depicting Chryses, a priest of
Apollo, sacrificing a bull to the god in order that he send a pestilence into the
ranks of the Trojans (inspired by the first verses of Homer, *Iliad*). Second half
of first century BC. Copy in the RGZM. Original in private ownership. Photo:
J. Rüpke, reproduced with the kind permission of the RGZM.

further comment the narrative voice of the authentic *Commentarii*,
reporting Caesar's deeds in the third person. This *Corpus Caesarianum*,
produced posthumously, may have been directed at those senators and
officers who were positioning themselves politically, and eventually
also militarily, as Caesar's heirs, providing them with a better basis for

establishing an identity than would have been possible by referencing a leading political figure of the day, such as Marcus Antonius. For all the sobriety of the earlier text, it is clear that religious elements were employed here. The final sentence of the compilation as it has come down to us (not necessarily as originally intended) reads: "Or do you not see that, after my death, the Roman people will have ten legions that will not only stand in your way, but may even tear down the heavens?"[34] However, in view of the rapidity of political and military developments, even the short-term contribution of these texts to the formation of groups or networks may have been limited.

The *Oracula Sibyllina*, already mentioned, were also calculated to define political boundaries; and here too, authors continued to add texts to a collection that was not completed until a foreword was added in the fifth or sixth century AD. At the core of these texts was a tradition of using oracles as a means of cultural and political resistance. They were known from the Hellenistic Age onward, and included the Ptolemaic Egyptian *Oracle of the Potter* and the *Oracle of Hystaspes*, which referred to conflicts with Rome in Persia and Asia Minor.[35] *Sibyllina* III to V were in the main compiled in stages, between the late first century BC and the Hadrianic Age. They vary widely in their content, but, beginning with 1.1–4, the books raise the claim to "prophesy" to "all people," or simply to the entire world.[36] The universal claim thus developed here, especially in criticism of Rome and Greco-Roman religious practices, does not imply a correspondingly universal public. The degree to which different individuals found their own contributions and those of others to be mutually compatible, however, is shown in the additions they made to the collection, which ranged eventually from the divine apparatus of classical epic to the *Christ Hymn*. Judging from the widespread quotes in Christian authors, including those writing in Latin (Lactantius in particular), the readership of the *Sibyllina* embraced widely disparate interests in both geographical and religious terms, although its readership may not have amounted to a mass public.

Elsewhere too, the reach of a text did not coincide with a single "textual" community. The letters collected under the name of Paul pose their argument against a background of Stoic and Platonic philosophy, while assuming an intensive knowledge of biblical writings, even on the part of noncircumcised recipients. This was another *bricolage* by intellectuals intent on their own legitimation. A collection of authentic letters between like-minded male and female correspondents in Jewish communities of the diaspora in Greece and Asia Minor would presumably have numbered in the hundreds. The extant corpus, on the other hand, has the character of a pseudepigraphical continuation of writings by Paul, to some extent going so far as to reflect the personal link in theological terms.[37] The writers' motivations were various, ranging from an interest in continuing Paul's work and providing contentious interpretations of it, to reverence for Paul and instrumentalization of his name (a process taken considerably further outside the corpus of letters, beginning in Luke's history of the apostles). In this manner, editors engaged in professional exegesis and in the formation of philosophical schools. But it was only with *Acts*, written deep into the first half of the second century, with its collective biography of the acts of the apostles, that we see the beginning of institutional history.[38] Here, Paul became the central link in a genealogy of groups that, from the mid-century onward, increasingly wished to see themselves primarily as *Christiani*.[39]

Even when authors worked in immediate geographical proximity, this was not necessarily a sufficient condition for a community held together by like-minded texts. The Nag Hammadi library discovered in 1945 comprised thirteen codices of the first half of the fourth century AD, reproducing a collection of older texts.[40] (Scattered) sub-groups of these texts appear to be gnostic, Valentinian, Sethianic, hermetic, or sapiential in nature; some appear to be non-gnostic Christian. They range from ritual texts (prayers) to apocalypses. It is not, therefore, concepts that unite the users of these texts, but solely their apparently consistent character as translations from Greek into Coptic dialects. Neither the nature of the original texts nor any desire on the part of their translators had sufficed to prevent their being brought together. The compilers modified the texts to make them fit their own situations. But there was also an interest in stressing the pan-Egyptian character of those texts that referred to Hermes Trismegistus in Codex VI.[41] The texts, the great majority of which had been translated into Sahidic, nevertheless remained elements in the discourse of intellectuals thinking within the categories of Greek and above all Platonic philosophy. Those intellectuals at the same time reckoned that epistemological advances could result from rituals of initiation and from ongoing revelation, although this took place within the individual, relocated to the inner consciousness, and derived, precisely, from books.[42]

Radical positions offered competing intellectuals opportunities to establish distinctive profiles This was true already in the first half of the second century AD, when, for example, the Epistle of Barnabas sought to derive every detail of a Christ-related doctrine from traditional biblical texts. It may have shared a public with texts advocating quite different theological positions.[43]

The Textualization of Religion

There is no doubt that in the Imperial Age more people acquired the ability to read written characters, even though advanced textual competence remained an elite phenomenon. Against this background, religion was increasingly regarded not only as something knowable, but also something that had to do with texts. A part of this process of the "textualization of religion"[44] saw religious rituals becoming the subject matter of texts. Familiarity with texts on religious activity also facilitated religious experiences and religious communication in writing as well as through reading and listening. During the second century AD, authors like Plutarch and Lucian, who had broad thematic orientations, devoted one fifth of their "moral texts," or a good quarter of their total oeuvre by title or content, to religious themes in the narrower sense.[45] For Varro and Cicero, religion had had no comparable importance. As textual production and communication increased in volume, moreover, participants developed new linguistic and communicative modes, and further developed old ones: myth, for example, was not exhausted as a genre with the advent of philosophy and historiography, although Varro and Cicero were fond of maintaining that it was in fact passé.[46] Quite the contrary; in conditions of increasing textuality, the narrative impulse flowered, giving rise to a number of new genres—in the religious sphere expressly in the writing of institution-related histories,[47] acts of the apostles and martyrs, and biographies such as that of Moses (Philo) and perhaps Abraham (Pseudo-Hecataeus).[48]

Professional exegesis came into being at the latest from the second century BC, with Aristarchus of Samothrace; attention was initially directed at Homer, but quickly turned to biblical texts, perhaps first with Aristarchus's contemporary Aristobulus. With Philo at the beginning of the first and Origen at the end of the second century AD, exegesis of central biblical texts had reached the same level as that of "classical" texts.

For the text-rich cultures of the Fertile Crescent, translation was an everyday practice, and this applied to religious texts as well, prominent among them the Septuagint (the Greek translation of the Hebrew Bible) and the Rosetta Stone. Important texts could be translated rapidly; perhaps copying in a foreign language was deemed to be scarcely less difficult than recasting the text in one's own. Moreover, such a translation process did not have to entail loss of identity: the creation of a new text in a target language does make for assimilation, but it also creates a distinct linguistic variant with its own peculiarities of syntax, semantics, and vocabulary.[49] A translation might also be given a deliberately alien air, allowing the foreign origin to show through. This was true not only of the Septuagint, but also of the Nag Hammadi texts and so-called Christian Latin.

But multilingualism required constant processes of translation. Despite the Septuagint, further biblical translations from Hebrew or Aramaic into Greek were undertaken until far into the Imperial Age. These were the projects of individuals, who allowed themselves to be identified as Jews or Christians only with difficulty, and on the basis of clues that changed constantly. This applied to the authors of Greek bible translations, such as Aquila, Symmachus, and Theodotion; it also applied to writers of biblical interpretations, who might, like

Philo, be identified as Christians, or, if writing in polemic mode, as Jews.[50] The Syriac language also enabled texts to be transported beyond the borders of the Roman Empire.[51]

The rabbinical movement demonstrated that the intentional renunciation of translation could be an instrument of control, bought at the price of forgoing expansion.[52] Conversely, translations such as the Celtic adoption of the Roman calendar at Coligny implied a loss of control for the creators of the original.[53] This also applied to a change of genre. With his tragedy *Exodus*, the Hellenistic author Ezekiel brought the bible to the stage; Flavius Josephus devoted ten of the twenty volumes of his *Jewish Antiquities* to a reformulation of biblical material, thus turning the Bible into a history book. And something similar is offered by the historical work of Pseudo-Philo.[54]

All of these instances took their impetus more from the specific interests and innovations of individual authors than from groups. The published corpora of letters did not give rise to networks, but, by affirming the existence of such networks, they made them a model for others. Only occasionally do we find accounts of pupil-teacher relationships in the areas of philosophy and philosophical "heresies" (*haereseis*); that is, accounts of "schools." Such narratives as we do have tell mostly about the history of the writer's own group, thus serving to reinforce its collective identity against external attack.[55] Accordingly, it was often not pupils wishing to acquire authority who wrote such narratives, but third parties.

Acknowledging authorship was by no means a given in the literature of antiquity. The claim that a particular narrative or prescriptive ethical standard was the work of a particular person rather than the product of an anonymous collective, orthonomy, meant taking responsibility and claiming authority. Such individual positioning was widespread among producers of religious texts. But sometimes authors—including females, but not groups!—resorted to the strategy of invisible authorship, often taking the pseudepigraphical route. This was especially frequent in the case of the apocalyptic writings previously mentioned, where claims might be made that texts had only just come to light. This method allowed the dissemination of content that was either of momentous originality or perhaps dangerously controversial. The texts took up minority opinions, but they were couched in language that was sufficiently diffuse to allow the reader latitude in choosing to agree or not. By giving the text a sympathetic reading, an individual could develop a collective identity and so become an informed observer. The facelessness of the writer thus empowered the reader.[56] From the first century AD onward, calls for action tended to be targeted at individuals as individuals. This made conspiracy theories and repressive actions by rulers, as repeatedly described by historians like Cassius Dio, appear paranoid.

Texts might of course be used within groups, for instance in those that were continually forming at Pergamum's Asclepius sanctuaries;[57] but only in quite exceptional cases did the texts actually create the groups. The Judaism that defined itself by reference to a collection of texts, and began to emerge in some places from the Hellenistic Period onward,[58] was one such subcategory of groups in which the recitation of texts must have played an increasingly important role. This was a widespread practice by the first century AD at the latest, certainly prior to the destruction of the Temple,[59] and one that was precisely *not* cued to higher literacy rates. Elsewhere, however, there were few signs of textual communities. Networks were quite local, or comprised weak ties between actors.[60] Typically, the texts involved either remained within elite confines this side of religious-group formation, or they enjoyed diffuse reception far beyond those confines. This was perceived by those who saw themselves to be threatened by such texts. The evidence for their reaction is ample: Augustus's burning of two thousand collections of Sibylline oracles; the suppression of particular unwelcome texts in the early Imperial Age; the specific seeking out of texts in the effort to destroy Christian structures in the late third century. Comparable practices continued into late antiquity.[61] Prior to this stage, however, destruction had always targeted individual owners or authors of texts, or rather their versions of past events and prognoses for the future. Texts were not vital in the developmental phase of a group.

2. Narratives

Texts did not create groups around them; but, in addition to hymns (whose authors were often known by name) and spoken prayers, reading and listening were important practices in the Imperial Age, and increasingly so.[62] Although distinct products, the texts involved called for particular modes of delivery, and, conversely, incorporated reflections of the practices and expectations that arose from such text-related interactions. The creators of these texts contributed to the religious changes of the period, and their texts were in turn changed by those very changes. Not all texts were or offered narratives, but it was narratives above all else that offered opportunities to affirm one's identity and one's relationship to the world in the mirror of others' lives, in their "histories." Narratives changed real or imagined processes, for example genealogies and rituals, into a knowledge that could be retold. The text that comes down to us is in this sense only a snapshot, a still frame from a narrative context that was constantly broadening, changing, and, often enough, in the process of dying. Textualized religion was subject to the full extent of such transformations.

Storytelling, either oral or written, but complicated by the absence of the narrator, was, moreover, independently of its content, a social phenomenon. The teller of the tale, whose credibility—and not only as a visionary—was precarious, had to achieve acceptance by coherence, or by testable reference to facts or to other narratives;[63] either under his own name or a plausible pseudonym. And the narratives eventually created communities, notional ones; they proffered a "we" that might be joined or opposed. Substantial historical narratives offered themselves to a quite specific group; brief fables, on the other hand, with their imperfectly defined or simply nonhuman actors, offered themselves to readers, male and female, of every hue.[64] An exploration of the structures of religious narratives of the Imperial Age therefore promises insight into this area of religious competencies and identities.[65]

The Roman Empire as a Narrative Framework

By their choice of where to set their beginnings and their endings, authors—or rather their circulating texts—not only determined a theme; they also defined conflicts, and specified whether these were to be regarded as resolved or as awaiting a solution. In his story of the banishment of the last Roman king, Tarquin the Proud, Ovid uses his subject matter to point to an example. He does not begin the narrative, in his commentary on the calendar, with Tarquin's plans for the immense Capitoline Temple, or with any instance of pride (or any other flaw of monarchy).[66] Instead, he has Tarquin steal away from the battlefield with the intention of raping Lucretia, thereby already setting the context for our assessment of the deed. The consequences: the rape, the victim's suicide, the revenge—and the rather incidental removal of the monarchy—communicated clear norms and exhortations to action. The producers of gospels and stories of martyrs and saints similarly offered conclusions that were readily comprehended by their readers and listeners. With their shaping of scenes, with suspense and plot twists, they made the stories entertaining and created the desire for more of the same.[67] Stories of the martyrs, on the model of interrogation and execution, and often enough with a voyeuristic treatment of violence—and especially violence toward women— were churned out like penny dreadfuls.[68]

In more sophisticated texts, however, multiple framings might increase the complexity of the narrative, and so prepare the ground for new approaches. A generation after Ovid, Valerius Maximus wrote nine books of *Memorable Deeds and Sayings*, beginning this collection of short tales with a treatise on religion. Surprisingly, where the reader might have expected at most something like an invocation of the Muses, Valerius opens with a prayer-like invocation of Augustus Tiberius. The end of the work again makes reference to the ruler or, more precisely, to his virtues of "imperial rectitude" and "the Caesar's unconquerable fortitude."[69] By this means, Valerius inserted into the new monarchic order a text that presents countless examples of commendable acts and virtues. For him, the new order of the Principate, reflecting a Republic that he could only imagine, as it already lay beyond his own power of recollection, allowed a glimpse of a kind of treasure house of solid values and individual initiative.[70]

An unknown author, writing in Rome in the first half of the second century AD, provides a similar and equally surprising framework for his so-called *First Epistle of Clement*. He opens with a formula in which the community in Rome recommends the text to the community in Corinth, and understands both of these "people's assemblies" (*ekklesiai*) as ephemeral groupings sanctified by God through the Lord Jesus Christ. In a substantial closing prayer, the author seeks safety and protection, with a nod also to terrestrial rulers and leaders (60.4). Their dominion is then justified theologically (61), before the writer eventually returns to the themes of insurrection and peace (63.1, 3). There is a matter that he initially tries to downplay, but then proceeds to address in his opening remarks, with sadness and inner turmoil (1.1), where he almost unwillingly concedes that the entire retelling of the biblical story, with accompanying ethical reflections, is framed by the imperial reality that both sender and addressee, in Rome and Corinth, share.

Perhaps a good decade later, Marcion in his "gospel" tells the story of Jesus's ministry, execution, and reappearance. The narrow timeframe of the narrative extends from the descent into Capernaum to the return to Jerusalem. This timeframe is expanded by an elaborate synchronization that aligns the fifteenth year of Tiberius's rule with Pontius Pilate's governorship of the province of Judaea.[71] Marcion, working in Rome, thus not only provides a dating, but also situates these provincial events within the Roman imperium.

All of these authors created fundamentally new texts. All fitted their religious ideas deftly into the framework of the Roman imperium.[72] What was at work here, however, was not a ruler cult, but rather an effort by individuals to appropriate for themselves the political identity that was central to their world. When numerous individuals had accepted this conceptualization, however, it altered perceptions.

Above all, it tended to the view of the Augusti as omnipresent. In their texts, these authors linked religion firmly to the imperium; and they proceeded to explore that relationship with care.

Biographical Schemata

Narration involves simplification. Details inevitably become lost. Complex events turn into sequences of simple actions. Complex casts of actors are reduced to names, and individuals are provided with stereotypical traits. Schemata emerge, types recognizable independent of specific narratives: there are unscrupulous rulers, wise Augusti, corrupt administrators, steadfast virgins. Such schemata help us today to follow unfamiliar stories, and to remember them. Terms such as "campaign," "war," "gospel," "passion story," "salvation" oriented audiences of the Imperial Age to just such structures. They also helped them to associate the stories they heard with other stories.[73] Virgil incorporated much-simplified narrative schemata from the *Iliad* and the *Odyssey* into his *Aeneid*,[74] and so was able to integrate local Italic narratives into a familiar framework. Christ's Passion served as a paradigm for the imagined martyrdom of Ignatius of Antioch, and retrospectively configured the narrative of the martyrdom of Bishop Polycarp of Smyrna in a way that made it more readily comprehensible.[75]

It was characteristic of the Imperial Age that many narratives relied on the schema of the biography. The brief narrative of a *vita* within a longer story was a widespread device all around the Mediterranean. In the Hellenistic Period its importance had grown to the point that the schema began to stand alone in autonomous texts, *bioi* of statesmen and writers, prophets, and the heads of schools.[76] Subsequently, serial biographies coincided with the interests of philosophical schools, and the genre was transposed to other fields by such writers as Suetonius. Encomiums and funeral orations were mined for what proved a wide range of themes characterizing the lifestyle of the biographical subject. Concentrating on one protagonist entailed neglecting other causalities, and overstressing the impact of that one character or divine actor on events. This might seem to be a deficiency, but it allowed listeners to bring their own thought processes to bear, to engage with the story, and so could heighten its attraction. Many storytellers took over-determination further by the introduction of portents. These gave the progress of events more transparency, but did not always support claims to historicity.[77]

Religious practices and ideas were only gradually brought within the remit of biographical narratives. It was probably shortly before the death of Domitian (AD 96) that Plutarch wrote the first proper biography of Rome's second king, Numa, to whom he also first ascribed the role of *pontifex*.[78] This was vexing, as Numa had previously been described as the founder of Rome's religious institutions, but not as an actor within them.[79] In making this attribution, Plutarch was probably responding to the Flavians' desire to conflate the ethical grounding of the ruler with his priestly roles, especially the supreme pontificate.[80] Numa, as a Pythagorean philosopher and a king, thus conformed to the ideal of a philosopher-king,[81] with the addition now, for the first time, of a religious element.

Flavius Josephus took up the biographical schema, turned it into autobiography, and set it within an imperial frame. He began with a reference to his priestly and royal origins (1), and ended by referring to his relationship with Augusta Domitia, and to the unremitting good services she had performed for him (429).[82] At the same time that Josephus in Rome expounded on the Jewish War,[83] Plutarch and soon also Suetonius were writing their multiple biographies. By the mid-second century at the latest, these texts were joined by many gospels and acts of the apostles, whose production continued without let-up through the third century.[84] Marcion's interest in biography was not exercised solely in his gospel, but also in his selection of Paul's letters, which allowed readers to follow the apostle from Jerusalem to Rome. Pythagorean *vitae* began to circulate.[85] To the already familiar types of narrative—stories of exemplary lives or of extraordinary phenomena, such as those of Apollonius of Tyana—were added conversion stories.[86] All of this literary activity likely reached only a small fraction of the people living around the Mediterranean; but in a rudimentary, paradigmatic form, the biographical schema certainly reached much further. By its clarity, capacity for extension, and flexibility, it permitted authors to impart religious knowledge in a way that facilitated an emotional relationship akin to identification with the life retold, thus easing the recipient's way to appropriating the values and lessons embodied in the texts. Biographical narrative was probably the most important form by which the personal, physical experience of individualization could be made a subject of reflection, and communicated.[87]

Discursive Diversification and the Extension of Networks

Did biographical narratives about common forebears or teachers serve other purposes besides consolidating group relationships? The texts themselves suggest two opposing tendencies. Those that have survived in the greatest numbers, martyrs' histories among them, have narratives that are schematized and generalized in such a way as to make them easily accessible to an ever greater number of people. As has been observed in the case of texts from North Africa and their reception by Donatists and Catholics in the fourth post-Christian century, homogenization generated consensus that went beyond the bounds of groups and interests. Authors who had the courage to abbreviate radically wrote summaries (*epitome, periochae*) that won a larger public than the original lengthy and sophisticated literary versions. Consider, for example, Julius Obsequens in relation to Livy. At the same time, the impulse to move away from such generalizations led some individuals to raise their own voices.[88] Such differentiation in reaction to generalization created differences between recipients: on the one hand, there were those who understood and were in sympathy with the change; and on the other stood the critics. Thus Ovid in his commentary on the calendar combined explanations of an almost tautological and correspondingly uncontroversial character with far-reaching assertions that he in part underpinned by citing deities who had appeared to him. Their fictional nature must have been clear to his cultured readers, who were thus enabled to arrive at varied and nuanced positions.[89] Since the mid-second century, experts had been bringing out a succession of new gospels, which clarified particular issues and defended their points of view at length in narrative form. This created followers and adversaries.

Such diversification was not necessarily intentional, and it might itself engender a new crop of variants that would be referenced and debated again and again. The more trivial and incoherent the detail, the more likely it was to imprint itself on the reader. So Numa could no longer be thought of in the Imperial Age without his books, which had been invented in the early second century BC in order to legitimize Pythagorean philosophy in Rome. Halachic *midrashim* concerned themselves with the smallest details in the narratives of the Pentateuch (the five books of Moses).[90] The same is true of Virgil commentators, especially in Late Antiquity.[91] On the one hand, the written form of the prototypes ensured that later generations could repeatedly refer back to them. In the absence of such an interest on their part, which would ensure that new copies were produced every century, texts could not survive.

The extension of networks, mentioned in the title of this section, may have owed more to multiple instances of diversification in the processes of telling and retelling than to the labors of a few scribes and copyists. Only in this way could new perspectives emerge, whose presence might then underpin the legitimacy of still newer perspectives. Women authors, even though we may not always be able to discern their presence as such, introduced tales of clever, resilient women, drawing on their own religious competence. We see this, for example, in traditions regarding widows in Jewish and, later, also Judeo-Christian texts.[92] Comparable traditions, and above all the desire to involve women in the network of storytelling, may have moved the (in all probability male) author of the *Acts of John* to give women a prominent role in his narrative.[93]

Many variants are also to be found in non-narrative texts, such as curses.[94] Other Judeo-Christian narrative texts, surviving in sufficient numbers for us to find variants at different locations, once again show us the boldness with which individual authors have introduced

new ideas into existing narrative schemata, going so far beyond reproduction as to justify the use of such descriptive terms as "rewritten
Bible" or "rewritten gospel."[95] The gospel described as the *Epistle of the
Apostles*, for example, is configured as a dialogue with the risen Jesus.
An apostolic pair, characterized simply as "we," learn from Jesus that
he appeared to the virgin Mary in the shape of the archangel Gabriel
and spoke with her in such a way that her heart received him, and she
believed and laughed. He was thus his own servant, and would assume that role again, in the guise of an angel, before returning to his
father.[96] There are similar new attempts at explanations in the *Ascension of Isaiah*, where Mary conceives upon catching sight of a baby.[97]
The author of the *Gospel of the Saviour*, again probably written in the
second century, and likewise in dialogue form, does not hesitate to
make Jesus announce that he will descend into "Hades."[98] Even Philo,
in his retelling of biblical material, did not bother much about details
in the texts before him.[99] And, in the first century AD, a narrative like
the *Thebaid* of the Flavian epic poet Statius could devise dramatic versions of the god Apollo that were far removed from the contemporary
conceptions of Plutarch.[100]

However, the existence of such texts does not signify unrestricted
openness. Potential recipients of the Gospel of Peter were included or
excluded on the ethnically defined basis of whether they were, respectively, Romans or Jews. In making such stipulations, a writer or writers
would supplant the leading figures in familiar narratives, thus opening a new page in anti-Jewish polemic.[101] Although women had long
been active as writers and copyists, and had influenced the form taken
by the texts they produced,[102] a new concept of authorship, which compared the authors in their labors with ascetics, significantly changed
the role of women and womanly virtues within the hierarchies of late
antique narrative.[103] Frequently, moreover, similar frameworks might
conceal different messages. It can scarcely be said of the beginning of
the *Gospel of the Ebionites* that it was less inclusive with regard to Jews
and non-Jews than the synchronism of Luke's gospel, or the genealogy in Matthew when it says of John that in the days of Herod, the
king of Judea, he came to the Jordan to baptize with a baptism of

penance, and that he himself came from the line of the priest Aaron and was a child of Zechariah and Elizabeth.[104] Such an opening offered many more connection points than Mark's gospel, which begins the story abruptly with the entrance of the Baptist.

It is beyond question that intellectual actors with their textualization of religion brought textual practices to population groups that had not been familiar with them prior to the Imperial Age. This had consequences that went beyond merely broadening communication about religion, and began to affect questions of dogma. But heady reflection about the fictionalization that narratives frequently entailed [105] could not gain traction in these new sub-cultural forums of communication. It was easier to take narratives at face value.[106] This may have created tensions or outright conflict about "truth." It is possible that, when intellectual discourse ventured beyond the elite, the threshold of intolerance was lowered: controversies in intellectual debate might now overlay and aggravate preexisting disputes and economic or political conflicts between social groups.[107] Here too, the ways in which texts were appropriated outnumbered the texts themselves. Reflections on the nature of narrative, on fictionality and authorship, remained the preserve of a few specialists, grammarians, and philosophers. Most readers and listeners enjoyed the stories and perhaps found in them stimulation for their own reflections, inspiration for action (whether religious or otherwise), or simply entertainment.

3. Historization and the Origin of Christianity

One of the ways in which religion in Rome was provided with a knowledge base in the second half of the first century BC was by history-telling, following a Greek model that had taken the same path long before. Varro, in his *Antiquitates rerum divinarum*, which regrettably has come down to us only in fragments, appears to have framed his work with historical sketches in Books 1 and 15 (thus prior to the concluding philosophical reflections), that recount the foundations of temples and rituals. These were mainly, but not exclusively, drawn from developments in the city of Rome. Varro's aim, in this novel undertaking is, as its title implies, to represent religion as something that had developed historically, and could have developed in other ways. He intended also to give space to the reception of non-Roman institutions: in the context of the imperial expansion of the first century, Rome had to be represented as an open city, with a culture that was potentially universal.[108] Two generations later, Ovid in his *Metamorphoses* (*Metamorphoseon libri*) offered a universal anthropology and cultural history with a Roman focus, while Valerius Maximus in the 30s of the first century AD demonstrated that models from outside Rome (*externi*) might also have relevance for ethics within the Roman imperium of the Principate. Strabo and Pompeius Trogus, from the perspective of outsiders from, respectively, Greece and Gaul, had already written universal narratives showing the territory freshly conquered by the Romans to be possessed of a long and many-stranded history.[109]

These narratives—in common with all historiography—were constructions by their authors. They reordered the past in order to relate it to the problems of the present, and in so doing were enabled directly to address the present, in the shape, say, of a provincial life within the Roman Empire. But they were also able to address particular consequences of the Roman imperium, either critically or approvingly. Pseudo-Philo, in his *Book of Biblical Antiquities*, offered a biblical history of the early days that was critical of the series of rulers, the genealogies, presented in the books of *Chronicles*. Himself confronted in the first century AD with a "Jewish" monarchy criticized by many as being Jewish in scarcely more than name and ruling by the good grace of the Romans, the anonymous author relates a history where succession is no longer by birthright, but by a series of divine elections that might alternate between prophets and kings.[110]

Jewish Contexts

The relating of history, especially when it is a people relating its own history, was and is one of the most important ways of finding an orientation in the present and for the future. This also applied to Mediterranean antiquity and its religious actors.[111] By relating what to the audience, or to some particular part of it, was a supposedly common past, it was possible to draw boundaries, either to exclude people or consciously to include them. In the ideal scenario, this might give rise to frameworks and schemata that could be repeated or represented figuratively, all the more tellingly if in simplified form, and thus given broader effect. The more self-evident such a construction was, the more far-reaching its effect: often extending into the present day. The emergence, or, better, the invention of Christianity within the framework of ancient Judaism provides an excellent example. Given the potency of the events in question, and the broad canvas on which they have already been retold, I intend to portray the process at a more succinct and summary level. In all other respects, however, I will follow the same narrative perspective, centered on Rome and oriented on known texts and concepts, as characterizes the rest of this book.

In the Mediterranean region during the period of Hellenistic and Roman dominance, Jews outside Palestine formed one minority among many.[112] With no common mother tongue, they yet saw themselves as part of one ethnic identity. Their center lay in Jerusalem, in Egypt in the recent foundation of Alexandria (where Greek was spoken), and in Mesopotamia, where, as in Palestine, Aramaic dominated. Under Persian rule, from broadly the fifth to the third century BC, Jewish intellectuals (scribes) busied themselves with the shaping of a literary tradition that provided a narrative bond between areas of Jewish settlement in the region. Under political conditions fundamentally similar to those described above for the later Roman Empire, practices related to the Pentateuch became ever more important, while, at the same time, the Temple in Jerusalem grew in significance.[113] Changes in everyday life outside the urban centres in Palestine, however, occurred only very gradually.[114] The more intensive dissemination of a political ideology comprising monotheism, Temple, and Torah may have had to await the establishment of a strong client kingdom, under first Macedonian and then Roman dominion, along with the support that was then extended to Jewish groups in the diaspora. Around Jerusalem at least, intellectual debate was set on a durable footing by the organization of substantial portions of the adult male population into distinct sects, although the cult of the Temple never fundamentally challenged.[115]

From as early as the third century BC, some intellectuals, perhaps drawn straight from the circles of the priests and scribes, were posing the question of evil in radical ways. Their answers remained substantially literary. Keeping as close as possible to the principle of the one God, they devised a dualistic element composed of minor divinities: demons and angels. In tune with this a vocabulary developed that could be heightened in apocalyptic directions by visionaries, or converted for use in cult practices or for purposes of a social-revolutionary character. Through the universalist historical perspective of the Torah, and the link made between God and earthly rule, this language itself had implications that were universalist, and thus at the same time critical of Rome. In about AD 30 there emerged among actors in Palestine a man called Jesus, of a prophetic and apocalyptic stamp, who was eventually executed.

Among Jewish networks, which by the early second century BC at the latest had also come to include Jews in Rome, an echo of this episode of the 30s of the previous century persisted, although on a scale that was not comparable with later uprisings. The main way in which this manifested itself was in conflicts within the Jewish community, which could escalate and cross into society at large when hostilities broke out between rival Jewish groups. It was probably by some process of this kind that the expression "followers of Christ" (*Christiani*) was coined, probably in Antioch, then to be used by Roman authorities such as Tacitus (perhaps already using sources for the Great Fire of Rome in AD 64), and Pliny in Asia Minor at the beginning of the second century AD.[116] What aspects of the Tiberian-age prophet were borrowed and assimilated to his person by commentators remains unclear. In the view of intellectuals, in any event, he was suited to a role in that newly emerged intermediate world, as "Son," "Name of God," or "Angel of God." Politically, his relevance was as a universalizing element in the growing marginal groups of Hellenistic Jewry wherein overlapping customs and identities had long clouded the question of what exactly being Jewish meant.

In the mid-first century AD, Paul, a Jewish intellectual, associated this figure of Jesus with the idea that Jewish identity might be detached from the practice of circumcision.[117] This expansive discourse of delimitation created more of a stir, but attracted a significantly smaller following, than, say, the cult of Theos or Zeus Hypsistos (and to some extent also that of Sabazius, often represented in a typical Jewish iconographic strategy only by a hand) (fig. 64). We must not imagine strongly separated groups with membership lists. In Asia Minor, however, and from the second century AD in particular, many who regarded themselves as Jews, or found Jewish practices such as the Sabbath attractive, adopted the name, the idea, and the image of the "most high God."[118] In the dedicatory offerings, inscriptions, and cult buildings by and within which they communicated with and about this God, they were solidly situated within the formal vocabulary of traditional ritual practice, connecting seamlessly with the practices of groups that were, in the above sense, biblically, not or only slightly Jewish. The groups of "Christians" observed by Pliny, with their ritual worship of "Christ" and their adherence to a set rhythm of days (*stato die*), may have belonged to just such a context.

Jews had been present in Rome at the latest by the time of the Roman expansion into the eastern Mediterranean in the early second century BC, the period when Judah the Hasmonean sent his delegation to Rome (161). As early as 139 BC, some of them, together with "Chaldeans," were compelled to leave Rome on the grounds that they had tried to disseminate "habits of worshipping Sabazius Jupiter."[119] This may have referred only to observance of the Sabbath, a core theme of protective agreements with foreign cities negotiated by figures such as Herod the Great. But those targeted in Rome, in common with the "Chaldeans," were banished not as members of an ethnic minority, but as suppliers of special services, as religious specialists.[120] Despite such episodes, Jews remained in Rome, enjoying, through political circumstances, closer contact with Jerusalem than was the case in many other places. In AD 64 in any event, representatives of a great variety of positions were present there at the center of the Empire, in the melting pot of a city with (almost) a million inhabitants.[121] It was

64. Hand used as a symbol for Sabazios in order to avoid full anthropomorphic representation, 13 cm, bronze, Imperial Age. Paris, Musée du Louvre, Dep. des Antiquités Grecques et Romaines. akg-images / Erich Lessing.

in just this context that Christ with his apocalyptic millennial expectations, redolent of ideas as potentially critical of Rome as they were universalistic, found followers of both sexes, and underwent a process of embourgeoisement in an immigrant community intent on advancement (if we do not wish to identify with Nero's accusation of them as incendiaries: which term at the time would probably have designated apocalyptic leanings).[122] It was in Rome that the Flavian Titus built his colorful triumphal arch with reliefs illustrating the removal of the seven-branched menorah from Jerusalem, thus memorializing the destruction of that city in the year AD 70, an event that elsewhere passed almost unnoticed.[123] It was in Rome that Josephus, who would after manumission adopt the name "Flavius," arrived, along with many other prisoners of war. They were faced with the great challenge of defining their relationship with their conqueror. Josephus had to call on all the resources of his ancestry, a recovered social position, and his personal self-mastery, before he came to the conclusion that the conflict between Rome and Jerusalem had been lost by the Judeans on account of their own avoidable errors.

To others, the figure of the crucified messianic visionary offered attractions of a different nature. One of these, from a Roman perspective perhaps the most critical, was the *ekklēsia*, an assembly, "a lawmaking body of God's people:"[124] in essence a world parliament to which all, male or female, regardless of status, would have access, under the leadership of a God of whom every individual could have certain knowledge. Another was the idea of a heavenly high priest, entirely on a par with the earthly Augustus and *pontifex maximus*, but, again, available to the individual.[125] As revealed by literary contexts, these ideas represented benefits that would have resonated with inhabitants of the Roman Empire, for they offered an extension of agency that was otherwise no longer open even to those of Roman citizenship. At the same time, it allowed speakers and their audiences in the lecture halls of bathhouse complexes, in workshops, or in the one-room habitations above the shops,[126] to place blame for real political catastrophes on failures by assimilated individuals, and not just on the old elites.

The Invention of Christianity

Rome's suppression of the uprising in Alexandria and the Bar Kochba uprising in Palestine, in AD 115–117 and 132–135 respectively,[127] shattered all hope for the restoration of a "Jewish" state of the sort imagined above, as well as any hope that the Temple might be rebuilt. The latter was probably more intensely desired, or at least more looked for, in Rome than in many other places. This, along with his own inner conflicts, may have been the last straw for a man who had in the meantime also settled in Rome: Marcion of Sinope, a shipowner from Asia Minor.[128]

Marcion organized his group of followers of Christ as a decidedly non-Jewish entity. He was perhaps not the first to undertake such a project, but he was certainly the first to give it a durable form, which in this case proved capable of persisting at least into the fifth century AD.[129] He found a theoretical, easily memorizable justification for his anti-Jewish position by reversing a prevailing dualistic narrative: evil was not to be identified with any kind of demon, but with the creator god as depicted in the Pentateuch. The god of Jesus Christ, as described in the available texts by Paul, was the positive antagonist of that ancient figure.[130] The most influential aspect of Marcionism, however, was neither the institutions it created nor any accompanying rituals, but its historiographical groundwork. In outlining a simple biographical schema, replete with current anecdotes and quotations—here I am following the increasingly mooted, even if still radical position of a second-century date for the canonical gospels and the Acts of the Apostles—Marcion's portrayal of the life of an apocalyptic visionary and peripatetic preacher, from his first emergence to his rather unusual execution, could be seen as the model of a life turning away from Judaism. He thus orchestrated a rupture that he relocated a century into the past, carefully keeping his narrative free of contemporary references.[131]

If the stunning absence of earlier biographical narratives of Jesus's life is not just an accident of transmission, but rather the consequence of such earlier narratives being nonexistent, the reason might be that there was no interest in biographies of "angels," "sons of god," or "names of gods," the identities most often ascribed to Jesus in Jewish contexts. The form chosen by Marcion for his writings depended neither on orally available narratives fed by biographical memory, nor on any form of oral transmission, which would have had to survive across more than the normally (barely) permissible three generations or seventy years.[132] Instead, Marcion invented something new. In the literary environment of the Roman Empire as described, nothing was more natural than to write a Greek-language "biography" as a founding document for a new religious network. Marcion's opponents reacted immediately with a weighty intellectual exchange of the sort that a metropolis like Rome made possible; and, as was usual in historiography, they reacted with competing versions.[133] Such a quick riposte was presumably possible (and I cannot conceal the hypothetical character of this reconstruction that locates decisive steps of an evolving Christianity in a religiously innovative capital) because Marcion's competitors were in fact also active in Rome, and, moreover, adopted substantial parts of his model. The author of the text that most plagiarized Marcion was identified a little later, by Marcion himself, as Luke, in an edition that featured the gospel along with some of Paul's letters. It concentrated on correcting Marcion's fundamental break with Judaism. With their narratives of Jesus's childhood, both Luke and Matthew demonstrate how familiar the biographical character of the template was, and also how scant the source background was as soon as one wanted to move beyond that template. Marcion, for his part, criticized their compositions (and that of Mark) as lying close to his own text.

Writings competing with Marcion's edition of the 140s AD, which was prefaced by his "Antitheses," could now only continue to accumulate. AD 160 saw a counter-edition that established the core of the future New Testament. The late addition of Luke's *Acts of the Apostles* rescued the philosophical core represented by Paul and took a direction that, while no longer avoiding the gray zones of Jewishness, also provided this orientation with a patron.[134] Within the same movement, however, spokesmen such as Luke (in *Acts of the Apostles*) and Justin (in his *Apology*)—and perhaps earlier the writer of the *Epistle of Barnabas*—persisted with the genealogy of exclusion, insisting that the destruction of the Temple in AD 70 was a consequence of the crucifixion of the "anointed one."[135] Still others in this same period, such as the author of the *Gospel of Peter*, did not shrink from obvious anti-Judaism and fawning to the Roman authorities.[136] For intellectuals in this area of Judaism, such schismatic polemics would remain a critical source of friction over the coming centuries, providing a forum where agendas of inclusion and exclusion could be exchanged. The polemic propagated by many Christian positions against the "gnosticism" of clearly anti-Judaic stances demonstrates the complexity that was emerging at the margins of a developing tradition.

This now historiographically constructed collective, this genealogy of Christ's apostles, had no basis in any historical reality of exclusive bonding. As was suggested by findings in the previous chapter, the various texts gave rise to no groups. Professional philosophers who taught for pay may well, like Justin, have read history, but it seldom played any important role in their argumentation. Tatian, Theophilus, and Athenagoras, in their "defenses" of their positions in the late second century, may often have addressed the Augusti formally, but in fact their primary goal was to reassure their students, freshly pressed into the fray, or to carry on disputes with critical colleagues. Christ (let alone Jesus) had no role to play. The same applies to Minucius Felix, a North African writing in Rome in the early third post-Christian century. Intellectuals who entered into the contests of the philosophers kept to their own circle, and it was a small one. Cassius Dio at the beginning of the third century noted that Hadrian Augustus, even at the beginning of his period in office, envied other philosophers like Favorinus, and so saw himself as in competition with them.[137] Dio records for the year 200 how Julia Augusta longed for the consolation of philosophy, and accordingly in 214 built a temple to Apollonius of Tyana.[138] Caracalla, on the other hand, was said to have hated

Aristotelian philosophy, and so—perhaps in 211—persecuted it; not least because in his view it had been responsible for the death of Alexander the Great, whom Caracalla revered.[139] Competition reigned here, not continuity.

Philosophy as the systematic involvement with other people's texts was thus above all a terrain reserved for the educated, thin upper crust of society. Only intellectuals possessed books.[140] And the new gospels gave rise to no text-based communities. The only exception was Marcion's group, founded by a typical, religious, small-scale entrepreneur: a well-traveled merchant, an organizer, an *arriviste* (at least by virtue of his move to Rome), and more successful with his money than with his writings. Beyond this group and the intellectual conversation circles (in which Marcion, at least since Justin's attack on him, was fully involved at a literary level), "God's people's assembly" (*ekklēsia*) had no lasting institutional basis: no one precisely knew where Peter and Paul had died, to say nothing of where their graves might be. The rituals that would, in subsequent centuries, be claimed by various groups as representing the core of a particular tradition that dated back to the founder were practiced only by a few individuals.[141] In short, to speak of Jews and Christians in the second century AD as distinct groups would be anachronistic.[142] At the same period, those responsible for the rebuilding of the Temple of Vesta after the fire of 191 insisted that it should be restored as far as possible to its original form.[143] This kind of continuity, which was valued in many settings, could be achieved only by conscious decision in an environment where institutions had long histories. There was nothing like this yet in Jewish Rome. Christianity had thus been invented historiographically by means of the gospels and the *Acts of the Apostles* complemented by collections of letters. There was as yet no actual community.

4. Religious Experiences and Identities

The people living in the territory of the Roman Empire in the second century had collective identities: they conceived of themselves as members of groups, many of which did not exist at all as social institutions or functioning networks. This does not detract from the importance of such conceptions in motivating the actions of these people in particular situations. Even in the absence of group pressure, identities could have implications. Important processes of identity-formation joined forces with experiences undergone in the context of rituals and with memories of rituals at particular places. While such experiences as a rule remained unspoken, once narrated, verbalized, they could take on additional solidity, so as to alter subsequent experiences, and also language.[144]

In epigraphical and literary portrayals of ancient rituals, most of them destined for public consumption, principals spoke little about the psychological mechanisms that we may now deduce with the aid of modern research methods. Great public rituals reflected social structures and power relationships, and served to build and stabilize normative and social systems, embedding more firmly such constructs as values, hierarchies, and political structures.[145] This was true even when the contribution made by such rituals in pluralistic urban and metropolitan societies remained limited.[146] Rituals appropriated by individuals for the configuration of their own efforts of religious communication had important effects,[147] even in quite spatially limited contexts:[148] they lent a routine element to fundamental social relationships, and corporealized memories that had their roots both in the individual's religious and biographical experience and in the communication of collective memories.[149]

As we have already seen, ritual experience took place most often in the close familial context of the apartment or house and the tomb. Some centralized rituals were presumably confined largely to cities, with most participants restricted to spectating, and many not participating at all. Only purpose-built structures such as theaters and amphitheaters had the acoustic capacity to reach an audience of more than a few hundred.[150] But even seeing without hearing could produce an intense experience, especially when those attending reacted emotionally. Journeys to trans-regional cult sites in order to consult oracles or to seek treatment for illnesses were expensive, and accordingly rare and for the most part available only to the wealthy. One had to know about such places, and that knowledge might form the basis for religious identity. Reference points for subsequent reflection engendered in such situations did not necessarily coincide with the loci of actual experiences; and this is also true of groups that have been no more than mentioned here.

Many of those who, especially from the second century AD onward, turned to Isis, Mithras, or Yahweh in their pursuit of religious communication assigned great importance to a distant "holy land," without thereby renouncing universalistic claims.[151] Jerusalem was a special case, conditioned by the real crisis of the city's destruction, and the ensuing crisis within the minds of those affected. But the evocation of Egypt in the early Imperial Age, which revolved around the worship of Serapis and Isis (securely dated by the Iseum in Pompeii), and the Rome-referenced construction of *capitolia* in the provinces during the first and second centuries AD, functioned in much the same way.[152] The Severan architectural program in both Rome and North Africa, and the extension of citizenship to all free inhabitants of the Roman Empire by the *Constitutio Antoniniana* of AD 212, also pointed in the same direction. It amounted to a new definition of the local and of the Roman imperium.[153]

The reasons for this lay at different levels. A great number of people had been displaced on military grounds. Slaves were traded throughout the Empire, if in reducing numbers. Other people had set out on their own account, for economic or social reasons: circumstances we have already considered here. The diasporas that resulted created the need for far-flung notional affiliations.[154] Over and above migration movements, the increasingly intensive experience of the rule of the Augusti and their provincial governors was fundamental at the local level.

In the new, multilayered—and thus uncertain—nature of political identities in the context of empire, Roman religion became an important instrument for the formation of collective identities and networks at a local level. In this new reality, the more effective religious signs and practices were at substituting for the all-embracing access to the world, the *Weltbeziehungen*, that political identities and institutions had previously mediated, the more successful they were. As in the process of incorporating the Augusti into religious communication, transregional connections, a point of reference to a location for the god worshipped that lay beyond the worshipper's everyday reality, became important. It was such a location that secured (on an imperial scale) extensive reach for a deity who had, of course, nevertheless, primarily to continue being effective locally, in the worshipper's own home and at the family gravesite.

But that distant location must not be merely notional. The interest in historization, as we saw it in Marcion, was not only an interest in achieving orientation in a city or world that had become more complex. The development of individuality, in religious communication in particular, arose from and itself in turn stimulated practices whereby a personal experience, facilitated by ritual, could lend verisimilitude to fictions:[155] "Here is the place where Mithras killed the bull." But the desire for authenticity might go still further. It might give rise to a wish to augment both experience and success in communication by presence at actual sites. Travelers' accounts and detailed reports of epiphanies experienced at such special places provide evidence that such experiences were perceived as distinctly different from the usual ritual, and were motivated by a desire for personal contact with the divine.[156] Historization in the sense of narration in an expressly nonfictional context might secure that desired object.[157]

However, such ritual references to places outside of one's present location could not be chosen at will. The selection always had a political dimension. "Locative" religious practices, those related to a particular locality, tended to stabilize local power relationships; whereas "utopian" practices tended to be critical of power, and to fortify religious actors.[158] This applied even under the conditions of hierarchy imposed by empire. Rulers might come to regard such locations as threatening. Rebellions with religious associations in Cyrenaica, Alexandria, Jerusalem, and Palmyra were accordingly treated with appropriate severity. The instances of Emesa (Homs), Doliche, and

Jerusalem demonstrate that such historical events did not necessarily detract from the notional image of such towns or landscapes in the mind.

But nobody could overlook the fact that, at least from the late first until the early third century AD, Rome was the symbolic and intellectual center of the Roman Empire. It was here that every school, every network of any size wanted to have some sort of presence; it was here that ideas were conveyed with great rapidity across cultural divides. This Roman intellectual arena was as open as Alexandria's had once been and would be again. For this very reason, Rome invited polemic and efforts to limit its influence. The *Oracula Sibyllina* condemned the place; texts with Hermes as their principal interlocutor decried the notion of the Syrian Orontes joining its flood to the Tiber, a confluence already lamented by Juvenal in the first century AD (if not explicitly in relation to religion), with the assertion that Egypt was "the whole world's temple."[159] Not only did many of the texts that later found their way into the New Testament canon arise in Rome, but Greek priests like Plutarch and Appian could be found there, also philosophers like Epictetus, Cornutus, and Marcus Aurelius, and religious intellectuals like Marcion, Justin, and Valentinus, scholars from Palestine like Matthatias, even priests of Isis from Alexandria. Here the emperor encouraged the worship of particular gods with games and temples and by showing preference for their networks. Here operated the lobbyists of the Jerusalem sect no less than those of the Syrian cults of Baal.

Anyone able to articulate his or her religious identity by reference to a distant location had an advantage in formulating a clear-cut identity. For the very reason that it lacked a firm location in the everyday world, such a reference permitted a monolithic classification (as we witness in certain discourses on Muslims in the U.S. and Europe): a black and white representation, in short. These others, one might say, are not different in one respect only: they are entirely different, and, of course, worse. It is clear that, if such an identity was met with imperial disdain on the one hand and provincial resistance on the other, the disconnect could easily accelerate to acrimony.[160] Rome (or, in the language of myth, "Babylon"), whether in the *Sibylline Oracles* or the *Apocalypse of John*, had, for the defeated, an identity that brooked no nuance. With historiographical constructions such as the doctrine of the four kingdoms, as formulated in the Hellenistic Period in the *Book of Daniel*, such an identity could be yet further loaded with notions of inevitability that legitimized action as much as they restricted options: Rome was the *final* kingdom. It is probably not by chance that a third-century AD commentary on Daniel is one of the earliest interpretations of biblical texts to have come down to us from Rome.[161] But these examples show that Rome's power of the imagination ran out at the borders of the Empire. Acceptable though the Persian god Mithras might be, the real-life Persian Mani (AD 216 to about 276) was certainly problematic, and in the end unacceptable. For all its expansion, the Empire was confined to territory west of the former empire of Alexander. In this respect, both notional and real communities were subject to similar borders, even though the Empire, and within it the city of Rome, facilitated the existence of a multitude of groups, both ideational and actual.

XII

Demarcations and Modes of Community

THE THIRD TO FOURTH CENTURIES AD

1. The Market Value of Religious Knowledge

Looking upon Rome from the vantage point of Gaulish Lugdunum in the 180s AD, the philosopher Irenaeus, probably, like Marcion, from Asia Minor, made a successful bid for fame. He compiled a list of systemically false lines of thinking (and correspondingly false practices). These he associated with Rome, where he had previously lived and perhaps also begun the work in question (*Against Heresies*). He moreover provided actors sympathetic to his way of thinking with a fictitious genealogy of *episkopoi* that traced the line of bishops back to Peter (not Paul, it should be noted), without himself ever raising any claim to being such an "overseer." The Greek text was then quickly translated into Latin, and in the tradition was handed on primarily in this mother tongue of the Romans. It is works such as those of Irenaeus, and a short while later Tertullian, with their polemic "against heresies," that have given rise to the impression that the history of ancient religion is that of a contest between competing groups. Less studied has been the question as to why and with what consequences authors have tried to create such an impression. My final chapter will accordingly take as its starting point not this prevalent assumption of competing groups, but rather the question as to how the actors and media we have already examined contributed either to the drawing of boundaries or the establishment of common ground. In at least one instance, where there is rather more documentation available than in most others, I will examine more fully the further question as to how religious "knowledge" was generated and employed in these contexts.

Anyone seeking to reach a wider public in Rome did well to avoid dwelling on philosophical trivia. Such was the strategy of a figure who, probably with a conception of himself as a teacher,[1] found a voice during the years after the *Constitutio Antoniniana* (AD 212), thus in a situation where "all were called Romans."[2] Hippolytus, later to be confused with the person and works of a bishop from the East of similar name, wrote a series of texts at the beginning of the third century AD,[3] among them a treatise on a book of the Bible that we have had occasion to mention, texts that must have had a certain currency in the circle of synagogue-attenders and followers of Christ: the Hellenistic tale of Daniel, his rescue of Susanna, his later visions, and his survival in the lion's den. Like few others, Hippolytus in his texts on the Book of Daniel provides us with credible insights into the goals, problems, and interactions of those we have referred to more than once in the previous chapter as "intellectuals."

An event that had excited great attention among the Roman public was perhaps the immediate factor that motivated Hippolytus to examine the Book of Daniel in particular, and especially the tale of how Daniel rescued Susanna from the two lecherous "elders," while it also provided him with an opportunity to reach a somewhat broader public within his Roman milieu. Shortly after the beginning of his sole reign as Augustus, Caracalla had had four Vestals executed. Cassius Dio, an immediate contemporary of the event, believed he knew that one of the Vestals, Clodia Laeta, had loudly protested against being buried alive, because she had been raped by Caracalla himself.[4]

Even though Hippolytus could claim a high degree of topicality for his selected theme, in that the story he addressed had a woman being rescued from a similar plight, like anyone taking to the written or spoken word he first had to assure his public of the relevance and credibility of his contribution. He accordingly announced that he would, within the historiographical form of his text, indicate the "precise period of the incarceration of the sons of Israel as prisoners of war" and would recount the "prophecies contained in the visions of the blessed Daniel," and in so doing would himself be "a witness for the prophets and witnesses [martyrs] of Christ" (1.1; 2.11). He thereby claimed for himself not only an eminently religious role, but also that of a knowledgeable and thoughtful historian,[5] all the while presumably being well aware that the historical dimension in this case might touch on end-time calculations (cf. 1.18). Already in about the year 202, an author named Judas—perhaps in Alexandria, where there had been a bloody uprising, or as a distant observer in Rome—had come up with a determination of the end-time on the basis of Daniel 9.[6] Sextus Iulius Africanus may also have been in Rome some ten years later, in 221/2, when he produced a world chronicle, a time-line of world events.[7] Hippolytus, in any event, proclaims himself to be a discerning chronographer (Hipp. *On Daniel* 1.5); but his text tends to drift from argumentation to narrative, interspersed with digressions that make for more exciting reading (1.7–9; 2.19). He not only relates the story of Susanna and the two lecherous elders, but remodels it, turning it into a variant that perhaps emerged only in Rome, for it is not found in other textual versions. The setting is now a bathhouse.[8] Inhabitants of Rome, who had ready access to public baths, would have had no difficulty in visualizing the scenes described.

Hippolytus configures the reading experience—and for the majority of his audience this would have meant listening as the written text was read out—with an intent to excite. In the biblical text, Daniel appears directly after Susanna's condemnation, the two witnesses having conspired to accuse her of adultery with an unknown third party, after they themselves had failed, even with the use of threats, to lure her into sexual relations. At this precise point, for a period of perhaps ten minutes (keeping in mind the scenario of an oral presentation) Hippolytus laments how very cruel it would be to kill such a young and beautiful woman. Only then does he introduce Daniel, who has had a vision (1.23–27). He is after all a prophet (1.28). Hippolytus points out in all fairness, however, that Daniel's vision springs from his own imagination as the teller of the story. The public, it would seem, deemed visions an acceptable reason for the young man's intervention (1.29.1).

But Hippolytus does not want merely to convince his audience of his skill as a storyteller. With a dazzling display of quotations, he represents himself also as a scholar well versed in the insightful reading of texts (e.g., 1.18, 1.29). For two hundred years, the philosophers described as Middle Platonic had taught that insights might be hidden under the surface of the words of an inspired text.[9] Daniel in the lion's den, the three youths in the fiery furnace, the handwriting on the wall in Belshazzar's (i.e., Nebuchadnezzar's) palace: these stories Hippolytus interprets in *precise* fashion, as required of one whose knowledge is directed toward the pursuit of truth (2.11).

But he does not turn his attention to this until his second book, which perhaps appeared in a later stage of composition. The finished text would include two further books or book rolls. But who is Hippolytus addressing here? In the first book he simulates a dialogue, with objections coming from a fictitious interlocutor (1.29.1, 2.35.8), but he also calls directly on his audience for their attention: "Women and maids, small and great [men]" (1.23.2). And he develops Susanna into a role model for the downtrodden: religious individualization was not only for male members of the elite.

The dialogue is accordingly intense. In his third and fourth books, Hippolytus then speaks explicitly to a public that is, in his opinion, all too interested in end-time calculations on the basis of old visions. This is such a mistake! Whole groups might succumb to hysteria, with catastrophic consequences. Just as we in the latter part of the twentieth century were captivated by the 1978 massacre and suicide at the People's Temple in Jonestown, so Hippolytus calls attention to a third-century-AD apocalyptic group that had been led into the Syrian desert. They would have perished there like bandits, if the leader's wife had not saved them. In Pontus, similar visions led a leader to fall into economic inactivity and moral abjection.[10] In Hippolytus's diagnosis these cases resulted from carelessness in the interpretation of texts.

But then, at last, in the second half of his fourth book, he gives his readers and listeners precisely what they are longing for: an end-time calculation. The result is sobering. The continued existence of the Roman Empire and its Augusti is not under threat. And, if there are indeed still three hundred years to wait, then those living now have nothing to worry about.[11]

Hippolytus advises his audience to concentrate on the present time and its problems. The direst threat he confronts them with is that of being brought before the court and condemned to death for disobedience to the Augusti. But this was rather a theoretical danger, for it would seem that there were scarcely any persecutions of Hippolytus's co-religionists in the twenty years before and after his book's appearance in Rome.[12] The writer's real concern was rather the situation within the *ekklēsia, the "people's assembly."*[13] And that is precisely what the two elders in the Susanna narrative stood for, emerging as they did from the center of the group to which all belonged. According to Hippolytus, these two symbolize the "circumcised" and the "nations," and are to be feared even within the present assembly (1.15). So where were lines to be drawn? Hippolytus is at a loss for an answer to this question. He occasionally cites and names *the* apostle Paul, occasionally too *the* Gospel: but this amounted to no more than the biography of Jesus. We are of course concerned here with followers of Christ; but, when it comes to describing others as "Jews," Hippolytus is very reticent.[14] The narratives that were most familiar to him and his people were evidently from the Book of Daniel and First and Second Maccabees,[15] stories of Jewish martyrs from the time of the Seleucid kings and their conflict with the Hasmoneans in 167/166 BC. These stories were regarded as helpful moral tales,[16] and in no way diverged from the interests of other Jews who did not include Christ in their world picture.[17] For Hippolytus, though, Christ had already been active as an angel in the fiery furnace.[18]

Hippolytus in his *Commentary on Daniel* provides an insider's view of a religious minority in which many, while aware of the possibility of individual persecution, and turning to narratives that told of salvation or steadfastness in the here and now, also asked themselves questions about fundamental change. The intellectual in this situation won himself an audience by dint of superior religious knowledge. Only thereby was it possible to avoid false radicalization, and locate the enemy where he had to be fought: inside a still very roughly defined gray zone within the one true *ekklēsia*. It was only by defining the conflict in this way that Hippolytus could attain the authority that he wanted.

2. Political Actors

In the third century AD more than ever, individualization and institutionalization were two sides of the same coin. Religious competence and responsibility were ascribed to individuals, who sought to secure their relationship to history and the world, to their fellow humans and to their own selves, but above all to the divine (whatever form it might take), by joining with others. It was not only Hippolytus who operated within this context, but also the many religious specialists: not only founders of cults, male and female priests, and visionaries, but also teachers and the producers of texts. In such a situation, where discrepancies of wealth were continually growing, specialists gathered other people around them using their own means, or by subscriptions, or with the support of patrons. These groupings might meet very occasionally, or newcomers might be required to follow the specialist for years at a time, or to engage in intensive interaction within the group. Even in the case of a singular ritual like the Taurobolium in temples of the Mater Magna, the idea arose that it should be repeated every twenty years, thus giving the participant a long biographical association with the ritual.[19]

There were many and varied ways of seeking community and knowledge, on either an occasional or a continuous basis. Many of these, such as the reading of texts, were in the purview of professionals only. Hippolytus for one repeatedly referred to his own texts. He worked in a tradition that no longer left to chance such techniques as reactualization (the reapplication of previously revealed religious truths to the present day). Exegetical strategies developed by Hellenistic philologists in Pergamum and Alexandria, Stoic techniques for creating etymologies and discovering analogies, and the awareness that spiritual messages might be hidden between the lines of a text (e.g., in Plato): all of these were grist to his mill. In the multicultural and contentious environment of the newly-founded Ptolemaic city of Alexandria, philologists worked side-by-side on both Homer and the *Tanakh*—here translated into Greek and extended as the *Septuaginta*[20]—and from this work schools emerged that gained far-flung reputations. Reading techniques were practiced and systematized across the boundaries of textual corpora. Ancient descriptions of conflicts, whether in the Iliad or the Pentateuch, gave up their secrets, revealing a spiritual world between the lines, upon which was built a sophisticated theology in a Middle- and Neoplatonic vein.[21]

Such exegetical techniques also served to prepare speakers in both religious and nonreligious contexts for tasks such as the delivery of "homilies," sermons. There was also the issue, as Hermas had shown, of how to reveal religious knowledge to individual readers of both sexes; for the battle between good and evil was above all an internal one, requiring intensive practice. To this end, a constant stream of new texts provided material that flowed into networks removed from any kind of control by institutions. People who read such texts were referred to as gnostics (those having knowledge) or Hermetics (followers of Hermes); but there were no groups that bore such names.[22] This absence of named groups is shared with Neoplatonism, which was the first system to provide the polytheistic traditions of antiquity with a theoretical underpinning that could stand on an equal footing in rational discourse with the tradition of (especially Platonic and Stoic) "philosophy," and its reception by Jewish-monotheistic thinkers (beginning with Philo in Alexandria in the first century AD).[23] Monotheism was at this period simply the normal form of "Greek philosophy;"[24] but there were elements of theurgy within Neoplatonism, and from these there also developed ritual forms of dealing with the gods.[25] But philosophical traditions were not the only determining factors.

Ruling Interests

In AD 212 in the *Constitutio Antoniniana*, Caracalla had made the majority of the inhabitants of the Roman Empire Roman citizens. He probably reminded them in the same decree of their duty to intercede with the gods for the common good.[26] With a central ruling apparatus that was only gradually consolidating—the first comprehensive body of law, the *Codex Theodosianus*, was not promulgated until two hundred years later, in AD 438—and given the difficulty of travel and communication in the ancient world, more importance accrued to the role of religious communication in providing support for imperial rule.[27] The process took a different direction now than a hundred years previously, when Pliny the Elder had declared that Roman and Italian leadership of the *oikoumene* had the effect of disempowering barbaric rituals.[28] Instead, the rising importance of religion, along with increasingly firm demarcations between religiously defined groups, laid the basis for the growing number and severity of religious conflicts in Late Antiquity. In the first two centuries of the Imperial Age, there was no clear conception of an empire unified through religion.[29] The Severan idea of granting citizenship to all was, however, to have incalculable consequences.

A decree of Decius in AD 249 (in a process lasting until 251) marks the first intervention of the central power into local religious practices. Conformity in the worship of local deities was made a matter of first importance and came under regulation.[30] Visible religious communication on behalf of the emperor, present in his image, may have been designed as a measure of reconciliation, to nullify previous accusations of religious deviance: whoever sacrificed was exonerated, no matter what he or she had done previously. For fundamentalists this constituted the *status confessionis*, the confessional moment.[31] Groups whose members, at the cost of their own lives, refused to make such sacrifices, gained an almost limitless power of agency. Indeed, it was in appropriating, imitating, and telling the stories of such acts of "resistance by confession" that a group might achieve stability.[32] Fellow

Christians would impose no limits on those condemned to death. Almost anything said or done by or about them was outside the normal rules governing history or truth. Tales of their heroism would in later periods become a central element of Christian imagination and Christian discipline.[33] But, already in the decade after the end of Decius's campaign, Valerian proceeded to target the institutional structures of the Christians, which were now becoming visible.[34] The correspondence of the *episcopus* Cyprian of Carthage tells of processes of professionalization among a group of individuals who had made the religious leadership of Christians their career. They called themselves *clerics*, after this "lot" (Greek *kleros*) they had chosen.

Against the background of a growing confluence of religious with political communication, even secessionist "emperors" began for the first time to claim for themselves the role of *pontifex maximus*; as, for example, under the "Gaulish Empire" of 260 to 274. In Rome, Aurelian (Augustus 270–275) gave central political status to the cult of the sun, installing a new type of *pontifex Solis*, "solar pontiff." The tetrarchs under Diocletian (Augustus 284–305), as "Man of Jupiter" (*Iovius*) and "Man of Hercules" (*Herculius*), assumed a close relationship with these protective deities, respectively at the levels of Augustus and of his assigned Caesar. When the problem of the succession became acute, Diocletian in 303 decided to destroy the Christian sect's financial, institutional, and intellectual base: the succession, assured as it was by religious motifs, had to be certain of a positive reception.[35] Maximinus Daia (Caesar/Augustus 305–313) declared that it was his intention too to bolster traditional religious structures, and especially priesthoods.[36]

The presence of all these mechanisms suggests that internal rivalries within the four-emperor regime should be understood to have included issues of religious preference. By means of "edicts of tolerance," between the years 311 and 313, Galerius, Licinius, and Constantine brought to an end *not* the conflict with the Christians, but their conflict among themselves.[37] It was probably after the Battle of the Milvian Bridge near Rome, and his victory there over Maxentius on October 28, 312, that Constantine (Augustus 306/7–337) began occasionally to use the Christogram (Chi-Rho, ☧) as his personal symbol.[38] Meanwhile, legal remedies in such contexts having scarcely changed since the Augustan Age (when in 27 BC Augustus and Agrippa issued a decree requiring that votive gifts should be returned to public and sacred establishments in Kyme without compensation), Constantine now ordered restitution to the legal representatives of the Christians.[39]

Constantine's decision in favor of the practices and institutions of the Christians and their God did not arise in a vacuum.[40] He made it clear in his edicts that he saw unity and peace in the Roman Empire as depending on correct religious convictions and appropriate actions, in furtherance of the intentions of Caracalla and Decius. The religious knowledge that he perceived in the circle of *episcopi* amicably disposed to him appeared to him to follow accurately the path set by the Sibyls and Virgil.[41] The fields of action open to him as Augustus were not in this regard unlimited. In the provinces, alongside occasional issues of coinage and the granting of favors to supporters, his most important actions were rulings obliging governors and any important interest groups to loyalty and continued cooperation.[42] Priority was given to the suppression of rivals, either external or from within his own family.

Constantine had more freedom of action, however, in three areas having to do with religious activity. The first was construction, above all in Rome. Building projects had for half a millennium served as a medium whereby short- or long-term imperial rulers signaled their religious preferences (although Diocletian's first visit to Rome came only after twenty years of his reign had elapsed). Here, Constantine competed first with Maxentius (Augustus 306/7–312), who in his few years in Rome had left his mark on the city.[43] This son of the former tetrarch Maximian had begun by strengthening the city walls and extending the Palatine so as to make of it a real palace. In rebuilding Hadrian's Temple of Venus and Roma, he had also created Rome's biggest temple. It stood adjacent to the enormous so-called Basilica of Maxentius. The temple to Maxentius's son Romulus, who had died and been deified in 309, may well be identified with the nearby round, domed structure; his actual mausoleum was situated near Maxentius's circus and villa complex on the Via Appia, perhaps signaling that even the country residence and tomb of this emperor should be linked to Rome.[44]

Constantine's construction program was directed against a predecessor branded by him an illegitimate ruler:[45] he was announcing a change of dynasty, not a change of religion. He built the enormous Lateran Basilica, in a gesture that, while especially calculated to demonstrate his ability to mobilize the city's planning resources, also removed one of Maxentius's important support bases, for it was built over the barracks of the *Equites singulares* cavalry unit. In at the same time erecting a structure dedicated to his favored deity, Constantine had tradition behind him. While the graves of Maxentius's knights under the Lateran were destroyed, both the new structure and the basilicas to follow (as far as possible using unencumbered sites for the sake of rapid construction and the avoidance of resentment) created new, urgently needed burial spaces, now for Constantine's own power base. Older Christian traditions were not essential to this project. Thus the "Constantinian" Basilica of San Sebastiano may have been the continuation of a project begun by Maxentius. No Christian tradition has been found for the structure on the Via Labicana. The Basilica of St. Peter in the Vatican was a very late undertaking. Constantine simply had no concern for the Pauline tradition.[46] Finally, however, he decided in favor of a radical break with the city of his predecessors. The foundation of "his" city, Constantinople, offered the possibility of a completely new beginning, one bathed in the spirit of a purified religious knowledge.[47]

The second area of action open to Constantine was in reacting to local problems by establishing legal norms. These were often not laws aimed at general implementation, even though they might have the coherence of such a program, and despite the fact that they found their way into everyday affairs against a background of increasing administrative penetration.[48] Besides the privileging of clerics, who were in particular relieved from the depredations of the decurions, the bearers of administrative authority, but freed too from financial burdens at a local level, prohibitions bore for the most part against divination, the generation of religious knowledge. This had been a concern of the Augusti since the Augustan Age. A distinction of long standing allowed private inquiry into the divine will (so long as it did not concern public matters such as the lifespan of the Augustus), while public inquiry was strictly forbidden.[49] Polemic against sacrifice increasingly entered this mainstream, for, from the perspective of criminal law, animal sacrifice appeared above all to be a technique of divination. Even a ban on visiting temples was probably formulated against such a background, in reaction to a series of events in the mid-fourth century.[50]

Thirdly, in the *episcopoi* Constantine gained a new group of supporters, and, by treating them as imperial advisers, he made them into those powerful officials who were subsequently to be associated with the term "bishop." It was in 313 and 314 that he first invited them to synods (meetings) in Rome and Arles.[51] The synod comprised the Emperor's personal network, not the structures of some "imperial Church," which in fact did not yet exist. But what at first had the air of an imperial advisory committee quickly became a battleground for conflicting factional power bases. The new forum strengthened particular bishops, while at the same time it signaled the institutionalization of *one* Church within the borders of the Roman Empire. Constantine saw himself as the bishop for those who stood outside the Church.[52] Members of the loftiest of those social strata that were oriented to advancement rapidly allowed themselves to be won over to the office of bishop, a position now growing in importance. These were the *curiales*, officials of the local and central administration, below the senatorial level, who came from a broad range of social classes.[53] It was not the tolerance laws, but the Augustus's own attitude, that made Christian activities no longer a social impediment, even for the elite.[54] It may have been at this same period that existing traditions, such as those of female "overseers" and annual offices, were brought to an end.[55]

In one respect, however, Constantine's strategy reached an impasse. The significance of "professions of faith" to these officers of the emerging Church on the one hand, in their attempts to establish permanent and reliable followings in a world of vague conceptions of membership, and excessive demands on followers on the other, appears to have escaped him. Moreover, one dimension of episcopal negotiating strategy uncongenial to an imperial "chief bishopric" was the assertion that one's own theological convictions were unalterable. Tensions between political calculation and conviction-based partisanship confined the emperor's options as much as they opened up new opportunities for other members of his court. The emperor's presence in such a negotiating climate—still his practice in Nicaea in 325—was on the whole deleterious to his authority. Constantine found a solution to this problem by sending legates to represent him.

Dogma, in the shape of rulings on questions of faith intended to be binding, was not mere pretext for some political or economic purpose in this kind of politics. Theological debate also revolved around the question of how to talk about the emperor. The problem now was not the tradition of ruler worship. On the contrary, court ceremonial only enhanced the prestige of bishops, a small circle of whom were able to participate at an elevated level. What was problematic was the place, between God the Father and the Son of Man, that particular definitions of the godhead and humanity left for imperial authority. Today's synod decision was tomorrow's political problem, and accordingly open to revision. Where political circumstances left a particular issue of theological conflict chronically unresolved, long-term consequences could not be ruled out. Thus those who were excluded owing to their view of the divine nature of Jesus as uniquely central (the so-called Monophysites) may have reappeared as central figures in a subsequent religious revolution: after Muhammad, they figured as those radically monotheistic theologians who, embracing a concept of "submission" (*islâm*), had the theological authority needed by the new movement.[56]

Even small events might thus have considerable long-term consequences. For the world at large, however, Constantine's activities were only one factor among many. In Africa, the change in direction, and Constantine's many undertakings, went virtually unnoticed.[57] Constantine's ruling strategy, maintaining the gradient from right knowledge at the center to not-entirely-right practice at the peripheries, held firm. He was thus consistently, constantly, but *selectively* invited to intervene. The effect was all the greater when he did make the occasional more clear-cut intervention. Prominent examples were the construction of the Church of the Sepulchre in Jerusalem after the discovery of the "true cross" by his mother Helena, and the construction of a basilica next to Abraham's Oak at Mamre, again after his mother had confirmed the presence of other cults there.[58] In terms of religious politics, the Roman Empire remained a patchwork,[59] in terms of religion it was a muddy, gray mix of many superimposed colors. And the same applied to the city of Rome.

3. The Treatment of Difference

But life in Rome was not gray. In 354, the calligrapher Furius Dionysius Philocalus handed a luxurious calendar in the form of a codex, known today as the *Chronograph of 354*, to its dedicatee.[60] The dedication gives the latter's name as Valentinus, probably a junior member of the Symmacchus family, consular of Campania from 364 to 375, and brother to the celebrated orator and priest Quintus Aurelius Symmachus.[61] The most probable patron, if not the originator of the text, was then presumably the father, Lucius Aurelius Avianus Symmachus, orator and perhaps poet, and at the time of his death in 376 a member of two prestigious priestly colleges.[62] Furius was the inventor of the elaborate "Philocaline" characters that dominate the epitaphs of martyrs and bishops commissioned by Bishop Damasus after 366.[63]

The title page identifies the codex as a collection of official documents. The work is thus the product of a process whereby thousands of rolls of literary texts from private and public libraries were transcribed into codices. At the same time, new texts were produced, such as the epic by the Roman aristocrat Faltonia Betitia Proba, who died before 380, on Magnentius's usurpation of 351 to 353, and her extant *cento* praising Christ in a pastiche of Virgilian verses and hemistichs.[64] Literary activities of this sort were not casual hobbies. A contemporary observer, the itinerant philosopher Iunior, characterized the senatorial class as being uninterested in political functions, much preferring to enjoy their country properties and to honor the gods. In this world, religion was not primarily an arena for political conflict, but a field of learning central to the senatorial way of life.[65]

Dedicated to Valentinus for his edification (*paideia*), the calendar contains chronological and historiographical information. Representations of four city deities, a dedication to the ruling emperors in the name of the book's owner (Valentinus), a list of emperors' birthdays in calendar form, and representations of planetary gods, are followed by astrological information on the twelve signs of the zodiac; these indicate which activities are to be preferred when the moon stands within the sign in question. Next comes the actual calendar on twelve double pages; in it the dates of Jewish and Christian festivals are absent. The portraits of two consuls—probably those for 354—separate the calendar from a list of "consuls" from 509 BC to the present, complemented by four chronicle-like references to the birth of Jesus Christ (AD 1), his death (29), the arrival of Peter and Paul in Rome "to take up the episcopacy" (33), and their deaths in 55. There follow the dates of Easter from 312 (and predicted up to 411) and a list of *praefecti urbis*. Philocalus then adds (or perhaps his clients had him add) a list, in calendar order, of the burial dates of bishops in the city of Rome, with their dates of death from 255 to 310/11, as well as "depositions," that is burials, from 336 and 352, and a similar list of funerals or "birthdays" (*dies natales*) of martyrs,[66] followed by a chronological list of Roman *episcopi*. The latter begins with the sequence of succession from the crucified Christ to Peter. Further elements were added to the chronograph in later editions.

This particular combination of elements did not come about by chance. An interest in astrology is at its core. Not only does the author dedicate the first ten pages of the codex to astrology; he also incorporates it in further lists. The list of consuls, containing information on planetary and lunar characteristics at the beginning of each year of office, is unparalleled. Astrological interest extends to the birth and death of Christ. By using rhythms such as the eighty-four-year cycle, which was also used to calculate the future dates of Easter, social events become part of natural history, linked to a cosmological order that transcends the contingencies of human history. Although it prompted criticism from some intellectuals, astrology was the era's most highly developed method for comprehending the cosmos.[67]

Within the cosmological framework, Valentinus was offered an imperial one as well. At the beginning of his codex, Philocalus has a winged Fortuna writing *salvis Augustis felix Valentinus* on a shield. The words imply that the wellbeing of the Augusti and individual happiness are mutually contingent. The geographical implications are illustrated by the inclusion of the Fortunae of Rome, Alexandria, Constantinople, and Trier. But the further focus remains fixed on Rome. The codex was produced shortly before Constantinople received more institutional weight and prestige, conveyed by important relics brought to the city in 357, by the office of *praefectus urbis* (established by analogy with Rome),[68] and perhaps also by a Curia, which was formed by Julian as the eastern capital's "second-level Senate."[69] The author of the codex takes up a stance in anticipation of such developments, perhaps even himself researching the list of city prefects and adding a list of bishops proclaiming a unique line of succession from Christ to the Roman incumbent of the time. This signifies a preeminent focus on the city of Rome: not a matter of course in a world of thousands of bishops, among them many significant office-holders, as we know from the *Church History* written decades before by Eusebius of Caesarea.

The codex also takes a religious stance by means of its selection and arrangement of texts. It makes reference, for example, to conflicts with the Novatianists, who, like the Donatists, had their own Roman bishop, and assuredly also their own succession lists, with names that differed from those on Philocalus's lists.[70] Contemporary Christian affairs were complicated. Thus the exiled bishop Liberius, who had espoused Magnentius's cause, returned to the city to find himself confronted by a rival, Felix, chosen in 335. And these were not isolated events. They were typical of the rivalries and the pluralism of Roman Christianity, as future developments under Bishop Damasus would demonstrate.[71] So a unified genealogy was as clear a statement as the decluttering of consular *fasti*. The traditions and legitimacy of particular martyr cults and their cult locales were debated at this time.[72] The question of the dates of Easter was current as well, and chronically controversial.[73] To give dates for the next half-century using the Roman method of calculation—for there were others!—was to adopt a position, and of course the winning position.

Valentinus's father (perhaps) and the chronograph's creator presented him with a private compilation of individualized versions of older traditions. Religious knowledge, especially historicized knowledge, was a matter of upbringing and reflection. New religious practices, institutions, and narratives were in this way bound into a fundamental structure marked by astrology, the classical iconography of the gods, and centuries-old Roman institutions. There were strict lines of demarcation in current conflicts—for example against the Novatianists—and a contrary tendency toward harmonization when dealing with more fundamental tensions, within a Christianity that itself stretched back to the beginnings of the imperial system. Both were part of the appropriation, by elite individuals, of a religion that could also be studied, reflected upon, and practiced in private.

Bible Epic

Others elsewhere were attempting, as in the case of the codex of 354, to combine new traditions with elite cultural practices, and so render them productive for the formation of the same elite—not only in the realm of philosophy, and not only in Rome.[74] The presbyter Gaius Vettius Aquilinus Iuvencus, himself "of the most genteel descent," lived in Spain, in the south of one of the most strongly Romanized provinces. He was still working on a version of the gospels in four verse volumes in the final years of Constantine.[75] In his preface, Iuvencus quite explicitly situates himself within the Greco-Latin epic tradition, the lineage of Homer and Virgil. In common with them, he associates his narrative with a river—in his case the Jordan—but he claims also to offer the "sure basis for faith" (*certa fides*) that is provided by the deeds of Christ: this in the place of lies about the deeds of humans. Iuvencus regarded poetic activity as a religious act that would figure in his life's final reckoning. The same motive was also central to the reception of Hermas, was responsible for the copying and writing of further biblical epics, and inspired the numerous acts of martyrs.

The work's four books constituted a biography that followed the basic line of Matthew's gospel, complemented by parts of Luke and John (Mark's gospel was still scarcely read at this time).[76] Contrary to the later assertion by the canonic expert Jerome, in writing a work in four volumes Iuvencus was not modeling his narrative on any canon, but rather on the classic model of the day's limits, the onsets of night and sunrise. Ivencus even sought a heroic tone for his versification by recasting his prose models.

In a literary subculture, such an opus was a gamble, and indeed it found no direct imitators for the next hundred years. Even when they did at last make an appearance, they modeled themselves on Iuvencus, no longer on Virgil. But the narrative retreated further and further into the background, while interpretation of the subtext came to the fore. The defining of a theological position was now regarded as a more appropriate source of distinction than using high-value texts to win over members of an upper class that had, in any case, by the fifth century, long adopted piecemeal the Christian paradigm.[77] On the other hand, the earlier generation of authors had included the above-mentioned Faltonia Betitia Proba, a member of the Roman upper classes and the wife of a *praefectus urbi*. Shortly before the mid-fourth century, she wrote a biblical epic barely seven hundred lines in length. The work depicted the period from the Creation to Noah and the exodus out of Egypt, directly followed by Christ's birth and life. By means of this atomization and recombination, and adopting the form of a Virgilian *cento*, she gave an entirely new sense to the ancient epic tradition. Her work raised the status of both the ancient source and the new product, which reached a larger audience than might be expected.[78] The dressing of modern texts in ancient costumes was explored more than a half-century later by Nonnus of Panopolis in his epic on Dionysus, which referred, in both length and structure, to Homer's *Iliad* and *Odyssey*, and at forty-two books ranks longest of all ancient epics.[79] The biblical epic had merely emerged alongside an existing tradition of retelling epic myth; it had not replaced it.

4. The Competitive Scene

Neither the mechanisms of private and criminal law by which the imperial administration tried to resolve many conflicts, nor messages from the center reduced to images on coins, proved equal to the complex variety of the actors whose acquaintance we have made in this and the two preceding chapters. Modes of religious communication, religious identities, and developing religious networks appear as opaque gray zones filling the available space. They went through contortions in order to fit gaps left by changes in social structures locally—often against the background of the delegitimization of local elites—and settled into the shrinking terrain not yet occupied by the Roman imperium and its growing central authority, which regularly made additional demands on those same elites. Upon closer inspection, however, these gray zones may be seen to conceal beds of glowing embers that should not simply be dismissed as meaningless anomalies. In aggregate, their sparks kindled religious transformations. If they fail to fit one unified pattern, I should nevertheless like to propose one model that seems to me generally fruitful.

The rapid increase in the number of inscriptions up to the time of the Severans at the beginning of the third century AD signifies a shift in the locus of possible social advancement in the urban public arena; even though, for many, this applied only to the more freely configured marginal zones of the necropoleis outside the city. "I write (my or my family's funerary inscription); therefore I remain": this was as much an expression of the development of the individual identity as its motor. Numerous small-scale religious entrepreneurs, service providers who promised more effective religious communication, specialists in astrology, divination, and healing, along with the removal of sexual or legal impediments, were parts of this phenomenon. Such entrepreneurs and specialists made themselves available in times of crisis; and, increasingly, also assisted in long-term developments, acting as guides in the making of religious choices and in the development of the religious identity. The body and its well-being were among the objects of religious reflection, and also media for religious communication. As the local political classes and their civic identities lost stature, and, in some cases, the old elites became increasingly distant both geographically and socially, the scope for religious activity widened, and its importance no longer necessarily required epigraphical proofs.

In addition to service providers of both sexes, and those "primitive intellectuals" whose mental putterings did not progress further than a private religious *bricolage*, the people I have repeatedly referred to as "intellectuals" became increasingly visible from the Late Hellenistic Period onward.[80] The spoken, and often written, word was their favored mode of operation. They shared a critical stance toward the elite and its religious practices, toward images and temples in particular, and animal sacrifice (especially in the East); and they objected in general to expensive religion. They were in the long term successful in their criticism, which was internalized by a sufficient number of political and religious actors.[81] Their positions nevertheless always remained ambivalent, as their deliberations on cult images make clear. The various positions taken up by the protagonists remained as a whole beholden to ontologies of a Platonic character, on the one hand stressing the problematic nature of the material representation of ideas, owing to the profound gulf between the two spheres, but on the other sensing a *representational relationship* behind all materiality. In actual theological deliberation, this provided scope for a broad spectrum of hypostases between the image and the actual godhead that could never adequately be plumbed by the concept of representation.[82]

The most important problem for these intellectuals, however, remained competition within their own ranks, the constant struggle for recognition and status.[83] Typically, but, as the rise of the rabbis tells us, not always, they pursued a double strategy here, which led to contradictions. On the one hand, they operated within a complex web of societies and associations that made even a rise from slavery to the summit of the Empire appear to be within the realm of possibility. This was consonant with the inherently universalist stance of many of their lines of argument, which grew from Greco-Hellenistic roots, and this was a tendency that could easily be intensified by the use of binary logics of the excluded third. Against such an appeal to the widest-possible public, often including a rhetorical address to the Augustus or Augusti, stood mechanisms of isolation: the exclusivity of master-pupil relationships, and the need to safeguard one's position within a school or within the lineage of heads of schools.[84] The professional status conferred by scholastic institutions could magnify this effect. The claim to regulate ever more aspects of everyday living by means of religious communication, extending even to the entirety of an individual's lifestyle, permitted the boundaries between membership and exclusion to be controlled by ritual and moral demands that could in principle not be fulfilled: whether one might still be just included or already beyond the pale was a subtle question of judgment. All this was directed as much internally as externally. It is not by chance that these texts give rise to the impression that the ancient world consisted of hundreds of mutually incompatible groups.

In such a competitive environment, religious knowledge obtained in the course of personal religious communication turned into a resource that was ever more useful: again, internally against competitors and externally in the contest for attention. Revelations obtained in visions were commonly claimed, as were inspired interpretations against a background of increasingly rigid textual traditions.[85] Here too, demonologies and counter-demonologies furnished the degree of complexity that reality seemed to call for, and helped make concrete problems understandable, whether by intellectuals in their consultancy practices or in the everyday domestic cult.[86]

The desire of intellectuals to combine together in their efforts to protect their own status quickly became problematic, however, when their rhetoric against the practices of the elite met with the resistance of a middle-class ethic. It was at this point that lines of argument either rapidly lost their focus, giving way to unnuanced assaults on *too much* wealth or social dependency, or degenerated into extremist rhetoric. In such situations, a combination of religious knowledge and institutional power proved to be the most successful remedy, at least in the medium term, whether applied by a rabbi in collaboration with the Jewish patriarchal administration, a theologian in the role of a bishop, or a teacher of philosophy operating in an academy. Such religious actors, both male and female, succeeded with increasing frequency and to ever greater effect in winning the resources that enabled them to expand their reach, even to the provision of charity and aid for the poor, and this on a large scale.[87]

In this manner, religion—and here, now as then, we may begin to use "our" concept of religion[88]—became increasingly important in many areas.[89] We begin to see religious institutions offering the sorts of benefits that they typically provide to their members: the preservation of status, exclusivity, the building of networks by the integration of common friendships, and the hardening of hierarchical distinctions. Individuals accordingly now saw themselves more frequently (if, overall, still rarely) as members of a religious group, and they more often ascribed such an affiliation to others as well (often pairing the identification with negatives, such as inferior worth, political unreliability, even criminality). Actors in conflicts now could and did formulate the lines of their disagreements in terms of religion.[90] This left problematic traces of supposedly religious conflicts and violence in the texts of this period: traces that are not easy to confirm in the archaeological record.[91] Since this time, for the people of the Mediterranean region and the geographical area that increasingly became "Europe," a religion has come to represent a collective identity, a marker by which groups are able to define themselves both internally and to the outside world, and also to make comparable assignments in respect of other groups. In brief, a religion is a polemical concept, but one that does not solely, or even particularly, target the *religious* practices and ideas of the antagonist. It is this understanding of religion that is required of us in the present day.

XIII

Epilogue

THIS BOOK HAS NARRATED a history. A world in which religion was an activity became a world in which it was possible to possess religious knowledge and to belong to one of several religions. By the mid-fourth century AD, where our narrative has now brought us, most people were not aware of this transformation, although some were already acting as if it were self-evident. All were equally unaware that the history of the Roman Empire would shortly come to a fork in the road. It would follow very different lines of development in the Latin West (through the agency of Germanic kingdoms) and the Byzantine East, and this, along with the Islamic expansion three hundred years later, would entail a long-term reduction in interchange across the Mediterranean. The main thing they did not know, however, was which religious knowledge was correct and which false, which religion would become legitimate and which not. And they also did not know that the seriousness of religion was now such that, however an individual's religious communication might be configured, in the future he or she would be restricted to membership in just one religion.

How great these changes were, and how vast the options for further development, becomes apparent when we look at institutions with which we have not so far become acquainted as motors of transformation. At about the turn of the third century AD, the *epulones* of the city of Rome, a priesthood responsible for particular rituals related to the supply of victuals, found themselves obliged as a body to set up dedicatory inscriptions to the Mater Deum Idaea and the (slightly modified) Capitoline Triad on the upper reaches of the Anio, a virtually inaccessible wilderness where the sources of important Roman aqueducts were located.[1] The accumulating of priestly offices now also became more frequent among the elite. In the second half of the fourth century, for example, Publius Vettius Agorius Praetextatus was augur, pontiff of Vesta, pontiff of the sun, *quindecimvir* (thus one of "the fifteen for sacral matters"), curial of Hercules, hierophant at Eleusis, and a temple warden, probably in the Isis cult of Serapis. Especial prominence is then given, at the end of the list, to his sacral functions as *pater patrum* in the cult of Mithras, with the formula "father of fathers in the true republic."[2] Here too we see something in the nature of a notional *ekklēsia*, whereby the social elite sought, by the intensification of their religious roles and activities, to gain a religious authority that was by this time no longer self-evident.[3]

In the East of the Roman Empire, the rhetorician Libanius and the bishop Synesius of Cyrene were in agreement insofar as the fundamentals and methods of their philosophical discourse were concerned, even if, perhaps with an eye to temples or to their own lifestyles, they arrived at very different conclusions.[4] The principles of textual interpretation do not vary with confessional boundaries.[5]

Constantine's grant of equal treatment to Christian clerics and teachers was in any case not irreversible. Julian as Augustus reintroduced discrimination in 361/2, even personally promoting cults that practiced animal sacrifice. This of course found no favor with the population of a culturally conservative city like Antioch.[6] At the same period, the population of Alexandria, especially the elite, still maintained about 2,500 small temples.[7] And, even after Gratian's rejection of the supreme pontificate (in about AD 380), Aurelius Symmachus mobilized his pontifical network to proceed against a fugitive Vestal suspected of so-called incest.

In the Judeo-Christian gray zone, despite episcopalization at one pole and the institutionalization of the rabbinate at the other—both still minority phenomena—many still espoused nonconformist positions. Shortly before the mid-fourth century, for example, the author of Pseudo-Clementine *Homily 11* observed followers of Christ "of foreign origin" who observed the law as "Judeans," in exactly the same way as Judean-born observers of the law.[8] Such blurring of differences did not reduce tensions. Quite the contrary. For his "polyphonic choir" of *episkopoi*, the historian and bishop Eusebius of Caesarea constructed a common genealogy that featured a separation from Judaism as early as the time of the apostles, Christ's immediate pupils. He saw confirmation of this in the events surrounding the ending of the rebellions of AD 70 and 135.[9] However, the rabbis, in their rival construction of a Judaism in which membership for intellectuals was defined by continued participation in a many-voiced discourse, rejected historization of this kind.[10]

The work of key actors in turning collective identities into institutions, and then further shaping those institutions by the creation of narratives and forms of knowledge, made it possible for attributions of religious affiliation to come into play in situations of conflict. These were legion, and as a rule did not depend on the coincidence of religious and social differences. Frequently, it was not only the initiators of conflicts who saw themselves as Christians, but also their antagonists.[11] It was bishops who extended their positions of power in the process, often in close accord with the central administration. For this they had not only their own clientele to rely on, but also groups such as the *fossores*, the cemetery workers, whom Constantine, for example, had put under the bishop's authority in Constantinople. Clearly, the administration of burial grounds—especially in the great cities—brought with it more than financial opportunities.[12] If, then, we seek the reasons why bishops in the western part of the Empire continued to exercise local dominion after "Rome" had fallen, it is to the context of the rise of more autonomous local and regional units that we should turn, not to some collective identification as a "Catholic Church" imagined by the very bishops we are talking about.

There was conflict, or rather competition, between Rome and Constantinople. After a thousand years of history, the new Rome threatened to sap the status of the old. Although this was not a religious conflict, it was a contest that was played out in the same religious forms as had facilitated place-related claims since the Early Iron Age.

Elites again and again put forward claims in the shape of sacral objects, statues, and reliquaries. This process culminated in the Palladium, supposedly transported from Troy as a token of the geographical transfer of dominion and its temporal permanence. When, as after the capture of Rome in AD 410, the object itself was not available, it was recreated in the form of knowledge, that is to say with the aid and in the medium of texts.[13]

Bishop Damasus's building program in Rome, beginning in the 360s, should be read in the same way. It affected central as well as peripheral locations. The Lateran Basilica itself was sited in a prime residential area, not hidden away at the edge of the city.[14] In the church of Santa Anastasia, Damasus built a substantial structure in a zone of great monuments that included the Palatine and the Forum, and he put his titular church of San Lorenzo in Damaso on the Field of Mars. His circle of martyrs' churches covered the cemetery zone outside the city. But even Damasus's projects became objects of inter-Christian conflicts that had to do with sites and their local traditions. Smaller churches, such as the basilica in Trastevere and the Titulus Marci, were occupied by rival groups and used for the holding of elections. Nearby, meanwhile, those texts that turned ancient religions into knowledge, and so have remained of major importance to us, works by Plautus and Cicero, Varro and Ovid, Virgil and Horace, Pliny and Suetonius, Gellius and Solinus, Livy and Lactantius, also Servius and Macrobius, to name only the Latin authors among them, were being transcribed into codices.

But this Roman Empire had diminished. It had turned inward. Beyond its borders, the world now had a different aspect. Mesopotamian Jews were able with impunity to mock "Romans" (i.e., "Christians"), who were regarded with mistrust by the ruling Sassanids; converts carried the texts of Mani—religion in pocketbook-form (remember the Mani Codex from Cologne)—along the Silk Road, and even further, beyond the mighty Iranian Empire and as far as China. If these travelers had spoken there about Numa or Jesus, either figure would surely have seemed rather insignificant to their listeners when compared to Zoroaster or Confucius. That they "belonged" to a religion would have struck the Chinese as a very odd idea, whereas accounts of religious discourses would have met with understanding in northern India. But, if they had spoken of their entirely practical attempts and strategies aimed at communicating with actors who were as a rule no longer humans, but still powerful; of whose existence they themselves were convinced, but not everyone else: then they would surely have initiated conversations that their interlocutors would have understood and might even have carried further. It was not the fact of religious activity that distinguished the people of the Roman Empire from the inhabitants of other parts of the world, but the specific names, the institutions, the specialists and their bodies of knowledge, and, finally, the forms of individual and collective identity that were acquired through religious practices. Rhea would have found this very strange indeed.

NOTES

Chapter I: A History of Mediterranean Religion

1. For an extensive treatment of the missionary phenomenon and its consequences: Fuchs, Linkenbach, and Reinhard 2015. The network concept in this context is expounded in Habermas 2008. On the frequently only short-term consequences of other imperialist adventures (excluding Central and South America), see Reinhard 2014.

2. This brings to mind the subject of our use of the eras before and after the birth of Christ [BC/AD]; while recognizing the existence of other eras in widespread use, this can no more be described as the "common era" than its specifically Christian origin should be concealed behind expressions such as the German *unserer Zeitrechnung*.

3. E.g., Meena 2013.

4. Durkheim 2007. Also Pickering 2008, Rosati 2009.

5. Asad 1993; McCutcheon 1997; Masuzawa 2000, 2005. For a detailed treatment of the following, see Rüpke 2015e.

6. See Nongbri 2013.

7. Luckmann 1991; also Dobbelaere 2011, 198 and Rüpke 2016d.

8. On the critique of a narrowing of perspectives associated with modernizing theories, see Rüpke 2012h; for a detailed treatment, see Rüpke 2013d.

9. On the concept of appropriation, see de Certeau and Voullié 1988, also Füssel 2006; the fragmentary aspect remains central for de Certeau 2009.

10. Rüpke 2012d, referring to McGuire 2008.

11. On ancient religious networks, see Rutherford 2007, Eidinow 2011, Rüpke 2013e, and Collar 2014.

12. On gods as "actors," see also Latour 2005b, 48.

13. Boyer 1994.

14. Archer 1996, 225–26.

15. See for example Kippenberg, Rüpke, and von Stuckrad 2009; on the nineteenth century, Nipperdey 1988, Hölscher 2005.

16. An example of a religious historiography taking individual actors as its starting point is Lane Fox 1988.

17. On the search for religious individualization beyond Christianity and so-called modernity, see Rüpke 2012h, Rüpke and Spickermann 2012, Rüpke 2013d, Fuchs and Rüpke 2015; and Fuchs, Linkenbach, and Reinhard 2015.

18. See Rüsen 1990 and de Certeau 1991.

19. E.g., in the work of Weber 1985 and Schütz 1981; more recently, Geertz 1973.

20. See Joas 1996.

21. Emirbayer and Mische 1998, also on what follows.

22. Ibid., 970.

23. Fundamental: Emirbayer and Mische 1998; taken up by Hitlin and Elder 2007, Dépelteau 2008, Campbell 2009, Noland 2009, Small 2011, and Silver 2011.

24. Emirbayer and Mische 1998, 975, 983, 993.

25. Ibid., 1004.

26. See e.g., Brelich 1969, Cancik 1973.

27. See Gill 2008, 2009b; Setaioli 2013; Rüpke and Woolf 2013b.

28. See Rüpke 1995a, 2006f.

29. See Gordon 2013d.

30. See e.g., Belayche et al. 2005, Santangelo 2013.

31. Rebillard 2012, 2–5, on "salient identity."

32. Ground-breaking for "social identity theory" was the work of Tajfel and Turner; see Tajfel 1974, 69. On the definition of the group; Turner 1975. Summarized in Ellemers, Spears, and Doosje 1999.

33. Ashmore, Deaux, and McLaughlin-Volpe 2004, 83, with an illustrative chart.

34. Beard 1991, cf. Woolf 2012a.

35. Ashmore, Deaux, and McLaughlin-Volpe 2004, 84.

36. Van Dommelen, Gerritsen, and Knapp 2005, 56.

37. Vásquez 2008, 167, with reference to Appadurai 2000.

38. The subject of religious communication is elaborated in Rüpke 2014e.

39. Sperber and Wilson 1987; Wilson and Sperber 2002, 2012.

40. See e.g., for Sparta, Richer 2012, ch. 5. On the absence of priests in rural Punic sanctuaries, López-Bertran 2011, 57.

41. See e.g., Fögen 1993 and Sear 2006.

42. Amply discussed in Otto 2011; for discussion of the research, Otto and Stausberg 2013.

43. On this dynamic concept of sacralization, and for a critique of the academic use of the concept of the sacral, see Rüpke 2013m. On definitions of religion that depend on "the holy," see briefly Dobbelaere 2011; Taves 2009 replaces it with "the special."

44. Cf. Cameron 2004, 257 (without reference to religion).

45. Punyanunt-Carter et al. 2008.

46. See Onorato and Turner 2004, Verkuyten and Martinovic 2012.

47. Taves (2011) rightly delivers this challenge to students of religious studies.

Chapter II: Revolutions in Religious Media in Iron Age Italy

1. See Scheid, Svenbro 1996 on the productivity of the metaphor of weaving. I take the concept of the "special" as a general determinant of religion from Taves 2009.

2. For a comprehensive account of animal sacrifice in the Mediterranean Bronze Age, see Wilkens 2012.

3. Zuchtriegel 2012; for significance at later periods, see Prayon 1990, Giontella 2011. For a general discussion of deposition, see Haynes 2013.

4. See e.g., Pezzoli-Olgiati and Rowland 2011, briefly at 11.

5. On the term and its research context, see Rüpke 2012h, 2013g, 2013f.

6. Meyer 2008.

7. A full treatment in Raja and Rüpke 2015b. For a brief treatment of "postprocessual archaeology," see Cazzella and Recchia 2013; on the theoretical construction of correlations with objects, their biography, and agency, see Latour 2005a and Hodder 2012.

8. On the Mediterranean region as a historical theater, see Horden and Purcell 2000, Woolf 2003, Abulafia 2005, Harris 2005, and Horden and Purcell 2005.

9. Ridgway 2000a, 181; Recchia 2011; and Alberti and Sabatini 2012.

10. Snodgrass 2000, 173.

11. Bietti Sestieri 2010.

12. Cazzella and Recchia 2009.

13. Perdigones Moreno 1991; on the contact, López Castro 2005.

14. See Bresson 2005, 100–102; on contacts between the Middle East and Greece in the religious sphere, see e.g., Auffarth 1991, Bremmer 2008, and Burkert 2011b.

15. Bietti Sestieri 2005, 16–17.

16. Malta: von Freeden 1993; Britain: Darvill 2010, 221.

17. Morris 2009, 66.

18. On the critique, Smith 2006.

19. E.g., Gilman et al. 1981.

20. Rathje 2005, 26.

21. Morgan 2009, 54.

22. Prayon 2004b, 88–89.

23. Mazarakis Ainian 1997, 394; Morris 2009, 73; de Polignac 2009, 429.

24. Morgan 2009, 53.

25. Dating according to Mazarakis Ainian 1988.

26. Mazzocchi 1997, 179.

27. Papadopoulos 1980.

28. Kyrieleis 2008.

29. de Polignac 2009, 440.

30. Bietti Sestieri 2005, 18–19; Tore 1983, 458.

31. Lo Schiavo 2002, 4.

32. Ibid., 12.

33. Tore 1983.

34. Lo Schiavo 2002; see also Torres Ortiz 2005 for Spain.

35. Kleibrink 2000, 443–44. There are similar finds for Rome, in the House of the Vestals: Argento, Cherubini and Gusberti 2010, 81.

36. Ibid., 441.

37. Kleibrink, Kindberg Jacobsen, and Handberg 2004, 48; see also Scheid and Svenbro 1996.

38. The basis for this interpretation is Mauss 1925.

39. See e.g., Beijer 1991.

40. For grave goods, see Laneri 2007, 2011; Rieger 2016.

41. Zuchtriegel 2012, 235; temple on 259.

42. Ibid., 269.

43. Di Giuseppe and Serlorenzi 2010.

44. Luckmann 1991.

45. Comella 1981 and 2005d.

46. Cf. for the Imperial Period, Rüpke and Woolf 2013b.

47. Van Rossenberg 2005, 90.

48. Wilkens 2002, 2012, 75–6.

49. I have Julie Casteigt, fellow at the Max Weber Center, to thank for this suggestion.

50. Gilman et al. 1981. Grave goods are interpreted in this way; e.g., the deposition of weapons as marking a change in social homogeneity in Vulci (Cherici 2005); see also Putz 1998.

51. Here I follow Smith 2005, 76–77, as applicable to Rome (78).

52. Wilkens 2012, 57.

53. Bartolini 2013, 80.

54. Van Rossenberg 2005, 88.

55. Pettitt 2011.

56. Buranelli 1983, 117; the chronology is subject to debate.

57. Sgubini and Ricciardi 2005, 526. Tabolli 2013 defined cremation temperatures of from 600 to 700 degrees Celsius for Faliscan Narce in the eighth and seventh centuries BC.

58. Van Rossenberg 2005, 87.

59. Cf. Van Rossenberg 2005, 87, and, more generally on strategies for the demarcation of religious space at this period, Van Dommelen, Gerritsen, and Knapp 2005; cf. for Syria in the 3rd millennium BC, Porter 2008. On forms of the necropolis over a limited period in Tarquinia, see Buranelli 1983, 117.

60. For Tarquinia, see Steingräber 1985a, 74.

61. For Orvieto, Prayon 1975, 179; for Cerveteri, Izzet 2007, 117.

62. Marín Ceballos, Belén 2005; Ridgway 2000a, 2000b; Prayon 2000.

63. Colonna 2000, 258–59, records such differences for the neighboring towns of Caere, Populonie, and Vetulonia, respecting access to graves and the frequency and duration of use of tumuli. See also Steingräber 1985b, 35, respecting orientation of graves.

64. Cuozzo 2005.

65. Smith 2006, 145; on problems, e.g., in identifying clients: D'Agostino 2005. Generally Laneri 2007, 9–10.

66. Rüpke 2012b.

67. Carroll 2006; Carroll, Rempel, and Drinkwater 2011; Hope and Huskinson 2011.

68. On the significance of this phase, Laneri 2011, 28–29.

69. Croucher 2012.

70. Van Rossenberg 2005, 88. For a possible practice in sixth-century BC Cortona of exposing the corpse on a burial tumulus, see Prayon 2010, 77.

71. Kleibrink 2000, 453.

72. Zuchtriegel 2012, 241.

73. de Grummond 2006; Radke 1970, 1979.

74. Pfiffig 1975, 240, 260, 277.

75. Maggiani 1997, 431–32; Pfiffig 1975, 24; stable language groups: Renfrew 1993, 48.

76. Rüpke 2012d. On de Certeau's concept of appropriation, see Füssel 2006 and de Certeau 2007.

77. Described for Veii by Maggiani 1997, 433–44.

78. Lorusso and Affuso 2008.

79. In particularly sophisticated form on those bronze vessels called *situla*, c.f. Wamers et al. 2011, 63–66. On the north Etruscan bronze figures of the eighth–sixth centuries BC, see Marchesi 2011.

80. Prayon 1998a, Prayon 2004b. However, isolated instances existed at several locations, e.g., the Giants of Mont'e Prama (ninth/eighth centuries BC) or the Lunigiana menhirs from the Neolithic into the eighth or even sixth century BC. For a more general discussion of the role of diffusion, see Wilkinson, Sherratt, and Bennet 2011.

81. Pliny, *Natural History*=Plin. *HN* 35.152. See also Dionysius of Halicarnassus 3.46.3–5, Strabo 5.2.2, and Roncalli 1985, 75. On the influx of craftsmen into Pithekoussai, the first Greek settlement in Italy, see Scatozza Höricht 2006.

82. Prayon 2004b. Misapprehensions evident in the production of such objects indicate the use of Punic models: Meissner 2004.

83. See Lemos 2000 for Lefkandi.

84. Mazzocchi 1997.

85. Kimmig 1985.

86. For this analogy, Holloway 2005, 34.

87. Torelli 2011, 3–4; Edlund-Berry 2011; Lulof 2011.

88. Torelli 2011, 5, fig. 4.

89. On the discussion of possible precursors, see Coarelli 2011, 49–50; but see also Zuchtriegel 2012, 293.

90. Izzet 2000, 2007, 130–42; see also 128–29 on walls and doorways. Cf. for Greece, on similar practices for diverting the gaze by the positioning of pictorial friezes or the construction of the temple pediment, see Osborne 2000.

91. Kleibrink, Kindberg Jacobsen, and Handberg 2004.

92. Bonghi Jovino 2005. On the discussion: Riva 2010; Fulminante 2014.

93. Berardi Priori 1997.

94. Aigner-Foresti 2000.

95. Roth-Murray 2005; a different position for Latium is held by Kleibrink 2000, 458, and Bietti Sestieri 2010, 274, and for Etruria by Bietti Sestieri 2011, 410. On the whole class of distaffs, see Gleba and Horsnaes 2011.

96. Rüpke 2013a.

97. Winther 1997, 424.

98. Botto 2005.

99. Batino 1998, 34–35.

100. Zuchtriegel 2012, 259–62. For contemporary and later ritual structures and findings in Anagni, see Gatti, Picuti 2008, 31–48.

101. See below, pp. 160–63.

Chapter III: Religious Infrastructure

1. The following relies on the discussion of Dutch excavations in Smith 1999. I favor the high chronology for "Temple 0."

2. See ibid., 466. These processes of differentiation can be discerned within the Villanovan culture from the eighth century BC at the latest (Giardino, Belardelli, and Malizia 1991).

3. On the concept of monumentality, see Meyers 2012.

4. As maintained in Smith 1999, 458.

5. Coldstream 2003, 317; the following typology is to be found on pp. 321–27.

6. See ibid., 328–29.

7. Ibid., 327.

8. Cf. ibid., 338.

9. Cf. Van Wees 2011, 19, for early coverage of Göbekli Tepe.

10. Coldstream 2003, 329–30.

11. As in the Tomba Castellani near Praeneste (briefly, Coarelli 2011, 30). We must also think here of the oversized Greek statues representing women (*korai*); see Franssen 2011, 402.

12. See ibid., 467.

13. Bouma 1996.

14. Ibid., ch. 8. See also Bouma and Prummel 1997.

15. Sinn 2005b, 88.

16. Lulof 2006, 239–40, makes a convincing case for this hypothesis.

17. Smith 1999, 465.

18. See ibid., 466.

19. See above, chapter II.5.

20. E.g., Meuli 1946; Burkert 1981, 1984; Cancik-Lindemaier 1987; Hultgård 1993; Kult 1997; Müller-Wille 1999; Gladigow 2000; Janowski and Welker 2000; Mylonopoulos 2006; Stroumsa 2009. See also Girard 1987, Hamerton-Kelly 1987.

21. Merely modified in Rüpke 2006b, 140–46.

22. Briefly, Comella 2005b, 226; also Comella 2005c, 2005e.

23. On the theory of self-world relations, see Rosa 2016.

24. Van Wees 2011, esp. 3–5 with the emphasis that competition does not take any constant direction as a historical "force."

25. See Franssen 2011, 397–98.

26. For an overview, see Ben Abed and Scheid 2003. On Etruria, see Prayon 1990; for northern central Italy as a whole, Giontella 2011.

27. See below on the Portonaccio complex. A cistern was also installed at Sant'Omobono. I am grateful to Marlis Arnold for the information.

28. Briefly, Attenni 2013.

29. Osanna and Sica 2005; taken up by Cerchiai 2008.

30. See chapter I.3 on the concept of collective religious identity.

31. See, for example, the "monotheism" of Minoan religion, formulated using these lines of argument in respect of Metapontum by Peatfield 1994, 34, and Barberis 2004, 195–99 (briefly, Barberis 2005). On the persistence of aniconic forms for symbols of gods, see Gaifman 2012.

32. Thus Prayon 2010, 75.

33. It is unclear how broadly such family ties may have been defined. It is certainly true that the seventh century BC saw the emergence of the gentilician name in central Italy, indicating relationship far beyond the Greek *patronymikon*: Rix 1972.

34. Unlike, e.g., in Pisa; see Prayon 2010, 76.

35. Prayon 2010, 78–81.

36. Ibid., 78–79.

37. Sinn 2005a, 15–16.

38. Colonna 1985, 23; for details, Bonghi Jovino and Bagnasco Gianni 2012, 31.

39. See already Cato, *On agriculture* 18.6.

40. Overview in Comella 2005a, Marcattili 2005, Menichetti 2005.

41. Argento, Cherubini, and Gusberti 2010, 86.

42. See Bomhard and Kerns 1994, 530, no. 381. Thus also the similarly sounding Hittite term for a hearth.

43. Cf. Matasović 2010 for the unusual formation, which uses an expression from the semantic field of "fire" for "hearth," whereas usually we find a generalization in the other direction.

44. Critical on previous research (but continuing the focus on sacrifice): Ekroth 2011, López-Ruiz 2013, and Naiden 2013.

45. Bell 1992, Humphrey and Laidlaw 1994; Rüpke 2013l.

46. See Scheid 1985, 1988, for treatments of the significance of the Roman festive meal against the background of Greek-orientated studies in respect of sacrifice.

47. For early Greece see Coldstream 2003, 332.

48. For the early period, the latter claim can only be extrapolated from Late Republican and Imperial Age evidence: Rüpke 2005d. See also Veyne 2000. For the importance of alterity in creating ritual space, see Mol 2015.

49. Linke 2003, Berg 2008, Estienne 2011.

50. Coldstream 2003, 321. The speed of dissemination depended on both the form of media and the theme. Themes of current importance "travelled" fast on ceramics in Greece, so that such themes were popular in Magna Graecia within a few years. Less politically pertinent fashions followed with a delay of about a quarter of a century (Giudice 1998, 147).

51. Greco 1998, 47–48. On the site on the Sele, also Greco 2008 and Cipriani 2008.

52. Ibid., 58; parallels, 62.

53. Breglia Pulci Doria 1998, 97 and 107.

54. Gaultier 2010, 121. I adhere to this account in the following.

55. Ibid., 122–23; on the Hercules, Plin. *HN* 35.157.

56. Gaultier 2010, 125, with reference to *Etruskische Texte* Ve 3.40, 37, 10, 9, 14. Vibenna: *Etruskische Texte* Ve 3.11; *Thesaurus linguae Etruscae* 35.

57. Gaultier 2010, 127–28.

58. On the depth of Etruscan gable ends in comparison with Greek architecture in stone, see Winter 2006. On the early independent development of terracotta architecture in central Italy, see also Winter 1993. The combination of wooden beams and terracotta plaques may itself have been a Corinthian invention (Coarelli 2011, 74).

59. Warden 2012, 97–99.

60. Gaultier 2010, 132, on forms from Falerii.

61. Ibid., 126.

62. Colonna 1985, 98.

63. Colonna 2002, 158.

64. Gaultier 2010, 135.

65. See Colonna 1985, 67–8.

66. On the nature of the setting, see Holloway 1994, 166–67.

67. Colonna 1991.

68. For a full discussion of the dating of this phase, Sommella Mura 1977b, especially 121, and Sommella Mura 1977a, 11. Overviews: Ioppolo 2000, Pisani Sartorio 2000. For a critical assessment of the historical reconstruction, see Brocato and Terrenato 2012. The first monumentalization of the Temple of Apollo at Pompeii should be set in the same period (Zevi 1998, 6).

69. Torelli 1997, 116. See also Lulof 1993.

70. Livy 5.19.6.

71. The date of about 509 BC for the expulsion of the Etruscan kings from Rome was a construct of early Roman historiography, and provides no basis for explanations prior to the third quarter of the 5th century BC (Bleicken 1988, 18).

72. See Livy 1.56.1 for forced labor on the Capitoline Temple of Jupiter.

73. In the long term, this called for specific decorative features on an isolated basis at the very least: Strazzulla 2006, 38–9.

74. See (although he does not use the term) Oakley 2014, 4.

75. Gaultier 2010, 129.

76. E.g. that of one Iana (*Année épigraphique*=AE 1995, 189).

77. Bartoloni 1989–90. See also the catalogue (for the entire Republic) in Marroni 2010, 43–206.

78. See Sciortino 2005, 92: deposits from the 7th century BC onwards.

79. Zeggio 2005, 69.

80. Pensabene et al. 2005, 105.

81. Bartoloni 1989–90, 758.

82. Sommella Mura 2000, 60.

83. Ibid. and Sommella Mura 2009. For a condensed construction history, Perry 2012.

84. Hopkins 2012, 124.

85. Plin. *HN* 35.154. On my characterization of the plebeians, see Oakley 2014, 8.

86. Livy 2.42.5; see also 4.20.12 and Dionysius of Halicarnassus 6.13.

87. For a reconstruction of the building, see Nielsen and Poulsen 1992, esp. 75–79.

88. For this observation, see Holloway 1994, 169. He is supported by the finds mentioned by Guzzo 1998. Cf. also the deposition of disks of graduated weight in the mid-sixth century BC, preceding the emergence of a money economy (ibid., 29–30).

89. Full coverage in Torelli 1997, and in the treatises in Palombi 2010.

90. Downey 1993, 243–45; a full treatment in Downey 1995.

91. Liou-Gille 2004, 249–51; Losehand 2007, 82–84; Coarelli 2011, 61–64.

92. See above, pp. 33–34.

93. Filippi 2007/8, 626–28 and 636; cf. Gallone 2008, 662–63.

94. See above, pp. 52–53.

95. On this process, see Rüpke 2012f, 19–20. On the history of the institution, see Bianchi 2010.

96. The latter hypothesis is in Zevi 1993.

Chapter IV: Religious Practices

1. On the central significance of music in ritual, see Michaels 2010, 20–21; Howes 2011, 95.

2. See Lacam 2011 for the Iguvine Tablets. On the problem of sources, Naerebout 2015; dance movements were possibly hardly ever portrayed because, although they occurred frequently, they conflicted with the values intended to be represented.

3. Romualdi 1990, concentrating especially on rural areas of northern Etruria (catalogue: 632–49).

4. Ibid., 626.

5. Comprehensively, but with unacceptable hypotheses, Torelli 1984 (critical appraisal: Ampolo 1988); Comella 2004, 332.

6. Steingräber 1980, 224–26; there too for what follows. I have to thank Marlis Arnhold for indications of the *possibility* of representations with staffs and robes.

7. Hofter 2010, 70. Hand-fashioned heads and portraits: 72–73.

8. Steingräber 1980, 234. On visibility and invisibility, Bagnasco Gianni 2005.

9. On this point, Söderlind 2005, 362; Comella 2004, 337, and see also 333 on the representation of covered heads in Latin-region statues.

10. On the concept of sacralization instead of "sanctuary," see Rüpke 2013m.

11. On the contrast, briefly, Steingräber 1980, 251; on Greek clay reliefs up to the end of the 5th century BC, Comella 2002. The situation is different within the ambit of the Asclepius cult.

12. For extreme examples, see Recke and Wamser-Krasznai 2008, 67–9; Charlier 2000.

13. Recke and Wamser-Krasznai 2008, cat. no. 25.

14. *CIL (Corpus Inscriptionum Latinarum)* 12,4=*ILS (Inscriptiones Latinae Selectae)* 8743=*ILLRP (Inscriptiones Latinae Liberae Rei Publicae)* 2; and most recently, *AE* 1992, 75; 1994, 102, and 1995, 89: *Iovesat deivos qoi med mitat nei ted endo cosmis uirco sied / asted noisi ope toitesiai pakari vois / Duenos med decet en manom einom dzenoine med malo statod* (cited after Clauss/Slaby).

15. See Ingrid E. Edlund-Berry, *ThesCRA 1* (2004), 372.

16. As evidenced in ibid., 375.

17. *ILLRP* 143=*AE* 1922, 97: *brat datas* (Lat. *parata data*, presumably relating to the donor, not the deity).

18. *ILLRP* 101=*CIL* 14.2863=*ILS* 3684.

19. Edlund-Berry 2004, 369, no. 343: from Satricum in hourglass form.

20. See Nonnis 2003.

21. See Comella 2005d; for a general view, de Hemmer Gudme 2012.

22. On the (omphalos) bowl, see Boardman, Mannack, and Wagner 2004, 305.

23. Overview in Edlund-Berry 2004, 369–70.

24. On method-related problems of verification, see e.g., Van Andringa and Lepetz 2003. Cf. overall Söderlind 2004, which stresses the frequent coincidence of representations of animals and humans in central Italy.

25. Bodel 2009, 18; Rüpke 2009a, 36.

26. Madigan 2013, Estienne 2014.

27. Plautus, *Rudens* 60; Titinius, *Comicorum Romanorum Fragmenta* 153.

28. Scheid 1981 has masterfully described the development of the situation that arose in Rome.

29. Adams 2007, 101–107.

30. *ILLRP* 238=*ILS* 3124=*AE* 1998, 506 (my translation). There is discussion as to whether the second "issued" refers to the formulation of the vow or indicates its realization (thus an abbreviated form of *donom dedit*; see Wachter 1987, 450–52). However, a correct formulation is necessary only for the prior contractual basis; the delivery speaks for itself.

31. *ILLRP* 136=*CIL* 10,5708=*ILS* 3411.

32. Livy 31.9.9–10.

33. Livy 28.38.8.

34. *ILLRP* 241.

35. *CIL* 11.5389; translation based on Langslow 2012, 304. For later frontier-defining rituals in Venetia, cf. Gambacurta 2005.

36. See Rüpke 2006a.

37. Gaius, *Institutions* 2.3–9.

38. Cf. Lacam 2010a, 215.

39. Coarelli 1977.

40. Aberson 2009.

41. For an overview, see Belayche and Pirenne-Delforge 2015; Elsner 2012a, 15, on the theological proportionality of material culture.

42. Bubenheimer-Erhart 2004, 58.

43. Krauskopf 2009, 506; here also on "urns."

44. Argento, Cherubini, and Gusberti 2010, 83. In the case of particular forms, this does not exclude the converse process by which forms used in a sacral context might be adopted into household use (see p. 84).

45. Ibid., 92.

46. See Rüpke 2016c, 110–14.

47. Stähli 2014, 135–36 (for Greece).

48. See Stibbe and Colonna 1980, Versnel 1982, Prosdocimi 1994.

49. Full accounts in Winter 2010, 128, and Lubtchansky 2010, 166.

50. Coarelli 2005; Rüpke 2012f, 19, with reference to the Tomba delle Bighe (Tarquinia) and the Tomba della Scimmia (Chiusi), as well as amphorae from Ponti di Micali (Bruni 2004, no. 29).

51. Huet 2015.

52. For an overview, see Toner 2014. For a comparative treatment of the hunt, and deer hunting in particular, Sykes et al. 2014.

53. Rüpke 2009b; for absinth, Plin. *HN* 27.45 (see Malavolta 1996, 261).

54. Wheeler 1982, Lonsdale 1993, Connelly 2011, Naerebout 2015 (on the archaeology).

55. Festus p. 212.15–214.3 Lindsay; see also Pasqualini 1996, 225–26; Kyle 1998, 36–37.

56. For a full account, see Rutherford 2007, 2013.

57. Dion. H. 7.72.

58. *Tabulae Iguvinvae* Ia.1–Ib.7, more detailed in VIa, 1–VIb, 46. Text and commentary, with Latin translation: Devoto 1940; with English translation, Poultney 1959.

59. See Lacam 2010b, 229, who, however, gives stronger emphasis to ritual scrupulousness and public control.

60. Livy 40.6.5 speaks of *lustratio* and the deployment of a military unit as *mos*, thus projecting it as a custom into the past (e.g., 3.22.4); already in 1.44, the assembled citizenry is in this way constituted. He first speaks of *lustrare urbem* in the extant books after 218 BC (21.62.7), and twice previously of the lustration of the Capitol after prodigies. Older literature: Bouché-Leclercq 1904, Boehm 1927, Ogilvie 1961, Scholz 1970, Gagé 1977. See now Scheid 2016b for a critique of interpreting *lustratio* as purification.

61. See e.g., Baudy 1998. *Suovetaurilia* are attested early on in Satricum: Bouma 1996, 1, 443.

62. For concise coverage of the development, see Rüpke 1990a, 216–17; important studies: Halkin 1953, Freyburger 1988, Linke 2003, Naiden 2006, Février 2009.

63. Rüpke 2006f; for a detailed treatment of Roman time, see Rüpke 2011d.

64. See e.g., de Grummond 2009.

65. See Pritchett 1968, Pritchett 2001.

66. On the *tabula Capuana*, see Stoltenberg 1952, Cristofani 1995, Rüpke 1999b.

67. On the calendar as an early element of the Republican rationalization process, see Rüpke 2012f, 94–110.

68. See Rüpke 2016c, 26–41.

69. On so-called sacrificial calendars (which did not document *all* days of the year), see Jameson 1965, Dow 1968, Scullion 1998, Pritchett 1999, Pritchett 2001, Gawlinski 2007.

70. Fasti Sacerdotum=FS (=Rüpke 2008a) no. 1172; Flavius: no. 1657.

71. Herz 1975.

72. For general studies of historical narratives, see Rüsen 1996, Straub 2001.

73. Wamers et al. 2011, 58–66, on the *situlae*.

74. Rüpke 2001a.

75. See Agelidis 2010; Steingräber 2002, on wooden heads 129–30.

76. Steingräber 1990a.

77. See Torelli 1997, 143: *locus medius.*

78. For an overview, see Chapman 2013.

79. Batino 1998, 25.

80. Prayon 2004a, 54, on the tomb of the Volumni at Perugia, and generally 57; here too on the nonhuman attendant figures.

81. Cf. the problematic attempt in Steiner 2004, 305–309.

82. Prayon 2004a.

83. Maggiani 2000, 264–66; see also Prayon 2004a, 66, with further literature in n. 80.

84. E.g., in the Tomba degli Scudi (Prayon 2004a, 50).

85. E.g., the Tomba degli Anina at Tarquinia or the Tomba degli Hescanas at Orvieto (Prayon 2004a, 65 and 48).

86. See Steuernagel 1998, 170.

87. Cf. Prayon 2004a, 51, on the Tomba del Tifone at Tarquinia.

88. For a full description, see Coarelli 1972.

89. Coarelli 1983. But on the interpretation, see Musti 2005, who points out that there is no parallelization of Greeks-Trojans and Etruscan-Romans. (On the problem of incipient narratives of the Trojan origin of the Romans, see Erskine 2001 and Battistoni 2010). Steingräber 1990b, 78, links the changes in tomb paintings with the emergence of a social stratum of *equites* below the political elite.

90. See Vollkommer 1990.

Chapter V: The Appropriation and Shaping of Religious Practices by Religious Actors

1. For a full account of the research, see Smith 2006.

2. Speculatively, but in an exhaustive account of historically possible religious associations: Palmer 1970; politically: Linke 1995; Jehne 2013b, 132–37; Smith 2005, 78–80, with reference to the Latin background; on the *lex curiata*, see also Rüpke 1990a, 47–51.

3. Paulus *ex Fest.* 56.7 and 21–22 L; Dion. H. 2.50.3.

4. Dion. H. 2.23.2; see also Fest. 180,32–3 L.

5. FS no. 2334: Livy 27.8.1–3 (election) and 41.21.8 (death).

6. On the end of the *curiae*, see Smith 2005, 81. On the blossoming of the *vici* in the Augustan Age see below, p. 192. The presence of the phratries and *genê* in Athens was more strongly defined; see e.g., Sourvinou-Inwood 2011, 340–53.

7. Holland 1953, Ampolo 1981, Frateantonio 2001. Ampolo is more inclined to surmise a shared ritual of the summits around the Palatine.

8. Terrenato 2011, 238–39.

9. Walter 2014b, 105.

10. Rüpke 1995b.

11. Hölkeskamp 2011. Developments in China, where comparable situations of threat led to durable monarchy, are discussed in Scheidel 2009. On the sense of commonality, see Jehne 2013a, Jehne and Lundgreen 2013.

12. See Hölkeskamp 2011, 109–11.

13. See Smith 2006, 290–95, on the *gens Fabia* and its defeat at the Cremera.

14. On Livy 1.24.4–6, see Rüpke 1990a, 100–103 and 97–121, and Santangelo 2008, 86–87, as well as Santangelo 2014 on the fetials and their historical status. On the motif of the soil of Rome, see also Ando 2015, 17–24.

15. See Scheid 2001, and for an exhaustive account of the consulate, Pina Polo 2011a, 21–57 and Pina Polo 2011b (under the inappropriate neologism *curatores pacis deorum*). On the immanent/performative character of Rome's political culture, see Hölkeskamp 2009, 47.

16. Pina Polo 2011b, 104–108. On the *feriae latinae*, Simón 2011.

17. See e.g., Propertius 4.8.

18. Simmel 1907.

19. According to Dong Zongshu, *Spring and Autumn Annals,* the cult of mountains and rivers was normatively reserved for officials (I am grateful to Heiner Roetz, Bochum, for the suggestion).

20. Schorn-Schütte 2012, 13. Cf. Linke 2009, 354, who confines this aspect too narrowly to a military context.

21. Cf. for Classical Greece, Chaniotis 2013, 42–43.

22. See Smith et al. 2015.

23. Holloway 2005, 34; on what follows, 35.

24. On the late reception history of these Italian palaces as a model for the spread of villas of this type as prestige buildings, see Terrenato 2001, 27–28. On the continuity of sumptuous elite tombs in Italy, briefly Terrenato 2010, 513.

25. See Bietti Sestieri 2006, 85.

26. FS s.v. Navius, Attus; Cicero, *On divination* 1.31–32; Livy 1.36.3–6; Dion. H. 3.70–1.

27. Thorough coverage in Brelich 1972, Vanggaard 1988, Simón 1996.

28. Problematic would be the change from the short *a* of the Sanskrit word to the long *a* of the Latin expression. A common reference, *bhlaghmen,* is thinkable.

29. Cicero, *Brutus* 56; FS no. 2807: *Laenas* from the woolen cloak, the *laena.*

30. Livy 1.21.4; Wissowa 1912, 134.

31. Rüpke 2010b.

32. Rüpke 2012c. On the ritual construct, see Schultz 2012.

33. Asconius pp. 39–40 Clark; see FS nos. 491, 2219, and 2361. For a full account, Rüpke 2012f, 122.

34. On Claudia and her father, Ap. Claudius Pulcher, see FS nos. 1152 and 1225; Valerius Maximus 5.4.6.

35. Central: Ovid, *Fasti* 4.629–40 and 721–40. Ovid claims to have fetched the ashes himself, encouraging his readers to do the same. On further examples of such material references, see Rüpke 2007a, 113–16.

36. E.g., Cn. Statilius Cerdo and Cn. Statilius Menander at around the turn of the second century AD (FS nos. 3129, 3135). Statue: *CIL* 6.32418 (FS no. 1668).

37. On the statues, see Lindner 2015.

38. For the classic discussion of the fundamental question, see Mitchell 1984 and Schiavone 2012, 56–78; on pontifical jurisprudence and its role in the Republican rationalization process, Rüpke 2012f, 94–110. *Pons*: e.g., Fest. 452.13–22 L.

39. A full account of the differentiation of competences may be found in Linderski 1986.

40. Harrison 2006, 139–40.

41. On the problem of the numbers in Livy 10.6.3–8, see Rüpke 2005c, 1621–22.

42. Thus Cicero, *On the agrarian law* 2.16–18; see *ibid.*, 1623–50. Augustus: *Res gestae* 10.

43. FS no. 507. *Roman Republican Coinage*=RRC 419/2 (*pontifex maximus*); Livy 32.7.15 (co-option); 40.42.12 (election as *pontifex maximus*); *Obsequens* 8; Livy, *Periochae* 48 (death). On opportunities for incurring such expense, cf. below, p. 140.

44. FS following no. 1322. Livy 40.42.8–11.

45. FS no. 3393. Central: Livy 27.8.4–10 and Val. Max. 6.9.3.

46. Only a coin of 48/47 indicates this membership with the depiction of an *ancile*, but Caesar must have been admitted according to the normal rules before the death of his father in 85.

47. FS no. 2003 (with sources; *salius*: RRC 452/3).

48. For an analysis in terms of rules and conflicts with rules, see Lundgreen 2011.

49. More detailed on what follows, see Arnhold and Rüpke 2016.

50. According to Rüpke 2006d.

51. Plin. *HN.* 36.43.

52. See e.g., Davies 2012.

53. Macrobius, *Saturnalia* 3.6.11. For all the following architectural details, see Arnhold in Arnhold and Rüpke 2016.

54. For a full account of the discussion, Coarelli 1992, 92–103 and 185–204.

55. FS no. 2308.

56. It must not be forgotten that the visibility of a temple depended primarily on the degree of development of its surroundings; Rome's narrow streets frequently allowed only short lines of sight (Betts 2011, 129).

57. On this level at the Largo Argentina, see Andreani, Moro, and Nuccio 2005.

58. This is perhaps the underlying reason why narrative friezes on temples played no great role in the pursuit of individual distinction (thus Rous 2011).

59. On the development, see Torelli 2012; Volpe 2012; Becker and Terrenato 2012.

60. Vitruvius 6.5.3. This sometimes conflicted with the commitment to temple construction: Plin. *HN* 36.5–6.

61. Sewell 2013.

62. On the consequences of such changes for ritual practice and experience, see especially Favro and Johanson 2010.

63. On the basic principles, Wallace-Hadrill 1997b, 239; see also Platt 2002. On religious use, see below Ch. VIII.4.

64. Macrob. *Sat.* 3.13.10–12. For further interpretation, see Rüpke 2016f.

65. Martialis 7.20.

66. Horace, *Satires* 1.15.10–11; Mart. 13.92 (also on hares); opinion of duck: Mart. 13.52.

67. Plin. *HN* 8.209.

68. Wallace-Hadrill 1994, 39, with reference to the Villa Oplontis.

69. See ibid., 31.

70. If, as indicated in Plutarch (*Lucullus* 41.5), Lucullus linked different dining rooms in his house with particular levels of cuisine, this would at least suggest the possibility of such references.

71. Varro, *Res rusticae* 3.6.6.

72. FS no. 985.

73. See Batino 1998, 27–28; Iaia 2006.

74. Maggiani 1997, 444.

75. Schlesier 1997, 653. On *Pacha*: Pfiffig 1975, 288–93.

76. Wiseman 2000.

77. Jaccottet 2011.

78. See Schneider 2009, 574. For a general view, Gilhus 1997.

79. Faraone 2013.

80. For Miletus, see Burkert 2011a, 434.

81. See Pfiffig 1975, 293.

82. Rüpke 1995a, 319–30.

83. See Rüpke 2010c.

84. Rosenberger 2003.

85. Fully covered in Rüpke 2007a, 31–34, with further literature and translation.

86. *Senatusconsultum de Bacchanalibus*: *CIL* 12.581=*ILS* 18=*ILLRP* 511.

87. Jannot 2009; Estienne 2010.

88. See Rüpke 2014b, 132–34, and Rüpke 2013j.

89. A full account in Rüpke 2012f, 28–50.

90. Leppin 1992. For the further history of chariot racing, Meijer 2010.

91. Classic analysis: Veyne 1988. For the Republican development: Bernstein 1998, 2007; further Clavel-Lévêque 1984, 1986; David 1998; Bell 2004; Toner 2014.

92. Bernstein 2007, 226–27.

93. On the increase in the census figures from an order of magnitude of 200,000 at the end of the Second Punic War to far more than 400,000 at the end of the second century BC, see Rosenstein 2012, 268.

94. Orlin 1997.

95. Albers 2010, 78, with reference to the capitol at Cosa.

96. Sear 2006, 48–52. On Greek-Hellenistic developments, Kotlinska-Toma 2015.

97. Sear 2006,54–55: Livy, *Periochae* 48; Varro in Servius, *Commentary on Vergil's Georgics* 3.24.

98. See Berg 2008. See also Estienne 2008 , 694–97.

99. See Fest. 348.27–350.12 L.

100. Livy *Per.* 16; Val. Max. 2.4.7

101. Livy 41.28.11.

102. Kajava 1998.

103. Val. Max. 2.4.7; Fulvius: Livy 39.22.2.

104. Leigh 2005, 187–90.

105. Cf. Keegan 1978, Lazenby 1991.

106. During the period of the Principate, the age of recruitment was between 17 and 21: Scheidel 1992. On the question of the involvement of other groups, see the unfortunately often uncritical work of Evans 1991.

107. Cato *Agr.* 141, see above, gives a detailed account.

108. Cf. the table in Rüpke 1990a, 243.

109. This hypothesis nevertheless remains decidedly more plausible than the existence of a local, colony-specific civil calendar (thus Reeves 2004).

110. Quite a different matter are the religious practices of soldiers on campaign, although primarily in the permanent garrisons of the Imperial Age; see Stoll 2001, esp. 133–209, for an account that, while broadly skeptical, and distinguishing between (official) "army religion" and "religions in the army," provides no crucial conceptual advances.

111. Gellius, *Attic Nights* 15.22.1–9.

112. Ferri 2010.

113. *AE* 1977, 816; see Rüpke 1990a, 164.

114. See Lonis 1979, 140–42.

115. On the Greek practice, see Jackson 1991.

116. A full account in in Valvo 1990. On the exceptions, see Amiotti 1990, Clementoni 1990, Sordi 1990. On Greek practice, see Vaughn 1991.

117. Flaig 1992.

118. Livy 22.42.7–9.

119. Cic. *Div.* 1.37.

120. Van Haeperen 2012; Smith 2006, 217–25.

121. Naiden 2006, 219–40.

122. On the aesthetic and performative aspect of the triumphal procession and preceding negotiations: Itgenshorst 2005, Beard 2007, Rüpke 2008c, Östenberg 2009; Lange and Vervaet 2014.

123. Rüpke 2012f, 62–81.

124. MacCormack 1981; McCormick 1987; Dufraigne 1994.

125. On Augustus's policy in this regard, see Hickson 1991. The emperor was a permanent victor; see e.g., Gratian in 369 (*ILS* 771). Scholars speak of a *théologie de la victoire* (Heim 1992).

126. Versnel 1981; González 1984.

127. On the absence of a negative effect of defeats on a general's further political career, see Rosenstein 1990.

128. For a programmatic account, see Terrenato 2010, 513.

129. Rosenberger 1998, 2005.

130. Rawson 1978.

131. Fr. 9 Scholz, Walter 2013 = Cic. *Div.* 1.72.

132. On the Italic lot oracles, see especially Champeaux 1986, 1987, 1990.

133. Rawson 1974, 157–8; Wiseman 1994; Bendlin 2002.

134. Suetonius, *Life of Augustus* 31, 1.

135. See Bleicken 1981.

136. Gladigow 1977, 20.

137. It is striking that the greatest act of disavowal, Bibulus's boycott of politics aimed against C. Iulius Caesar, was associated with a permanent *obnuntiatio* (Cicero, *On his house* 40; Suet. *Iul.* 20.1 et passim). Cf. however, Scheid 2012a.

138. See Burckhardt 1988, 192.

139. Linderski 1986, 2162–68. See Burckhardt 1988, 193–94 with concrete examples.

140. See the examples in Linderski 1986, 2168–73.

141. Flaig 1995b, 92 emphasizes this.

Chapter VI: Speaking and Writing about Religion

1. Cancik 1973.

2. See e.g., Massa 2013.

3. Rüpke 1996a.

4. Rüpke 2012g, 50–51; on 249 BC, 53.

5. FS no. 1399.

6. Rüpke 2008a, 43.

7. I cannot concur with the symbolic interpretation in Rodriguez-Mayorgas 2011, that it is the college's control over Rome's fate and its crucial importance in maintaining the *pax deorum* that find expression here. That phrase is first attested in the middle of the 1st cent. BC in Lucretius 5, 1229: *divum pacem*.

8. See also Cicero, *On Laws* 2.47.

9. For a reconstruction and reading of *CIE* = *Corpus Inscriptionum Etruscarum* 5385, see Morandi 1987.

10. Text and commentary: Torelli 1975; see Cornell 1978.

11. Steuernagel 1998, 171.

12. Thus Steuernagel's emphatic thesis.

13. See Prayon 1998b, 173.

14. On this characterization of divination see Rüpke, Stagl, and Winiwarter 2012.

15. Bloch 1966, 1968.

16. Steuernagel 1998, 177. Hellenistic influence: Briquel 1990; see e.g., Furley and Gysembergh 2015. Cf. Briquel 1985, Capdeville 1989, Gaultier and Briquel 1997.

17. Steuernagel 1998, 176. But the representation of hepatoscopy from the end of the fifth century BC expressly shows the Greek seer Calchas, cf. Van der Meer 2011, 37. Liver: Van der Meer 1987, 18. See also Van der Meer 2010.

18. For details, see Turfa 2012, and of course the collection of fragments, Thulin 1906a, 1906b, 1906c.

19. See on this (but with no radical conclusion), Siewert 2012.

20. For an understanding of the conflicts in question, see De Sanctis 2015.

21. FS no. 2367.

22. Rosen 1985, Willi 1998, Rosenberger 2003.

23. Gagarin 2011. Collections of texts for Greece: Sokolowski 1955, 1962, 1969; see also Zimmermann 2000, Ennabli and Scheid 2007–2008.

24. See González 1984, González and Arce 1988, Lebek 1990, Wolters 1990.

25. On genres, see Manuwald 2001, 2011.

26. Panayotakis 2010.

27. Fr. 7 = Charisius, *gramm.* 204.22 Keil. Contrary to Panayotakis, this was a private function as augur, not a supposedly official one.

28. See Giancotti 1967, 22–26. On the following ibid., 31: urbane individualism.

29. Jerome, *Epistle* 107.8 = *CSEL* 55, p. 299.

30. Thom 2012. See also Mikalson 2010. On moral discourse with a suitably broad social reach, see Morgan 2007, 2015.

31. See the typology in Dunsch 2014, 639. Agents: 650.

32. Aricó 2001.

33. Accius, *Scaenica* 169–70 Ribbeck; see Rüpke 2012f, 57–60.

34. Rüpke 2012f, 55–56.

35. Comprehensively on what follows, Rüpke and Rüpke 2010 and Rüpke 2014d. Cf. the fundamental treatment of the relationship between myth and ritual in the introduction to Bierl, Lämmle, and Wasselmann 2007.

36. See Müller 1993; Winiarczyk 2002; Whitmarsh 2013, 49–62; on the euhemeristic interpretation of myth: Roubekas 2012, Hawes 2014, 25-28.

37. See Battistoni 2010, 79–111.

38. See generally: Bickerman 1968, Samuel 1972, Möller and Rüpke 2002.

39. Rüpke 2009b.

40. Erskine 2001.

41. See Feeney 2016, 243.

42. Xenophanes, frs. 11, 14, and 15 Diels-Kranz.

43. See Hawes 2014, 28–35.

44. Cf. ibid., 35–66.

45. Cornutus 35.7 (tr. D.M.B. Richardson).

46. Essler 2011, 262 (col. 10). Further essential texts by Cornutus: Obbink 1996, Philodemus 2009.

47. On the critique of imagery, see e.g., Graf 2001, 233.

48. See Piano 2013; for Nyx/Night, see Piano 2010.

49. Overview: Rüpke 2014f, 69–70, 97–101.

50. See e.g., frs. 3 and 5 Beck/Walter (Dreams of Aeneas); fr. 7a (Plut. *Rom.* 7.2); 7b (Dion. Hal. 1.79.13) (ritual practices of Romulus); fr. 15 (Livy 1.55.8) (financing of the Capitoline Temple).

51. See Levene 1993, Davies 2004.

52. For full accounts of the phenomenon, Ma 2013. For Rome, Stewart 2003.

53. Miano 2011.

54. Plin. *HN* 34.30–1; Sehlmeyer 1999, 152–61.

55. Polybius 6.53. On this interpretation of the *funus publicum*, see Rüpke 2006e, Rüpke 2008c.

56. See Sallustius, *Iugurtha* 4.5–6 on the *memoria* and its incentive effect within the great families.

57. See Cancik 2012a.

58. For a brief account of Atthidography, see Rhodes 1990; briefly on Philochorus, Brodersen 2013.

59. A variation on the theories of Ungern-Sternberg 1988, 262–65. See also Ungern-Sternberg 2008, 528.

60. Fabius Pictor *Iur.* fr. 6 Seckel/Kübler (Serv. auct. *Georg.* 1.21).

61. For a full account of this identification, FS no. 1600.

62. See a more complete account in Rawson 1985; Rüpke 2012f.

63. On these conflicts, see Beard 1994 and Beard, North, and Price 1998, 108–13.

64. Rüpke 2012f, 111–25.

65. Yarrow 2007, 76–77; Rüpke 2012a, 112–13; Rüpke 2012f, 218.

66. See Rüpke 1990b; Flower 2015; and for a general treatment, Smith 2009; Scholz and Walter 2013.

67. Greece: Chaniotis 1988; Peró 2012 (on internal orientation: 25). Ennius: Rüpke 2006c; Rüpke 2011d, 105–108. Further instances: Rüpke 2012g, 95–110.

68. Rüpke 1995a, 391–416, and Rüpke 2011d, 121–39.

69. See above, Ch. IV.3.

70. Cautiously: Belfiore 2010.

71. On archaic elements, see Gabba 1988, 162–3.

72. On Cicero's second book *On laws*, see Rüpke 2016c, 21–31.

73. See Crawford 1996b, 362. At ibid., 396, an attempt is made to reconstruct a vague concept of religion for the *lex Ursonensis*.

74. Gabba 1988, 158.

75. Thus also Raggi 2011, 342–43.

76. See chs. 65, 69–72; also central to ch. 128. For more details, see Rüpke 2014b, 113–36. Cf. Raggi 2006, 719, on the self-evidence of such public financing in the later *lex Irnitana*.

77. What follows is based on Rüpke 2012f, 192–202.

78. Thus also the reading of Feil 1986.

79. Cic. *Nat. D.* 1.118–19; similarly Lactantius, *Institutions* 5.14. On the concept of *pietas* as an essentially social relationship, see Schröder 2012.

80. See Henrichs 2010.

81. My inference. This is the philosophical agenda that is repeated in Cicero's following work, *On divination* (2.148–9).

82. So far as we can tell, Cicero is here making a polemical point, which fails adequately to acknowledge the broad acceptance of traditional gods by both earlier and contemporary Epicureans (see Obbink 2001).

83. Cf. Henderson 2006 and Krostenko 2000, 357.

84. Henderson 2006.

85. Van Nuffelen 2010, 2011. The Stoical idea of rational coherence may be a factor in the background here (Long 2010, 53).

Chapter VII: The Redoubling of Religion in the Augustan Saddle Period

1. On the work itself, see esp. Cardauns 1976, Jocelyn 1982, Traver 1997, Rüpke 2005e, 2014c.

2. Varro, *Antiquitates rerum divinarum* fr. 4 Cardauns. On the etymological method in theology, see Blank 2012, 279–88.

3. Ibid., fr. 2a.

4. Wallace-Hadrill 2008, 236.

5. Varro, *Ant. rer. div.* fr. 206 Cardauns; aniconism: fr. 18.

6. Rüpke 2012f; similarly Wallace-Hadrill 2008, 215–51 (see Wallace-Hadrill 1997a, 5–6). No expectation comparable with Cicero's claims for consistency existed in the normal legislative process (Walter 2014a, 17).

7. See Cramer 1954, Barton 1994, Wendt 2015.

8. Deshours 2011, 303–16.

9. See Gentili 2005.

10. On the Campana reliefs (*lastra Campana*), see Strazzulla 1993.

11. Groups of statuary: Ellinghaus 2004, 119.

12. Bubenheimer-Erhart 2004, 58–9.

13. Plin. *HN* 35.160. For the biography, Sallmann 2002.

14. Caesar, *Bellum civile* 1.22.5; also, for the opposition, *Bellum Africanum* 22.

15. Bleicken 1998, 297–369. See also Walter 2010.

16. Thus August. *Gest.* 1.1.

17. For a suggested structure, see Scheid 2007b, xxxvii–xl.

18. *FS* no. 1012.

19. See *FS* for 35 BC. Up until the late Augustan Age, we know of fewer members of the pontifical college than of the other ancient colleges. For the role of Lepidus, see the recently discovered *Fasti Privernati*.

20. Tacitus, *Annals* 1.10.5. Nero (*FS* no. 1216) was the father of the future emperor Tiberius, whom Augustus adopted in AD 4.

21. See Albert 1980; Rüpke 1990a, 97–127; Santangelo 2008, 2014.

22. Wiedemann 1986; Rüpke 1987.

23. Cassius Dio 43.24.4; as in Tacitus's account of the pontifical opinion on Octavian's marriage, here too we find sarcastic language in the historiographical verdict on the event (Pascal 1981, 263). For a full account of the ritual, see Rüpke 2009b.

24. Rüpke 1993a.

25. See Cass. Dio 51.20.3. Scheid 1978, 632–39 dates the beginning of the process to 36 BC; i.e., after the end of the Sicilian War and the capitulation of Lepidus. On "invented tradition," see Hobsbawm and Ranger 1983.

26. August. *Gest.* 25.3.

27. For a full account, Scheid 1990.

28. See ibid., 149. On the archaeology, see Broise and Scheid 1987, Broise, Scheid, et al. 2017.

29. Rüpke 1995a, 45.

30. Rüpke 2016c, 110–14. On the effects of inscriptions on bullets and missiles on those throwing them. Cf. Ma 2010.

31. Scheid 1990, 700, referring to Cass. Dio 53.6.79.

32. Galinsky 2013, 32–36.

33. See Berthelet 2015, 287–88; his assumption of particular *auctoritas* on the part of the augurs (ibid., 215–17), on the other hand, should be rejected.

34. Thus e.g., *Acta Arvalia* 1 Scheid (with integrations).

35. See Bremmer 1993, on the Salii; Demougin 1992, 170, on the Luperci. For the Latin priesthoods, especially the *sacerdotes Caeninenses*, see Scheid 2009, 287; but cf. Rüpke 2008a, 10–11.

36. Rüpke 2012g, 114–15.

37. A full account in Tarpin 2002, 137–73, here 161; and Lott 2004, 81–171. On the pre-history, see Niebling 1956, Flambard 1981. For the development of the image, Rosso 2014.

38. Simon 1986.

39. Varro, *Ling.* 5.165, with reference to Piso; on what follows, Rüpke 1990a,136–41.

40. Cf. Norden 1915 (written in the middle of World War I!). Repetitions: Suet. *Nero* 36.1; Orosius 7.3.7.

41. Cf. Tiberius's remark about Augustus, cited by Galinsky 1996, 292, to the effect that he had adapted something for the present out of the deepest past (Tac. *Ann.* 4.16).

42. A full account in Censorinus, *Dies Natalis* 17.

43. Weiß 1973.

44. Galinsky 2012, 100.

45. Text and commentary: Schnegg-Köhler 2002 (*ILS* 5050); on the ritual, see also Can-cik 1996.

46. Alföldy 1991.

47. Ma 2012, 142–43.

48. Galinsky 1996, 385.

49. See Berthelet 2015, 290–92 and 318–21.

50. Gurval 1995, 135.

51. See Hölkeskamp 2001 and Miano 2009, the latter on p. 367 mentioning above all Augustan evidence. More generally, Smith 2015.

52. A full account is in Kolb 1993.

53. Zevi 1979; Ley and Struß 1982; AAVV 1989; Meyboom 1995; Quilici and Quilici Gigli 1995. See also Meusel 1923, Buchet 2012. For theatrical ritual in Pompeii, see Gasparini 2013.

54. See below, Ch. IX.2.

55. Mattern 2000, 153.

56. A full account in Gros 1976; Galinsky 2007, 73–74.

57. Zink and Piening 2009.

58. See Prop. 2.31.

59. Bradley 2006, 2009.

60. Zanker 2010.

61. Ibid., but without reference to temples.

62. Varro, *Res rusticae* the framing plot of the dialogue.

63. Eck 2010, 96–98: *trapezophora*.

64. Richardson 1992, 157. On the occasion for the structure, see Bleicken 1998, 362.

65. For the description, see Andersen 2003; on the reliefs, Simon 1967; Koeppel 1987, 1988; Settis 1988; Elsner 1991; Billows 1993. On the floral ornamental theme, Pollini 2012, chs. 5–6.

66. See Bleicken 1998, 381.

67. De Cazanove 2011, 36–38; see also Nava and Cracolici 2005.

68. On the evolution of population numbers, see de Ligt 2012; de Ligt and Garnsey 2012; Hin 2013.

69. Crawford 1985, Wallace-Hadrill 1986, Meadows and Williams 2001, Norena 2001; summarized in Williams 2007.

70. *RRC* 540/2; (36 BC); *RRC* 480/21 (44 BC).

71. *RRC* 436/1 and 543/1. The genitive, perhaps formally also present here, was used in representations of buildings, but the nominative was usual for heads.

72. *Roman Imperial Coinage* Augustus 365–66 and 170.

73. Shaya 2013, 95–100.

74. Crawford 1996a, 424.

75. Rüpke 2003b; cf. Feeney 2007.

76. On changes of date associated with restorations, briefly, see Rüpke 2011d, 124.

77. Winter 2013, 192.

78. Ibid., 194.

79. See Rüpke 2017a.

80. See Berger 2011, 350. For full accounts of Livy, see Levene 1993, briefly Scheid 2015, who on page 87 rightly emphasizes the individual character of his position. On Dionysius: Gabba 1982, Mora 1995; see also Clarke 1999 on Strabo. Cf. Simon 2011, 437, on Livy's concern to minimize the role of Greek culture in Rome's history.

81. Mittag 2012, 25, on the coin series and its dating around 23 BC.

82. E.g., Tibullus 2.5.

83. On Philo, see e.g., Barraclough 1984, Sandmel 1984, Walter 1987, Williamson 1989, Dyck 2002, Bloch 2011. On the Maccabees, Bickerman 1979, Honigman 2014.

84. Prop. 2.31, here 4.6.

85. Prop. 4.9.

86. Cf. Fantham 2009, 5–33.

87. See Rüpke 1996b, 2006f; Gee 2000. Cf. on the *parapegmata* associated with such data, Lehoux 2007. For a general treatment of the *Libri fastorum*, Wallace-Hadrill 1988, Scheid 1992, Herbert-Brown 1994, Fantham 2002.

88. On Manilius, see Abry 2011.

89. The following paragraphs summarize Rüpke 2016a.

90. Ibid.

91. Val. Max. 1, pr.

92. Cf. Varro, *Ant. rer. div.* fr. 3: *pro ingenti beneficio ... iactat praestare se ciuibus suis, quia non solum commemorate deos, quos coli oporteat a Romanis, uerum etiam dicit, quid ad quemque pertineat.*

93. Suet. *Aug.* 31.1.

94. Suet. *Tib.* 14.2 and 4. See the general judgement in 69: *Circa deos ac religiones negle-gentior, quippe addictus mathematicae ...*

95. See Rüpke 2011a, 105–109 and Fögen 1993, on the radicalization of the problem from the third century AD onward.

96. Suet. *Tib.* 36.

97. Tac. *Ann.* 2.32.

98. Suet. *Tib.* 63.

99. Cowan 2011, x.

100. Val. Max. 1.4.1.

101. Val. Max. 1.8. ext. 18; cf. the repetition of the notion "nature" in 2, pr.

102. Val. Max. 1.8.1; see 2–10 for the following.

103. Mueller 2002, 175.

104. Wardle 2000, 489–90.

Chapter VIII: Lived Religion

1. Plato, *Res publica* 427bc; Cic. *Leg.* 2.20 and 25 (see also 2.21 in respect of ritual errors).

2. John Scheid has proposed the best defense of this interpretation (Scheid 2016a), differing from Rüpke 2016e and Rüpke 2016c.

3. On the term, see above, p. 10.

4. On this dynamic, see Raja and Rüpke 2015a, Rüpke 2015d.

5. Köves-Zulauf 1990, 11, with full discussion of the misunderstanding.

6. More details: Kajava 1994.

7. See the résumé by Dondin-Payre (2011); on the historical development, Salway 1994.

8. Freedmen with fictitious "Latin" status, the so-called *Latini Iuniani*, constituted a special case; they too possessed the *tria nomina*, but did not have citizenship (and so suffrage rights); they must have made up a not inconsiderable portion of the total: de Ligt and Garnsey 2012.

9. See Plutarch, *Roman questions* 101; and Stupperich 1985, Goette 1986a, 1990. On the communicative dimension of clothing, Edmondson and Keith 2009.

10. Thus Varro, *Res rusticae* 1.17.1.

11. Unfortunately, evidence for painted wooden tablets scarcely exists (see, for references in wall painting, Stewart 2014, 357).

12. For the different, even negative associations of simple but not archaic representations, see Mylonopoulos 2014, 281.

13. A full account is in Rosa 2016.

14. See above, p. 133.

15. Gury 2008.

16. See e.g., Boehm and Hübner 2011, Green 2014.

17. Volk 2009.

18. Denzey Lewis 2013; see also Schildgen 2012.

19. Horden and Purcell 2000. I am grateful to Greg Woolf for reference to the severe quantitative limits imposed on mobility by transport capacities and routes over long distances.

20. Stowers 2008, 10.

21. For classic portrayals of domestic cults, see Bakker 1994; Bodel, Olyan 2008; Boedeker 2008; Giacobello 2008; Nevett 2010.

22. See Wallace-Hadrill 2003.

23. General: Waltzing 1895, Poland 1909, Liebenam 1964, Ausbüttel 1982, Kolb 1995, Kloppenborg and Wilson 1996, Bollmann 1998, Harland 2003, Kloppenborg 2006, Bendlin 2011, Harland 2014. With particular regard to this context, Steuernagel 2004.

24. For an introduction, see Hunt 1984, Adams and Laurence 2011; see also Wachsmuth 1967 for discussion of religious aspects.

25. Cic. *Leg.* 2.25–6.

26. Bodel 2008b, 251. On the accustomed harmonious conception of household cults, cf. e.g., Gherchanoc 2012 for Greece.

27. Flower 1996, 2002, but see also Rüpke 2006e.

28. Bowes 2015a, 217.

29. See ibid., 212.

30. Stirling 2008; on the Roma, 131.

31. Ibid., 133.

32. Photographs of individual objects: http://www.augustonemetum.fr/News/Info-24/Religion-et-culte.html (20 October 2017).

33. Kaufmann-Heinimann 2007. On an ensemble found in Kaiseraugst, see Kaufmann-Heinimann 1998, Schmidt and Kaufmann-Heinimann 1999.

34. After Boyce 1937 now Cicala 2007; Bassani 2008; images: Fröhlich 1991; in the provinces: Kaufmann-Heinemann 1998 and briefly Schmidt, Kaufmann-Heinimann 1999. For what follows I refer to Rüpke 2012i.

35. See Van Andringa 2009, 265–69.

36. Ibid., 265; Bodel 2008a, 261.

37. Aelius Aristides, *Sacred Tales* 2.27; tr.Behr 1968, vol. 2.

38. E.g., ibid., 4.43; see the following section.

39. Inscriptions: Graf 2010a. Urns: Davies 2011, 28.

40. Morciano 2009.

41. Only limited use was made of the possibility of using this in the sense of theophoric personal names. Examples in Paganini 2009; *contra* Frankfurter 2014

42. Rives 1995, 186–93, with reference to *Corpus Inscriptionum Latinarum* 8.999; 24528, and 24518, as well as *Inscriptiones Latinae Africae* 354.

43. See ibid., 190 and 192. Here it would be possible to speak of pragmatic cult individuality. For a differentiation of different types of religious individuality see Rüpke 2013g, 2015d, 2016d.

44. For a general treatment, see Collins 2008.

45. See the case studies in Clarke 2012.

46. Fundamental: Petzl 1994; important in respect of their place in the history of religion: Belayche 2006, Belayche 2008. On the collaboration, see Gordon 2016.

47. Thus Marco Galli with reference to *Inscriptiones Graecae* 4.88.

48. Zosimus 4.18 (I have Silviu Anghel, Göttingen, to thank for the suggestion).

49. Nilsson 1940, 68: Athenaeus 11.473b=Antikleides 140 F 22. Objects: Kaufmann-Heinimann 2007, 195–97; on the coin bank, see also Robinson 1924 (illustrations).

50. On children's participation in religious practices, see Van der Leeuw 1939, Brelich 1969, Mantle 2002. Explicit religious instruction is unusual at Rome: Cancik 1973. For Greece see Bremmer 1995a, Auffarth 2012.

51. Plato, *Laws* 887d, cited in Prescendi 2010, 78; ibid., 77, also the following quote.

52. Prudentius, *Contra Symmachum* 1.197–214.

53. On their respective *De superstitione* and *Peri deisidaimonias*, see Rüpke 2016e, 45–48. On the concept, Eitrem 1955.

54. Prudent. *Contra Symm.* 1.207. 215–44.

55. On the lack of a clear distinction in the concept of the *carmen*, see Hickson Hahn 2007, 236–27. For a general view, Brulé and Vendries 2001.

56. This also applies to research studies; e.g., Gordley 2011; for an alternative view, see Habinek 2005 and Eberhardt and Franz 2012, 261, with reference to Kowalzig 2007, 393. For a full account, see Brulé and Vendries 2001; Garelli 2007, esp. 145–294.

57. Emphasized as the central content of Christian hymns by Gordley 2011, 391.

58. See e.g., Zanker 1976, 20, on architectural painting.

59. Larcher 1990.

60. See Lorenz 2008.

61. For a general view, see Esposito 2014.

62. See Feldherr 2010, esp. 243–92.

63. See Elsner 1995.

64. Thus Trimble 2011, also in criticism of Squire 2009, who investigates the variety of references of text and image.

65. This form of reencounter too was important, as there was no canon of texts to serve as a point of reference (Gordon 1979).

66. Bergmann 1994.

67. See above, p. 51. See also Rüpke 2013c.

68. Steuernagel 2009b, 124–26; Steuernagel 2009a, 238–39.

69. Hesberg 2007. Pliny (*HN* 36.185) relates the introduction of mosaics into the Capitoline Temple of Jupiter in 149 BC.

70. Hesberg 2007, 458–59.

71. Ibid., 456.

72. See Moormann 2011.

73. See generally Gordon 1979, Rüpke 2010d.

74. Bowes 2008, 2015a, 2015b.

75. Walde 2001; Weber 2005–2006; Frenschkowski 2006; Renberg 2010a; rich in material: Harris 2009.

76. See Deubner 1900, LiDonnici 1995, Renberg 2015.

77. Aristid. 4.45–6; tr. Behr 1968, vol. 2.

78. *Shepherd of Hermas* 8.1, 9.1; on the text, Peterson 1959, Hellholm 1980, Rüpke 2005b, 2015b.

79. See e.g., Rieger 2017.

80. Varro, *On Latin Language* 5.152 and 5.49. On Roman woodlands, see Stara-Tedde 1905, Goodhue 1975, Broise and Scheid 1993, Scheid 1993b, Häuber 2001.

81. On the evidence and its interpretation, see Neudecker 2015, 226–27; here too on the following.

82. Ibid., 228, with reference to texts from the *Corpus Tibullianum* (3.3.15) and from the Augustan poet Tibullus himself (2.5, 95–96).

83. Stackelberg 2009, 87.

84. Inventory: http://www.stoa.org/projects/ph/house?id=21 (20 October 2017). Full account: Seiler 1992.

85. See Stackelberg 2009, 87–88.

86. Comella 2011, 104–10.

87. See also Messalina's Bacchic garden design in AD 48: Tac. *Ann.* 11.31.2–3.

88. See Dräger 1994.

89. Briefly, Neudecker 2015, 229–30.

90. On their mobility, see Esposito 2005.

91. E.g., in Lanuvium, Wyler 2006.

92. Cf. on the principle, Gosden 2005; on the creation of emotions by interactions between humans and objects, see Riis and Woodhead 2010, 208.

93. Some aspects of change in Late Antiquity are discussed in Morvillez 2016.

94. Rebenich 2008, 192–98; Laforge 2009, 199–203.

95. On the grave cult as a family affair, see e.g., Shaw 1984, Hope 2001, Carroll 2006, Carroll, Rempel, and Drinkwater 2011.

96. Rome: Cic. *Leg.* 2.58: Twelve-Table laws; Campanian laws (especially Puteoli): *AE* 1971.88; Libitina 2004, Schrumpf 2006, Castagnetti 2012; on child burial, see also Varro, fr. 109 Riposati; Serv. *Aen.* 12.142–43.

97. Varro, *Ling.* 5.25. On the problem, see Hope 2009, 158.

98. On burial in costly clothes, see Blanchard et al. 2007.

99. On the *laudatio funebris*, see Vollmer 1892, Mommsen 1905, Kierdorf 1980. On reconstruction of the procession via the Forum, Favro and Johanson 2010.

100. Rüpke 2006e; for an alternative view, see Flower 1996; see also Flaig 1995a.

101. A full account in Degelmann 2017.

102. *Twelve-Table-Law* 10.3; Cic. *Leg.* 2.59, with Dyck 2004; Crawford 1996b, 2, 705–706.

103. Ibid.

104. Cf. Porter and Boutin 2014; in the provinces, Pearce 2011.

105. See for Rome, e.g., Grossi and Mellace 2007; for the provinces, further articles in Faber et al. 2007 and Scheid 2008; for Palmyra, Henning 2013.

106. Bodel 2004, 157. See also Cic. *Leg.* 2.60: *sumptuosa respersio; longae coronae; acerrae,* with Dyck *ad loc.* Lucian, *Luct.* 12 provides a contrasting emphasis.

107. Varro, *Vita populi Romani* fr. 111 Riposati.

108. Tac. *Ann.* 3.2.2; Buccellato, Catalano, and Musco 2008, 86.

109. See Verg. *Aen.* 11.201.

110. Cf. Prop. 4.7 with Cic. *Leg.* 2.60 (*Twelve-Table-Law*). On this material aspect of memory, see Graham 2011b. *Ossifragus* was a term for a specific trade or function: a person who broke up the larger bones so that they would fit into the urn; see *AE* 2007, 260, A21–24 as an image of the underworld on a curse tablet in the necropolis on the via Ostiense outside Rome.

111. Bel 2010.

112. The approach to the *os resectum,* a small bone that features in the antiquarian literature as a minimum when it comes to covering the body with earth, appears accordingly inconsistent (see Graham 2011a, 92–103).

113. Scheid 1993a.

114. McCane 2007.

115. Hesberg 1992.

116. Plin. *HN* 35.160. On the contemporary perception of the Pythagorean tradition, see Flinterman 2014, 343–50.

117. On the person, FS no. 1139.

118. Thus the interpretation in Petersen 2003, 245–47.

119. Ibid., 234.

120. Ibid., 251. The inscription is well explained in Kolb and Fugmann 2008, 120–24. Something similar is to be found in textual form in the second century AD in *The Shepherd of Hermas* (Rüpke 1999a).

121. Petronius 71.5–12; on the legal arrangements, see Ulpianus, *Digestae* 11.7.6.

122. *ICG* 1598. For the text of the *Life*, cf. Thonemann 2012; text: 258–59; with Engl. tr. https://en.wikipedia.org/wiki/Inscription_of_Abercius; with German tr., Seeliger and Wischmeyer 2015, 464–45. I am grateful to Markus Vinzent for sharing his new analysis and his desire to analyze the texts separately.

123. On the chronology, see Hesberg 1992, briefly, 242–43.

124. See Hope 1997, 81–82.

125. Examples in Van Andringa 2013.

126. Hesberg, Nowak, and Thiermann 2015, 246.

127. See e.g., outside Rome, Hesberg 2006.

128. Carroll 2013.

129. Champlin 1991, 183. See also 184 on burial costs.

130. Graham 2009 overlooks this vital point in her stimulating essay. Generally on the practice of funerary inscriptions, Eck 1987.

131. For the Epicurean Philodemus too, in his treatise *On death*, provision for friends and family is an honorable motif for legacies (Tsouna 2007, 261–62).

132. See Carroll 2011.

133. On the terminology of "cultural technique," see Maye 2010.

134. D'Ambra 2002, 240–41. On instances where the quality of work suffered, see Pollini 2007, 261. Generally on the function of roads lined with tombs, Hesberg and Zanker 1987.

135. Mouritsen 2011, 284–89.

136. Borbonus 2014. Cf. Penner 2012, 146, for concentration on the Julian-Claudian Age and the unusually high presence of female corpses (30–41 percent).

137. Borg 2013, 273.

138. *CIL* 6.37965; for a brief account, Hope 2011, 178–79.

139. Lamotte 2010. On the attitude to premature death, see Graf 2010b.

140. Mielsch 2009, 30; without reference to Mielsch, Davies 2011. Here also on the proactive role of purchasers (48–49). A general view is in Rawson 2003.

141. See Koch 1993.

142. Nielsen 2009, 87. The same applies to the regional traditions of the Abruzzi: Benelli and Rizzitelli 2010, 137.

143. Newby 2011, 224.

144. D'Ambra 1988.

145. Borg 2011, 60. Also on the temple projects.

146. Ibid., esp. 64–65. The Haterii too, of course, chose such a form, judging from the well-known relief (62).

147. The following is encapsulated in Borg 2013, 271–78.

148. See on the Vatican, Liverani and Spinola 2010 (I owe this suggestion and many others to Richard Gordon).

149. See Pirson 1997; Gering 2002.

150. Rebillard 2003; Rüpke 2005a; Borg 2013, 274.

151. Cf. Borg 2013, 276–77, with Scott 1997, 58, and Trimble 2011, 324.

152. *Inscriptions Latines d'Afrique=ILAfr* 225; see Vigourt 2011.

153. Jastrzeboska 1981, Février 1990, McDonough 2004.

154. For an excellent treatment of archaeological grave finds, Van Andringa 2013.

155. Pseudo-Quintilian, *Declamationes Maiores* 10.

156. *Digests* 11.7.6.1; see also *Dig.* 11.7.2 on further attributes of a genuine grave. According to Ulp. *Dig.* 11.8.4, it can never become personal property by virtue of long-standing actual possession.

157. Ov. *Fast.* 5.419–46, in the interpretation of Bettini 2009, 124–26.

158. Cic. *Leg.* 2.22, in the textual reconstruction by Andrew Dyck.

159. Bettini 2009, 109–18.

160. See Norden and Kytzler 1966; Bauckham 1988, Colpe and Habermehl 1996; Markley 2013.

161. King 2013.

162. Graf and Johnston 2007, no. 9. Further texts: Edmonds 2011.

163. On this characterization of Orphism, see Edmonds 2013; for closer discussion of leaves of gold, Edmonds 2009, Calame 2011, de Jáuregui 2011, Faraone 2011a, 2011a, 2011b, Riedweg 2011a.

164. Cuneo 2012: to Constantine II in the fourth century.

165. See S. Fine 2010 on the weak correlation between the archaeological evidence and "beliefs." On the latter and their vagueness, see Cavallin 1979.

166. Plautus, *Aulularia*, pr.; Dion. Hal. 4.2 and 4.14. The textual tradition in the last-mentioned reference is mistakenly held to be unreliable, as Dionysius's attempt to bring the various strands together fails to say what was expected by interpreters.

167. I thus follow the line of Samter 1901, 105–28, *contra* Wissowa (briefly, Wissowa 1912, 174–75); positions discussed fully in Boehm 1927, and most recently also Mastrocinque 1999. For a comprehensive treatment of the *lares*, Flower 2017.

168. Myth: Dion. Hal. 4.2. Pompeii: Foss 1997, 217.

169. See Weiss 2009 on Egypt in the Roman period; for a full account, Weiss 2015b. On Pompeiian niches, especially in workspaces, see Kastenmeier 2007.

170. On the concept, Weiss 2015a.

171. See Niebling 1956, Flambard 1981. For a prosopography of *vicomagistri*, Rüpke 2008a.

172. See e.g., *CIL* 10.1235: *Genio et Laribus* (from Nola).

173. Giacobello 2005, 242; *lararium*: Scriptores Historiae Augustae, *Marcus Aurelius* 3.5; *Alexander Severus* 29.2–3 and 31.4.5.

174. See above, p. 219.

175. Discarding: Suet. *Cal.* 5.

176. The material is there in Linderski 2000, but the consequences are not drawn.

177. Here, against a background of comparable textual knowledge, the intuition of Charles César Boudelot in his *Utilités des voyages* (1686) lay nearer to ancient understanding than the attempt by Wissowa and his disciples (and still Hersch 2010, 278–79) to perceive firm distinctions more convergent with the idea of a systematic state cult (for the suggestion I thank Martin Mulsow, Gotha Research Centre).

178. Although it is a claim still made in Laforge 2009.

179. Bielfeldt 2014, 202.

180. Ibid., 221. On the ancient conception of seeing by the active projection of light, 213–14.

181. Dräger 1994.

182. Lacam 2008. I owe reference to widespread non-documentary representations of bull sacrifices in the Roman Imperial Age to Günther Schörner, Vienna.

183. Rüpke 2005d; see also Foss 1997, 217 and Estienne 2011; *contra* Scheid 1985. On the ambivalence of meat consumption, see Corbier 1989, Kearns 2011. Cf. on imperial practice in the East, Petropoulou 2008.

184. On the *visceratio* as reflected in the New Testament, see Standhartinger 2012.

185. Stern 2014, esp. 146. In houses: Scheibelreiter-Gail 2012, 161, with instances from the first century BC to the fourth century AD.

186. Exemplary: Scapaticci 2010, esp. 107.

187. Dasen 2015.

188. For protective deities, Potter and Mattingly 1999, 165–66; for the interplay of forms of knowledge, Gordon 2011; Faraone 2011b. For gems, see Michel 2000, 2001; Nagy 2011.

189. Gaillard-Seux 1998.

190. Mastrocincque 2009.

191. For basilicas, Scott 1997, 54; private chapels, Bowes 2015b, see above, pp. 227–28.

192. Gordon 2013d; see also Gordon 1999. Deposition in graves in Rome, e.g., Bevilacqua 1998.

193. *DTM* 1 Blänsdorf.

Chapter IX: New Gods

1. Fully covered in Rüpke 2011e, 2011c.

2. Examples from Thessaloniki, see Steimle 2007.

3. See e.g, Rieger 2007, Bricault 2007. Books: Rüpke 2011e, 133–41. Pattern books: Gordon 2011.

4. On the concept of "intellectuals," see Bendlin 2006, 170–81. On textual production, see de Certeau 1988.

5. See e.g., Dirven 1999, 190–95; Egelhaaf-Gaiser 2000; Steuernagel 2004, 2007; Gasparini 2007.

6. Bremmer 2017, Denzey Lewis 2017.

7. Cf. Eidinow 2016; on the conditions for *epideixis*, see Staden 1997, 54.

8. Wedekind 2012.

9. Bricault 2006, 34.

10. Meyboom 1995; Meyboom and Versluys 2000 (not necessarily a sanctuary of Isis).

11. For an overview of the process, see Gasparini 2007; Pompeii: Gasparini 2011, 82. Metellus: Mora 1990, 73, after Coarelli; for a dating as early as the second century BC, see Fontana 2010, 27.

12. See not only Versluys 2010, but also Mol 2012. On the name in Egypt, see Quack 2016.

13. See Varro, *Ant. rer. div.* fr. 46 Cardauns.

14. Cass. Dio 42.26.1; see Santangelo 2013, 260, but without his conclusion as to the character of Isis.

15. Cic. *Nat. D.* 3.47 (animal worship); Cic. *Div.* 1.132.

16. Catull. 74.4 and 102.4. But cf. Matthey 2011.

17. Briefly Cramer 1954, Barton 1994; on developmental mechanisms of further bodies of knowledge of this kind, see Gordon 2010, 2013a.

18. Dio 47,16,1.

19. Tac. *Ann.* 2.85.4. See Versluys 2004, 446.

20. On such "orientalization," see Versluys 2013.

21. More radical, Scheid 2004b. For a structural description, see Egelhaaf-Gaiser 2000, 176–82; comprehensively treated in Lembke 1994.

22. See Egelhaaf-Gaiser 2000, 252, and on the contrasting everyday reality of a dress practice that was *socially* strictly hierarchized and visible, Allorge-Courtin 2011. Emotional participation is posited on the basis of satirical comment, see Kardos 2011. On initiation, see Bremmer 2014a.

23. Martzavou 2012b.

24. Soler 2011, 17.

25. For an exemplary treatment, Gasparini 2013. For temples, e.g., the "Red Hall" at Pergamum, see Hoffmann 2005; or at Thurii (Sybaris), Greco and Gasparini 2014.

26. *Recueil des Inscriptions concernants les Cultes Isiaques*=RICIS 501/0101. I take this and the following examples from Rüpke 2016h.

27. *RICIS* 501/0122.

28. *RICIS* 501/0112.

29. Val. Max. 9.15.1. Livy, *Per.* 116, which speaks of a "son" sprung from the humblest of backgrounds.

30. Cicero, *Letters to Atticus* 14.6–8 (12–15 April 44 BC).

31. Appianus, *Bellum Civile* 3.1.2–3.

32. Seneca, *On anger* 3.18.1–2; see also Gradel 2002, 51.

33. Plautus, *Asinaria* 711–18.

34. *CIL* 9.1556. On the individual, see Cass. Dio 54.23.1–6.

35. *CIL* 11.7431; further examples in Hänlein-Schäfer 1985, 89–93.

36. Silvestrini 1992, Abramenko 1993, Pappalardo 1995; Gasparini 2014.

37. For a general treatment of the emperor's referentiality, see Ando 2003.

38. *CIL* 11.1420=*ILS* 139; see also the subsequent resolution after the death of Lucius's brother Gaius Caesar in AD 4 (*CIL* 11.1421=*ILS* 140).

39. On this color system, see Rüpke 1993b.

40. On the spectrum of relevant aristocratic traditions of ritual performance, see Scheid 1993a, 2007a, 2009.

41. Várhelyi 2010, 166.

42. E.g., Varro, *Ling.* 7.45; *Fasti Praenestini, Inscr. It.* 13.2.139; Ov. *Am.* 3.637, *Fast.* 5.148; Plin. *HN* 3.65; Solinus 1.6; Augustine, *De Civitate Dei* 6.10 (Varro).

43. Cic. *Leg.* 2.22 in the reconstruction of the text by Andrew Dyck.

44. This is still valid in the early fourth century: Rosenbaum-Alföldi 2015b.

45. For the topographical context and development, see Albers 2013, 206–11.

46. Thus Jaccottet 2013.

47. See Fishwick 2002. On the nexus of tradition around the deification of Antinous, see Renberg 2010b.

48. On Hercules/Herakles, see Jaczynowska 1981, Ritter 1995, Schultz 2000.

49. Ennius, *Annals* 99–100 Skutsch; for the interpretation, Gell. *NA* 13.23.7, 15 and 19.

50. *ILS* 119–21. In Juno and Ceres, two goddesses associated with maternal roles are invoked here; Imperial Age theorizing over the "Juno" in every woman (Seneca, *Letters* 110.1; Plin. *HN* 2.16) is extraneous here.

51. On the other hand, the utmost variety of local conceptions could lie concealed behind a concept such as "angel" (*angelos*; Cline 2011, 75); see also Fauth 2014; Muehlberger 2013.

52. Varro, *Ling.* 7.85; cf. Livy 7.6.8–11.

53. See Fishwick 2002, 234.

54. See e.g., Serv. *Aen.* 1.8, 5.241; *Georgica* 1.21; cf. Pötscher 1978, Fishwick 1991, Fenechiu 2008 (the latter with painstaking analysis of preimperial sources).

55. There is an exception perhaps in *CIL* 10.3920=*ILS* 6307: *numen Capuae.*

56. Reynolds 1962. This also applies to writers in a Christian context, such as Tertullian (*Apology* 29–30) and Lactantius (e.g., *On the deaths of the persecutors* 34.5); see also Kahlos 2011, 261–66.

57. See e.g., the comprehensive list of beneficiaries and principals in *CIL* 6.225=*ILS* 2186: *pro salute, itu, reditu et victoria imp(eratorum)* ...

58. On the emergence of this concept see Wardle 2009, 480–83 and McIntyre 2016. On the formula *in honorum domus divinae*, see Cesarano 2015; generally on the family as *domus*, Saller 1984, Hölkeskamp 2014.

59. See e.g., Eck 1995.

60. Price 1984.

61. Rutherford 2013, 440–41, Text G4.

62. Friesen 1993; *theoriai:* Rutherford 2007, 2013.

63. Norena 2001, Chancey 2004, Williams 2007.

64. Cicero, *Phillipica* 2.110; on Antonius's appointment in Caesar's lifetime, Cass. Dio 44.6.4.

65. Plutarch, *Antonius* 33.1.

66. See FS no. 669, with further sources.

67. *CIL* 8.24583=*ILS* 8963, with FS no. 687 on the identification.

68. Augustus's membership and presumably thus also his initiative is attested only in the August. *Gest.* 7, see FS no. 1012.

69. See above, pp. 190–91.

70. The only Republican source is Varro, *Ling.* 5.85, where the more precise description until the beginning of the exposition [. . . *augures ab avibus] quas in auguriis certis observare solent* is omitted from the tradition of the *Codex unicus*. Scheid 1990, 252, establishes the connection with the *curia*.

71. Dion. Hal. *Ant. Rom.* 2.52.5; there too the information about the five years in shared office.

72. Tac. *Ann.* 1.54.1.

73. See Rüpke 2005c, 24.

74. See Tac. *Ann.* 2.41.1; similarly Wissowa 1912, 565.

75. Thus with Wissowa from Tac. *Ann.* 15.23.2.

76. Ibid. 3.64, esp. 4.

77. Rüpke 2005c, 1587–1600.

78. Pleket 1965; Gagé 1981, 1986; Clauss 1999, 339–41 (the phenomenon does not feature in the study by Engster 2002, otherwise rich in material).

79. Jarrett 1971, Alföldy 1973, Fishwick 1981. Christians: *CIL* 8.450; Marcillet-Jaubert 1987.

80. Di Vita-Évrard 1997; Cébeillac-Gervasoni 2000; Gasparini 2014, 267–72.

81. Further developed by Ando 2001, 2003, 2013b. Demonstrated, for instance, for Paul by Maier 2013.

82. Hekster 2011.

83. See e.g., Seneca, *On clemency* 1.10.3: no belief in divinity on command. On changes in genres and themes, see also Haake 2011.

84. Horace, *Songs* 1.2.

85. Ibid., 4.5.1–8.

86. Ibid., 4.5.33–36.

87. Val. Max. 1, *pr.* See also above, Ch. VI.3. On the limits to the ecumenical view, see Nguyen 2008, 72–76.

88. See Gallia 2012; and, esp., Orlin 2016.

89. Tac. *Ann.* 1.10.8, tr. 2004 by A. J. Woodman: Hacket, Indianapolis and Cambridge, modified. On practices of the ruler cult, see Cancik and Hitzl 2003.

90. Tac. *Ann.* 1.11.1.

91. Cf. Scheid 2012b, 210: "timeless, ancient Rome." For the ruler cult in contemporary Greece, see Camia 2011; Lozano 2011, 512 indicates a ruler cult heralded by the phenomenon of Romanization.

92. Lapatin 2010, 150; see also Pollini 2012.

93. On the beginning of dynastic strategies, see Hurlet 2009.

94. Rüpke 2011d, 140–45. See above, p. 204.

95. Cooley 2014.

96. An exception was widespread acceptance of "August 1," which was centrally decreed in the cult of the *lares* in the *vici*; see e.g., *AE* 1980.57.

97. Garthwaite 2009, 320–21, on Calpurnius, *Eclogues* 7.

98. See generally Scheid 2004a, 248; Pompeii: Torelli 1998; Gasparini 2016 (an alternative view in Marcattili 2015); Ostia: Calandra 2000.

99. See Saddington 2009, 98.

100. On the comparison, see Clauss 1994. On the cults, Gordon 2012, Dorcey 1992.

101. Marginal phenomenon: Bremmer 1994, 2011.

102. Gill 2009a, 82.

103. Sellars 2004, 171–72. See also Bartsch and Wray 2009.

104. Sellars 2004.

105. Gill 2009a, 77–8.

106. This also applies to Plotinus: Kühn 2008, 140.

107. Richter 2011, 82–85; Reydams-Schils 2005, 53–63, 140–41, 174–76.

108. For Seneca in the first century AD, see Setaioli 2007. On Plutarch and Seranus of Ephesus in the second century AD, Brenk 1998, 170–81; Podolak 2010. On the concept of transformation in Prudentius in late antiquity, Mastrangelo 2008.

109. See e.g., Van Hoof 2010 on Plutarch. See also Seim and Œkland 2009.

110. See Markschies 1997.

111. Ildefonse 2008, 233; Aubry 2008. Cf. Song 2009.

112. Sfameni Gasparro 2007, Israelowich 2015.

113. Harris and Holmes 2008, Petridou 2015; see also Fields 2008, Petsalis-Diomidis 2010. On narratives of healing, see also Martzavou 2012a.

114. On the special role in the military, see Wesch-Klein 2009. For organized worshippers, see Petridou 2016.

115. See e.g. Plin. *Letters* 7.27 (I owe the suggestion to the late Veit Rosenberger).

116. Athanassiadi 1993, Harris 2009, Renberg 2010a, Pizzone 2013. On Artemidorus, see also Weber 1999; Brakke, Satlow, and Weitzman 2005; du Bouchet and Chandezon 2012; Downie 2015. On Hermas, see Miller 1988. Elegists of the Augustan Age had also tried to convey dream experiences to their readers, Scioli 2015.

117. As regards references to dreams, Gil Renberg estimates for Silvanus more than two thirds of all inscriptions, with Asclepius's share lying at only 40 percent (lecture at Erfurt University on November 13, 2009); briefly, Renberg 2015, 257.

118. Bendlin 2006; Stoneman 2011, 174–89; Kindt 2015. See also Eidinow 2007, 42–55.

119. Smadja 1986.

120. See ibid., 509–14.

121. Frankfurter 1998, 242.

122. Schörner 2013.

123. Haensch 1997, 2006.

124. Herz 2003.

125. Horden and Purcell 2000.

126. See Bernstein 2007.

127. For Gaul, see Lobüscher 2002.

128. See Sartre 2005, 299–318; more broadly comparative, Raja 2015.

129. Raja 2013a, 40. See generally, Andrade 2013, Butcher 2013.

130. Van Andringa 2011.

131. See Rüpke 2008b.

132. Ameling 2009. On the significance of linguistic boundaries, Kaizer 2009.

133. Richert 2005, 16.

134. Ando 2005; see also Richter 2011, 207–42. On epigraphic competence and altered conditions for it in the Greek-speaking world, see e.g. Chaniotis 2009; with regard to the special case of non-lingual *charakteres*, see Gordon 2014.

135. See Rüpke 2001b, Haeussler 2012, Spickermann 2015.

136. See Caes. *B Gall.* 6.17 and 6.21: *Germani multum ab hac consuetudine differunt.* Cf. Woolf 2011, on the logic of the observer. On Tacitus: Rives 2011b.

137. Ducoeur 2011: King Pṛthu.

138. Cf. Woolf 2015.

Chapter X: Experts and Providers

1. On the determination that prayer rather than sacrifice was the key characteristic of Roman religion, see Patzelt 2017. On the long continuity and essential role of prayer from Hellenistic to rabbinical Judaism, see Chazon 2012, 387; see also Jonquière 2007.

2. Mauss 1925 (trans. Mauss 2002) is fundamental. See Moebius and Papilloud 2006; Hoffmann, Link-Wieczorek, and Mandry 2016.

3. This is what is termed "embedded religion."

4. *Acta Arvalia* 49.8–32 Scheid.

5. *Simulatrices:* Paul. *Fest.* 455.15–16 L; the only *popa* known by name was a woman: FS no. 1419. On the multitude of overlooked religious (and cultural) roles of women, see Keegan 2014, 121–34; see previously Momigliano 1992a.

6. *Fest.* 472.19–23 L.

7. Goette 1986b, 64, surmises a *pontifex minor*; evidence for this is lacking.

8. See Gordon 1990.

9. Keegan 2014, 133.

10. On the role, see Vinzent 2016.

11. Ullucci 2012; for the wider context, see Knust and Várhelyi 2011, Faraone and Naiden 2012.

12. Eckhardt 2014, referring to Plut. *Numa* 16.2. Cf. Stroumsa 2009, where, though, too much stress is put on the role of Jews and Christians in these processes.

13. Elsner 2012b.

14. Gordon 2009a, 640; Meier 2009, 207–208. For the regionally varying ends of other games, see Remijsen 2015.

15. See Rüpke 2016e. On the choice of the term *episkopoi*, see Eck 2014, 344–5.

16. On the problematic nature of the term, see Ando and Rüpke 2006b, 2006a.

17. Radin 1927. I am greatly beholden to Richard Gordon for my argument here (an exemplary treatment in Gordon 2005).

18. See above, p. 217.

19. Wilburn 2012. Here generally on the constraints governing the tradition, and the resulting gaps in *our knowledge* of these practices. On sounds in general, see Vendries 2015.

20. On the term, see Mulsow 2012. For literary notions in so-called personal poetry, see e.g., Luck 1992, Phillips III 1994, Phillips 1995, O'Neill 1998, Janowitz 2001, Murray 2007, Rüpke 2016c, 65–79.

21. Fest. 232.33–234.2 L; here too the following synonyms. Definition of *saga* in Cic. *Div.* 1.65.

22. Exception: Keegan 2014, 129.

23. See Varro, *Ling.* 6.14: *sacerdotes Liberi*. Only two male *libarii* are known, from Pompeiian graffiti (*CIL* 4.1768–9); the normal assumption that these were secular bakers is questionable.

24. Mart. 10.24.4. The great variety of different cakes for rituals included the *arculata*: Paul. *Fest.* 15.10 L.

25. Belayche 2013, 114–22, rightly challenges any categorical separation between priests male or female and specialists in divination.

26. See Rüpke 2013i, Eidinow 2013, and Bowden 2013, 54–56, on the increasing importance of the latter aspect during the course of the Imperial Age.

27. Cato *Agr.* 5.4; critical voices also in Plaut. *Amph.* 1132.

28. Plautus, *Miles gloriosus* 693.

29. See above, p. 184.

30. Thus generally Van Nuffelen 2011 (cf. Adluri 2013: longer-term trend); on Manilius, Volk 2009.

31. Schmid 2005; Green 2014, here too for the following.

32. Firmicus, *Contra mathematicos* 2.30.5.

33. *Declamationes maiores* 4.17.1. On the text, Stramaglia 2013.

34. On techniques and client groups, see Demandt 1990, Brodersen 2006, Nollé 2007. For Italy: Bouché-Leclercq 1882; Champeaux 1986, 1990; Buchholz 2013. In general: Bouché-Leclercq 1879; Belayche et al. 2005. Manual: Mowat 2016.

35. Epictetus 1.31; rivalry with soothsayers: 1.32.

36. See Denzey Lewis 2017, with reference to Irenaeus and the Hippolytus of the *Refutatio*; later to be joined by Epiphanius.

37. Kemezis 2014.

38. Cass. Dio 72.23.1–2.

39. Cass. Dio 53.1.5; 58.12.5.

40. Cass. Dio 56.46.1.

41. Cass. Dio 55.22.5.

42. E.g., Cass. Dio 52.30.4–6, 54.8.5, 55.6.5; esp. 56.46.5 and 59.6.4.

43. For a full account of the following, Rüpke 2011b.

44. Rüpke 2010b.

45. *ILS* 8380; see Van Haeperen 2002, 198–201.

46. *CIL* 6.31034.

47. *CIL* 6.709, 6.52.

48. *CIL* 6.40684.

49. Cf. *Dig.* 1.2.2.49, on the granting of *ius publice respondendi* by the *Augusti*.

50. Esmonde Cleary 2013, 226–30. However, the "confessional inscriptions" are a rural phenomenon (stressed by G. Horsley, lecture at Erfurt on October 1, 2015).

51. Thus Gordon 2016. The texts are freely available in Petzl 1994. See also Rostad 2002, Chaniotis 2009, and Belayche 2013, on the role of priests.

52. Cass. Dio 55.31.2–3.

53. Cass. Dio 59.9.3.

54. Cass. Dio 79.4.1–5, 79.31.1–2.

55. Thus Smith 1978b, ch. 2. Generally on apocalyptic writings, Momigliano 1992b. On sibyls, Collins 1987; Parke 1988; Potter 1990, 1994; Neujahr 2012, 195–242. On apocalyptic texts, Nagel, Schipper, and Weymann 2008, Jones 2011.

56. Cass. Dio 57.18.4–5. Fire of Rome: 62.18.3.

57. Satake 2008, 126; Malina 2002; see Taeger and Bienert 2006, 162–63.

58. Osiek 1999, 24; Rüpke 2013b.

59. Rüpke 2005b.

60. On the following see Gordon 2013b.

61. *Shepherd of Hermas* 8.3.

62. *Shepherd* 7.4; see Leutzsch 1989, 70–71.

63. *Shepherd* 8.3.

64. Lieu 2004, 243. Cf. Cicero, *On the laws* 2.5, and the discussions of the Alexandrian Jews in Josephus, *Against Apion* 2.6, and Diognetus 5–6.

65. *Apocalypse* 17–18; *4 Esra* 11–12; *Sibylline Oracles* 5.408–27; Jones 2011.

66. On the Flavians: Boyle and Dominik 2003; cf. Rüpke 2012i for a somewhat earlier text in Rome, and Nasrallah 2010 for eastern Mediterranean cities. Cf., on the other hand, modes of reference in John's *Apocalypse*, Karrer 2012.

67. *Shepherd* 9 (*visio* 3.1), 4, and *vis* 1.4.1 and 3; *vis* 3.1.6 and 10.1.

68. *Shepherd* 50.8–10.

69. Waldner 2012.

70. See e.g., Lucian, *Alexandros,* or *Peregrinus* 11; Origenes, *Contra Celsum* 7.9 (for the suggestion I thank Maria dell'Isola, who is preparing for publication a work on the historiographical construction of Montanism).

71. Fronto, *Epistulae* 2, p. 10 (226 N): *epularum dictator, cenarum libator, feriarum promulgator.*

72. Lucian, *Peregr.* 13.

73. See e.g., *AE* 1997, 857; Chaniotis 2005, 163; a full account is in Alföldy 1997.

74. Irenaeus, *Adversus haereses* 1.23; Allen Brent in a paper presented at the British Patristics Conference, London, 2014. E.g., Lucius Aelius Moles Iunior and his son Lucius Aelius Terentianus Moles built at Keraia (Belören), in the late first or the second century AD, a small cult locale intended only for libations to the god Men Keraeiton (Horsley 2007, no. 110).

75. The following is based essentially on Gordon 2012, here 971–72. On the Iranian origin of the concept of a cosmic founding sacrifice, see Gordon 2017.

76. On the spread of images of Mithras, see Boschung 2014.

77. White 2012, 481–86. On the invocation of "Mithras" in other contexts; e.g., *Inscriptiones Graecae ad Res Romanas Pertinentes* 1.79, with Gordon 1994, 471; Sanzi 2005; Latteur 2011.

78. Gordon 2017, 980. Against a location in the military: Gordon 2009b.

79. Gordon 2017; see also Martens 2015; generally on the finds at Tienen and similar (such as the snake vessel from the "Ballplatz" Mithraeum in Mainz), see Martens and Boe 2004.

80. See Gordon 2013c, extrapolating on Chalupa and Glomb 2013. On a Cautes with a bull's head, Szabó 2015.

81. Cf. Gordon 2013c. This poses major problems for an "archaeology of ritual" (see e.g. Van Andringa and Lepetz 2003; Scheid 2008) and the interpretation of animal bones and the remains of meals: chicken bones too can indicate the sacrifice of bulls.

82. The latter factor applies similarly to occurrences of the name Jupiter Dolichenus, largely absent in Gallia and Hispania (Schwarzer 2012); on this so-called cult, see e.g., Merlat 1960, Hörig, Schwertheim 1987, Blömer, Winter 2012, Sanzi 2013.

83. Auffarth 2013.

84. On the experiences thus facilitated, see Gordon 2015. On the use of light in mysteries, see also Patera 2010.

85. See the exemplary treatment by Gawlinski (2012).

86. Rogers 2012. E.g., Horsley 2007, no. 21 (first half of first century AD).

87. See e.g., Pappalardo 2012, on the Villa of the Mysteries in Pompeii. Central here is Pausanias's text; on Pausanias's own religious experiences, see Funke 2010, 226.

88. Simón 2010; Harland 2011; see also Klotz 2012, 404, on Thebes. On journeys by Italics to Greek temples as early as the Republican period, see Naso 2011.

89. Full coverage in Van der Horst 1982.

90. Cic. *Leg.* 2.20–21; Rüpke 2016e, 29–31.

91. See above, p. 178. Tacitus the *quindecimvir* did not write on religion.

92. For details, see Rüpke 2014b, 239–49; *contra* Cameron 2007, 2011.

93. See Ullucci 2012, although he provides no more precise social differentiation. As established by Rebillard 2010, Christian criticism until the fifth century extended almost exclusively to participation in sacrifices, not to enjoyment of the resulting "sacrificial meat."

94. Thus the important finding in Schörner 2011, 94. On translatability, see Richter 2011, 211.

95. Auffarth 2013, 434. See e.g., Galen, *Diff. puls.* 2.4.

96. Thus Van Nuffelen 2011. On the role of religious "knowledge" and the authority lent by it, see North 2010, 47; see also Sanders 1992, 191.

97. Branham 2012, 222–23; Swartz 2016.

98. On processes of religious individualization in the Imperial Age, see Rüpke and Spickermann 2012; Rüpke 2013g, 2013k; Rüpke and Woolf 2013a.

99. Rüpke 2016c. On examples of religious consequences of geographical mobility, see Hekster, Schmidt-Hofner, and Witschel 2009.

100. Thus Richard Gordon. On the Roman situation, see Orlin 2010.

101. *Shepherd* 8.3. For this idea, as for the opportunity to develop it further, I thank Jos Verheyden, Leuven.

102. Schellenberg 2011, 156–58; Baslez 2011, 25.

103. Here I am conveying considerations proposed by Richard Gordon in respect of the perceived functioning of curse tablets: Gordon 1995, 2007, 2013e, and, esp., Gordon 2013d.

104. Briefly, Ando 2008, 2013b, 2013a; Woolf 2009, 2012b; Rüpke 2014b, 1–21.

105. Hurlet 2011, 134. On the unsystematic character of the regime, see Eck and Müller-Luckner 1999.

106. For the central argument, Price 1984.

107. Cf. generally, G. A. Fine 2010.

108. See Martin 1995, 723; on the superimposition, Picard 2012.

109. On the lack of reinvestment in public temples in northwestern Europe from the second half of the third century AD onward, see Van Andringa 2014a and the instances cited in Van Andringa 2014b.

110. Bazzana 2010, 108–109; Schwartz 2010, 170.

111. Harland 2014, no. 95 from AD 81.

112. On differences in the complexity of political/cultural identities, see Demougin 2012, 109; on the situation in the eastern Mediterranean, see e.g., Jones 2004; Raja 2013b, 169. On synagogues as associations, Richardson 2004.

113. Lieu 2004, DePalma Digeser 2006, Schott 2008, Perkins 2009, Nigdelis 2010, Rebillard 2012.

114. This entices us today to indulge in homogenizing talk of "cults," where stress is laid on the sought-after identical features, while no account is taken of the countless local variations.

Chapter XI: Notional and Real Communities

1. On the context, see Gordon 2013b, 165. For the foundation of an association overseas in Nicomedia in northwestern Asia Minor by the carpenter Papos from Phoenicia to provide for burial, see Price 2012, 8 (referring to *Bulletin de Correspondence Hellénique* 102, 1978, 413–15).

2. See Ausbüttel 1982, 35–37.

3. See e.g., Harland 2014, no. 103: a shared dedication to Roma secured the local population and the Roman merchants a common basis for trading. For a similar situation at Kozluca, Horsley 2007, no. 328 (Myliadeis, Roman merchants, resident Thracians).

4. Exemplary: Bendlin 2011.

5. Fully covered in Egelhaaf-Gaiser 2000, 272–329.

6. Bollmann 1998; with particular reference to religious groups, see White 1990, Nielsen 2014.

7. Rohde 2012, 359. On the dating, cf. Trimble 2011, 337.

8. Ando 2013b, 92–100.

9. *Dig.* 47.22.1.2; White 1990, 26–28. On an association at the cusp between household and neighborhood: *CIL* 6.455 (*collegium Larum*).

10. See *Dig.* 47.22.1.1; also Bendlin 2005, 80–82.

11. Noy 2010, 211. See in general Belayche, Dubois 2011.

12. The following section 1 relies on Rüpke 2016g.

13. Ascough 2005, 2007.

14. König 2011.

15. Cf. de Certeau 1991 on historians.

16. On the critical process, see Stowers 2011, Urciuoli 2013. On particular problems resulting, as in the discourse regarding Pythagoreans, see Cornelli 2013.

17. See Iricinschi and Zellentin 2008; Denzey Lewis 2017.

18. King 2008, 35.

19. See Stock 1983 for the Middle Ages; for antiquity, Brakke 2012.

20. See Quinn 1982, here 79–93.

21. Starr 1987.

22. For late antiquity, see Mratschek 2010.

23. Johnson 2012, here Ch. 2.

24. Schmidt 2001, here 940.

25. Johnson 2012, 42–56.

26. Juvenal 7.36–47.

27. Hoffer 1999, 10–13; Gibson and Morello 2012, 136–38; on the indirect inclusion of women, see Shelton 2013. Sherwin-White 1966 (in many reprints) remains irreplaceable for prosopographical aspects of the network.

28. 3 John: 9–10, English Standard Version.

29. Musonius in his Diatribes III and IV directly encourages women to philosophize; see Ramelli 2008 *ad loc.*

30. See Vinzent 2011.

31. Eusebius, *Historia ecclesiae* 5.13.5–7; I thank Markus Vinzent 2011, 126, for the reference.

32. E.g., Galen, *De usu partium* 11.14; see Tieleman 2005.

33. Rüpke 2012g, 74–8.

34. Ps.-Caesar, *Bellum Hispaniense* 42.7.

35. Momigliano 1992b; Potter 1990, 1994; Gauger 1998, 412–18.

36. E.g., *Oracula Sibyllina* 1.2, 3.163; cf. 4.1 and 5.1. People/world: 1.4, 2.21, 3.7, 8.1.3. Cf. Usher 2013 on possible reception, critical of the imperial regime, in the *Octavia* praetexta.

37. See Henderson 2012.

38. Thus Cancik 2011.

39. See Arnal 2011 and below. On their designation by others, and then also by themselves, as "Christians," see Trebilco 2012, 272–311.

40. Scopello 2010, here 253 (see also 270); Schenke in Schenke, Bethge, and Kaiser 2007, 2.

41. Thus Ramelli 2005, 1358–59, compared against the texts of the post-antique collection in the *Corpus Hermeticum.*

42. Cf. ibid. 1344 and 1362–64. For discussion of monastic use, see Lundhaug and Jenott 2015.

43. Cf. Vielhauer 1975, 602: without a real public.

44. Schaper 2009, here relating to the seventh to fifth centuries BC.

45. In the case of Lucian, it is possible to relate some twenty out of seventy available texts to religion, in the case of Plutarch some fifteen of the seventy-eight assembled in the *Moralia*.

46. Rüpke 2013h.

47. See Cancik 2011; Rüpke 2012g; cf. Becker 2005.

48. On the latter, see Rajak 2009.

49. Ibid., 152–75; "foreignizing": 153.

50. See Rajak 2009, 311.

51. Millar 2010, Takahashi 2014.

52. On the thesis of the "split diaspora," for the extensive loss of contact with the communities of the western diaspora before the Islamic era, and possibly far-reaching Latin-Christian assimilations, see Edrei and Mendels 2007, 2008, 2012. In treating the question of the rise of Jewish communities in the West, both authors remain on the whole reticent, and fail to address the problem of a Greek-speaking minority in a Latin-speaking environment.

53. Stern 2012, 303–13.

54. Rajak 2009, 223–24.

55. Watts 2010, 45–52. See generally Cancik-Lindemaier 2012; Cancik 2012b, 103, on the role of such narratives in the field of transition between Judaism and Christianity.

56. Cf., with a different emphasis, Brakke 2012, 275.

57. Martzavou 2012a, 195; Petridou 2016.

58. Kratz 2013; Sharon 2012, 439, on the development of synagogues in Egypt from the third century BC onward.

59. Rajak 2009, 234–35. See below, p. 350.

60. On the concept, see Granovetter 1973.

61. Suet. *Aug.* 31.1; Teja Casuso and Marcos 2012.

62. The following relies on Rüpke 2016b.

63. Verdoner 2011, 19.

64. Generally, Dithmar 1995.

65. In the following I am guided by Koschorke 2012, 27–110, for analytic terminology.

66. Ov. *Fast.* 2.721–852. Full treatment in Rüpke 2010a.

67. Koschorke 2012, 61–74. For the gospels, King 2015.

68. See the overview in Seeliger and Wischmeyer 2015, 1–45; see also Waldner 2004.

69. Val. Max. 9.15.5 and 9.15, ext. 1.

70. Wardle 2000, 2002, Lucarelli 2007. On the concept of *post-memory*, see Hirsch 2012.

71. Marcion 1:2 Klinghardt=Luke 3:1.

72. See Bowersock 1994, Whitmarsh 2010, Woolf 2010.

73. On this connectivity, see Koschorke 2012, 29–38.

74. Knauer 1964 (repr. 1979).

75. E.g., Bremmer 1991, Hartmann 2013; on the later importation into the Polycarp narrative, see Zwierlein 2014 and Seeliger and Wischmeyer 2015, 29.

76. Especially helpful on ancient biography: McGing and Mossman 2006, Shuttleworth Kraus 2007, Radke-Uhlmann 2008, Hägg 2012. On religious biography, see Talbert 1978, Cox 1983, Momigliano 1987, Dihle 1993, Dillon 2006, König 2006, Debié 2010.

77. On Caesar and Tacitus, see e.g., Krauss 1930, Kröger 1940, Rüpke 2012g, 74.

78. Plut. *Numa* 9.1.

79. On older conceptions of Numa, see most recently Deremetz 2013.

80. Rüpke 2012i.

81. Lombardi 2012, 391.

82. On Josephus, cf. Hadas-Lebel 1993. On autobiography, see Engels 1993, Pelling 2009, Smith 2009.

83. McLaren 2013.

84. For discussion of the biographical character of the gospels, see Cancik 1984b, 1984a; Dormeyer and Frankemölle 1984; skeptical treatment in Becker 2006; a variant assessment in Baum 2013.

85. See e.g., Stefaniw 2012, Johnston 2012.

86. Demoen, and Praet 2009 on Apollonius; Lipsett 2011 on Hermas and the *Acts of Paul and Thecla*, as well as the romance of *Joseph and Aseneth*. On the rare instances of conversion as a specific biographical narrative, see Bremmer 2014c and 2016a.

87. Cf. the development of the Clementine Romance and its evolution into a first-person narrative, in Syria, Wehnert 2015.

88. Generally Koschorke 2012, 38–51, esp. 41.

89. Rüpke 2015a.

90. Ben-Eliyahu, Cohn, and Millar 2012, 62.

91. See even for the 19th century, Lersch 1843.

92. Standhartinger 2010, summary at 25.

93. Bremmer 1995b.

94. See above, p. 261.

95. See Henderson 2011, 224, on the concept's application to some of the following texts. On the concept itself, see Schiffman 1985, Feldman 1998.

96. *Epistula apostolorum* 14; Ehrman 2003, 75.

97. *Ascensio Iesaiae* 11.8–9; Vinzent 2011, 119–22.

98. *Evangelium soteros* 7 = *P. Berol.* 22220; ed. Ehrman 2003.

99. Niehoff 2012.

100. Cf. Newlands 2009, 372–33, with Nikolaidis 2009.

101. E.g., 1, 25, 49; see Henderson 2011.

102. Haines-Eitzen 2012.

103. Krueger 2004, 191; for the later period, Krueger 2010.

104. *Gospel of the Ebionites* 1 = Epiphanius, *Panarion* 30.13.6.

105. Exemplary: Feldherr 2010 on Ovid.

106. Stressed by Frenschkowski 2009, there too on the concept of a subculture (230–32).

107. See Brown in Brown and Lizzi Testa 2011, 607.

108. Fully covered in Rüpke 2014c.

109. See e.g., Nicolet 1988, Clarke 1999, Dueck 2012; on Trogus, Widevoort Crommelin 1993.

110. Gillet-Didier 2002, 391–92.

111. On religious practices of memorialization and historiography in Rome, see Rüpke 2012g. Generally on the phenomenon, Rüsen 1996, 2001; Straub 2001.

112. Gruen 2011, 227.

113. Schwartz 2001, 19–21.

114. For Egypt, especially Elephantine and Leontopolis, see Kratz 2013. On the following, see Schwartz 2001, 32–99, although the author neglects to reflect on universalist implications.

115. Tuval 2012, 238.

116. Tac. *Ann.* 15.44.2–3; Plin. *Ep.* 10.96–97. Cf. Zetterholm 2003.

117. On the ambivalent character of circumcision as a distinctive characteristic and means of control, see Jacobs 2012; see also Neutel and Anderson 2014 on the ambivalence of the masculine symbol in Philo and Paul. On Paul's "imperial" program, see Arnal 2011.

118. Mitchell 1999, 2010; Belayche 2011a.

119. Val. Max. 1.3.2 in connection with the suppression of foreign religious practices (come down to us only by the epitome of Iulius Paris).

120. Thus, convincingly, Wendt 2015.

121. See Tac. *Ann.* 15.44.3.

122. On the latter, see Baudy 1991, with critique in Rüpke 1994. Generally, Shaw 2015.

123. For the discussion, Goodman 2012, Clements 2012. Colorful: Fine 2015. See also Weikert 2016, 75–76, for the addressees of the arch; and for a narrative of the conflict at Judaea, Rudich 2015.

124. Ebner 2012, 85–91, with reference to Paul and the *First Epistle of Clement*. Cf. Maier 2015 on Hermas; Neutel 2015 on Paul.

125. Rüpke 2012i on the *Letter to the Hebrews*.

126. Thus Ebner 2012, 91, with reference to *Acts* 18:1–3; the same applies to Justin.

127. Briefly on Alexandria: Clauss 2004, 161–64; see also Bland 1996. For Bar Kochba, Eck 2012.

128. In the following I follow the reconstruction of the priority of Marcion's gospel most recently adopted by Vinzent 2014a, 2014b, and there too obtained my sources (10–133). Textual reconstruction: Klinghardt 2015, who, though, leaves open the question of the authorship of the gospel used by Marcion, and the interval between it and the time when Marcion was active.

129. Frenschkowski 2002, Monnot 2003, Nicklas 2014, 97.

130. On the central work of Harnack and his earlier position, see Harnack 1921, Steck and Harnack 2003, Kinzig 2004. The most important source is Tertullian (see Moreschini 2014).

131. Cf. the observations in Becker 2011, 143, on Matthew and Mark (dating them much earlier).

132. Generally, Foley 1987, 1988.

133. See in general Ankersmit 2002, Ascough 2008.

134. Vinzent 2014a, 73. 272–76; for the same dating of the collection on a different basis, see Zwierlein 2010, 143; Zwierlein 2009, 299–301. Nicklas 2014, 218, characterizes Paul's orientation as a new focus in a Jewish matrix.

135. Clements 2012. On the *Acts of the* Apostles as a tale of schism, see Cancik 2011, 328–33.

136. Henderson 2011.

137. Cass. Dio 69.2.3.

138. Cass. Dio 76.15.7, 78.18.3.

139. Cass. Dio 78.7.1–3, Xiphilinus.

140. Ameling 2011, 485; see also Rizzi 2010, 20. On Christianity as a popular form of Judaism, see Hezser 2013.

141. Absence of local tradition: Zwierlein 2010, Ameling 2011. Central on the liturgy, Bradshaw 2014; see also Leonhard 2017.

142. Nicklas 2014, 61.

143. Caprioli 2007, 288–93.

144. For a full account of this process, see Jung 1999, 2004, 2005, 2006. On language, Schlette and Jung 2005.

145. Ritual theories have obtained these outcomes on the basis of highly varied positions; see e.g., Staal 1980, Burkert 1981, Bernardi 1984; Heesterman 1986; Rappaport 1992.

146. See critique in Rüpke 2013l.

147. On the reinterpretation and affective loading of social ritual scripts, see Schechner 1985, Kranemann and Rüpke 2003, Rüpke 2003a.

148. Des Bouvrie 2011, 171, characterized public rituals (and dramatic productions in particular) as "a programme of performances . . . producing a sequence of prescribed emotions." See also Woolf 2013.

149. Grimes 1990, Rappaport 1999, Assmann 1999, Brandt and Iddeng 2012, Rüpke 2012e.

150. Rüpke 2012e.

151. Petsalis-Diomidis 2007, 252.

152. See e.g., Kuhfeldt 1882, Lomas 1997, Lackner 2013; Quinn and Wilson 2013. Time after time, such construction projects followed the change to colony status by decades or even a century.

153. *Cf.* Petsalis-Diomidis 2007, 252.

154. See e.g. Woolf 2009.

155. On the suspension of disbelief, see Eco 1999, 103. On the cognitive basis, see Boyer 1994.

156. Petsalis-Diomidis 2007, 289.

157. I thank Georgia Petridou, Liverpool/Erfurt, for the suggestion.

158. Smith 1978a.

159. *Asclepius* 24; Juv. 3.62.

160. Momigliano 1992b, Frankfurter 1998; cf. Webster and Cooper 1996, Chakrabarty 2008.

161. See Bracht 2014 and the next chapter. Heracleon's commentary on John's Gospel may also have originated in Rome, if so from as early as the 170s, immediately after the compilation of a first "Christian" textual corpus; on author and text, see Pagels 1973.

Chapter XII: Demarcations and Modes of Community

1. See the contrasting of teachers on the one hand and *episkopoi*, priests, and Levites on the other in Hippolytus, *Commentary on Daniel* 1.18.

2. See ibid., 4.8.7 and 4.9.2. On the dating as well as details of the following interpretation, see Rüpke 2017b. For a defense of the traditional dating of AD 204 *cf.* on the other hand Bracht 2014, 58–64.

3. On the identification of the different respective authors, see Scholten 1991; Brent 1995, 2004; Volp 2009; Heintz 2011; cf. Cerrato 2002, 2004; Heine 2004.

4. Cass. Dio 77.16.1–2.

5. Thus also Markschies 1999.

6. On Judas, known only from Eus. *HE* 6.7, see Strobel 1993, 113–15, locating him in Alexandria, although the argument is by no means compelling. Origen too spent some time in Rome in 212/3.

7. Briefly, Burgess and Kulikowski 2013, 110–17, with my review in the 2015 *Journal for the History of Astronomy*. For a full account of Africanus, see Wallraff 2006, Wallraff et al. 2007, Wallraff and Mecella 2009.

8. On the possibility that he may have used Theodotion's text, see the discussion in Bracht 2014, 17, 43–47.

9. Berchman 1984, Dillon 1996, Turner and Corrigan 2010, J. M. Dillon 2012.

10. Hippol. *Dan.* 4.18; for another example; 4.19. For a critique of the approach, 4.16.6, 21.4–22.1.

11. See Magny 2006, 430.

12. Cf. Rebillard 2016.

13. Cf. Marcus 2011, esp. 395–96.

14. Hippol. *Dan.* 1.22.2, 2.34, 4.50.3; cf. though 1.15: "Jews by circumcision." Cf. on the terms "Jews" and "Hellenes" or *pagani* as group-internal differentiations, Boin 2014.

15. E.g., ibid., 2.20 (2 Maccabees) or 4.42 (1 Maccabees). On the resumption of interest in the Maccabees in 4 Maccabees, written in the early second century AD, see Spieckermann 2014, 165–83, esp. 172–73.

16. On interest in *Daniel* in the (early) Imperial Age, see Theodoretus 2006, Hill 2007, Tilly 2007, Oegema 2008. Critically on the events of 167/6, Honigman 2014.

17. See Van Henten 2010. See also Shelton 2003, 69–78; 2008.

18. Briefly on Hippolytus's angelological christology, Bracht 2014, 291, 296–97; generally: Bucur 2009.

19. *CIL* 6.502=*ILS* 4150=*Corpus Cultus Cybelis Attidisque*=*CCCA* 231 (similar: 6.504=*CCCA* 233). Cf. 6.510=*ILS* 4152=*CCCA* 242: *in aeternum renatus.* The Taurobolia were often performed with wives present, but might also be given a *pro salute imperatoris* flavor: *CIL* 12.1745 (Valentia); *AE* 1910, 217 (Nemausus).

20. Rajak 2009.

21. See Stefaniw 2011.

22. See Jenott and Pagels 2010.

23. Niehoff 2011a, 2011b; Rajak 2013.

24. Cf. the contributions in Mitchell and Van Nuffelen 2010.

25. Berchman 1998; Frede 1999. Girgenti and Muscolino 2011; D'Anna 2011; Addey 2014; Agosti 2015. On the ritual, see esp. Janowitz 2002; Smith 1997, 2011. See also Marx-Wolf 2014.

26. *Papyrus Gissensis* 40. New translation and interpretation of the papyrus as a local product, Bryen 2016.

27. Ando 2008, 2010, 2013b, 2015; overview: Ando 2012.

28. Plin. *HN* 3.39.

29. See Rüpke 2011e, 157–75. But see at the end of the fourth century, Ambrosius; e.g. Ambrosius, *Letters* 72.3 (CSEL 82.3) to Valentinian II: *fides . . . quae servat imperium.*

30. Rives 1999, 152. On reactions to the situation in letters by those affected, see Luijendijk 2008, 216–26.

31. See, more generally, North 1994, North 2011.

32. For a detailed account of the persecution in Carthage, see Brent 2011.

33. Seeliger and Wischmeyer 2015, 9–13. Shortly, Ando 2017.

34. Rives 2011a, 212.

35. Schwarte 1994.

36. On the very limited goals of the project, see Belayche 2011b.

37. Schmidt-Hofner 2016.

38. See Rosenbaum-Alföldi 2015a on the coin perhaps minted as early as AD 313 (ibid., 24).

39. See *Supplementum epigraphicum graecum* 18.555.

40. The literature on Constantine is vast. Important contributions to the discussion are: Cameron 2006, Bleckmann 2007, Eck 2007, Schuller and Wolff 2007, Van Dam 2009, Barnes 2011, Potter 2013, Lenski 2016.

41. Here I follow the interpretation of Schott 2008, 110–28.

42. On the emotional element in the publication of imperial norms, see Hahn 2011, 216.

43. In the following I follow Curran 2000 (using Rüpke 2007a).

44. Curran 2000, 59–63.

45. Ibid., 70.

46. Ibid., 99–115.

47. Bauer 2001, Isele 2010, Lønstrup Dal Santo 2012, Ward-Perkins 2012, Ando 2013b, Mulryan 2013.

48. J. N. Dillon 2012. Fundamental: Ando 2000, 2011.

49. *Codex Theodosianus* 16.10.1, pr. (AD 320/1); see also 9.16.9 of AD 319. On this in detail, Rüpke 2011a, 77–116. On the prehistory, Fögen 1993.

50. See *Cod. Theod.* 16.10.4, with 16.10.7 (of AD 381).

51. On the following: Barceló 2013, with Rüpke 2014a. See also Clark 2004, 95–100; Thompson 2015.

52. Lenski 2016, 93–94.

53. Rapp 2000.

54. For the idea I thank Jan Bremmer. See Salzman 1992, 2002.

55. Cf. for the period around AD 200, Tertullian, *De praescriptione haereticorum* 41.5 and 8.

56. Cf. Stroumsa 2015.

57. Rebillard 2012; this does not signify an absence of conflicts: Shaw 2011.

58. Schott 2008, 128–35, with further examples. On the further context of the remodelling of cities, see Lenski 2016, 147–78. On Helena, see Cooper 2013, 131–37; Dirschlmayer 2015, 50–52 (never attested as sponsor).

59. Barnes 2011, 142.

60. On the text and its social context, Stern 1953, Salzman 1990, Divjak 2002, Wischmeyer 2002, Burgess 2012, Rüpke 2015c (which I use in the following).

61. Rüpke 2005c, no. 876. Salzman 2002, 201 suggests the nephew.

62. Symmachus, *Letters* 1.2; ibid., no. 808.

63. Jerome, *De viris Illustribus* 103.

64. Clark and Hatch 1981, Jensen 1991, Matthews 1992, Harich-Schwarzbauer 2001; Cooper 2013, 140–46. On the significance of the codex for Christian practices, see Wallraff 2013.

65. Iunior, *Expositio totius mundi et gentium* 55. On the latter, Demandt 2007, 341.

66. On the conception and the banquet ritual, see Carletti 2004.

67. von Stuckrad 2000a, 2000b.

68. Demandt 2007, 112.

69. Demandt 2007, 447 n. 62.

70. On them: Hirschmann 2015.

71. Ammianus Marcellinus 27.3.12–13; Guyon 1996, 886–87.

72. Pietri 1976, 376–80.

73. Briefly in Piétri and Markschies 1996, 316; for details see Mayr 1955, Mosshammer 2008.

74. Cf. Leppin 2012, 260, on the phase of "neutralization" in the context of his conception of a process of Christianization.

75. Brief biography in Jer. *Vir. Ill.* 84. For full coverage of the following, Rüpke 2012a, 233–44. See also Flieger 1993.

76. See Stökl Ben Ezra 2012.

77. Generally: Kartschoke 1975, Roberts 1985, Nodes 1993, Speyer 1996.

78. Agosti 2013.

79. Shorrock 2011, 119. On Nonnus: Newbold 2003; Auger 2003; Accorinti 2009, 2013; Spanoudakis 2014. See also Massa 2014, de la Fuente 2013, and Kirkpatrick 2013, on the presence of Dionysus in the Judaeo-Christian tradition.

80. There is no possibility of quantifying any greater prominence in the body of surviving texts, which is not representative.

81. Cf. Giradet 2011, 225. On images, see e.g., Lightfoot 2007, 83; Rebillard 2009, 325.

82. Ando 2008, 21–42; Deligiannakis 2015. Examples in van den Kerchove 2012.

83. Good observations on this in Eshleman 2012.

84. See e.g., Stroumsa 2005; Johnston 2012; Stefaniw 2012; Ulucci 2014. On the rabbis, briefly, Reed 2013.

85. See Stefaniw 2011.

86. Frankfurter 1998, 131–44.

87. Clark 2004, 107–8; for further developments in this direction, see Brown 2015. On the centrality of generosity and benefaction in Mediterranean societies, cf. Schwartz 2010.

88. Rüpke 2010e, 2011c.

89. On the (limited) effect in private letters, see Choat 2006, esp. 143 on polytheistic formulae.

90. Gotter 2011, 152; see also Goldhill 2006, 161–62. On a popular view of traditional religion see Ps.-Meliton (Lightfoot 2007). Actual implementations of such demarcations always required a consensus among relevant local actors: Meyer-Zwiffelhoffer 2011, 128; Wiemer 2011, 176 (for Antioch).

91. Ward-Perkins 2011.

Chapter XIII: Epilogue

1. *CIL* 14.3469.

2. *CIL* 6.1778–9.

3. Rüpke 2014b, 238–241, *contra* Cameron 2011. Leppin 2008, on the other hand, assumes the development of a coherent "paganism."

4. Cf. Nesselrath 2012; Cribiore 2013, with Tanaseanu-Döbler 2008.

5. See Fuhrer 2011, Stefaniw 2011; previously, Niehoff 2011a.

6. Important inputs in Bowersock 1978, Athanassiadi 1992, Wojaczek 1992, Smith 1995, Mastrocinque 2005, Rosen 2007, Tanaseanu-Döbler 2008, Marcos 2009, Riedweg 2011b, Baker-Brian and Tougher 2012, Harrington 2012, Elm 2012.

7. Hahn 2004, 22.

8. Pseudo-Clement, *Homilies* 11.16; see Reed 2008, 181. On the patriarchate, Curran 2011.

9. See e.g., Harries 1986, Chesnut 1992, Morgan 2005, Grafton and Williams 2006, Willing 2008, Bazzana 2010, Verdoner 2011.

10. For debate on the ahistoricity of the Mishnah and the formation of the rabbis, see e.g. Green 1979; Neusner 1979, 1997, 2004; Stemberger 1999; Lightstone 2002; Boyarin 2004, 2008; Yuval, Harshav, and Chipman 2008; Goodman and Alexander 2010; Lapin 2012; Dohrmann 2013; Goldhill 2015. On the separation of "law" and "truth" developed in this discourse, see Hayes 2015, 244–45.

11. See Hahn 2004, 275 and 285, on interaction with provincial administrations; Haas 1997, 278–330. Generally: Sizgorich 2009; Isele 2010. An overview with further literature is in Bremmer 2014b.

12. On the limited role of monks, see Hahn 2004, 267. A detailed account is in Watts 2010. Constantinople: Bond 2013.

13. Ando 2008, 149–97. Reliquaries: Lønstrup Dal Santo 2012; for justification of the reliquary cult, see Constas 2002.

14. Curran 2000, 96. On the following, see 155–77, 129ff.; 139 (schisms).

REFERENCES

AAVV 1989. *Urbanistica ed architettura dell'antica Praeneste: Atti del convegno di studi archelologici, Palestrina 16/17 Aprile 1988*. Palestrina.

Aberson, M. 2009. "Le statut des dépôts d'offrandes dans l'Italie du Ve au Ier siècle av. J.-C. : l'apport de l'épigraphie et des textes normatifs." In S. Bonnardin and C. Hamon, eds., *Du Matériel au Spirituel: Réalités archéologiques et historiques des "dépôts" de la Préhistoire à nos jours. XXIXe Rencontres Internationales d'Archéologie et d'Histoire d'Antibes (Antibes, France, du 16 au 18 octobre 2008)*. Antibes. 97–104.

Abramenko, A. 1993. *Die munizipale Mittelschicht im kaiserzeitlichen Italien: Zu einem neuen Verständnis von Sevirat und Augustalität*, Europäische Hochschulschriften; Reihe 3, Histoire, sciences auxiliares de l'histoire 57. Frankfurt am Main.

Abry, J. H. 2011. "La place des Astronomiques de Manilius dans la poésie astrologique antique." In I. Boehm and W. Hübner, eds., *La poésie astrologique dans l'Antiquité: Actes du colloque organisé les 7 et 8 décembre 2007 par J.-H. Abry*. Paris. 95–114.

Abulafia, D. 2005. "Mediterraneans." In W. V. Harris, ed., *Rethinking the Mediterranean*. Oxford. 64–93.

Accorinti, D. 2009. "Poèsie et Poétique dans l'Oeuvre de nonnos de Panopolis." In P. Odorico, P. A. Agapitos, and M. Hinterberger, eds., *"Doux Remède..." Poèsie et Poétique à byzance*. Paris. 67–98.

———. 2013. "Nonnos von Panopolis." *Reallexikon für Antike und Christentum* 25: 1107–29.

Adams, C., and R. Laurence, eds. 2011. *Travel and Geography in the Roman Empire*. London.

Adams, J. N. 2007. *The Regional Diversification of Latin, 200 BC–AD 600*. Cambridge.

Addey, C. 2014. *Divination and Theurgy in Neoplatonism: Oracles of the Gods*, Ashgate Studies in Philosophy and Theology in Late Antiquity. Farnham.

Adluri, V. P., ed. 2013. *Philosophy and Salvation in Greek Religion*, Religionsgeschichtliche Versuche und Vorarbeiten 60. Berlin.

Agelidis, S. 2010. "Tod und Jenseits." In V. Kästner, ed., *Etrusker in Berlin: Etruskische Kunst in der Berliner Antikensammlung—Eine Einführung*. Berlin. 41–56.

Agosti, G. 2013. "Classicism, Paideia, Religion." In R. L. Testa, ed., *The Strange Death of Pagan Rome: Reflections on a Historiographical Controversy*. Giornale Italiano di Filologia Bibliotheca 16. Turnhout, Belgium. 123–40.

———. 2015. "Chanter les dieux dans la société chrétienne: les Hymnes de Proclus dans le contexte culturel et religieux de leur temps." In N. Belayche and V. Pirenne-Delforge, eds., *Fabriquer du divin: Constructions et ajustements de la représentation des dieux dans l'Antiquité*. Collection Religions: Comparatisme—Histoire—Anthropologie 5. Liège. 183–211.

Aigner-Foresti, L. 2000. "Orientalische Elemente im etruskischen Königtum?" In F. Prayon and W. Röllig, eds., *Akten des Kolloquiums zum Thema "Der Orient und Etrurien": Zum Phänomen des "Orientalisierens" im westlichen Mittelmeerrum (10.—6. Jh. v. Chr.)*. Pisa. 275–86.

Albers, J. 2010. "Tempel, Terrasse und Altar. Untersuchungen zum etruskischen Temenos." In A. Kieburg and A. Rieger, eds., *Neue Forschungen zu den Etruskern—Beiträge der Tagung vom 07. bis 09. November 2008 am Archäologischen Institut der Universität Bonn*. Oxford. 73–82.

———. 2013. *Campus Martius: Die urbane Entwicklung des Marsfeldes von der Republik bis zur mittleren Kaiserzeit*, Studien zur antiken Stadt 11. Wiesbaden.

Albert, S. 1980. *Bellum iustum: Die Theorie des "gerechten Krieges" und ihre praktische Bedeutung für die auswärtigen Auseinandersetzungen Roms in republikanischer Zeit*, Frankfurter Althistorische Studien 10. Kallmünz.

Alberti, M. E., and S. Sabatini, eds. 2012. *Exchange Networks and Local Transformations: Interaction and Local Change in Europe and the Mediterranean from the Bronze Age to the Iron Age*. Oxford.

Alföldy, G. 1973. *Flamines provinciae Hispaniae citerioris*, Anejos de Archivo Español de Arqueologia 6. Madrid.

———. 1991. "Augustus und die Inschriften: Tradition und Innovation: Die Geburt der imperialen Epigraphik." *Gymnasium* 98: 289–324.

———. 1997. "Die Mysterien von Panóias (Vila Real, Portugal)." *Mitteilungen des deutschen archäologischen Instituts, Madrid* 38: 176–246.

Allorge-Courtin, M. 2011. "La rue à Rome, spectable des apparences d´après Martial et Juvénal." In M.-J. Kardos and L. Voinson, eds., *Habiter en ville au temps de Vespasien: Actes de la table ronde de Nancy, 17 octobre 2008*. Etudes d'archéologie classique 14. Nancy, Paris.

Ameling, W. 2009. "The Epigraphic Habit and the Jewish Diasporas of Asia Minor and Syria." In H. Cotton, ed., *From Hellenism to Islam: Cultural and Linguistic Change in the Roman Near East*. Cambridge. 203–34.

———. 2011. "Petrus in Rom: Zur Genese frühchristlicher Erinnerung." In S. Heid, ed., *Petrus und Paulus in Rom: Eine interdisziplinäre Debatte*. Freiburg i. Br. 468–91.

Amiotti, G. 1990. "Il 'monumento ai caduti' di Adamklissi." In M. Sordi, ed., *"Dulce et decorum est pro patria mori": La morte in combattimento nell'antichità*. Milano. 207–13.

Ampolo, C. 1981. "La città arcaica e le sue feste: Due ricerche sul Septimontium e l'Equus October." *Archeologia laziale* 4: *Quarto incontro di studio del comitato per l'archeologia laziale*: 233–40.

———. 1988. "Lavinium and Rome." *Classical Review* 38 (1): 117–20.

Andersen, W. 2003. *The Ara Pacis of Augustus and Mussolini: An Archeological Mystery*. Geneva.

Ando, C. 2000. *Imperial Ideology and Provincial Loyalty in the Roman Empire*, Classics and Contemporary Thought 6. Berkeley.

————. 2001. "The Palladium and the Pentateuch: Towards a Sacred Topography of the Later Roman Empire." *Phoenix* 55: 369–411.

————. 2003. "A Religion for the Empire." In A. J. Boyle and W. J. Dominik, eds., *Flavian Culture: Culture, Image, Text.* Leiden.

————. 2005. "Interpretatio Romana." *Classical Philology* 100/1: 41–51.

————. 2008. *The Matter of the Gods: Religion and the Roman Empire,* Transformation of the Classical Heritage 44. Berkeley.

————. 2010. "Imperial Identities." In T. Whitmarsh, ed., *Local Knowledge and Micro-identities in the Imperial Greek World. Greek Culture in the Roman World.* Cambridge. 17–45.

————. 2011. *Law, Language, and Empire in the Roman Tradition.* Philadelphia.

————. 2012. *Imperial Rome, AD 193–284: The Critical Century,* Edinburgh History of Ancient Rome. Edinburgh.

————. 2013a. "Cities, Gods, Empire." In T. Kaizer et al., eds., *Cities and Gods: Religious Space in Transition.* Babesch Supplement 22. Leuven. 51–57.

————. 2013b. "Subjects, Gods, and Empire, or Monarchism as a Theological Problem." In J. Rüpke, ed., *The Individual in the Religions of the Ancient Mediterranean.* Oxford. 85–111.

————. 2015. *Roman Social Imaginaries: Language and Thought in Contexts of Empire,* The Robson classical lectures. Toronto.

————. 2017. *The Holy Man and his Holy Fools.* Berkeley.

Ando, C. and J. Rüpke. 2006a. "Introduction: Religion and Law in Classical and Christian Rome." In C. Ando and J. Rüpke, eds., *Religion and Law in Classical and Christian Rome.* Potsdamer altertumswissenschaftliche Beiträge 15. Stuttgart. 9–13.

Ando, C. and J. Rüpke, eds. 2006b. *Religion and Law in Classical and Christian Rome,* Potsdamer altertumswissenschaftliche Beiträge 15. Stuttgart.

Andrade, N. J. 2013. *Syrian Identity in the Greco-Roman World,* Greek Culture in the Roman World. Cambridge.

Andreani, C., M.P.D. Moro, and M. D. Nuccio. 2005. "Contesti e materiali votivi dell' 'area sacra' di Largo Argentina." In A. Comella and S. Mele, eds., *Depositi Votivi e Culti dell'Italia Antica dall'Età Arcaica a Quella Tardo-Repubblicana—Atti del Convegno di Studi Perugia, 1–4 giugno 2000.* Bibliotheca archaeologica 16. Bari. 111–25.

Ankersmit, F. R. 2002. *Historical Representation.* Repr. Stanford, Calif.

Appadurai, A. 2000. "Grassroots Globalization and the Research Imagination." *Public Culture* 12/1: 1–19.

Archer, M. S. 1996. *Culture and Agency: The Place of Culture in Social Theory.* Orig. 1988 ed. Cambridge.

Argento, A., S. Cherubini, and E. Gusberti. 2010. "I reperti." In N. Arvanitis, ed., *Il santuario di Vesta: La casa delle vestali e il tenpio di Vesta VIII sec. A.C.–64 D.C. Rapporto preliminare.* Pisa. 60–95.

Aricó, G. 2001. "Ennio e la divinazione." In S. Faller, ed., *Studien zur antiken Identitäten* 9: Identitäten und Alteritäten. Würzburg. 53–58.

Arnal, W. 2011. "The Collection and Synthesis of "Tradition" and the Second-Century Invention of Christianity." *Method & Theory in the Study of Religion* 23 (3–4): 193–215.

Arnhold, M., and J. Rüpke. 2016. "Appropriating and Shaping Religious Practices in the Roman Republic." In Matthias Haake and Ann-Cathrin Harders, eds., *Politische Kultur und soziale Struktur der Römischen Republik: Bilanzen und Perspektiven.* Stuttgart. 413-28.

Asad, T. 1993. *Genealogies of Religion: Discipline and Reasons of Power in Christianity and Islam.* Baltimore.

Ascough, R. S., ed. 2005. *Religious Rivalries and the Struggle for Success in Sardis and Smyrna,* Studies in Christianity and Judaism 14. Waterloo, Ont.

———. 2007. "Defining Community-Ethos in Light of the 'Other': Recruitment Rhetoric Among Greco-Roman Associations." *Annali di stroia dell'esegesi* 24 (1): 59–75.

———. 2008. "Bringing Chaos to Order: Historical Memory and the Manipulation of History." *Religion & Theology* 15: 280–303.

Ashmore, R. D., K. Deaux, and T. McLaughlin-Volpe. 2004. "An Organizing Framework for Collective Identity: Articulation and Significance of Multidimensionality." *Psychological Bulletin* 130, 1: 80–114.

Assmann, J. 1999. *Das kulturelle Gedächtnis: Schrift, Erinnerung und politische Identität in frühen Hochkulturen.* München.

Athanassiadi, P. 1992. *Julian: An Intellectual Biography.* London.

———. 1993. "Dreams, Theurgy, and Freelance Divination: The Testimony of Iamblichus." *Journal of Roman Studies* 83: 115–30.

Attenni, L. 2013. "The Pantanacci Votive Deposit: New Anatomical Discoveries." *Etruscan News* 15: 1, 6.

Aubry, G. 2008. "Démon et intériorité d'Homère à Plotin: esquisse d'une histoire." In G. Aubry, ed., *Le moi et l'intériorité.* Textes et traditions 17. Paris. 255–68.

Auffarth, C. 1991. *Der drohende Untergang: "Schöpfung" in Mythos und Ritual im Alten Orient und in Griechenland am Beispiel der Odyssee und des Ezechielbuches,* Religionsgeschichtliche Versuche und Vorarbeiten 39. Berlin.

———. 2012. "Religious Education in Classical Greece." In I. Tanaseanu-Döbler and M. Döbler, eds., *Religious Education in Pre-Modern Europe.* Leiden. 39-61.

———. 2013. "Mysterien." *Reallexikon for Antike und Christentum* 25: 422–71.

Auger, D. L. 2003. "Le monde des rêves dans les Dionysiaques de Nonnos." In D. Accorinti, and P. Chuvin, eds., *Des Géants à Dionysos. Mélanges de mythologie et de poésie grecques offerts à Francis Vian* 10. Alexandria. 415–32.

Ausbüttel, F. M. 1982. *Untersuchungen zu den Vereinen im Westen des Römischen Reiches,* Frankfurter Althistorische Studien 11. Kallmünz.

Bagnasco Gianni, G. 1996. *Ogetti iscritti di epoca orientalizzante in Etruria,* Istituto Nazionale di studi etruschi e italici—Biblioteca di "Studi Etruschi" 30. Firenze.

———. 2005. "Sui 'contenitori' arcaici di ex-voto nei santuari etruschi." In A. Comella and S. Mele, eds., *Depositi votivi e culti dell'Italia antica dall'età arcaica a quella tardorepubblicana: Atti del Convegno di Studi, Perugia, 1–4 giugno 2000.* Bari. 351–58.

Baker-Brian, N. J., and S. Tougher, eds. 2012. *Emperor and Author: The Writings of Julian the Apostate.* Swansea. Classical Press of Wales.

Bakker, J. T. 1994. *Living and Working with the Gods: Studies of Evidence for Private Religion and Its Material Environment in the City of Ostia (100–500 AD).* Dutch Monographs on Ancient History and Archaeology 12. Amsterdam.

Barberis, V. 2004. *Rappresentazioni di divinitá e di devoti dall'area sacra urbana di Metaponto: La coroplastica votiva dalla fine del VII all'inizio del V sec. a.C.*, Facoltá di Lettere e Filosofia Fondo Studi Parini—Chirio. Torino.

———. 2005. "Terrecotte votive e culti nel santuario urbano di Metaponto: l'etá arcaica e severa." In M. L. Nava and M. Osanna, eds., *Lo spazio del rito: Santuari e culti in Italia Meridionale tra indigeni e Greci* 1. Bari. 55–67.

Barceló, P. 2013. *Das Römische Reich im religiösen Wandel der Spätantike: Kaiser und Bischöfe im Widerstreit*. Regensburg.

Barnes, T. D. 2011. *Constantine: Dynasty, Religion and Power in the Later Roman Empire*. Chichester.

Barraclough, R. 1984. "Philo's Politics: Roman Rule and Hellenistic Judaism." *ANRW* II.21,1: 417–553.

Bartolini, G. 2013. "The Villanovan Culture: At the Beginning of Etruscan History." In J. M. Turfa, ed., *The Etruscan World*. London. 79–98.

———. 1989–90. "I depositi votivi di Roma arcaica." *Scienze dell'Antichità: Storia, acheologia, antropologia* 3–4 (Anathema: Regime delle offerte e vita dei santuari nel Mediterraneo antico): 747–59.

Barton, T. 1994. *Ancient Astrology*. London.

Bartsch, S., and D. Wray, eds. 2009. *Seneca and the Self*. Cambridge.

Baslez, M.-F. 2011. "Voyages et Médiation culturelle: L'exemple de Paul de Tarse." In A. Gangloff, ed., *Médiateurs culturels et politiques dans L'empire romain—Voyages, conflits, identités*. Paris. 23–35.

Bassani, M. 2008. *Sacraria: ambienti e piccoli edifici per il culto domestico in area vesuviana*. Antenor Quaderni 9. Roma.

Batino, S. 1998. "Contributo alla costruzione di una ideologia funeraria etrusca arcaica: I corredi ceretani tra l'orientalizzante recente e l'età arcaia." *Ostraka* 7: 7–38.

Battistoni, F. 2010. *Parenti dei romani: mito troiano e diplomazia*. Pragmateiai 20. Bari.

Bauckham, R. J. 1988. "The Apocalypse of Peter: An Account of Research." *ANRW* II.25,6: 4712–50.

Baudy, D. 1998. *Römische Umgangsriten: Eine ethologische Untersuchung der Funktion von Wiederholung für religiöses Verhalten*. Religionsgeschichtliche Versuche und Vorarbeiten 43. Berlin.

Baudy, G. J. 1991. *Die Brände Roms: Ein apokalyptisches Motiv in der antiken Historiographie*. Spudasmata 50. Hildesheim.

Bauer, F. A. 2001. "Urban Space and Ritual: Constantinople in Late Antiquity." *Acta ad Archaeologiam et Artium Historiam pertinentia* 15: 27–61.

Baum, A. D. 2013. "Biographien im alttestamentlich-rabbinischen Stil: Zur Gattung der neutestamentlichen Evangelien." *Biblica* 94 (4): 534–64.

Bazzana, G. B. 2010. "The Bar Kokhba Revolt and Hadrian's Religious Policy." In M. Rizzi, ed., *Hadrian and the Christians*. Millennium-Studien. Studien zu Kultur und Geschichte des ersten Jahrthausends n. Chr. 30. Berlin. 85–110.

Beard, M. 1991. "Writing and Religion: Ancient Literacy and the Function of the Written Word in Roman Religion." In M. Beard, ed., *Literacy in the Roman World*. Journal of Roman Archaelogy Suppl. 3. Ann Arbor. 35–58.

———. 1994. "Religion." In J. A. Crook, A. Lintott, and E. Rawson, eds., *The Cambridge Ancient History* 9: *The Last Age of the Roman Republic, 146–43 B. C.* Cambridge. 729–68.

———. 2007. *The Roman Triumph.* Cambridge, Mass.

Beard, M., J. North, and S. Price. 1998. *Religions of Rome.* 1: *A History.* 2: *A Sourcebook.* Cambridge.

Becker, E.-M., ed. 2005. *Die antike Historiographie und die Anfänge der christlichen Geschichtsschreibung. [Forschungskolloquium am 23./24. Januar 2004 unter dem Titel: "Die Wirkung des Anfangs—Die antike Historiographie und die Anfänge der christlichen Geschichtsschreibung" im Institut für Neues Testament der Friedrich-Alexander-Universität Erlangen-Nürnberg],* Beihefte zur Zeitschrift für die neutestamentliche Wissenschaft und die Kunde der älteren Kirche 129. Berlin.

———. 2006. *Das Markus-Evangelium im Rahmen antiker Historiographie,* Wissenschaftliche Untersuchungen zum Neuen Testament 194. Tübingen.

———. 2011. "Dating Mark and Matthew as Ancient Literature." In E.-M. Becker and A. Runesson, eds., *Mark and Matthew* I: *Comparative Readings: Understanding the Earliest Gospels in their First-Century Settings.* Tübingen. 123–43.

Becker, J. A., and N. Terrenato, eds. 2012. *Roman Republican Villas: Architecture, Context, and Ideology.* Papers and monographs of the American Academy in Rome 32. Ann Arbor.

Behr, C. A. 1968. *Aelius Aristides and the Sacred Tales.* Amsterdam.

Beijer, A. J. 1991. "Impasto Pottery and Social Status in Latium Vetus in the Orientalising Period." In E. Herring, R. Whitehouse, and J. Wilkins, eds., *Papers of the Fourth Conference of Italian Archaeology* 2: *The Archaeology of Power* 2. London. 21–39.

Bel, V. 2010. "Evolution des pratiques funéraires à Nîmes entre le IIe siècle av. J.-C. et le IIIe siècle ap. J.-C." In J. Rüpke, and J. Scheid, eds., *Bestattungsrituale und Totenkult in der römischen Kaiserzeit/Rites funéraires et culte des morts aux temps impériales.* Potsdamer altertumswissenschaftliche Beiträge 27. Stuttgart.

Belayche, N. 2006. "Rites et 'Croyances' dans l'Épigraphie Religieuse de l'Anatolie Impériale." *Entretiens sur l'Antiquité Classique* 53 (Rites et Croyances dans les Religions du Monde Romain): 73–115.

———. 2008. "Du texte à l'image: les reliefs sur les stèles 'de confession' d'Anatolie." In S. Estienne, et al., eds., *Image et Religion dans l'Antiquité Gréco-Romaine: actes du colloque de Rome, 11–13 décembre 2003.* Collection du Centre Jean Bérard 28. Naples. 181–94.

———. 2011a. "Hypsistos: A Way of Exalting the Gods in Graeco–Roman Polytheism." In J. A. North, and S.R.F. Price, eds., *The Religious History of the Roman Empire: Pagans, Jews, and Christians.* Oxford. 139–74.

———. 2011b. "La politique religieuse 'Païenne' de Maximin Daia. De l'historiographie à l'histoire." In G. A. Cecconi and C. Gabrielli, eds., *Politiche religiose nel mondo antico e tardoantico.* Bari. 235–59.

———. 2013. "Priests as Diviners: An Impact on Religious Changes in Imperial Anatolia?" In B. Dignas, R. Parker, and G. G. Stroumsa, eds., *Priests and Prophets among Pagans, Jews and Christians.* Studies in the History and Anthropology of Religion 5. Leuven. 112–35.

Belayche, Nicole, and Jean-Daniel Dubois, eds. 2011. *L'oiseau et le poisson: cohabitations religieuses dans les mondes grec et romain.* Religions dans l'histoire, Paris: PUPS.

Belayche, N., and V. Pirenne-Delforge, eds. 2015. *Fabriquer du divin: Constructions et ajustements de la représentation des dieux dans l'antiquité.* Collection Religions: Comparatisme—Histoire—Anthropologie 5. Liège.

Belayche, N., et al. 2005. "Divination romaine." *ThesCRA* 3: 79–104.

Belfiore, V. 2010. *Il Liber linteus di Zagabria: Testualità e contenuto.* Biblioteca di Studi etruschi 50. Pisa.

Bell, C. 1992. *Ritual Theory, Ritual Practice.* New York.

Bell, S., ed. 2004. *Games and Festivals in Classical Antiquity: Proceedings of the Conference held in Edinburgh 10–12 July 2000,* BAR: International Series 1220. Oxford.

Ben Abed, A., and J. Scheid. 2003. "Sanctuaire des eaux, sanctuaire de sources, une catégorie ambigue: l'exemple de Jebel Oust (Tunisie)." In O. de Cazanove and J. Scheid, eds., *Sanctuaires et sources dans l'antiquité: Les sources documentaires et leurs limites dans la description des lieux de culte.* Collection du Centre Jean Bérard 22. Napoli. 7–14.

Ben-Eliyahu, E., Y. Cohn, and F. Millar. 2012. *Handbook of Jewish Literature from Late Antiquity, 135–700 CE.* Oxford.

Bendlin, A. 2002. "Vates." *Neuer Pauly* 12/1: 1150–1.

———. 2005. " 'Eine Zusammenkunft um der religio willen ist erlaubt . . . ?' Zu den politischen und rechtlichen Konstruktionen von (religiöser) Vergemeinschaftung in der römischen Kaiserzeit." In H. G. Kippenberg and G. F. Schuppert, eds., *Die verrechtlichte Religion: Der Öffentlichkeitsstatus von Religionsgemeinschaften.* Tübingen. 65–107.

———. 2006. "Vom Nutzen und Nachteil der Mantik: Orakel im Medium von Handlung und Literatur in der Zeit der Zweiten Sophistik." In D. von Elm, J. Rüpke, and K. Waldner, eds., *Texte als Medium und Reflexion von Religion im römsichen Reich.* Stuttgart. 159–207.

———. 2011. "Associations, Funerals, Sociality, and Roman Law: The collegium of Diana and Antinous in Lanuvium (CIL 14.2112) Reconsidered." In M. Öhler, ed., *Aposteldekret und antikes Vereinswesen: Gemeinschaft und ihre Ordnung.* Tübingen. 207–96.

Benelli, E., and C. Rizzitelli 2010. *Culture funerarie d'Abruzzo (IV-I secolo A.C.).* Mediterranea 5. Pisa.

Berardi, M. C., and G. F. Priori. 1997. "Viterbo, località Norchia: Tome doriche. Campagne di scavo 1992–1993." *Notizie degli scavi di antichità* 7: 331–63.

Berchman, R. M. 1984. *From Philo to Origen: Middle Platonism in Transition.* Brown Judaic studies 69. Chico, Calif.

———. 1998. *Mediators of the Divine: Horizons of Prophecy, Divination, Dreams and Theurgy in Mediterranean Antiquity.* South Florida Studies in the History of Judaism 163. Atlanta.

Berg, C.V.D. 2008. "The 'Pulvinar' in Roman Culture." *Transactions of the American Philological Association* (1974-) 138 (2): 239–73.

Berger, V. 2011. "Orality in Livy's Representation of the Divine: The Construction of a Polyphonic Narrative." In A.P.M.H. Lardinois. World, ed., *Sacred Words: Orality,*

Literacy and Religion; Orality and Literacy in the Ancient World 8 Mnemosyne suppl. 332. Leiden. 311–27.

Bergmann, B. 1994. "The Roman House as Memory Theater: The House of the Tragic Poet in Pompeii." *Art Bulletin* 76 (2): 225–56.

Bernardi, A. 1984. "Homo ritualis." *RSI* 96: 784–810.

Bernstein, F. 1998. *Ludi publici: Untersuchungen zur Entstehung und Entwicklung der öffentlichen Spiele im republikanischen Rom.* Historia Einzelschriften 119. Stuttgart.

———. 2007. "Complex rituals: Games and Processions in Republican Rome." In J. Rüpke, ed., *A Companion to Roman Religion.* Oxford. 222–34.

Berthelet, Y. 2015. *Gouverner avec les dieux: Autorité, auspices et pouvoir, sous la République romaine et sous Auguste.* Paris.

Bettini, M. 2009. *Affari di famiglia.* Bologna.

Betts, E. 2011. "Towards a Multisensory Experience of Movement in the City of Rome." In R. Laurence, ed., *Rome, Ostia, and Pompeii: Movement and Space.* Oxford. 118–32.

Bevilacqua, G. 1998. "Due nuove defixiones greche da Roma." *Epigraphica* 60: 113–34.

Bianchi, E. 2010. *Il rex sacrorum a Roma e nell'Italia antica.* Milano.

Bickerman, E. J. 1968. *Chronology of the Ancient World.* London.

———. 1979. *The God of the Maccabees: Studies on the Meaning and Origin of the Maccabean Revolt.* Studies in Judaism in Late Antiquity 32. Leiden.

Bielfeldt, R. 2014. "Lichtblicke—Sehstrahlen: Zur Präsenz römischer Figuren- und Bildlampen." In R. Bielfeldt, ed., *Ding und Mensch in der Antike: Gegenwart und Vergegenwärtigung.* Heidelberg. 195–238, 350–66.

Bierl, A., R. Lämmle, and K. Wasselmann, eds. 2007. *Literatur und Religion: Wege zu einer mythisch-rituellen Poetik bei den Griechen.* 2 vols., MythosEikonPoiesis. Berlin.

Bietti Sestieri, A. M. 2005. "A Reconstruction of Historical Powers in Bronze and Early Iron Age Italy based on recent archeological research." In P. Attema et al., eds., *Papers in Italian Archaeology* VI : *Communities and Settlements from the Neolithic to the Early Medieval Period; Proceedings of the 6th Conference of Italian Archaeology held at the University of Groningen, Groningen Institute of Archaeology, the Netherlands, April 15–17, 2003* Vol. 1. Oxford. 9–24.

———. 2006. "Il rituale funerario nel Lazio tra età del bronzo finale e prima età del ferro." In P. v. Eles, ed., *La ritualità funeraria tra età del ferro e orientalizzante in Italia: Atti del Convegno Verucchio, 26–26 Giugno 2002.* Pisa. 79–93.

———. 2010. *L'Italia nell'età del bronzo e del ferro: Dalle palafitte a Romolo (2200–700 a.C.),* Manuali universitari (Rome, Italy) 92. Roma.

———. 2011. "Archeologia della morte fra età del bronzo ed età del ferro in Italia: implicazioni delle scelte relative alla sepoltura in momenti di crisi o di trasformazione politico-organizzativa." In V. Nizzo, ed., *Dalla nascita alla morte: antropologia e archeologia a confronto: Atti dell'incontro internazionale di studi in onore di Claude Lévi-Strauss. Roma, Museo nazionale preistorico etnografico "Luigi Pigorini," 21 maggio 2010.* Roma. 397–417.

Billows, R. 1993. "The Religious Procession of the Ara Pacis Augustae: Augustus' Supplicatio in 13 B. C." *Journal of Roman Archaeology* 6: 80–92.

Blanchard, P. et al. 2007. "A mass grave from the Catacomb of Saints Peter and Marcellinus in Rome, second–third century AD." *Antiquity* 81 (314): 989–98.

Bland, R. 1996. "The Roman Coinage of Alexandria, 30 B.C.–A.D.296: Interplay between Roman and Local Designs." In D. M. Bailey, ed., *Archaeological Research in Roman Egypt: The Proceedings of the Seventeenth Classical Colloquium of the Department of Greek and Roman Anitiquities, British Museum, held on 1–4 December, 1993. Journal of Roman Archaeology*, Suppl. 19. Portsmouth, RI. 113–27.

Blank, D. 2012. "Varro and Antiochus." In D. Sedley, ed., *The Philosphy of Antiochus.* Cambridge. 250–89.

Bleckmann, B. 2007. "Konstantin der Große: Reformer der römischen Welt." In F. Schuller, and H. Wolff, eds., *Konstantin der Große: Kaiser einer Epochenwende.* Lindenberg. 26–68.

Bleicken, J. 1981. "Zum Begriff der römischen Amtsgewalt: auspicium—potestas—imperium." *Nachrichten der Akademie der Wissenschaften in Göttingen, phil.-hist. Kl.*: 255–300.

———. 1988. *Geschichte der römischen Republik*, Oldenbourg-Grundriß der Geschichte 2. München.

———. 1998. *Augustus: Eine Biographie.* Berlin.

Bloch, R. 1966. "Liberté et déterminisme dans la divination étrusque et romaine." *La divination en Mésopotamie ancienne et dans les régions voisines: XIVe Rencontre Assyriologique Internationale.* Paris. 159–70.

———. 1968. "La divination en Étrurie et à Rome." In A. Caquot and M. Leibovici, eds., *La divination* 1. Paris. 197–232.

Bloch, R. S. 2011. *Moses und der Mythos: Die Auseinandersetzung mit der griechischen Mythologie bei jüdisch-hellenistischen Autoren.* Supplements to the *Journal for the Study of Judaism* 145. Leiden.

Blömer, M., and E. Winter, eds. 2012. *Iuppiter Dolichenus: Vom Lokalkult zur Reichsreligion.* Tübingen.

Boardman, J., T. Mannack, and C. Wagner 2004. "II. Greek Votive Objects." *Thesaurus Cultus et Rituum Antiquorum* 1: 281–318.

Bodel, J. 2004. "The Organization of the Funerary Trade at Puteoli and Cumae." In *Libitina e dintorni : Libitina e luci sepolcrali; le leges libitinariae campane; Iura sepulcrorum; vecchie e nuove iscrizioni; atti dell'XI Rencontre Franco-Italienne sur l'Epigraphie.* Libitina 3. Roma. 147–72.

———. 2008. "Cicero's Minerva, *Penates*, and the Mother of the *Lares*: An Outline of Roman Domestic Religion." In J. Bodel and S. M. Olyan, eds., *Household and Family Religion in Antiquity.* Oxford. 248–75.

———. 2009. "'Sacred dedications': A Problem of Definitions." In J. Bodel and M. Kajava, eds., *Dediche sacre nel mono greco-romano: Diffusione, funzioni, tipologie/Religious Dedications in the Greco-Roman World: Distribution, Typology, Use.* Acta Instituti Romani Finlandiae 35. Roma. 17–30.

Bodel, J., and S. M. Olyan, eds. 2008. *Household and Family: Religion in Antiquity.* The Ancient World: Comparative Histories. Malden, Mass.

Boedeker, D. 2008. "Family Matters: Domestic Religion in Classical Greece." In J. Bodel and S. M. Olyan, eds., *Household and Family Religion in Antiquity.* The Ancient World: Comparative Histories. Malden, Mass. 229–47.

Boehm, F. 1927. "Lustratio." *RE* 13,2: 2029–39.

Boehm, I., and W. Hübner 2011. *La poésie astrologique dans l'Antiquité: Actes du colloque organisé les 7 et 8 décembre 2007 par J.-H. Abry (Université Jean Moulin Lyon 3) avec la collaboration d'I. Boehm (Université Frères Lumière Lyon 2).* Collection du Centre d'Études et de Recherches sur l'Occident Romain NS 38. Paris.

Boin, D. 2014. "Hellenistic 'Judaism' and the Social Origins of the Christian-Pagan Debate." *Journal of Early Christian Studies* 22 (2): 167–96.

Bollmann, B. 1998. *Römische Vereinshäuser: Untersuchungen zu den Scholae der römischen Berufs-, Kult- und Augustalen-Kollegien in Italien.* Mainz.

Bomhard, A. R., and J. C. Kerns 1994. *The Nostratic Macrofamily: A Study in Distant Linguistic Relationship.* Trends in Linguistics: Studies and Monographs 74. Berlin.

Bond, S. E. 2013. "Mortuary Workers, the Church, and the Funeral Trade in Late Antiquity." *Journal of Late Antiquity* 6 (1): 135–51.

Bonghi Jovino, M. 2005. "Tarquinia: Monumenti urbani." In M. Bonghi Jovino, ed., *Dinamiche di Sviluppo delle cittá nell'etruria Meridionale: Veio, Caere, Tarquinia, Vulci* 1. Pisa. 309–22.

Bonghi Jovino, M., and G. Bagnasco Gianni. 2012. *Tarquinia: Il santuario dell'Ara della Regina; i templi arcaici,* Tarchna 4. Roma.

Borbonus, D. 2014. *Columbarium Tombs and Collective Identity in Augustan Rome.* New York.

Borg, B. E. 2011. "What's in a Tomb: Roman Death, Public and Private." In J. Andreu, D. Espinosa, and S. Pastor, eds., *Mors omnibus instat: Aspectos arqueológicos, epigráficos y rituale de la muerte en el Occidente Romano.* Madrid. 51–78.

———. 2013. *Crisis and Ambition: Tombs and Burial Customs in Third-Century CE Rome.* Oxford Studies in Ancient Culture and Representation. Oxford.

Boschung, D. 2014. "Mithras: Konzeption und Verbreitung eines neuen Götterbildes." In Id. and A. Schäfer, eds., *Römische Götterbilder der mittleren und späten Kaiserzeit.* München. 217-34.

Botto, M. 2005. "Considerazioni sul periodo orientalizzante nella penisola italica: la documentazione del Latium vetus." *Anejos de Archivo Español de Arqueología* 35: 47–74.

Bouché-Leclercq, A. 1879. *Histoire de la divination dans l'antiquité* 1: *Introduction, divination hellénique.* Paris.

———. 1882. *Histoire de la divination dans l'antiquité* 4: *Divination italique.* Paris.

———. 1904. "Lustratio." *DA*: 1405–32.

Bouma, J. 1996. *Religio votiva: The Archaeology of Latial Votive Religion: 5th–3rd c. BC.* Vol. 3. Groningen.

Bouma, J., and W. Prummel. 1997. "Animal Offerings at Borgo Le Ferriere (Latium, Italy)." *Anthropozoologica* 25/26: 531–37.

Bowden, H. 2013. "Seeking Certainty and Claiming Authority: The Consultation of Greek Oracles from the Classical to the Roman Imperial Periods." In V. Rosenberger, ed., *Divination in the Ancient World: Religious Options and the Individual.* Potsdamer Altertumswissenschaftliche Beiträge 46. Stuttgart. 41–59.

Bowersock, G. W. 1978. *Julian the Apostate.* Cambridge, Mass.

————. 1994. "Greek Intellectuals and the Imperial Cult in the Second Century A. D." In G. W. Bowersock, ed., *Studies on the Eastern Roman Empire: Social, Economic and Administrative History, Religion, Historiography*. Goldbach. 293–326.

Bowes, K. 2008. *Private Worship, Public Values, and Religious Change in Late Antiquity.* Cambridge.

————. 2015a. "At Home." In R. Raja and J. Rüpke, eds., *A Companion to the Archaeology of Religion in the Ancient World*. Malden, Mass. 209–19.

————. 2015b. "Sixth-Century Individual Rituals: Private Chapels and the Reserved Eucharist." In É. Rebillard and J. Rüpke, eds., *Group Identity and Religious Individuality in Late Antiquity.* CUA Studies in Early Christianity. Washington, DC. 54–88.

Boyarin, D. 2004. "The Christian Invention of Judaism: The Theodosian Empire and the Rabbinic Refusal of Religion." *Representations* 85: 21–57.

————. 2008. "The Christian Invention of Judaism: The Theodosian Empire and the Rabbinic Refusal of Religion." In H. d. Vries, ed., *Religion: Beyond a Concept.* New York. 150–77.

Boyce, G. K. 1937. *Corpus of the Lararia of Pompeii.* Monographs of the Amercan Academy in Rome 14. Rome.

Boyer, P. 1994. *The Naturalness of Religious Ideas: A Cognitive Theory of Religion.* Berkeley.

Boyle, A. J., and J. W. Dominik, eds. 2003. *Flavian Rome: Culture, Image, Text.* Leiden.

Bracht, K. 2014. *Hippolyts Schrift In Danielem: Kommunikative Strategien eines frühchristlichen Kommentars.* Studien und Texte zu Antike und Christentum 85. Tübingen.

Bradley, M. 2006. "Colour and Marble in Early Imperial Rome." *Cambridge Classical Journal* 52: 1–22.

————. 2009. *Colour and Meaning in Ancient Rome.* Cambridge.

Bradshaw, P. F. 2014. "What Do We Really Know about the Earliest Roman Liturgy?" *Studia patristica* 71: 7–19.

Brakke, D. 2012. "Scriptural Practices in Early Christianity: Towards a New History of the New Testament Canon." In A.-C. Jacobsen, J. Ulrich, and D. Brakke, eds., *Invention, Rewriting, Usurpation—Discursive Fights over Religious Traditions in Antiquity* 11. Early Christianity in the Context of Antiquity. Frankfurt am Main. 263–80.

Brakke, D., M. L. Satlow, and S. Weitzman, eds. 2005. *Religion and the Self in Antiquity.* Bloomington, Ind.

Brandt, J. R., and J. W. Iddeng, eds. 2012. *Festivals in the Ancient World.* Oxford.

Branham, J. R. 2012. "Mapping Sacrifice on Bodies and Spaces in Late-Antique Judaism and Early Christianity." In B. D. Wescoat and R. G. Ousterhout, eds., *Architecture of the Sacred: Space, Ritual, and Experience from Classical Greece to Byzantium.* Cambridge. 201–30.

Breglia Pulci Doria, L. 1998. "Atena e il mare: problem e ipotesi sull'Athenaion di Punta della Campanella." In *I culti della Campania antica: Atti del Convegno Internazionale di Studi in ricordo di Nazarena Valenza Mele, Napoli 15–17 Maggio 1995. II 3,3.* Pubblicazioni scientifiche del Centro di Studi della Magna Grecia dell'Università degli studi di Napoli Federico 3,3. Roma. 97–108.

Brelich, A. 1969. *Paides e parthenoi* 1, Incunabula graeca 36. Roma.

———. 1972. "Appunti sul flamen dialis." *ACD* 8: 17–21.

Bremmer, J. N. 1991. " 'Christianus sum': The Early Christian Martyrs and Christ." In G. J. Barteling, A. Hilhorst, and C. H. Kneepkens, eds., *Eulogia: Mélanges offerts à Antoon A. R. Bastiaensen à l'occasion de son soixante-cinquième anniversaire.* Den Haag. 11–20.

———. 1993. "Three Roman Aetiological Myths." In F. Graf, ed., *Mythos in mythenloser Gesellschaft: Das Paradigma Roms.* Stuttgart. 158–74.

———. 1994. "The Soul, Death and the Afterlife in Early and Classical Greece." In J. M. Bremer, T. P. van den Hout, and R. Peters, eds., *Hidden Futures: Death and Immortality in Ancient Egypt, Anatolia, the Classical, Biblical and Arabic-Islamic World.* Amsterdam. 91–106.

———. 1995a. "The Family and Other Centres of Religious Learning in Antiquity." In J. W. Drijvers and A. A. MacDonald, eds., *Centres of Learning.* Leiden. 29–38.

———. 1995b. "Women in the Apocryphal Acts of John." In J. N. Bremmer, ed., *The Apocryphal Acts of John.* Kampen. 37–56.

———. 2008. *Greek Religion and Culture, the Bible and the Ancient Near East,* Jerusalem Studies in Religion and Culture 8. Leiden.

———. 2011. "Tours of Hell: Greek, Jewish, Roman and Early Christian." In W. Ameling, ed., *Topographie des Jenseits—Studien zur Geschichte des Todes in Kaiserzeit und Spätantike.* Altertumswissenschaftliches Kolloquium 21.

———. 2014a. *Initiation into the Mysteries of the Ancient World,* Münchener Vorlesungen zu antiken Welten 1. Berlin.

———. 2014b. "Religious Violence between Greeks, Romans, Christians and Jews." In A. C. Geljon and R. Roukema, eds., *Violence in Ancient Christianity: Victims and Perpetrators.* Leiden.

———. 2014c. "Conversion in the Oldes Apocryphal Acts." In B.S. Bøgh, ed., *Conversion and Initiation in Antiquity: Shifting Identities—Creating Change.* Berne. 59–76.

———. 2016. "Arthur Darby Nock's Conversion (1933): A Balance." In J. Weitbrecht, W. Röcke, and R. von Bernuth, eds., *Zwischen Ereignis und Erzählung: Konversion als Medium der Selbstbeschreibung in Mittelalter und Früher Neuzeit.* Berlin. 9–29.

———. 2017. "Lucian on Peregrinus and Alexander of Abonuteichos: A Sceptical View of Two Religious Entrepreneurs." In G. Petridou, R. Gordon, and J. Rüpke, eds., *Beyond Priesthood: Religious Entrepreneurs and Innovators in the Roman Empire.* Religionsgeschichtliche Versuche und Vorarbeiten 66. Berlin. 49–78.

Brenk, F. E. 1998. *Relighting the Souls: Studies in Plutarch, in Greek Literature, Religion, and Philosophy, and in the New Testament Background.* Potsdamer altertumswissenschaftliche Beiträge 21. Stuttgart.

Brent, A. 1995. *Hippolytus and the Roman Church in the Third-Century Communities in Tension before the Emergence of a Monarch Bishop.* Supplements to Vigiliae Christianae 31. Leiden.

———. 2004. "St. Hippolytus, Biblical Exegete, Roman Bishop, and Martyr." *St. Vladimir's Theological Quarterly* 48 (2).

———. 2011. *Cyprian and Roman Carthage.* Cambridge.

Bresson, A. 2005. "Ecology and Beyond: The Mediterranean Paradigm." In W. V. Harris, ed., *Rethinking the Mediterranean.* Oxford. 94–114.

Bricault, L. 2006. *Isis, Dame des flots*, Aegyptiaca Leodiensia 7. Liège.

———. 2007. "Fonder un lieu de culte." *Mediterranea* 4: 49–64.

Briquel, D. 1985. "'Etrusca disciplina' et origines étrusques." *La divination dans le monde étrusco-italique 1*. Caesarodunum supplement. 3–22.

———. 1990. "Divination étrusque et mantique grecque: la recherche d'une origine hellénique de l'Etrucsa disciplina." *Latomus* 49: 321–42.

Brocato, P., and N. Terrenato, eds. 2012. *Nuove ricerche nell'area archaeologica di S. Omobono a Roma*. Arcavacata di Rende.

Brodersen, K. 2006. *Astrampsychos: Das Pythagoras-Orakel*. Texte zur Forschung 88. Darmstadt.

———. 2013. "Philochoros of Athens." *Encyclopedia of Ancient History* 9: 5271–72.

Broise, H., and J. Scheid. 1987. *Recherches archéologiques à la Magliana: Le balneum des frères arvales*, Roma antica 1. Rome.

———. 1993. "Etude d'un cas: le lucus deae Diae à Rome." *Les bois sacrés: Actes du colloque international de Naples*: 145–57.

Broise, H., J. Scheid, et al. 2017. *Recherches archéologiques à la Magliana 3: La topographie générale du site*. Roma antica. Rome. Forthcoming.

Brown, P. 2015. *The Ransom of the Soul: Afterlife and Wealth in Early Western Christianity*. Cambridge, Mass.

Brown, P.R.L., and R. Lizzi Testa, eds. 2011. *Pagans and Christians in the Roman Empire: The Breaking of a Dialogue (4th–6th Century A. D.)*. Christianity and History 9. Münster.

Brulé, P., and C. Vendries, eds. 2001. *Chanter les dieux: Musique et religion dans l'Antiquité grecque et romaine*. Rennes.

Bruni, S. 2004. "Le processioni in Etruria." In J. C. Balty, ed., *Thesaurus cultus et rituum antiquorum (ThesCRA) 1*. Los Angeles. 21–32.

Bryen, A. Z. 2016. "Reading the Citizenship Papyrus (P. Giss. 40)." In C. Ando, ed., *Citizenship and Empire in Europe 200–1900: The Antonine Constitution after 1800 years*. Potsdamer altertumswissenschaftliche Beiträge 54. Stuttgart. 29–43.

Bubenheimer-Erhart, F. 2004. "Räuchergeräte aus Etrurien und ihre Beziehungen zum östlichen Mittelmeerraum." In R. Bol and D. Kreikenbom, eds., *Sepulkral- und Votivdenkmäler östlicher Mittelmeergebiete (7. Jh. v. Chr.–1. Jh. v. Chr.): Kulturbegegnungen im Spannungsfeld von Akzeptanz und Resistenz*. Paderborn. 51–59.

Buccellato, A., P. Catalano, and S. Musco 2008. "Alcuni aspetti rituali evidenziati nel corso dello scavo della necropoli Collatina (Roma)." In J. Scheid, ed., *Pour une archéologie du rite: nouvelles perspectives de l'archéologie funéraire*. Collection de l'École francaise de Rome 407. Rome. 59–88.

Buchet, E. 2012. "Tiburnus, Albunea, Hercules Victor: The Cults of Tibur between Integration and Assertion of Local Identity." In S. T. Roselaar, ed., *Processes of Integration and Identity Formation in the Roman Republic*. Mnemosyne Supplements: History and Archaeology of Classical Antiquity 342. Leiden. 355–64.

Buchholz, L. 2013. "Identifying the Oracular *sortes* of Italy." In M. Kajava, ed., *Studies in Ancient Oracles and Divination*. Acta instituti Romani Finlandiae 40. Rome. 111–44.

Bucur, B. G. 2009. *Angelomorphic Pneumatology: Clement of Alexandria and Other Early Christian Witnesses*, Supplements to Vigiliae Christianae 95. Leiden

Buranelli, F. 1983. *La Necropoli Villanoviana "Le Rose" di Tarquinia*. Quaderni del Centro di Studio per l'archeologia Etrusco—Italica 6. Roma.

Burckhardt, L. A. 1988. *Politische Strategien der Optimaten in der späten römischen Republik*, Historia Einzelschriften 57. Stuttgart.

Burgess, R. W. 2012. "The Chronograph of 354: Its Manuscripts, Contents, and History." *Journal of Late Antiquity* 5 (2): 345–96.

Burgess, R. W., and M. Kulikowski 2013. *Mosaics of Time: The Latin Chronicle Traditions from the First Century BC to the Sixth Century AD 1: A Historical Introduction to the Chronicle Genre from Its Origins to the High Middle Ages*, Studies in the Early Middle Ages 33. Turnhout.

Burkert, W. 1981. "Glaube und Verhalten: Zeichengehalt und Wirkungsmacht von Opfer-ritualen." *Le Sacrifice dans l'antiquité*: 91–125.

———. 1984. *Die Anthropologie des religiösen Opfers: Die Sakralisierung der Gewalt*, C. F. v. Siemens Stiftung. Themen 40. München.

———. 2011a. *Griechische Religion der archaischen und klassischen Epoche*, 2nd revised and expanded ed. Die Religionen der Menschheit 15. Stuttgart.

———. 2011b. "Varianten der Kulturbegegnung im 8. und 7. Jahrhundert v. Chr." In C. Ulf and R. Rollinger, eds., *Lag Troia in Kilikien? Der aktuelle Streit um Homers Ilias*. Darm-stadt. 409–23.

Butcher, K. 2013. "Continuity and Change in Lebanese Temples." In A. Gardner, ed., *Creating Ethnicities and Identities in the Roman World*. Bulletin of the Institute of Classical Studies Suppl. 120. London. 195–211.

Calame, C. 2011. "Funerary Gold Lamellae and Orphic Papyrus Commentaries: Same Use, Different Purpose." In R. G. Edmonds, ed., *The "Orphic" Gold Tablets and Greek Religion : Further along the Path*. Cambridge. 203–18.

Calandra, E. 2000. "Documenti inediti sul tempio di Roma e di Augusto a Ostia." *Mitteilungen des Deutschen Archäologischen Instituts, Römische Abteilung* 107: 417–45.

Cameron, A. 2006. "Constantine and Christianity." In E. Hartley, J. Hawkes, and M. Henig, eds., *Constantine the Great—York's Roman Emperor*. York. 96–103.

———. 2007. "The Imperial Pontifex." *Harvard Studies in Classical Philology* 103: 341–84.

———. 2011. *The Last Pagans of Rome*. Oxford.

Cameron, J. E. 2004. "A Three-Factor Model of Social Identity." *Self and Identity* 3 (3): 239–62.

Camia, F. 2011. THEOI SEBASTOI: *Il Culto degli Imperatori Romani in Grecia (Provincia Achaia) nel Secondo Secolo D.C.* Athens.

Campbell, C. 2009. "Distinguishing the Power of Agency from Agentic Power: A Note on Weber and the 'Black Box' of Personal Agency." *Sociological Theory* 27 (4): 407–18.

Cancik, H. 1973. "Römischer Religionsunterricht in apostolischer Zeit: Ein pastoralge-schichtlicher Versuch zu Statius, Silve V 3,176–184." In H. Feld and J. Nolte, eds., *Wort Gottes in der Zeit: Festschrift für K.H. Schelkle*. Düsseldorf. 181–97.

———. 1984a. "Bios und Logos: Formengeschichtliche Untersuchungen zu Lukians 'Leben des Demonax'." In H. Cancik, ed., *Markus-Philologie: Historische, literargeschicht-liche und stilistische Untersuchungen zum zweiten Evangelium*. Tübingen. 115–30.

———. 1984b. "Die Gattung Evangelium: Das Evangelium des Markus im Rahmen der antiken Historiographie." In H. Cancik, ed., *Markus-Philologie: Historische, literarge-schichtliche und stilistische Untersuchungen zum zweiten Evangelium.* Tübingen. 85–113.

———. 1996. "Carmen und sacrificium: Das Saecularlied des Horaz in den Saecularakten des Jahres 17 v. Chr." In R. Faber and B. Seidensticker, eds., *Worte, Bilder, Töne: Studien zur Antike und Antikerezeption.* Würzburg. 99–113.

———. 2011. "Hairesis, Diatribe, Ekklesia: Griechische Schulgeschichte und das Lu-kanische Geschichtswerk." *Early Christianity* 2 (3): 312–34.

———. 2012a. "The Awareness of Cultural Diversity in Ancient Greece and Rome." In M. I. Spariosu and J. Rüsen, eds., *Exploring Humanity: Intercultural Perspectives on Human-ism.* Göttingen/Taipei. 123–44.

———. 2012b. "Lehrer—Charismatiker—Philosoph: Zum Rollenverständnis intellektu-eller und religiöser Vergemeinschaftung im römischen Imperium (2. Jh. n. Chr.)." In A.-B. Renger, ed., *Meister und Schüler in Geschichte und Gegenwart. Von Religion der An-tike bis zur modernen Esoterik.* Göttingen. 97–113.

Cancik, H., and K. Hitzl, eds. 2003. *Die Praxis der Herrscherverehrung in Rom und seinen Provinzen.* Tübingen.

Cancik-Lindemaier, H. 1987. "Opferphantasien: Zur imaginären Antike der Jahrhundert-wende in Deutschland und Österreich." *Altsprachlicher Unterricht* 30,3: 90–104.

———. 2012. "*Contubernium.* Schüler und Lehrer der Philosophie in neronischer Zeit." In A.-B. Renger, ed., *Meister und Schüler in Geschichte und Gegenwart. Von Religion der An-tike bis zur modernen Esoterik.* Göttingen. 81–96.

Capdeville, G. 1989. "Les dieux fulgurants dans la doctrine étrusque." In *Secondo congresso internazionale etrusco, Firenze 26 Maggio-2 Giugno: Atti* 3. Roma. 1171–90.

Caprioli, F. 2007. *Vesta Aeterna—L'aedes Vestae e la sua Decorazione Architettonica.* Studia Archaeologica 154. Roma.

Cardauns, B. 1976. *M. Terentius Varro, Antiquitates rerum divinarum.* 1: *Die Fragmente.* 2: *Kommentar.* Akademie der Wissenschaften und der Literatur, Mainz, Abhandlungen der Geistes- und sozialwissenschaftlichen Klasse 1. Wiesbaden.

Carletti, C. 2004. "Dies mortis-depositio: un modulo 'profano' nell'epigrafia tardoantica." *Vetera Christianorum* 41 (1): 21–48.

Carroll, M. 2006. *Spirits of the Dead—Roman Funerary Commemoration in Western Europe.* Oxford Studies in Ancient Documents. Oxford.

———. 2011. "*Memoria* et *Damnatio Memoriae:* Preserving and Erasing Identities in Roman Funerary Commemoration " In M. Carroll, ed., *Living through the Dead: Burial and Com-memoration in the Classical World.* Studies in Funerary Archaeology 5. Oxbow. 64–90.

———. 2013. "Ethnicity and Gender in Roman Funerary Commemoration: Case Studies from the Empire's Frontiers." In S. Tarlow and L. Nilsson Stutz, eds., *The Oxford Hand-book of the Archaeology of Death and Burial.* Oxford. 559–79.

Carroll, M., J. Rempel, and J. Drinkwater, eds. 2011. *Living Through the Dead: Burial and Commemoration in the Classical World.* Studies in Funerary Archaeology 5. Oxford.

Castagnetti, S. 2012. *Le "Leges Libitinariae" flegree: Edizione e comment.* Pubblicazioni del dipartimento di diritto Romano, storia e teoria del diritto "F. de Martino" dell'università degli studi di Napoli "Federico II" 34. Napoli.

Cavallin, H. C. 1979. "Leben nach dem Tode im Spätjudentum und im frühen Christentum: I. Spätjudentum." *ANRW* II.19,1: 240–345.

Cazzella, A., and G. Recchia 2009. "The 'Mycenaeans' in the Central Mediterranean: A comparison between the Adriatic and the Tyrrhenian seaways." *Pasiphae* 3: 27–40.

———. 2013. "The Human Factor in the Transformation of Southern Italian Bronze Age Societies: Agency Theory and Marxism Reconsidered." *Origini* 35: 191–209.

Cébeillac-Gervasoni, M., ed. 2000. *Les élites municipales de l'Italie péninsulaire de la mort de César à la mort de Domitien entre continuité et rupture: Classes sociales dirigeantes et pouvoir central.* Collections de l'École Française de Rome. 271. Rome.

Cerchiai, L. 2008. "Cerimonie di chiusura nei santuari italici dell'Italia meridionale." In G. Greco and B. Ferrera, eds., *Doni agli dei, Il sistema dei doni votivi nei santuari: atti del seminario di studi, Napoli 21 aprile 2006.* Napoli. 23–27.

Cerrato, J. A. 2002. *Hippolytus between East and West: The Commentaries and the Provenance of the Corpus.* Oxford Theological Monographs. Oxford.

———. 2004. "The Association of the Name Hippolytus with a Church Order now known as the Apostolic Tradition." *St Vladimir's Theological Quarterly* 48:2.

Cesarano, M. 2015. *In honorem domus divinae: Introduzione allo studio dei cicli statuari giulio-claudii a Roma e in occidente.* Roma.

Chakrabarty, D. 2008. *Provincializing Europe: Postcolonial Thought and Historical Difference.* Reissue, with a new preface by the author. Princeton, NJ.

Chalupa, A. and T. Glomb. 2013. "The Third Symbol of the Miles Grade on the Floor Mosaic of the Felicissimus Mithraeum in Ostia: A New Interpretation." *Religio* 21: 9–32.

Champeaux, J. 1986. "Oracles institutionnels et formes populaires de la divination italique." *La divination dans le monde étrusco-italique:* 90–113.

———. 1987. *Fortuna: Recherches dur le culte de la fortune à Rome et dans le monde romain des origines à la mort de César.* II: *Les transformations de Fortuna sous la république.* Collections de l'École française de Rome 64. Rome.

———. 1990. "Sors oraculi: Les oracles en Italie sous la république et l'empire." *MEFR* 102: 271–302.

Champlin, E. 1991. *Final Judgments: Duty and Emotion in Roman Wills, 200 B. C.–A. D. 250.* Berkeley.

Chancey, M. A. 2004. "City Coins and Roman Power in Palestine: From Pompey to the Great Revolt " In D. R. Edwards, ed., *Religion and Society in Roman Palestine: Old Questions, New Approaches.* New York. 103 12.

Chaniotis, A. 1988. *Historie und Historiker in den griechischen Inschriften: Epigraphische Beiträge zur griechischen Historiographie.* Heidelberger Althistorische Beiträge und Epigraphische Studien 4. Stuttgart.

———. 2005. "Ritual Dynamics in the Eastern Mediterranean: Case Studies in Ancient Greece and Asia Minor." In W. V. Harris, ed., *Rethinking the Mediterranean.* Oxford. 141–66.

———. 2009. "Ritual Performances of Divine Jusitice: The Epigraphy of Confession, Atonement and Exaltation in Roman Asia Minor." In H. Cotton, ed., *From Hellenism to Islam: Cultural and Linguistic Change in the Roman Near East.* Cambridge. 115–53.

———. 2013. "Processions in Hellenistic Cities. Contemporary Discourses and Ritual Dynamics." In R. Alston, O. M. van Nijf, and C. G. Williamson, eds., *Cults, Creeds and Identities in the Greek City after the Classical Age*. Groningen-Royal Holloway Studies on the Greek City after the Classical Age. Leuven; Paris; Walpole, Mass. 21–48.

Chapman, R. 2013. "Death, Burial, and Social Representation." In S. Tarlow and L. Nilsson Stutz, eds., *The Oxford Handbook of the Archaeology of Death and Burial*. Oxford. 47–57.

Charlier, P. 2000. "Nouvelles hypothèses concernant la représentation des uterus dans les ex-voto etrusco-romains: anatomie et Histoire de l'Art." *Ocnus* 8: 33–46.

Chazon, E. G. 2012. "Liturgy before and after the Temple's Destruction: Change or Continuity?" In D. R. Schwartz and Z. Weiss, eds., *Was 70 CE a Watershed in Jewish History? On Jews and Judaism before and after the Destruction of the Second Temple*. Ancient Judaism and Early Christianity: Arbeiten zur Geschichte des antiken Judentums und des Urchristentums 78. Leiden. 371–92.

Cherici, A. 2005. "Dinamiche sociali a Vulci: Le Tombe con Armi." In Cherici, ed., *Dinamiche di sviluppo delle città nell'Etruria meridionale: Veio, Caere, Tarquinia, Vulci. Atti del XXIII Convegno di Studi Etruschi ed Italici, 1–6 ottobre 2001*, II. Pisa. 531–49.

Chesnut, G. F. 1992. "Eusebius, Augustine, Orosius, and the Later Patristic and Medival Christian Historians." In H. W. Attridge and G. Hata, eds., *Eusebius, Christianity and Judaism*. Köln. 687–713.

Choat, M. 2006. *Belief and Cult in Fourth-Century Papyri*. Studia antiqua australiensia 1. Turnhout/Sydney.

Cicala, V. 2007. "Tradizione e culti domestici " In J. Ortalli and D. Neri, eds., *Immagini divine: devozioni e divinità nella vita quotidiana ei Romani, testimonianze archeologiche dall´Emilia Romagna*. Quaderni di Archeologia dell´Emilia Romagna 18. Firenze. 43–55.

Cipriani, M. 2008. "Il santuario settentrionale di Poseidona: la documenatzione archaeologica dei culti dalla fondazione della città al tramonto dell'egemonia lucana." In G. Greco and B. Ferrera, eds., *Doni agli dei, Il sistema dei doni votivi nei santuari: atti del seminario di studi, Napoli 21 aprile 2006* Napoli. 113—39.

Clark, E. A., and D. F. Hatch. 1981. *The Golden Bough, the Oaken Cross: The Virgilian Cento of Faltonia Betitia Proba*. Chico, Calif.

Clark, G. 2004. *Christianity and Roman Society*. Cambridge.

Clarke, J. R. 2012. "Representations of Worship at Rome, Pompeii, Heraculaneum, and Ostia in the Imperial Period—A Model of Production and Consumption." In D. L. Balch and A. Weissenrieder, eds., *Contested Spaces: Houses and Temples in Roman Antiquity and the New Testament* 285. Wissenschaftliche Untersuchungen zum Neuen Testament. Tübingen. 3–20.

Clarke, K. 1999. *Between Geography and History: Hellenistic Constructions of the Roman World*. Oxford.

Clauss, M. 1994. "Die Anhängerschaft des Silvanus-Kultes." *Klio* 76: 381–87.

———. 1999. *Kaiser und Gott: Herrscherkult im römischen Reich*. Stuttgart.

———. 2004. *Alexandria: Schicksale einer antiken Weltstadt*. 2nd ed. Stuttgart.

Clavel-Lévêque, M. 1984. *L'Empire en jeux: Espace symbolique et pratique sociale dans le monde romain*. Paris.

————. 1986. "L'espace des jeux dans le monde romain: hégémonie, symbolique et pratique sociale." *ANRW* II.16,3: 2405–563.

Clementoni, G. 1990. "Germanico e i caduti di Teutoburgo." In M. Sordi, ed., *"Dulce et decorum est pro patria mori": La morte in combattimento nell'antichità*. Milano. 197–206.

Clements, R. A. 2012. "Epilogue: 70 CE after 135 CE—The Making of a Watershed?" In D. R. Schwartz and Z. Weiss, eds., *Was 70 CE a Watershed in Jewish History? On Jews and Judaism before and after the Destruction of the Second Temple*. Ancient Judaism and Early Christianity: Arbeiten zur Geschichte des antiken Judentums und des Urchristentums 78. Leiden. 517–36.

Cline, R. H. 2011. *Ancient Angels: Conceptualizing Angeloi in the Roman Empire*. Religions in the Graeco-Roman World 172. Leiden.

Coarelli, F. 1972. "Il sepolcro degli Scipioni." *Dialoghi d'Archeologia* 6: 36–106.

————. 1977. "Il comizio dalle origini alla fine della repubblica: Cronologia e topographia." *Parola di Passato* 32: 166–238.

————. 1983. "Le pitture della tomba François a Vulci: una proposta di lettura." *Dialoghi d'Archeologia* ser. 3,1: 43–69.

————. 1992. *Il Foro Boario: Dalle origine alla fine della repubblica*. Roma.

————. 2005. "I percorsi cerimoniali a Roma in età regia." In E. Greco, ed., *Teseo e Romolo: Le origini di Atene e Roma a confronto*. Tripodes 1. Athens. 29–42.

————. 2011. *Römische Kunst: Von den Anfängen bis zur mittleren Republik*. Darmstadt/Mainz.

Coldstream, J. N. 2003. *Geometric Greece, 900–700 BC*. London.

Collar, A. 2014. *Religious Networks in the Roman Empire: The Spread of New Ideas*. Cambridge.

Collins, J. J. 1987. "The Development of the Sibylline Tradition." *ANRW* II.20,1: 421–59.

Collins, P. 2008. "Accommodating the Individual and the Social, the Religious and the Secular: Modelling the Parameters of Discourse in 'Religious' Contexts." In A. Day, ed., *Religion and the Individual: Belief, Practice, Identity*. Aldershot. 143–67.

Colonna, G., ed. 1985. *Santuari d'Etruria*. Milano.

————. 1991. "Le due fasi del tempio arcaico di S. Omobono." In M. Gnade, ed., *Stips votiva: Papers presented to C. M. Stibbe*. Amsterdam. 51–59.

————. 2000. "Populonia e l'architettura funeraria etrusca." In A. Zifferero, ed., *L'architettura funaria a Populonia tra IX e VI secolo a.C.* Firenze. 253–60.

————, ed. 2002. *Il Santuario di Portonaccio a Veio*, Monumenti Antichi: Serie Miscellanea VI-3. Rome.

Colpe, C., and P. Habermehl. 1996. "Jenseitsreise (Reise durch das Jenseits)." *RAC* 17: 490–543.

Comella, A. 1981. "Tipologia e diffusione dei complessi votivi in Italia in epoca medio- e tardo-repubblicana: Contributo alla storia dell'artigianato antico." *MEFRA* 93: 717–803.

————, ed. 2002. *I relievi votivi greci di periodo arcaico e classico: Diffusione, ideologia, committenza*. Bibliotheca Archaeologica 11. Bari.

————. 2004. "I. Italien. A. Offerte in forma di figura umana." *Thesaurus Cultus et Rituum Antiquorum* 1: 330–59.

————. 2005a. "Altare (Etruria)." *Thesaurus Cultus et Rituum Antiquorum* 4: 166–71.

———. 2005b. "Deposito votivo." *Thesaurus Cultus et Rituum Antiquorum* 4: 226–8.

———. 2005c. "Favisae." *Thesaurus Cultus et Rituum Antiquorum* 4: 240–41.

———. 2005d. "Il messaggio delle offerte dei santuari etrusco-italici di periodo medio- e tardo-repubblicano." In A. Comella and S. Mele, eds., *Depositi Votivi e Culti dell'Italia Antica dall'Età Arcaica a Quella Tardo-Repubblicana—Atti del Convegno di Studi Perugia, 1–4 giugno 2000.* Bibliotheca archaeologica 16. Bari. 47–59.

———. 2005e. "Stips." *Thesaurus Cultus et Rituum Antiquorum* 4: 336–37.

———. 2011. *Da anathema a ornamenta: Rilievi votivi greci riutilizzati in Italia in epoca romana.* Collezione Archeologica. Roma.

Connelly, J. B. 2011. "Ritual Movement Through Greek Sacred Space: Towards an Archaeology of Performance." In A. Chaniotis, ed., *Ritual Dynamics in the Ancient Mediterranean: Agency, Emotion, Gender, Representation.* Heidelberger althistorische Beiträge und epigraphische Studien 49. Stuttgart. 313–46.

Constas, N. 2002. "An Apology for the Cult of Saints in Late Antiquity: Eustratius Presbyter of Constantinople, On the State of the Soul after Death (CPG 7522)." *Journal of Early Christian Studies* 10 (2): 267–85.

Cooley, A. 2014. "Paratextual Readings of Imperial Discourse in the *Res Gestae Divi Augusti*." *Cahiers du centre Gustave Glotz* 25: 215–30.

Cooper, K. 2013. *Band of Angels: The Forgotten World of Early Christian Women.* London.

Corbier, M. 1989. "The Ambiguous Status of Meat in Ancient Rome." *Food and Foodways* 3 (3): 223–64.

Cornell, T. J. 1978. "Principes of Tarquinia." Review of Torelli 1975. *Journal of Roman Studies* 68: 167–73.

Cornelli, G. 2013. *In Search of Pythagoreanism.* Studia Praesocratica 4. Berlin.

Cowan, E., ed. 2011. *Velleius Paterculus: Making History.* Swansea.

Cox, P. 1983. *Biography in Late Antiquity: A Quest for the Holy Man.* Transformation of the Classical Heritage 5. Berkeley.

Cramer, F. H. 1954. *Astrology in Roman Law and Politics.* Memoirs of the American Philosophical Society 37. Philadelphia.

Crawford, M. 1985. *Coinage and Money under the Republic: Italy and the Mediterranean Economy.* London.

Crawford, M. H. 1996a. "Italy and Rome from Sulla to Augustus." In A. K. Bowman, E. Champlin, and A. Lintott, eds., *The Cambridge Ancient History* 10: *The Augustan Empire, 43 B.C.–A.D. 69.* Cambridge. 414–33.

———, ed. 1996b. *Roman Statutes* 2. Bulletin of the Institute of Classical Studies, Suppl. 64. London.

Cribiore, R. 2013. *Libanius the Sophist: Rhetoric, Reality, and Religion in the Fourth Century.* Ithaca.

Cristofani, M. 1995. *Tabula Capuana: Un calendario festivo di età arcaica,* Istituto nazionale di studi etruschi e italici: biblioteca di Studi Etruschi 29. Firenze.

Croucher, K. 2012. *Death and Dying in the Neolithic Near East.* Oxford.

Cuneo, P. O. 2012. *Anonymi graeci oratio funebris in Constantinum II.* Collana della Rivista di diritto romano, Saggi. Milano.

Cuozzo, M. 2005. "Community Norms and Inter-Group Dialectics in the Necropoleis of Campania, during the Orientalizing Period." In P. Attema, A. Nijboer, and A. Zifferero, eds., *Papers in Italian Archaeology 6: Communities and Settlements from the Neolithic to the Early Medieval Period; Proceedings of the 6th Conference of Italian Archaeology held at the University of Groningen, Groningen Institute of Archaeology, the Netherlands, April 15–17, 2003*, 1. BAR International Series 1452. Oxford. 92–102.

Curran, J. 2011. "The Jewish Patriarchate: A State within a State?" In C. Kelly, ed., *Unclassical Traditions 2: Perspectives from East and West in Late Antiquity:* Suppl. vol. 35. Cambridge. 15–28.

Curran, J. R. 2000. *Pagan City and Christian Capital: Rome in the Fourth Century.* Oxford Classical Monographs. Oxford.

D'Agostino, B. 2005. "La cittá." In D'Agostino, ed., *Dinamiche di Sviluppo delle cittá nell'etruria Meridionale—Veio, Caere, Tarquinia, Vulci* 1. Pisa/Roma. 21–25.

D'Ambra, E. 1988. "A Myth for a Smith: A Meleager Sarcophagus from a Tomb in Ostia." *AJA* 92: 85–99.

———. 2002. "Acquiring an Ancestor: The Importance of Funerary Statuary among the Non-Elite Orders of Rome." In J. M. Højte, ed., *Images of Ancestors.* Aarhus Studies in Mediterranean Aniquity (ASMA) 5. Aarhus. 223–46.

D'Anna, N. 2011. *Il Neoplatonismo: Significato e dottrine di un movimento spirituale*, Homo absconditus. [Rimini].

Darvill, T. C. 2010. *Prehistoric Britain.* London.

Dasen, V. 2015. "Probaskania: Amulets and Magic in Antiquity." In D. Boschung and J. N. Bremmer, eds., *The Materiality of Magic.* Morphomata 20. Paderborn. 177–203.

David, J.-M. 1998. "Les enjeux de l'exemplarité à la fin de la République romaine et au début du principat " In J.-M. David, ed., *Valeurs et mémoire à Rome: Valère Maxime ou la vertu recomposée.* Collections de l'Université des Sciences Humaines de Strasbourg : Études d'archéologie et d'histoire ancienne. Paris. 9–17.

Davies, G. 2011. "Before Sarcophagi." In Elsner, J., and J. Huskinson, eds., *Life, Death and Representation: Some New Work on Roman Sarcophagi.* Millennium-Studien 29. Berlin. 21–54.

Davies, J. P. 2004. *Rome's Religious History: Livy, Tacitus and Ammianus on Their Gods.* Cambridge.

Davies, P.J.E. 2012. "On the Introduction of Stone Entablatures in Republican Temples in Rome." In M. L. Thomas and G. E. Meyers, eds., *Monumentality in Etruscan and Early Roman Architecture: Ideology and Innovation.* Austin. 139–65.

Debié, M. 2010. "Writing History as "Histories": The Biographical Dimension of East Syriac Historiography." In A. Papaconstantinou, ed., *Writing "True Stories": Historians and Hagiographers in the Late Antique and Medieval Near East.* Turnhout. 43–75.

De Cazanove, O. 2011. "Sanctuaries and Ritual Practices in Lucania from the 3rd c. B.C. to the Early Empire." In F. Colivicchi, ed., *Local Cultures of South Italy and Sicily in the Late Republican Period: Between Hellenism and Rome* 83. Portsmouth, Rhode Island. 30–43.

de Certeau, M. 1984. *The Practices of Everyday Life.* Berkeley.

———. 1987. *La faiblesse de croire.* Seuil, Paris.

———. 1988. *The Writing of History.* T. Conley, trans. New York.

———. 2007. *Arts de faire*. 2nd ed., Luce Giard, ed. Paris.

Degelmann, C. 2017. *Prekäres Handeln: Trauerszenen im republikanischen und frühkaiserzeitlichen Rom*. Potsdamer altertumswissenschaftliche Studien. Stuttgart.

de Grummond, N. T. 2006. *Etruscan Myth, Sacred History and Legend*. Philadelphia.

———. 2009. "The Sacred Day on Etruscan Mirrors." In S. Bruni, ed., *Etruria e Italia Preromana: studi in onore die Giovannangelo Camporeale*. Pisa. 287–94.

de Hemmer Gudme, A. K. 2012. "Out of Sight, Out of Mind? Dedicatory Inscriptions as Communication with the Divine." In C. M. Crouch, ed., *Mediating between Heaven and Earth: Communication with the Divine in the Ancient Near East*. London. 1–15.

de Jáuregui, M. H. 2011. "Dialogues of Immortality from the *Iliad* to the Gold Leaves." In R. G. Edmonds, ed., *The "Orphic" Gold Tablets and Greek Religion: Further along the Path*. Cambridge. 270–90.

de la Fuente, D. H. 2013. "Parallels between Dionysos and Christ in Late Antiquity: Miraculous Healings in Nonnus' Dionysiaca." In A. Bernabé et al., eds., *Redefining Dionysos*. MythosEikonPoiesis 5. Berlin/Boston. 464–87.

Deligiannakis, G. 2015. "Religious Viewing of Sculptural Images of Gods in the World of Late Antiquity: From Dio Chrysostom to Damaskios." *Journal of Late Antiquity* 8 (1): 168–94.

de Ligt, L. 2012. *Peasants, Citizens and Soldiers: Studies in the Demographic History of Roman Italy 225 BC–AD 100*. Cambridge.

de Ligt, L., and P. Garnsey 2012. "The Album of Herculaneum and a Model of the Town's Demography." *Journal of Roman Archaeology* 25: 69–94.

Demandt, A. 1990. "Die Sortes Sangallenses: Eine Quelle zur spätantiken Sozialgeschichte." In G. Crifò and S. Giglio, eds., *Atti dell'Accademia Romanistica Costantiniana: VIII convegno internazionale*. Napoli. 635–50.

———. 2007. *Die Spätantike: Römische Geschichte von Diocletian bis Justinian 284–565 n. Chr.*, 2nd ed. Handbuch der Altertumswissenschaft 3,6. München.

Demoen, K., and D. Praet, eds. 2009. *Theios Sophistes: Essays on Flavius Philostratus' Vita Apolloni*. Mnemosyne Suppl. 305 Leiden.

Demougin, S. 1992. *Prosopographie des chevaliers romains julio-claudiens (43 av. J.-C.–70 ap. J.-C.)*, Collection de l'École française de Rome 153. Rome.

———. 2012. "Citoyennetés multiples en Occident?" In A. Heller and A.-V. Pont, eds., *Patrie d'origine et patries électives: les citoyennetés multiples dans le monde grec d'époque romaine. Actes du colloque international de Tours, 6–7 novembre 2009*. Ausonius Éditions: Scripta Antiqua 40. Paris. 99–109.

Denzey Lewis, N. 2013. *Cosmology and Fate in Gnosticism and Graeco-Roman Antiquity: Under Pitiless Skies*. Nag Hammadi and Manichaean Studies 81. Leiden.

———. 2017. "Lived Religion Among Second-Century Gnostic Hieratic Specialists." In G. Petridou, R. Gordon, and J. Rüpke, eds., *Beyond Priesthood: Religious Entrepreneurs and Innovators in the Roman Empire*. Religionsgeschichtliche Versuche und Vorarbeiten 66. Berlin. 79-102.

DePalma Digeser, E. 2006. "Christian or Hellene? The Great Persecution and the Problem of Identity." In R. M. Frakes, E. DePalma Digeser, eds., *Religious Identity in Late Antiquity*. Toronto. 36–57.

Dépelteau, F. 2008. "Relational Thinking: A Critique of Co-Deterministic Theories of Structure and Agency." *Sociological Theory* 26 (1): 51–73.

de Polignac, F. 2009. "Sanctuaries and Festivals." In K. A. Raaflaub and H. van Wees, eds., *A Companion to Archaic Greece.* Blackwell Companions to the Ancient World. Malden, Mass. 427–43.

Deremetz, A. 2013. "Numa in Augustan Poetry." In J. Farrell and D. P. Nelis, eds., *Augustan Poetry and the Roman Republic.* Oxford. 228–43.

De Sanctis, G. 2015. *La logica del confine: Per un'antropologia dello spazio nel mondo romano.* Roma.

Des Bouvrie, S. 2011. "Continuity and Change without Individual Agency: The Attic Ritual Theatre and the 'Socially Unquestionable' in the Tragic Genre." In A. Chaniotis, ed., *Ritual Dynamics in the Ancient Mediterranean: Agency, Emotion, Gender, Representation.* Heidelberger althistorische Beiträge und epigraphische Studien 49. Stuttgart. 139–78.

Deshours, N. 2011. *L'été indien de la religion civique—Étude sur les cultes civiques dans le monde égéen à l'époque hellénistique tardive,* Ausonius Éditions—Scripta Antiqua. Paris.

Deubner, L. 1900. *De incubatione capita quattuor.* Leipzig.

Devoto, G. 1940. *Tabulae Iguvinae.* Ed. altera ed., Scriptores Graeci et Latini. Romae.

Di Giuseppe, H., and M. Serlorenzi, eds. 2010. *I riti del costruire nelle acque violate: Atti del Convegno Internazionale Roma, Palazzo Massimo 12–14 giugno 2008.* Roma.

Dihle, A. 1993. "Antike Grundlagen." In W. Berschin, ed., *Biographie zwischen Renaissance und Barock.* Heidelberg. 1–22.

Dillon, J. M. 1996. *The Middle Platonists: A Study of Platonism, 80 BC to AD 220.* Rev. ed. London.

———. 2006. "Holy and Not So Holy: On the Interpretation of Late Antique Biography." In B. McGing and J. Mossman, eds., *The Limits of Ancient Biography.* Swansea. 155–67.

———. 2012. *The Platonic Heritage: Further Studies in the History of Platonism and Early Christianity.* Variorum collected studies series 1008. Farnham.

Dillon, J. N. 2012. *The Justice of Constantine: Law, Communication, and Control.* Law and Society in the Ancient World. Ann Arbor, Mich.

Dirschlmayer, M. 2015. *Kirchenstiftungen römischer Kaiserinnen vom 4. bis zum 6. Jahrhundert: Die Erschließung neuer Handlungsspielräume.* Jahrbuch für Antike und Christentum, Kleine Reihe 13. Münster.

Dirven, L. 1999. *The Palmyrenes of Dura-Europos: A Study of Religious Interaction in Roman Syria,* Religions in the Graeco-Roman World 138. Leiden.

Dithmar, R. 1995. *Fabeln, Parabeln und Gleichnisse,* UTB 1892. Paderborn.

Di Vita-Évrard, G. 1997. "Les fastes des Sodales Augustales." In M. Mayer, ed., *Religio deorum.* Sabadell (Barcelona). 471–84.

Divjak, J. 2002. "Der sogenannte Kalender des Filocalus." In A. Primmer, ed., *Textsorten und Textkritik: Tagungsbeiträge.* Wien. 19–38.

Dobbelaere, K. 2011. "The Contextualization of Definitions of Religion." *Revue Internationale de Sociologie* 21 (1): 191–204.

Dohrmann, N. B. 2013. "Law and Imperial Idioms: Rabbinic Legalism in the Roman World." In N. B. Dohrmann and A. Y. Reed, eds., *Jews, Christians, and the Roman*

Empire: The Poetics of Power in Late Antiquity. Jewish Culture and Contexts. Philadelphia. 63–78, 272–88.

Dondin-Payre, M. 2011. "Conclusion: Dis-moi ton nom . . ." In M. Dondin-Payre, ed., *Les noms de personnes dans l'Empire romain: Transformation, adaption, évolution.* Scripta Antiquita 36. Paris. 275–77.

Dorcey, P. F. 1992. *The Cult of Silvanus: A Study in Roman Folk Religion.* Columbia Studies in the Classical Tradition 20. Leiden.

Dormeyer, D., and H. Frankemölle. 1984. "Evangelium als literarische Gattung und als theologischer Begriff: Tendenzen und Aufgaben der Evangelienforschung im 20. Jahrhundert, mit einer Untersuchung des Markusevangeliums in seinem Verhältnis zur antiken Biographie." *ANRW* II.25.2: 1543–704.

Dow, S. 1968. "Six Athenian Sacrificial Calendars." *Bulletin de Correspondance Hellénique* 92: 170–86.

Downey, S. 1993. "Archaic Architectural Terracottas from Regia." In E. Rystedt, C. Wikander, and Ö. Wikander, eds., *Deliciae Fictiles—Proceedings of the First International Conference on Central Italic Architectural Terracottas at the Swedish Institute in Rome, 10–12 December, 1990.* Stockholm. 233—47.

———. 1995. *Architectural Terracottas from the Regia.* Papers and Monographs of the American Academy in Rome 30. Ann Arbor.

Downie, J. 2015. "Narrative and Divination: Artemidorus and Aelius Aristides." *Archiv für Religiongeschichte* 15: 97–116.

Dräger, O. 1994. *Religionem significare: Studien zu reich verzierten römischen Altären und Basen aus Marmor,* Mitteilungen des deutschen archäologischen Instituts Rom, Ergänzungsheft 33. Mainz.

du Bouchet, J., and C. Chandezon, eds. 2012. *Études dur Artémidore et l'interprétation des rêves.* Paris.

Ducoeur, G. 2011. "Interpretatio, relectures et confusions chez les auteurs gréco-romains: le cas du Dionysos indien." In C. Bonnet, A. Declercq, and I. Slobodzianek, eds., *Les représentations des dieux des autres* 2. Palermo. 143–58.

Dueck, D. 2012. *Geography in Classical Antiquity.* Cambridge.

Dufraigne, P. 1994. *Adventus Augusti, adventus Christi: Recherche sur l'exploitation idéologique et littéraire d'un cérémonial dans l'antiquité tardive.* Collection des études augustiniennes : Série antiquité 141. Paris.

Dunsch, B. 2014. "Religion in Roman Comedy." In M. Fontaine and A. C. Scafuro, eds., *The Oxford Handbook of Greek and Roman Comedy.* Oxford. 633–52.

Durkheim, É. 2007. *Die elementaren Formen des religiösen Lebens.* L. Schmidts, trans. Frankfurt am Main.

Dyck, A. R. 2004. *A Commentary on Cicero, De Legibus.* Ann Arbor.

Dyck, J. 2002. "Philo, Alexandria und Empire: The Politics of Allegorical Interpretation." In J. R. Bartlett, ed., *Jews in the Hellenistic and Roman Cities.* London. 149–74.

Eberhardt, J., and A. Franz. 2012. "Musik II (Vokalmusik)." *RAC* 25: 247–83.

Ebner, M. 2012. *Die Stadt als Lebensraum der ersten Christen,* Das Urchristentum in seiner Umwelt 1. Göttingen.

Eck, W. 1987. "Römische Grabinschriften: Aussageabsicht und Aussagefähigkeit im funerären Kontext." In Henner von Hesberg and Paul Zanker, eds., Römische Gräberstrassen: Selbstdarstellung—Status—Standard. Munich. 61–84.

———. 1995. "'Tituli honorarii,' curriculum vitae und Selbstdarstellung in der Hohen Kaiserzeit." In H. Solin, O. Salomies, and U.-M. Liertz, eds., Acta Colloquii Epigraphici Latini: Helsingiae 3.–6. Sept. 1991 habiti. Helsinki. 211–37.

———. 2007. "Eine historische Zeitenwende: Kaiser Constantins Hinwendung zum Christentum und die gallischen Bischöfe." In F. Schuller and H. Wolff, eds., Konstantin der Große: Kaiser einer Epochenwende. Lindenberg. 69–94.

———. 2010. "Emperor and Senatorial Aristocracy in Competition for Public Space." In B. C. Ewald, and C. F. Noreña, eds., The Emperor and Rome: Space, Representation, and Ritual. Yale Classical Studies 35. Cambridge. 89–110.

———. 2012. "Der Bar Kochba-Aufstand der Jahre 132–136 und seine Folge für die Provinz Judea/Syria Palestina." In G. Urso, ed., Iudea Socia—Iudea Capta: Atti del convegno internazionale Cividale del Friuli, 22–24 settembre 2011. Pisa. 249–65.

———. 2014. "Die Entwicklung des Bischofsamtes in den ersten drei Jahrhunderten: Strukturelle Ähnlichkeiten oder Vorbilder bei Priesterämtern der paganen Welt?" In G. Urso, ed., Sacerdos: Figure del sacro nella società romana. Atti del convegno internazionale Cividale del Friuli, 26–28 settembre 2012. Pisa. 341–54.

Eck, W., and E. Müller-Luckner. 1999. Lokale Autonomie und römische Ordnungsmacht in den kaiserzeitlichen Provinzen vom 1. bis 3. Jahrhundert. Schriften des Historischen Kollegs Kolloquien 42. München.

Eckhardt, B. 2014. "'Bloodless sacrifice': A Note on Greek Cultic Language in the Imperial Era." Greek, Roman, and Byzantine Studies 54 (2): 255–73.

Eco, U. 1999. Im Wald der Fiktionen sechs Streifzüge durch die Literatur. 2nd ed. Munich.

Edlund-Berry, I.E.M. 2004. "C. Other Votive Objects." Thesaurus Cultus et Rituum Antiquorum 1: 368–78.

———. 2011. "Akroteria in Ancient Italy: Images and Architectural Traditions." In P. Lulof and C. Rescigno, eds., Deliciae Fictiles IV—Architectural Terracottas in Ancient Italy—Images of Gods, Monsters and Heroes. Oxford. 16–22.

Edmonds III, R. G. 2009. "Who Are You? Mythic Narrative and Identity in the "Orphic" Gold Tablets." In G. Casadio and P. A. Johnston, eds., Mystic Cults in Magna Graecia. Austin. 73–94.

———, ed. 2011. The "Orphic" Gold Tablets and Greek Religion: Further along the Path. Cambridge.

———. 2013. Redefining Ancient Orphism: A Study in Greek Religion. Cambridge.

Edmondson, J., and A. Keith, eds. 2009. Roman Dress and the Fabrics of Roman Culture, Phoenix Suppl. 46. Toronto.

Edrei, A., and D. Mendels. 2007. "A Split Jewish Diaspora: Its Dramatic Consequences." Journal for the Study of the Pseudepigrapha 16.2: 91–137.

———. 2008. "A Split Jewish Diaspora: Its Dramatic Consequences II." Journal for the Study of the Pseudepigrapha 17.3: 163–87.

———. 2012. "Reaction to Fergus Millar's article 'A Rural Community in Late Roman Mesopotamia, and the Question of a "Split" Jewish Diaspora.' " *Journal for the Study of Judaism* 43: 78–9.

Egelhaaf-Gaiser, U. 2000. *Kulträume im römischen Alltag: Das Isisbuch des Apuleius und der Ort von Religion im kaiserzeitlichen Rom*, Potsdamer altertumswissenschaftliche Beiträge 2. Stuttgart.

Ehrman, B. D. 2003. *Lost Scriptures: Books That Did Not Make It into the New Testament.* Oxford.

Eidinow, E. 2007. *Oracles, Curses, and Risk among the Ancient Greeks.* Oxford.

———. 2011. "Networks and Narratives: A Model for Ancient Greek Religion." *Kernos* 24: 9–38.

———. 2013. "Oracular Consultation, Fate, and the Concept of the Individual." In V. Rosenberger, ed., *Divination in the Ancient World: Religious Options and the Individual.* Potsdamer Altertumswissenschaftliche Beiträge 46. Stuttgart. 21–39.

———. 2017. "In Search of the 'Beggar-Priest.'" In G. Petridou, R. Gordon, and J. Rüpke, eds., *Beyond Priesthood: Religious Entrepreneurs and Innovators in the Roman Empire.* Religionsgeschichtliche Versuche und Vorarbeiten 66. Berlin. 255–76.

Eitrem, S. 1955. "Zur Deisidämonie." *Symbolae Osloenses* 31: 155–69.

Ekroth, G. 2011. "Meat for the Gods." In V. Pirenne-Delforge and F. Prescendi, eds., *"Nourrir les dieux?" Sacrifice et représentation du divin.* Liége. 15–41.

Ellemers, N., R. Spears, and B. Doosje, eds. 1999. *Social Identity: Context, Commitment, Content.* Oxford.

Ellinghaus, C. 2004. "Der Giebel des Apollon Sosianus Tempel in Rom—wirklich ein Giebel?" In J. Gebauer et al., eds., *Bildergeschichte—Festschrift für Klaus Stähler.* Möhnesee. 111–23.

Elm, S. 2012. *Sons of Hellenism, Fathers of the Church: Emperor Julian, Gregory of Nazianzus, and the Vision of Rome.* Transformation of the Classical Heritage 49. Berkeley.

Elsner, J. 1991. "Cult and Sculpture: Sacrifice in the Ara Pacis Augustae." *Journal of Roman Studies* 81: 50–61.

———. 1995. *Art and the Roman Viewer: The Transformation of Art from the Pagan World to Christianity.* Cambridge.

———. 2012a. "Material Culture and Ritual: State of the Question." In B. D. Wescoat and R. G. Ousterhout, eds., *Architecture of the Sacred: Space, Ritual, and Experience from Classical Greece to Byzantium.* Cambridge. 1–26.

———. 2012b. "Sacrifice in Late Roman Art." In C. A. Faraone and F. S. Naiden, eds., *Greek and Roman Animal Sacrifice: Ancient Victims, Modern Observers.* Cambridge. 120–63.

Emirbayer, M., and A. Mische. 1998. "What Is Agency?" *American Journal of Sociology* 103, 4: 962–1023.

Engels, J. 1993. "Die Ὑπομνήματα-Schriften und die Anfänge der politischen Biographie und Autobiographie in der griechischen Literatur." *ZPE* 96: 19–36.

Engster, D. 2002. *Konkurrenz oder Nebeneinander: Mysterienkulte in der hohen römischen Kaiserzeit.* Quellen und Forschungen zur Antiken Welt 36. München.

Ennabli, L., and J. Scheid. 2007–2008. "Une lex sacra de Carthage relative au culte des Cereres? Nouvelles observations sur les fragments découverts dans la basilique de Carthagena." *Rendiconti Pontificia Accademia Romana di Archeologia* 80: 37–75.

Erskine, A. 2001. *Troy between Greece and Rome: Local Tradition and Imperial Rome.* Oxford.

Eshleman, K. 2012. *The Social World of Intellectuals in the Roman Empire: Sophists, Philosophers, and Christians.* Greek Culture in the Roman World. Cambridge.

Esmonde Cleary, S. 2013. "The City as Preferred Written Space: The Case of Aquitania." In G. Sears, P. Keegan, and R. Laurence, eds., *Written Space in the Latin West, 200 BC to AD 300.* London. 217–30.

Esposito, D. 2005. "Breve nota su pitture di giardino da Ercolano." *Cronache Ercolanesi* 35: 223–30.

———. 2014. *La pittura di Ercolano.* Studi della Soprintendenza archeologica di Pompeii 33. Roma.

Essler, H. 2011. *Glückselig und Unsterblich: Epikureische Theologie bei Cicero und Philodem.* Schwabe Epicurea 2. Basel.

Estienne, S. 2008. "Èléments pour une définition rituelle des 'espaces consacrés' à Rome." In X. D. Raventós and S. Ribichini, eds., *Saturnia Tellus—definizioni dello spazio consacrato in ambiente etrusco, otalico, fenicio-punico, iberico e celtico.* Roma. 687–99.

———. 2010. "Simulacra deorum versus ornamenta aedium: The Status of Divine Images in the Temples of Rome." In J. Mylonopoulos, ed., *Divine Images and Human Imaginations in Ancient Greece and Rome.* Religions in the Graeco-Roman World 170. Leiden. 257–71.

———. 2011. "Les dieux á table: lectisternes romains et représentation divine." In V. Pirenne-Delforge and F. Prescendi, eds., *"Nourrir les dieux?" Sacrifice et représentation du divin.* Liége. 443–57.

———. 2014. "Aurea pompa venit: Présences divines dans les processions romaines." In S. Estienne et al., eds., *Figures de dieux: Construire le divin en images.* Rennes. 337–49.

Evans, J. K. 1991. *War, Women and Children in Ancient Rome.* New York.

Faber, A. et al. 2007. *Körpergräber des 1.–3. Jahrhunderts in der römischen Welt: Internationales Kolloquium Frankfurt am Main 19.–20. November 2004.* Schriften des Archäologischen Museum Frankfurt 21. Frankfurt am Main.

Fantham, E. 2002. "Ovid's Fasti: Politics, History, and Religion." In B. W. Boyd, ed., *Brill's Companion to Ovid.* Leiden. 197–233.

———. 2009. *Latin Poets and Italian Gods.* Robson Classical Lectures. Toronto.

Faraone, C. A. 2011a. "Rushing into Milk: New Perspectives on the Gold Tablets." In R. G. Edmonds, ed., *The "Orphic" Gold Tablets and Greek Religion: Further along the Path.* Cambridge. 308–309.

———. 2011b. "Text, Image and Medium: The Evolution of Graeco-Roman Magical Gemstones." In C. Entwistle and N. Adams, eds., *'Gems of heaven': Recent Research on Engraved Gemstones in Late Antiquity, AD 200–600.* British Museum Research Publication 177. London. 50–61.

————. 2013. "Gender Differentiation and Role Models in the Worship of Dionysos: The Thracian and Thessalian Pattern." In A. Bernabé et al., eds. *Redefining Dionysos*. Mytho-sEikonPoiesis 5. Berlin. 120–43.

Faraone, C. A., and F. S. Naiden, eds. 2012. *Greek and Roman Animal Sacrifice: Ancient Victims, Modern Observers*. Cambridge.

Fauth, W. 2014. *Jao-Jahwe und seine Engel Jahwe-Appellationen und zugehörige Engelnamen in griechischen und koptischen Zaubertexten*. Studien und Texte zu Antike und Christentum 74. Tübingen.

Favro, D., and C. Johanson. 2010. "Death in Motion: Funeral Processions in the Roman Forum." *Journal of the Society of Architectural Historians* 69 (1): 12–37.

Feeney, D. 2007. *Caesar's Calendar: Ancient Time and the Beginnings of History*. Sather Classical Lectures 65. Berkeley.

————. 2016. *Beyond Greek: The Beginnings of Latin Literature*. Cambridge, Mass.

Feil, E., ed. 1986. *Religio: Die Geschichte eines neuzeitlichen Grundbegriffs vom Frühchristentum bis zur Reformation*. Forschungen zur Kirchen- und Dogmengeschichte 36. Göttingen.

Feldherr, A. 2010. *Playing Gods: Ovid's Metamorphoses and the Politics of Fiction*. Princeton.

Feldman, L. H. 1998. *Studies in Josephus' Rewritten Bible*. Supplements to the *Journal for the Study of Judaism* 58. Leiden.

Fenechiu, C. 2008. *La notion de numen dans les textes littéraires et épigraphiques*. Cluj-Napoca.

Ferri, G. 2010. *Tutela urbi: il significato e la concezione della divinità tutelare cittadina nella religione romana*. Potsdamer altertumswissenschaftliche Beiträge 32. Stuttgart.

Février, C. 2009. *Supplicare deis. La supplication expiatoire à Rome*. Recherches sur les rhétoriques religieuses 10. Turnhout.

Février, P.-A. 1990. "Kult und Geselligkeit: Überlegungen zum Totenmahl." In J. Martin and B. Quint, ed., *Christentum und antike Gesellschaft*. Darmstadt. 358–90.

Fields, D. 2008. "Aristides and Plutarch on Self-Praise." In W. V. Harris and B. Holmes, eds., *Aelius Aristides between Greece, Rome, and the Gods*. Leiden. 151–72.

Filippi, D. 2007/8. "Dalla domus Regia al foro: Depositi di fondazione e di obliterazione nella prima età regia." *Scienze dell'Antichità: Storia Archeologia Antropologia* 14: 617–38.

Fine, G. A. 2010. "Sociology of the Local: Action and Its Publics." *Sociological Theory* 28 (4): 355–76.

Fine, S. 2010. "Death, Burial, and Afterlife." In C. Hezser, ed., *The Oxford Handbook of Jewish Daily Life in Roman Palestine*. Oxford. 440–63.

————. 2015. "Polychromy and Jewish Visual Culture of Roman Antiquity." In R. Raja and J. Rüpke, eds., *A Companion to the Archaeology of Religion in the Ancient World*. Malden, Mass. 133–43.

Fishwick, D. 1981. "From Flamen to Sacerdos: The Title of the Provincial Priest of Africa Proconsularis." *B A Paris* 17, B: 337–43.

————. 1991. "Sanctissimum Numen: Emperor or God?" *ZPE* 89: 196–200.

————. 2002. *The Imperial Cult in the Latin West: Studies in the Ruler Cult of the Western Provinces of the Roman Empire* 3 (Pt. 1: "Institution and Evolution"). Religions in the Graeco-Roman World 145. Leiden.

Flaig, E. 1992. *Den Kaiser herausfordern: Die Usurpation im römischen Reich.* Historische Studien 7. Frankfurt a. M.

————. 1995a. "Die Pompa Funebris: Adlige Konkurrenz und annalistische Erinnerung in der Römischen Republik." In O. G. Oexle, ed., Memoria *als Kultur.* Göttingen. 115–48.

————. 1995b. "Entscheidung und Konsens: Zu den Feldern der politischen Kommunikation zwischen Aristokratie und Plebs." In M. Jehne, ed., *Demokratie in Rom? Die Rolle des Volkes in der Politik der römischen Republik.* Stuttgart. 77–127.

Flambard, J.-M. 1981. "Collegia Compitalicia: phénomène associatif, cadres territoriaux et cadres civiques dans le monde romain à l'époque républicaine." *Ktema* 6: 143–66.

Flieger, M. 1993. *Interpretationen zum Bibeldichter Juvencus.* Berlin.

Flinterman, J.-J. 2014. "Pythagoreans in Rome and Asia Minor around the Turn of the Common Era." In C. A. Huffman, ed., *A History of Pythagoreanism.* Cambridge. 341–59.

Flower, H. I. 1996. *Ancestor Masks and Aristocratic Power in Roman Culture.* Oxford.

————. 2002. "Were Women ever "Ancestors" in Republican Rome?" In J. Munk Højte, ed., *Images of Ancestors.* Aarhus. 159–290.

————. 2015. "Sulla's Memoirs as an Account of Individual Religious Experience." *Religion in the Roman Empire* 1 (3): 297–320.

————. 2017. *The Dancing Lares.* Princeton.

Fögen, M.-T. 1993. *Die Enteignung der Wahrsager: Studien zum kaiserlichen Wissensmonopol in der Spätantike.* Frankfurt a. M.

Foley, J. M., ed. 1987. *Comparative Research on Oral Traditions: A Memorial for Milman Parry.* Columbus, Ohio.

————. 1988. *The Theory of Oral Composition: History and Methodology.* Bloomington.

Fontana, F. 2010. *I culti isiaci nell'Italia settentrionale* 1: *Verona, Aquileia, Trieste. Con un contributo di Emanuela Murgia.* Trieste.

Foss, P. 1997. "Domestic Space in the Roman World: Pompeii and Beyond." *Journal of Roman Archaeology.* Suppl. Series 22: 196–240.

Frankfurter, D. 1998. *Religion in Roman Egypt: Assimilation and Resistance.* Princeton.

————. 2014. "Onomastic Statistics and the Christianization of Egypt: A Response to Depauw and Clarysse." *Vigiliae Christianae* 68: 284–89.

Franssen, J. 2011. *Votiv und Repräsentation—Statuarische Weihungen archaischer Zeit aus Samos und Attika.* Archäologie und Geschichte 13. Heidelberg.

Frateantonio, C. 2001. "Septimontium." *Neuer Pauly* 11: 436.

Frede, M. 1999. "Monotheism and Pagan Philosophy in Later Antiquity." In P. Anthanassiadi and M. Frede, eds., *Pagan Monotheism in Late Antiquity.* Oxford. 41–67.

Freeden, J. v. 1993. *Malta und die Baukunst seiner Megalith-Tempel.* Darmstadt.

Frenschkowski, M. 2002. "Marcion in arabischen Quellen." In G. May and K. Greschat, eds., *Marcion und seine kirchengeschichtliche Wirkung.* Berlin. 39-63.

———. 2006. "Vision als Imagination: Beobachtungen zum differenzierten Wirklichkeit-sanspruch frühchristlicher Visionsliteratur." In N. Hömke and M. Baumbach, eds., *Fremde Wirklichkeiten: Literarische Phantastik und antike Literatur*. Kalliope 6. Heidelberg.

———. 2009. "Erkannte Pseudepigraphie? Ein Essay über Fiktionalität, Antike und Christentum." In J. Frey and J. Herzer, eds., *Pseudepigraphie und Verfasserfiktion in frühchristlichen Briefen: Pseudepigraphie and Author Fiction in Early Christian Letters*. Tübingen. 181–232.

Freyburger, G. 1988. "Supplication grecques et supplication romaine." *Latomus* 47: 501–25.

Friesen, S. J. 1993. *Twice Neokoros: Ephesus, Asia and the Cult of the Flavian Imperial Family*. Religions in the Graeco-Roman World 116. Leiden.

Fröhlich, T. 1991. *Lararien- und Fassadenbilder in den Vesuvstädten: Untersuchungen zur "volkstümlichen" pompejanischen Malerei*. Mitteilungen des deutschen archäologischen Instituts Rom, Ergänzungsheft 32. Mainz.

Fuchs, M., A. Linkenbach, and W. Reinhard, eds. 2015. *Individualisierung durch christliche Mission?* Studien zur außereuropäischen Christentumsgeschichte (Asien, Afrika, Lateinamerika) / Studies in the History of Christianity in the Non-Western World 24. Wiesbaden.

Fuchs, M., and J. Rüpke. 2015. "Religious Individualisation in Historical Perspective." *Religion* 45 (3): 323-29.

Fuhrer, T. 2011. "Allegorical Reading and Writing in Augustine's Confessions." In J. A. v. d. Berg et al., eds., *"In Search of Truth": Augustine, Manichaeism, and Other Gnosticism: Studies for Johannes van Oort at Sixty*. Leiden. 25–45.

Fulminante, F. 2014. *The Urbanisation of Rome and Latium Vetus: From the Bronze Age to the Archaic Era*. Cambridge.

Funke, P. 2010. "Pausanias und die griechischen Heiligtümer und Kulte." In F. Marco Simón, F. Pina Polo, and J. Remesal Rodríguez, eds., *Viajeros, peregrinos y aventureros en el Mundo Antiguo*. Barcelona. 219–26.

Furley, W., and V. Gysembergh. 2015. *Reading the Liver: Papyrological Texts on Ancient Greek Extispicy*. Studien und Texte zu Antike und Christentum 94. Tübingen.

Füssel, M. 2006. "Die Kunst der Schwachen: Zum Begriff der 'Aneignung' in der Geschichtswissenschaft." *Sozial. Geschichte* 21 (3): 7–28.

Gabba, E. 1982. "La 'storia di Roma arcaica' di Dionigi di Alicarnasso." *ANRW* II.30,1: 799–816.

———. 1988. "Reflessioni sulla Lex Coloniae Genetivae Iuliae." *Anejos de Archivo Español de Arqueología* 9: 157–68.

Gagarin, M. 2011. "Sacred Laws in Archaic and Classical Crete." In A. Lardinois, ed., *Sacred Words: Orality, Literacy and Religion*. Orality and Literacy in the Ancient World 8. Leiden. 101–11.

Gagé, J. 1977. "Les rites anciens de lustration du populus et les attributs 'triomphaux' des censeurs." In J. Gagé, ed., *Enquêtes sur les structures sociales et religieuses de la Rome primitive*. Bruxelles. 338–66.

———. 1981. "La mystique impériale et l'épreuve des 'jeux': Commode-Hercule et l'anthropolgie héracléenne." *ANRW* II.17,2: 662–83.

———. 1986. "Les pratiques magiques d'épiphanie royale—basiléia—et la mystique impériale aux IIe et IIIe siècles." *ANRW* II.16,3: 2382–403.

Gaifman, M. 2012. *Aniconism in Greek Antiquity.* Oxford Studies in Ancient Culture and Representation. Oxford.

Gaillard-Seux, P. 1998. "Les amulette gynécologiques dans les textes latins médicaux de l'Antiquité." In C. Deroux, ed., *Maladie et maladies dans les textes latins antiques et médiévaux: Actes du Ve Colloque International "Textes médicaux latins" (Bruxelles, 4–6 septembre 1995).* Collection Latomus 242. Bruxelles. 70–84.

Galinsky, K. 1996. *Augustan Culture: An Interpretive Introduction.* Princeton, NJ.

———. 2007. "Continuity and Change: Religion in the Augustan Semi-Century." In J. Rüpke, ed., *A Companion to the Roman Religion.* Malden, Mass. 71–82.

———. 2012. *Augustus: Introduction to the Life of an Emperor.* Cambridge.

———. 2013. "La costruzione del mito augusteo: Some Construction Elements." In M. Labate and G. Rosati, eds., *La costruzione del mito augusteo.* Heidelberg. 29–47.

Gallia, A. B. 2012. *Remembering the Roman Republic: Culture, Politics and History under the Principate.* Cambridge.

Gallone, A. 2008. "Sepolti tra le mura della prima Roma: Il caso delle tombe sulla pendice Palatina." In *Sepolti tra i Vivi—Buried among the Living: Atti del Convegno Internazionale.* Roma. 653–66.

Gambacurta, G. 2005. "Il bothros di Asolo: una cerimonia pubblica in epoca di romanizzazione." In A. Comella and S. Mele, eds., *Depositi votivi e culti dell'Italia antica dall'età arcaica a quella tardo-repubblicana: Atti del Convegno di Studi, Perugia, 1–4 giugno 2000.* Bari. 491–505.

Garelli, M.-H. 2007. *Danser le mythe: la pantomime et sa réception dans la culture antique.* Bibliothèque d'études classiques 51. Louvain.

Garthwaite, J. 2009. "Visions of Gold: Hopes for the New Age in Calpurnius Siculus' Eclogues." In W. J. Dominik, J. Garthwaite, and P. A. Roche, eds., *Writing Politics in Imperial Rome.* Leiden. 307–22.

Gasparini, V. 2007. "Santuari isiaci in Italia: Criteri e contesti di diffusione." *Mediterranea* 4: 65–88.

———. 2011. "Cronologia ed Architettura dell'iseo di Pompei: Una proposta di schema verificabile." *Vesuviana: An International Journal of Archaeological and Historical Studies on Pompeii and Herculaneum* 3: 66–88.

———. 2013. "Staging Religion: Cultic Performances in (and around) the Temple of Isis in Pompeii." In N. Cusamano et al., eds., *Memory and Religious Experience in the Graeco-Roman World.* Potsdamer altertumswissenschaftliche Beiträge 45. Stuttgart. 185–212.

———. 2014. "Les cultes isiaques et les pouvoirs locaux en Italie." In L. Bricault and M. J. Versluys, eds., *Power, Politics and the Cults of Isis: Proceedings of the Vth International Conference of Isis Studies, Boulogne-sur-Mer, October 13–15, 2011.* Leiden. 260–99.

———. 2016. "Engineering of the Sacred: The Mechanics of Introducing the Cult of Fortuna Augusta in Pompeii." In M. Bolder-Boos and D. Maschek, eds., *Orte der Forschung, Orte des Glaubens: Neue Perspektiven für Heiligtümer in Italien von der Archaik bis zur Späten Republik.* Bonn. 43–67.

Gatti, S., and M. R. Picuti, eds. 2008. *Regio I: Alatri, Anagni, Capitulum Hernicum, Ferentino, Veroli*, Fana, templa, delubra: Corpus dei luoghi di culto dell'Italia antica (FTD) 1.

Gauger, J.-D. 1998. *Sibyllinische Weissagungen: Griechisch—deutsch*. Darmstadt.

Gaultier, F. 2010. "Sanctuaires et territoires en pays étrusque: le cas de Véies." In J. de la Genière, A. Vauchez, and J. Leclant, eds., *Colloque: Les sanctuaires et leur rayonnement dans le monde méditerranéen de l'antiquité à l'époque moderne*. Cahiers de la Villa "Kérylos" 21. Paris. 115–39.

Gaultier, F., and D. Briquel, eds. 1997. *Les Étrusques: Les plus religieux des hommes: État de la recherche sur la religion étrusque: Actes du colloque internationale du Grand Palais 17–18–19 novembre 1992*. Paris.

Gawlinski, L. 2007. "The Athenian Calendar of Sacrifices: A New Fragment from the Athenian Agora." *Hesperia* 76 (1): 37–55.

———. 2012. *The Sacred Law of Andania: A New Text with Commentary*. Sozomena 11. Berlin.

Gee, E. 2000. *Ovid, Aratus and Augustus: Astronomy in Ovid's Fasti*. Cambridge.

Geertz, C. 1973. "Thick Description: Toward an Interpretive Theory of Culture." In Geertz, ed., *The Interpretation of Culture*. New York. 3–30.

Gentili, M. D. 2005. "Riflessioni sul fenomeno storico dei depositi votivi di tipo etrusco-laziale-campano." In A. Comella and S. Mele, eds., *Depositi Votovi e culti dell'italia antica a quella tardo-Republicana*. Bari. 367–78.

Gering, A. 2002. *Ostia: Wohnen in der Insula*. Diss. München.

Gherchanoc, F. 2012. *L'oikos en fête: célébrations familiales et sociabilité en Grèce ancienne*. Publications de la Sorbonne Histoire ancienne et medievale 111. Paris.

Giacobello, F. 2005. "Lararium (mondo romano)." *ThesCRA* 4: 262–64.

———. 2008. *Larari pompeiani. Iconografia e culto dei Lari in ambito domestico*, Il filarete; 251: Sezione di archeologia. Milano.

Giancotti, F. 1967. *Mimo e gnom: Studio su Decimo Laberio e Publilio Siro*, Biblioteca di cultura contemporanea (Casa editrice G. D'Anna) 98. Messina, Firenze.

Giardino, C., C. Belardelli, and A. Malizia. 1991. "Power and the Individual in Funerary Ideology." In E. Herring, R. Whitehouse, and J. Wilkins, eds., *Papers of the Fourth Conference of Italian Archaeology* 2: *The Archaeology of Power* 2. London. 9–19.

Gibson, R. K., and R. Morello. 2012. *Reading the Letters of Pliny the Younger: An Introduction*. Cambridge.

Gilhus, I. S. 1997. *Laughing Gods, Weeping Virgins: Laughter in the History of Religion*. London.

Gill, C. 2008. "The Self and Hellenstic-Roman Philosophical Therapy." In A. Arweiler and M. Möller, eds., *Vom Selbst-Verständnis in Antike und Neuzeit: Notions of the Self in Antiquity and Beyond*. Transformationen der Antike 8. Berlin. 359–80.

———. 2009a. "Seneca and Selfhood: Integration and Disintegration." In S. Bartsch and D. Wray, eds., *Seneca and the Self*. Cambridge. 65–83.

———. 2009b. *The Structured Self in Hellenistic and Roman Thought*. Oxford.

Gillet-Didier, V. 2002. "Passé généalogique et passé électif: usage comparé des généalogies dans les livres des Chroniques et le Livre des antiquités bibliques du Pseudo-Philon." *Revue des Études juives* 161 (3–4): 357–92.

Gilman, A. et al. 1981. "The Development of Social Stratification in Bronze Age Europe [and Comments and Reply]." *Current Anthropology* 22 (1): 1–23.

Giontella, C. 2011. *"... nullus enim fons non sacer ...": Culti idrici di epoca preromana e romana (Regiones VI-VII)*. Pisa.

Giradet, K. M. 2011. "Libertas religionis: 'Religionsfreiheit' bei Tertullian und Laktanz. Zwei Skizzen." In K. Muscheler, ed., *Römische Jurisprudenz—Dogmatik, Überlieferung, Rezeption: Festschrift für Detlef Liebs zum 75. Geburtstag*. Berlin. 205–66.

Girard, R. 1987. *Das Heilige und die Gewalt*. Zürich.

Girgenti, G., and G. Muscolino 2011. *La filosofia rivelata dagli oracoli: Con tutti i frammenti di magia, stregoneria, teosofia e teurgia ; testi greci e latini a fronte*, Il pensiero occidentale. Milano.

Giudice, F. 1998. "Le divinitá della ceramica attica in Magna Grecia ed il problema della "velocità" delle immagini." In Giudice, ed., *I culti della Campania antica: Atti del Convegno Internazionale di Studi in ricordo di Nazarena Valenza Mele, Napoli 15–17 Maggio 1995*. Pubblicazioni scientifiche del Centro di Studi della Magna Grecia dell'Università degli studi di Napoli Federico 3,3. Roma. 143–47.

Gladigow, B. 1977. "Macht und Religion: Formen der Herrschaftslegitimierung in den antiken Religionen." *Humanistische Bildung* 1: 1–31.

———. 2000. "Opfer und komplexe Kulturen." In B. Janowski and M. Welker, eds., *Das Opfer: Theologische und kulturelle Kontexte*. Frankfurt a. M. 86–107.

Gleba, M., and H. W. Horsnaes. 2011. *Communicating Identity in Italic Iron Age Communities*. Oxford.

Goette, H. R. 1986a. "Die Bulla." *Bonner Jahrbücher* 186: 133–64.

———. 1986b. "Kuh und Stier als Opfertier: Zur 'probatio victimae'." *Bullettino Comunale* 91: 61–68.

———.1990. *Studien zu römischen Togadarstellungen*. Beiträge zur Erschliessung hellenistischer und kaiserzeitlicher Skulptur und Architektur 10. Mainz.

Goldhill, S. 2006. "Rethinking Religious Revolution." In S. Goldhill and R. Osborne, eds., *Rethinking Revolutions Through Ancient Greece*. Cambridge. 141–63.

———. 2015. "Lived Experience, History, and Narrative Form in the Rabbinical Writings." *Religion in the Roman Empire* 1 (3): 343–77.

González, J. 1984. "Tabula Siarensis, Fortunales Siarenses et Municipia civium Romanorum." *ZPE* 55: 55–100.

González, J., and J. Arce, eds. 1988. *Estudios sobre la tabula Siarensis: Actas de las jornadas celebradas en Sevilla en 1986*. Anejos de archivo español de arqueología 9. Madrid.

Goodhue, N. 1975. *The Lucus Furrinae and the Syrian Sanctuary on the Janiculum*. Amsterdam.

Goodman, M. 2012. "Religious Reactions to 70: The Limitations of the Evidence." In D. R. Schwartz and Z. Weiss, eds., *Was 70 CE a Watershed in Jewish History? On Jews and Judaism before and after the Destruction of the Second Temple*. Ancient Judaism and Early Christianity 78. Leiden. 509–16.

Goodman, M., and P. Alexander 2010. *Rabbinic Texts and the History of Late-Roman Palestine*. A. British, trans. Proceedings of the British Academy. 165. Oxford.

Gordley, M. E. 2011. *Teaching through Song in Antiquity: Didactic Hymnody among Greeks, Romans, Jews, and Christians.* Wissenschaftliche Untersuchungen zum Neuen Testament, Series 2, 302. Tübingen.

Gordon, R. 1979. "The Real and the Imaginary: Production and Religion in the Graeco-Roman World." *Art History* 2: 5–34.

———. 1990. "The Veil of Power: Emperors, Sacrificers and Benefactors." In M. Beard and J. North, eds., *Pagan Priests: Religion and Power in the Ancient World.* London. 201–31.

———. 1994. "Who Worshipped Mithras?" *Journal of Roman Archaeology* 7: 459–74.

———. 1995. "The Healing Event in Graeco-Roman Folk-Medicine." In P. J. van der Eijk, W.F.J. Horstmanshoff, and P. H. Schrijvers, eds., *Ancient Medicine in its Socio-Cultural Context: Papers Read at the Congress held at Leiden University, 13–15 April 1992.* Vol. 2. Amsterdam. 363–76.

———. 1999. "Imagining Greek and Roman Magic." In B. Ankarloo and S. Clark, eds., *The Athlone History of Witchcraft and Magic in Europe* 2: *Ancient Greece and Rome.* London. 159–275.

———. 2005. "Competence and 'Felicity Conditions' in Two Sets of North African Curse-Tablets (DTAud nos. 275–85; 286–98)." *MHNH* 5: 61–86.

———. 2007. "The Coherence of Magical-Herbal and Analogous Recipes." *MHNH* 7: 115–46.

———. 2009a. "Animal-Lore and the Role of Animals." Review of Ingvild, Saelid Gilhus, *Animals, Gods and Humans . . .* 2006. *Journal of Roman Archaeology* 22: 637–42.

———. 2009b. "The Roman Army and the Cult of Mithras: A Critical View." In C. Wolff, and Y. LeBohec, eds., *L'armée romaine et la religion sous le Haut-Empire romain* 33. Paris. 397–450.

———. 2010. "Magian Lessons in Natural History: Unique Animals in Graeco-Roman Natural Magic." In J. Dijkstra, J. Kroesen, and Y. Kuiper, eds., *Myths, Martyrs, and Modernity—Studies in the History of Religions in Honour of Jan N. Bremmer.* Leiden. 249–69.

———. 2011. "Archaeologies of Magical Gems." In C. Entwistle and N. Adams, eds., *"Gems of Heaven": Recent Research on Engraved Gemstones in Late Antiquity c. AD 200–600.* British Museum Research Publication 177. London. 39–49.

———. 2012. "Mithras." *Reallexikon für Antike und Christentum* 24: 964–1009.

———. 2013a. "Cosmology, Astrology, and Magic: Discourse, Schemes, Power, and Literacy." In L. Bricault and C. Bonnet, eds., *Panthée: Religious Transformations in the Graeco-Roman Empire.* Religions in the Graeco-Roman World 177. Leiden. 85–111.

———. 2013b. "Individuality, Selfhood and Power in the Second Century: The Mystagogue as a Mediator of Religious Options." In J. Rüpke and G. Woolf, eds., *Religious Dimensions of the Self in the Second Century CE.* Studien und Texte zu Antike und Christentum 76. Tübingen. 146–71.

———. 2013c. "The Miles-frame in the Mitreo di Felicissimo and the Practicalities of Sacrifice." *Religio* 21: 33–38.

———. 2013d. "The Religious Anthropology of Late-Antique 'High' Magical Practice." In J. Rüpke, ed., *The Individual in the Religions of the Ancient Mediterranean.* Oxford. 163–86.

———. 2013e. " 'Will My Child Have a Big Nose?': Uncertainty, Authority and Narrative in Katarchic Astrology." In V. Rosenberger, ed., *Divination in the Ancient World: Religious Options and the Individual*. Potsdamer Altertumswissenschaftliche Beiträge 46. Stuttgart. 93–137.

———. 2014. "Charaktêres between Antiquity and Renaissance: Transmission and Re-Invention." In V. Dasen, and J.-M. Spieser, eds., *Les savoirs magiques et leur transmission de l'Antiquité à la Renaissance*. Micrologus' Library 60. Firenze. 253–300.

———. 2015. "Temporary Deprivation: Rules and Meaning." In R. Raja and J. Rüpke, eds., *A Companion to the Archaeology of Religion in the Ancient World*. Malden, Mass. 194–206.

———. 2016. "Negotiating the Temple-Script: Women's Narratives among the Mysian-Lydian 'Confession-Texts'." *Religion in the Roman Empire* 2 (2): 227–55.

———. 2017. "From East to West: Staging Religious Experience in the Mithraic Temple." In S. Nagel, J.-F. Quack, and C. Witschel, eds., *Entangled Worlds: Religious Confluences Between East and West in the Roman Empire*. Orientalische Religionen in der Antike 22. Tübingen. 413–42.

Gosden, C. 2005. "What Do Objects Want?" *Journal of Archaeological Method and Theory* 12 (3): 193–211.

Gotter, U. 2011. "Zwischen Christentum und Staatsraison: Römisches Imperium und religiöse Gewalt." In J. Hahn, ed., *Spätantiker Staat und religiöser Konflikt: Imperiale und lokale Verwaltung und die Gewalt gegen Heiligtümer*. Millennium-Studien 34. Berlin. 133–58.

Gradel, I. 2002. *Emperor Worship and Roman Religion*. Oxford.

Graf, F. 2001. "Der Eigensinn der Götterbilder in antiken religiösen Diskursen." In G. Boehm, eds., *Homo Pictor*. Colloquium Rauricum 7. München. 227–43.

———. 2010a. "Gods in Greek Inscriptions: Some Methodological Questions." In J. N. Bremmer and A. Erskine, eds., *The Gods of Ancient Greece: Identities and Transformations*. Edinburgh Leventis Studies 5. Edinburgh. 55–80.

———. 2010b. "Victimology: Or, How to Deal with Untimely Death." In S. P. Ahearne-Kroll, P. A. Holloway, and J. A. Kelhoffer, eds., *Women and Gender in Ancient Religions: Interdisciplinary Approaches*. Tübingen. 227–40.

Graf, F., and S. I. Johnston. 2007. *Ritual Texts for the Afterlife*. New York.

Grafton, A., and M. Williams. 2006. *Christianity and the Transformation of the Book—Origen, Eusebius, and the Librara of Caesarea*. Camdridge, London.

Graham, E.-J. 2009. "Becoming Persons, Becoming Ancestors: Personhood, Memory and the Corpse in Roman Rituals of Social Remembrance." *Archeological Dialogues* 16 (1): 51–74.

———. 2011a. "From Fragments to Ancestors: Re-defining the Role of *os resectum* in Rituals of Purification and Commemoration in Republican Rome." In M. Carroll. ed., *Living through the Dead: Burial and Commemoration in the Classical World*. Studies in Funerary Archaeology 5. Oxford. 91–109.

———. 2011b. "Memory and Materiality: Re-embodying the Roman Funeral." In V. M. Hope and J. Huskinson, eds., *Memory and Mourning: Studies on Roman Death*. Oxford. 21–39.

Granovetter, M. 1973. "The Strength of Weak Ties." *American Journal of Sociology* 78 (6): 1360–80.

Greco, E., and V. Gasparini. 2014. "Il santuario di Sibari—Casa Bianca." In L. Bricault and R. Veymiers, eds., *Bibliotheca Isiaca* III. Bordeaux. 55–72.

Greco, G. 1998. "Da Hera argiva ad Hera pestana." In *I culti della Campania antica: Atti del Convegno Internazionale di Studi in ricordo di Nazarena Valenza Mele, Napoli 15–17 Maggio 1995* Vol. III. Pubblicazioni scientifiche del Centro di Studi della Magna Grecia dell'Università degli studi di Napoli Federico II 3,3. Roma. 45–62.

———. 2008. "Strutture per un sacrificio." In G. Greco and B. Ferrera, eds., *Doni agli dei, Il sistema dei doni votivi nei santuari: atti del seminario di studi, Napoli 21 aprile 2006*. Napoli. 29–48.

Green, S. J. 2014. *Disclosure and Discretion in Roman Astrology: Manilius and His Augustan Contemporaries*. Oxford.

Green, W. S. 1979. "Palestinian Holy Men: Charismatic Leadership and Rabbinic Tradition." *ANRW* II.19,2: 619–47.

Grimes, R. L. 1990. *Ritual Criticism: Case Studies in Its Practice, Essays on Its Theory*, Studies in Comparative Religion. Columbia, SC.

Gros, P. 1976. *Aurea Templa: Recherches sur l'architecture religieuse de Rome à l'époque d'Auguste*. Bibliothèque des écoles françaises d'Athènes et de Rome 231. Rome.

Grossi, M. C., and V. S. Mellace. 2007. "Roma, Via Portuense: la necropoli di vigna pia." In A. Faber, ed., *Körpergräber des 1.–3. Jahrhunderts in der römischen Welt*. Schriften des Archäologischen Museums Frankfurt 21. Frankfurt a. M. 185–200.

Gruen, E. S. 2011. "Beyond Anti-Judaism: Louis Feldman and the "Lachrymose Version" of Jewish History." In A. W. Astell and S. Goodhart, eds., *Sacrifice, Scripture, and Substitution: Readings in Ancient Judaism and Christianity*. Christianity and Judaism in Antiquity 18. Notre Dame, Ind. 227–31.

Gurval, R. A. 1995. *Actium and Augustus: The Politics and Emotions of Civil War*. Ann Arbor.

Gury, F. 2008. "Les perles et les imperatores: Caligula in litore oceani." In J. Napoli, ed., *Actes du colloque international Ressources et activités maritimes des peuples de l'Antiquité*. Boulogne. 401–26.

Guyon, J. 1996. "Die Kirche Roms vom Anfang des 4. Jahrhunderts bis zu Sixtus III. (312–432)." In C. Piétri and L. Piétri, eds., *Die Geschichte des Christentums 2: Das Entstehen der einen Christenheit (250–430)*. Freiburg. 877–917.

Guzzo, P. G. 1998. "Doni preziosi agli dei." In *I culti della Campania antica: Atti del Convegno Internazionale di Studi in ricordo di Nazarena Valenza Mele, Napoli 15–17 Maggio 1995*. Pubblicazioni scientifiche del Centro di Studi della Magna Grecia dell'Università degli studi di Napoli Federico 3,3. Roma. 27–36.

Haake, M. 2011. "Zwischen Alexander dem Großen und Arcadius, von Anaxarchos von Abdera zu Synesios von Kyrene: Die Gattung über das Königtum im Kontext antiker Alleinherrschaften—eine Skizze." *Quaestio* 11: 65–82.

Haas, C. 1997. *Alexandria in Late Antiquity: Topography and Social Conflict*. 2006 ed. Baltimore.

Habermas, R. 2008. "Mission im 19. Jahrhundert—Globale Netze des Religiösen." *Historische Zeitschrift* 287: 629–78.

Habinek, T. 2005. *The World of Roman Song: From Ritualized Speech to Social Order.* Baltimore.

Hadas-Lebel, M. 1993. "Le double récit autobiographique chez Flavius Josèphe." In M.-F. Baslez, P. Hoffmann, and L. Pernot, eds., *L'invention de l'autobiographie d'Hésiode à Saint Augustin: Actes du deuxième colloque de l'Équipe de recherche sur l'hellénisme postclassique (Paris, École normale supérieure, 14–16 juin 1990).* Paris. 125–32.

Haensch, R. 1997. *Capita provinciarum: Statthaltersitze und Provinzialverwaltung in der römischen Kaiserzeit.* Kölner Forschungen 7. Mainz.

———. 2006. "'Religion' und Kulte im juristischen Schrifttum und in rechtsverbindlichen Verlautbarungen der Hohen Kaiserzeit." In D. von Elm, J. Rüpke, and K. Waldner, eds., *Texte als Medium und Reflexion von Religion im römischen Reich.* Stuttgart. 233–47.

Haeussler, R. 2012. "Interpretatio indigena: Re-Inventing Local Cults in a Global World." *Mediterraneo Antico* 15 (1–2): 143–74.

Hägg, T. 2012. *The Art of Biography in Antiquity.* Cambridge.

Hahn, J. 2004. *Gewalt und religiöser Konflikt: Studien zu den Auseinandersetzungen zwischen Christen, Heiden und Juden im Osten des Römischen Reiches (von Konstantin bis Theodosius II).* Beihefte Klio NF 8. Berlin.

———. 2011. "Gesetze als Waffe? Die kaiserliche Religionspolitik und die Zerstörung der Tempel." In J. Hahn, ed., *Spätantiker Staat und religiöser Konflikt: imperiale und lokale Verwaltung und die Gewalt gegen Heiligtümer.* Millennium-Studien 34. Berlin. 201–20.

Haines-Eitzen, K. 2012. *The Gendered Palimpsest: Women, Writing, and Representation in Early Christianity.* Oxford.

Halkin, L. 1953. *La supplication d'action de graces chez les Romains.* Bibliothèque de la Faculté de Philosophie et Lettres de l'Université de Liège 128. Paris.

Hamerton-Kelly, R. G., ed., 1987. *Violent Origins: Walter Burkert, René Girard, and Jonathan Z. Smith on Ritual Killing and Cultural Formation,* with an introd. by Burton Mack and a comm. by Renato Rosaldo. Stanford, Calif.

Hänlein-Schäfer, H. 1985. *Veneratio Augusti: Eine Studie zu den Tempeln des ersten römischen Kaisers.* Archaeologica 39. Roma.

Harich-Schwarzbauer, H. 2001. "Proba." *Neuer Pauly* 10: 356.

Harland, P. A. 2003. *Associations, Synagogues, and Congregations—Claiming a Place in Ancient Mediterranean Society.* Minneapolis.

———. 2011. "Journeys in Pursuit of Divine Wisdom: Thessalos and Other Seekers." In P. A. Harland, ed., *Travel and Religion in Antiquity.* Studies in Christianity and Judaism 21. Waterloo, Ont. 122–40.

———. 2014. *Greco-Roman Associations: Texts, Translations, and Commentary.* Beiheft zur Zeitschrift für die neutestamentliche Wissenschaft 204. Berlin/Boston.

Harnack, A. v. 1921. *Marcion: Das Evangelium vom fremden Gott. Eine Monographie zur Geschichte der Grundlegung der katholischen Kirche.* Texte und Untersuchungen zur Geschichte der altchristlichen Literatur 45=R. 3, 15. Leipzig.

Harries, J. 1986. "Sozomen and Eusebius: The Lawyer as Church Historian in the Fifth Century." In C. Holdsworth and T. P. Wiseman, eds., *The Inheritance of Historiography 350–900*. Exeter. 45–52.

Harrington, M. 2012. "The Emperor Julian's Use of Neoplatonic Philosophy and Religion." In K. Corrigan, J. D. Turner, and P. Wakefield, eds., *Religion and Philosophy in the Platonic and Neoplatonic Traditions: From Antiquity to the Early Medieval Period*. Sankt Augustin. 65–79.

Harris, W. V. 2005. "The Mediterranean and Ancient History." In W. V. Harris, ed., *Rethinking the Mediterranean*. Oxford. 1–42.

———. 2009. *Dreams and Experience in Classical Antiquity*. Cambridge, Mass.

Harris, W. V., and B. Holmes, eds. 2008. *Aelius Aristides between Greece, Rome, and the Gods*. Columbia Studies in the Classical Tradition 33. Leiden.

Harrison, T. 2006. "Religion and the Rationality of the Greek City." In S. Goldhill and R. Osborne, ed., *Rethinking Revolutions through Ancient Greece*. Cambridge. 124–40.

Hartmann, N. 2013. *Martyrium: Variationen und Potenziale eines Diskurses im Zweiten Jahrhundert*, Early Christianity in the Context of Antiquity 14. Frankfurt a.M.

Häuber, C. 2001. "Wald und Siedlung im antiken Rom: Spuren heiliger Haine auf dem Mons Oppius." *Geographie* 19: 57–94.

Hawes, G. 2014. *Rationalizing Myth in Antiquity*. Oxford.

Hayes, C. E. 2015. *What's Divine about Divine Law? Early Perspectives*. Princeton.

Haynes, I. 2013. "Advancing the Systematic Study of Ritual Deposition in the Greco-Roman World." In A. Schäfer and M. Witteyer, eds., *Rituelle Deponierungen in Heiligtümern der hellenistisch-römischen Welt: International Tagung Mainz 28.–30. April*. Mainzer Archäologische Schriften 10. Mainz. 7–19.

Heesterman, J. C. 1986. "Ritual, Revelation, and the Axial Age." In S. N. Eisenstadt, ed., *The Origins and Diversity of Axial Age Civilizations*. Albany. 393–406.

Heim, F. 1992. *La théologie de la victoire de Constantin à Théodose*, Théologie historique 89. Paris.

Heine, R. H. 2004. "Hippolytus, Ps.-Hippolytus and the Early Cannon." In F. Young, L. Ayres, and A. Louth, eds., *The Cambridge History of Early Christian Literature*. Cambridge. 142–51.

Heintz, M. 2011. "Martyrdom from Exegesis in Hippolytus: An Early Church Presbyteré Commentary on Daniel." *Religious Studies Review* 37 (2): 139–40.

Hekster, O. 2011. "Imagining Power: Reality Gaps in the Roman Empire." *Babesch* 86: 111–24.

Hekster, O., S. Schmidt-Hofner, and C. Witschel, eds. *Ritual Dynamics and Religious Change in the Roman Empire: Proceedings of the Eighth Workshop of the International Network on the Impact of Empire (Heidelberg, July 5–7, 2007)*. Impact of Empire 9. Leiden.

Hellholm, D. 1980. *Das Visionenbuch des Hermas als Apokalypse: Formgeschichtliche und texttheoretische Studien zu einer literarischen Gattung 1: Methodologische Vorüberlegungen und makrostrukturelle Textanalyse*. Coniectanea biblica, New Testament Series 13:1. Lund.

Henderson, I. 2012. "'. . . Hidden with Christ in God' (Colossians 3:3): Modes of Personhood in Deutero-Pauline Tradition." In J. Rüpke and W. Spickermann, eds., *Reflections* on *Religious Individuality: Greco-Roman and Judaeo-Christian Texts and Practices*. Religionsgeschichtliche Versuche und Vorarbeiten 62. Berlin. 43–67.

Henderson, J. 2006. "From ΦΙΛΟΣΟΦΙΑ into Philosophia: Classicism and Ciceronianism." In J. I. Porter, ed., *Classical Pasts: The Classical Traditions of Greece and Rome*. Princeton. 173–203.

Henderson, T. P. 2011. *The Gospel of Peter and Early Christian Apologetics: Rewriting the Story of Jesus' Death, Burial, and Resurrection*. Wissenschaftliche Untersuchungen zum Neuen Testament 2. Reihe 301. Tübingen.

Henning, A. 2013. *Die Turmgräber von Palmyra: Eine lokale Bauform im kaiserzeitlichen Syrien als Ausdruck kultureller Identität*. Orient-Archäologie 29. Rahden.

Henrichs, A. 2010. "What Is a Greek God?" In J. N. Bremmer and A. Erskine, eds., *The Gods of Ancient Greece: Identities and Transformations*. Edinburgh Leventis Studies 5. Edinburgh. 19–39.

Herbert-Brown, G. 1994. *Ovid and the Fasti: An Historical Study*. Oxford.

Hersch, K. K. 2010. *The Roman Wedding: Ritual and Meaning in Antiquity*. Cambridge.

Herz, P. 1975. *Untersuchungen zum Festkalender der römischen Kaiserzeit nach datierten Weih- und Ehreninschriften* 2. Diss. Mainz.

———. 2003. "Neue Forschungen zum Festkalender der römischen Kaiserzeit." In H. Cancik and K. Hitzl, eds., *Die Praxis des Herrscherkults*. Tübingen. 47–67.

Hesberg, H. v. 1992. *Römische Grabbauten*. Darmstadt.

———. 2006. "Die Torre del Breny—ein Monumentales Altargrab der frühen Kaiserzeit." In D. Vaquerizo and J. F. Murillo, eds., *El concepto de lo provincial en el mundo antiguo: Homenaje a la profesora Pilar León Alonso* 2. Córdoba. 295–316.

———. 2007. "Die Statuengruppe im Tempel der Dioskuren von Cori: Bemerkungen zum Aufstellungskontext von Kultbildern in spätrepublikanischer Zeit." *Mitteilungen des Deutschen Archäologischen Instituts, Römische Abteilung* 113: 443–61.

Hesberg, H. v., C. Nowak, and E. Thiermann, eds. 2015. "Religion and Tomb." In R. Raja and J. Rüpke, eds., *A Companion to the Archaeology of Religion in the Ancient World*. Malden, Mass. 235–49.

Hesberg, H. v., and P. Zanker, eds. 1987. *Römische Gräberstraßen: Selbstdarstellung, Status, Standard*. Abhandlungen Bayerische Akademie der Wissenschaften, Phil.-hist. Kl. NF 96. München.

Hezser, C. 2013. "The Jesus Movement as a 'Popular' Judaism for the Unlearned." In P. Gemuenden, D. G. Horrell, and M. Kuechler, eds., *Jesus—Gestalt und Gestaltungen: Rezeptionen des Galilaeers in Wissenschaft, Kirche und Gesellschaft*. Göttingen. 79–104.

Hickson [Hahn], F. V. 1991. "Augustus Triumphator: Manipulation of the Triumphal Theme in the Political Program of Augustus." *Latomus* 50: 124–38.

———. 2007. "Performing the Sacred: Prayer and Hymns." In J. Rüpke, ed., *A Companion to Roman Religion*. Oxford. 235–48.

Hill, R. C. 2007. "The Commentary on Daniel by Theodoret of Cyrus." In K. Bracht, and D. S. du Toit, eds., *Die Geschichte der Daniel-Auslegung in Judentum, Christentum und Islam: Studien zur Kommentierung des Danielbuches in Literatur und Kunst*. Beihefte zur Zeitschrift für die alttestamentliche Wissenschaft 371. Berlin. 151–63.

Hin, S. 2013. *The Demography of Roman Italy: Population Dynamics in an Ancient Conquest Society (201 BCE–14 CE)*. Cambridge.

Hirsch, M. 2012. *The Generation of Postmemory: Writing and Visual Culture after the Holocaust*. New York.

Hirschmann, V. 2015. *Die Kirche der Reinen: Kirchen- und sozialhistorische Studie zu den Novatianern im 3. bis 5. Jahrhundert*. Studien und Texte zu Antike und Christentum 96. Tübingen.

Hitlin, S., and G. H. Elder. 2007. "Time, Self, and the Curiously Abstract Concept of Agency." *Sociological Theory* 25 (2): 170–91.

Hobsbawm, E. J., and T. Ranger, eds. 1983. *The Invention of Tradition*. Past and Present Publications. Cambridge.

Hodder, I. 2012. *Entangled: An Archaeology of the Relationships between Humans and Things*. Malden, Mass.

Hoffer, S. E. 1999. *The Anxieties of Pliny the Younger*. American Classical Studies 43. Atlanta, Ga.

Hoffmann, A., ed. 2005. *Ägyptische Kulte und ihre Heiligtümer im Osten des römischen Reiches. Internationales Kolloquium, 5./6. September 2003 in Bergama (Türkei)*. Byzas 1. [Istanbul].

Hoffmann, V., U. Link-Wieczorek, and C. Mandry, eds. 2016. *Die Gabe: Zum Stand der interdisziplinären Diskussion*. Freiburg i. Br.

Hofter, M. R. 2010. "Etruskische und italische Votivplastik aus Ton." In V. Kästner, ed., *Etrusker in Berlin—Etrsukische Kunst in der Berliner Antikensammlung—Eine Einführung*. Berlin. 69–76.

Hölkeskamp, K.-J. 2001. "Capitol, Comitium und Forum: Öffentliche Räume, sakrale Topographie und Erinnerungslandschaften der römischen Republik." In S. Faller, ed., *Studien zu antiken Identitäten*. Würzburg. 97–132.

———. 2009. "Mythos und Politik—(nicht nur) in der Antike: Anregungen und Angebote der neuen 'historischen Politikforschung'." *Historische Zeitschrift* 288: 1–50.

———. 2011. *Die Entstehung der Nobilität: Studien zur sozialen und politischen Geschichte der Römischen Republik im 4. Jh. v. Chr*. 2nd ed. Alte Geschichte. Stuttgart.

———. 2014. "Under Roman Roofs: Family, House, and Household." In H. Flower, ed., *The Cambridge Companion to the Roman Republic*. Cambridge. 101–26.

Holland, L. A. 1953. "Septimontium or Saeptimontium." *TAPhA* 84: 16–34.

Holloway, R. Ross. 1994. *The Archaeology of Early Rome and Latium*. London.

———. 2005. "Urbanism—Etruscan, Italic and Latin in the Light of Recent Developments." In P. Attema et al., eds., *Papers in Italian Archaeology* VI: *Communities and Settlements from the Neolithic to the Early Medieval Period; Proceedings of the 6th Conference of Italian Archaeology held at the University of Groningen, Groningen Institute of Archaeology, the Netherlands, April 15–17, 2003* 1. Oxford. 32–58.

Hölscher, L. 2005. *Geschichte der protestantischen Frömmigkeit in Deutschland*. München.

Honigman, S. 2014. *Tales of High Priests and Taxes: The Books of the Maccabees and the Judean Rebellion against Antiochos IV*. S. Mark Taper Foundation Book in Jewish Studies. Oakland.

Hope, V. M. 1997. "A Roof over the Dead: Communal Tombs and Family Structure." In R. Laurence and A. Wallace-Hadrill, eds., *Domestic Space in the Roman World: Pompeii and Beyond.* Journal of Roman Archaeology, Suppl. 22. Portsmouth, RI. 69–88.

———. 2001. *Constructing Identity: The Roman Funerary Monuments of Aquileia, Mainz and Nîmes,* BAR International Series 960. Oxford.

———. 2009. *Roman Death: The Dying and the Dead in Ancient Rome.* London.

———. 2011. "Remembering to Mourn: Personal Mementos of the Dead in Ancient Rome." In V. M. Hope and J. Huskinson, eds, *Memory and Mourning: Studies on Roman Death.* Oxford. 176–95.

Hope, V. M., and J. Huskinson, eds. 2011. *Memory and Mourning: Studies on Roman Death.* Oxford.

Hopkins, J. N. 2012. "The Capitoline Temple and the Effects of Monumentality on Roman Temple Design." In M. L. Thomas and G. E. Meyers, eds., *Monumentality in Etruscan and Early Roman Architecture: Ideology and Innovation.* Austin. 111–38.

Horden, P., and N. Purcell. 2000. *The Corrupting Sea: A Study of Mediterranean History.* Oxford.

———. 2005. "Four Years of Corruption: A Response to Critics." In W. V. Harris, ed., *Rethinking the Mediterranean.* Oxford. 348–75.

Hörig, M., and E. Schwertheim. 1987. *Corpus Cultus Iovis Dolicheni (CCID).* EPRO 106. Leiden.

Horsley, G.H.R. 2007. *The Greek and Latin Inscriptions in the Burdur Archaeological Museum.* Regional Epigraphic Catalogues of Asia Minor 5. Ankara.

Howes, D. 2011. "Sensation." *Material Religion* 7: 92–98.

Huet, V. 2015. "Watching Rituals." In R. Raja and J. Rüpke, eds., *A Companion to the Archaeology of Religion in the Ancient World.* Malden, Mass. 144–54.

Hultgård, A. 1993. "Altskandinavische Opferrituale und das Problem der Quellen." In T. Ahlbäck, ed., *The Problem of Ritual.* Åbo/Stockholm. 221–59.

Humphrey, C. and J. Laidlaw. 1994. *The Archetypal Actions of Ritual: A Theory of Ritual Illustrated by the Jain Rite of Worship.* Oxford.

Hunt, E. D. 1984. "Travel, Tourism and Piety in the Roman Empire: A Context for the Beginning of Christian Pilgrimage." *Echos du monde classique* 28: 391–417.

Hurlet, F. 2009. "Le statut posthume de Caius et Lucius César." In M. Christol and D. Darde, eds., *L' expression du pouvoir au début de l'Empire: autour de la Maison Carrée à Nîmes; actes du colloque organisé à l'initiative de la ville de Nîmes et du Musée Archéologique (Nîmes, Carré d'Art, 20–22 octobre 2005).* Paris. 75–82.

———. 2011. "(Re)penser l'Empire romain. Le défi de la comparaison historique." *Dialogues d'histoire ancienne. Supplément* 5: 107–40.

Iaia, C. 2006. "Servizi cerimoniali e da 'simposio' in bronzo del primo ferro in Italia centro-settentironale." In P. v. Eles, ed., *La ritualità funeraria tra età del ferro e orientalizzante in Italia: Atti del Convegno Verucchio, 26–26 Giugno 2002.* Pisa. 103–10.

Ildefonse, F. 2008. "Questions pour introduire à une histoire de l'intériorité." In G. Aubry, ed., *Le moi et l'intériorité.* Textes et traditions 17. Paris. 223–39.

Ioppolo, G. 2000. "Il tempio arcaico." In Ioppolo, ed., *Il viver quotidiano in Roma arcaica: Materiali dagli scavi del Tempio Arcaico nell'area sacra di S. Omobono*. Roma. 28–33.

Iricinschi, E., and H. M. Zellentin 2008. "Making Selves and Marking Others: Identity and Late Antique Heresiologies." In E. Iricinschi and H. M. Zellentin, eds., *Heresy and Identity in Late Antiquity*. Texts and Studies in Ancient Judaism 119. Tübingen. 1–27.

Isele, B. 2010. *Kampf um Kirchen: Religiöse Gewalt. Heiliger Raum und christliche Topographie in Alexandria und Konstantinopel (4. Jh.)*. Jahrbuch für Antike und Christentum—Ergänzungsband Kleine Reihe 4. Münster.

Israelowich, I. 2015. *Patients and Healers in the High Roman Empire*. Baltimore.

Itgenshorst, T. 2005. *Tota illa pompa: der Triumph in der römischen Republik; mit einer CD-ROM: Katalog der Triumphe von 340 bis 19 vor Christus*. Göttingen.

Izzet, V. 2000. "Tuscan Order: The Development of Etruscan Sanctuary." In E. Bispham and C. Smith, eds., *Religion in Archaic and Republican Rome and Italy: Evidence and Experience*. Edinburgh. 34–53.

———. 2007. *The Archaeology of Etruscan Society*. Cambridge.

Jaccottet, A.-F. 2011. "Integrierte Andersartigkeit: Die Rolle der dionysischen Vereine." In R. Schlesier, ed., *A Different God? Dionysos and Ancient Polytheism*. Berlin. 413–31.

———. 2013. "Du Corps Humain au Corps Divin: L'apothéose dans l'imaginaire et les représentations figurées." In P. Borgeaud and D. Fabiano, eds., *Reception et Construction du Divine dans l'Antiquité*. Recherches et Rencontres 31. Genève. 293–322.

Jackson, A. H. 1991. "Hoplites and the Gods: The Dedication of Captured Arms and Armours." In V. D. Hanson, ed., *Hoplites: The Classical Greek Battle Experience*. London. 228–49.

Jacobs, A. 2012. *Christ Circumcised: A Study in Early Christian History and Difference*. Divinations: Reading Late Ancient Religion. Philadelphia.

Jaczynowska, M. 1981. "Le culte de l'Hercule romain au temps du Haut-Empire." *ANRW* II.17,2: 631–61.

Jameson, M. 1965. "Notes on the Sacrificial Calendar from Erchia." *Bulletin de Correspondance Hellénique* 89: 154–72.

Jannot, J.-R. 2009. "Une barque pour l'au-delà: à propos d'une urne cinéraire d'Arezzo." In S. Bruni, ed., *Etruria e Italia Preromana: Studi in Onore di Giovannangelo Camporeale* 2. Pisa. 491–94.

Janowitz, N., ed. 2001. *Magic in the Roman World: Pagans, Jews and Christians*. Religion in the First Christian Centuries. London.

———. 2002. *Icons of Power: Ritual Practices in Late Antiquity*. Magic in History. University Park, Penn.

Janowski, B., and M. Welker, eds. 2000. *Das Opfer: Theologische und kulturelle Kontexte*. Frankfurt a. M.

Jarrett, M. G. 1971. "Decurions and Priests." *American Journal of Philology* 92: 513–38.

Jastrzeboska, E. 1981. *Untersuchungen zum christlichen Totenmahl aufgrund der Monumente des 3. und 4. Jahrhunderts unter der Basilika des Hl. Sebastian in Rom*. Europäische Hochschulschriften, Series 38 (Archäologie), 2. Frankfurt a. M.

Jehne, M. 2013a. "Der römische Senat als Hüter des Gemeinsinns." In M. Jehne and C. Lundgreen, eds., *Gemeinsinn und Gemeinwohl in der römischen Antike*. Stuttgart. 23–50.

———. 2013b. "Konsensfiktionen in römischen Volksversammlungen: Überlegungen zur frührepublikanischen Curienversammlung und zu den kaiserzeitlichen Destinationscenturien." In E. Flaig and E. Müller-Luckner, eds., *Genesis und Dynamiken der Mehrheitsentscheidung*. Schriften des Historischen Kollegs: Kolloquien 85. München. 129–52.

Jehne, M., and C. Lundgreen. 2013. "Einleitung: Gemeinsinn und Gemeinwohl in der römischen Antike." In M. Jehne and C. Lundgreen, eds., *Gemeinsinn und Gemeinwohl in der römischen Antike*. Stuttgart. 11–9.

Jenott, L., and E. Pagels. 2010. "Antony's Letters and Nag Hammadi Codex I: Sources of Religious Conflict in Fourth-Century Egypt." *Journal of Early Christian Studies* 18: 557–89.

Jensen, A. 1991. "Faltonia Betitia Proba: eine Kirchenlehrerin der Spätantike." In H. Pissarek-Hudelist and L. Schottroff, eds., *Mit allen Sinnen glauben: feministische Theologie unterwegs, für Elisabeth Moltmann-Wendel zum 65. Geburtstag*. Güterloh. 84–93.

Joas, H. 1996. *Die Kreativität des Handelns*. Frankfurt a. M.

Jocelyn, H. D. 1982. "Varro's antiquitates rerum diuinarum and Religious Affairs in the Late Roman Republic." *Bulletin of the John Rylands University Library of Manchester (BRL)* 65: 148–205.

Johnson, W. A. 2012. *Readers and Reading Culture in the High Roman Empire: A Study of Elite Communities*. Oxford.

Johnston, S. I. 2012. "Sosipatra and the Theurgic Life: Eunapius Vitae Sophistorum 6.6.5–6.9.24." In J. Rüpke and W. Spickermann, eds., *Reflections on Religious Individuality: Greco-Roman and Judaeo-Christian Texts and Practices*. Religionsgeschichtliche Versuche und Vorarbeiten 62. Berlin. 99–117.

Jones, C. P. 2004. "Multiple Identities in the Age of the Second Sophistic." In B. E. Borg, ed., *Paideia: The World of the Second Sophistic*. Millennium-Studien 2. Berlin. 13–21.

Jones, K. R. 2011. *Jewish Reactions to the Destruction of Jerusalem in A.D. 70: Apocalypses and Related Pseudepigrapha*, Suppl. to the *Journal for the Study of Judaism* 151. Leiden.

Jonquière, T. M. 2007. *Prayer in Josephus*. Ancient Judaism and Early Christianity 70. Leiden.

Jung, M. 1999. *Erfahrung und Religion: Grundzüge einer hermeneutisch-pragmatischen Religionsphilosophie*. Freiburg i. Br.

———. 2004 "Qualitative Erfahrung in Alltag, Kunst und Religion " In G. Mattenklott, ed., *Ästhetische Erfahrung im Zeichen der Entgrenzung der Künste: Epistemische, ästhetische und religiöse Erfahrungsformen im Vergleich*. Hamburg. 31–53.

———. 2005 "'Making Us Explicit'—Artikulation als Organisationsprinzip von Erfahrung." In M. Schlette and M. Jung, eds., *Anthropologie der Artikulation*. Würzburg. 103–42.

———. 2006 "Making Life Explicit—The Symbolic Pregnance of Religious Experience." *Svensk Teologisk Kvartalskrift* vol. "Ernst Cassirer." 16–23.

Kahlos, M. 2011. "Who Is a Good Roman? Settings and Resetting Boundaries for Romans, Christians, Pagans, and Barbarians in the Late Roman Empire." In M. Kahlos, ed., *The*

Faces of the Others: Religious Rivalry And Ethnic Encounters in the Later Roman World. Cursor Mundi 10. Turnhout. 259–74.

Kaizer, T. 2009. "Religion and Language in Dura-Europos." In H. Cotton, ed., *From Hellenism to Islam: Cultural and Linguistic Change in the Roman Near East.* Cambridge. 235–53.

Kajava, M. 1994. *Roman Female praenomina: Studies in the Nomenclature of Roman Women.* Acta Instituti Romani Finlandiae 14. Rome.

———. 1998. "Visceratio." *Arctos* 32: 109–31.

Kardos, M.-J. 2011. "La satire des cultes égyptiens chez Martial et Juvénal et l'*Iseum* du Champ de Mars" [Pl. XI-XIII]. In M.-J. Kardos and L. Voinson, eds., *Habiter en ville au temps de Vespasien: actes de la table ronde de Nancy, 17 octobre 2008.* Études d'archéologie classique 14. Nancy. Paris.

Karrer, M. 2012. "Apoll und die apokalyptischen Reiter." In Michael Labahm and M. Karrer, eds., *Die Johannesoffenbarung, Ihr Text und ihre Auslegung.* Arbeiten zur Bibel und ihrer Geschichte 8. Leipzig. 223–51.

Kartschoke, D. 1975. *Bibeldichtung: Studien zur Geschichte der epischen Bibelparaphrase von Iuvencus bis Otfried von Weißenburg.* München.

Kastenmeier, P. 2007. *I luoghi del lavoro domestico nella casa pompeiana.* Studi della Soprintendenza Archeologica di Pompei 23. Roma.

Kaufmann-Heinimann, A. 1998. *Götter und Lararien aus Augusta Raurica: Herstellung, Fundzusammenhänge und sakrale Funktion figürlicher Bronzen in einer römischen Stadt.* Forschungen in August.

———. 2007. "Religion in the House." In J. Rüpke, ed., *A Companion to Roman Religion.* Oxford. 188–201.

Kearns, E. 2011. "The Rationale of Cakes and Bloodless Offerings in Greek Sacrifice." In V. Pirenne-Delforge and F. Prescendi, eds., *"Nourrir les dieux?" Sacrifice et représentation du divin.* Liége. 89—103.

Keegan, J. 1976. *The Face of Battle.* Harmondsworth.

Keegan, P. 2014. *Roles for Men and Women in Roman Epigraphic Culture and Beyond: Gender, Social Identity and Cultural Practice in Private Latin Inscriptions and the Literary Record.* BAR International Series 2626. Oxford.

Kemezis, A. M. 2014. *Greek Narratives of the Roman Empire under the Severans: Cassius Dio, Philostratus and Herodian.* Greek Culture in the Roman World. Cambridge.

Van den Kerchove, A. 2012. *La voie d'Hermés—Pratiques rituelles et traités hermétique.* Leiden.

Kierdorf, W. 1980. *Laudatio funebris: Interpretationen und Untersuchungen zur Entwicklung der römischen Leichenrede.* Beiträge zur Klassischen Philologie 106. Meisenheim a. Glan.

Kimmig, W. 1985. "Eisenzeitliche Grabstelen in Mitteleuropa." In M. Liverani, A. Palmieri, and R. Peroni, eds., *Studi die Paletnologia in onore di Salvatore M. Puglisi.* Roma. 591–615.

Kindt, J. 2015. "Oracular Shrines as Places of Religious Experience." In R. Raja and J. Rüpke, eds., *A Companion to the Archaeology of Religion in the Ancient World.* Malden, Mass. 268–78.

King, K. L. 2008. "Social and Theological Effects of Heresiological Discourse." In E. Iricinschi and H. M. Zellentin, eds., *Heresy and Identity in Late Antiquity*. Texts and Studies in Ancient Judaism 119. Tübingen. 28–49.

———. 2013. "Mary, Gospel of." *Encyclopedia of Ancient History* 8: 4337–38.

———. 2015. "Endings: The Gospel of Mark and the Gospel of Judas." In I. Ramelli and J. Perkins, eds., *Early Christian and Jewish Narrative: The Role of Religion in Shaping Narrative Forms*. Tübingen. 55–72.

Kinzig, W. 2004. *Harnack, Marcion und das Judentum nebst einer kommentierten Edition des Briefwechsels Adolf von Harnacks mit Houston Stewart Chamberlain*. Arbeiten zur Kirchen- und Theologiegeschichte 13. Leipzig.

Kippenberg, H., J. Rüpke, and K. v. Stuckrad, eds. 2009. *Europäische Religionsgeschichte: Ein mehrfacher Pluralismus*. 2 vols. Göttingen.

Kirkpatrick, J. 2013. "The Jews and Their God of Wine." *Archiv für Religiongeschichte* 15: 167–85.

Kleibrink, M. 2000. "The Miniature Votive Pottery Dedicated at the 'Laghetto del Monsignore', Campoverde." *Palaeohistoria* 39–40 (1997–98): 441–63.

Kleibrink, M., J. Kindberg Jacobsen, and S. Handberg. 2004. "Water for Athena: Votive Gifts at Lagaria (Timpone della Motta, Francavilla Marittima, Calabria)." *World Archaeology* 36 (1): 43–67.

Klinghardt, M. 2015. *Das älteste Evangelium und die Entstehung der kanonischen Evangelien*. 2 vols. Texte und Arbeiten zum neutestamentlichen Zeitalter 60,1–2. Tübingen.

Kloppenborg, J. S. 2006. "Associations in the Ancient World." In A. J. Levine, D.C.J. Allison, and J. D. Crossan, eds., *The Historical Jesus in Context*. Princeton Readings in Religions. Princeton. 323–38.

Kloppenborg, J. S., and S. G. Wilson, eds. 1996. *Voluntary Associations in the Graeco-Roman World*. London.

Klotz, D. 2012. *Caesar in the City of Amun: Egyptian Temple Construction and Theology in Roman Thebes*. Monographies Reine Élisabeth 15. Turnhout.

Knauer, G. N. 1964. *Die Aeneis und Homer: Studien zur poetischen Technik Vergils mit Listen der Homerzitate in der Aeneis*. Hypomnemata 7. Göttingen.

Knust, J. W., and Z. Várhelyi, eds. 2011. *Ancient Mediterranean Sacrifice*. New York.

Koch, G. 1993. *Sarkophage der römischen Kaiserzeit*. Darmstadt.

Koeppel, G. M. 1987. "Die historischen Reliefs der römischen Kaiserzeit V: Ara Pacis Augustae, Teil 1." *Bonner Jahrbücher* 187: 101–57, 54 ill.

———. 1988. "Die historischen Reliefs der römischen Kaiserzeit V: Ara Pacis Augustae Teil 2." *Bonner Jahrbücher* 188: 97–106.

Kolb, A. 1993. *Die kaiserliche Bauverwaltung in der Stadt Rom: Geschichte und Aufbau der cura operum publicorum unter dem Prinzipat*. Heidelberger Althistorische Beiträge und Epigraphische Studien 13. Stuttgart.

———. 1995. "Vereine 'kleiner Leute' und die kaiserliche Verwaltung." *ZPE* 107: 201–12.

Kolb, A., and J. Fugmann 2008. *Tod in Rom: Grabinschriften als Spiegel römischen Lebens*. Mainz.

König, J. 2006. "The Cynic and Christian Lives of Lucian's 'Peregrinus'." In B. McGing and J. Mossman, eds., *The Limits of Ancient Biography*. Swansea. 227–54.

———. 2011. "Competitiveness and Anti-Competitiveness in Philostratus' Lives of the Sophists." In N. Fisher and H. v. Wees, eds., *Competition in the Ancient World*. Swansea. 279–300.

Koschorke, A. 2012. *Wahrheit und Erfindung: Grundzüge einer Allgemeinen Erzähltheorie*. Frankfurt/Main.

Kotlinska-Toma, A. 2015. *Hellenistic Tragedy: Texts, Translations and a Critical Survey*. London.

Köves-Zulauf, T. 1990. *Römische Geburtsriten*. Zetemata 87. München.

Kowalzig, B. 2007. *Singing for the Gods: Performances of Myth and Ritual in Archaic and Classical Greece*. Oxford.

Kranemann, B., and J. Rüpke, eds. 2003. *Das Gedächtnis des Gedächtnisses: Zur Präsenz von Ritualen in beschreibenden und reflektierenden Texten*. Europäische Religionsgeschichte 2. Marburg.

Kratz, R. G. 2013. "Elephantine und Alexandria: Nichtbiblisches und biblisches Judentum in Ägypten." In T. Georges, F. Albrecht, and R. Feldmeier, eds., *Alexandria*. Tübingen. 193–208.

Krauskopf, I. 2009. "Etruskische Kultgeräte zwischen Griechenland und Rom: Einige Überlegungen." In S. Bruni, ed., *Etruria e Italia Preromana: studi in onore die Giovannangelo Camporeale* 2. Pisa. 501–506.

Krauss, F. B. 1930. *An Interpretation of the Omens, Portents, and Prodigies Recorded by Livy, Tacitus, and Suetonius*. Philadelphia.

Kröger, H. 1940. *Die Prodigien bei Tacitus*. Diss. Münster.Krostenko, B. A. 2000. "Beyond (Dis)belief: Rhetorical Form and Religious Symbol in Cicero's *de Divinatione*." *Transactions and Proceedings of the American Philological Association* 130: 353–91.

Krueger, D. 2004. *Writing and Holiness: The Practice of Authorship in the Early Christian East*. Divinations. Philadelphia.

———. 2010. "Early Byzantine Historiography and Hagiography as Different Modes of Christian Practice " In A. Papaconstantinou, ed., *Writing "True Stories": Historians and Hagiographers in the Late Antique and Medieval Near East*. Turnhout. 13–30.

Kuhfeldt, O. 1882. *De Capitoliis imperii Romani*. Berlin.

Kühn, W. 2008. "Se connaître soi-même: la contribution de Plotin à la compréhension du moi." In G. Aubry, ed., *Le moi et l'intériorité*. Textes et traditions 17. Paris. 127–49.

Kult 1997. *der Vorzeit: Opfergaben—Opferplätze—Opferbrauchtum*. Innsbruck.

Kyle, D. G. 1998. *Spectacles of Death in Ancient Rome*. London.

Kyrieleis, H. 2008. "Sphyrelata: Überlegungen zur frürharchaischen Bronze-Großplastik in Olympia." *Mitteilungen des deutschen archäologischen Instituts, Athen* 123: 177–98.

Lacam, J.-C. 2008. "Le sacrifice du chien dans les communautés grecques, étrusques, italiques et romaines: Approche comparatiste." *MEFRA* 120 (1): 29–80.

———. 2010a. "Les Jupiter infernaux: Variations divines en terres italienne et sicilienne (époques pré-romaine et romaine)." *Archiv für Religiongeschichte* 12: 197–242.

———. 2010b. *Variations rituelles: Les pratiques religieuses en Italie centrale et méridionale au temps de la deuxième guerre punique*. Collection de l'École Française de Rome 430. Roma.

———. 2011. "Le 'prêtre dansur' de Gubbio: Étude ombrienne (IIIe–IIe s. av. J.-C.)." *Revue de l'histoire des religions* 228 (1): 5–26.

Lackner, E.-M. 2013. "Arx und Capitolinischer Kult in den Latinischen und Bürgerkolonien Italiens als Spiegel römischer Religionspolitik." In M. Jehne, B. Linke, and J. Rüpke, eds., *Religiöse Vielfalt und soziale Integration: Die Bedeutung der Religion für die kulturelle Identität und politische Stabilität im republikanischen Italien.* Studien zur Alten Geschichte 17. Heidelberg. 163–201.

Laforge, M.-O. 2009. *La religion privée à Pompéi,* Études 7. Naples.

Lamotte, H. 2010. "Le rôle de l'épitaphe das la commémoration des enfants défunts: l'exemple des carmina Latina epigraphica paiens." In A.-M. Guimier-Sorbets, and Y. Morizot, eds., *L'Enfant et la mort dans l'Antiquité I: Nouvelles recherches dans les nécropoles grecques. Le singalement des tombes d'enfants.* Paris. 363–96.

Lane Fox, R. 1988. *Pagans and Christians in the Mediterranean World from the Second Century AD to the Conversion of Constantine.* London.

Laneri, N. 2007. *Performing Death: Social Analyses of Funerary Traditions in the Ancient Near East and Mediterranean.* Oriental Institute Seminars 3. Chicago.

———. 2011. "Dall'archeologia funeraria alla *new archaelogy.*" In Laneri, ed., *Archaelogia della morte.* Roma. 20–31.

Lange, C. H., and F. J. Vervaet, eds. 2014. *The Roman Republican Triumph: Beyond the Spectacle,* Analecta Romana Instituti Danici Supplementum 45. Roma.

Langslow, D. 2012. "Integration, Identity, and Language Shift: Strengths and Weaknesses of the 'Linguistic' Evidence." In S. T. Roselaar, ed., *Processes of Integration and Identity Formation in the Roman Republic.* Mnemosyne Suppl.: History and Archaeology of Classical Antiquity 342. Leiden. 289–309.

Lapatin, K. 2010. "New Statues for Old Gods." In J. N. Bremmer and A. Erskine, eds., *The Gods of Ancient Greece: Identities and Transformations.* Edinburgh Leventis Studies 5. Edinburgh. 142–51.

Lapin, H. 2012. *Rabbis as Romans: The Rabbinic Movement in Palestine, 100–400 CE.* New York.

Larcher, A. 1990. "Gemalte Götterstatuen—Ein Beitrag zur Ikonographie der pompejanischen Wandmalerei." In B. Otto and F. Ehrl, eds., *ECHO—Beiträge zur Archäologie des mediterranen und alpinen Raumes Vol. 27.* Innsbruck.

Latour, B. 2005a. *Reassembling the Social: An Introduction to Actor-Network-Theory.* Clarendon Lectures in Management Studies. Oxford, New York.

———. 2005b. *Reassembling the Social: An Introduction to Actor-Network-Theory.* Pb. 2007 ed. Oxford.

Latteur, O. 2011. "Le culte de Mithra a-t-il été intégré dans certains panthéons?" *Latomus* 70 (3): 741–54.

Lazenby, J. 1991. "The Killing Zone." In V. D. Hanson, ed., *Hoplites: The Classical Greek Battle Experience.* London. 87–109.

Lebek, W. D. 1990. "Welttrauer um Germanicus: Das neugefundene Originaldokument und die Darstellung des Tacitus." *Antike und Abendland* 36: 93–102.

Lehoux, D. 2007. *Astronomy, Weather, and Calendars in the Ancient World: Parapegmata and Related Texts in Classical and Near-Eastern Societies.* Cambridge.

Leigh, M. 2005. *Comedy and the Rise of Rome.* Oxford.

Lembke, K. 1994. *Das Iseum Campense in Rom: Studie über den Isiskult unter Domitian.* Archäologie und Geschichte 3. Heidelberg.

Lemos, I. 2000. "Songs for Heroes: The Lack of Images in Early Greece." In N. K. Rutter and B. A. Sparkes, eds., *Word and Image in Ancient Greece* 1. Edinburgh Leventis Studies. Edinburgh. 11–21.

Lenski, N. 2016. *Constantine and the Cities: Imperial Authority and Civic Politics, Empire and After.* Philaldelphia.

Leonhard, C. 2017. "Establishing Short-Term Communities in Eucharistic Celebrations of Antiquity." *Religion in the Roman Empire* 3 (1): 66-86.

Leppin, H. 1992. *Histrionen: Untersuchungen zur sozialen Stellung von Bühnenkünstlern im Westen des Römischen Reiches zur Zeit der Republik und des Principats.* Antiquitas R. 1 (Abhandlungen zur Alten Geschichte) 41. Bonn.

———. 2008. "Zum Wandel des spätantiken Heidentums." *Millennium* 4: 59–81.

———. 2012. "Christianisierungen im Römischen Reich: Überlegungen zum Begriff und zur Phasenbildung." *Zeitschrift für Antikes Christentum* 16 (2): 247–78.

Lersch, L. 1843. *Antiquitates Vergilianae ad vitam populi Romani descriptae.* Bonn.

Leutzsch, M. 1989. *Die Wahrnehmung sozialer Wirklichkeit im "Hirten des Hermas."* Forschungen zur Religion und Literatur des Alten und Neuen Testaments 150. Göttingen.

Levene, D. S. 1993. *Religion in Livy.* Mnemosyne Suppl. 127. Leiden.

Ley, A., and R. Struß. 1982. "Gegenarchitektur: Das Heiligtum der Fortuna Primigenia als Symbol der politischen Selbstbehauptung Praenestes." *Hephaistos* 4: 117–38.

Libitina. 2004. *Libitina e dintorni: Libitina e luci sepolcrali; le leges libitinariae campane; Iura sepulcrorum; vecchie e nuove iscrizioni. Atti dell'XI Rencontre Franco-Italienne sur l'Epigraphie.* Libitina 3. Roma.

LiDonnici, L. R. 1995. *The Epidaurian Miracle Inscriptions: Text, Translation, and Commentary.* Atlanta, Ga.

Liebenam, W. 1964. *Zur Geschichte und Organisation des römischen Vereinswesens: Drei Untersuchungen.* Aalen.

Lieu, J. M. 2004. *Christian Identity in the Jewish and Graeco-Roman World.* Oxford.

Lightfoot, J. L. 2007. "The Apology of Ps. Meliton." *Studi epigrafici e lingustici sul Vicino Oriente antico* 24: 59–110.

Lightstone, J. N. 2002. *Mishnah and the Social Formation of the Early Rabbinic Guild: A Socio-Rhetorical Approach.* Studies in Christianity and Judaism 11. Waterloo, Ont.

Linderski, J. 1986. "The Augural Law." *ANRW* II.16,3: 2146–312.

———. 2000. "Penates (Di Penates)." *Neuer Pauly* 9: 514–16.

Lindner, M. M. 2015. *Portraits of the Vestal Virgins, Priestesses of Ancient Rome.* Ann Arbor.

Linke, B. 1995. *Von der Verwandtschaft zum Staat: Die Entstehung staatlicher Organisationsformen in der römischen Frühgeschichte.* Stuttgart.

———. 2003. "Emotionalität und Status: zur gesellschaftlichen Funktion von supplicationes und lectisternia in der römischen Republik " In A. Kneppe and D. Metzler, eds., *Die emotionale Dimension antiker Religiösität.* Forschungen zur Anthropologie und Religionsgeschichte 37. Münster. 65–86.

———. 2009. "Jupiter und die Republik: Die Entstehung des europäischen Republikanismus in der Antike." *Chiron* 39: 339–58.

Liou-Gille, B. 2004. "Comment cinquante années de découvertes archéologiques ont permis une interprétation plus riche et plus précise de la tradition annalistique concernant la Rome archaique (II partie)." *Euphrosyne* 32: 243–63.

Lipsett, B. D. 2011. *Desiring Conversion : Hermas, Thecla, Aseneth*. New York.

Liverani, P., and G. Spinola. 2010. *Die Nekropolen im Vatikan*. From the Ital. ed., Monumenta Vaticana selecta. Città del Vaticano/Stuttgart.

Lobüscher, T. 2002. *Tempel- und Theaterbau in den tres Galliae und den germanischen Provinzen: Ausgewählte Aspekte*, Kölner Studien zur Archäologie der römischen Provinzen 6. Rahden.

Löhr, W. 2012. "Christian Gnostics and Greek Philosophy in the Second Century." *Early Christianity* 3: 349–77.

Lomas, K. 1997. "The Idea of a City: Élite Ideology and the Evolution of Urban Form in Italy, 200 BC–AD 100." In H. M. Parkins, ed., *Roman Urbanism: Beyond the Consumer City*. London. 21–41.

Lombardi, N. 2012. "[Plutarco, Vite parallele: Numa] Introduzione." In B. Scardigli, ed., *Plutarco, Licurgo e Numa*. Milano. 383–411.

Long, A. A. 2010. "Cosmic Craftsmanship in Plato and Stoicism." In R. D. Mohr and B. M. Sattler, eds., *One Book, the Whole Universe: Plato's Timaeus Today*. Las Vegas, Nev. 37–53.

Lonis, R. 1979. *Guerre et religion en Grèce a l'époque classique: Recherches sur les rites, les dieux, l'idéologie de la victoire*, Centre de recerces d'histoire ancienne 33=Annales littéraires de l'Université de Besançon 238. Paris.

Lonsdale, S. H. 1993. *Dance and Ritual Play in Greek Religion*. Baltimore.

Lønstrup Dal Santo, G. 2012. "Bishop and Believers—Patrons and Viewers: Appropriating the Roman Patron Saints Peter and Paul in Constantinople." In S. Birk and B. Poulsen, eds., *Patrons and Viewers in Late Antiquity*. Aarhus. 237–57.

López-Bertran, M. 2011. "Where Are the Priests? Ritual Mastery in Punic Shrines." In A. Chaniotis, ed., *Ritual Dynamics in the Ancient Mediterranean: Agency, Emotion, Gender, Representation*. Heidelberger althistorische Beiträge und epigraphische Studien 49. Stuttgart. 43–54.

López Castro, J. L. 2005. "Aristocracia fenicia y aristocracia autóctonas: Relaciones de intercambio." *Anejos de Archivo Español de Arqueología* 35: 405–22.

López-Ruiz, C. 2013. "Sacrifice and the City: Administration and Religion in the Eastern Mediterranean Bronze Age." *Asdiwal* 8: 59–82.

Lorenz, K. 2008. *Bilder machen Räume: Mythenbilder in pompeianischen Häusern*. Image & Context 5. Berlin.

Lorusso, P., and A. Affuso. 2008. "Anthropomorphic Images of the Early and Middle Neolithic Apulo-Lucano: Aspects and Interpretative Problems." In O. Menozzi, M. L. Di Marzio, and D. Fossataro, eds., *SOMA 2005: Proceedings of the IX Symposium on Mediterranean Archaeology, Chieti (Italy), 24–26 February 2005*. BAR International Series 1739. Oxford. 97–103.

Lo Schiavo, F. 2002. "Uomini e dei: Ripostigli ed offerte nella Sardegna nuragica." *Rendiconti della pontificia Accademia Romana d'Archeologia* 75: 3–32.

Losehand, J. 2007. *Häuser für die Herrscher Roms und Athens?—Überlegungen zu Funktion und Bedeutung von Gebäude F auf der Athener Agora und der Regia auf dem Forum Romanum* 42. Antiquitates: Archäologische Forschungsergebnisse. Hamburg.

Lott, J. B. 2004. *The Neighborhoods of Augustan Rome.* Cambridge.

Lozano, F. 2011. "The Creation of Imperial Gods: Not Only Imposition versus Spontaneity." In P. P. Iossif, A. S. Chankowski, and C. C. Lorber, eds., *More Than Men, Less Than Gods: Studies on Royal Cult and Imperial Worship—Proceeding of the International Colloquium Organized by the Belgian School at Athens (November 1–2, 2007)* 51. Studia Hellenistica. Leuven. 474—519.

Lubtchansky, N. 2010. "Les petits chevaux de Pometia: Les significations du programme iconographique des frieses de Caprifico." In P. Domenico, ed., *Il Tempio Arcaico di Caprifico di Torrecchia (Cisterna di Latina) I Materiali e il Contesto.* Roma. 133–71.

Lucarelli, U. 2007. *Exemplarische Vergangenheit: Valerius Maximus und die Konstruktion des sozialen Raumes in der frühen Kaiserzeit.* Hypomnemata 172. Göttingen.

Luck, G. 1992. *Arcana mundi: Magic and the Occult in the Greek and Roman Worlds: A Collection of Ancient Texts.* Philadelphia.

Luckmann, T. 1991. *Die unsichtbare Religion.* Frankfurt a. M.

Luijendijk, A. 2008. *Greetings in the Lord: Early Christians and the Oxyrhynchus Papyri,* Harvard Theological Studies 60. Cambridge, Mass.

Lulof, P. S. 1993. "Reconstruction and Architectural Setting of Large Terracotta Statues in Late Archaic Central Italy: The Case of Satricum." In E. Rystedt, C. Wikander, and Ö. Wikander, eds., *Deliciae Fictiles—Proceedings of the First International Conference on Central Italic Architectural Terracottas at the Swedish Institute in Rome, 10–12 December, 1990.* Stockholm. 277–86.

———. 2006. " 'Roofs from the South': Campanian Architectural Terracottas in Satricum." In I. Edlund-Berry, G. Greco, and J. Kenfield, eds., *Deliciae Fictiles* III: *Architectural Terracottas in Ancient Italy: New Discoveries and Interpretations.* Oxford. 235–42.

———. 2011. "The Late Archaic Miracle. Roof Decoration in Central Italy between 510 and 450 B.C." In P. Lulof and C. Rescigno, eds., *Deliciae Fictiles* IV—*Architectural Terracottas in Ancient Italy—Images of Gods, Monsters and Heroes.* Oxford. 23–31.

Lundgreen, C. 2011. *Regelkonflikte in der römischen Republik: Geltung und Gewichtung von Normen in politischen Entscheidungsprozessen,* Historia-Einzelschriften 221. Stuttgart.

Lundhaug, H. and L. Jenott. 2015. *The Monastic Origins of the Nag Hammadi Codices,* Studien und Texte zu Antike und Christentum 97. Tübingen.

Ma, J. 2010. "Autour des balles de fronde 'camiréennes'." *Chiron* 40: 155–73.

———. 2012. "Epigraphy and the Display of Authority." *Proceedings of the British Academy* 177: 133–58.

———. 2013. *Statues and Cities: Honorific Portraits and Civic Identity in the Hellenistic World.* Oxford Studies in Ancient Culture and Representation. Oxford.

MacCormack, S. G. 1981. *Art and Ceremony in Late Antiquity.* Berkeley.

McIntyre, Gwynaeth. 2016. *A Family of Gods: The Worship of the Imperial Family in the Latin West*. Ann Arbor.

Madigan, B. 2013. *The Ceremonial Sculptures of the Roman Gods*, Monumenta Graeca et Romana 20. Leiden.

Maggiani, A. 1997. "Réflexions sur la religion étrusque 'primitive': de l'époque villanovienne à l'époque archaique." In *Les plus religieux des hommes: état de la recherche sur la religion étrusque*. Paris. 431–47.

———. 2000. "Tipologia tomabale e società: Chiusi in età orientalizzante." *Annali della Fondazione per il Museo Claudio Faina* 7: 249–75.

Magny, A. 2006. "Prophyre, Hippolyte et Origène commenten sur Daniel." In I. H. Henderson and G. S. Oegema, eds. *The Changing Face of Judaism, Christianity, and Other Greco-Roman Religions in Antiquity, Jüdische Schriften aus hellenistisch-römischer Zeit.* Studien zu den Jüdischen Schriften aus hellenistisch-römischer Zeit 2. Gütersloh. 427–51.

Maier, H. O. 2013. *Picturing Paul in Empire: Imperial Image, Text and Persuasion in Colossians, Ephesians and the Pastoral Epistles*. London.

———. 2015. "From Material Place to Imagined Space: Emergent Christian Community as Thirdspace in the 'Shepherd of Hermas'." In M.R.C. Grundeken and J. Verheyden, eds., *Early Christian Communities between Ideal and Reality*. WUNT. Tübingen. 143–60.

Malavolta, M. 1996. "I ludi delle feriae a Roma." In A. Pasqualini, ed., *Alba Longa: Mito, storia, archeologia*. Studi pubblicati dall'Istituti Italiano per la Storia Antica 60. Roma. 255–73.

Malina, B. J. 2002. *Die Offenbarung des Johannes: Sternvisionen und Himmelsreisen*. Stuttgart.

Mantle, I. C. 2002. "The Roles of Children in Roman Religion." *Greece & Rome* 49 (1): 85–106.

Manuwald, G. 2001. *Fabulae praetextae: Spuren einer literarischen Gattung der Römer*, Zetemata 108. München.

———. 2011. *Roman Republican Theatre*. Cambridge.

Marcattili, F. 2005. "Altare (mondo italico)." *Thesaurus Cultus et Rituum Antiquorum* 4: 171–73.

———. 2015. "L'altare del Vicus Sandaliarius e il culto della Fortuna Augusta. Da Roma a Pompei nel 2 a.C." *Vesuviana* 7: 35–54.

Marchesi, M. 2011. *Le sculture di età orientalizzante in Etruria padana: Cathaloghi delle collezioni del Museo civicoarcheologico di Bologna*. Bologna.

Marcillet-Jaubert, J. 1987. "Sur des flamines perpétuels de Numide." *ZPE* 69: 207–23.

Marcos, M. 2009. "'He forced with gentleness': Emperor Julian's Attitude to Relgious Coercion." *Antiquité Tardive* 17: 191–204.

Marcus, J. 2011. "Israel and the Church in the Exegetical Writings of Hippolytus." *Journal of Biblical Literature* 130 (1): 385–406.

Marín Ceballos, M. C., and M. Belén. 2005. "El fenómeno orientalizante en su vertiente religiosa." *Anejos de Archivo Español de Arqueología* 35: 441–66.

Markley, J. R. 2013. *Peter—Apocalyptic Seer.* Wissenschaftliche Untersuchungen zum Neuen Testament 348. Tübingen.

Markschies, C. 1997. "Innerer Mensch." *RAC* 18: 266–312.

———. 1999. "Origenes und die Kommentierung des paulinischen Römerbriefs: Bemerkungen zur Rezension von antiken Kommentartechniken im Christentum des dritten Jahrhunderts und zu ihrer Vorgeschichte." In G. W. Most, ed., *Commentaries—Kommentare*. Göttingen. 66–94.

Marroni, E. 2010. *I culti dell'Esquilino*, Archaeologia perusina 17. Roma.

Martens, M. 2015. "Communal Dining: Making Things Happen." In R. Raja and J. Rüpke., eds., *A Companion to the Archaeology of Religion in the Ancient World*. Malden, Mass. 167–80.

Martens, M., and G. d. Boe, eds. 2004. *Roman Mithraism: The Evidence of the Small Finds*, Archeologie in Vlaanderen 4. Brussels.

Martin, J. 1995. "The Roman Empire: Domination and Integration." *Journal of Institutional and Theoretical Economics* 151/4: 714–24.

Martzavou, P. 2012a. "Dream, Narrative, and the Construction of Hope in the 'Healing Miracles' of Epidauros." In A. Chaniotis, ed., *Unveiling Emotions: Sources and Methods for the Study of Emotions in the Greek World*. Heidelberger althistorische Beiträge und epigraphische Studien 52. Stuttgart. 177–204.

———. 2012b. "Isis Aretalogies, Initiations, and Emotions: The Isis Aretalogies as a Source for the Study of Emotions." In A. Chaniotis, ed., *Unveiling Emotions: Sources and Methods for the Study of Emotions in the Greek World*. Heidelberger althistorische Beiträge und epigraphische Studien 52. Stuttgart. 267–91.

Marx-Wolf, H. 2014. "Phythagoras the Theurgist." In J. D. Rosenblum, L. C. Vuong, and N. P. DesRosiers, eds., *Religious Competition in the Third Century CE: Jews, Christians, and the Greco-Roman World. Journal of Ancient Judaism:* Suppl. 15. Göttingen. 32–38.

Massa, F. 2013. "Écrire pour Dionysos: la présence de textes écrits dans les rituels dionysiaques." *Revue de l'histoire des religions* 230 (2): 20–232.

———. 2014. *Tra la vigna e la croce: Dioniso nei discorsi letterari e figurativi cristiani (II-IV secolo)*, PawB 47. Stuttgart.

Mastrangelo, M. 2008. *The Roman Self in Late Antiquity: Prudentius and the Poetics of the Soul*. Baltimore.

Mastrocinque, A. 1999. "Laren." *Neuer Pauly* 6: 1147–50.

———. 2005. "Cosmologia e impero in Giuliano l'Apostata." *Klio* 87 (1): 154–76.

———. 2009. "Le gemme votive." In J.-P. Brun, ed., *Artisanats antiques d'Italie et de Gaule: Mélanges offerts à Maria Francesca Buonaiuto*. Collection du Centre Jean Bérard 32. Naples. 53–65.

Masuzawa, T. 2000. "The Production of 'Religion' and the Task of the Scholar: Russell McCutcheon among the Smiths." *Culture and Religion* 1 (1): 123–30.

———. 2005. *The Invention of World Religions: Or, How European Universalism Was Preserved in the Language of Pluralism*. Chicago.

Matasović, R. 2010. "The Etymology of Latin Focus and the Devoicing of Final Stops before *s in Proto-Indo-European." *Historische Sprachforschung / Historical Linguistics* 123: 212–16.

Mattern, T. 2000. "Der Magna-Mater-Tempel und die augusteische Architektur in Rom." *Mitteilungen des deutschen archäologischen Instituts, Rom* 107: 141–53.

Matthews, J. 1992. "The Poetess Proba and Fourth-Century Rome: Questions of Interpretation." In M. Christol, ed., *Institutions, société et vie politique dans l'empire romain au IVe siècle ap. J.-C.* Roma. 277–304.

Matthey, P. 2011. "'Chut!' Le signe d'Harpocrate et l'invitation au silence." In F. Prescendi and Y. Volokhine, eds., *Dans le laboratoire de l'historien des religions.* Geneva. 541–65.

Mauss, M. 1925. "Essai sur le don." *Année sociologique* ns 1: 30–186.

———. 2002. *The Gift: The Form and Reason for Exchange in Archaic Societies.* Routledge Classics. London.

Maye, H. 2010. "Was ist eine Kulturtechnik?" *Zeitschrift für Medien- und Kulturforschung* 1 (1): 121–35.

Mayr, J. 1955. "Der Computus ecclesiasticus." *Zeitschrift für Katholische Theologie* 77: 301–30.

Mazarakis Ainian, A. J. 1988. "Early Greek Temples: Their Origin and Function." In R. Hägg, N. Marinatos, and G. C. Nordquist, eds., *Early Greek Cult Practice: Proceedings of the Fifth International Symposium at the Swedish Institute at Athens, 26–29 June, 1986.* Stockholm. 105–19.

———. 1997. *From Rulers' Dwellings to Temples: Architecture, Religion and Society in Early Iron Age Greece (1100–700 B.C.).* Studies in Mediterranean Archaeology 121. Jonsered.

Mazzocchi, A. 1997. "Bronzetti votivi a figura umana di età arcaica di Roma e del Lazio." In *Miscellanea etrusco italica* 2. QuadAEI 26. Roma.

McCane, B. R. 2007. "Jewish Ossuaries of the Early Roman Period: Continuity and Change in Death Ritual." In D. R. a. C.T.M.C. Edwards, ed., *The Archaeology of Difference: Gender, Ethnicity, Class and the "Other" in Antiquity—Studies in Honor of Eric M. Meyers.* Boston. 235–42.

McCormick, M. 1987. *Eternal Victory: Triumphal Rulership in Late Antiquity, Byzantium, and the Early Medieval West.* Cambridge.

McCutcheon, R. T. 1997. *Manufacturing Religion: The Discourse on sui generis Religion and the Politics of Nostalgia.* New York.

McDonough, C. M. 2004. "The Hag and the Household Gods: Silence, Speech, and the Family in Mid-February (Ovid, *Fasti* 2.533–638)." *Classical Philology* 99: 354–69.

McGing, B., and J. Mossman, eds. 2006. *The Limits of Ancient Biography.* Swansea.

McGuire, M. B. 2008. *Lived Religion: Faith and Practice in Everyday Life.* Oxford.

McLaren, J. S. 2013. "The Jews in Rome during the Flavian period." *Antichthon* 47: 156–72.

Meadows, A. and J. Williams. 2001. "Moneta and the Monuments: Coinage and Politics in Republican Rome." *Journal of Roman Studies* 91: 27–49.

Meena, S. S. 2013. "Maritime Trade with Rome in Ancient India." In R. Pande, ed., *Trade Routes and Trade Centers in Ancient and Medieval India.* Jaipur, India. 46–49.

Meier, M. 2009. "Die Abschaffung der venationes durch Anastasios im Jahr 499 und die 'kosmische' Bedeutung des Hippodroms." In H. Beck and H.-U. Wiemer, eds., *Feiern und Erinnern: Geschichtsbilder im Spiegel antiker Feste.* Studien zur Alten Geschichte 12. Berlin. 203–32.

Meijer, F. 2010. *Chariot Racing in the Roman Empire*. L. Waters, trans. Baltimore.

Meissner, N. 2004. "Die Inszenierung des Jenseits: Die Reaktion in Etrurien auf den sog. Priestersarkophag in Tarquinia." In R. Bol and D. Kreikenbom, eds., *Sepulkral- und Votivdenkmäler östlicher Mittelmeergebiete (7. Jh. v. Chr.–1. Jh. v. Chr.): Kulturbegegnungen im Spannungsfeld von Akzeptanz und Resistenz*. Möhnesee. 183–92, pls. 77–81.

Menichetti, M. 2005. "Altare (romano-repubblicano)." *Thesaurus Cultus et Rituum Antiquorum* 4: 173–76.

Merlat, P. 1960. *Jupiter Dolichenus: Essai d'interprétation et de synthèse*. Publications de l'Institut d'art et d'archéologie de l'Université de Paris 5. Paris.

Meuli, K. 1946. "Griechische Opferbräuche." *Phyllobolia für Peter von der Mühll zum 60. Geburtstag*. Basel. 185–288.

Meusel, E. 1923. *De sacris Tiburtinis et Praenestinis*, Diss. Halle (Wissowa).

Meyboom, P. G. 1995. *The Nile Mosaic of Palestrina: Early Evidence of Egyptian Religion in Italy*. Religions in the Graeco-Roman World 121. Leiden.

Meyboom, P. G., and M. J. Versluys. 2000. "Les scènes dites nilotiques et les cultes Isiaques: une interprétation contextuelle." In L. Bricault, ed., *De Memphis à Rome. Actes du Ier Colloque international sur les études isiaques, Poitiers, Futuroscope, 8–10 avril 1999*. Leiden. 111–27.

Meyer, B. 2008. "Media and the Senses in the Making of Religious Experience: An Introduction." *Material Religion* 4: 124–35.

Meyer-Zwiffelhoffer, E. 2011. "Mala desidia iudicum? Zur Rolle der Provinzstatthalter bei der Unterdrückung paganer Kulte (von Constantin bis Theodosius II.)." In J. Hahn, ed., *Spätantiker Staat und religiöser Konflikt: imperiale und lokale Verwaltung und die Gewalt gegen Heiligtümer*. Millennium-Studien 34. Berlin. 93–131.

Meyers, G. E. 2012. "Introduction: The Experience of Monumentality in Etruscan and Early Roman Architecture." In M. L. Thomas and G. E. Meyers, eds., *Monumentality in Etruscan and Early Roman Architecture: Ideology and Innovation*. Austin. 1–20.

Meyer-Zwiffelhoffer, E. 2011. "Mala desidia iudicum? Zur Rolle der Provinzstatthalter bei der Unterdrückung paganer Kulte (von Constantin bis Theodosius II.)." In J. Hahn, ed., *Spätantiker Staat und religiöser Konflikt: imperiale und lokale Verwaltung und die Gewalt gegen Heiligtümer*. Millennium-Studien 34. Berlin. 93–131.

Miano, D. 2009. "Loci memoriae: Spazio e memoria nella Roma repubblicana." *Mediterraneo antico* 12 (1–2): 361–80.

———. 2011. *Monimenta: Aspetti storico-culturali della memoria nella Roma mediorepubblicana*. Mos maiorum 6. Roma.

Michaels, A. 2010. "The Grammar of Rituals." In A. Michaels et al. (eds.), *Grammars and Morphologies of Ritual Practices in Asia*. Ritual Dynamics and the Science of Ritual 1. Wiesbaden. 9–28.

Michel, S. 2000. *Magische Gemmen im Britischen Museum*. London.

———. 2001. *Die magischen Gemmen im Britischen Museum 2*. London.

Mielsch, H. 2009. *Überlegungen zum Wandel der Bestattungsformen in der römischen Kaiserzeit*. Paderborn.

Mikalson, J. D. 2010. *Greek Popular Religion in Greek Philosophy*. Oxford.

Millar, F. 2010. *Religion, Language and the Community in the Roman Near East: Constantine to Muhammad.* Oxford.

Miller, P. C. 1988. " 'All the Words were Frightful': Salvation by Dreams in the 'Shepherd of Hermas'." *Vigiliae Christianae* 42: 327–38.

Mitchell, R. E. 1984. "Roman History, Roman Law, and Roman Priests: The Common Ground." *University of Illinois Law Review* 1984, 3: 541–60.

Mitchell, S. 1999. "The Cult of Theos Hypsistos between Pagans, Jews, and Christians." In P. Athanassiadi and M. Frede, eds., *Pagan Monotheism in Late Antiquity.* Oxford. 81–148.

———. 2010. "Further Thoughts on the Cult of Theos Hypsistos." In S. Mitchell and P. van Nuffelen, eds., *One God: Pagan Monotheism in the Roman Empire.* Cambridge. 167–208.

Mitchell, S., and P. van Nuffelen, eds. 2010. *One God: Pagan Monotheism in the Roman Empire.* Cambridge.

Mittag, P. F. 2012. *Römische Medaillons: Caesar bis Hadrian,* 2nd. rev. ed. Stuttgart.

Moebius, S., and C. Papilloud, eds. 2006. *Gift: Marcel Mauss' Kulturtheorie der Gabe.* Wiesbaden.

Mol, E. 2012. "The Perception of Egypt in Networks of Being and Becoming: A Thing Theory Approach to Egyptianising Objects in Roman Domestic Contexts." In A. Bokern et al., eds., *TRAC 2012: Proceedings of the Twenty-Second Annual Theoretical Roman Archaeology Conference.* Oxford. 117–31.

———. 2015. "Romanising Oriental Cults? A Cognitive Approach to Alterity and Religious Experience in the Roman Cults of Isis." In A. Nikoloska and S. Müskens, eds., *Romanising Oriental Gods? Religious Transformations in the Balkan Provinces in the Roman Period: New Finds and Novel Perspectives.* Skopje. 89–111.

Möller, A., and J. Rüpke. 2002. "Zeitrechnung I. Allgemein. V. Klassische Antike." *Neue Pauly* 12/2: 717–19, 23–24.

Momigliano, A. 1987. "Ancient Biography and the Study of Religion in the Roman Empire." In A. Momigliano, ed., *Ottavo contributo alla storia degli studi classici e del mondo antico.* Roma. 193–210.

———. 1992a. "Men and Women in Roman Religion." *Nono contributo alla storia degli studi classici e del mondo antico:* 577–91.

———. 1992b. "Some Preliminary Remarks on the 'Religious Opposition' to the Roman Empire." *Nono contributo alla storia degli studi classici e del mondo antico:* 681–99.

Mommsen, T. 1905. "Zwei Sepulcralreden aus der Zeit Augusts und Hadrians." In T. Mommsen, ed., *Gesammelte Schriften* 1: *Juristische Schriften* 1. Berlin. 194–240.

Monnot, G. 2003. "Les marcionites dans l'hérésiographie musulmane." In A. von Harnack, *Marcion, l'évangile du Dieu étranger: Contribution à l'histoire de la fondation de l'Église catholique.* B. Lauret, trans. Patrimoines, christianisme. Paris. 403-17.

Moormann, E. M. 2011. *Divine Interiors: Mural Paintings in Greek and Roman Sanctuaries.* Amsterdam Archaeological Studies 16. Amsterdam.

Mora, F. 1990. *Prosopografia Isiaca* 2: *Prosopografia storica e statistica del culto Isiaco.* EPRO 113. Leiden.

———. 1995. *Il pensiero storico-religioso antico: Autori greci e Roma* 1: *Dionigi d'Alicarnasso.* Roma.

Morandi, A. 1987. "La Tomba degli Scudi di Tarquinia: Contributo epigrafico per l'esegesi dei soggetti." *MEFRA* 99 (1): 95–110.

Morciano, M. M. 2009. "Il culto capitolini nella sfera del privato." *Mitteilungen des Deutschen Archäologischen Instituts. Römische Abteilung* 115: 57–91.

Moreschini, C. 2014. *[Tertullianus] Contro Marcione: Libri I—III, 1=Adversus Marcionem*, Scrittori cristiani dell'Africa romana: edizione latino-italiana 3,1. Roma.

Morgan, C. 2009. "The Early Iron Age." In K. A. Raaflaub and H. van Wees, ed., *A Companion to Archaic Greece*. Blackwell Companions to the Ancient World. Malden, Mass. 43–63.

Morgan, T. 2005. "Eusebius of Caesarea and Christian Historiography." *Athenaeum* 93 (1): 193–208.

———. 2007. *Popular Morality in the Early Roman Empire*. Cambridge.

———. 2015. "Living with the Gods in Fables of the Early Roman Empire." *Religion in the Roman Empire* 1 (3): 378–402.

Morris, I. 2009. "The Eighth-Century Revolution." In K. A. Raaflaub and H. van Wees, eds., *A Companion to Archaic Greece*. Blackwell Companions to the Ancient World. Malden, Mass. 64–80.

Morvillez, E. 2016. "Le jardin privé conserve-t-il dans l'Antiquité tardive une forme de sacralité paienne?" In Y. Lafond and V. Michel, eds., *Espaces sacrés dans la Méditerranée antique: Actes du colloque des 13 et 14 octobre 2011, Université de Poitiers*. Rennes. 317–45.

Mosshammer, A. A. 2008. *The Easter Computus and the Origins of the Christian Era*. Oxford.

Mouritsen, H. 2011. *The Freedman in the Roman World*. Cambridge.

Mowat, C. 2016. "A Study on Spontaneity: Some Notes on the Divinatory Handbook P.Ryl. 28." *Religion in the Roman Empire* 2 (3): 415–40.

Mratschek, S. 2010. "Zirkulierende Bibliotheken: Medien der Wissensvermittlung und christliche Netzwerke bei Paulinus von Nola." In J. Desmulliez, ed., *L'étude des correspondances dans le monde romain de l'Antiquité classique*. Collection UL3. Travaux & recherche. Lille. 325–50.

Muehlberger, E. 2013. *Angels in Late Ancient Christianity*. Oxford.

Mueller, H.-F. 2002. *Roman Religion in Valerius Maximus*. London.

Müller, R. J. 1993. "Überlegungen zur Ἱερὰ Ἀναγραφή des Euhemeros von Messene." *Hermes* 121: 276–300.

Müller-Wille, M. 1999. *Opferkulte der Germanen und Slawen*. Archäologie in Deutschland: Sonderheft 1999. Darmstadt.

Mulryan, M. 2013. "Religion on the Ground: Rome and Constantinople: A Comparative Topographical Study." In R. Alston, O. M. Van Nijf, and C. G. Williamson, eds., *Cults, Creeds and Identities in the Greek City after the Classical Age*. Groningen-Royal Holloway Studies on the Greek City after the Classical Age. Leuven, Paris, Walpole, Mass. 331–52.

Mulsow, M. 2012. *Prekäres Wissen: Eine andere Ideengeschichte der Frühen Neuzeit*. Berlin.

Murray, M. 2007. "The Magical Female in Graeco-Roman Rabbinic Literature." *Religion and Theology* 14 (3): 284–309.

Musti, D. 2005. "Temi etici e politici nella decorazione pittorica della Tomba François." In *Dinamiche di sviluppo delle città nell'Etruria meridionale: Veio, Caere, Tarquinia, Vulci. Atti del XXIII Convegno di Studi Etruschi ed Italici, 1–6 ottobre 2001*, vol. II. Pisa. 485–505.

Mylonopoulos, J. 2006. "Griechische und römische Opferrituale als Medien der Kommunikation." *Polifemo* 6: 191–208.

———. 2014. "Simplicity and Elaboration in the Visual Construction of the Divine in Ancient Greece." In S. Estienne et al., eds., *Figures de dieux: Construire le divin en images*. Rennes. 269–91.

Naerebout, F. 2015. "Dance." In R. Raja and J. Rüpke, eds., *A Companion to the Archaeology of Religion in the Ancient World*. Malden, Mass. 107–19.

Nagel, A. K., B. U. Schipper, and A. Weymann, eds. 2008. *Apokalypse: Zur Soziologie und Geschichte religiöser Krisenrhetorik*. Frankfurt.

Nagy, Á. M. 2011. "Magical Gems and Classical Archaeology." In C. Entwistle and N. Adams, eds., *"Gems of Heaven": Recent Research on Engraved Gemstones in Late Antiquity, AD 200–600*, vol. 177. London. 75–81.

Naiden, F. S. 2006. *Ancient Supplication*. Oxford.

———. 2013. *Smoke Signals for the Gods: Ancient Greek Sacrifice from the Archaic through Roman Periods*. New York.

Naso, A. 2011. "Reperti italici nei santuari greci." In R. H. Neudecker, ed., *Krise und Wandel: Süditalien im 4. und 3. Jahrhundert v. Chr.—Internationaler Kongress anlässlich des 65. Geburtstages von Dieter Mertens, Rom 26. bis 28. Juni 2006*. Wiesbaden. 39–53.

Nasrallah, L. S. 2010. *Christian Responses to Roman Art and Architecture: The Second-Century Church amid the Spaces of Empire*. New York.

Nava, M. L., and V. Cracolici. 2005. "Il santuario lucano di Rossano di Vaglio." In M. L. Nava and M. Osanna, eds., *Lo Spazio del Rito Santuari E Culti in Italia Meridionale Tra Indigeni E Greci* 1. 103–12.

Nesselrath, H.-G. 2012. *Libanios: Zeuge einer schwindenden Welt*. Stuttgart.

Neudecker, R. 2015. "Gardens." In R. Raja and J. Rüpke, eds., *A Companion to the Archaeology of Religion in the Ancient World*. Malden, Mass. 220–34.

Neujahr, M. 2012. *Predicting the Past in the Ancient Near East: Mantic Historiography in Ancient Mesopotamia, Judah, and the Mediterranean World*. Brown Judaic Studies 354. Providence.

Neusner, J. 1979. "The Formation of Rabbinic Judaism: Yavneh (Jamnia) from A.D. 70 to 100." *ANRW* II.19,2: 3–42.

———. 1997. "Paradigmatic versus Historical Thinking: The Case of Rabbinic Judaism." *History and Theory* 36 (3): 353–77.

———. 2004. *The Idea of History in Rabbinic Judaism*, The Brill Reference Library of Judaism 12. Leiden, Boston.

Neutel, K. B. 2015. *A Cosmopolitan Ideal: Paul's Declaration "Neither Jew nor Greek, Neither Slave nor Free, nor Male and Female" in the Context of First-Century Thought*. The Library of New Testament Studies 513. London.

Neutel, K. B., and M. R. Anderson. 2014. "The First Cut Is the Deepest: Masculinity and Circumcision in the First Century." In P.-B. Smit and O. Creanga, eds., *Biblical Masculinities Foregrounded*. Sheffield. 228–44.

Nevett, L. C. 2010. *Domestic Space in Classical Antiquity.* Cambridge.

Newbold, R. F. 2003. "The Power of Sound in Nonnus' Dionysiaca." In D. Accorinti and P. Chuvin, eds., *Des Géants à Dionysos: Mélanges de mythologie et de poésie grecques offerts à Francis Vian.* Alexandria. 457–68.

Newby, Z. 2011. "In the Guise of Gods and Heroes." In J. Elsner and J. Huskinson, eds., *Life, Death and Representation: Some New Work on Roman Sarcophagi.* Millennium-Studien 29. Berlin. 189–228.

Newlands, C. 2009. "Statius' Programmatic Apollo and the Ending of Book 1 of the Thebaid." In L. Athanasaki, R. P. Martin, and J. F. Miller, eds., *Apolline Politics and Poetics.* Athens. 353–78.

Nguyen, V.H.T. 2008. *Christian Identity in Corinth—A Comparative Study of 2 Corinthians, Epictetes and Valerius Maximus.* Wissenschaftliche Untersuchungen zum neuen Testament 243. Tübingen.

Nicklas, T. 2014. *Jews and Christians? Second Century "Christian" Perspectives on the "Parting of the Ways."* Tübingen.

Nicolet, C. 1988. *L'Inventaire du monde: Geographie et politique aux origines de l'empire romain.* Paris.

Niebling, G. 1956. "Laribus Augustis Magistri Primi: Der Beginn des Compitalkultes der Lares und des Genius Augusti." *Historia* 5: 303–31.

Niehoff, M. R. 2011a. *Jewish Exegesis and Homeric Scholarship in Alexandria.* Cambridge.

———. 2011b. "Philo's Exposition in a Roman Context." *The Studia Philonica Annual* 23: 1–21.

———. 2012. "Philons Beitrag zur Kanonisierung der griechischen Bibel." In E.-M. Becker and S. Scholz, eds., *Kanon in Konstruktion und Dekonstruktion: Kanonisierungsprozesse religiöser Texte von der Antike bis zur Gegenwart. Ein Handbuch.* Berlin. 329–44.

Nielsen, I. 2014. *Housing the Chosen: The Architectural Context of Mystery Groups and Religious Associations in the Ancient World.* Contextualizing the Sacred 2. Turnhout.

Nielsen, I., and B. Poulsen. 1992. *The Temple of Castor and Pollux: The Pre-Augustan Temple Phases with Related Decorative Elements.* Lavori e studi di archeologia 17. Roma.

Nielsen, M. 2009. "United in Death: The Changing Image of Etruscan Couples." In Nielsen, ed., *Gender Identities in Italy in the First Millennium BC.* Oxford. 79–95.

Nigdelis, P. M. 2010. "Voluntary Associations in Roman Thessalonike: In Search of Identity and Support in a Cosmopolitan Society." In L. S. Nasrallah, C. N. Bakirtzis, and S. J. Friesen, eds., *From Roman to Early Christian Thessalonike: Studies in Religion and Archaeology.* Cambridge, Mass. 1–47.

Nikolaidis, A. G. 2009. "What Did Apollo Mean to Plutarch?" In L. Athanasaki, R. P. Martin, and J. F. Miller, eds., *Apolline Politics and Poetics.* Athens. 569–86.

Nilsson, M. P. 1940. *Greek Popular Religion,* Lectures on the History of Religions NS 1. New York.

Nipperdey, T. 1988. *Religion im Umbruch Deutschland, 1870–1918.* Beck'sche Reihe 363. München.

Nodes, D. J. 1993. *Doctrine and Exegesis in Biblical Latin Poetry.* Arca 31. Leeds.

Noland, C. 2009. *Agency and Embodiment: Performing Gesture/Producing Culture.* Cambridge, Mass.

Nollé, J. 2007. *Kleinasiatische Losorakel: Astragal- und Alphabetchresmologien der hochkaiserzeitlichen Orakelrenaissance.* Vestigia 57. München.

Nongbri, B. 2013. *Before Religion: A History of a Modern Concept.* New Haven.

Nonnis, D. 2003. "Dotazioni funzionali e di arredo in luoghi di culto dell'Italia repubblicana: L'apporto della documentazione epigrafica." In O. de Cazanove and J. Scheid, eds., *Sanctuaires et sources dans l'antiquité: Les sources documentaires et leurs limites dans la description des lieux de culte.* Collection du Centre Jean Bérard 22. Napoli. 25–54.

Norden, E. 1915. *Ennius und Vergilius: Kriegsbilder aus Roms grosser Zeit.* Leipzig.

———. 1966. "Die Petrusapokalypse und ihre antiken Vorbilder (1893)." In B. Kytzler, ed., *Eduard Norden. Kleine Schriften zum klassischen Altertum.* Berlin. 218–33.

Norena, C. F. 2001. "The Communication of the Emperor's Virtues." *Journal of Roman Studies* 91: 146–68.

North, J. A. 1994. "The Development of Religious Pluralism." In J. Lieu, J. North, and T. Rajak, eds., *The Jews among Pagans and Christians: In the Roman Empire.* London. 174–93.

———. 2010. "Pagan Ritual and Monotheism." In S. Mitchell and P. Van Nuffelen, eds., *One God: Pagan Monotheism in the Roman Empire.* Cambridge. 34–52.

———. 2011. "Pagans, Polytheists, and the Pendulum." In J. A. North and S.R.F. Price, eds., *The Religious History of the Roman Empire: Pagans, Jews, and Christians.* Oxford. 479–502.

Noy, D. 2010. "Immigrant and Jewish Families at Rome in the 2nd–5th Centuries." In É. Rebillard and C. Sotinel, eds., *Les frontières du profane dans l'antiquité tardive.* Collection de l'école francaise de Rome 428. Rome. 199–211.

Oakley, S. P. 2014. "The Early Republic." In H. I. Flower, ed., *The Cambridge Companion to the Roman Republic.* New York. 3–18.

Obbink, D., ed. 1996. *Philodemus, On Piety Pt. 1: Critical Text with Commentary.* Oxford.

———. 2001. "Le livre I du *De Natura Deorum* de Cicéron et le *De Pietate* de Philodème." In C. Auvray-Assayas, ed., *Cicéron et Philodème: la polémique en philosophie.* Études de littérature ancienne 12. Paris. 203–25.

Oegema, G. S. 2008. "Back to the Future in the Early Church: The Use of the Book of Daniel in the Early Patristic Eschatology." In P. G. Kirkpatrick and T. D. Goltz, eds., *The Function of Ancient Historiography in Biblical and Cognate Studies.* New York. 186–98.

Ogilvie, R. M. 1961. "'Lustrum Condere'." *Journal of Roman Studies* 51: 31–39.

O'Neill, K. 1998. "Symbolism and Sympathetic Magic in Propertius 4.5." *Classical Journal* 94 (1): 49–80.

Onorato, R. S., and J. C. Turner 2004. "Fluidity in the Self-Concept: the Shift from Personal to Social Identity." *European Journal of Social Psychology* 34: 257–78.

Orlin, E. M. 1997. *Temples, Religion and Politics in the Roman Republic,* Mnemosyne Suppl. 164. Leiden.

———. 2010. *Foreign Cults in Rome—Creating a Roman Empire.* Oxford.

———. 2016. "Augustan Reconstruction and Roman Memory." In K. Galinsky, ed., *Memory in Ancient Rome and Early Christianity.* Oxford. 115–44.

Osanna, M., and M. M. Sica. 2005. "Articolazione dello spazio e pratiche rituali nel santuario lucano di Torre di Satriano." In M. L. Nava and M. Osanna, eds., *Lo spazio del rito: Santuari e culti in Italia meridionale tra indigeni e greci* 1. 125–39.

Osborne, R. 2000. "Archaic and Classical Greek Temple Sculpture and the Viewer." In N. K. Rutter and B. A. Sparkes, eds., *Word and Image in Ancient Greece* 1. Edinburgh. 228–46.

Osiek, C. 1999. *Shepherd of Hermas: A Commentary.* Hermeneia. Minneapolis.

Östenberg, I. 2009. *Staging the World: Spoils, Captives, and Representations in the Roman Triumphal Procession.* Oxford.

Otto, B.-C. 2011. *Magie: Rezeptions- und diskursgeschichtliche Analysen von der Antike bis zur Neuzeit.* Religionsgeschichtliche Versuche und Vorarbeiten 57. Berlin.

Otto, B.-C., and M. Stausberg. 2013. *Defining Magic: A Reader.* Critical Categories in the Study of Religion. Sheffield.

Paganini, M.C.D. 2009. "Theophoric Personal Names in Graeco-Roman Egypt: The Case of Sarapis." *Archiv für Papyrusforschung* 55 (1): 68–89.

Pagels, E. H. 1973. *The Johannine Gospel in Gnostic Exegesis: Heracleon's Commentary on John.* Society of Biblical Literature Monograph Series 17. Nashville.

Palmer, R. E. 1970. *The Archaic Community of the Romans.* Cambridge.

Palombi, D., ed. 2010. *Il Tempio Arcaico di Caprifico di Torrecchia (Cisterna di Latina): I Materiali e il Contesto.* Roma.

Panayotakis, C. 2010. *Decimus Laberius: The Fragments.* Cambridge Classical Texts and Commentaries 46. Cambridge.

Papadopoulos, J. 1980. *Xoana e Sphyrelata: Testimoniana delle fonti scritte.* Roma.

Pappalardo, O. 2012. "How the Romans saw the Frieze in the Villa of the Mysteries at Pompeii." In D. L. Balch and A. Weissenrieder, eds., *Contested Spaces: Houses and Temples in Roman Antiquity and the New Testament.* Wissenschaftliche Untersuchungen zum neuen Testament 285. Tübingen. 261–64.

Pappalardo, U. 1995. "Spazio sacro e spazio profano: Il Collegio degli Augustali ad Ercolano." In E. M. Moormann, ed., *Functional and Spatial Analysis of Wall Painting.* Leiden. 90–95.

Parke, H. W. 1988. *Sibyls and Sibylline Prophecy in Classical Antiquity.* London.

Pascal, C. B. 1981. "October Horse." *Harvard Studies in Classical Philology* 85: 261–91.

Pasqualini, A. 1996. "I miti albani e l'origine delle feriae Latinae." In A. Pasqualini, ed., *Alba Longa—Mito Storia archeologia.* Roma. 217–54.

Patera, I. 2010. "Light and Lighting Equipment in the Eleusinian Mysteries: Symbolism and Ritual Use " In M. Christopoulo, ed., *Light and Darkness in Ancient Greek Myth and Religion.* Lanham 261–75.

Patzelt, M. 2017. *Beten bei den Römern.* Religionsgeschichtliche Versuche und Vorarbeiten. Berlin.

Pearce, J. 2011. "Marking the Dead: Tombs and Topography in the Roman Provinces." In M. Carroll, ed., *Living through the Dead: Burial and Commemoration in the Classical World.* Studies in Funerary Achaeology 5. Oxford.

Peatfield, A. 1994. "After the "Big Bang"–What? or Minoan Symbols and Shrines beyond Palatial Collapse." In S. E. Alcock and R. Osborne, eds., *Placing the Gods—Sanctuaries and Sacred Space in Ancient Greece.* Oxford. 19–36.

Pelling, C. 2009. "Was There an Ancient Genre of 'Autobiography'? or, Did Augustus Know What He Was Doing?" In C. Smith, ed., *The Lost Memoirs of Augustus and the Development of Roman Autobiography*. Swansea 41–123.

Penner, L. 2012. "Gender, Household Structure and Slavery: Re-Interpreting the Aristocratic Columbaria of Early Imperial Rome." In R. Laurence and A. Strömberg, eds., *Families in the Greco-Roman World*. London. 143–58.

Pensabene, P. et al. 2005. "Testimonianze die attività cultuali nell'area sud-ovest del Palatino dalla fine del VII al V secolo a.C." In A. Comella and S. Mele, eds., *Depositi Votivi e Culti dell'Italia Antica dall'Età Arcaica a Quella Tardo-Repubblicana—Atti del Convegno di Studi Perugia, 1–4 giugno 2000*. Bibliotheca archaeologica 16. Bari. 95–109.

Perdigones Moreno, L. 1991. "Hallazgos recientes entorno al santuario de Melkart en la isla de Sancti Petri (Cádiz)." In E. Acquarino and P. Bartoloni, eds., *Atti del II Congresso Internazionale di Studi Fenici e Punici, Roma, 9–14 Novembre 1987*, 3. Collezione di studi fenici 30. Roma. 1119–32.

Perkins, J. 2009. *Roman Imperial Identities in the Early Christian Era*. Routledge Monographs in Classical Studies. London.

Peró, A. 2012. *La statua di Atena: Agalmatofilia nella "Cronaca" di Lindos*. Pubblicazioni della Facoltá di lettere e filosofia dell'Universitá degli Studi di Milano 278. Milano.

Perry, E. 2012. "The Same, but Different: The Temple of Jupiter Optimus Maximus Through Time." In B. D. Wescoat and R. G. Ousterhout, eds., *Architecture of the Sacred: Space, Ritual, and Experience from Classical Greece to Byzantium*. Cambridge. 175–200.

Petersen, Lauren Hackworth. 2003. "The Baker, His Tomb, His Wife, and Her Breadbasket: The Monument of Eurysaces in Rome." *Art Bulletin* 85 (2), 230–57.

Peterson, E. 1959. "Beiträge zur Interpretation der Visionen im Pastor Hermae." In E. Peterson, *Frühkirche, Judentum und Gnosis: Studien und Untersuchungen*. Freiburg i. Br. 254–70.

Petridou, G. 2015. "Emplotting the Divine: Epiphanic Narratives as Means of Enhancing Agency." *Religion in the Roman Empire* 1 (3): 321–42.

———. 2017. "Contesting Medical and Religious Expertise in the Hieroi Logoi: Aristides as Therapeutes and the Therapeutai of Asclepius at Pergamum." In G. Petridou, R. Gordon, and J. Rüpke, eds., *Beyond Priesthood: Religious Entrepreneurs and Innovators in the Roman Empire*. Religionsgeschichtliche Versuche und Vorarbeiten 66. Berlin. 185-214.

Petropoulou, M.-Z. 2008. *Animal Sacrifice in Ancient Greek Religion, Judaism, and Christianity, 100 BC to AD 200*, Oxford Classical Monographs. Oxford.

Petsalis-Diomidis, A. 2007. "Landscape, Transformation, and Divine Epiphany." In S. Swain, S. Harrison, and J. Elsner, eds., *Severan Culture*. Cambridge. 250–89.

———. 2010. *Truly beyond Wonders: Aelius Aristides and the Cult of Asklepios*. Oxford.

Pettitt, P. 2011. *The Palaeolithic Origins of Human Burial*. Milton Park, Abingdon.

Petzl, G. 1994. *Die Beichtinschriften Westkleinasiens*. Epigraphica Anatolica 22. Bonn.

Pezzoli-Olgiati, D., and C. Rowland, eds. 2011. *Approaches to the Visual in Religion*. Research in Contemporary Religion 10. Göttingen.

Pfiffig, A. J. 1975. *Religio Etrusca*. Graz.

Phillips III, C. R. 1994. "Seek and Go Hide: Literary Source Problems and Graeco-Roman Magic." *Helios* 21,2: 107–14.

Phillips, O. 1995. "Singing Away Snakebite: Lucan's Magical Cures." In M. Meyer and P. Mirecki, eds., *Ancient Magic and Ritual Power*. Leiden. 391–400.

Philodemus 2009. *On Death*. Writings from the Greco-Roman World 29. Atlanta.

Piano, V. 2010. " '. . . e quella profetizzò dall'antro': Mitologia e cosmologia di Notte nel papiro di Derveni." *Atti e memorie dell'Accademia Toscana di scienze e lettere* 75 (ns 61): 9–48.

———. 2013. "Le papyrus de Derveni et son contexte de découverte: parole écrite et rituels funéraires dans la Macédoine grecque antique." *Revue de l'histoire des religions* 230 (2): 233–52.

Picard, O. 2012. "De la citoyenneté classique à al citoyenneté d'époque romaine: essai de conclusion." In A. Heller and A.-V. Pont, eds., *Patrie d'origine et patries électives: les citoyennetés multiples dans le monde grec d'époque romaine. Actes du colloque international de Tours, 6–7 novembre 2009*. Ausonius Éditions: Scripta Antiqua 40. Paris. 341–45.

Pickering, W.S.F. 2008. "Emile Durkheim." In J. Corrigan. ed., *The Oxford Handbook of Religion and Emotion*. Oxford. 438–56.

Piétri, C. 1976. *Roma christiana: Recherches sur l'Église de Rome, son organisation, sa politique, son idéologie, de Miltiade à Sixte III (311–440)*, 2. Bibliothèque des écoles françaises d'Athènes et de Rome 224. Rome.

Piétri, C., and C. Markschies. 1996. "Theologische Diskussionen zur Zeit Konstantins: Arius, der 'arianische Streit' und das Konzil von Nizäa, die nachnizänischen Auseinandersetzungen bis 337." In C. Piétri and L. Piétri, eds., *Die Geschichte des Christentums* 2: *Das Entstehen der einen Christenheit (250–430)*. Freiburg. 271–344.

Pina Polo, F. 2011a. *The Consul at Rome: The Civil Functions of the Consuls in the Roman Republic*. Cambridge.

———. 2011b. "Consuls as curatores pacis deorum." In H. Beck, ed., *Consuls and res publica: Holding High Office in the Roman Republic*. Cambridge. 97–115.

Pirson, F. 1997. "Rented Accomodation at Pompeii: The Evidence of the Insula Arriana Polliana VI 6." In R. Laurence and A. Wallace-Hadrill, eds., *Domestic Space in the Roman World: Pompeii and Beyond* 22. *Journal of Roman Archaeology* Suppl. Portsmouth, RI. 165–82.

Pisani Sartorio, G. 2000. "La scoperta dei Templi della Fortuna e della Mater Matuta." In *Il viver quotidiano in Roma arcaica: Materiali dagli scavi del Tempio Arcaico nell'area sacra di S. Omobono*. Roma. 13–15.

Pizzone, A.M.V. 2013. "The Tale of a Dream: Oneiros and Mythos in the Greek Novel." In M. P. Futre Pinheiro, A. Bierl, and R. Beck, eds., *Intende, Lector—Echoes of Myth, Religion and Ritual in the Ancient Novel*. MythosEikonPoiesis 6. Berlin. 67–81.

Platt, V. 2002. "Viewing, Desiring, Believing: Confronting the Divine in a Pompeian House." *Art History* 25 (1): 87–112.

Pleket, H. W. 1965. "An Aspect of the Emperor Cult: Imperial Mysteries." *Harvard Theological Review* 58: 331–47.

Podolak, P. 2010. *Soranos von Ephesos, Περὶ ψυχῆς: Sammlung der Testimonien, Kommentar und Einleitung*, Beiträge zur Altertumskunde 279. Berlin.

Poland, F. 1909. *Geschichte des griechischen Vereinswesens*. Leipzig.

Pollini, J. 2007. "Ritualizing Death in Republican Rome: Memory, Religion, Class Struggle, and the Wax Ancestral Mask Tradition's Origin and Influence on Veristic Portraiture." In N. Laneri, eds., *Performing Death: Social Analyses of Funerary Traditions in the Ancient Near East and Mediterranean.* Oriental Institute Seminars 3. Chicago. 237–85.

———. 2012. *From Republic to Empire: Rhetoric, Religion, and Power in the Visual Culture of Ancient Rome.* Oklahoma Series in Classical Culture 48. Norman.

Porter, A. 2008. "Evocative Topography: Experience, Time and Politics in a Landscape of Death." In *Sepolti tra i Vivi—Buried among the Living: Atti del Convegno Internazionale.* Roma. 195–214.

Porter, B. W., and A. T. Boutin, eds. 2014. *Remembering the Dead in the Ancient Near East.* Boulder.

Pötscher, W. 1978. "'Numen' und 'numen Augusti'." *ANRW* II.16,1: 355–92.

Potter, D. S. 1990. *Prophecy and History in the Crisis of the Roman Empire: A Historical Commentary on the Thirteenth Sibylline Oracle.* Oxford Classical Monographs. Oxford.

———. 1994. *Prophets and Emperors: Human and Divine Authority from Augustus to Theodosius.* Revealing Antiquity 7. Cambridge, Mass.

Potter, D. S. 2013. *Constantine the Emperor.* Oxford.

Potter, D. S., and D. J. Mattingly, eds., 1999. *Life, Death, and Entertainment in the Roman Empire.* Ann Arbor.

Poultney, J. W. 1959. *The Bronze Tables of Iguvium.* Philological Monographs XVIII. Oxford.

Prayon, F. 1975. *Frühetruskische Garb—und Hausarchitektur.* Heidelberg.

———. 1990. "Wasserkulte in Etrurien." In H. Heres and M. Kunze, eds., *Die Welt der Etrusker: Internationales Kolloquium 24.–26. Oktober in Berlin.* Berlin. 77–81.

———. 1998a. "Die Anfänge großformatiger Plastik in Etrurien." In P. Schauer, ed., *Archäologische Untersuchungen zu den Beziehungen zwischen Altitalien und der Zone Nordwärts der Alpen während der frühen Steinzeit Alteuropas 4.* Regensburg. 191–206.

———. 1998b. "Die etruskische Grabarchitektur und Rom." In A. Foresti, ed., *Die Integration der Etrusker und das Weiterwirken etruskischen Kulturgutes im republikanischen und kaiserlichen Rom.* Wien. 165–76.

———. 2000. "Aspekte zum Thema 'Kunst und Handwerk'." In F. Prayon and W. Röllig, eds., *Akten des Kolloquiums zum Thema: Der Orient und Etrurien—Zum Phänomen des "Orientalisierens" im westlichen Mittelmeerraum (10.–6. Jahrhundert v. Chr.).* Tübingen. 107–12.

———. 2004a. "Reditus as maiores: Ein Aspekt etruskischer Jenseitsvorstellungen." *Mitteilungen des Deutschen Archäologischen Instituts, Römische Abteilung* 111: 45–67.

———. 2004b. "Überlegungen zur Monumentalität frühetruskischer Plastik und Architektur." In M. Novák, F. Prayon, and A.-M. Wittke, eds., *Die Außenwirkung des späthethitischen Kulturraumes: Güteraustausch—Kulturkontakt—Kulturtransfer* 323. Münster. 85–105.

———. 2010. "The Tomb as Altar." In L. B. v. d. Meer, ed., *Material Aspects of Etruscan Religion: Proceedings of the International Colloquium, Leiden, May 29 and 30, 2008.* Leuven. 75–82.

Prescendi, F. 2010. "Children and the Transmission of Religious Knowledge." In V. Dasen and T. Späth, eds., *Children, Memory, and Family Identity in Roman Culture.* Oxford. 73–94.

Price, S. 2012. "Religious Mobility in the Roman Empire." *Journal of Roman Studies* 102: 1–19.

Price, S.R.F. 1984. *Rituals and Power: The Roman Imperial Cult in Asia Minor.* Cambridge.

Pritchett, W. K. 1968. "The Intercalary Month at Athens." *CP* 63: 53–54.

———. 1999. "Postscript: The Athenian Calendars." *ZPE* 128: 79–93.

———. 2001. *Athenian Calendars and Ekklesias,* ΑΡΧΑΙΑ ΗΕΛΛΑΣ 8. Amsterdam.

Prosdocimi, A. 1994. "Satricum: I sodales del Publicola steterai a Mater (Matuta?)." *Parola di Passato* 49: 365–77.

Punyanunt-Carter, N. M. et al. 2008. "An Examination of Reliability and Validity of the Religious Communication Apprehension Scale." *Journal of Intercultural Communication Research* 37 (1): 1–15.

Putz, U. 1998. "Gesellschaftlicher Wandel in Mittelitalien im Spiegel villanovazeitlicher Prunkgräber." In P. Schauer, ed., *Archäologische Untersuchungen zu den Beziehungen zwischen Altitalien und der Zone Nordwärts der Alpen während der frühen Steinzeit Alteuropas* 4. Regensburg. 49–68.

Quack, J. F. 2017. "What Is a Priest of Ēse, of Wusa, and of Isis in the Egyptian and Nubian World?" In V. Gasparini and R. Veymiers, eds., *The Greco-Roman Cults of Isis: Agents, Images and Practices.* Religions in the Graeco-Roman World. Leiden.

Quilici, L., and S. Quilici Gigli. 1995. "Un grande santuario fuori la porta occidentale di Tusculum." *Archeologia Laziale* 12: 509–34.

Quinn, J. C., and A. Wilson 2013. "Capitolia." *Journal of Roman Studies* 103: 117–73.

Quinn, K. 1982. "The Poet and his Audience in the Augustan Age." *ANRW* II.30,1: 75–180.

Radin, P. 1927. *Primitive Man as Philosopher.* J. Dewey, trans. New York.

Radke, G. 1970. "Das Wirken der römischen Götter." *Gymnasium* 77: 23–46.

———. 1979. *Die Götter Altitaliens.* Fontes et Commentationes 3. Münster.

Radke-Uhlmann, G. 2008. "Aitiologien des Selbst: Moderne Konzepte und ihre Alternativen in antiken autobiographischen Texten." In A. Arweiler and M. Möller, eds., *Vom Selbst-Verständnis in Antike und Neuzeit: Notions of the Self in Antiquity and Beyond.* Transformationen der Antike 8. Berlin. 107–29.

Raggi, A. 2006. "Le norme sui sacra nelle leges municipales." In L. Capogrossi and E. Gabba, eds., *Gli statuti municipali.* Pavia. 701–21.

———. 2011. "'Religion' in Municipal Laws." In J. Richardson and F. Santangelo, eds., *Priests and State in the Roman World.* Potsdamer Altertumswissenschaftlich Beiträge 33. Stuttgart. 333–46.

Raja, R. 2013a. "Changing Spaces and Shifting Attitudes: Revisiting the Sanctuary of Zeus in Gerasa." In T. Kaizer et al., eds., *Cities and Gods: Religious Space in Transition.* Leuven. 31–43.

———. 2013b. "Expressing Public Identities in Urban Spaces: The Case of Aphrodisias in Caria." In C. P. Dickenson and O. M. Van Nijf, eds., *Public Space in the Post-Classical City.* Leuven; Paris; Walpole, Mass. 148–72.

———. 2015. "Complex Sanctuaries in the Roman Period." In R. Raja and J. Rüpke, eds., *A Companion to the Archaeology of Religion in the Ancient World.* Malden, Mass. 307–19.

Raja, R., and J. Rüpke. 2015a. "Appropriating Religion: Methodological Issues in Testing the 'Lived Ancient Religion' Approach." *Religion in the Roman Empire* 1 (1): 11–19.

Raja, R., and J. Rüpke, eds. 2015b. *A Companion to the Archaeology of Religion in the Ancient World*. Boston.

Rajak, T. 2009. *Translation and Survival: The Greek Bible and the Jewish Diaspora*. Oxford.

———. 2013. "The Individual and the Word in Hellenistic Judaism: Cases in Philo and Josephus." In J. Rüpke, ed., *The Individual in the Religions of the Ancient Mediterranean*. Oxford. 298–314.

Ramelli, I. 2005. "L'ermetismo filosofico conservato in copto: saggio introduttivo." In I. Ramelli, ed., *Corpus Hermeticum: Edizione e commento di A.D. Nock e A.-J. Festugière; edizione dei testi ermetici copti e commento di I. Ramelli. Testo greco, latino e copto*. Milano. 1267–407.

———. 2008. *Stoici romani minori: Testi greci e latini a fronte. Introduzione di Roberto Radice*. Bompiani, Il pensiero occidentale. Milano.

Rapp, C. 2000. "The Elite Status of Bishops in Late Antiquity in Ecclesiastical, Spiritual, and Social Contexts." *Arethusa* 33: 379–99.

Rappaport, R. A. 1992. "Ritual, Time, and Eternity." *Zygon* 27: 5–30.

———. 1999. *Ritual and Religion in the Making of Humanity*. Cambridge.

Rathje, A. 2005. "Reconstracting the Orientralizing and Archaic Periods." In P. Attema et al., eds., *Papers in Italian Archaeology 6: Communities and Settlements from the Neolithic to the Early Medieval Period; Proceedings of the 6th Conference of Italian Archaeology held at the University of Groningen, Groningen Institute of Archaeology, the Netherlands, April 15–17, 2003*, 1. Oxford. 25–31.

Rawson, B. 2003. "Death, Burial and Commemoration of Children in Roman Italy." In D. L. Balch and C. Osiek, eds., *Early Christian Families in Context—An Interdisciplinary Dialogue*. Grand Rapids, Mich. 277–97.

Rawson, E. 1974. "Religion and Politics in the Late Second Century B. C. at Rome." *Phoenix* 28: 193–212.

———. 1978. "Caesar, Etruria and the Disciplina Etrusca." *Journal of Roman Studies* 68: 132–52.

———. 1985. *Intellectual Life in the Late Roman Republic*. London.

Rebenich, S. 2008. "Garten, Gräber und Gedächtnis: Villenkultur und Bestattungspraxis in der römischen Kaiserzeit." In H. Börm, N. Ehrhardt, and J. Wiesehöfer, eds., *Monumentum et instrumentum inscriptum: Beschriftete Objekte aus Kaiserzeit und Spätantike als historische Zeugnisse. Festschrift Peter Weiß zum 65. Geburtstag*. Stuttgart. 187–201.

Rebillard, É. 2003. "Groupes religieux et élection de sépulture dans l'Antiquité tardive." In N. Belayche and S. C. Mimouni, eds., *Les communautés religieuses dans le monde gréco-romain: Essais de définition*. Turnhout. 259–77.

———. 2009. "Augustin et le culte des statues." In G. Partoens, A. Dupont, and M. Lamberigts, eds., *Ministerium sermonis: Philological, Historical, and Theological Studies on Augustine's Sermones ad populum*. Instrumenta patristica et mediaevalia 53. Turnhout. 299–325.

———. 2010. " 'Vivre avec les païens, mais non mourir avec eux': Le problème de la commensalité des chrétiens et des non-chrétiens (I–V siècles)." In É. Rebillard and C.

Sotinel, eds., *Les frontières du profane dans l'antiquité tardive*. Collection de l'école francaise de Rome 428. Rome. 151–76.

———. 2012. *Christians and Their Many Identities in Late Antiquity, North Africa, 200–450 CE*. Ithaca.

———. 2016. "Everyday Christianity in Third-Century Carthage." *Religion in the Roman Empire* 2 (1): 91–102.

Recchia, G. 2011. "Burial Mounds and 'Specchie' in Apulia During the Bronze Age: Local Developments and Transadriatic Connections." In *Ancestral Landscapes*. TMO 58. Lyon. 475–84.

Recke, M., and W. Wamser-Krasznai. 2008. *Kultische Anatomie: Etruskische Körperteil-Votive aus der Antikensammlung der Justus-Liebig-Universität Gießen (Stiftung Ludwig Stieda)*. Kataloge des Deutschen Medizinhistorischen Museums Ingolstadt 31. Ingolstadt.

Reed, A. Y. 2008. "'Jewish Christianity' as Counter-History? The Apostolic Past in Eusebius' Ecclesiastical History and the Pseudo-Clementine Homilies." In G. Gardner and K. L. Osterloh, eds., *Antiquity in Antiquity—Jewish and Christian Pasts in the Greco-Roman World*. Texts and Studies in Ancient Judaism 123. Tübingen.

———. 2013. "When Did Rabbis Become Pharisees? Reflections on Christian Evidence for Post-70 Judaism." In R. a. S. Boustan et al., eds., *Envisioning Judaism: Studies in Honor of Peter Schäfer on the Occasion of his Seventieth Birthday* 2. Tübingen. 859–95.

Reeves, Barbara. 2004. *The feriale Duranum, Roman Military Religion, and Dura-Europos: A Reassessment*. Diss. Buffalo.

Reinhard, W., ed. 2014. *Geschichte der Welt 1350–1750: Weltreiche und Weltmeere*. Geschichte der Welt. München, Cambridge, Mass.

Remijsen, S. 2015. *The End of Greek Athletics in Late Antiquity*. Greek Culture in the Roman World. Cambridge.

Renberg, G. 2010a. "Dream-Narratives and Unnarrated Dreams in Greek and Latin Dedicatory Inscriptions." In E. Scioli and C. Walde, eds., *Sub imagine somni: Nighttime Phenomena in the Greco-Roman World*. Testi e studi di cultura classica 46. Pisa. 33–61.

———. 2010b. "Hadrian and the Oracles of Antinous (SHA Hadr. 14.7): With an Appendix on the So-called Antinoeion at Hadrian's Villa and Rome's Monte Pincio Obelisk." *MAAR* 55: 159–98.

———. 2015. "The Role of Dream-Interpreters in Greek and Roman Religion." In G. Weber, ed., *Artemidor von Daldis und die antike Traumdeutung: Texte—Kontexte—Lektüren* Colloquia Augustana 33. Berlin. 233–62.

Renfrew, C. 1993. *The Roots of Ethnicity: Archaeology, Genetics and the Origins of Europe*. Conferenze 10. Roma.

Reydams-Schils, G. J. 2005. *The Roman Stoics: Self, Responsibility, and Affection*. Chicago.

Reynolds, J. M. 1962. "Vota Pro Salute Principis." *BSA* 30 (ns 17): 33–36.

Rhodes, P. J. 1990. "The Atthidographers." In H. Verdin, G. Schepens, and E. de Keyser, eds., *Purposes of History: Studies in Greek Historiography from the 4th to the 2nd Centuries B.C. Proceedings of the International Colloquium Leuven, 24–26 May 1988*. Studia Hellenistica 30. Leuven. 73–81.

Richardson, L. 1992. *A New Topographical Dictionary of Ancient Rome*. Baltimore.

Richardson, P. 2004. *Building Jewish in the Roman East.* Suppl. to the *Journal for the Study of Judaism* 92. Waco, Tex.

Richer, N. 2012. *La Religion des Spartiates: Croyances et cultes dans l'Antiquité.* Paris.

Richert, E. A. 2005. *Native Religion under Roman Domination: Deities, Springs and Mountains in the North-West of the Iberian Peninsula.* BAR/International series 1382. Oxford.

Richter, D. S. 2011. *Cosmopolis: Imagining Community in Late Classical Athens and the Early Roman Empire.* Oxford.

Ridgway, D. 2000a. "The First Western Greeks Revisited." In D. Ridgway et al., eds., *Ancient Italy in Its Mediterranean Setting—Studies in Honour of Ellen Macnamara.* Accordia Specialist Studies on the Mediterranean 4. London. 179–91.

———. 2000b. "Seals, Scarabs and People in Pithekoussai I." In G. R. Tsetskhladze, A.J.N.W. Prag, and A. M. Snodgrass, eds., *Periplous: Papers on Classical Art and Archaeology Presented to Sir John Boardman.* London. 235–43.

Riedweg, C. 2011a. "Initiation—Death—Underworld. Narrative and Ritual in the Gold Leaves." In R. G. Edmonds, ed., *The "Orphic" Gold Tablets and Greek Religion: Further along the Path.* Oxford. 219–56.

———. 2011b. "Teilt Kaiser Julian die kritische Sicht auf monströse orphische Mythologeme mit den Christen? Beobachtungen zu Adversus Galilaeos fr. 4 Masaracchia (=OF 59 VII=Kyrill von Alexandrien Contra Iulianum 2.11)." In M. Herrero de Jáuregui et al., eds., *Tracing Orpheus.* Sozomena 10. Berlin. 77–84.

Rieger, A.-K. 2007. "Lokale Tradition versus überregionale Einheit: Der Kult der Magna Mater." *Mediterranea* 4: 89–120.

———. 2016. "Waste Matters: Life Cycle and Agency of Pottery Employed in Graeco-Roman Sacred Spaces." *Religion in the Roman Empire* 2 (3): 307–39.

———. 2017. "Approaches to an Interpretation of Visual and Material Cultural Remains from the Cave Sanctuary at Caesarea Philippi/Bania (Gaulantis)." In M. Arnhold, H. O. Maier, and J. Rüpke, eds., *Seeing the Gods.* Tübingen.

Riis, O., and L. Woodhead. 2010. *A Sociology of Religious Emotion.* Oxford.

Ritter, S. 1995. *Hercules in der römischen Kunst von den Anfängen bis Augustus.* Archäologie und Geschichte 5. Heidelberg.

Riva, C. 2010. *The Urbanisation of Etruria: Funerary Practices and Social Change, 700–600 BC.* Cambridge.

Rives, J. B. 1995. *Religion and Authority in Roman Carthage from Augustus to Constantine.* Oxford.

Rives, J. B. 1999. "The Decree of Decius and the Religion of Empire." *Journal of Roman Studies* 89: 135–54.

———. 2011a. "The Persecution of Christians and Ideas of Community in the Roman Empire." In G. A. Cecconi and C. Gabrielli, eds., *Politiche religiose nel mondo antico e tardo antico: poteri e indirizzi, forme del controllo, idee e prassi di tolleranza.* Bari. 199–216.

———. 2011b. "Roman Translation: Tacitus and Ethnographic Interpretation." In P. A. Harland, ed., *Travel and Religion in Antiquity.* Studies in Christianity and Judaism 21. Waterloo, Ont. 165–81.

Rix, H. 1972. "Zum Ursprung des römisch-mittelitalischen Gentilnamensystems." *ANRW* I.2: 700–58.

Rizzi, M. 2010. "Hadrian and the Christians." In M. Rizzi, ed., *Hadrian and the Christians*. Millennium-Studien 30. Berlin. 7–20.

Roberts, M. 1985. *Biblical Epic and Rhetorical Paraphrase in Late Antiquity*. ARCA 16. Liverpool.

Robinson, D. M. 1924. "Some Roman Terra-Cotta Savings-Banks." *American Journal of Archaeology* 28 (3): 239–50.

Rodriguez-Mayorgas, A. 2011. "Annales Maximi: Writing, Memory, and Religious Performance in the Roman Republic." In A.P.M.H. Lardinois, ed., *Sacred Words: Orality, Literacy and Religion. Orality and Literacy in the Ancient World* 8 = Mnemosyne Suppl. 332. Leiden. 235–54.

Rogers, G. M. 2012. *The Mysteries of Artemis of Ephesos: Cult, Polis, and Change in the Graeco-Roman World*. Synkrisis. New Haven.

Rohde, D. 2012. *Zwischen Individuum und Stadtgemeinde: Die Integration von Collegia in Hafenstädten*. Studien zur Alten Geschichte 15. Mainz.

Romualdi, A. 1990. "Luoghi di culto e depositi votivi nell'etruria settentrionale in epoca arcaica: considerazioni sulla tipologia e sul significato delle offerte votive." In *Scienze dell'antichità: storia archeologia antropologia* 3. Roma. 619–49.

Roncalli, F. 1985. "Zum historischen, sozioökonomischen und religionsgeschichtlichen Hintergrund." In S. Steingräber, ed., *Etruskische Wandmalerei*. Stuttgart. 73–78.

Rosa, H. 2016. *Resonanz: Eine Soziologie der Weltbeziehung*. Frankfurt a.M.

Rosati, P.D.M. 2009. *Ritual and the Sacred: A Neo-Durkheimian Analysis of Politics, Religion and the Self*. Rethinking Classical Sociology. England.

Rosen, K. 1985. "Die falschen Numabücher: Politik, Religion und Literatur in Rom, 181 v. Chr." *Chiron* 15: 65–90.

———. 2007. "Kaiser Julian Apostata (361–363): Die alten Götter gegen das junge Christentum." In F. Schuller and H. Wolff, eds., *Konstantin der Große: Kaiser einer Epochenwende*. Lindenberg. 200–15.

Rosenbaum-Alföldi, M. 2015a. "Der Name—nicht das Symbol: Gedanken zum Silbermultiplum Constantins des Grossen mit dem Christogramm auf dem Helm." In T. Khidesheli and N. Kavvadas, eds., *Bau und Schrift: Studien zur Archäologie und Literatur des antiken Christentums für Hans Reinhard Seeliger*. Jahrbuch für Antike und Christentum, Suppl. 12. Münster. 1–37.

———. 2015b. "Die consecratio des Constantius I. und der Sol-Kult." *Geldgeschichtliche Nachrichten* 50: 136–41.

Rosenberger, V. 1998. *Gezähmte Götter: Das Prodigienwesen der römischen Republik* HABES 27. Stuttgart.

———. 2003. "Die verschwundene Leiche: Überlegungen zur Auffindung des Sarkophags Numas im Jahre 181 v. Chr." In B. Kranemann and J. Rüpke, eds., *Das Gedächtnis des Gedächtnisses: Zur Präsenz von Ritualen in beschreibenden und reflektierenden Texten*. Marburg. 39–59.

——. 2005. "Prodigien aus Italien: geograophische Verteilung und religiöse Kommunikation." *Cahiers Glotz* 16: 235–57.

Rosenstein, N. 1990. *Imperatores victi: Military Defeat and Aristocratic Competition in the Middle and Late Republic.* Berkeley.

——. 2012. *Rome and the Mediterranean 290 to 146 BC: The Imperial Republic.* Edinburgh.

Rosso, E. 2014. "Genius Augusti: Construire la divinté impériale en images." In S. Estienne et al., eds., *Figures de dieux: Construire le divin en images.* Rennes. 39–76.

Rostad, A. 2002. "Confession or Reconciliation? The Narrative Structure of the Lydian and Phrygian 'Confession Inscriptions'." *Symbolae Osloenses* 77: 145–64.

Roth-Murray, C. 2005. "A Disclosure of Power: Elite Etruscan Iconography during the 8th–6th Centuries BC." In P.A.J. Attema, ed., *Papers in Italian Archaeology 6: Communities and Settlements from the Neolithic to the Early Medieval Period; Proceedings of the 6th Conference of Italian Archaeology held at the University of Groningen, Groningen Institute of Archaeology, the Netherlands, April 15–17, 2003,* 1. BAR International Series 1452. Oxford. 186–95.

Rous, B. 2011. "An Age without Images: Architectural Decoration in the Late Republican Period." In P. Lulof and C. Rescigno, eds., *Deliciae Fictiles IV—Architectural Terracottas in Ancient Italy—Images of Gods, Monsters and Heroes.* Oxford. 84–94.

Rudich, V. A. 2015. *Religious Dissent in the Roman Empire: Violence in Judaea at the Time of Nero,* Routledge Monographs in Classical Studies. London.

Rüpke, J. 1987. "Kriegserklärung und Fahnenweihe: Zwei Anmerkungen zu einem 'historischen Experiment'." *Altsprachlicher Unterricht* 30,3: 105–107.

——. 1990a. *Domi militiae: Die religiöse Konstruktion des Krieges in Rom.* Stuttgart.

——. 1990b. "Gerechte Kriege—gerächte Kriege: Die Funktion der Götter in Caesars Darstellung des Helvetierfeldzuges (Gall. 1,12)." *Altsprachlicher Unterricht* 33,5: 5–13.

——. 1993a. "Vergil's Laokoon." *Eranos* 91: 126–28.

——. 1993b. "Vexillum caeruleum." *Rheinisches Museum* 136: 374–76.

——. 1994. "Rez. Gerhard J. Baudy, Die Brände Roms . . . 1991." *Gnomon* 66: 40–44.

——. 1995a. *Kalender und Öffentlichkeit: Die Geschichte der Repräsentation und religiösen Qualifikation von Zeit in Rom.* Religionsgeschichtliche Versuche und Vorarbeiten 40. Berlin.

——. 1995b. "Wege zum Töten, Wege zum Ruhm: Krieg in der römischen Republik." In H. v. Stietencron and J. Rüpke, eds., *Töten im Krieg.* Freiburg. 213–40.

——. 1996a. "Charismatics or Professionals? Analyzing Religious Specialists." *Numen* 43: 241–62.

——. 1996b. "Quis vetat et stellas . . . ? Les levers des étoiles et la tradition calendaire chez Ovide." In B. Bakhouche, A. Moreau, and J.-C. Turpin, eds., *Les astres 1: Les astres et les mythes, la description du ciel.* Publications de la Recherche Université Paul Valéry. Montpellier. 293–306.

——. 1999a. "Apokalyptische Salzberge: Zum sozialen Ort und zur literarischen Strategie des 'Hirten des Hermas'." *Archiv für Religiongeschichte* 1: 148–60.

——. 1999b. "[Rez.] Cristofani, Mauro: Tabula Capuana . . . 1995." *Gnomon* 71 (3): 272–74.

———. 2001a. "Kulturtransfer als Rekodierung: Überlegungen zum literaturgeschichtlichen und sozialen Ort der frühen römischen Epik." In J. Rüpke, ed., *Von Menschen und Göttern erzählen: Formkonstanzen und Funktionswandel vormoderner Epik*. Stuttgart. 42–64.

———. 2001b. "Religiöse Kommunikation im provinzialen Raum." In W. Spickermann, ed., *Religion in den germanischen Provinzen Roms*. Tübingen. 71–88.

———. 2003a. "Acta aut agenda: Text-Performanz-Beziehungen in der römischen Religionsgeschichte." In B. Kranemann and J. Rüpke, eds., *Das Gedächtnis des Gedächtnisses: Zur Präsenz von Ritualen in beschreibenden und reflektierenden Texten*. Marburg. 11–38.

———. 2003b. "L'histoire des fasti romains: aspects médiatiques." *Revue historique de droit francais et étranger* 81: 125–39.

———. 2005a. "Bilderwelten und Religionswechsel." In R. v. Haehling, ed., *Griechische Mythologie und frühes Christentum*. Darmstadt.

———. 2005b. "Der Hirte des Hermas: Plausibilisierungs- und Legitimierungsstrategien im Übergang von Antike und Christentum." *Zeitschrift für antikes Christentum* 8: 276–98.

———. 2005c. *Fasti sacerdotum: Die Mitglieder der Priesterschaften und das sakrale Funktionspersonal römischer, griechischer, orientalischer und jüdisch-christlicher Kulte in der Stadt Rom von 300 v. Chr. bis 499 n. Chr*. Potsdamer altertumswissenschaftliche Beiträge 12/1–3. Stuttgart.

———. 2005d. "Gäste der Götter—Götter als Gäste: zur Konstruktion des römischen Opferbanketts." In S. Georgoudi, R. Koch Piettre, and F. Schmidt, eds., *La cuisine et l'autel: Les sacrifices en questions dans les sociétés de la Méditerranée ancienne (Bibliothèque des Hautes Études)*. Turnhout. 227–39.

———. 2005e. "Varro's tria genera theologiae: Religious Thinking in the Late Republic." *Ordia prima* 4: 107–29.

———. 2006a. "Communicating with the Gods." In R. Morstein-Marx and N. Rosenstein, eds., *The Blackwell Companion to the Roman Republic*. Oxford. 215–35.

———. 2006b. *Die Religion der Römer. Eine Einführung*. 2nd rev. ed. Munich.

———. 2006c. "Ennius' Fasti in Fulvius' Temple: Greek Rationality and Roman Tradition." *Arethusa* 39: 489–512.

———. 2006d. "Tempel, Daten, Rituale: die Götter als Langzeitgedächtnis der Gesellschaft." In E. Stein-Hölkeskamp and K.-J. Hölkeskamp, eds., *Erinnerungsorte der Antike: Die römische Welt*. München. 554–69.

———. 2006e. "Triumphator and Ancestor Rituals between Symbolic Anthropology and Magic." *Numen* 53: 251–89.

———. 2006f. *Zeit und Fest: Eine Kulturgeschichte des Kalenders*. München.

———. 2007a. *Religion of the Romans*. R. Gordon, trans. Cambridge.

———. 2007b. "Römische Religion und religiöser Wandel in der Spätantike." *Verkündigung und Forschung* 52 (2): 7–19.

———. 2008a. *Fasti sacerdotum. A Prosopography of Pagan, Jewish, and Christian Religious Officials in the City of Rome, 300 BC to AD 499*. D.M.B. Richardson, trans. Oxford.

———. 2008b. "Göttliche Macht ohne Gesicht: Eine religionswissenschaftliche Sondierung." In R. G. Kratz and H. Spieckermann, eds., *Vorsehung, Schicksal und göttliche Macht: Antike Stimmen zu einem aktuellen Thema*. Tübingen. 1–22.

————. 2008c. "Neue Perspektiven auf alte Statuenrituale. Überlegungen zu *Res gestae Divi Augusti* 4." *Triplici invectus triumpho* 2008: 11–26.

————. 2009a. "Dedications Accompanied by Inscriptions in the Roman Empire: Functions, Intentions, Modes of Communication." In J. Bodel and M. Kajava, eds., *Dediche sacre nel mono greco-romano: Diffusione, funzioni, tipologie / Religious Dedications in the Greco-Roman World: Distribution, Typology, Use.* Acta Instituti Romani Finlandiae 35. Roma. 31–41.

————. 2009b. "Equus October und ludi Capitolini: Zur rituellen Struktur der Oktoberiden und ihren antiken Deutungen." In U. Duell and C. Walde, eds., *Antike Mythen: Medien, Transformationen und Konstruktionen: FS Fritz Graf zum 65. Geburtstag.* Berlin. 97–121.

————. 2010a. "'Königsflucht' und Tyrannenvertreibung: Zur Historisierung des Regifugium in augusteischer Zeit." In R. Gröschner and W. Reinhard, eds., *Tage der Revolution—Feste der Nation.* Politika 3. Tübingen. 29–41.

————. 2010b. "Performanzkultur: Zur Sichtbarkeit von Religion und religiösen Spezialisten im antiken Rom." In B. Beinhauer-Köhler, D. Pezzoli-Olgiati, and J. Valentin, eds., *Religiöse Blicke—Blicke auf das Religiöse: Visualität und Religion.* Zürich. 149–63.

————. 2010c. "Radikale im öffentlichen Dienst: Status und Individualisierung unter römischen Priestern republikanischer Zeit." In P. Barceló, ed., *Religiöser Fundamentalismus in der römischen Kaiserzeit.* Potsdamer altertumswissenschaftliche Beiträge 29. Stuttgart. 11–21.

————. 2010d. "Representation or Presence? Picturing the Divine in Ancient Rome." *Archiv für Religionsgeschichte* 12: 183–96.

————. 2010e. "Wann begann die europäische Religionsgeschichte? Der hellenistisch-römische Mittelmeerraum und die europäische Gegenwart." *Historia religionum* 2: 91–102.

————. 2011a. *Aberglauben oder Individualität? Religiöse Abweichung im römischen Reich.* Tübingen.

————. 2011b. "Individual Appropriations and Institutional Changes: Roman Priesthoods in the Later Empire." In G. A. Cecconi and C. Gabrielli, eds., *Politiche religiose nel mondo antico e tardoantico: Poteri e indirizzi, forme del controllo, idee e prassi di tolleranza: Atti del Convegno internazionale di studi (Firenze, 24–26 settembre 2009).* Munera 33. Bari. 261–73.

————. 2011c. "Reichsreligion? Überlegungen zur Religionsgeschichte des antiken Mittelmeerraums in römischer Zeit." *Historische Zeitschrift* 292: 297–322.

————. 2011d. *The Roman Calendar from Numa to Constantine: Time, History and the Fasti.* D.M.B. Richardson, trans. Malden, Mass.

————. 2011e. *Von Jupiter und Christus: Religionsgeschichte in römischer Zeit.* Darmstadt.

————. 2012a. *Antike Epik. Eine Einführung von Homer bis in die Spätantike.* 2nd. ammended ed., Nova Classica 1. Marburg.

————. 2012b. "Der Tod als Ende der Sterblichkeit: Praktiken und Konzeptionen in der römischen Antike." In A. Lang and P. Marinkovic, eds., *Bios—Cultus—(Im)mortalitas: Zur Religion und Kultur—Von den biologischen Grundlagen bis zu Jenseitsvorstellungen:*

Beiträge der interdisziplinären Kolloquium vom 10.–11. März 2006 und 24.–25. Juli 2009 in der Ludwig-Maximilians-Universität München. Rahden/Westf. 199–209.

———. 2012c. "Flamines, Salii, and the Priestesses of Vesta: Individual Decision and Differences of Social Order in the Late Republic." In A. Mastrocincque and C. G. Scibona, eds., *Demeter, Isis, Vesta, and Cybele: Studies in Greek and Roman Religion in Honour of Giulia Sfameni Gasparro,* Potsdamer altertumswissenschaftliche Beiträge 36. Stuttgart. 183–94.

———. 2012d. "Lived Ancient Religion: Questioning 'Cults' and 'Polis Religion'." *Mythos* ns 5 (2011) 191–204.

———. 2012e. "Public and Publicity: Long-Term Changes in Religious Festivals during the Roman Republic." In J. R. Brandt and J. W. Iddeng, eds., *Festivals in the Ancient World.* Oxford. 305–22.

———. 2012f. *Religion in Republican Rome: Rationalization and Ritual Change.* Philadelphia.

———. 2012g. *Religiöse Erinnerungskulturen: Formen der Geschichtsschreibung in der römischen Antike.* Darmstadt.

———. 2012h. "Religiöse Individualität in der Antike." In B. Janowski, ed., *Der ganze Mensch: Zur Anthropologie der Antike und ihrer europäischen Nachgeschichte.* Berlin. 199–219.

———. 2012i. "Starting Sacrifice in the Beyond: Flavian Innovations in the Concept of Priesthood and Their Repercussions in the Treatise 'To the Hebrews'." *Revue d'histoire des religions* 229: 5–30.

———. 2013a. "Archaic Roman Religion through the Republic." In M. R. Salzman and M. A. Sweeney, eds., *Cambridge History of Religions in the Ancient World* 1: *From the Bronze Age to the Hellenstic Age.* Cambridge. 336–63.

———. 2013b. "Fighting for Differences: Forms and Limits of Religious Individuality in the 'Shepherd of Hermas'." In J. Rüpke, ed., *The Individual in the Religions of the Ancient Mediterranean.* Oxford. 315–41.

———. 2013c. "Heiliger und öffentlicher Raum: Römische Perspektiven auf private Religion." In B. Edelmann-Singer and H. Konen, eds., *Salutationes—Beiträge zur Alten Geschichte und ihrer Diskussion: Festschrift für Peter Herz zum 65. Geburtstag.* Region im Umbruch 9. Berlin. 159–68.

———. 2013d. *The Individual in the Religions of the Ancient Mediterranean.* Oxford.

———. 2013e. "Individuals and Networks." In L. Bricault and C. Bonnet, eds., *Panthée: Religious Transformations in the Graeco-Roman Empire.* Religions in the Graeco-Roman World 177. Leiden. 261–77.

———. 2013f. "Individuelle Religion." In A. Schäfer and M. Witteyer, eds., *Rituelle Deponierungen in Heiligtümern der hellenistisch-römischen Welt: International Tagung Mainz 28.–30. April.* Mainzer Archäologische Schriften 10. Mainz. 25–34.

———. 2013g. "Introduction: Individualisation and Individuation as Concepts for Historical Research." In J. Rüpke, ed., *The Individual in the Religions of the Ancient Mediterranean.* Oxford. 3–28.

———. 2013h. "Leistung und Grenze von Mythen in religionswissenschaftlicher Perspektive." In A. Zgoll and R. G. Kratz, eds., *Arbeit am Mythos: Leistung und Grenze des Mythos in Antike und Gegenwart.* Tübingen. 35–58.

————. 2013i. "New Perspectives on Ancient Divination." In V. Rosenberger, ed., *Divina-tion in the Ancient World: Religious Options and the Individual*. Potsdamer Altertum-swissenschaftliche Beiträge 46. Stuttgart. 9–19.

————. 2013j. "Regulating and Conceptualizing Religious Plurality: Italian Experiences and Roman Solutions." In M. Jehne, B. Linke, and J. Rüpke, eds., *Religiöse Vielfalt und soziale Integration: Die Bedeutung der Religion für die kulturelle Identität und politische Stabilität im republikanischen Italien*. Studien zur Alten Geschichte 17. Heidelberg. 275–95.

————. 2013k. "Religiöse Individualität." In B. Kracke, R. Roux, and J. Rüpke eds., *Die Re-ligion des Individuums*. Vorlesungen des Interdisziplinären Forums Religion 9. Münster. 13–29.

————. 2013l. "Überlegungen zur öffentlichen Festkultur aus ritualtheoretischer Perspe-ktive." In H. Groschopp, ed., *Humanismus—Laizismus—Geschichtskultur*. Schriften-reihe der Humanistischen Akademie Berlin 6. Aschaffenburg. 123–38.

————. 2013m. "Was ist ein Heiligtum? Pluralität als Gegenstand der Religionswissen-schaft." In A. Adogame, M. Echtler, and O. Freiberger, eds., *Alternative Voices: A Plural-ity Approach for Religious Studies: Essays in Honor of Ulrich Berner*. Critical Studies in Religion/Religionswissenschaft 4. Göttingen. 211–25.

————. 2014a. "Der Kaiser ist kein Vollzeitchrist." Review of Pedro Barceló, *Das Römische Reich im religiösen Wandel der Spätantike: Kaiser und Bischöfe im Widerstreit . . . 2013. Frankfurter Allgemeine Zeitung* 45 (25.2.2014): 30.

————. 2014b. *From Jupiter to Christ: On the History of Religion in the Roman Imperial Pe-riod*. D.M.B. Richardson, trans. Oxford.

————. 2014c. "Historicizing Religion: Varro's Antiquitates and History of Religion in the Late Roman Republic." *History of Religions* 53 (3): 246–68.

————. 2014d. *Il crocevia del mito: Religione e narrazione nel mondo antico*. G. Cerro, trans. Bologna.

————. 2014e. "Religiöses Handeln: Kommunikation mit göttlichen Mächten." In Bad-isches Landesmuseum, ed., *Imperium der Götter: Isis—Mithras—Christus. Religionen im römischen Reich*. Stuttgart. 32–39.

————. 2014f. *Römische Geschichtsschreibung*. Marburg.

————. 2015a. "The 'Connected Reader' as a Window into Lived Ancient Religion: A Case Study of Ovid's Libri fastorum " *Religion in the Roman Empire* 1 (1): 95–113.

————. 2015b. "Der Hirte des Hermas: Visionsliteratur als Anleitung zu religiöser Praxis in Textproduktion und -rezeption." In P. Eich et al., eds., *Alejandro, Aníbal y Constan-tino. Tres personajes históricos y una vida dedicada a conocerlos mejor (Homenaje a Pedro Barceló en su jubilación académica)—Alexander, Hannibal und Constantin. Drei histo-rische Persönlichkeiten und ein Forscher, der sich ihnen widmet (Festschrift für Pedro Bar-celó)*. Institut des Sciences et Techniques de l'Antiquité, Lyon.

————. 2015c. "Geteilte und umstrittene Geschichten: Der Chronograph von 354 und die Katakombe an der Via Latina." In H. Leppin, ed., *Antike Mythologie in christlichen Kon-texten der Spätantike*. Berlin. 221–38.

————. 2015d. "Individual Choices and Individuality in the Archaeology of Ancient Reli-gion." In R. Raja and J. Rüpke, eds., *A Companion to the Archaeology of Religion in the Ancient World*. Malden, Mass. 437–50.

———. 2015e. "Religious Agency, Identity, and Communication: Reflecting on the History and Theory of Religion." *Religion* 45 (3): 344–66.

———. 2016a. "Knowledge of Religion in Valerius Maximus' Exempla: Roman Historiography and Tiberian Memory Culture." In K. Galinsky, ed., *Memory in Ancient Rome and Early Christianity*. Oxford. 89–111.

———. 2016b. "Narratives as a factor and indicator of religious change in the Roman Empire (1st and 2nd centuries)." *Studia Patristica* 75.

———. 2016c. *On Roman Religion: Lived Religion and the Individual in Ancient Rome*, Townsend Lectures/Cornell Studies in Classical Philology. Ithaca, NY.

———. 2016d. "Privatization and Individualization." In S. Engler and M. Stausberg, ed., *The Oxford Handbook of the Study of Religion*. Oxford. 702–17.

———. 2016e. *Religious Deviance in the Roman World: Superstition or Individuality*. D.M.B. Richardson. Cambridge.

———. 2016f. "Römische Priestermähler." In D. Hellholm and D. Sänger, eds., *The Eucharist—Its Origins and Contexts: Sacred Meal, Communal Meal, Table Fellowship, and the Eucharist* 3. WUNT. Tübingen. 1527–37.

———. 2016g. "Textgemeinschaften und die Erfindung von Toleranz in der römischen Kaiserzeit (2./3. Jh. n. Chr.)." In M. Wallraff, ed., *Religiöse Toleranz. 1700 Jahre nach dem Edikt von Mailand*. Colloquium Rauricum 14. Berlin. 141–57.

———. 2016h. "Theorizing Religion for the Individual." In V. Gasparini and R. Veymiers, eds., *The Greco-Roman Cults of Isis: Agents, Images and Practices*. Religions in the Graeco-Roman World. Leiden.

———. 2017a. "Doubling Religion in the Augustan Age: Shaping Time for an Empire." In J. Ben-Dov and L. Doering, eds., *The Construction of Time in Antiquity*. Cambridge.

———. 2017b. "Writing the First Christian Commentary on a Biblical Book in Ancient Rome: Hippolytus." In C. Altini, P. Hoffmann, J. Rüpke, *Interpretazione—Interpretation*. Stuttgart.

Rüpke, J., and W. Spickermann, eds. 2012. *Reflections on Religious Individuality: Greco-Roman and Judaeo-Christian Texts and Practices*. Religionsgeschichtliche Versuche und Vorarbeiten 62. Berlin.

Rüpke, J., J. Stagl, and V. Winiwarter. 2012. "Formen des Wissens über die Zukunft." *Saeculum* 62 (2): 183–7.

Rüpke, J. and G. Woolf, eds. 2013a. "Introduction." In J. Rüpke and G. Woolf, eds., *Religious Dimensions of the Self in the Second Century CE*. Studien und Texte zu Antike und Christentum 76. Tübingen. vii–xi.

———. 2013b. *Religious Dimensions of the Self in the Second Century CE*. Studien und Texte zu Antike und Christentum 76. Tübingen.

Rüpke, U. and J. Rüpke. 2010. *Die 101 wichtigsten Fragen—Götter und Mythen der Antike*. Beck'sche Reihe 7028. München.

Rüsen, J. 1990. *Zeit und Sinn: Strategien historischen Denkens*. Frankfurt a. M.

———. 1996. "Some Theoretical Approaches to Intercultural Comparative Historiography." *History and Theory* 35 (4): 5–22.

———, ed. 2001. *Geschichtsbewußtsein: psychologische Grundlagen, Entwicklungskonzepte, empirische Befunde*, Beitäge zur Geschichtskultur 21. Köln.

Rutherford, I. 2007. "Network Theory and Theoric Networks." *Mediterranean Historical Review* 22 (1): 23–37.

———. 2013. *State Pilgrims and Sacred Observers in Ancient Greece: A Study of Theōriā and Theōroi.* Cambridge.

Saddington, D. B. 2009. "Deities Chosen for Worship by Soldiers in a Provincial Army— the Case of Roman Britain." In Catherine Wolff and Y. L. Bohec, eds., *L'armée romaine et la religion sous le Haut-Empire romain* 33. Collection du Centre d'Etudes et de Recherches sur l'Occident Romain. Paris. 87–98.

Saller, R. P. 1984. "Familia, domus, and the Roman Conception of the Family." *Phoenix* 38: 336–55.

Sallmann, K. 2002. "Varro [2] Terentius, M. (Reatinus)." *Neuer Pauly* 12/2: 1130–44.

Salway, B. 1994. "What's in a Name? A Survey of Roman Onomastic Practice from c. 700 BC to AD 700." *Journal of Roman Studies* 84: 124–45.

Salzman, M. R. 1990. *On Roman Time: The Codex-Calendar of 354 and the Rhythms of Urban Life in Late Antiquity.* The Transformation of the Classical Heritage 17. Berkeley.

———. 1992. "How the West Was Won: The Christianization of the Roman Aristocracy in the West in the Years after Constantine." In C. Deroux, ed., *Studies in Latin Literature and Roman History* 6. Brussels. 451–79.

———. 2002. *The Making of a Christian Aristocracy: Social and Religious Change in the Western Roman Empire.* Cambridge, Mass.

Samter, E. 1901. *Familienfeste der Griechen und Römer.* Berlin.

Samuel, A. E. 1972. *Greek and Roman Chronology: Calendars and Years in Classical Antiquity.* Handbuch der Altertumswissenschaft 1,7. München.

Sanders, E. P. 1992. *Judaism: Practice and Belief, 63 BCE—66 CE.* 4th repr. 2005 ed. London.

Sandmel, S. 1984. "Philo Judaeus: An Introduction to the Man, His Writings, and His Significance." *ANRW* II.21,1: 3–46.

Santangelo, F. 2008. "The Fetials and Their Ius." *Bullentin of the Institute of Classical Studies* 54: 63–93.

———. 2013. *Divination, Prediction and the End of the Republic.* Cambridge.

———. 2014. "I feziali fra rituale, diplomazia e tradizioni inventate." In G. Urso, ed., *Sacerdos: Figure del sacro nella società romana. Atti del convegno internazionale Cividale del Friuli, 26–28 settembre 2012.* Pisa. 83–103.

Sanzi, E. 2005. "Magia e Culti orientali V: Che ci fa dio Mithra in un papiro magico-oracolare? Ovverosia note storico-religiose intorno a PGM V, 1–53." In G. Sfameni Gasparro, ed., *Modi di comunicazione tra il divino e l'umano: Tradizioni profetiche, divinazione, astrologia e magia nel ondo mediterraneo antico.* Themes and Problems of the History of Religions in Contemporary Europe 2. Cosenza. 355–83.

———. 2013. *Iuppiter Optimus maximus Dolichenus: Un 'culto orientale' fra tradizione e innovazione: riflessioni storico-religose.* Roma.

Sartre, M., ed. 2005. *The Middle East under Rome.* Cambridge.

Satake, A. 2008. *Die Offenbarung des Johannes.* Göttingen.

Scapaticci, M. G. 2010. "Vetralla: Un santuario a 'Macchia delle Valli'." In P. A. Gianfrotta and A. M. Moretti, eds., *Archeologia nella Tuscia: Atti dell'Incontro di Studio (Viterbo, 2 marzo 2007)* 10. DAIDALOS—Studi e ricerche del Dipartimento di Scienze del Mondo Antico 10. Tuscia. 101–36.

Scatozza Höricht, L. A. 2006. "Modellino votivo e rivestimenti fittili di Pithekoussai." In I. Edlund-Berry, G. Greco, and J. Kenfield, eds., *Deliciae Fictiles* III: *Architectural Terracottas in Ancient Italy: New Discoveries and Interpretations.* Oxford. 249–57.

Schaper, J. 2009. *Die Textualisierung der Religion.* Forschungen zum Alten Testament 62. Tübingen.

Schechner, R. 1985. *Between Theater and Anthropology.* Foreword by Victor Turner. Philadelphia.

Scheibelreiter-Gail, V. 2012. "Inscriptions in the Late Antique Private House: Some Thoughts about Their Function and Distribution." In S. Birk and B. Poulsen, eds., *Patrons and Viewers in Late Antiquity.* Aarhus. 135–65.

Scheid, J. 1978. "Les prêtres officiels sous les empereurs julio-claudiens." *ANRW* II.16,1: 610–54.

———. 1981. "Le délit religieux dans la Rome tardo-républicaine." In Scheid, ed., *Le délit religieux dans la cité antique.* Rome. 117–71.

———. 1985. "Sacrifice et banquet à Rome: Quelques problèmes." *MEFRA* 97: 193–206.

———. 1988. "La spartizione sacrificale a Roma." In M. G. Amadasi Guzzo, ed., *Sacrificio e società nel mondo antico.* Bari. 267–92.

———. 1990. *Romulus et ses frères: Le collège des frères arvales, modèle du culte public dans la Rome des empereurs.* Bibliothèque des Écoles françaises d'Athènes et de Rome 275. Rome.

———. 1992. "Myth, Cult and Reality in Ovid's Fasti." *PCPhS* 38: 118–31.

———. 1993a. "Die Parentalien für die verstorbenen Caesaren als Modell für den römischen Totenkult." *Klio* 75: 188–201.

———. 1993b. "Lucus, nemus: Qu'est-ce qu'un bois sacré?" *Les bois sacrés: Actes du colloque international de Naples*: 13–20.

———. 2001. *Religion et piété à Rome.* Paris.

———. 2004a. "Comprendre le culte dit impérial: Autour de deux livres récents." Review of Liertz, *Kult und Kaiser* and Gradel, *Emperor Worship. L'Antiquité classique* 73: 239–49.

———. 2004b. "Quand fut construit l'Iseum Campense?" In L. Ruscu, ed., *Orbis Antiquus: Studia in honorem Ioannis Pisonis.* Bibliotheca Musei Napocensis 21. Cluj-Napoca. 308–11.

———. 2007a. "Körperbestattung und Verbrennungssitte aus der Sicht der schriftlichen Quellen." In A. u. a. H. Faber, ed., *Körpergräber des 1.–3. Jahrhunderts in der römischen Welt.* Schriften des Archäologischen Museums Frankfurt 21. Frankfurt a. M. 19–25.

———. 2007b. *Res gestae divi Augusti: Hauts faits du divin Auguste.* Collection Budé. Paris.

———. ed. 2008. *Pour une archéologie du rite: nouvelles perspectives de l'archéologie funéraire.* Collection de l'École francaise de Rome 407. Rome.

———. 2009. "To Honour the Princeps and Venerate the Gods: Public Cult, Neighbourhood Cults, and Imperial Cult in Augustan Rome." In J. Edmondson, ed., *Augustus.* Edinburgh. 275–99.

———. 2012a. "Le rite des auspices à Rome: quelle évolution? Réflexions sur la transformation de la divination publique des Romains entre le IIIe et le Ier siècle avant notre ère." In S. Georgoudi, R. Koch Piettre, and F. Schmidt, eds., *La Raison des signes: Présages, rites, destin dans les sociétés de la Méditerranée ancienne*. Religions in the Graeco-Roman World 174. Leiden. 109–28.

———. 2012b. *Plutarch, Römische Fragen: Ein virtueller Spaziergang im Herzen des alten Rom*. Darmstadt.

———. 2015. "Livy and Religion." In B. Mineo, ed., *A Companion to Livy*. Malden, Mass. 78–89.

———. 2016a. *The Gods, the State, and the Individual: Reflections on Civic Religion in Rome*. C. Ando, trans. Empire and After. Philadelphia.

———. 2016b. "Le lustrum et la lusratio: En finir avec la 'purification'." In V. Gasparini, ed., *Vestigia: Studii Filippo Coarelli*. PawB. Stuttgart. 203–10.

Scheid, J., and J. Svenbro. 1996. *The Craft of Zeus: Myths of Weaving and Fabric*. Translated by C. Volk, Revealing Antiquity 9. Cambridge, Mass.

Scheidel, W. 1992. "Inschriftenstatistik und die Frage des Rekrutierungsalters römischer Soldaten." *Chiron* 22: 281–97.

———. 2009. "Introduction." In W. Scheidel, ed., *Rome and China: Comparative Perspectives on Ancient World Empires*. Oxford. 3–51.

Schellenberg, R. S. 2011. "'Danger in the wilderness, danger at sea': Paul and the Perils of Travel." In P. A. Harlan, ed., *Travel and Religion in Antiquity*. Studies in Christianity and Judaism 21. Waterloo, Ont. 141–61.

Schenke, H.-M., H.-G. Bethge, and U. U. Kaiser, eds. 2007. *Nag Hammadi Deutsch: Studienausgabe*. Eingeleitet und übers. von Mitgliedern des Berliner Arbeitskreises für Koptisch-Gnostische Schriften. Berlin.

Schiavone, A. 2012. *The Invention of Law in the West*. Cambridge.

Schiffman, L. H. 1985. "The Sacrificial System of the Temple Scroll and the Book of Jubilees." *Society of Biblical Literature Seminar Papers No* 24: 217–33.

Schildgen, B. D. 2012. *Divine Providence. A History: The Bible, Virgil, Orosius, Augustine, and Dante*. London.

Schlesier, R. 1997. "Dionysos I. Religion." *Neuer Pauly* 3: 651–62.

Schlette, M., and M. Jung, eds. 2005. *Anthropologie der Artikulation: Begriffliche Grundlagen und transdiziplinäre Perspektiven*. Würzburg.

Schmid, A. 2005. *Augustus und die Macht der Sterne: Antike Astrologie und die Etablierung der Monarchie in Rom*. Köln.

Schmidt, D., and A. Kaufmann-Heinimann. 1999. *Götter im Haus*, Augster Museumshefte 21. August.

Schmidt, P. L. 2001. "Rezitation(en), öffentliche." *Neuer Pauly* 10: 940–42.

Schmidt-Hofner, S. 2016. "Die Kaiser und das Risiko der Toleranz: Zur Funktion der sogenannten 'Toleranzedikte'." In M. Wallraff, ed., *Religiöse Toleranz. 1700 Jahre nach dem Edikt von Mailand*. Colloquium Rauricum 14. Berlin. 159–92.

Schnegg-Köhler, B. 2002. *Die augusteischen Säkularspiele*. Archiv für Religionsgeschichte 4. München.

Schneider, R. M. 2009. "Gegen die Norm? Lachen im Medium antiker Bilder." In A. Nitschke, ed., *Überraschendes Lachen, gefordertes Weinen: Gefühle und Prozesse; Kulturen und Epochen im Vergleich*. Veröffentlichungen des Instituts für Historische Anthropologie 11. Wien.

Scholten, C. 1991. "Hippolytos II (von Rom)." *RAC* 15: 492–551.

Scholz, P., and U. Walter. 2013. *Fragmente Römischer Memoiren*. Studien zur Alten Geschichte 18. Heidelberg.

Scholz, U. W. 1970. *Studien zum altitalischen und altrömischen Marskult und Marsmythos*. Heidelberg.

Schörner, G. 2011. "Sacrifice East and West: Experiencing Ritual Differences in the Roman Empire." In U. Simon et al., eds. *Reflexivity, Media, and Visuality*. Ritual Dynamics and the Science of Ritual 4. Wiesbaden. 81–99.

———. 2013. "Wie integriert man Rom in die Polis? Der Kult des Senats in Kleinasien." In G. de Kleijn and S. Benoist, eds., *Integration in Rome and in the Roman World: Proceedings of the Tenth Workshop of the International Network Impact of Empire*. Leiden. 217–42.

Schorn-Schütte, L. 2012. "Einleitung: Das Politische als Argument." In A. De Benedictis et al., eds., *Das Politische als Argument: Beiträge zur Forschungsdebatte aus dem Internationalen Graduiertenkolleg "Politische Kommunikation von der Antike bis in das 20. Jahrhundert."* Göttingen. 7–15.

Schott, J. M. 2008. *Christianity, Empire, and the Making of Religion in Late Antiquity*. Philadelphia.

Schröder, B. 2012. "Römische pietas—kein universelles Postulat." *Gymnasium* 119 (4): 335–58.

Schrumpf, S. 2006. *Bestattung und Bestattungswesen im Römischen Reich: Ablauf, soziale Dimension und ökonomische Bedeutung der Totenfürsorge im lateinischen Westen*. Bonn.

Schuller, F., and H. Wolff, eds. 2007. *Konstantin der Große: Kaiser einer Epochenwende*. Lindenberg.

Schultz, C. E. 2000. "Modern Prejudice and Ancient Praxis: Female Worship of Hercules at Rome." *Zeitschrift für Papyrologie und Epigrafik* 133: 291–97.

———. 2012. "On the Burial of Unchaste Vestal Virgins." In M. Bardley, ed., *Rome, Pollution and Propriety: Dirt, Disease and Hygiene in the Eternal City from Antiquity to Modernity*. Cambridge. 122–36.

Schütz, A. 1981. *Der sinnhafte Aufbau der sozialen Welt: Eine Einleitung in die verstehende Soziologie*. Frankfurt a. M.

Schwarte, K.-H. 1994. "Diokletians Christengesetz." In R. Günther and S. Rebenich, eds., *E fontibus haurire: Beiträge zur römischen Geschichte und zu ihren Hilfswissenschaften*. Paderborn. 203–40.

Schwartz, S. 2001. *Imperialism and Jewish Society, 200 B.C.E. to 640 C.E. Jews, Christians, and Muslims from the Ancient to the Modern World*. Princeton.

———. 2010. *Were the Jews a Mediterranean Society? Reciprocity and Solidarity in Ancient Judaism*. Princeton.

Schwarzer, H. 2012. "Die Heiligtümer des Iuppiter Dilochenus." In M. Blömer and E. Winter, eds., *Iuppiter Dilochenus. Vom Lokalkult zur Reichsreligion*. Tübingen. 143–210.

Scioli, E. 2015. *Dream, Fantasy, and Visual Art in Roman Elegy*. Wisconsin Studies in Classics. Madison, Wisconsin.

Sciortino, I. 2005. "Roma, Foro Romano: Il deposito votivo presso el Clivo Capitolino." In A. Comella and S. Mele, eds., *Depositi votivi e culti dell'Italia antica dall'età arcaica a quella tardo-repubblicana: Atti del Convegno di Studi Perugia, 1–4 giugno 2000*. Bibliotheca archaeologica 16. Bari. 85–93.

Scopello, M. 2010. "Les Milieux Gnostiques." In M. J.-P. Mahé, M. P.-H. Poirier, and M. Scopello, eds., *Les Textes de Nag Hammadi: Histoire des Religions et approches contemporaines: Actes du colloque international réuni á Paris, le 11 décembre 2008, á la fondation Simone et Cino del Duca, le 12 décembre 2008, au palais de l'Institut de France*. Paris. 251–67.

Scott, S. 1997. "The Power of Images in the Late Roman House." In R. Laurence and A. Wallace-Hadrill, eds., *Domestic Space in the Roman World: Pompeii and Beyond. Journal of Roman Archaeology*, Suppl. 22. Portsmouth, RI. 53–67.

Scullion, S. 1998. "Three Notes on Attic Sacrificial Calendars." *Zeitschrift für Papyrologie und Epigraphik* 12. 116–22.

Sear, F. 2006. *Roman Theatres: An Architectural Study*. Repr. 2010 ed. Oxford.

Seeliger, H. R., and W. Wischmeyer. 2015. *Märtyrerliteratur*. Texte und Untersuchungen zur Geschichte der altchristlichen Literatur 172. Berlin.

Sehlmeyer, M. 1999. *Stadtrömische Ehrenstatuen der republikanischen Zeit: Historizität und Kontext von Symbolen nobilitären Standesbewusstseins*, Historia Einzelschriften 130. Stuttgart.

Seiler, F. 1992. *Casa degli Amorini dorati (VI 16, 7.38)*. Häuser in Pompeji 5. München.

Seim, T. K., and J. Økland, eds. 2009. *Metamorphoses: Resurrection, Body and Transformative Practices in Early Christianity*. Ekstasis 1. Berlin.

Sellars, J. 2004. *The Art of Living: The Stoics on the Nature and Function of Philosophy*. Burlington, VT.

Setaioli, A. 2007. "Seneca and the Divine: Stoic Tradition and Personal Developments." *International Journal of the Classical Tradition* 13: 333–68.

———. 2013. "Cicero and Seneca on the Fate of the Soul: Private Feelings and Philosophical Doctrines." In J. Rüpke, ed., *The Individual in the Religions of the Ancient Mediterranean*. Oxford. 455–88.

Settis, S. 1988. "Die Ara Pacis." In Settis, ed., *Kaiser Augustus und die verlorene Republik*. Berlin. 400–26.

Sewell, J. 2013. "New Observations on the Planning of Fora in the Latin Colonies during the Mid-Republic." In C. P. Dickenson and O. M. Van Nijf, eds., *Public Space in the Post-Classical City*. Leuven, Paris, Walpole, MA. 76–112.

Sfameni Gasparro, G. 2007. "ΘΕΟΣ ΣΩΤΗΡ: Aspetti del culto di Asclepio dell'eta ellenistica alla tarda antichita." In H. Brandenburg, S. Heid, and C. Markschies, eds., *Salute e guarigione nella tarda antichità: atti della giornata tematica dei Seminari di Archeologia Cristiana, Roma, 20 maggio 2004*. Sussidi allo studio delle antichità cristiane 19. Città del Vaticano. 245–71.

Sgubini, A. M., and M., L. Ricciardi 2005. "Usi funerari a Vulci." In Sgubini and Ricciardi, eds., *Dinamiche di sviluppo delle città nell'Etruria meridionale: Veio, Caere,*

Tarquinia, Vulci. Atti del XXIII Convegno di Studi Etruschi ed Italici, 1–6 ottobre 2001, 2. Pisa. 523–27.

Sharon, N. 2012. "Setting the Stage: The Effects of the Roman Conquest and the Loss of Sovereignty." In D. R. Schwartz and Z. Weiss, eds., *Was 70 CE a Watershed in Jewish History? On Jews and Judaism before and after the Destruction of the Second Temple*. Ancient Judaism and Early Christianity: Arbeiten zur Geschichte des antiken Judentums und des Urchristentums 78. Leiden. 415–45.

Shaw, B. D. 1984. "Latin Funerary Epigraphy and Family Life in the Later Roman Empire." *Historia* 33: 457–97.

———. 2011. *Sacred Violence: African Christians and Sectarian Hatred in the Age of Augustine*. 1st ed. Cambridge.

———. 2015. "The Myth of the Neronian Persecution." *Journal of Roman Studies* 105: 73–100.

Shaya, J. 2013. "The Public Life of Monuments: The Summi Viri of the Forum of Augustus." *American Journal of Archaeology* 107: 83–110.

Shelton, J.-A. 2013. *The Women of Pliny's Letters*. Women of the Ancient World. London.

Shelton, W. B. 2003. *Exegesis and the Role of Martyrdom in Hippolytus' Commentary on Daniel*. Ann Arbor.

———. 2008. *Martyrdom from Exegesis in Hippolytus: An Early Church Presbyter's Commentary on Daniel*. Studies in Christian History and Thought. Milton Keynes.

Sherwin-White, A. N. 1966. *The Letters of Pliny: A Historical and Social Commentary*. Oxford.

Shorrock, R. 2011. *The Myth of Paganism: Nonnus, Dionysus and the World of Late Antiquity*. Classical Literature and Society. London.

Shuttleworth Kraus, C. 2007. "Historiography and Biography." In S. J. Harrison, ed., *A Companion to Latin Literature*. Blackwell Companions to the Ancient World, Literature and Culture. Malden, Mass. 241–56.

Siewert, P. 2012. "Zum politischen Hintergrund des etruskisch-römischen 'Donnerkalenders' bei Johannes Lydos, de ostentiis 27–38." In P. Amann, ed., *Kulte–Riten—religiöse Vorstellungen bei Etruskern und ihr Verhältnis zu Politik und Gesellschaft: Akten der 1. Internationalen Tagung der Sektion Wien/Österreich des Instituto di Studi Etruschi ed Italici (Wien, 4.–6. 12. 2008)* 440. Philosophisch-Historische Klasse Denkschriften. Wien. 153–61.

Silver, D. 2011. "The Moodines of Action." *Sociological Theory* 29 (3): 199–222.

Silvestrini, M. 1992. "L'augustalità alla luce di una nuova iscrizione per i Lari Augusti." *Quaderni di storia* 35: 83–110.

Simmel, G. 1907. "Das Geheimnis: Eine sozialpsychologische Skizze." *Der Tag* 626: 1.

Simon, E. 1967. *Ara Pacis Augustae*. Tübingen.

———. 1986. "Ianus Curiatius und Ianus Geminus im frühen Rom." In R. Altheim-Stiehl and M. Rosenbach, eds., *Beiträge zur altitalischen Geistesgeschichte: Festschrift Gerhard Radke zum 18. Februar 1984*. Münster. 257–68.

Simón, F. M. 1996. *Flamen Dialis: El sacerdote de Júpiter en la religión romana*. Madrid.

———. 2010. "From Thessalos of Tralles to Nicagoras of Athens: Religious Pilgrimage to Egypt in the Roman Empire." In F. M. Simón, F. P. Polo, and J. R. Rodriguez, eds., *Viajero, Peregrinos y Aventureros en el mundo antigua*. Barcelona. 227–40.

———. 2011. "The Feriae Latinae as Religious Legitimation of the Consuls' Imperium." In H. Beck et al., eds., *Consuls and res publica: Holding High Office in the Roman Republic.* Cambridge. 116–32.

Simon, M. 2011. *Le rivage grec de l'Italie romaine: La grande Grèce dans l'historiographie augustéenne,* Collection de l'École française de Rome 442. Rome.

Sinn, U. 2005a. "Altar." *Thesaurus Cultus et Rituum Antiquorum* 4: 14–21.

———. 2005b. "Tempel I. Typologie und Funktion." *Thesaurus Cultus et Rituum Antiquorum* 4: 87–100.

Sizgorich, T. 2009. *Violence and Belief in Late Antiquity: Militant Devotion in Christianity and Islam.* Divinations: Rereading Late Ancient Religion. Philadelphia.

Smadja, E. 1986. "La Victoire et la religion impériale dans les cités d'Afrique du nord sous l'empire romain." *Figures religieuses 1986*: 503–19.

Small, D. B. 2011. "Contexts, Agency, and Social Change in Ancient Greece." In N. Terrenato and D. C. Haggis, eds., *State Formation in Italy and Greece: Questioning the Neoevolutionist Paradigm.* Oxford. 135–61.

Smith, A. 1997. "Porphyry and Pagan Religious Practice." In J. J. Clearly, ed., *The Perennial Tradition of Neoplatonism.* Leuven. 29–35.

———. 2011. *Plotinus, Porphyry and Iamblichus: Philosophy and Religion in Neoplatonism.* Farnham.

Smith, C. 2009. *The Lost Memoirs of Augustus and the Development of Roman Autobiography.* Swansea.

Smith, C. J. 1999. "Reviewing Archaic Latium: Settlement, Burials, and Religion at Satricum." *Journal of Roman Archaeology* 12: 453–75.

———. 2005. "Festivals of Community in Rome and Latium." In P. Attema et al., eds., *Papers in Italian Archaeology 6: Communities and Settlements from the Neolithic to the Early Medieval Period; Proceedings of the 6th Conference of Italian Archaeology held at the University of Groningen, Groningen Institute of Archaeology, the Netherlands, April 15–17, 2003,* 1. BAR International Series 1452. Oxford. 76–83.

———. 2006. *The Roman Clan: The gens from Ancient Ideology to Modern Anthropology.* The W.B. Stanford Memorial Lectures. Cambridge.

———. 2015. "Urbanization and Memory." In R. Raja and J. Rüpke, eds., *A Companion to the Archaeology of Religion in the Ancient World.* Malden, Mass. 362–75.

Smith, J. Z. 1978a. "Map Is Not Territory." In J. Z. Smith, ed., *Map Is Not Territory: Studies in the History of Religion.* Leiden. 289–309.

———. 1978b. *Map Is Not Territory: Studies in the History of Religion.* Studies in Judaism in Late Antiquity 23. Leiden.

Smith, M. E. et al. 2015. "Conceptual Approaches to Service Provision in Cities throughout History." *Urban Studies*: 1–17.

Smith, R. 1995. *Julian's Gods: Religion and Philosophy in the Thought and Action of Julian the Apostate.* London.

Snodgrass, A. 2000. "Prehistoric Italy: A View from the Sea." In D. Ridgway et al., eds., *Ancient Italy in Its Mediterranean Setting—Studies in Honour of Ellen Macnamara.* Accordia Specialist Studies on the Mediterranean 4. London. 171–77.

Söderlind, M. 2004. "Man and Animal in Antiquity: Votive Figures in Central Italy from the 4th to 1st Centuries B.C." In B. Santillo Frizell, ed., *Pecus: Man and Animal in Antiquity. Proceedings of the Conference at the Swedish Institute in Rome, September 9–12, 2002.* Swedish Institute in Rome. Projects and Seminars 1. Rome. 277–94.

———. 2005. "Heads with Velum and the Etrusco-Latial-Campanian Type of Votive Deposit." In A. Comella and S. Mele, eds., *Depositi votivi e culti dell'Italia antica dall'età arcaica a quella tardo-repubblicana: Atti del Convegno di Studi, Perugia, 1–4 giugno 2000.* Bari. 359–66.

Sokolowski, F. 1955. *Lois sacrées de l'Asie Mineure,* École française d'Athènes. Travaux et mémoires des anciens membres étrangers de l'École et de divers savants 9. Paris.

———. 1962. *Lois sacrées des cités grecques supplement.* Travaux et mémoires des anciens membres étrangers de l'école et de divers savants 11. Paris.

———. 1969. *Lois sacrées des cités grecques.* École française d'Athènes: Travaux et mémoires des anciens membres étrangers 18. Paris.

Soler, J. 2011. "La Désse Syrienne, dea peregrina: la mise en récit de l'altérité religieuse dans les Métamorphoses d'Apulée." In C. Bonnet, A. Declercq, and I. Slobodzianek, eds., *Les représentation des dieux des autres* 2. Supplemento a MYTHOS 2: Rivista di Storia delle Religioni. Caltanissetta. 21–30.

Sommella Mura, A. 1977a. "L''introduzione di Eracle all'Olimpo' in un gruppo arcaico in terracotta dall'area sacra di S. Omobono: Note su una bottega coroplastica a Roma nella 2a metà del VI sec. a.C." *Bollettino dei musei comunali di Roma* 24: 3–15.

———. 1977b. "La decorazione architettonica del tempio arcaico." *Parola del Passato* 32: 62–128.

———. 2000. "Le recenti scoperte sul campidoglio e la fondazione del tempio di Giove Capitolino." *Rendiconti della Pontificia Accademia Romana di Archeologia* 70, 1997–1998: 57–79.

———. 2009. "Il tempio di Giove Capitolino: Una nuova proposta di lettura." *Annali della Fondazione per il Museo Claudio Faina* 16: 333–72.

Song, E. 2009. *Aufstieg und Abstieg der Seele: Diesseitigkeit und Jenseitigkeit in Plotins Ethik der Sorge.* Hypomnemata 180. Göttingen.

Sordi, M. 1990. "Cicerone i il primo epitafio romano." In M. Sordi, ed., *"Dulce et decorum est pro patria mori": La morte in combattimento nell'antichità.* Milano. 171–79.

Sourvinou-Inwood, C. 2011. *Athenian Myths and Festivals: Aglauros, Erechtheus, Plynteria, Panathenaia, Dionysia.* Robert Parker, ed. Oxford.

Spanoudakis, K. 2014. *Nonnus of Panopolis in Context: Poetry and Cultural Milieu in Late Antiquity.* Trends in Classics: Suppl. 24. Berlin.

Sperber, D., and D. Wilson 1987. "Précis of Relevance." *Behavioral & Brain Sciences* 10.4: 697–710.

Speyer, W. 1996. "Der Bibeldichter Dracontius als Exeget des Sechstagewerkes Gottes." In G. Schöllgen and C. Scholten, eds., *Stimuli: Exegese und ihre Hermeneutik in Antike und Christentum: Festschrift für Ernst Dassmann.* Münster. 464–84.

Spieckermann, H. 2014. *Lebenskunst und Gotteslob in Israel: Anregungen aus Psalter und Weisheit für die Theologie.* Forschungen zum Alten Testament 91. Tübingen.

Spickermann, W. 2015. "Monumental Inscriptions." In R. Raja and J. Rüpke, eds., *A Companion to the Archaeology of Religion in the Ancient World*. Malden, Mass. 412–24.

Squire, M. 2009. *Image and Text in Graeco-Roman Antiquity*. Cambridge.

Staal, J. F. 1980. "Ritual Syntax." In M. Nagatome, ed., *Sanskrit and Indian Studies: Essays in Honor of Daniel H. H. Ingalls*. Dordrecht. 119–42.

Stackelberg, K. T. v. 2009. *The Roman Garden: Space, Sense, and Society*. London.

Staden, H. v. 1997. "Galen and the 'Second Sophistic'." In R. Sorabji, ed., *Aristotle and After*. Bulletin of the Institute of Classical Studies: Suppl. 68. London. 33–54.

Stähli, A. 2014. "Sprechende Gegenstände." In R. Bielfeldt, ed., *Ding und Mensch in der Antike. Akademiekonferenzen* 16. Heidelberg. 113–41.

Standhartinger, A. 2010. 'Mehr als 'nutzlos, geschwätzig und neugierig' (1 Tim 5,13): Religiöse Frauentraditionen am Beispiel der Witwen im antiken Judentum und entstehenden Christentum." In C. Bertelsmeier-Kierst, ed., *Zwischen Vernunft und Gefühl: Weibliche Religiosität von der Antike bis heute*. Kulturgeschichtliche Beiträge zum Mittelalter und zur frühen Neuzeit 3. Frankfurt a. M. 11–25.

———. 2012. " 'And all ate and were filled' (Mark 6:42 par.): The Feeding Narratives in the Context of Hellenistic-Roman Banquet Culture." In N. MacDonald, K. Ehrensperger, and L. S. Rehmann, eds., *Decisive Meals: Table Politics in Biblical Literature*. 62–82.

Stara-Tedde, G. 1905. "I boschi sacri dell'antica Roma." *BCAR* 33: 189–232.

Starr, R. J. 1987. "The Circulation of Literary Texts in the Roman World." *Classical Quarterly* 37: 213–23.

Steck, F., and A. v. Harnack 2003. *Adolf Harnack: Marcion; der moderne Gläubige des 2. Jahrhunderts, der erste Reformator; die Dorpater Preisschrift (1870); kritische Edition des handschriftlichen Exemplars mit einem Anhang*. Texte und Untersuchungen zur Geschichte der altchristlichen Literatur 149. Berlin.

Stefaniw, B. 2011. *Mind, Text, and Commentary: Noetic Exegesis in Origen of Alexandria, Didymus the Blind, and Evagrius Ponticus*. Early Christianity in the Context of Antiquity 6. Frankfurt a.M.

———. 2012. "Gregory Taught, Gregory Written: The Effacement and Definition of Individualization in the Address to Origen and the Life of Gregory the Wonderworker." In J. Rüpke and W. Spickermann, eds., *Reflections on Religious Individuality: Greco-Roman and Judaeo-Christian Texts and Practices*. Religionsgeschichtliche Versuche und Vorarbeiten 62. Berlin. 119–43.

Steimle, C. 2007. *Religion im römischen Thessaloniki*. Studien und Texte zu Antike und Christentum 47. Tübingen.

Steiner, D. 2004. *Jenseitsreise und Unterwelt bei den Etruskern: Untersuchung zur Ikonographie und Bedeutung*. Quellen und Forschungen zur antiken Welt 42. München.

Steingräber, S. 1980. "Zum Phänomen der etruskisch—italischen Votivköpfe." In Steingräber, ed., *Mitteilungen des deutschen archäologischen Instituts römische Abteilung* 87. Mainz am Rhein. 215—53.

———. 1985a. *Etruskische Wandmalerei*. Stuttgart.

———. 1985b. "Grabarchitektur." In S. Steingräber, ed., *Etruskische Wandmalerei*. Stuttgart. 35–40.

———. 1990a. "Die etruskisch-hellenistische Grabmalerei: Probleme und Perspektiven." In H. Heres and M. Kunze, eds., *Die Welt der Etrusker: Internationales Kolloquium 24.–26. Oktober in Berlin*. Berlin. 315–20.

———. 1990b. "Traditionelle und innovative Elementen der frühhellenistischen Grabarchitektur und -malerei Unteritaliens." In E. Schwinzer and S. Steingräber, eds., *Kunst und Kultur in der Magna Graecia: Ihr Verhältnis zum griechischen Mutterland und zum italienischen Umfeld*. Schriften des Deutschen Archäologen-Verbandes 11. Tübingen. 78–87.

———. 2002. "Ahnenkult und bildliche Darstellungen von Ahnen in etruskischen und unteritalischen Grabgemälden aus vorrömischer Zeit." In J. M. Hojte, ed., *Images of Ancestors*. Aarhus Studies in Mediterranean Antiquity (ASMA) V. Aarhus. 127–58.

Stemberger, G. 1999. "Die Umformung des palästinischen Judentums nach 70: Der Aufstieg der Rabbinen." In A. Oppenheimer, ed., *Jüdische Geschichte in hellenistisch-römischer Zeit: Wege der Forschung: vom alten zum neuen Schürer*. München. 85–99.

Stern, H. 1953. *Le calendrier de 354: Étude sur son texte et ses illustrations*. Institut français d'archéologie de Beyrouth: Bibliothèque archéologique et historique 55. Paris.

Stern, K. B. 2014. "Inscription as Religious Competition in Third-Century Syria." In J. D. Rosenblum, L. C. Vuong, and N. P. DesRosiers, eds., *Religious Competition in the Third Century CE: Jews, Christians, and the Greco-Roman World. Journal of Ancient Judaism*: Suppl. 15. Göttingen. 141–52.

Stern, S. 2012. *Calendars in Antiquity: Empires, States, and Societies*. New York.

Steuernagel, D. 1998. *Menschenopfer und Mord am Altar: Griechische Mythen in etruskischen Gräbern*. Palilia 3. Wiesbaden.

———. 2004. *Kult und Alltag in römischen Hafenstädten: soziale Prozesse in archäologischer Perspektive*. PawB 11. Stuttgart.

———. 2007. "Hafenstädte: Knotenpunkte religiöser Mobilität?" *Mediterranea* 4: 121–34.

———. 2009a. "Romanisierung und hellenismós: Drei Fallstudien zur Gestaltung und Nutzung griechischer Tempel in den römischen Provinzen Achaia und Cyrenaica." *Jahrbuch des Deutschen Archäologischen Instituts* 124: 279–345.

———. 2009b. "Wozu brauchen Griechen Tempel? Fragen und Perspektiven." In H. Cancik and J. Rüpke, eds., *Die Religion des Imperium Romanum: Koine und Konfrontationen*. Tübingen. 115–38.

Stewart, P. 2003. *Statues in Roman Society: Representation and Response*. Oxford.

———. 2014. "Ephemerality in Roman Votive Images." In S. Estienne et al., eds., *Figures de dieux: Construire le divin en images*. Rennes. 351–60.

Stibbe, C. M., G. Colonna, et al. 1980. *Lapis Satricanus*. Archeologische Studien van het Nederlands Instituut te Rome, Scripta minora 5.

Stirling, L. 2008. "Pagan Statuettes in Late Antique Corinth: Sculpture from the Panayia Domus." *Hesperia* 77: 89–161.

Stock, B. 1983. *The Implications of Literacy: Written Language and Models of Interpretation in the Eleventh and Twelfth Centuries*. Princeton.

Stökl Ben Ezra, D. 2012. "Markus-Evangelium." *Reallexikon für Antike und Christentum* 24: 173–208.

Stoll, O. 2001. *Zwischen Integration und Abgrenzung: Die Religion des Römischen Heeres im Nahen Osten. Studien zum Verhältnis von Armee und Zivilbevölkerung im römischen Syrien und den Nachbargebieten.* Mainzer Althistorische Studien 3. St. Katharinen.

Stoltenberg, H. L. 1952. "Uebersetzung der Tontafel von Capua." *Studi Etruschi* 22: 157–65.

Stoneman, R. 2011. *The Ancient Oracles: Making the Gods Speak.* New Haven, CT.

Stowers, S. K. 2008. "Theorizing the Religion of Ancient Households and Families." In J. Bodel and S. M. Olyan, ed., *Household and Family: Religion in Antiquity.* The Ancient World: Comparative Histories. Malden, Mass. 5–19.

———. 2011. "The Concept of 'Community' and the History of Early Christianity." *Method and Theory in the Study of Religion* 23: 238–56.

Stramaglia, A. 2013. *[Quintiliano] L'astrologo (Declamazioni maggiori, 4).* Collana di studi umanistici 4. Cassino.

Straub, J. 2001. "Temporale Orientierung und narrative Kompetenz: Zeit- und erzähltheoretische Grundlagen einer Psychologie biographischer und historischer Sinnbildung." In J. Rüsen, ed., *Geschichtsbewußtsein: Psychologische Grundlagen, Entwicklungskonzepte, empirische Befunde.* Beiträge zu Geschichtskultur 21. Köln, Weimar, Wien. 15–44.

Strazzulla, M. J. 1993. "L'ultima fase decorativa dei santuari etrusco-italici: le lastre "Campana." In E. Rystedt, C. Wikander, and Ö. Wikander, eds., *Deliciae Fictiles—Proceedings of the First International Conference on Central Italic Architectural Terracottas at the Swedish Institute in Rome, 10–12 December, 1990.* Stockholm. 299–306.

———. 2006. "Le terrecotte architettoniche nei territori italici." In I. Edlund-Berry, G. Greco, and J. Kenfield, eds., *Deliciae Fictiles III: Architectural Terracottas in Ancient Italy: New Discoveries and Interpretations.* Oxford. 25–42.

Strobel, K. 1993. *Das Imperium Romanum im "3. Jahrhundert": Modell einer historischen Krise? Zur Frage mentaler Strukturen breiterer Bevölkerungsschichten in der Zeit von Marc Aurel bis zum Ausgang des 3. Jh. n. Chr,* Historia Einzelschriften 75. Stuttgart.

Stroumsa, G. G. 2005. "From Master of Wisdom to Spiritual Master in Late Antiquity." In D. Brakke, M. L. Satlow, and S. Weitzman, eds., *Religion and the Self in Antiquity.* Bloomington, Ind. 183–96.

———. 2009. *The End of Sacrifice: Religious Transformations in Late Antiquity.* Chicago.

———. 2012. *Das Ende des Opferkults: Die religiösen Mutationen der Spätantike.* Berlin.

———. 2015. "Jewish Christianity and Islamic Origins." In B. Sadeghi et al., eds., *Islamic Cultures, Islamic Contexts: Essays in Honor of Professor Patricia Crone.*

Stuckrad, K. v. 2000a. "Jewish and Christian Astrology in Late Antiquity: A New Approach." *Numen* 47: 1–40.

———. 2000b. *Das Ringen um die Astrologie: Jüdische und christliche Beiträge zum antiken Zeitverständnis.* Religionsgeschichtliche Versuche und Vorarbeiten 49. Berlin.

Stupperich, R. 1985. "Zur bulla auf römischen Grabreliefs." *Epigraphia Anatolica* 6: 103–108.

Swartz, M. D. 2017. "Rhetorical Indications of the Poet's Craft in the Ancient Synagogue." In G. Petridou, R. Gordon, and J. Rüpke, eds., *Beyond Priesthood: Religious Entrepreneurs and Innovators in the Roman Empire.* Religionsgeschichtliche Versuche und Vorarbeiten 66. Berlin. im Erscheinen. 231–50.

Sykes, N. et al., eds. 2014. *Deer and People.* Havertown.

Szabó, C. 2015. "Notes on a New Cautes Statue from Apulum (Jud. Alba/Ro)." *Archäologisches Korrespondenzblatt* 45 (2): 237–47.

Tabolli, J. 2013. *Narce tra la prima età del ferro e l'orientalizzante antico: L'abitato, i Tufi e la Petrina* 1. suppl. 9. Pisa.

Taeger, J.-W., and D. C. Bienert. 2006. *Johanneische Perspektiven: Aufsätze zur Johannesapokalypse und zum johanneischen Krei,s 1984–2003.* Göttingen.

Tajfel, H. 1974. "Social Identity and Intergroup Behaviour." *Social Science Information* 13, N. 2: 65–93.

Takahashi, H. 2014. "Syriac as a Vehicle for Transmission of Knowledge across Borders of Empires." *Horizons* 5 (1): 29–52.

Talbert, C. H. 1978. "Biographies of Philosophers and Rulers as Instruments of Religious Propaganda in Mediterrean Antiquity." *ANRW* II.16,2: 1619–51.

Tanaseanu-Döbler, I. 2008. *Konversion zur Philosophie in der Spätantike. Kaiser Julian und Synesios von Kyrene* Potsdamer altertumswissenschaftliche Beiträge 23. Stuttgart.

Tarpin, M. 2002. *Vici et pagi dans l'occident romain.* Paris.

Taves, A. 2009. *Religious Experience Reconsidered: A Building Block Approach to the Study of Religion and Other Special Things.* Princeton, NJ.

———. 2011. "2010 Presidential Address: 'Religion' in the Humanities and the Humanities in the University." *Journal of the American Academy of Religion* 79 (2): 287–314.

Teja Casuso, R., and M. Marcos. 2012. "Circulación y quema de libros en la antigüedad tardía en el ámbito de la polémica cristianismo-paganismo." In J. Alturo, M. Torras, and A. Castro, eds., *La producció i circulació de llibres clandestins des de l'antiguitat fins als nostres dies.* Barcelona. 33–56.

Terrenato, N. 2001. "The Auditorium Site and the Origin of the Roman Villas." *JRA* 14: 5–32.

———. 2010. "Early Rome." In A. Barchiesi and W. Scheidel, eds., *The Oxford Handbook of Roman Studies.* Oxford. 507–18.

———. 2011. "The Versatile Clans: Archaic Rome and the Nature of Early City-States in Central Italy." In N. Terrenato and D. C. Haggis, eds., *State Formation in Italy and Greece: Questioning the Neoevolutionist Paradigm.* Oxford. 231–44.

Theodoretus 2006. *Commento a Daniele / Teodoreto di Cirro. Introduzione, traduzione e note a cura di Daniela Borrelli.* Roma.

Thom, J. C. 2012. "Popular Philosophy in the Hellenistic-Roman World." *Early Christianity* 3 (3): 279–95.

Thompson, Glen L. 2015. "The Pax Constantiniana and the Roman Episcopate." In Goffrey D. Dunn, ed., *The Bishop of Rome in Late Antiquity.* Burlington: Ashgate. 19–36.

Thonemann, P. 2012. "Abercius of Hierapolis: Christianization and Social Memory in Late Antique Asia Minor." In B. Dignas and R.R.R. Smith, ed., *Historical and Religious Memory in the Ancient World.* Oxford. 257–82.

Thulin, C. O. 1906a. *Die etruskische Disciplin II: Die Haruspizin.* Göteborgs Högskolos Årsskrift 12,1. Göteborg.

———. 1906b. *Die etruskische Disziplin 1: Die Blitzlehre.* Göteborgs Högskolas Årsskrift 11 (1905), 5. Göteborg.

————. 1906c. *Scriptorum disciplinae Etruscae fragmenta* 1. Berlin.

Tieleman, T. 2005. "Galen and Genesis." In G. H. van Kooten, ed., *The Creation of Heaven and Earth: Re-interpretations of Genesis in the Context of Judaism, Ancient Philosophy, Christianity, and Modern Physics.* Leiden. 125–45.

Tilly, M. 2007. "Die Rezeption des Danielbuches im hellenistischen Judentum." In K. Bracht and D. S. du Toit, eds., *Die Geschichte der Daniel-Auslegung in Judentum, Christentum und Islam: Studien zur Kommentierung des Danielbuches in Literatur und Kunst.* Beihefte zur Zeitschrift für die alttestamentliche Wissenschaft 371. Berlin. 31–54.

Toner, J. P. 2014. *The Day Commodus Killed a Rhino: Understanding the Roman Games.* Witness to Ancient History. Baltimore.

Tore, G. 1983. "I bronzi figurati fenicio-punici in Sardegna." In *Atti del I Congresso Internazionale di Studi Fenici e Punici, Roma, 5–10 Novembre 1979, vol. 2.* Roma. 449–61, pls. 81–82.

Torelli, M. 1975. *Elogia Tarquiniensia. Studi e materiali di etruscologia e antichità italiche* 15. Firenze.

————. 1984. *Lavinio e Roma: Riti iniziatici e matrimonio tra archeologia e storia.* Roma.

————. 1997. *Il rango, il rito e l'immagine: Alle origini della rappresentazione storica romana.* Milano.

————. "Il culto imperiale a Pompei." In G. Bretschneider, ed., *I culti della Campania antica* III. Roma. 245–70.

————. 2011. "Fictilia tecta: Riflessioni storiche sull'arcaismo etrusco e romano." In P. Lulof and C. Rescigno, eds., *Deliciae Fictiles* IV: *Architectural Terracottas in Ancient Italy: Images of Gods, Monsters and Heroes.* Oxford. 3–16.

————. 2012. "The Early Villa: Roman Contributions to the Development of a Greek Prototype." In J. A. Becker and N. Terrenato, eds., *Roman Republican Villas: Architecture, Context, and Ideology.* Papers and Monographs of the Amercan Academy in Rome 32. Ann Arbor. 8–31.

Torres Ortiz, M. 2005. "Las necrópolis orientalizantes del sudoeste de la Península Ibérica." *Anejos de Archivo Español de Arqueología* 35: 423–40.

Traver, T. 1997. "Varro and the Antiquarianism of Philosophy." In J. Barnes and M. Griffin, eds., *Philosophia Togata* II: *Plato and Aristotle at Rome.* Oxford. 130–64.

Trebilco, P. 2012. *Self-Designations and Group Identity in the New Testament.* Cambridge.

Trimble, J. 2011. *Women and Visual Replication in Roman Imperial Art and Culture.* Cambridge.

Tsouna, V. 2007. *The Ethics of Philodemus.* Oxford.

Turfa, J. M. 2012. *Divining the Etruscan World: The Brontoscopic Calendar and Religious Practice.* Cambridge.

Turner, J. C. 1975. "Social Comparison and Social Identity: Some Prospects for Intergroup Behaviour." *European Journal of Social Psychology* 5 (1): 5–34.

Turner, J. D., and K. Corrigan, eds. 2010. *Plato's Parmenides and Its Heritage* 1: *History and Interpretation from the Old Academy to Later Platonism and Gnosticism.* Writings from the Greco-Roman World Suppl., series 2. Atlanta.

Tuval, M. 2012. "Doing without the Temple: Paradigms in Judaic Literature of the Diaspora." In D. R. Schwartz and Z. Weiss, eds., *Was 70 CE a Watershed in Jewish History? On Jews and Judaism before and after the Destruction of the Second Temple*. Ancient Judaism and Early Christianity: Arbeiten zur Geschichte des antiken Judentums und des Urchristentums 78. Leiden. 181–239.

Ullucci, D. C. 2012. *The Christian Rejection of Animal Sacrifice*. Oxford.

———. 2014. "What Did He Say? The Ideas of the Experts and the 99%." In J. D. Rosenblum, ed., *Religious Competition in the Third Century CE: Jews, Christians, and the Greco-Roman World*. *Journal of Ancient Judaism*: Suppl. 15. Göttingen. 21–31.

Ungern-Sternberg, J. v. 1988. "Überlegungen zur frühen römischen Überlieferung im Lichte der Oral-Tradition-Forschung." In J. v. Ungern-Sternberg and H. Reinau, eds., *Vergangenheit in mündlicher Überlieferung*. Stuttgart. 237–65.

———. 2008. "[Rez.] Emilio Gabba: Roma arcaica . . . 2000 . . ." *Gnomon* 80: 526–69.

Urciuoli, E. R. 2013. "La comunità ubiqua: Considerazioni sull'onnipresenza comunitaria nella storia del cristianesimo antico." *Studi e Materiali di Storia delle Religioni* 79 (2): 557–83.

Usher, M. D. 2013. "Teste Galba cum Sibylla: Oracles, Octavia, and the East." *Classical Philology* 108 (1): 21–40.

Valvo, A. 1990. " 'Legibus soluti virtutis causa' nelle disposizioni della x 'tabula'." In M. Sordi, ed., *"Dulce et decorum est pro patria mori": La morte in combattimento nell'antichità*. Milano. 145–55.

Van Andringa, W. 2009. *Quotidien des dieux et des hommes: la vie religieuse dans les cités du Vésuve à l'époque romaine*. BEFRAR 337. Rome.

———. "Les dieux, la cité et le pouvoir impérial: Religions et intégration des provinces de l'Occident romain." In G. Moosbauer and R. Wiegels, eds., *Fines Imperii—imperium sine fine? Römische Okkupations- und Grenzpolitik im frühen Prinzipat*. Osnabrücker Forschungen zu altertum und Antike-Rezeption 14. Rahden/Westf. 219–26.

———. 2013. *Mourir à Pompéi: Fouille d'un quartier funéraire de la nécropole romaine de Porta Nocera (2003—2007)*. 2 vols. Collection de l'École Française de Rome 468. Rome.

———. 2014a. "Les dieux changent en Occident (IIIe-IVe siècle apr. J.-C.): Archéologie et mutations religieuses de l'Antiquité tardive." *Gallia* 71 (1): 3–10.

———. 2014b. *La fin des dieux: Les lieux de culte du polythéisme dans la pratique religieuse du IIIe au Ve s. apr. J.-C. (Gaules et provinces occidentales)* = *Gallia* 71.1. Paris.

Van Andringa, W., and S. Lepetz. 2003. "Le ossa animali nei santuari: per un'archeologia del sacrificio." In O. de Cazanove and J. Scheid, eds., *Sanctuaires et sources dans l'antiquité: Les sources documentaires et leurs limites dans la description des lieux de culte*. Collection du Centre Jean Bérard 22. Napoli. 85–96.

Van Dam, R. 2009. *The Roman Revolution of Constantine*. Cambridge.

Van den Kerchove, A. 2012. *La voie d'Hermés—Pratiques rituelles et traités hermétique*. Leiden.

Van der Horst, P. W. 1982. "The Way of Life of the Egyptian Priests according to Chaeremon." In M. H. van Voss, ed., *Studies in Egyptian Religion*. Leiden. 61–71.

Van der Leeuw, G. 1939. *Virginibus puerisque: A Study on the Service of Children in Worship.* Mededeelingen der Koninklijke Nederlandsche Akademie van Wetenschappen, afd. Letterkunde, NR 2,12. Amsterdam.

Van der Meer, L. B. 1987. *The Bronze Liver of Piacenza. Analysis of a Polytheistic Structure.* Amsterdam.

————. 2010. *Material Aspects of Etruscan Religion. Proceedings of the International Colloquium, Leiden, May 29 and 30, 2008.* Babesch: Suppl. 16. Leuven.

————. 2011. *Etrusco ritu: Case Studies in Etruscan Ritual Behaviour.* Monographs on Antiquity 5. Leuven.

Van Dommelen, P., F. Gerritsen, and B. Knapp. 2005. "Common Places: Archaeologies of Community and Landscape." In P.A.J. Attema, ed., *Papers in Italian Archaeology 6: Communities and Settlements from the Neolithic to the Early Medieval Period; Proceedings of the 6th Conference of Italian Archaeology held at the University of Groningen, Groningen Institute of Archaeology, the Netherlands, April 15–17, 2003,* 1. BAR International Series 1452. Oxford. 55–63.

Vanggaard, J. H. 1988. *The Flamen: A Study in the History and Sociology of Roman Religion.* Copenhagen.

Van Haeperen, F. 2002. *Le Collège pontifical (3ième s. a. C.–4ième s. p. C.): Contribution à l'étude de la religion publique romaine* Belgisch historisch Instituut te Rome: Studies over oude Filologie, Archeologie en Geschiedenis 39. Bruxelles.

————. 2012. "Auspices d'investitutre, loi curiate et légitimité des magistrats romains." *Cahiers du Centre Gustave-Glotz* 23: 71–112.

Van Henten, J. W. 2010. "The Reception of Daniel 3 and 6 and the Maccabean Martyrdoms in Hebrews 11:33–38." In J. Dijkstra, J. Kroesen, and Y. Kuiper, eds., *Myths, Martyrs, and Modernity—Studies in the History of Religions in Honour of Jan N. Bremmer.* Leiden. 359–77.

Van Hoof, L. 2010. *Plutarch's Practical Ethics: The Social Dynamics of Philosophy.* Oxford.

Van Nuffelen, P. 2010. "Varro's Divine Antiquities: Roman Religion as an Image of Truth." *Classical Philology* 105: 162–88.

————. 2011. *Rethinking the Gods—Philosophical Readings of Religion in the Post-Hellenistic Period.* Cambridge.

Van Rossenberg, E. 2005. "Between Households and Communities: Layers of Social Life in the Later Bronze Age and Early Iron Age of Central Italy." In P. Attema, A. Nijboer, and A. Zifferero, eds., *Papers in Italian Archaeology VI: Communities and Settlements from the Neolithic to the Early Medieval Period. Proceedings of the 6th Conference of Italian Archaeology held at the University of Groningen, Groningen Institute of Archaeology, The Netherlands, April 15–17, 2003.* BAR International Series 1452, vol. 1. Oxford. 84–91.

Van Wees, H. 2011. "Rivalry in History: An Introduction." In N. Fisher and H. v. Wees, eds., *Competition in the Ancient World.* Swansea. 1–36.

Várhelyi, Z. 2010. *The Religion of Senators in the Roman Empire.* Cambridge.

Vásquez, M. A. 2008. "Studying Religion in Motion: A Networks Approach." *Method and Theory in the Study of Religion* 20: 151–84.

Vaughn, P. 1991. "The Identification and Retrieval of the Hoplite Battle-Dead." In V. D. Hanson, ed., *Hoplites: The Classical Greek Battle Experience.* London. 38–62.

Vendries, C. 2015. "Du bruit dans la cité: L'invention du 'paysage sonore' et l'antiquité romaine." In S. Emerit et al., eds., *Le paysage sonore de l'antiquité: Méthodologie, historiographie et perspectives.* Châtillon. 209-56.

Verdoner, M. 2011. *Narrated Reality: The Historia ecclesiastica of Eusebius of Caesarea.* Early Christianity in the Context of Antiquity 9. Frankfurt am Main.

Verkuyten, M., and B. Martinovic 2012. "Social Identity Complexity and Immigrants' Attitude toward the Host Nation: The Intersection of Ethnic and Religious Group Identification." *Personality and Social Psychology Bulletin* 38: 1165-77.

Versluys, M. J. 2004. "Isis Capitolina and the Egyptian Cults in Late Republican Rome." In L. Bricault, ed., *Isis en Occident: Actes du IIème Colloque international sur les études isiaques, Lyon III 16-17 mai 2002.* Religions in the Graeco-Roman World 151. Leiden. 421-48.

———. 2010. "Understanding Egypt in Egypt and Beyond." In L. Bricault and M. Malaise, eds., *Isis on the Nile: Egyptian Gods in Hellenistic and Roman Egypt.* Religions in the Graeco-Roman World 171. Leiden. 7-36.

———. 2013. "Orientalising Roman Gods." In L. Bricault and C. Bonnet, eds., *Panthée: Religious Transformations in the Graeco-Roman Empire.* Religions in the Graeco-Roman World 177. Leiden. 235-59.

Versnel, H. S. 1981. "Destruction, Devotio and Despair in a Situation of Anomy: The Mourning for Germanicus in Triple Perspective." *Perennitas: Studi in onore di Angelo Brelich.* 541-618.

———. 1982. "Die neue Inschrift von Satricum in historischer Sicht." *Gymnasium* 89: 193-235.

Veyne, P. 1988. *Brot und Spiele: Gesellschaftliche Macht und politische Herrschaft in der Antike.* K. Laermann and H. R. Brittnacher, trans. Theorie und Gesellschaft 11. Frankfurt a. M./Paris.

———. 2000. "Inviter les dieux, sacrifier, banqueter: Quelques nuances de la religiosité gréco-romaine." *Annales HSS* 2000: 3-42.

Vielhauer, P. 1975. *Geschichte der urchristlichen Literatur: Einleitung in das Neue Testament, die Apokryphen und die Apostolischen Väter.* Berlin.

Vigourt, A. 2011. "Normes religieuses et piété privée vers le milieu du IIe siècle ap. J.-C." In B. Cabouret-Laurioux and M.-O. Charles-Laforge, eds., *La norme religieuse dans l'antiquité.* Paris. 73-84.

Vinzent, M. 2011. "Give and Take amongst Second Century Authors: The Ascension of Isaiah, the Epistle of the Apostles, and Marcion of Sinope." *Studia Patristica* 50: 105-29.

———. 2014a. *Marcion and the Dating of the Synoptic Gospels.* Studia patristica suppl. 2. Leuven.

———. 2014b. "Marcion's Roman Liturgical Traditions, Innovations and Counter-Rites: Fasting and Baptism." *Studia patristica* 71: 187-211.

———. 2017. "Christians, the 'more obvious' representatives of the religion of Israel than the Rabbis?" In G. Petridou, R. Gordon, and J. Rüpke, eds., *Beyond Priesthood: Religious Entrepreneurs and Innovators in the Roman Empire.* Religionsgeschichtliche Versuche und Vorarbeiten 66. Berlin. 215-30.

Volk, K. 2009. *Manilius and His Intellectual Background*. Oxford.

Vollkommer, R. 1990. "Tendenzen in der attischen und apulischen Vasenmalerei des 4. Jhs. v. Chr. anhand der Heraklesdarstellungen." In E. Schwinzer and S. Steingräber, eds., *Kunst und Kultur in der Magna Graecia: Ihr Verhältnis zum griechischen Mutterland und zum italienischen Umfeld*. Schriften des Deutschen Archäologen-Verbandes 11. Tübingen. 35–45.

Vollmer, F. 1892. "Laudationum funebrium Romanorum historia et reliquiarum editio." *Jahrbücher für classische Philologie* suppl. 18: 445–528.

Volp, U. 2009. "Hippolytus." *Expository Times* 120 (11): 521–59.

Volpe, R. 2012. "Republican Villas in the *Suburbium* of Rome." In J. A. Becker and N. Terrenato, eds., *Roman Republican Villas: Architecture, Context, and Ideology* 32. Ann Arbor. 94–110.

Wachsmuth, D. 1967. Πομπιμὸς ὁ δαίμων: *Untersuchung zu den antiken Sakralhandlungen bei Seereisen*. Diss. Tübingen.

Wachter, R. 1987. *Altlateinische Inschriften: Sprachliche und epigraphische Untersuchungen zu den Dokumenten bis etwa 150 v. Chr.* Europäische Hochschulschriften 15 (Klass. Sprachen und Literaturen), 38. Bern.

Walde, C. 2001. *Die Traumdarstellungen in der griechisch-römischen Dichtung*. München.

Waldner, K. 2004. "Zur narrativen Technik der Körperdarstellung." In B. Feichtinger and H. Seng, eds., *Die Christen und der Körper: Aspekte der Körperlichkeit in der christlichen Literatur der Spätantike*. München. 29–74.

———. 2012. "Vision, Prophecy, and Authority in the *Passio Perpetuae*." In J. N. Bremmer and M. Formisano, eds., *Perpetua's Passions: Multidisciplinary Approaches to the Passio Perpetuae et Felicitatis*. Oxford. 201–19.

Wallace-Hadrill, A. 1986. "Image and Authority in the Coinage of Augustus." *Journal of Roman Studies* 76: 66–87.

———. 1988. "Time for Augustus: Ovid, Augustus and the Fasti." In M. Whitby, P. Hardie, and M. Whitby, eds., *Homo Viator: Classical Essays for John Bramble*. Bristol. 221–30.

———. 1994. *Houses and Society in Pompeii and Herculaneum*. Princeton.

———. 1997a. "Mutatio morum: The Idea of a Cultural Revolution." In T. N. Habine and A. Schiesaro, eds., *The Roman Cultural Revolution*. Cambridge. 3–22.

———. 1997b. "Rethinking the Roman Atrium House." In R. Laurence and A. Wallace-Hadrill, eds., *Domestic Space in the Roman World: Pompeii and Beyond*. Journal of Roman Archaeology suppl. series 22. Portsmouth, RI. 219–40.

———. 2003. "Domus und Insulae in Rome: Families and Housefuls." In D. L. Balch and C. Osiek, eds., *Early Christian Families in Context—An Interdisciplinary Dialogue*. Grand Rapids. 3–18.

———. 2008. *Rome's Cultural Revolution*. Cambridge.

Wallraff, M., ed. 2006. *Julius Africanus und die christliche Weltchronik*. Texte und Untersuchungen zur Geschichte der altchristlichen Literatur 157. Berlin.

———. 2013. *Kodex und Kanon: Das Buch im frühen Christentum*. Hans-Lietzmann-Vorlesungen 12. Berlin.

Wallraff, M. et al. 2007. *Iulius Africanus Chronographiae: The Extant Fragments*. Die griechischen christlichen Schriftsteller der ersten Jahrhunderte N.F. 15. Berlin.

Wallraff, M., and L. Mecella, eds. 2009. *Die Kestoi des Julius Africanus und ihre Überlieferung*, Texte und Untersuchungen zur Geschichte der altchristlichen Literatur 165. Berlin.

Walter, N. 1987. "Jüdisch-hellenistische Literatur vor Philon von Alexandrien (unter Ausschluß der Historiker)." *ANRW* II.20,1: 67–120.

Walter, U. 2010. "Prinzipat, Kopflastig: Jochen Bleickens *Augustus*: eine Nachwort." In J. Bleicken, ed., *Augustus eine Biographie*. Hamburg 801–16.

———. 2014a. "Einleitung." In U. Walter. ed., *Gesetzgebung und Politische Kultur in der römischen Republik*. Studien zur Alten Geschichte 20. Mannheim. 9–30.

———. 2014b. "Meister der Macht ohne Formierung von Staatlichkeit: Die römische Aristokratie." In C. Lundgreen, ed., *Staatlichkeit in Rom? Diskurse und Praxis (in) der römischen Republik*. Stuttgart. 91–116.

Waltzing, J. P. 1895. *Étude sur les corporations professionnelles chez les romains depuis les origines jusqu'à la chute de l'Empire d'Occident*. 1: *Le droit d'association à Rome. Les collèges professionnels considérés comme associations privées*. 2: *Les collèges professionnels considérés comme institutions officielles*. 3: *Recueil des inscriptions grecques et latines relatives aux corporations des Romains*. 4: *Indices. Liste des collèges connus, leur organisation intérieure, leur caractère religieux, funéraires et public, leurs finances*. Louvain.

Wamers, E. et al. 2011. *Fürsten—Feste—Rituale—Bilderwelten zwischen Kelten und Etruskern*. Frankfurt am Main.

Warden, P. G. 2012. "Monumental Embodiment: Somatic Symbolism and the Tuscan Temple." In M. L. Thomas and G. E. Meyers, eds., *Monumentality in Etruscan and Early Roman Architecture: Ideology and Innovation*. Austin. 82–110.

Wardle, D. 2000. "Valerius Maximus on the Domus Augusta, Augustus and Tiberius." *Classical Quarterly* 50: 479–93.

———. 2002. "The Heroism and Heroicisation of Tiberius: Valerius Maximus and His Emperor." *Prose et linguitstique, médicine* 2: 433–40.

Ward-Perkins, B. 2011. "The End of the Temple: An Archaeological Problem." In J. Hahn, ed., *Spätantiker Staat und religiöser Konflikt: imperiale und lokale Verwaltung und die Gewalt gegen Heiligtümer*. Millennium-Studien 34. Berlin. 187–99.

———. 2012. "Old and New Rome Compared: The Rise of Constantinople." In L. Grig and G. Kelly, eds., *Two Romes: Rome and Constantinople in Late Antiquity*. Oxford Studies in Late Antiquity. Oxford 53–78.

Watts, E. J. 2010. *Riot in Alexandria: Tradition and Group Dynamics in Late Antique Pagan and Christian Communities*. The Transformation of the Classical Heritage 46. Berkeley.

Weber, G. 1999. "Artemidor von Daldis und sein 'Publikum'." *Gymnasium* 106: 209–29.

———. 2005–2006. "Träume und Visionen im Alltag der römischen Kaiserzeit: Das Zeugnis der Inschriften und Papyri." *Quaderni Catanesi* 4–5: 55–121.

Weber, M. 1985. *Wirtschaft und Gesellschaft: Grundriss der verstehenden Soziologie*. Tübingen.

Webster, J., and N. J. Cooper, eds. 1996. *Roman Imperialism: Post-Colonial Perspectives: Proceedings of a Symposium held at Leicester University in November 1994*, 3. Leicester Archaeology Monographs. Leicester.

Wedekind, K. 2012. *Religiöse Experten im lokalen Kontext: Kommunikationsmodelle in christlichen Quellen des 1.–3. Jh. n. Chr.* Gutenberg.

Wehnert, J. 2015. *Der Klemensroman.* Kleine Bibliothek der antiken jüdischen und christlichen Literatur. Göttingen.

Weikert, C. 2016. *Von Jerusalem zu Aelia Capitolina: Die römische Politik gegenüber den Juden von Vespasian bis Hadrian.* Hypomnemata 200. Göttingen.

Weiss, L. 2009. "Personal Religious Practice: House Altars at Deir El-medina." *Journal of Egyptian Archaeology* 95: 193–208.

———. 2015a. "Perpetuated Action." In R. Raja and J. Rüpke, eds., *A Companion to the Archaeology of Religion in the Ancient World.* Malden, Mass. 60–70.

———. 2015b. *Religious Practice at Deir el-Medina.* Egyptologische Uitgaven 29. Leuven.

Weiss, P. 1973. "Die 'Säkularspiele' der Republik—eine annalistische Fiktion? Ein Beitrag zum Verständnis der kaiserzeitlichen Ludi saeculares." *Mitteilungen des deutschen archäologischen Instituts, Rom* 80: 205–17.

Wendt, H. 2015. "A Rereading of Judean Expulsions from Rone." *Journal of Ancient Judaism* 6: 97–126.

Wesch-Klein, G. 2009. "Gesundheit spendende Gottheiten des römischen Herres." In C. Wolff and Y. L. Bohec, eds., *L'armée romaine et la religion sous le Haut-Empire romain* 33. Paris. 99—120.

Wheeler, E. L. 1982. "Hoplomachia and Greek Dances in Arms." *Greek, Roman and Byzantine Studies* 123: 223–33.

White, L. M. 1990. *Building God's House in the Roman World: Architectural Adaptation among Pagans, Jews, and Christians.* American Schools of Oriental Research. Baltimore.

———. 2012. "The Changing Face of Mithraism at Ostia: Archaeology, Art, and the Urban Landscape." In D. L. Balch and A. Weissenrieder, eds., *Contested Spaces: Houses and Temples in Roman Antiquity and the New Testament.* Wissenschaftliche Untersuchungen zum Neuen Testament 285. Tübingen. 435–92.

Whitmarsh, T., ed. 2010. *Local Knowledge and Microidentities in the Imperial Greek World,* Greek Culture in the Roman World. Cambridge.

———. 2013. *Beyond the Second Sophistic Adventures in Greek Postclassicism.* Berkeley.

Widevoort Crommelin, B. R. 1993. *Die Universalgeschichte des Pompeius Trogus: Herculea Audacia Orbem Terrarum Adgressus.* Beiträge zur Geschichtskultur 7. Hagen.

Wiedemann, T. 1986. "The Fetiales: A Reconsideration." *Classical Quarterly* 36 (1986/87): 478–90.

Wiemer, H.-U. 2011. "Für die Tempel? Die Gewalt gegen heidnische Heiligtümer aus der Sicht städtischer Eliten des spätrömischen Ostens." In J. Hahn, ed., *Spätantiker Staat und religiöser Konflikt: imperiale und lokale Verwaltung und die Gewalt gegen Heiligtümer.* Millennium-Studien 34. Berlin. 159–85.

Wilburn, A. T. 2012. *Materia magica: The Archaeology of Magic in Roman Egypt, Cyprus, and Spain.* New texts from ancient cultures. Ann Arbor.

Wilkens, B. 2002. "The Sacrifice of Dogs in Ancient Italy." In L. M. Snyder and E. M. Moore, eds., *Dogs and People in Social, Working, Economic or Symbolic Interaction.* 9th ICAZ Conference, Durham 2002. Oxford. 131–36.

―――. 2012. *Archeozoologia: Il Mediterraneo, la storia, la Sardegna.* 3rd ed. Sassari.

Wilkinson, T. C., S. Sherratt, and J. Bennet, eds. 2011. *Interweaving Worlds: Systemic Interactions in Eurasia, 7th to 1st Millennia BC.* Oakville, CT.

Willi, A. 1998. "Numa's Dangerous Books: The Exegetic History of a Roman Forgery." *Museum Helveticum* 55: 139–72.

Williams, J. 2007. "Religion and Roman Coins." In J. Rüpke, ed., *A Companion to Roman Religion.* Oxford. 143–63.

Williamson, R. 1989. *Jews in the Hellenistic World: Philo.* Cambridge.

Willing, M. 2008. *Eusebius von Cäsarea als Häreseograph.* Patritische Texte und Studien 63. Berlin.

Wilson, D., and D. Sperber. 2002. "Relevance Theory." *UCL Working Papers in Linguistics* 13: 249–87.

―――. 2012. *Meaning and Relevance.* Cambridge.

Winiarczyk, M. 2002. *Euhemeros von Messene: Leben, Werk und Nachwirkung,* Beiträge zur Altertumskunde 157. München.

Winter, E. 2013. *Zeitzeichen* 1: Text; 2: Katalog.

Winter, N. A. 1993. "The Greek Background for Archaic Architectural Terracottas of Central Italy." In E. Rystedt, C. Wikander, and Ö. Wikander, eds., *Deliciae Fictiles—Proceedings of the First International Conference on Central Italic Architectural Terracottas at the Swedish Institute in Rome, 10–12 December, 1990.* Skrifter utgivna av Svenska Institutet i Rom 4°.50. Stockholm. 17–20.

―――. 2006. "The Origin of the Recessed Gable in Etruscan Architecture." In I. Edlund-Berry, G. Greco, and J. Kwenfield, eds., *Deliciae Fictiles III—Architectural Terracottas in Ancient Italy: New Discoveries and Interpretations* 3. Oxford. 45–48.

―――. 2010. "The Caprifico Roof in Its Wider Context." In P. Domenico, ed., *Il Tempio Arcaico di Caprifico di Torrecchia (Cisterna di Latina) I Materiali e il Contesto.* Roma. 113–31.

Winther, H. C. 1997. "Princely Tombs of the Orientalizing Period in Etruria and Latium vetus." *Acta hyperborea* 7: 423–46.

Wischmeyer, W. 2002. "Die christlichen Texte im sogenannten Filocalus-Kalender." In A. Primmel, ed., *Textsorten und Textkritik: Tagungsbeiträge.* Wien. 45–67.

Wiseman, T. P. 1994. "Lucretius, Catiline, and the Survival of Prophecy." In T. P. Wiseman, ed., *Historiography and Imagination: Eight Essays on Roman Culture.* Exeter. 49–67, 133–39.

―――. 2000. "Liber: Myth, Drama and Ideology in Republican Rome." In C. Bruun, ed., *The Roman Middle Republic: Politics, Religion, and Historiography c. 400–133 B. C.* Rome. 265–99.

Wissowa, G. 1912. *Religion und Kultus der Römer.* Handbuch der Altertumswissenschaft 5,4. 2nd ed. München.

Wojaczek, G. 1992. "Die Heliosweihe des Kaisers Julian: Ein initiatorischer Text des Neuplatonismus." *Würzburger Jahrbücher* NF 18: 207–36.

Wolters, R. 1990. "Der Gamanicus-Dupondius, die Tabula Siarensis und der römische Verzicht auf die Okkupation Germaniens." *Numismatische Zeitschrift* 101: 7–16.

Woolf, G. 2003. "A Sea of Faith." *Mediterranean Historical Review* 18, 2: 126–43.

———. 2009. "Found in Translation: The Religion of the Roman Diaspora." In O. Hekster, S. Schmidt-Hofner, and C. Witschel, eds., *Ritual Dynamics and Religious Change in the Roman Empire: Proceedings of the Eighth Workshop of the International Network Impact of Empire (Heidelberg, July 5–7, 2007)*. Impact of Empire 9. Leiden 239–52.

———. 2010. "Afterworld: The Local and the Global in the Graeco-Roman East." In T. Whitmarsh, ed., *Local Knowledge and Microidentities in the Imperial Greek World*. Greek Culture in the Roman World. Cambridge. 189–200.

———. 2011. *Tales of the Barbarians: Ethnography and Empire in the Roman West*. Malden, Mass.

———. 2012a. "Reading and Religion in Rome." In J. Rüpke and W. Spickermann, eds., *Reflections on Religious Individuality: Greco-Roman and Judaeo-Christian Texts and Practices*. Religionsgeschichtliche Versuche und Vorarbeiten 62. Berlin. 193–208.

———. 2012b. *Rome: An Empire's Story*. Oxford.

———. 2013. "Ritual and the Individual in Roman Religion." In J. Rüpke, ed., *The Individual in the Religions of the Ancient Mediterranean*. Oxford. 136–60.

———. 2015. "Ritual Traditions of Non-Mediterranean Europe." In R. Raja and J. Rüpke, eds., *A Companion to the Archaeology of Religion in the Ancient World*. Malden, Mass. 465–77.

Wyler, S. 2006. "Images dionysiaques à Rome: à propos d'une fresque augustéenne de Lanuvium." In C. Bonnet, J. Rüpke, and P. Scarpi, eds., *Religions orientales—culti misterici: Neue Perspektiven—nouvelles perspectives—prospettive nuove*. Potsdamer altertumswissenschaftliche Beiträge 16. Stuttgart. 135–46.

Yarrow, L. M. 2007. *Historiography at the End of the Republic: Provincial Perspectives on Roman Rule*. Oxford Classical Monograph. Oxford.

Yuval, I. J., B. Harshav, and J. Chipman. 2008. *Two Nations in Your Womb. Perceptions of Jews and Christians in Late Antiquity and the Middle Ages*. 1st pb. ed., A Mark Taper Foundation Book in Jewish Studies. Berkeley.

Zanker, P. 1976. "Einleitung." In P. Zanker, ed., *Hellenismus in Mittelitalien: Kolloquium in Göttingen vom 5. bis 9. Juni 1974*. Abhandlungen der Akademie der Wissenschaften Göttingen, Phil.-hist. Kl. 3. Folge, 97/I-II. Göttingen. 11–20.

———. 2010. "By the emperor, for the people: 'Popular' Architecture in Rome." In B. C. Ewald and C. F. Noreña, eds., *The Emperor and Rome: Space, Representation, and Ritual*. Yale Classical Studies 35. Cambridge. 45–87.

Zeggio, S. 2005. "Un santuario alle pendici nord-orientali del Palatino ed i suoi depositi votivi fra età arcaica e medio-repubblicana." In A. Comella and S. Mele, eds., *Depositi Votivi e Culti dell'Italia Antica dall'Età Arcaica a Quella Tardo-Repubblicana—Atti del Convegno di Studi Perugia, 1–4 giugno 2000*. Bibliotheca archaeologica 16. Bari. 63–76.

Zetterholm, M. 2003. *The Formation of Christianity in Antioch: A Social-Scientific Approach to the Separation between Judaism and Christianity*. London, New York.

Zevi, F. 1979. "Il santuario della Fortuna Primigenia a Palestrina." *ivi* 16: 2–22.

———. 1993. "Gli altari di Lavinio: un'ipotesi." In R. T. Scott and A. Reynolds Scott, eds., *Eius Virtutis Studiosi: Classical and Postclassical Studies in Memory of Frank Edward Brown (1908–1988)*. Hanover.

———. 1998. "I Greci, gli Etruschi, il Sele (Note sui culti arcaici di Pompei)." In *I culti della Campania antica: Atti del Convegno Internazionale di Studi in ricordo di Nazarena Valenza Mele, Napoli 15–17 Maggio 1995*. Pubblicazioni scientifiche del Centro di Studi della Magna Grecia dell'Università degli studi di Napoli Federico 3, 3. Roma. 3–25.

Zimmermann, K. 2000. "Späthellenistische Kultpraxis in einer karischen Kleinstadt. Eine neue lex sacra aus Bargylia." *Chiron* 30: 451–85.

Zink, S., and H. Piening. 2009. "Haec aurea templa: The Palatine Temple of Apollo and Its Polychromy." *Journal of Roman Archaeology* 22: 109–22.

Zuchtriegel, G. 2012. *Gabii I—Das Santuario Orientale im Zeitalter der Urbanisierung—Eisenzeitliche und archaische Funde der Ausgrabungen 1976/77*. Venosa.

Zwierlein, O. 2009. *Petrus in Rom: Die literarischen Zeugnisse. Mit einer kritischen Edition der Martyrien des Petrus und Paulus auf neuer handschriftlicher Grundlage*. UaLG 96. Berlin.

———. 2010. "Kritisches zur Römischen Petrustradition und zur Datierung des Ersten Clemensbriefes." *Göttinger Forum für Altertumswissenschaft* 13: 87–157.

———. 2014. *Die Urfassungen der Martyria Polycarpi et Pionii und das Corpus Polycarpianum*. 2 vols. Untersuchungen zur antiken Literatur und Geschichte 116. Berlin.

INDEX

The indexed practices, cognitions, and roles always concern/include both female and male agents as well as their agency.

121, 135, 186, 195, 262, 264, 298, 374, 376,
382, 388
Ayia Irini, 60

Bacchus, 134–36, 253
Baetica, 30, 177
Baghdad, 216
banquet, 61, 64, 72–76, 104–6, 133–34, 148,
274, 297, 314, 317, 328; banquet culture,
54, 133; banqueting utensils, 88, 97
Bar Kochba uprising, 355
Bellona, 126, 188, 222
benefactor and liturgy, 103, 137, 242, 257
Betitia Proba, Faltonia, 377, 381
bible, 13, 337–38, 365; rewritten, 347.
    See also Pentateuch; Septuagint
biography 28, 122, 176, 290, 307, 329,
    343–45, 359, 369, 381; of the apostles,
    335, 337; autobiography, 122, 152, 176, 311,
    344; of the emperors, 204, 288; of the
    god, 315, 356; of Jesus, 368; of objects,
    36; schema of, 343–45, 355
bishop, 260, 343, 364–65, 375–79, 385,
    387–89. *See also* specialists
Bithynia, 307
body, 37, 82, 213–14, 235, 249, 383, 386;
    body parts, 37, 44–45, 87–88, 129, 306
Bona Dea, 13, 126, 277
Bona Diva, 277
Boscotrecase, 232
bricolage, 335, 383
Britannia, 285, 293
Bulla, 213
burial, 32–33, 37–46, 53, 61, 67, 160, 174, 179,
    235–37, 246, 250, 287, 308, 327, 378; admin-
    istration of b. grounds, 388; collective, 39;
    cremation, 46; infant, 39, 82, 244; luxuri-
    ous, 77; mounds for, 52; multilayered,
    246; public, 145, secondary, 45; solitary,
    45; sites for, 39, 41, 45, 63, 82, 236, 374

Caecilius Metellus Pius, Quintus, 134, 264
Caesareum, 189–91, 274

Calabria, 52
calendar, 13, 101–3, 143, 150, 159, 161, 176–77,
    190, 198, 203–7, 288, 301, 341, 345,
    377–79; reform of, 123, 204
Calpurnius Rufinus, Gaius, 314
Calpurnius Siculus, Titus, 231, 289
Campania, 41, 62, 73, 139, 234–35, 264, 377
Campetti, 76, 84
Campoverde, 35, 55
Cannae, 146
Canopus, 267
Capernaum, 342
Capitol, 98, 112, 118, 147, 198, 265, 297
Caprifico di Torrecchia (Suessa Pometia),
    76
Capua, 62, 102
Caracalla (Marcus Aurelius Severus
    Antoninus Augustus), 195, 310, 357–58,
    365, 371, 373
carmina Marciana, 152, 161
Carthage, 29, 168, 222, 262
Casa degli Amorini Dorati, 229
Casa delle pareti rosse, 219, 253
Cassius Dio, Lucius, 307, 310, 365
Castor, 79, 126, 131, 209, 287
Castration, 18
Catullus, Gaius Valerius, 267
Ceius Privatus, Lucius, 269–70
Celsus, 312
cena aditialis, 131. *See also* banquet
ceramics, 25, 28, 35, 48, 84, 90, 214, 225
Ceres, 79, 138, 175, 280
Cernunnos, 219
Cerveteri (Caere), 41, 48, 67
Cestius Epulo, Gaius, 238
Chaeremon, 319
changes in religion, 6–7, 10, 77, 183–85,
    262, 290, 340, 374
charity, 385. *See also* benefactor
Cisterna di Latina, 76
Claudius Caecus, Appius, 103, 173
Claudius Nero, Tiberius (praetor 42 BC),
    187

Numa Pompilius, 135, 161, 181, 205–6, 300, 314, 344, 346, 389
numen, 280–81, 287; *Augusti*, 280
Numisius Vitalis, Lucius, 247
nymphus, 317. *See also* specialists

objects, 2, 18, 21, 28, 33, 35–37, 45–48, 55, 57–60, 63–66, 70, 72, 74–76, 79, 83, 87, 89–91, 95–97, 102, 104, 118, 129, 197, 214, 216, 218–19, 221, 223, 227, 230, 234, 237, 254, 257, 259, 263, 270, 316, 389; biographies of, 35
obnuntiatio, 146, 153–55
Octavius Herennus, Marcus, 127, 129
Octavius Rufus, Gnaeus, 276
October equus, 99, 188
oracles, 13, 121, 152–53, 209, 228, 266–67, 291–92, 303, 310–12, 359; by lot, 306; oracular sanction, 75; *Oracle of the Potter*, 334; Sibylline, 121, 152, 161, 194, 334, 339, 362–63; unauthorized, 20. *See also* divination
Orceria (wife of Numerius), 89
organ, 18. *See also* music
organization, 7, 19, 32, 44, 98–99, 141, 161, 178, 189, 192, 246, 318, 328, 350
Orientalizing Period, 41, 54, 63, 96
Origen, 337
Orontes, 362
Orvieto, 41
Osiris, 264–65, 269
ossuaries, 237
Ostia, 176, 289, 316–17
Ovidius Naso, Publius, 207, 215, 225, 231, 248, 341, 345, 349, 389

Pacha, 134
paideia, 246, 378
Palatine, 78, 197–98, 206–7, 308, 373, 389
Palestine, 174, 237, 350–51, 355, 362
Panayia Domus, 218, 226
pantheon, 4, 10, 20, 22, 48, 125, 221, 290

pater patratus, 112. *See also* specialists
patricians, 32, 103, 110, 123, 125, 184, 189, 213. *See also* plebeians
Paul, 249, 324, 334–35, 344, 352, 355–56, 358, 364, 368, 374, 378
Paulinus of Nola, 331
Peking, 5
Peleus, 185
penates, 117, 126, 184, 209, 250, 253–54
Pentateuch, 346, 350, 355, 370
Pergamum, 167, 200, 206, 339, 370
Perge, 314
Perpetua (visionary), 312
Perugia, 100, 402
Peter, 249, 347, 357–58, 364, 378
Petronius Arbiter, Titus, 240, 323
Philippi, 185, 196
Philo of Alexandria, 206
Philochorus of Athens, 175
Philodemus of Gadara, 172, 306
philosopher, 4, 170–71, 179, 181, 184, 227, 272, 290, 299, 301, 306, 314, 321, 324, 344, 348, 357, 362, 364, 367, 377. *See also* specialists
philosophy, 3–4, 16, 164, 166, 170–72, 181, 183, 224, 227, 272, 290, 303–4, 306, 311, 332, 335–36, 338, 348, 356–58, 370, 380, 385, 387; Greek, 179; natural, 170; Pythagorean, 346; Roman, 182; Stoic, 13, 171, 335
Philostratus, Flavius, 329
piatrix, 302
pietas, 90, 126, 180
Pietrabbondante, 139
Pisa, 68, 275–76
pit, 19, 24, 35–36, 45, 55–57, 61, 63–64, 84, 86, 96, 129, 314; longitudinal, 40
Plato, 166, 178, 211, 224–25, 290, 332, 335–36, 370, 383
Plautus, Titus Maccius, 92, 139, 152, 165, 170, 250, 273, 303, 389
plebeians, 32, 78, 103, 110, 116, 121, 123, 125, 159, 189. *See also* patricians

temples, 9, 14, 27, 36, 51, 61–65, 81, 92, 94, 97–98, 101, 115, 135, 143–45, 151, 158, 260, 387; of Apollo, 185, 198, 206; of Bellona, 188; of Castor, 131; construction of, 126–30, 137, 186, 196–201, 275, 293, 357; criticism against, 172, 375, 383; of Dea Dia, 189; dedications in, 221, 309; donations in, 178, 185; Etruscan, 75–79, 105, 294; freestanding, 52; foundations of, 176, 197, 203, 210, 267, 279, 287, 314, 348; Greek, 52, 58, 73; of Hercules, 176, 229; innovations in, 126–30, 175, 199, 226–29, 257–58, 260; of Isis, 264; of Janus, 193; in Jerusalem, 299, 321, 339, 350–57; of Jupiter, 74, 78, 98, 122, 127, 147, 161, 341; of Mars, 198, 203; of Mater Magna, 198, 261, 301, 369; miniature, 219; personnel in, 227, 270, 303, 387; as places of experience, 226–29, 246, 257, 269, 298, 328, 362, 369; podiums for, 137, 226; rectangular, 246; restoration of, 196, 204; round, 127; of Venus, 373; of Vesta, 358; of the Winged Horses, 70. *See also* architecture; space; synagogue

Teotihuacán, 216

territoriality, 34, 39

Tertullian, Quintus Septimius Florens, 139, 364

theater, 99, 136–39; 166, 170, 194–97, 199, 217, 269, 293, 330–31, 359; amphitheater, 20, 98–99, 217, 293, 359; theater-temple, 200

Theocritus, 231

Theodotion, bible translator, 337

theology, 172, 205, 216, 277, 370

Theophilus, 357

Thesan, 47

Thessaloniki, 272

Thessalus, 319

Thessaly, 172

Thetis, 185

theurgy, 370

Thuburbo Maius, 247

Thucydides, 166, 170

Tiber, 3, 76, 83, 122, 127, 189, 207, 362

Tiberius Iulius Caesar Augustus, 205, 208–9, 284, 310, 341–42

Tibur, 197

Tienen, 316

Timaeus, historian, 168

Tinia, 47

Titinius (poet), 92

Titus Tatius, 284

toga, 18, 112, 147, 213, 251, 276, 308

Tomba Castellani, 396

Torre di Satriano, 66

traditions, 3, 5, 147, 183, 186, 209, 224, 229, 310, 334, 358, 364, 369, 374–75; of action, 275; alteration of, 125, 176; appropriation of, 10, 125; Christian, 374; connection with, 17; consolidation of, 65; craft, 222; creation of, 12, 84, 225, 380; development of, 39, 76, 90, 357; elite, 218; epic, 189, 381; of expertise, 302; family, 159; hegemonic, 58; historiographical, 78; local, 90, 143, 275, 389; maintenance of, 34; martyr, 379–80; Mediterranean, 156; narrative, 79; polytheistic, 370; prophetic, 311; reference to, 129; reinforcement of, 125; reinvention of, 185; religious, 186, 225, 294, 315; research, 31; ritual 41, 161; of ruler-worship, 376; social, 11; song, 173; stabilization of, 67; textual, 273, 277, 350, 384; transient, 105; involving women, 346

transcendence, 37, 118, 215–16; transcendent actors, 8–9; transcendent worldview, 216

transformation: individual 311; into public action, 98; religious, 5, 22, 340, 382, 386

Trastevere, 309, 389

Trestina, 83–84

tribus, 110, 121, 283

Trier, 379

tripudium, 144, 153

Troy, 117, 167–68, 189, 389

A NOTE ON THE TYPE

This book has been composed in Arno, an Old-style serif font in the classic Venetian tradition, designed by Robert Slimbach at Adobe.